RESOURCE ECONOMICS

Resource Economics

An Economic Approach to Natural Resource and
Environmental Policy, Third Edition

John C. Bergstrom

The University of Georgia, Athens, USA

Alan Randall

The Ohio State University, USA

Edward Elgar
Cheltenham, UK • Northampton, MA, USA

Published by
Edward Elgar Publishing Limited
The Lypiatts
15 Lansdown Road
Cheltenham
Glos GL50 2JA
UK

Edward Elgar Publishing, Inc.
William Pratt House
9 Dewey Court
Northampton
Massachusetts 01060
USA

A catalogue record for this book
is available from the British Library

Library of Congress Control Number: 2009941152

Mixed Sources
Product group from well-managed
forests and other controlled sources
www.fsc.org Cert no. SA-COC-1565
© 1996 Forest Stewardship Council
FSC

ISBN 978 1 84844 253 5 (cased)
ISBN 978 1 84980 248 2 (paperback)

Printed and bound by MPG Books Group, UK

Contents

Preface

The overall theme of this book is the role that economics plays in helping society to understand, analyze, and address natural resource and environmental issues and problems and, along the way, to develop thoughtful policies and management actions for making things better. Natural Resource and Environmental Economics (we use the imprecise but at least brief term "Resource Economics" for short in the title of this book) is an applied, policy-oriented field of inquiry. We see it as so thoroughly policy oriented that it would not exist as an identifiable subdiscipline of economics if unfettered competitive markets achieved, on their own, economically efficient and socially acceptable allocations of natural resources to economic production and consumption *plus* a clean and healthy environment. Simultaneously meeting economic, environmental, and equity (for example, justice) goals – sometimes referred to as the "triple bottom line" of "profit, planet, and people" – is a tall order for the market, but in some cases it can be done. When it comes to using natural resources and protecting the environment, the unique characteristics of the systems involved often raise additional challenges concerning one or more aspects of the "triple bottom line." Often there are calls for public policies and management actions to "fix or prevent the problem." If there was no cry or need for natural resource policies and management actions, there would be no need for the study of applied resource economics (or resource economics professors and students!)

People are very concerned about present and future natural resource use and environmental protection, and markets – although amazingly effective and resilient – do not seem to have all the answers. For example, as this book is being completed in 2010, newspaper and Internet headlines and stories around the world are focusing on the environmental and economic damages associated with a current, huge oil spill along the Louisiana, USA coast resulting from a blow-out during offshore drilling for oil. Many policy and management concerns related to this developing environmental and economic disaster have already been voiced, and will continue to arise for many years to come. As we hope will become clear to the reader of this book, natural resource and environmental economists are in a unique and important position to help evaluate and develop policies and management actions that meet "triple bottom line" goals in the case of this oil spill and other natural resource and environmental issues and problems that society will surely face in the future.

The organization of this book reflects the authors' philosophy of teaching natural resource and environmental economics, and preparing students to help resolve practical natural resource and environmental issues and problems. We believe that it is important to begin with a strong understanding of economic theory and methods, but effective applied problem-solvers will need to call upon a broader range of knowledge and ideas – economics alone cannot do the job. The careful reader of this book will indeed gain a strong and complete understanding of basic microeconomic theory and tools needed to understand, analyze, and resolve natural resource and environmental issues and problems. The diligent student will also learn how to apply the things in his or her economics "tool box" to real-world natural resource and environmental issues and problems in a way that integrates economic, environmental, and equity considerations and concerns. Towards these ends, although the focal point and unifying theme of this book is economics, the reader will gain important complementary knowledge in the physical sciences (for example, ecology, ecosystem goods and services), social institutions (for example, the legal system, property rights, government entities), and ethical systems. By presenting natural resource and environmental economics in an integrated policy-oriented framework, we hope to equip the reader not just to be a well-prepared "knower," but to also be a passionate and effective "doer" who will make a positive difference in a world that needs people committed to being part of the solution, rather than just part of the problem. Let the journey begin!

Acknowledgments

The authors have been on their own journey revising and writing this third edition. Alan Randall deserves the credit for the first and second editions, along with contributors he acknowledged in these editions. John Bergstrom took the lead and did most of the work in preparing this third edition, and both authors contributed new material that updated and extended the reach of this book.

Both authors owe a huge debt of gratitude to their teachers, mentors, professional colleagues, and students for sharing their knowledge and experiences in the field of natural resource and environmental economics – each in their own way has prepared us to produce this book. Converting the last paper-copy-only edition of this book to a modern, electronic format was no easy task and could not have been completed without the dedicated, masterful, and cheerful contributions of professional staff in the Department of Agricultural and Applied Economics at the University of Georgia, especially Jo Anne Norris and Karina Koppius – thanks so much to you all! We also gratefully acknowledge professional "shepherding" and editing provided by Edward Elgar editors including Caroline Cornish, Alexandra Mandzak, and Alan Sturmer, who were all a great pleasure to work with and who helped to improve the final product tremendously.

Personal acknowledgments
I would like to sincerely thank Alan Randall here for the special opportunity and great pleasure to work with him on the third edition. I give deep and heartfelt thanks to my wife Jodi and our four children, Erin, Lora, Anna, and Luke, for all of their wonderfully incredible support, help, and love over the years, especially when I have needed it most. I hope this book helps you and others understand more about what a resource economist does (since, as you know, it is sometimes hard to explain!) and how we all can become better stewards of what we have, including natural resources and the environment.

John Bergstrom

I am so grateful to John Bergstrom for convincing me to attempt a third edition of *Resource Economics* so long after the second edition appeared – it would not have happened without his persistence – and for undertaking the lion's share of the hard work involved. Many teachers, mentors, and professional colleagues have contributed to my understanding of economics as a theoretical framework, a coherent set of methods, and a (rather particular) kind of ethical system, but I have learned more from my distinguished group of graduate advisees over the years and from some of their advisees (John Bergstrom is in that group), than from any other source. The support of my wife Beverley, the encouragement of our adult children Glenn and Nicole, and the joy that our grandchildren Isabel and Kendall bring to our lives were all essential to the effort – without a strong family foundation, things would have been so much harder.

Alan Randall

PART I

NATURAL RESOURCE AND ENVIRONMENTAL POLICY AND NATURAL RESOURCE SUPPLY AND SCARCITY

1 Economic growth, resource scarcity, and environmental degradation: where have we been and where are we going?

The complex relationships, dependencies, and feedbacks between people and the environment in which we live were not always as we see them in the world today. For most of our relatively brief history, people were preoccupied with the endless struggle merely to survive: to find food and shelter and to protect ourselves as best we could from disease, pestilence, and the depredations of wild animals and hostile interlopers. In those days, the connection between humans and the environment was very up close and personal! Although humans were winning the struggle for survival, it was not by a comfortable margin. The continued existence of the human race must have seemed precarious. Humans were, even then, set apart from the rest of the ecosystem by our superior intellect, abilities of communication, inquisitiveness, aesthetic sensibility, and spirituality which enabled us to pose and seek answers to great metaphysical questions of the meaning of life.

Applying our unique set of abilities and skills, people slowly began to bend the environment to their needs and to develop a social structure to better communicate and organize systems for directing our collective energies. We banded together in groups for defense, domesticating animals, and cultivating crops. We learned to use hides, wood, stone, bronze, and iron. We developed civilizations, cultures, art and literature, myth, and religion. We also played a part in the creation of deserts and the demise of ecosystems. And we refined techniques for torture, destruction, warfare, and the domination and enslavement of our fellow human beings. Great civilizations grew, flourished, and when they outgrew their resource bases and social structures, decayed.

What we now call progress came slowly and painfully. The limits seemed always close at hand. The historian, looking back across centuries and millennia, could discern key developments in social organization, which permitted increases in the scale and changes in the nature of the extended family, the tribe, the feudal domain, the state, the nation, and the empire. Pivotal technical inventions including the wheel, the stirrup, and the cannon could be identified, along with the incremental developments in weaponry, land transportation, and navigation that permitted people to exploit more effectively their environment (which always included more primitive human populations). Nevertheless, although life was surely eventful, most individuals could expect to see little technological change and little change in the real incomes of their communities (unless through redistribution by plunder or conquest) in their lifetimes. For most of human history, then, change came slowly. Increasing affluence was seldom hoped for, let alone expected as a right. Social, cultural, and political institutions were geared to ensuring stability rather than facilitating change.

The Four-Hundred-Year Boom

Sometime about 500 or 600 years ago, the rates of technical, economic, social, political, and cultural change began to increase rapidly, first in Western Europe and later around the world. These changes established the conditions that permitted the unprecedented economic progress of the last 400 years.

The first manifestation of this abrupt change was the development of transoceanic navigation, which facilitated trade and the growth of economic opportunities related to global trade. Even more importantly, large sailing vessels, equipped with the more potent weaponry made possible by the development of military uses for gunpowder, expanded the resource base of Western Europe. There followed an age of intercontinental exploration and plunder, and piracy to redistribute the spoils. Initially, gold and precious objects were simply taken from Asia and the Americas to enrich the homeland. Later, it was spices, oils, and minerals. Then a broad range of food, fiber, mineral, and human resources were exploited to supply European economies with raw materials and enslaved labor. Colonies were established to serve as bases for plunder, to operate mines, and, especially in the warmer climates, to produce food and fiber under the plantation system.

Back home, rapidly increasing wealth and ease of travel, which permitted the cross-fertilization of ideas, encouraged technical developments at an exponentially increasing rate. First the agrarian revolution and then the industrial revolution radically changed both the techniques and the social organization of production. The domestic resource base was expanded as uses were found for things like petroleum that were previously undiscovered or were known but considered useless. Developments in science and medicine permitted population growth at unprecedented rates. The non-European world increased, rather than decreased, in importance to Europe. It continued to provide food, fiber, minerals, and slaves. In addition, the colonies provided markets for the industrial surplus of Europe and homes for its population surplus. Areas sparsely settled and with premodern indigenous populations including North America, Australia, southern Africa, and parts of South America, became the frontier to be tamed and developed by European populations. The resource base of the New World was huge, especially in North America. Drawing on its European technology and cultural heritage, a steady flow of immigrants from Europe, and a massive resource base ripe for exploitation, the United States became in less than three centuries the dominant economic power in the world.

The European populations in Europe and the New World entered an age of increasing affluence. Some other populations, notably the Japanese, joined them. Technological progress continued apace, with developments unimaginable only a few centuries ago in electronics, computer science, air transportation, nuclear engineering, genetics, and medicine. Food, clothing, shelter, and protection from predators demanded an ever-decreasing proportion of real income, and discretionary consumption beyond the necessities of life now provided the incentive for people to work and to invest in increasing their own technical skills. Production and marketing were organized on a global scale. A combination of increasing discretionary income and the incentives provided by the international economic system freed individuals from the bonds of family, community, and place and encouraged individualism and mobility. For many, location and interpersonal relationships became transitory, but income continued to grow. The range of choice seemed to be expanding exponentially.

The social organization mechanisms, the legal system, and the institutional structure that developed during the Four-Hundred-Year Boom no longer promoted stability. Instead, they promoted industrial progress, resource exploitation, and the transfer of resources to those best able to utilize them. As one small example, in the face of the new possibilities of air transportation, the centuries-old common-law concept of landowner-ship was summarily changed. No longer did landownership apply to the air space above land to the extent that a landowner could deny passage of an airplane through that air. When the old concepts of ownership could impede development of air transportation, it was the legal construct rather than air transportation that had to go. More generally, laws of nuisance and legal standing were interpreted to encourage industry and new resource uses even when these imposed costs on others such as water contamination, foul odors, and noise.

The point of this thumbnail sketch of history is that the Four-Hundred-Year Boom is not typical of human history. It was a most unusual time; yet it shaped the aspirations and expectations of contemporary populations in the developed countries. It shaped their lifestyles and intellectual orientations. It shaped the institutions under which pro-duction and human interaction are organized. And it provided the experience on which the technologists, economists, lawyers, and political scientists base their projections for the future.

What is the assurance that the trends of the Four-Hundred-Year Boom can be con-tinued indefinitely? Rather than attempt a definitive answer, it might be appropriate to consider three important characteristics of the boom. First, it was based to a signifi-cant degree on plunder, colonialism, and the exploitation of the resource base of non-European lands by technically advanced European peoples. It was not self-supporting in geographical space, but depended on the exploitation of the world's resources for the primary and immediate benefit of a fraction of the world's population. Second, it was based to a significant degree on the exploitation of exhaustible and non-renewable resources. Conservation of resources was not important, and recycling of resources was costly compared with the costs of using newly extracted resources, and fundamentally limited by the laws of physics. The use of exhaustible resources represents withdrawals from the store of such resources. Thus the boom was not self-supporting over time but depended on the exploitation of resources that when used would become unavailable for future generations. Third, it depended to a significant degree on the progressive and irreversible modification of ecosystems. Land was converted to uses that were thought productive regardless of the changes wrought in its plant and animal commu-nities. Agricultural and industrial wastes were released without concern for, and often without knowledge of, their ecological impacts. Thus, the boom was not ecologically self-supporting. These considerations do not prove that the Four-Hundred-Year Boom cannot be continued indefinitely. However, these three conditions cannot themselves be continued indefinitely on the planet Earth. Continued progress and prosperity, as we have come to define them, depend on substantial changes in the bases of economic activity.

The New Globalization Era
The Four-Hundred-Year Boom initiated an era of globalization characterized by increased trade primarily driven by the colonialism model. In the colonialism model,

more technically advanced "mother" countries used colonies as sources of raw materials including natural resources. The mother country, in turn, provided manufactured goods to the colony along with other political, social, and military support and protection. The colonialism era lasted for a good part of the Four-Hundred-Year Boom, but eventually died out as former colonies gained their independence from mother countries through wars of independence (e.g., the American Revolution in the 1770s) and more recently through diplomatic action. Thus, although some developed countries still have semblances of colonies throughout the world, colonialism is no longer a dominant driver of global trade and relations.

By the end of World War II the heyday of colonial expansion had passed, and the trend turned towards transitioning colonies toward independence.[1] During the next several decades after World War II, global trade continued to grow. Advancements in transportation technology during the Four-Hundred-Year Boom made moving raw materials (e.g., crude oil), agricultural commodities (e.g., corn, wheat) and manufactured goods (e.g., electronic goods) between countries much more technically feasible and cost-effective on a global scale. Thus, in the several decades following World War II, US imports of crude oil greatly increased, especially from Middle Eastern countries such as Saudi Arabia. US imports of electronic goods (e.g., TVs) and cars also greatly increased, especially from Japan. The US also increased its exports of some manufactured goods and agricultural commodities to other countries.

However, during the several decades following World War II, global trade and relations were constrained by Cold War superpower country politics and communication technology. After World War II, the United States and the Soviet Union quickly became the two world superpowers in terms of economic and military might. The competition and tension between these two superpowers led to Cold War politics driven by the appropriately named MAD (mutual assured destruction) policy. The ongoing Cold War and looming threat of the MAD policy forced many other countries to choose sides, and put a political damper on global trade and cooperative relations.

Although transportation technology had improved immensely during the Four-Hundred-Year Boom, communication technology lagged behind in comparison. Although it will be hard for college students reading this book to believe, there once was a time when the Internet, World Wide Web and cellular phones did not exist. Before the Internet and cellphones, the business, education and government communities relied on land telephone lines and snail mail services to communicate within and across countries. In the 1970s, alternatives to snail mail including private overnight express mail services became well established, but were expensive. Long-distance landline telephone services were also relatively expensive and often times an inefficient means for communication with people around the US and the world who lived in different time zones. The inability to communicate efficiently and inexpensively with people throughout the world also dampened global trade and relations.

Beginning in the late 1980s, a series of events literally changed the world, leading to a new globalization era. In 1989, the Berlin Wall separating US-backed West Germany and Soviet Union-backed East Germany was literally taken down. This action destroyed the "Iron Curtain" separating democratic Western nations from communist Eastern nations. The collapse of the Soviet Union in 1991 left the US as the world's sole superpower, and ended the Cold War. These events opened up new opportunities for improved global relations and trade between countries that had been held apart by Cold War alliances.

Around the same time as the collapse of the Soviet Union, a communications revolution was also about to hit the world. Although the Internet had been under development by US military and academic cooperators since the 1960s, it did not become practical to expand this technology to the general public until the World Wide Web (WWW) was added to the Internet platform in 1991. In 1992, the US government began turning over network management to private companies, which then offered expanded Internet and World Wide Web services to the general public. The rest, as they say, "is history" and now most of us take for granted having the world literally at our fingertips via the Internet and World Wide Web.

But the Internet and World Wide Web are only part of the recent communications revolution. Who could forget about cellular phones or "cellphones" (mobile phones)? The first commercial cellular phone networks in the world date back to the 1970s. However, cellular phones did not become widely available to the general public until the 1980s; even then, the phones that were available were bulky, expensive to buy and expensive to operate (you've seen them in those old 1980s' movies and TV shows). Since the 1990s, cellular phone technology and networks have exploded across the world, and now almost everyone, especially in developed countries, can afford to own and operate a cellphone. As a result, international phone calls have become quick, easy, and relatively inexpensive compared to the old, landline-only days.

The upshot of the communication revolution involving the Internet, World Wide Web, and cellular phones is that the world is now a much more "connected" place, which has opened up immense opportunities for increased global cooperation and trade. In the authors' own academic field, collaborating on projects between Georgia (where one of the authors currently lives) and Ohio (where the other author currently lives) is very easy. Both of the authors also use the Internet, World Wide Web, and cellular phones to work with collaborators throughout the US and the world in ways that simply were not possible prior to the turn of the twenty-first century. Of course, business opportunities have also increased throughout the world as producers and consumers from different, faraway places can now easily communicate with each other no matter which time zone they are located in.

The communications revolution has favored international finance even more than trade – after all, trade in goods still requires shipping and handling, whereas global financial transactions are all about communications. Capital has become even more mobile than goods, while labor remains relatively immobile due to restrictions on international migration. Here, we draw attention to just two of the many implications of these trends: the distribution of personal incomes and wealth has become even more unequal; and it has become harder to regulate financial markets effectively (one major cause of the global recession that began in autumn 2007 was the emergence and rapid growth of an unregulated shadow banking system).

In addition to the fall of the Iron Curtain and the communications revolution, the new globalization era is characterized by a shifting in economic and political power from the US, Russia, and European Union nations to Asian nations, especially China and India. Some South American nations, particularly Brazil, are also becoming major players in the global economy. According to the World Bank, as of 2008, the US still has the largest economy of any single country, Japan ranks second, and China has the third-largest single-country economy. India has the twelfth-largest economy on the single country list, with Canada, Spain, Russia, Brazil, Italy, the United Kingdom, France and Germany filling out the top 12. The combined economy of the European Union member countries is about the same size as the US economy.

China and India are the focus of much current attention because of their huge populations, their rapidly growing economic power and political influence, and their potentially huge demands on natural resources and environmental assimilative capacity. Both countries have been experiencing rapid economic growth and increasing per capita consumption rates of material goods and services during the 1990s and 2000s. Since total consumption equals total population times per capita consumption, increasing per capita consumption rates in China and India translate to potentially enormous increases in global consumption of material goods and services and raw materials (including natural resources) used to produce these goods and services. Such potential increases in global consumption of material goods and services and raw materials presents a "good news, bad news" scenario. The good news is that the global economy may grow, providing opportunities for increased jobs, income, and standards of living throughout the world. The bad news, as discussed more in the next section, is that there may be negative natural resource and environmental consequences. Darn those economists who are always reminding us that "there ain't no such thing as a free lunch"!

We cannot conclude a discussion of the New Globalization Era without recognizing the profound political changes in the world which were brought to a head on September 11, 2001 – the day, of course, the World Trade Center Twin Towers in New York City came crashing down as the result of terrorism. Since then, the US and much of the rest of the world have been engaged in new types of politics and warfare involving tensions and conflicts not just between nations, but between nations and non-state terrorist groups that operate beyond the control and influence of national governments and the United Nations. The new politics and warfare have put new constraints on global relations, the implications of which are playing out as the book is being completed in 2010.

Some benefits and costs of economic growth
For its beneficiaries, the affluent citizens of the developed countries and the emerging economic powers, the Four-Hundred-Year Boom has brought prosperity, freedom from anxiety about food and shelter, an extended life expectancy and a modicum of relief from pain, education to develop skills and the capacity for self-fulfillment, and leisure time. Common people own products of industry and technology and can to some extent indulge a desire for status through consumption. They are typically educated beyond the mere needs of employment and have the time to indulge their creative instincts in hobbies, literature, and popular culture through print, film, the broadcast media, and the Internet. Though largely protected from constant crises of survival, they can indulge their need for excitement by contriving adventure through travel, sports, and all kinds of challenging and risky activities undertaken not from necessity but for fun. The well-educated middle and upper-middle classes are freed from drudgery to a degree enjoyed by only the very rich of past societies. They seem surrounded by choices, and if indeed they exercise little real power, they have always the hope and the expectation that their command over material goods will increase with time.

This condition has not been achieved without cost. The ecosystem of vast expanses of the globe has been irreversibly changed, and its balance and diversity have diminished. This is not all bad: human civilization (which on balance, we have seen as a good thing) is incompatible with the ecosystem in which prehistoric people survived. Yet something of value, we instinctively feel, has been lost. In addition, there is evidence indicating that the gene pool has diminished and that, in many ways, the capacity of the environment to absorb wastes, handle extremes of weather (for example, the run-off from unusually heavy rains), and provide natural competition for pests has been reduced.

The pollution of land, air, and water has increased alarmingly. Although it has been correctly observed that the concentration of some kinds of pollution in large cities has been reduced by the replacement of coal furnaces in the home with oil, gas, and electric heat, and by improved sanitation practices, new forms of pollution are becoming important, and pollution has spread across the landscape. Although emissions from the internal combustion engine have become notorious, the rapid increase in the production of nearly indestructible synthetic chemicals and nuclear wastes poses perhaps a greater threat. Modern methods of agricultural production have accelerated the loss of topsoil due to the erosion of broad expanses of the finest cropland and have made pollution from animal wastes, fertilizers, and pesticide residues almost ubiquitous. Congestion in commercial centers and places of mass entertainment, in residential agglomerations, on the highways, and even in outdoor recreation sites intended to provide opportunities to "get away from it all" has become a source of increasing frustration.

Although anxieties about food, shelter, and predators have largely disappeared, it seems they have been replaced by other anxieties about physical appearance, health, job status, social status, and alienation and lack of attachments to place, community, and family caused by a mobile society and global, dynamic economy. Some have expressed the view that the expansion of choice brought about by affluence is largely illusory. The famous economist E.J. Mishan wrote (and we paraphrase) that as the carpet of choice is unrolled before us by the foot, it is rolled up behind us by the yard.[2] Beyond these anxieties and neuroses, there is another set of concerns that are perplexing to the thoughtful. These include the rapid increases in the population of many already overpopulated countries in the early stages of economic modernization, the fears of resource exhaustion every time there is an upward spike in energy prices, and the concern for the effects of nearly indestructible wastes on the environment.

As economic development reaches many of the world's middle-income countries, per capita consumption of material goods and services is increasing rapidly in some of the most populated countries in the world including China and India. There is concern that, as per capita consumption rates in these modernizing countries become comparable to those in the rich countries, global consumption of raw materials will soar, along with global emissions and effluents. Today, most of the world's economy still runs on non-renewable, carbon-based fossil fuels such as crude oil, coal, and natural gas. So the obvious question arises: How long and at what prices can the supplies of these limited natural resources last in the face of increasing global demand and consumption?

In addition to natural resource depletion, environmental system degradation is another major concern related to increased global demand and consumption of material goods and services and fossil fuels. For example, burning fossil fuels emits carbon dioxide into the atmosphere which contributes to global warming (we have more to say on this topic in Chapter 2). For most of the past several decades, the US and European Union countries have been the major emitters of carbon dioxide in the world because of their large economies. However, in 2006 China surpassed them all, due to its recent rapid economic growth. China and other emerging industrial nations such as India and Brazil are also contributing more of other kinds of pollutants to the world's ecosystems. These countries are also undergoing massive landscape changes (e.g., deforestation) which have ecologists and economists alike worried about sustaining the health of both ecosystems and economies in the future.

Although all is not rosy in the affluent nations and some middle-income countries such as China, India, and Brazil are experiencing an economic boom of their own, there are still many countries with much of the world's population that have yet to obtain the benefits of the Four-Hundred-Year Boom and the New Globalization Era. Some of these countries are perhaps poised to join other developing countries on the path to economic growth and developed-country status. However, in other countries there seems to be little hope in sight for relief from poverty, malnutrition, poor sanitation, and short life expectancy. Some of these countries have always been poorly endowed with resources. Some are also battling outbreaks of deadly diseases which not only take human lives by the thousands, but also render others too sick to work and take care of themselves and their families. Others have seen much of their resource base plundered, exploited by foreign corporations paying only a pittance to domestic menial labor, or exchanged for imported manufactured products in an international monetary system that favored the industrial nations. The Four-Hundred Year Boom not only diminished the store of exhaustible resources in the lands that enjoyed its benefits but also irreversibly limited the economic prospects of many countries that did not. The desperate state of affairs faced by those people in the world who seem, through no apparent fault of their own, to bear a disproportionate share of the environmental costs of economic growth while others enjoy the majority of the benefits, raises a number of ethical questions and issues that thoughtful economists cannot simply ignore.

An uncertain future
We live in a time when future prospects are uncertain. The pioneering natural resource and environmental economist William J. Baumol once argued that it made little sense for present generations to forgo current consumption to invest in projects designed to benefit future generations, as history suggested that future generations would surely be richer than present generations anyway.[3] However, many other thoughtful individuals, laypersons and specialists alike, question whether or not future generations will always be better off. It is clear that the bases that supported the Four-Hundred-Year Boom cannot continue to exist forever. Resource exhaustion and overloading of the environmental mechanisms to assimilate wastes are serious concerns with respect to future economic growth and prosperity. Increasing resource scarcity, ecosystem degradation, and the loss of environmental amenities also threaten to reduce overall quality-of-life.

In spite of all our advances in technology and the policy sciences, extrapolation of past trends remains the customary method of predicting future trends. Yet history is anything but linear. Instead it reveals patterns of growth, stagnation, decay, and abrupt changes in direction. Turning points are positively identified only in retrospect. During the Four-

Hundred-Year Boom, there have been periods of uncertainty and pessimism, economic stagnation and depression, and concern about overpopulation and resource exhaustion. The present time may be (and the technological optimists tell us it is) just another of these temporary pauses in our progress toward an age of plenty for all.

There are several possible solutions to the world's resource and environmental problems, but it is nearly impossible to evaluate them all in advance. New deposits of exhaustible resources may be found, and more efficient techniques of extraction may bring lower-grade deposits into production. Production processes and consumption habits may be modified to permit substitution of more plentiful resources for those that are approaching exhaustion. Ways may be found for economically utilizing things that now seem useless; those things would thus become valuable resources. Solar radiation from the sun and wind generated by the earth's magnetic forces represents renewable resources. Technological developments to harness these resources would not only allow substitution of these energy sources for non-renewable energy stocks, but could also provide the energy to permit more efficient recycling of non-renewable mineral resources.

Increasing scarcity and higher prices of resources may encourage conservation and making do with less of some kinds of resources. People may find it relatively easy to change wasteful habits when waste becomes much more costly. Similarly, increasing awareness and immediacy of the real costs of environmental degradation may encourage greater effort in preserving the quality of the environment. Finally, those whose thought processes are most deeply rooted in the Four-Hundred-Year Boom look to high technology and interplanetary travel for the solution. They dream of orbiting solar generators beaming electricity back to earth, and of mining and even colonizing the moon and the other planets. And, who knows, these may eventually occur.

A fairly well-balanced viewpoint may be something like the following. Although there is no need to be totally despondent about the future of humankind, neither is there reason to place our faith with those who believe technology will solve all problems. All too often, it seems, technology helps solve a recognized problem but at the cost of introducing totally new problems, such as nuclear waste disposal, whose solutions are not evident. Solutions will not come easily, and will require some combination of technology, resource substitution, conservation, and even rethinking our per capita consumption rates (e.g., how much happiness can money and consumption really buy?). Hard decisions will need to be made, as every feasible course of action will have its costs as well as its benefits. Some courses of action will preclude others. There will be agonizing trade-offs among goals, as the pursuit of some goals will involve the sacrifice of others. We will also have to deal continually with the constraints imposed by limited capital, whether it be natural capital, physical capital, financial capital or human capital.

But problems always provide opportunities for change. When facing tough problems at the local, national, and global levels, we often see motivated and talented people rise up to the challenge and develop innovative solutions nobody else has even dreamed of. The need to find solutions to pressing problems often spurs on great achievements from unlikely sources (most of the computer operating software in use today had its start in an ordinary neighborhood garage). In a society that values democratic government and individual decision-making, the roles of the technologist, the physicist, the chemist, and the engineer will be important but limited. Sound solutions will also require the services of management experts, social scientists, and policy analysts. Among these, the role of the natural resource and environmental economist will continue to increase in importance. Each person, including the one reading this page now, will also need to be engaged and involved as significant change requires all of us "ordinary citizens" to do our part. It is our hope that the following chapters will provide you, the reader, with knowledge, tools, and insight needed to make a difference in the way we use and manage our natural resources and the environment for our own good and the good of others now and in the future.

Questions for discussion

1. In what ways do the last 400 years represent an unusual period in the history of humanity? Is it reasonable to expect the trends of rapid technological innovation and increasing material wealth, established in the developed countries during that period, to continue (e.g., consider the growth of the Internet and World Wide Web in the 1990s)?
2. In what ways do you expect ethics, customs, and institutions developed during the agrarian, industrial, and technological revolutions to change in the future? (Your answer will surely be influenced by the way you answered question 1.)
3. How has the New Globalization Era affected your life so far? How do you expect globalization including the communications revolution to affect the balance of global economic and political power in the future? (e.g., think about how people obtain information about global happenings these days including the Internet and cellphones). How will these changes affect global trade, finance, and relations, and life in your hometown?
4. During any campaign for President of the United States, candidates from both major political parties (Democrats and Republicans) will say that they are for taking actions to keep the American economy growing, providing jobs and income to the American people. Why is this? What do you think would happen if a candidate came out with a "no economic growth" (or steady-state economy) platform?
5. Read the articles by Robert Ayres ("Limits to Growth Paradigm") and Nancy Stokey ("Are There Limits to Growth") which relate to economic growth, natural resources, and the environment. Can these two authors be talking about the same world? Why or why not?

Notes

1. For example, India gained its independence from England in 1947.
2. Ezra J. Mishan (1967), *The Costs of Economic Growth*, New York: Praeger, p. 85.
3. William J. Baumol (1968), "On The Social Rate of Discount," *American Economic Review* **58**: 788–802.

Suggested reading: classic and contemporary

Ayres, R.U. (1996), "Limits to Growth Paradigm," *Ecological Economics* **19** (2): 117–34.
Howe, C.W. (1990), "The Social Discount Rate," *Journal of Environmental Economics and Management* **18**: S1–S2.
Meadows, D.H., J. Randers, and D.L. Meadows (2004), *Limits to Growth: The 30 Year Update*, White River Junction, VT: Chelsea Green Publishing Company.
Stokey, N.L. (1998), "Are There Limits to Growth?," *International Economic Review* **39**: 1–31.

2 Ecosystem goods and services: how does a healthy environment support economic production, consumption, and quality of life?

Since the Four-Hundred-Year Boom discussed in Chapter 1, we have come a long way in the world with respect to our understanding of the role of natural resources in economic production and consumption. We now realize that for much of history up to the present time, we have taken for granted the support that natural ecosystems and the environment provides us not only for life itself, but for enjoying a high quality of life. We now realize that we cannot ignore the interdependence between a healthy environment and a healthy economy. A healthy economy is dependent upon a healthy environment and the ecosystem goods and services it provides. In this chapter, we define the meaning of ecosystem goods and services (the "natural gifts of nature") and how a healthy environment provides these goods and services. A healthy environment is also dependent upon a healthy economy – one which uses and manages the environment and ecosystems wisely. We learn in this chapter that the misuse and mismanagement of the environment and ecosystems may imperil their ability to continue providing us with valuable ecosystem goods and services. We show at the end of the chapter that the interdependencies between a healthy environment and a healthy economy are important to each one of us because natural capital and ecosystem goods and services are essential for the production of consumer goods and services (e.g., food, clothes, cars, computers) which give us utility or satisfaction. Moreover, we enjoy natural capital and ecosystem goods and services directly such as when we breathe in clean, crisp air and enjoy the feeling of warm sunshine on our faces.

Ecosystem structure

Ecosystem goods and services, of course, come from ecosystems. In this book, an ecosystem is defined generally as a community of plants, animals, and people interacting in a given physical environment with each other and the environment and operating as a unit. The boundaries of a particular ecosystem, like the boundaries of a particular economy, are rather vague and varied. An ecosystem, like an economy, can be relatively small and local, or relatively large and global. Whatever boundary we put around different ecosystems, these ecosystems share common characteristics related to ecosystem structure, ecosystem processes and functions, and ecosystem goods and services.

Ecosystem structure refers to the components of an ecosystem and the connections between these components. Ecosystem components are divided into two basic categories: biotic components and abiotic components. Abiotic components of ecosystems are the non-living components of ecosystems including energy, chemicals, and physical features. Chemicals in ecosystems include inorganic chemicals and organic chemicals. Major inorganic chemicals include H_2O (water), O_2 (molecular oxygen), C (carbon), N (nitrogen), CO_2 (carbon dioxide), and various minerals. Organic chemicals include proteins, carbohydrates, lipids, and vitamins. Major physical features in ecosystems include temperature, humidity, wind, and light.

Energy in an ecosystem and its surroundings is governed by the laws of thermodynamics. The first law of thermodynamics (first law of energy, law of conservation of energy) states that energy is neither created nor destroyed as it moves through a system and its surroundings – rather, it just changes from one form to another. For example, suppose we define your college campus as the system of interest. Energy comes into the campus every day in the form of food for students, fossil fuels to power campus vehicles, and electricity to light the buildings. This energy then changes form as it moves through the system and its surroundings. For example, when a student eats an apple and later walks across campus, the energy stored in the apple is transformed to kinetic energy in the student's body that is used to power the walk across campus. As the student walks across campus, this kinetic energy is transformed into waste heat that flows out from the student's body in to the surrounding atmosphere. According to the first law of thermodynamics, the amount of energy entering the campus (A) plus the amount of energy used on campus (B) plus waste heat flowing into the atmosphere from the campus (C) is a constant amount (e.g., A + B + C = Energy Constant).

The second law of thermodynamics states that any system plus its surroundings tends spontaneously towards disorder or randomness. Relative randomness is measured by entropy; something with more entropy is more disorderly. For example, an apple before it is eaten by a student has relatively low entropy (e.g., is more orderly) as compared to the ultimate waste heat produced after the student burns off the calories in the apple walking across campus. The waste heat generated from the student's body during the walk across campus has relatively high entropy (e.g., is more disorderly). An implication of the second law of thermodynamics is that we must expend effort and energy to keep things orderly. For example, your professor's office will tend to get messier and more disorderly unless he or she expends effort and energy trying to keep it tidy and orderly (a never-ending battle against the second law of thermodynamics).

Biotic components are the living components of ecosystems. These biotic components include producers, macroconsumers, and microconsumers. In the ecologic systems, natural producers act much like human producers in economic systems. Natural producers, termed autotrophs (literally "self-nourishing"), naturally manufacture food from simple inorganic substances (e.g., H_2O, CO_2, nitrates) through photosynthesis powered by solar energy. Examples of natural producers include all forms of plant life and some types of bacteria. In ecologic systems, macroconsumers, termed heterotrophs, are organisms that cannot manufacture their own food and therefore must consume the organic compounds found in other organisms (e.g., plants and animals). Primary macroconsumers are composed of herbivores or plant-eaters such as deer, ducks, grass carp, and people who are vegetarians. Secondary macroconsumers include carnivores or meat-eaters such as mountain lions, eagles, and sharks; and omnivores who are both plant- and meat-eaters such as grizzly bears, crows, catfish, and the majority of people on Planet Earth. In ecologic systems, microconsumers, termed saprotrophs or decomposers, break down complex compounds in dead plants and animals, releasing chemicals for reuse by natural producers.

Some of the major connections between abiotic and biotic components of an ecosystem are illustrated by the food chain (food web). In a simple food chain, natural producers start the chain by combining solar energy, water, and simple inorganic chemicals to manufacture more complex organic compounds such as carbohydrates found in living plants. Herbivores such as deer eat these plants and turn the carbohydrates into other complex organic compounds such as proteins. These proteins (and other chemicals) are then transferred to carnivores (e.g., mountain lion) and omnivores (e.g., grizzly bear) when they eat the deer. When the mountain lion or grizzly bear dies, microorganisms decompose the body, releasing chemicals back into the ecosystem which can then again be taken up by natural producers back at the beginning of the chain.

Ecosystem processes
We identify two major ecosystem processes: (1) the one-way flow of energy through the system; and (2) the cycling of chemicals in the system.

One-way energy flow
Solar energy is the ultimate, external source of energy powering everything that goes on in an ecosystem. For example, solar energy provides the ultimate, external source of energy powering the food chain or web. This energy changes form as it moves through the food chain or web, ultimately leaving the chain or web as relatively high-entropy waste heat. This waste heat is not reused – it is lost forever to the system. But as long as the sun shines this is not a worry since more relatively lower entropy solar energy is provided to the system each and every day.

The flow of energy through all of the planet Earth's ecosystems and their surroundings follows a global atmospheric energy balance illustrated by Figure 2.1. As the sun burns, it sends a flow of solar radiation (solar energy) towards the earth. For a given time period (e.g., hour, day, week, month, year) this flow represents 100 percent of the solar

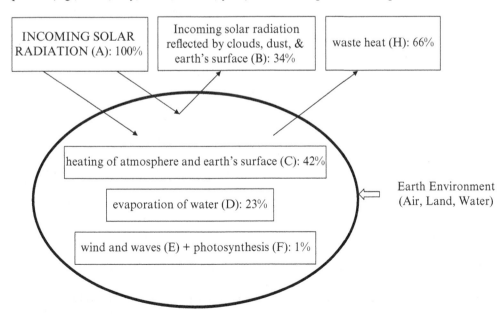

Figure 2.1   The global energy balance

radiation from the sun which reaches the earth's atmosphere (A). Some of this incoming radiation is reflected back into outer space by clouds, dust, and other particulates in the atmosphere, and the earth's surface – call this "percent reflected" (B). Some of the incoming solar radiation is used to heat the atmosphere and earth's surfaces – call this "percent used for heating" (C). Some is used to evaporate water – call this "percent used for evaporation" (D). Some is used to power wind and waves – call this "percent used for wind and waves" (E). Finally, some is used to power photosynthesis – call this "percent used for photosynthesis" (F). After being used in different forms for heating (C), evaporation (D), wind and waves (E), and photosynthesis (F), the original energy from the sun which was not reflected back into the atmosphere (B) leaves the earth's ecosystems and their surroundings and goes back into outer space as waste heat (H). Following the first law of thermodynamics, in the global atmospheric energy balance, A = B + H and C + D + E + F = H.

Figure 2.1 and the global atmospheric energy balance illustrate the fundamental difference between a closed system and an open system. In a closed system, only energy is exchanged between the system and its surroundings. The "earth environment," defined as the earth itself and the atmosphere which surrounds it,[1] is an example of a closed system since only energy is exchanged between the earth environment and its surroundings in outer space (except for the occasional meteor). In an open system, both matter and energy are exchanged between the system and its surroundings. An example of an open system is a forest ecosystem since trees, for instance, absorb CO_2 from the surrounding atmosphere and emit O_2 back into the atmosphere. Another example of an open system is a lake ecosystem since H_2O, for instance, enters the lake from the surrounding atmosphere in the form of rain and goes back into the atmosphere in the form of water vapor when water evaporates from the lake. The earth's terrestrial and aquatic ecosystems are all open systems. There have been attempts to engineer artificial closed ecosystems on the earth's surface and under water.[2]

Chemical cycles
The major chemical cycles in ecosystems include the following: carbon and oxygen cycle, phosphorous cycle, nitrogen cycle, sulfur cycle, and hydrologic cycle.

Carbon and oxygen cycle   Carbon (C) is the basic building block for plant, animal, and human life – all are "carbon-based" organisms. Plants, animals, and humans all also depend on oxygen (O_2) for survival. The cycling of carbon and oxygen in ecosystems is ultimately powered by solar energy. In photosynthesis, plants combine carbon dioxide (CO_2), water (H_2O), and solar energy to produce sugars, oxygen, and energy. In cellular respiration, animals and humans combine sugars and oxygen (O_2) to produce carbon dioxide (CO_2), water (H_2O) and energy. Carbon–oxygen–hydrogen compounds (e.g., sugars) pass through the food chain or web in ecosystems via herbivores, carnivores, and omnivores. In the food chain, some of the carbon and oxygen stored in organic compounds is returned to the environment in the form of CO_2 and H_2O via cellular respiration. When a large organism such as a plant or animal dies and is decomposed by microorganisms, more of the CO_2 and H_2O stored within the plant or animal is returned to the environment where it can be taken up again by plants to produce more carbon–oxygen–hydrogen compounds which can then be taken up again by animals and humans.

Not all carbon and oxygen is recycled in the relatively short-term cycle described above. Some carbon and oxygen from decomposing plants and animals is converted by relatively long-term geologic processes into rocks (e.g., carbonate rock formations such as limestone) and minerals (e.g., coal, oil, natural gas) stored in the earth's crust. When coal, oil and natural gas enter economic systems, they are termed fossil fuels. The "fossil" part of this term derives from the fact that they come from fossilized remains of plants and animals. The "fuel" part is derived from the fact that coal, oil and natural gas and their processed derivatives (e.g., gasoline) are burned as fuel in engines and other machinery found throughout our economic system (e.g., planes, trains, automobiles, electricity power plants, home furnaces).

When fossil fuels are burned, CO_2 stored in these minerals is released back into the environment. The release of CO_2 from fossil fuel burning is at the center of recent concern and debate over global climate change. According to the theory of human-induced global climate change, the rapid increase in fossil fuel burning since the industrial revolution in the late 1800s has elevated CO_2 levels in the atmosphere to a point sufficient to induce non-marginal changes in global climate. The primary mechanism for change is what is known commonly as the "greenhouse effect" theory. According to the greenhouse effect theory, elevated levels of CO_2 increase the capacity of the atmosphere to retain solar energy in the form of waste heat for longer periods of time before this waste heat eventually emanates into outer space (e.g., recall the global atmospheric energy balance illustrated in Figure 2.1). An expected effect of keeping waste heat in the atmosphere for longer periods of time is to raise mean annual global atmospheric temperatures – as in an artificial greenhouse. The knowledgeable gardeners out there know that an artificial greenhouse used to grow plants stays warm by trapping heat from solar radiation entering the greenhouse through many window panels.

The theory of human-induced climate change has many proponents in the academic, political, and even entertainment arenas. There are, however, also skeptics within the same arenas. In the academic arena at least, most skeptics do not deny that atmospheric CO_2 levels have risen over the past century or so and that real evidence of global climate changes exists. The skepticism and debate center primarily on the causes of global climate change and the relative effects of different causes. For example, one alternative to the human-induced theory of global climate change is the theory of nature-induced global climate change. According to this theory, the primary causes of global climate change are changes in natural processes which affect the carbon–oxygen cycle and the global atmospheric energy balance. These natural causes include periodic changes in the amount of solar radiation generated by the sun, periodic changes in the earth's orbit around the sun, and periodic natural changes in the amount of CO_2 absorbed by the earth's vast saltwater oceans. It should be noted that the theory of human-induced global climate change and the theory of nature-induced global climate change are not mutually exclusive and one can accept tenets from both theories without jettisoning one's intellectual (and social) sense and sensibilities. For example, most climate scientists agree that global climate change is a result of both natural and human causes. Where scientists and others differ is with respect to the relative strength of various natural and human causes.[3] Much rides on this apparently benign difference of opinion. Because reducing emissions of greenhouse gases (GHGs) including CO_2 on a global scale would be enormously expensive, failure to get it right could cause massive harm if it turns out that we have underestimated the damage from GHG accumulation and enacted an inadequate policy response, or if it turns out that we have overestimated the benefits of reducing GHG emissions and implemented an overblown policy response.

At any rate, there seems little doubt that the earth's global climate is undergoing change. This really should not be surprising since the long-term geologic evidence indicates that the earth's global climate has never been static – that is, it is always changing (for one reason or another). Recent scientific studies suggest that, on average across the globe, mean surface temperatures have risen 0.35°F from the 1910s to the 1940s and 0.55°F from the 1970s to the mid-2000s. The same studies suggest that global atmospheric temperatures up to 10 km from the earth's surface have risen at a slightly greater rate as compared to surface temperatures. However, recent past and projected future climate change trends are not uniform across the globe: some regions of the world have experienced cooler temperatures in recent years and some are projected to become cooler in the future, even under the assumption of increasing global mean temperatures.[4]

As indicated in the discussion above, human activities affect global climate change through impacts on the carbon and oxygen cycle. Burning of fossil fuels is a major contributor to releasing more CO_2 into the atmosphere, primarily from terrestrial sources of stored carbon (e.g., coal deposits, oil deposits, trees). Human activities can also help to remove CO_2 from the atmosphere, with one of the primary means being increasing the storage of carbon in terrestrial plants. For example, taking actions to protect "green space" including farmland from development (e.g., see Chapter 17) and managing forests in a sustainable manner following an optimal harvest and replanting schedule (e.g., see Chapter 15) helps to remove CO_2 in the atmosphere through carbon sequestration in plants via photosynthesis. Farms, forests, and other green space areas thus act as "carbon sinks" helping to counteract the greenhouse effect.

Phosphorous cycle   In the phosphorous cycle, plants absorb inorganic phosphates found in the soil and water bodies and convert these simple inorganic compounds into more complex organic phosphates. These organic phosphate compounds are then passed along the food chain through herbivores, carnivores, and omnivores. Some organic phosphates are directly returned to the soil and water bodies through animal wastes (manure). When plants and animals die and are decomposed by microorganisms, stored organic phosphates are broken down and returned to the soil and water bodies as inorganic phosphates, which are then available to be taken up again by plants. Some of the phosphates stored in animals, however, temporarily (where "temporary" may be a long time) leave the cycle and are deposited in ocean-floor sediments in the form of fossilized animal bones and teeth and phosphate rocks. Eventually, geologic forces result in some of the phosphates in phosphate rock and fossil deposits being dissolved and returned to the soil and water bodies in the form of inorganic phosphates.

Humans interact with the phosphorous cycle in many ways. For example, seabird waste deposits (guano) and phosphate rock and fossil deposits are mined to obtain phosphates for use in the manufacturing of artificial fertilizers and detergents. When these artificial fertilizers are used in human activities (e.g., applying fertilizers to agricultural crops, golf courses and home lawns, and washing clothes and linens with detergents) dissolved inorganic phosphates are returned to the soil and water bodies. Phosphates in fertilizers applied to plants in excessive quantities may end up washing into surface water bodies (e.g., lakes and rivers) and leaching into ground water (e.g. aquifers). Phosphates in detergents and human wastes also re-enter surface and groundwater through home septic tank systems and municipal waste-treatment plants.

Additional phosphates entering surface water bodies act as nutrients for aquatic plants and algae which in warm water may cause an "algal bloom." As the elevated population of algae dies and decomposes, much oxygen is taken out of the water, say, in a lake or pond. This reduction of dissolved oxygen in the lake or pond may then result in relatively large fish and shellfish kills. Excessive aquatic plant and algae growth in a surface water body due to large influxes of nutrients into the water body from human sources is known as cultural or anthropocentric eutrophication which causes the premature "aging" of the surface water body.[5] Cultural or anthropocentric eutrophication was first widely studied as a water quality problem in the US in the 1960s and was recognized as a water pollution problem by the US Environmental Protection Agency in the 1970s.

In order to counteract negative impacts from human activities on the phosphorous cycle, humans can take actions to reduce emission of phosphates into surface and water bodies. For example, farmers, golf course managers, and homeowners should apply fertilizers to crops, grass and other plants following a "nutrient budget" which provides only as much additional nutrients as plants need and are able to absorb – this not only makes ecologic sense, but it makes good economic sense since application of excess fertilizers which end up washing into lakes or rivers or leaching into aquifers is a waste of money. Municipalities and homeowners can also work to ensure that sewage treatment plants and home septic tank systems are in good operating order. Residential and commercial users (e.g., hotels, laundry services) of laundry detergent can also use phosphate-free detergents or simply wash clothes and linens less. For example, most hotels these days give guests the option of reusing linens over a multiple-day stay rather than using fresh linen every day (this also saves the hotel money and may help to keep lodging room fees down).

Nitrogen cycle   In the nitrogen cycle, nitrogen in the atmosphere is deposited into soil and surface water bodies. For example, lightning strikes in the atmosphere convert gaseous nitrogen to nitric oxide (NO) and nitrogen dioxide (NO_2). Nitrogen dioxide may then react with water vapor in the atmosphere to form nitric acid (HNO_3) which then falls into soil and surface water bodies as a constituent of "acid rain." Inorganic nitrogen compounds deposited from the atmosphere into soil and surface water bodies are converted by nitrogen-fixing bacteria to organic nitrates which can be taken up by plants. Nitrogen-fixing bacteria live in the soil or on the root nodules of plants called legumes. Legumes include many agricultural crops such as alfalfa, beans, peanuts, and peas. Other soil bacteria convert nitrates in the soil to gaseous nitrogen which is released back into the atmosphere. The nitrates taken up by plants are passed through the food chain in protein molecules by herbivores, carnivores and omnivores. When plants and animals die and decompose, nitrogen compounds, for example in the form of ammonia (NH_3), are returned to the soil and water bodies. Ammonia can be taken up by plants directly or is first converted by bacteria to nitrates which are then taken up by plants. Nitrogen compounds also enter into the soil and water through animal wastes.

Human activities contribute large amounts of nitrogen compounds to the soil, air, and water. For example, the burning of fossil fuels, wood or any other fuel releases nitric oxide (NO) into the atmosphere. In the atmosphere, NO combines with O_2 to form NO_2 which then combines with water vapors to form nitric acid (HNO_3) contributing to "acid rain" reaching the Earth's surface. High levels of acid rain can cause considerable ecologic and economic damage. For example, acid rain may result in lakes and rivers becoming "toxic" to aquatic life. The loss of fish life in a lake or river due to acid rain is an ecological loss which may result in economic losses, such as reductions in recreational and commercial fishing opportunities. Acid rain can also damage the exterior of buildings and cars and any other artificial structures exposed to the elements. Acid rain can also damage plants, including agricultural crops.

The overapplication of nitrogen fertilizers to agricultural fields, golf courses, and home lawns may result in run-off of nitrates into surface water bodies and leaching of nitrates into groundwater. Nitrates from human wastes are also released into surface and groundwater through municipal sewage treatment plants and home septic systems. Nitrates in drinking water are a health concern, especially for infants who may experience "blue baby syndrome" from ingesting high levels of nitrates. Since nitrogen is a plant nutrient, run-off of nitrates into lakes, ponds, and rivers may also contribute to the cultural or anthropocentric eutrophication problem discussed above under the phosphorous cycle.

What can be done to counteract the emission of more nitrogen into the nitrogen cycle by human activities? Driving our automobiles less, using more wind and solar power, and any other action which reduces fossil fuel burning will help to reduce NOx levels in the atmosphere.[6] Planting more legumes, including rotating legume crops with non-legume crops in agricultural operations, will help to fix and store more nitrogen in the soil and plants. Nitrogen fertilizers should be applied to agricultural crops, grass, and other plants following a "nutrient budget" where the amount of additional nutrient added is only as much as is needed and can be absorbed by the target plants – this is good for both the ecologic and economic "bottom line." Organic farming methods can also reduce the amount of excess nitrogen (and phosphorous) entering the soil and water from agricultural operations.

Sulfur cycle   In the sulfur cycle, volcanoes and hot springs send sulfur into the atmosphere in the form of hydrogen sulfide (H_2S) and sulfur dioxide (SO_2). Decomposition of organic matter in swamps, bogs, and marshes also adds hydrogen sulfide to the atmosphere (that's where that "rotten egg" odor comes from that you may smell around coastal wetlands areas and natural hot springs). In the atmosphere, sulfur dioxide (SO_2) reacts with oxygen (O_2) producing sulfur trioxide gas (SO_3).

SO_3 then reacts with water (H_2O) vapor producing sulfuric acid (H_2SO_4) droplets. SO_2 also reacts with other chemicals in the atmosphere, producing sulfate salts. Sulfuric acid and sulfate salts then fall to the earth's surface as part of acid rain. Plants and animals then take up sulfuric acid and sulfate salt compounds which are passed through the food chain. When plants and animals die and are decomposed by microorganisms, hydrogen compounds are returned to the atmosphere, completing the cycle.

One of the major ways in which human activities impact the sulfur cycle is by adding additional hydrogen sulfide (H_2S) and sulfur dioxide (SO_2) to the atmosphere through the burning of fossil fuels. For example, coal-fired and oil-fired electricity power plants are a major industrial source of SO_2 entering the atmosphere. Industrial petroleum refining (e.g., processing crude oil to produce gasoline) and industrial smelting (e.g., extracting metals such as copper, lead, nickel, silver, and zinc from sulfide ore deposits) also adds more SO_2 to the atmosphere. By adding more SO_2 to the atmosphere, fossil fuel burning, smelting, and other industrial processes contribute to acid rain deposition on the earth's surface. Sulfur compounds contribute in many ways to economic production and consumption including uses as a food preservative, bleaching agent for paper and clothes, solvent in various industrial processes, and medicine component.

Hydrologic cycle   In the hydrologic cycle, solar energy from the sun evaporates liquid water (H_2O) from surface water bodies (e.g., oceans, lakes, rivers) releasing water vapor into the atmosphere. Water vapor in the atmosphere then falls back to the earth's surface in the form of rain, snow, or hail. Some of the water reaching the earth's surface runs off into ponds, lakes, streams, and rivers and eventually into the oceans, and some percolates down through the soil into groundwater aquifers. This percolation of water into aquifers is referred to as "groundwater recharge" or "aquifer recharge." Some groundwater flows underground into ponds, lakes, streams, rivers, and the oceans. Thus, there is a natural inflow and outflow of water to and from groundwater and surface water bodies.

Human activity interacts with and affects the hydrologic cycle in many ways. For example, water is withdrawn from surface and groundwater bodies for municipal, industrial, agricultural, and recreational purposes (see Chapter 18). If withdrawals from a groundwater aquifer for human uses exceeds natural groundwater or aquifer recharge, water deposits in the aquifer can be exhausted. Likewise, surface water bodies (e.g., reservoirs) can be exhausted if outflows (withdrawals) for human use exceed natural inflows (e.g., rainfall, inflow from groundwater). Aquifer water deposits and surface water (e.g., reservoir) stocks can be renewed if natural inflow (recharge) increases and/ or human use withdrawals decrease. In some regions, excessive human use withdrawals from groundwater aquifers can increase salt levels in the water. For example, in coastal areas, excessive withdrawals of groundwater from aquifers can increase the underground flow of salt water from oceans into freshwater aquifers; this saltwater intrusion can result in groundwater becoming too salty for humans to drink, with obvious economic and social consequences (e.g., contaminated drinking water has adverse health effects and is a barrier to economic development).

In the United States, land use changes also have major impacts on the hydrologic cycle. For example, clearing vegetation from land and replacing it with impervious surfaces (e.g., concrete and asphalt surfaces) reduces groundwater or aquifer recharge, contributing to the depletion of groundwater supplies and to potential water shortage problems. More impervious surfaces also contribute to additional run-off of rainfall into surface water bodies, increasing flooding risks. These potential problems resulting from impervious surfaces can be mitigated by incorporating more green space into residential, commercial, and industrial developments and taking proactive measure to protect forests, farmland, and other green space (e.g., public parks) in a community (see Chapter 17).

Ecosystem functions
The broad ecosystem processes of energy transfer and chemical cycling discussed in the previous section support ecosystem functions. Ecosystem functions are defined as major

environmental tasks performed by ecosystems at the scale of a specific ecosystem type (e.g., forest, lake, ocean, river).[7] An example of an ecosystem function is natural development of wildlife. Natural development is defined as natural changes in the quantity and/or quality of biotic and abiotic components of ecosystems. Thus, natural development of wildlife refers to changes in the quantity and/or quality of wildlife in an ecosystem. Natural development can be viewed at different geographic and temporal scales. For example, transition of a single, individual deer from a fawn to a doe in a local forest would involve a relatively small geographic scale and short time-frame. Alternatively, we may consider natural development of a deer herd over relatively broader geographic and temporal scales such as how the entire deer herd in a given state (e.g., Georgia or Ohio) changes over 20 years. The term "natural development" also applies to abiotic ecosystem components; for example, changes in the quantity or quality of soil nutrients in a particular forest over a one-year time period, or changes in the quantity or quality of underground crude oil deposits across the planet Earth over thousands or millions of years.

Having defined natural development, we identify two major biotic functions of ecosystems, and three major abiotic functions. The biotic functions are: (1) natural plant development; and (2) natural development of wildlife. The abiotic functions are: (1) natural development of water supplies; (2) natural development of air supplies; and (3) natural development of minerals. Natural development of plants, wildlife, water, air, and minerals is governed by the one-way energy transfer and chemical cycling processes (including the food chain) discussed in the previous section. Through our intervention into and influence on energy transfer and chemical cycling processes, human activities can have negative or positive impacts on the natural development functions of ecosystems. For example, when human development starts to dominate a landscape or ecosystem, large predator species (e.g., wolves) tend to disappear. Without these large predator species, the food chain is altered and prey species such as deer may proliferate, resulting in deer herd overpopulation in a particular ecosystem. This overpopulation changes the natural development of wildlife function in the ecosystem – a greater quantity of deer in the herd, but with lower-quality attributes (e.g., smaller deer with more sickness). In this situation, the introduction of human deerhunters (predators) into the ecosystem may help to improve the natural development of wildlife function. For example, thinning out the herd and reducing overpopulation via human hunting may result in a lesser quantity of deer with higher-quality attributes (e.g., larger, healthier deer).

The biotic and abiotic functions of ecosystems are dynamic, making measurement of the direct biotic and abiotic outputs of these functions (e.g., wildlife populations, air quality in a particular airshed) difficult. In practice, scientists typically make static measurements of the direct biotic and abiotic outputs of ecosystem functions during a given developmental phase. A developmental phase is defined as the state of natural development during a specific period of time at a specific place (e.g., state of fish populations in a particular lake in the State of Georgia in the year 2010). During a particular developmental phase, the biotic and abiotic outputs of ecosystem functions have given quantity and quality dimensions. Quantitative measures of these dimensions give a snapshot of the quantity of and quality of biotic and abiotic components of an ecosystem at a given time and place (e.g., number, length, and weight of fish species in a particular lake at a given point in time).

Ecosystem goods and services

Ecosystem processes and functions generate ecosystem goods and services with given quantity and quality dimensions. Following Brown, Bergstrom, and Loomis,[8] we define ecosystem goods as generally tangible materials generated by ecosystem processes and functions such as trees, fish, birds, deer, coal, crude oil, and natural gas which are useful and valuable to humans. Also following Brown, Bergstrom and Loomis, we define ecosystem services as improvements in the condition or location of things which are useful and valuable to people. Thus, ecosystem services may improve the condition or location of ecosystem goods. For example, ecosystem services associated with the natural plant development function could include a landscape-level change in the quantity and quality of trees available at a National Forest for wildlife habitat, on-site photography, and/or harvest for commercial lumber.

A key feature of the definition of ecosystem goods and services in the paragraph above is the emphasis on materials and things generated by ecosystems which are useful and valuable to people, which is consistent with our definition of natural resources in Chapter 3. Thus, our definition of ecosystem goods and services, as with our definition of natural resources, is anthropocentric or human-centered. Anthropocentrism is in keeping with an economic perspective on the environment since, as a social science, the focus of economics is on human actions and values. The anthropocentric focus inherent in economic studies of the environment does not mean that other less human-centered perspectives or ethics are not important. We discuss some of the more common environmental ethics perspectives in Chapter 20.

Ecosystem goods and services may often be confused with ecosystem processes and functions. In this book, ecosystem processes refer to the one-way flow of energy through an ecosystem, and the chemical cycles discussed previously. Ecosystem functions refer to natural development of plants, wildlife, rocks and minerals, and air and water. Ecosystem processes and functions involve complex physical and biological relationships and interactions that work together for a particular ecological purpose such as nutrient cycling. Ecosystem goods and services are the specific results of ecosystem processes and functions that either directly or indirectly contribute to human well-being. For example, solar energy and nutrient cycling promote tree growth – trees can then be harvested as timber (an ecosystem good), or provide natural shade in cities, lowering surface temperatures (an ecosystem service). As another example, solar energy and the hydrologic cycle contribute to rainfall. Some of the rainfall flows into rivers and lakes resulting in natural surface water supplies (an ecosystem good). In a river or lake, living organisms such as shellfish and microorganisms act as filters to remove contaminants and purify water (an ecosystem service).

To some readers, the difference between ecosystem processes and functions on the one hand, and ecosystem goods and services on the other hand, may seem merely semantic. Indeed this may especially seem to be the case when the terms used to define an ecosystem good or service and the ecosystem processes and functions from which it is derived sound very similar. The important conceptual difference to keep in mind is that ecosystem goods and services are defined as goods and services which are useful and valuable to people (e.g., an economic perspective), whereas ecosystem processes and functions are useful and valuable to plants, animals, and the ecosystem itself (e.g., an ecologic perspective). From an ecologic perspective, ecosystem process and functions may be viewed

Table 2.1   Ecosystem goods and services

Ecosystem goods	Ecosystem services
Non-renewable	Air and water purification
Metal Minerals (e.g., iron, tungsten, silver, gold)	Nutrient translocation
Non-metallic Industrial Minerals (e.g., gypsum, limestone, clay)	Pollen dispersal (e.g., to aid in crop pollination)
Fossil Fuels (e.g., petroleum, coal, natural gas)	Seed dispersal (e.g., to aid in natural growth of plants)
Renewable	Pest and disease control and prevention
Wildlife (e.g., food, medicines, viewing)	Erosion control and prevention
Plants (e.g., food, fiber, fuel, medicines)	Flood control and prevention
Water (e.g., potable drinking water, crop irrigation water)	Protection from the sun's UV rays
Air (e.g., oxygen, clear visibility)	Flow energy (e.g., solar and wind energy)
Soil (e.g., prime agricultural soils)	Maintenance of chemical content in soil and water
Outdoor recreation resources and opportunities	Maintenance of temperature, moisture, light
Aesthetic enjoyment resources and opportunities	Maintenance of biodiversity
Spiritual contentment resources and opportunities	Environmental education and learning services

Sources: Based on: T.C. Brown, J.C. Bergstrom, and J.B. Loomis (2007), "Defining, Valuing and Providing Ecosystem Goods and Services," *Natural Resources Journal* **47** (2): 329–76; Wallace, K.J. (2007), "Classification of Ecosystem Services: Problems and Solutions," *Biological Conservation* **139** (3–4): 235–46.

as ends in themselves (e.g., the ends would include maintaining ecosystem health and integrity). However, from an economic perspective, ecosystem processes and functions are viewed as means to ends – the ends of interest are goods and services or "outputs" which are useful and valuable to people. Thus, within the economic perspective, eco-system processes and functions have instrumental value as inputs into the generation of outputs (ecosystem goods and services) which impact human utility or well-being (e.g., by entering into a person's utility function).

Table 2.1 lists ecosystem goods and services identified by Brown, Bergstrom and Loomis. Ecosystem goods are grouped in two broad categories: renewable and non-renewable. With continual use, the supply of non-renewable ecosystem goods will even-tually be used up over time, but with some potential for reuse through recycling (e.g., aluminum recycling). The supply of renewable ecosystem goods can be maintained at a constant level over time, even with continual use, provided the stock is managed in a sustained yield fashion (i.e., fish harvest equals fish growth).

The ecosystem goods listed in Table 2.1 are things we as society are generally aware of – a tree or a forest is hard to miss. However, the ecosystem services listed in Table 2.1 include life and quality-of-life services that the average person going about his or her daily life may be less aware of and take for granted. For example, it is hard for us to see and be aware of living organisms purifying water before it is piped into our homes where we drink it, cook with it, and wash in it. We may also be generally unaware of how a healthy ecosystem works to pollinate plants which we enjoy looking at (e.g., flowers) or the fruits and nuts of which we enjoy eating (e.g., apples, pecans, blueberries).

How do ecosystem goods and services affect utility?
As indicated in the above discussion, ecosystem goods and services are something of value to people which are generated from natural capital (*N*) through ecological processes and functions according to an ecological–economic (EE) transformation function:

$$E = r(N) \tag{2.1}$$

where, *E* = ecosystem good and services, *N* = natural capital (ecosystem structure), *r(.)* = EE transformation function. For example, solar radiation, hydrologic and nutrient cycling processes and functions in ecosystems generate naturally pure drinking water from energy and natural matter (e.g., precipitation, terrain, soils, aquifers, biota).

   In traditional neoclassical economic theory, the firm-level production function for a good or service, such as agricultural products, is typically shown by the standard production function:

$$Q = Q(D, K, L) \tag{2.2}$$

where *Q* = firm-level production of a good or service (e.g., production of corn by a single farm), *D* = land input (e.g., farm acres devoted to corn production), *K* = capital input (e.g., farm equipment devoted to corn production), and *L* = labor input (e.g., farm labor hours devoted to corn production). With our more modern understanding of ecosystem goods and services discussed in this chapter, as well as more modern formulations of different forms of capital, we can modify equation (2.2) to specify the following neoclassical/ecosystems production function:

$$Q = Q(E, H, B, F, S) \tag{2.3}$$

where, *E* = ecosystem goods and services (replacing *D* in equation 2.2), *H* = human capital (replacing *L* in equation 2.2), *B* = built capital, *F* = financial capital, and *S* = social capital (*B*, *F*, and *S* replace *K* in equation 2.2). Human capital (*H*) in equation 2.3 represents not just physical labor, but also the skills, knowledge, experience and ingenuity of laborers. Built capital (*B*) in equation 2.3 represents all constructed and manufactured goods used in production including equipment, buildings, and infrastructure (e.g., water distribution and treatment facilities, power production and distribution facilities, buildings, roads and bridges). Financial capital (*F*) in equation 2.3 represents cash and credit and other financial instruments (e.g., stocks, bonds, etc.) available to a producer. Social capital (*S*) in equation 2.3 represents the ability of people, say in a firm and community, to get along and work together to produce *Q*.

   There is another form of capital that we need to consider: *N* = natural capital which we introduced in equation 2.1. Natural capital (*N*) refers to biotic and abiotic components of ecosystems and the environment including living macroorganism (e.g., wildlife), microorganisms (e.g., bacteria), plants, solar radiation, air, water, rocks, minerals, and physical space. Substituting equation 2.1 into equation 2.3 gives the following neoclassical/neocapital production function:

$$Q = Q\left(r(N), H, B, F, S\right) \tag{2.4}$$

Equation 2.4 shows that firm-level production of goods and services is ultimately dependent on the quantity and quality of various forms of capital available to the producer, including natural capital. For example, to produce corn, a farmer must have access to natural capital of sufficient quantity and quality including solar energy (e.g., to power photosynthesis), air (e.g., CO_2 in air needed for photosynthesis, and air of the correct temperature needed to grow crops), water (e.g., for photosynthesis and nutrient transport), minerals (e.g., fertilizers), and physical space in which to plant and harvest crops.

Why do producers produce Q? (For instance, why does a farmer produce corn?) In a market economy, producers produce Q to meet consumers' needs and wants – that is, Q is used by consumers to generate utility or satisfaction. In traditional neoclassical economic theory, the manner in which a consumer generates utility from goods and services is typically shown by the standard utility function:

$$U = U(Q) \tag{2.5}$$

where, U = an individual's utility or satisfaction, and Q = produced goods and services. How do natural capital and ecosystem goods and services affect utility? One avenue is indirectly through the production of Q as shown in equations 2.3 and 2.4. However, natural capital and ecosystem goods and services can also directly affect a consumer's utility or satisfaction. For example, an individual consumer may enjoy solar radiation directly, as in enjoying a nice sunny day or sunbathing at the beach. An individual consumer may also directly enjoy breathing clean, crisp air, and a certain air temperature. An individual consumer can also gain utility or satisfaction by drinking directly from a cold, clear, and clean natural spring or stream.

With our better understanding of how natural capital and ecosystem goods and services directly and indirectly affect utility, we can modify equation 2.5 to specify a neoclassical/ecosystems utility function as:

$$U = U(E, Q(E, H, B, F, S)) \tag{2.6}$$

By substituting equation 2.1 into equation 2.6, we specify a neoclassical/neocapital utility function as:

$$U = U(r(N), Q(r(N), H, B, F, S)) \tag{2.7}$$

Equations 2.6 and 2.7 illustrate that natural capital and ecosystem goods and services affect an individual consumer's utility or satisfaction: (1) indirectly through the production of Q which then enters into the consumer's utility function; and (2) directly by entering into the consumer's utility function – or directly affecting utility such as enjoyment of a warm, sunny day.

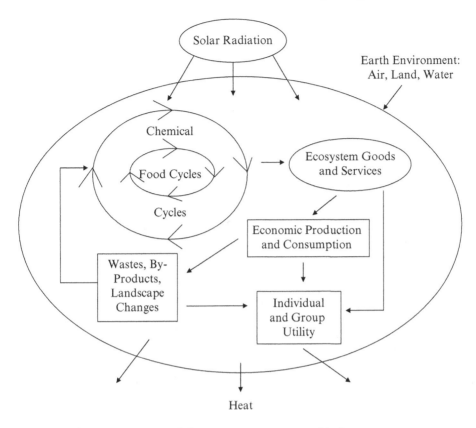

Figure 2.2 The environment and the economy: summary of linkages

The relationships and connections between the environment and the economy are summarized in Figure 2.2. The figure illustrates that economic production and consumption, and individual and group utility, are dependent upon ecosystem goods and services which are supported by chemical and food cycles. Ecosystem goods and services may also impact individual and group utility directly. The ability of chemical and food cycles to continue providing ecosystem goods and services may be impacted by wastes, by-products, and landscape changes. Wastes, by-products, and landscapes changes may also impact individual and group utility directly. The whole system is ultimately powered by energy from the sun. A fundamental proposition arising from the relationships and connections shown in Figure 2.2 is that a healthy economy is based on a healthy environment, and a healthy environment is based on a healthy economy. More insight on this fundamental proposition, including the role of ethics and ethical systems, is provided in subsequent chapters of this book.

Questions for discussion

1. Do you believe that a healthy economy is dependent upon a healthy environment? Why or why not? Do you believe that a healthy environment is dependent upon a healthy economy? Why or why not?
2. Distinguish between an ecosystem good and an ecosystem service. Why, in general, is it more difficult

to recognize ecosystem services? (For instance, why would we tend to take ecosystem services more for granted as compared to ecosystem goods?)

3. Describe some ways through use (misuse) and management (mismanagement) that people can positively or negatively impact the provision of ecosystem goods and services from the environment.
4. Describe the relationship between natural capital and ecosystem goods and services? What is an ecologic–economic transformation function? Give an example.
5. How do natural capital and ecosystem goods and services directly and indirectly affect your own utility or satisfaction and quality of life?

Notes

1. The atmosphere is a layer of gases surrounding planet Earth containing approximately 78 percent nitrogen, 21 percent oxygen, 1 percent argon, 0.04 percent carbon dioxide and trace amounts of other gases; it also contains a variable amount of water vapor, averaging about 1 percent.
2. For example, Biosphere 2 is a University of Arizona research project attempting to establish a land-based, artificial closed-system environment with human occupants.
3. For a more detailed discussion of natural and human causes of global climate change, see United States Environmental Protection Agency, "Climate Change," http://www.epa.gov/climatechange/.
4. Intergovernmental Panel on Climate Change (2007), *Climate Change 2007: The Physical Science Basis*, Cambridge, UK and New York, USA: Cambridge University Press.
5. Natural eutrophication is a process in which a surface water body such as a lake or pond gradually ages, becomes more ecologically productive, and eventually "dies out," converting to a terrestrial ecosystem following ecologic succession.
6. NOx is a generic designation for a group of different gases made up of nitrogen and oxygen such as nitric oxide (NO) and nitrogen dioxide (NO_2).
7. For an earlier presentation of the ecosystem function concepts discussed in this section, see John C. Bergstrom and John B. Loomis (1999), "Economic Dimensions of Ecosystem Management," in *Integrating Social Sciences with Ecosystem Management*, ed. H. Ken Cordell and John C. Bergstrom, Champaign, IL: Sagamore Publishing Co., Chapter 11.
8. Much of the discussion of ecosystem goods and services in this section is a summary of a more complete and comprehensive discussion provided in Thomas C. Brown, John C. Bergstrom, and John B. Loomis (2007), "Defining, Valuing and Providing Ecosystem Goods and Services," *Natural Resources Journal* **47** (2): 329–76.

Suggested reading: classic and contemporary

Boyd, J. and S. Banzhaf (2007), "What are Ecosystem Services? The Need for Standardized Environmental Accounting Units," *Ecological Economics* **63**: 616–26.

Daily, G.C. (1997), "Introduction: What are Ecosystem Services?," *Nature's Services: Societal Dependence on Natural Ecosystems*, Washington, DC: Island Press.

England, R.W. (2000), "Natural Capital and the Theory of Economic Growth," *Ecological Economics* **34**: 425–31.

Heal, G.M., E.B. Barbier, K.J. Boyle, A.P. Covich, S.P. Gloss, C.H. Hershner, J.P. Hoehn, C.M. Pringle, S. Polasky, K. Segerson, and K. Shrader-Frechette (2005), *Valuing Ecosystem Services: Toward Better Environmental Decision-Making*, Washington, DC: National Academies Press.

Millennium Ecosystem Assessment (2005), *Ecosystems and Human Well-Being: Synthesis Report*, Washington, DC: Island Press.

Wallace, K.J. (2007), "Classification of Ecosystem Services: Problems and Solutions," *Biological Conservation* **139**: 235–46.

3 Resource supply and scarcity: how do we define, measure, and monitor natural resource supply and scarcity?

Some things seem obvious. Here are a few examples. Considering the amount of mineral raw materials we use and how little we recycle, reserves must be declining at an alarming rate. The continuing loss of farmland to urban and similar uses is surely reflected in increasing scarcity of food. Air and water pollution is still a pervasive problem across the globe, and getting worse. With each passing year, opportunities for experiencing "wild" natural environments untrammeled by human contact diminish. All in all, our voracious appetite for raw materials and environmental services is making them increasingly scarce and expensive. A simple projection of population growth, per capita consumption trends and environmental degradation patterns suggests that future generations will have fewer opportunities than we have today. One obvious solution is to rely more on nature's renewable resources. Surely, because they reproduce themselves and use the sun as their fundamental energy source, the raw materials produced by farms, forests, and fisheries are exempt from the increasing scarcity and rising costs that beset the mineral resources.

As it turns out, none of the above statements is completely true. Each is wrong or, at best, highly contentious. Nevertheless, the truth about the concerns raised in the previous paragraph is quite elusive. It is not easy to get to the bottom of these issues. Evidence that would resolve these questions is not easy to obtain, and evidence is meaningless without a conceptual basis for its interpretation. In the next section of this chapter, the concepts of scarcity and exhaustion are introduced and given economic definitions. The distinctions among resource types – exhaustible, flow, fund, and biological – are essential to analyzing resource scarcity issues. The history of economic thought regarding scarcity is briefly reviewed so as to show how economics has influenced and been influenced by the events of the day. With these concepts as background, we then turn to the evidence about resource use and consumption, reserves, raw materials prices, and resource costs. Two conclusions emerge: first, resource scarcity is an economic concept, and the economic evidence is more informative than are the data confined to physical quantities; and second, even the economic evidence can be confusing and occasionally contradictory. Nevertheless, the evidence for impending catastrophe is thin and weak. There are forces at work mitigating resource scarcity, many of which operate through price signals that encourage conservation, substitution, and technical innovation.

Natural resource and scarcity concepts

A natural resource is something that is useful and valuable in the condition in which we find it. In the terminology of the previous chapter, natural resources include natural capital and ecosystem goods and services. As discussed in the previous chapter, a natural resource (natural capital, ecosystem good or service) in its raw or unmodified state may be an input into the process of producing something of economic value, or it may enter consumption processes directly and thus acquire economic value. "Natural resource" is a dynamic concept, and the possibility always exists that changes in information, technology, and relative scarcity may make an economically valuable resource out of something that previously had no economic value. Things that are produced under human guidance in processes that combine resources, capital, technology, and/or labor, are not themselves called natural resources, although natural resources are always among the inputs used to produce them. For example, copper ore is a natural resource, but copper wire is not.

Scarcity (of anything) means simply that the amount available is limited relative to the amount demanded. Any resource with a positive explicit or implicit price must be scarce: if its availability were unlimited relative to demand, it would be free. Note, however, that the argument does not work in the opposite direction. Some scarce natural resources are unpriced because there are no functioning markets in which to trade them.

It is simple to define what is scarce, as opposed to what is not scarce. The concepts of "more scarce" and "less scarce" are more difficult. Most good economists will tell you that if all markets functioned well, a rise in the price of X relative to other goods would indicate that X had become relatively scarcer. The idea is that an indicator of relative scarcity should summarize the sacrifices required to obtain the good concerned. However, as we shall see, this fairly simple concept is not easily implemented in the form of a universally reliable scarcity indicator.

Natural resources are multi-attribute and thus have quantity, quality, time, and space dimensions. Air is a useful example. It is available in most places in such vast quantities relative to demand that it is essentially a free good. Yet in many places, the quality of air is impaired to some degree, and thus air of better quality has a positive value (that is, individuals and/or society are willing to spend money to obtain air of higher quality). In certain small, enclosed places – for example, manned space capsules – air (or its oxygen component) is very scarce and is highly valued. In the open environment, air quality may change as time passes. In a space capsule or station, the flow of oxygen is strictly limited by the amount initially available and the rate at which stocks can be replenished; the exhaustion of the oxygen supply as time passes is possible. As this example suggests, the concept of scarcity is not confined to the quantity dimension but pertains to each of the dimensions of resources.

Natural resource classification
When considering human use and management, natural resources are generally classified as fund resources or flow resources. A fund resource is a resource which for a given time period exists as a fixed stock with given quantity and quality dimensions. A fund resource is analogous, say, to a monetary college fund set up by Joe College-Student's parents at a local bank to cover his tuition, fees, and other expenses for a certain time period (e.g., semester, school year). The parents deposit money into the fund in the bank at the beginning of the time period; thus, on day one of the semester the college fund exists as a fixed stock of money of a certain amount. During the time period (e.g., semester, school year), Joe makes withdrawals from the fund to pay his college bills and cover his living expenses. In the case of a natural fund resource, resources are deposited into the fund by ecosystem processes and functions. For example, as mentioned above, over

long periods of time the carbon and oxygen cycle deposits coal, crude oil, and natural gas into natural storage areas in the ground where they are "banked." Humans then tap into these natural storage areas and make withdrawals from the natural resource fund.

Fund resources are divided into exhaustible, non-renewable resources and exhaustible, renewable resources. An exhaustible, non-renewable resource is characterized by a depletable supply that cannot be renewed within a meaningful human time horizon. For example, suppose Joe College-Student's parents set up a monetary college fund of $X to cover Joe's tuition, fees and other expenses for his entire undergraduate college education and say to Joe: "Once the $X is gone, that's the end of your college fund and you pay the rest." Joe's college fund then would be exhaustible and non-renewable. The same goes for natural resources such as coal, crude oil and natural gas. Once we use up the natural deposits of these resources, they are gone and cannot be renewed within a meaningful human time horizon (the carbon and oxygen cycle, for example, is continually producing more crude oil, but over thousands or millions of years, which doesn't do current generations or even their great, great-grandchildren much good).

An exhaustible, renewable resource is characterized by a depletable supply that can be renewed in a relatively short time period. For example, suppose Joe College-Student's parents set up a monetary college fund of $Y per semester to cover Joe's tuition, fees and other expenses for his undergraduate college education and say to Joe: "You can make withdrawals from the fund for the semester and we will add more funds at the beginning of each semester based on your costs and expenditures the previous semester." In this case, Joe's college fund is exhaustible and renewable. He can deplete the fund one semester, but it will be replenished the next semester. A forest of pine trees is an example of an exhaustible, renewable resource. We can make withdrawals of trees from the forest, thereby depleting the forest, but ecosystem processes and functions (e.g., natural plant development) will add trees back to the forest through natural regeneration. Humans can also supplement the natural regeneration of trees by planting tree seeds and saplings.

A flow resource is a resource which for a given time period exists as a continuous stream with given quantity and quality dimensions. Flow resources are divided into non-storable flow resources and storable flow resources. A non-storable flow resource is a resource which cannot be captured and stored for future use, given present technology. Wind and solar radiation are examples of non-storable flow resources since we cannot capture the wind or solar radiation itself, store it, and then release it for later use. We can convert wind and solar radiation to electricity and then store the electricity in batteries, but this is not the same as storing the resource itself (e.g., capturing and storing wind in a box). A storable flow resource is a resource which can be captured and stored for future use, given present technology. Rainfall is an example of a storable flow resource since we can capture and store rainfall in reservoirs for future use. The classification of resources into exhaustible, non-renewable fund resources, exhaustible, renewable fund resources, non-storable flow resources, and storable flow resources is imperfect. There are overlaps, and some kinds of resources do not fit very well into any category. Fossil fuels are usually classified as exhaustible, non-renewable resources and for good reason. Yet the carbon and oxygen cycle is in fact continually adding to the Earth's store of fossil fuels. Why, then, are they not called exhaustible, renewable resources (or even flow resources)? The answer is that deposits of fossil fuels occur over geological time, whereas the rate of withdrawal is limited only by capital, technology, and human restraint. It is the human concept of time that makes the fossil fuels exhaustible and non-renewable for all relevant policy purposes. The supply of the different types of fund and flow resources from an economic perspective is discussed in more detail in the following sections.

Exhaustible, non-renewable resource supply
The best examples of exhaustible, non-renewable resources are mineral deposits which are classified as ecosystem goods in Table 2.1. For all intents and purposes, they can be withdrawn and used up, but no more can be made or recreated. If we use S to denote the stock, H to denote the amount extracted to provide raw materials, and the subscript $\tau = 0, \ldots, t, \ldots, \infty$ to indicate time, the current stock of an exhaustible, non-renewable resource can be expressed as:

$$S_t = S_0 - \sum_{\tau=1}^{t-1} H_\tau \qquad (3.1)$$

That is, the current stock at time t, S_t, is equal to the initial stock, S_0, minus the sum of all previous withdrawals through time $t - 1$.

Although the notion of a given stock is valid, not all of that stock has been identified. If $\hat{S}$ indicates the known stock, discovery can add to known stocks just as extraction subtracts from them. Thus:

$$\hat{S}_t = \hat{S}_0 - \sum_{\tau=1}^{t-1} (H_\tau - R_\tau) \qquad (3.2)$$

where $R\tau$ is the amount discovered in period τ. If we introduced recycling, the known stock can be extended by both discovery and recycling, so that:

$$\hat{S}_t = \hat{S}_0 - \sum_{\tau=1}^{t-1} (H_\tau - R_\tau - C_\tau) \qquad (3.3)$$

where $C\tau$ is the amount recycled in period τ and is limited by the amount of resources previously used but not recycled.

The quantity and time dimensions of exhaustible, non-renewable resources have been addressed in these equations. Recognition that these resources are seldom homogenous introduces the quality and space/place dimensions. Quantity is measurable, usually in terms of mass or volume. Quality is often measurable in terms of chemical composition (for example, mineral content of ores, or ash content of coal) but may also have more nearly intangible aspects, such as aesthetic properties. The distinction between the concepts of quantity and quality is simply that quantity is usually unidimensional (that is, mass or volume), whereas quality is multi-attribute and may refer to any dimension or composite of dimensions (for example, chemical composition, physical structure, and aesthetic attributes) that affects the value of the resource in use. Resource quality will be perceived differently for different uses, and the less tangible (for example, aesthetic) aspects of quality will be perceived differently by different users.

The space/place dimension is the location of the deposit (which influences extraction costs) and its relationship to processing facilities, transportation, and markets (which influence the profits that can be made from exploiting that deposit). Although the equations address the time dimension – especially as it relates to the timing of discovery and withdrawal – there is another aspect of time. Even in the absence of human interven-

Cumulative Production	IDENTIFIED			UNDISCOVERED	
	Demonstrated		Inferred	Probability Range	
	Measured	Indicated		Hypothetical	Speculative
ECONOMIC	Reserves		Inferred Reserves		
MARGINALLY ECONOMIC	Marginal Reserves		Inferred Marginal Reserves		
SUB-ECONOMIC	Demonstrated subeconomic resources		Inferred subeconomic resources		

Decreasing Degree of Feasibility (vertical axis, downward)

Decreasing Degree of Geologic Assurance ⟶

Source: US Bureau of Mines and US Geological Survey (1980), Circular 831. Based on McKelvey's classification system, V.E. McKelvey (1972), "Mineral Resource Estimates and Public Policy," *American Scientist* **60** 1: 32–40.

Figure 3.1   Classification of mineral resources

tion, the natural processes of entropic degradation will change the quantity and quality dimensions over time.

Reserves

The concepts of "known stock," S, and discovery (already introduced) hint at the complexity of the idea of reserves. The nature of reserves is dynamic and reflects prices, technology, and exploration effort, as well as the pattern of previous extraction and use. What counts as reserves is only a portion of total physical supply or total potential resources (Figure 3.1). An increase in raw materials prices will increase extraction, thus diminishing reserves; but it may also increase reserves, as some of the previously subeconomic resources become profitable to extract. Exploration may be encouraged by higher raw materials prices. Technological developments in extraction and processing may bring subeconomic resources into the economic picture. And improvements in exploration technology may increase the rate at which new reserves are identified.

Exhaustion

Exhaustion, like scarcity and reserves, is an economic concept. By definition, no more of a non-renewable resource is being made or created; continued extraction subtracts from the stock. Exhaustion is defined as a state in which the extraction rate falls to zero. Obviously, a resource is exhausted when there is literally none left. But it could be exhausted well before then. When the costs of extraction and preparation of one more unit for market exceed its price, so that there is no incentive for further extraction, the resource is exhausted. Like reserves, exhaustion is a dynamic concept. Anything that would reduce unit extraction costs or increases its price would encourage further extraction of a once exhausted resource.

Exhaustible, renewable resource supply
Examples of exhaustible, renewable resources include crops, forests, and wildlife populations. As compared to exhaustible, non-renewable resources, an added complexity of exhaustible, renewable resources is that the latter are living, biological resources. The biological reproduction and growth of these resources use the flow of solar radiation, the flow (or fund) of hydrological resources, and the fund of soil nutrients. Fragile equilibriums may be established independently of humankind, and people may manipulate the complex system to establish and maintain different equilibriums. Given the flow of solar radiation and the biological capacity for reproduction and growth, biological resources are renewable: not automatically self-renewing, but renewable given human restraint and sound management.

At any given time the stock of an exhaustible, renewable resource, its biomass, is determined by:

$$S_t = S_0 - \sum_{\tau=1}^{t-1} (H_\tau - R_\tau) \tag{3.4}$$

where R refers, in this context, to net recruitment (the excess of additions from reproduction and growth over losses from mortality and the like occurring independently of harvest, H). In bad times, R could be negative, and at other times, it could exceed H, for a net increase in biomass.

Generally, R is determined by:

$$R_t = h(S_t, N_t, X_t) \tag{3.5}$$

where N and X define the support provided by the environment, N being the inputs provided by nature and X the inputs under the control of people. Assuming, for the moment, that X and N are given and constant across time periods, we can consider the relationship between R_t and S_t. In a stable unmanaged ecosystem, the biomass of any species tends toward $\overline{S}$, the carrying capacity as illustrated in Figure 3.2. If for some reason the biomass were to fall below $\underline{S}$ in Figure 3.2, it would continue to fall to zero. $\underline{S}$ is the extinction threshold. Net recruitment is negative for a biomass of less than $\underline{S}$ as illustrated in Figure 3.3. At $\overline{S}$ in Figure 3.3, the maximum sustainable biomass has been achieved, and net recruitment stabilizes at zero. This is exactly what Thomas Malthus had in mind when he wrote of the natural tendency of populations to increase up to the limits of the support system, until each surviving member obtains a mere subsistence living.[1] Recruitment is maximized, R^*, at some intermediate biomass level, S^* (Figure 3.3). This has important implications for managed biological systems.

Once the biomass level, S^*, is attained, it can be maintained at that level by harvesting $H^* = R^*$ in each period thereafter. H^* is thus the maximum sustainable yield. If the biological system is integrated into the economy and has economic value as a capital asset, consideration of the costs of alternative strategies may lead to selection of an

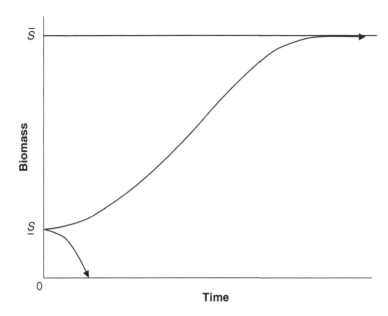

Figure 3.2   Biomass production as a function of time

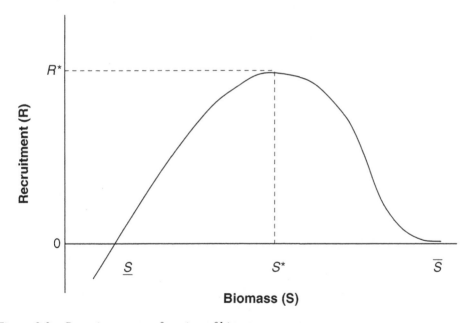

Figure 3.3   Recruitment as a function of biomass

economically optimal biomass level and harvest rate deviating a little from S^* and H^*. The maximum sustained yield is not likely to be an optimal management strategy (in a later chapter, we find that a zero cost of capital – a zero real interest rate – is necessary for it to be optimal). There are some cases in which an economically optimal strategy would permit local extinction (for example, when the growth rate in value of the resource is lower than the rate of interest). As economists, however, we would hesitate to endorse policies leading to the global extinction of a species unless we were convinced that the costs of avoiding extinction were intolerably high (see Chapter 19).

The complexity of exhaustible, renewable biological resources, evident in our discussion of the time dimension, extends to the quantity, quality, and space/place dimensions. Quantity is elusive: biomass is a well-defined quantity indicator, but it does not necessarily capture the economically important quantity dimensions. For people's various uses of biological resources, other quantity measures will be relevant: mass, volume, and population size, for example. Quality is defined in terms of intended use, and notions of what constitutes high quality may conflict, given different valuations of alternative uses. A monoculture of an artificially bred variety of some species may be considered "high quality" for uses emphasizing the production of food for human consumption, but "low quality" for uses emphasizing ecological continuity and natural aesthetics. The space/place dimension is complicated by incompletely mapped habitats and territorial ranges, the possibility of successfully transplanting some species, and the elaborate migratory patterns of others.

Flow resource supply

Flow resources are closely related to ecosystem processes, functions, and services. Solar radiation resulting from the one-way flow of energy through an ecosystem and rainfall resulting from the hydrologic cycle are good examples of flow resources. Their distinguishing characteristics are that they are provided in some predetermined quantity and quality beyond human control and must be used when provided or otherwise wasted (i.e., "use it or lose it").

Non-storable flow resource supply
Abstracting from quality, we can express the relationship between a non-storable flow resource and its use:

$$F_t = R_t + W_t \geq R_t \qquad (3.6)$$
$$W_t \geq 0$$

where F_t is the flow provided in period t and W indicates the amount wasted. There are no relevant concepts of stocks and storage. Examples of non-storable flow resources include solar radiation and wind. But, the reader may question, can we not store energy (e.g., electricity in batteries) from solar energy and wind? Yes, we can convert solar radiation and wind to some other form of energy (e.g., electricity stored in batteries), but we are not storing the solar radiation or wind itself (e.g., we do not capture and store wind in a box, then release the wind from the box at a later date). Thus, the term "non-storable" means that we cannot store the natural resource itself. Returning to the real world, we recognized the quality and space/place dimensions. Air pollution can reduce the quality of incident solar radiation for some uses, and the amount received varies with location.

Storable flow resource supply
Some flow resources, rainfall being perhaps the best example, can be captured and stored for later use. Storage actually changes a flow resource into a fund resource, in that

deposits and withdrawals can be made and manipulated by people, subject to the rule expressed in the following equation:

$$S_t = \sum_{\tau=1}^{t-1} (F_\tau - R_\tau - W_\tau) + F_t \geq R_t \qquad (3.7)$$

The current period's use cannot exceed the cumulative net storage from previous periods plus this period's flow.

For example, consider a managed reservoir such as the large reservoirs managed by the US Army Corps of Engineers in the eastern US and the US Bureau of Reclamation in the western US. In the case of managed reservoirs, F_t in equation (3.7) represents the flow of water into the reservoir in the current time period and F_τ represents the flow of water into the reservoir in all previous time periods. F_t and F_τ are determined by rainfall and the physical (e.g., hydrologic) conditions of the reservoir's watershed which determine the inflow of water to the reservoir. The amount of water wasted, W_τ, is determined, for example, by the amount of stored water lost from the reservoir because of evaporation and seepage into the soil and groundwater supplies. The total amount of water used, R_τ, is determined by the amounts of water withdrawn or released for various human uses (e.g., drinking water, hydropower, navigation, irrigation) as well as downstream environmental flows (e.g., water released to support downstream fish and wildlife habitat). A little thought reveals the importance of the quantity, quality, time, and space/place dimensions in describing water flow, storage, and use in various regions of the country with different climates, topography, ecologies, and economies.

Scarcity viewpoints or philosophies

Natural resource scarcity has been a major theme of economics since its emergence as an identifiable discipline more than two centuries ago. Mainstream economics is largely an artifact of the post-industrial age in the so-called Western world, and its practitioners tend to see things from a Western perspective. Nevertheless, each generation of economists has had to come to terms with this question: To what extent do natural resource limitations restrain the prospects for humankind? In each generation, not all economists have agreed, but the terms of the economic debate have reflected (and, in turn, influenced) the prevailing attitudes toward technology, economic growth, and the human prospect.

The classical economists and the Malthusian Doctrine

The classical economists were writing in England as the first phase of the industrial revolution drew to a close. Their experience of everyday life made them accustomed to technological progress and aware of the importance of capital to productivity. Nevertheless, famine was not unheard of, and industrial progress had as yet done little to improve the lot of the common people.

Imagine an aggregate production function for a whole society, relating the total productivity to the amounts of various inputs used. Obviously, output and inputs would need to be defined broadly. The classical economists conceptualized the aggregate production function as taking the form:

$$Y = f(D, K, L) \qquad (3.8)$$

Land, *D*, was defined broadly to include soil and mineral resources (and thus was a synonym for "natural resources" as natural resources were understood at the time). Land was thought to be not only important but also fundamentally limiting. David Ricardo was concerned that expanding populations and growing demands would force the exploitation of progressively poorer land resources for agriculture and (at least implicitly) for minerals. Thomas Malthus (ironically, a distinctly poorer intellect than Ricardo) gained greater fame beyond the economics profession with his analysis of population pressures. Malthus thought that food output would be limited to no better than an arithmetic rate of increase (2, 4, 6, 8, . . .), whereas population would tend to grow geometrically (2, 4, 8, 16, . . .), thus, humankind was doomed to a standard of living at the mere subsistence level. Although modern economists can find plenty of gaps in the Malthusian argument (e.g., it failed to recognize the potential roles of capital and technology, the possibilities of resource discovery and resource substitution, and the emergence of voluntary restraint on human reproduction), it is not difficult to see how Malthus and his fellow classical economists earned for economics the name the "dismal science."

The rather pessimistic viewpoint or philosophy which holds that limited resources combined with tenacious human population growth will eventually lead to a "crash" with much environmental destruction and human suffering has become commonly known as the "Malthusian Doctrine." When it comes to natural resource scarcity and human well-being, there are many followers of this doctrine today (even though they may not actually realize it). This viewpoint or philosophy may be summed up by the statement: "We are headed towards a catastrophic shortage of resources and there's not much we can do about it." Whether this statement is right or wrong, and for whom, is an empirical question and only time will reveal the answer.

The neoclassicals and the neoclassical/human capital perspective
As time passed, the industrial revolution continued apace, increasing the importance of capital in production and substituting mineral raw materials for animal and vegetable materials. As technological progress continued, it became built into expectations and into the institutional framework. Colonization supplied raw materials and inexpensive labor to the colonial powers. Although there were frequent warnings that known reserves of particular resources were perilously low, new reserves always seemed to be discovered or substitute resources found and utilized. Standards of living were improving, and for the first time it could be claimed that industrialization had made the common people in industrial societies better off.

Land, broadly defined as natural resources, seemed less of a constraint. Perhaps more important, land itself responded to investment, and so there seemed nothing special or unique about land. The neoclassical aggregate production function was usually expressed as:

$$Y = g(K, L) \tag{3.9}$$

For the current generation of economists, everyday life experiences have left impressions different from those that formed the attitudes of the classical economists. For the ordinary citizens of advanced countries, prosperity is the norm: technological progress pervades the whole economy from the farms to the information industries; and the acquisition of education and training is a lifelong process.

The modern economist T.W. Schultz, who like many of his contemporary colleagues has a strong neoclassical intellectual heritage, has been associated with two ideas: (1) even for agriculture, land no longer has any unique significance; and (2) labor is responsive to investment; that is, investment in developing "human capital" increases skills, thus permitting continued increases in output and further technological progress. Thus, the "Schultzian" production function could read, in its most aggregate form, as:

$$Y = h(K) \tag{3.10}$$

In this formulation, K is given a modern interpretation. Capital is seen as whatever is created by the act of investment and thus includes physical plant, educated human minds and bodies, farms and forests that respond to investment and management, and the technologies embodied in all of these productive facilities. The point is that investment is considered the only fundamental limitation to the capacity of the human population to support itself on this earth. Equation 3.10 representing economic growth for the economy as a whole is akin to the neoclassical/neocapital production function (equation 2.4) discussed in Chapter 2, representing production at the firm level.

According to this "neoclassical/human capital" perspective, natural resource limitations are simply not fundamental. They can be overcome by substituting capital (physical and human) and the technological innovations the capital generates and embodies for limited natural resources. The neoclassical/human capital perspective also implicitly assumes that the environment has an unlimited capacity to absorb and dilute wastes. The neoclassical/human capital perspective also assumes there is a one-way flow of wastes from economic production and consumption into the environment where these wastes are absorbed, diluted, or otherwise "cleaned up" (e.g., through the actions of microorganisms). Thus, because of its faith in technology and the unlimited capacity of the environment to deal with wastes, the neoclassical/human capital approach is a more optimistic perspective or viewpoint on natural resource scarcity which may be summed up by the statements: "human ingenuity and technology will come to the rescue" and "environmental dilution is the solution to pollution." Whether or not these statements are true, and for whom, is also an empirical question and only time will tell us the answer.

The materials balance approach and neo-Malthusians
We do not mean to leave the impression that all modern economists take the very optimistic (with respect to resource scarcity) neoclassical/human capital perspective. High gasoline prices, polluted air and water, chemically contaminated food supplies, and global climate change concerns have encouraged more modern economists to take a "materials balance approach" to resource scarcity issues. Allen Kneese, Robert Ayres, and Ralph d'Arge emphasized the first law of thermodynamics (energy matter is neither created nor destroyed) and introduced the "materials balance" concept to economists.[2] Materials are not "consumed," as economists had conveniently assumed, but merely transformed in the process of providing for human wants. From this perspective, the management of wastes, or residuals from production and consumption processes, has

a legitimate call upon resources. Overloads of residuals threaten the capacity of the environment to cleanse and renew itself. The concept of scarcity is broadened to include limitations on the environmental system.

The second law of thermodynamics (the entropy law) informs us that the energy matter in a system is inexorably transformed from more to less available states. This process occurs in nature but is accelerated by human-directed production and consumption processes. In the materials balance approach, the planet Earth environment is thought of as a closed system (even though some matter is exchanged between outer space and the planet Earth environment (e.g., meteorites, satellites). Within the planet Earth environment, the second law focuses our attention on the costs (in physical terms) of the energy matter transformation processes. Some economists (particularly Nicolas Georgescu-Roegen and Herman Daly) have drawn attention to these costs, the remainder of which will come due at some future time when it will be too late to undo the damage already done. This "too late to undo the damage" view is consistent with a Malthusian perspective; thus proponents of the materials balance approach sometimes are referred to as neo-Malthusians.

The materials balance approach or perspective on resource scarcity may be summed up by the statement: "a healthy environment and a healthy economy both require that we need to maintain a proper balance between what we take from the environment and what we put back." The viewpoint expressed in this statement is what differentiates classical Malthusians from neo-Malthusians. The former believe resource scarcity catastrophes are inevitable, whereas the latter believe that with enough foresight and deliberate action taken before the "point of no return," a proper materials balance may be restored and resource scarcity catastrophes avoided. Thus, the material balance approach, unlike the neoclassical/human capital perspective, does not hold that the environment has an unlimited capacity to absorb, dilute, or otherwise clean up wastes from economic production and consumption – too much pollution in too short a time, for example, could overload environmental systems and seriously degrade ecosystem processes, functions, and services. When it comes to the ultimate effects of resource scarcity on human well-being, the materials balance approach is somewhat in between the very pessimistic Malthusian Doctrine and the very optimistic neoclassical/human capital perspective. Again, only time will reveal if the material balance approach is a more realistic scarcity viewpoint and for whom.

Assessing resource scarcity

Having defined some important terms and reviewed the history of thought regarding natural resource supply and scarcity, we are now in a better position to consider the issues raised at the beginning of this chapter. Let us look briefly at the empirical evidence concerning resource use and scarcity.

Rates of use and consumption

With economic growth and rising standards of living, consumption of raw materials has increased dramatically in the US, as illustrated in Figure 3.4 which shows consumption of selected raw materials from 1900 to 2007. Cement mixed with water, sand, gravel and/or lime forms concrete, plaster, or mortar used in the construction of buildings, roads and other infrastructure.[3] Gypsum is used to produce wallboard used in building

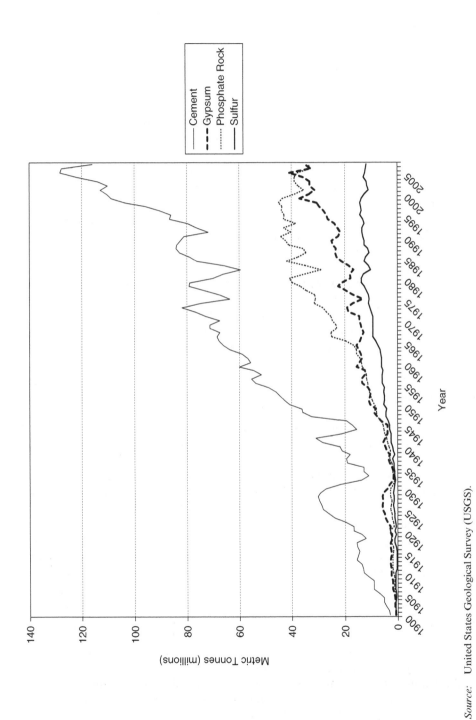

Source: United States Geological Survey (USGS).

Figure 3.4 Select raw materials consumption in the US

41

construction – the walls in your house and college classrooms are probably made of gypsum wallboard. Phosphate rock is used to produce agricultural fertilizers and cleaning detergents. Sulfur is used in many industrial manufacturing processes. Thus, as we build more houses, manufacture more consumer goods, grow more food, and send more young people off to college, all to increase our standard of living, our consumption of raw materials is expected to increase. The link between materials consumption and standard of living is reinforced by the observation in Figure 3.4 of the declines in raw material consumption during the "Great Depression" in the 1930s, a major economic recession in the early 1980s, and the start of a serious economic recession in 2007.

Energy consumption has also steadily increased in the US with economic growth and rising standards of living. Figure 3.5 shows energy consumption in the US from 1949 to 2007 by fuel source. During this time period, petroleum was the source of most of our energy consumption. From the late 1950s to the mid-1980s, natural gas was the source of more energy consumption as compared to coal. From the mid-1980s to 2007, coal and natural gas have accounted for about the same amount of energy consumption. Commercial nuclear energy came online in the US in 1958. Consumption of energy generated by nuclear power plants increased for about 30 years, leveling off in the 1990s and 2000s. Consumption of energy from all renewable sources (biomass, geothermal, hydropower, solar, and wind) was relatively flat during the 1950s, slowly increased in the 1960s and 1970s (especially during the 1970s' energy crisis and rise of the environmentalism era), and has basically leveled off since the early 1980s.

Over the 100-plus-year time period from 1900 to 2007, the rate of consumption in the US of the representative raw materials illustrated in Figure 3.4 and many others was far greater than the rate of population growth during the same time period. The rate of total energy consumption in the US illustrated in Figure 3.5 from 1949 to 2007 was also far greater than population growth in the US during this same time period. Thus, it is clear that throughout its relatively young history, economic growth and rising standards of living in the US has meant high per capita consumption of raw materials and energy, as is the general case with other countries as they become more industrialized and developed.

When speaking about consumption patterns and trends of raw materials, energy, or anything else for that matter in the US and the world, we must always keep in mind that total consumption is a function of both the size of the population and per capita consumption. Thus, a country with a relatively large population and low per capita consumption rate (e.g., developing country) and a country with a relatively small population and high per capita consumption rate (e.g., developed country) may consume about the same amount of raw materials. In fact, a smaller (in terms of population) developed country may consume more than the larger (in terms of population) country as evidenced by the observation that although all the developed countries in the world comprise only 22 percent of the world's population, they consume more than 60 percent of the industrial raw materials. One of these developed countries, the United States, consumes about 30 percent of industrial raw materials produced in the world each year even though it has only about 5 percent of the world's population.[4]

As indicated in Figure 3.5, most of the energy consumed in the US currently comes from mineral, fossil fuel sources. The natural source of fossil fuels is the carbon–oxygen cycle. As discussed earlier in this book, because the carbon–oxygen cycle generates coal,

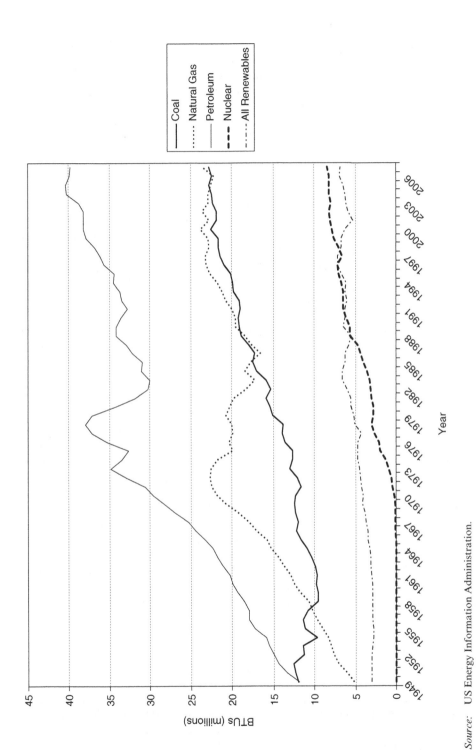

Source: US Energy Information Administration.

Figure 3.5   US energy consumption by fuel source

natural gas, and crude oil very slowly over time, these resources are considered exhaustible and non-renewable from a policy and management perspective. Many industrial raw materials are also in the nature of exhaustible, non-renewable resources. For example, phosphate rock is generated by the phosphate cycle over long periods of geologic time – so long, in fact, that for practical policy and management purposes, we consider it non-renewable. We also consider the amounts of gypsum, sulfur, and cement ingredients (predominately calcium) cycling through the environment to be fixed and thus exhaustible and non-renewable from a policy and management perspective.

Taking a naive view, the mere fact that increasing per capita and total consumption over time has been heavily dependent on non-renewable mineral resources would seem a cause for concern about resource scarcity and economic growth. Surely we cannot consume without limit what is exhaustible and non-renewable. However, the possibilities of exploration and discovery, recycling, substitution, and conservation suggest that the consumption data alone are not sufficient to tell us much about future resource scarcity and economic growth, even of mineral resources.

This emphasis on raw materials and energy, however, should not leave the impression that modern improvements in the standard of living have bequeathed to us a society obsessed with materials and manufactured goods. Higher standards of living have given us the time and the wherewithal to indulge our preferences for leisure. Our choices show a strong preference for outdoor enjoyment, nature study, and the pursuit of natural beauty and tranquility. As one piece of evidence, notice that the number of visits to US National Parks started a very steep increase after the end of World War II as Americans took to the highways and public parks in search of recreation and leisure during the post-war era of peace and prosperity. This steep increase lasted for several decades before leveling off in the 250–300 million visit range in the late 1980s to 2007 (Figure 3.6).

Although the growth in the use of outdoor recreation sites offers flattering testimony to human nature, it too contains a threat. The well-off citizens of the modern economies seem to be well on the way to "loving their parks and natural areas to death." While demand for outdoor recreation in aggregate has leveled off since the late 1980s, demand at the most highly valued sites continues to grow, exposing those environments to ever-increasing invasions of people who, perhaps without intending to, inevitably destroy much of what is natural. The use of these environments imposes pressures on them from which they may be unable to recover. Human enjoyment of these places is likely to entail congestion, as more and more people get in one another's way, diminishing the enjoyment of each. Thus, there is the threat of possibly destroying what would otherwise be much appreciated by future generations. However, with proper management, recreational use of natural environments is, in principle, renewable over time.

Reserves

Data about consumption and use may be suggestive, but they are not enough to tell us all we need to know about resource adequacy for the future. For the exhaustible, non-renewable mineral resources that can be used up but not created, it might be useful to examine the ratio between reserves and mine extraction. Suppose the reserves in a given year of copper are 1000 million metric tonnes, and 1000 million metric tonnes are extracted from these reserves during the same year. The reserves-to-extraction ratio is equal to 1, implying that reserves will be totally exhausted in one year. Hence, a

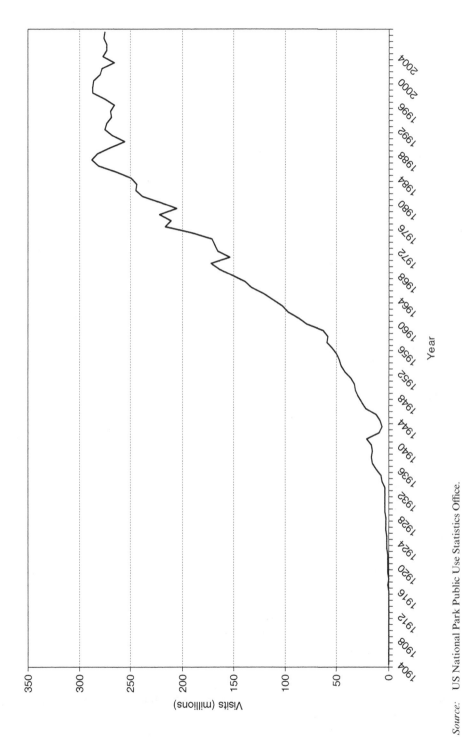

Source: US National Park Public Use Statistics Office.

Figure 3.6   Recreation visits to US national parks

45

Table 3.1   Mineral reserves to extraction ratios

Mineral	Year		
	1995	2000	2007
Copper	2	3	3
Gypsum	42	36	39
Phosphate rock	28	26	40
Platinum group metals	78	127	54
Crude oil	10	12	13

Source: United States Geological Survey (USGS).

reserves-to-extraction ratio of two indicates reserves will be exhausted in 2 years and so forth. If we are running out of a natural resource because of the continuing process of consumption, we would expect to see diminishing reserves-to-extraction ratios over time. Yet that is not the picture that always emerges.

Reserves-to-extraction ratios for copper, gypsum, phosphate rock, platinum-group metals, and crude oil are shown in Table 3.1. The reserves-to-extraction ratio for copper increased from 1995 to 2000 and stayed steady in 2007. The ratios for gypsum and phosphate rock fell from 1995 to 2000, and then increased from 2000 to 2007. Platinum-group metals are used in many manufacturing processes including computers, televisions, and other electronics. The reserves-to-extraction ratio of these metals showed a high increase from 1995 to 2000, and then an almost equally high decrease from 2000 to 2007. For crude oil, the ratio increased from 1995 to 2000 and from 2000 to 2007, suggesting a decrease in the scarcity of crude oil from 1995 to 2007. Notice also that according to the reserves-to-extraction ratio of 2 for copper in 1995, we should have run out of copper in the US in 1997. The ratio of 10 for crude oil in 1995 indicates that we should have run out of crude oil in 2005. But, 1997 and 2005 have come and gone, and we did not run out of copper and crude oil; we still are extracting copper and crude oil in the US as this book is being completed in 2010.

Changes in the reserves-to-extraction ratio in Table 3.1 are caused predominately by changes in reserves, since extraction and consumption of the minerals shown in Table 3.1 have generally increased over time (with fluctuations). For example, consider crude oil. Figure 3.7 shows proven US crude oil reserves over time. These reserves steadily increased from 1900 to 1970 even though crude oil consumption increased at about the same rate during this 70-year time period as indicated in Figure 3.5. How could this be? For minerals such as crude oil, there is theoretically some fixed initial stock – for example, the totality of all that the carbon–oxygen cycle has deposited in the earth's environment. Reserves, however, are different. The nature of reserves is dynamic. What counts as reserves changes with time, depending on prices, technology, and exploration effort, as illustrated by Figure 3.1.

Knowledge from exploration is cumulative, as past discoveries make new discoveries more likely. Often it pays to explore in places near, or similar to, the sites of previous finds. For some range of quantities, it may be true that: "the more we've already found, the easier it will be to find still more." Nevertheless, that cannot be true forever,

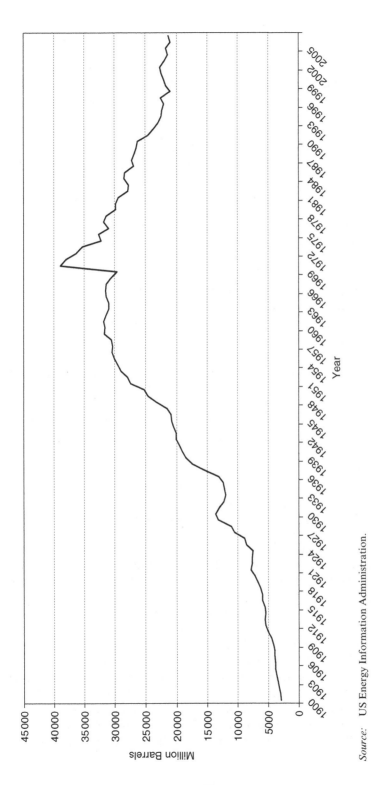

Source: US Energy Information Administration.

Figure 3.7   US crude oil reserves

as eventually the limits of nature's providence are reached. For example, the drop in US crude oil reserves since 1970 observed in Figure 3.7 reflects the fact that crude oil is becoming harder to find and extract in the US, especially in the 48 contiguous states.

The possibility of literally running out of minerals, so that there is none to be had at any price, is remote. The least economically attractive resources that are available in very low concentrations in ordinary rocks, sand, and soil are present in enormous quantities and could be used if the price were high enough to make their extraction feasible. These constitute the ultimate backstop against resources exhaustion. Furthermore, recycling offers the possibility of extending indefinitely some kinds of resource (metals especially). Major increases in recycling will come only with price increases or technological breakthroughs. Recycling for many kinds of materials is energy-intensive, which limits its current application. Price increases for materials would encourage recycling, as would price reductions for energy. The latter may result if flow resources (the sun or the wind) can be inexpensively tapped for useable energy, or if nuclear fusion technology is implemented.

Economic indicators of scarcity
Examination of consumption patterns and time trends in reserves has provided no real information about the prospects of adequate resources for the future. Perhaps there is another, more meaningful way to ask the question. Are raw materials becoming more scarce? If so, that might provide a warning; if not, that would offer some comfort. As indicated earlier in this chapter, a good indicator or resource scarcity would summarize the sacrifices required to obtain a unit of the resource. But the perfect economic indicator is not easy to find. Next, we consider some indicators that have been used.

Real prices of raw materials   Prices contain some information about scarcity, although that information is not always helpful without some further analysis. A single price observation by itself tells us nothing. Movements in prices, as time passes, are more useful but may be distorted by general inflation. Thus, to compare price trends over time, we must use real prices adjusted for inflation rather than nominal prices.

Basic economic theory suggests that as the supply of a resource becomes more scarce relative to demand, its price should increase. In his seminal article on the economics of exhaustible resources, Harold Hotelling predicted that because of scarcity, mineral prices should be observed to increase over time at the going rate of interest – this predicted price relationship has become well known as "Hotelling's Rule."[5] In a recent study, Lin and Wagner used econometric models to examine real-world price trends over time for 13 minerals. They conclude that growth rates of real prices have remained zero for more than 30 years (1970–2004).[6] Zero growth rates in real prices in the US for ten minerals for more than a century up to 2004 are also reported in a recent study by Gaudet.[7] These recent studies fail to support Hotelling's prediction of increasing mineral prices over time, suggesting that the minerals studied are not becoming scarcer.

If crude oil supplies were becoming scarcer over time, we would expect the retail price of gasoline to increase over time (since gasoline is derived from crude oil). Yet, as Figure 3.8 shows, the retail price of gasoline in the US has been relatively stable for the more than 30-year time period from the early 1970s to the mid-2000s. Thus, retail gasoline price trends also fail to support the expectation of increasing crude oil scarcity over time.

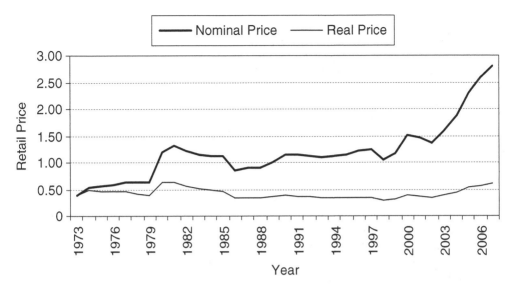

Source: US Energy Information Administration.

Figure 3.8   Nominal and real retail gasoline price trends in the US

The mineral price trend studies described above basically confirm an earlier classic study of resource scarcity by W.D. Nordhaus. Nordaus examined the time pattern of relative prices, which would tell us more about whether some things are becoming scarcer relative to other things. He considered the prices of 11 extracted and processed minerals relative to the hourly wage in manufacturing.[8] In the time period 1900–1970, his results showed that the relative price of mineral raw materials fell significantly in every case and dramatically in some cases. These results suggest that for most of the twentieth century, mineral raw materials were becoming less scarce or, at least, less scarce than is labor for manufacturing.

The "real cost" of raw materials   In a classic study of resource scarcity, Harold J. Barnett and Chandler Morse reasoned that the increasing scarcity of raw materials would be reflected in the increasing real costs of obtaining them.[9] They calculated the real unit cost for agriculture, fishing, forestry, and minerals, and traced its path from 1870 to 1957. Their results suggest that for the almost 100-year period examined, the real costs of obtaining mineral raw materials decreased, indicating declining scarcity. During the same time period, the real unit cost of agricultural products remained constant, and the real unit cost of forestry and fishery products showed a slight upward trend. Thus, of all the categories studied, only the products of forests and fisheries appeared to become scarcer during the time period studied. Ironically, their results seem to indicate that increasing scarcity beset not the exhaustible mineral resources (where one might at first expect to find it), but the biological resources.

More recently, Barnett updated the earlier analysis through 1970 without overturning its basic conclusions. V. Kerry Smith re-examined the Barnett–Morse statistical analysis with more sophisticated methods.[10] He found that the basic trend of decreasing minerals scarcity between 1870 and 1957 could not be refuted, although for some minerals there were briefer periods when real costs were rising.

Economic rent   Economic rent measures the real value of resources *in situ*. It seems clear that the sacrifices required to obtain mineral raw materials have diminished as consumption has increased. But that is insufficient reason for economists to dismiss all concerns about increasing scarcity. The prices, or costs, of raw materials are composed of two elements: the price of mineral resources *in situ* (that is, in the ground) and the costs of extraction and processing.

If there were continued cost-reducing technological advances in the mining and processing industries, that might be sufficient to drive down the price of raw materials even if the price of resources *in situ* were increasing over time. If that were happening, the consumption of raw materials would be encouraged by falling prices, even though mineral resources were becoming scarcer.

The perfect economic indicator of increasing scarcity would trace the real value of resources *in situ*. Because this value emerges from scarcity alone, it is often called rent, and it is closely related to the Ricardian concept of land rent (see Chapter 17). Unfortunately, resource rents can seldom be directly observed and are not recorded in readily available statistical series. So the preferred scarcity indicator, resource rents corrected for inflation, is unavailable. Furthermore, there is the possibility that if it were, it might tell a different story than that told by the relative prices and real costs of raw materials.

Summary and interpretation of the economic evidence

As the preceding discussion suggests, there is some cause for concern that the economic evidence is incomplete. It is, nevertheless, more informative than are those indicators, like consumption rates and reserves, that focus most directly on physical quantities. Questions of scarcity cannot be usefully addressed by reference to physical quantities alone. Scarcity is an economic concept, and it can be understood and observed only by considering economic entities such as prices, costs, and economic rents.

Although economists are aware of the caveats that must be applied to indicators such as relative prices and costs of raw materials, most interpret the available data as showing that there is no irrefutable evidence that resource scarcity is becoming more severe. Certainly, the relatively calming message that one gets from the available economic indicators of scarcity is in sharp contrast to the panic expressed by some who focus on consumption rates and current reserves.

Our discussion of scarcity has concentrated mostly on raw materials. But a complete treatment must also consider environmental resources and amenities, for two reasons. First, real cost calculations of the kind used by Barnett and Morse largely ignore the environmental damages (equally real) that accompany resource extraction and processing. An accounting of environmental costs may or may not cast a different light on the raw materials scarcity picture. Second, the quality of the environment is itself an important resource and one that may well be increasing in scarcity.

It is well to remember that all of the data we have been considering are historical and therefore predictive only to the extent that the future is predictable from the past. Some catastrophists believe that the future will be very different from the past. The evidence summarized in this chapter can scarcely address this concern. Those of us who have lived through the 1970s saw the first world energy crisis characterized by rapidly increasing oil prices and long waiting lines at fuel pumps due to physical shortages. However, in the late 1980s, the world experienced a glut of oil supplies and world oil prices crashed, ushering in a new era of relatively cheap energy and low gasoline prices which lasted through the 1990s and helped to drive one of the largest expansions of the US and world economies in history. Nobody, however, will forget the events of September 11, 2001 when terrorists flew hi-jacked US airplanes into the World Trade Center in the city of New York. This led to conflict and war in the Middle East and another spike in oil prices in the US because of fears of disruptions to oil imports from that region of the world.

Driven by fears of supply disruptions and also increasing demand from rapidly industrializing countries, primarily China, US and world oil and gasoline prices continued an upward trend in the 2000s, reaching dizzying highs in 2008. Almost everyone interpreted these high oil and gasoline prices as signaling a new energy crisis, sparking great fears of running out of oil, and frantic calls by government and private industry to replace energy produced from fossil fuels with energy produced from wind, solar radiation, and other renewable resources. As we write this chapter now, in 2009, the prices of oil and gasoline have dropped dramatically from their highs in 2008 primarily because of a global economic recession tied to the bursting of the US housing market bubble and the resulting credit market crisis. In fact, when adjusted for inflation, average gasoline prices in the US in January 2009 are lower than at any other point in time in the US since the 1970s – including during the 1970s' energy crisis. Are we now entering another era of cheap oil and gasoline prices when running out of oil is not a major concern in most people's minds? "Yes," you might say, "and bring back the Hummers and other gas-guzzlers!" Once again, however, it is possible that short-term trends will soon turn out to have been ephemeral.

What mitigates scarcity?
The evidence seems to show that at least some natural resources are, in general, not becoming more scarce. That seems at first glance to be counterintuitive, especially for the minerals. If we are using them up and not replacing them, how can they fail to grow scarcer? The answer lies in the responsiveness of human beings to the incentives provided by prices. The increasing scarcity of some resource is signaled by a rise in its relative price. This offers incentives for a variety of activities, all of which tend to mitigate scarcity. Final users find products made with the resource more expensive, and so make do with fewer of them by reducing their total consumption a little and switching to substitutes. Processors and manufacturers seek substitute raw materials. Thus on the demand side, a price increase induces conservation and substitution. On the supply side, a price increase encourages exploration, extraction from reserves that were previously unattractive, and investment in technological developments that may make discovery, extraction, and processing less costly.

Thus increasing scarcity induces price increases, which establish incentives that tend to mitigate the scarcity. That is, prices are a signaling and incentive system providing feedback that tends to stabilize the resource economy and correct any aberrations therein. The price system does not operate painlessly and cannot offer instant stability to a jolted system: witness the slow and painful adjustments to the rising prices of fuel for heating and transportation during the oil and gasoline price hikes and shortages in the 1970s and 2000s. Nevertheless, price-induced conservation dramatically reduced the growth in the consumption of gasoline and electricity, for example, and the supply of oil and coal proved responsive to price incentives. Can an economic system that uses non-renewable resources maintain its standard of living forever? The discussion in this chapter provides some insight to this question. A more complete answer, however, requires a more detailed discussion of the sustainability issue which we provide in Chapter 19.

Questions for discussion

1. It has been said that "resources are not, they become." What does this mean?
2. "Solar energy research is an effort to find ways to convert a flow resource into a stored form of energy so that it may more effectively substitute for exhaustible, non-renewable resources." So, if you had some extra money today, would you invest in solar energy company stock rather than oil company stock? Explain your reasoning.
3. "The differences among the Malthusian Doctrine, neoclassical/human capital perspective, and materials balance approach viewpoints on resource scarcity boil down to different views about the substitutability of natural resources, capital, labor, population growth, and the ability of the environment to absorb wastes." Explain and discuss this statement.
4. What are some factors that might explain the anomaly that the "renewable" resources seem to be growing scarcer relative to the exhaustible resources?
5. How would you explain to someone who is not an economist that scarcity and resource exhaustion are economic concepts?

Notes

1. Malthus wrote his original famous population essay in 1798. It is reprinted in Thomas R. Malthus (Author) and Geoffrey Gilbert (ed.) (2008), *An Essay On The Principle Of Population*, Oxford World's Classics, Oxford: Oxford University Press.
2. Allen V. Kneese, Robert U. Ayres, and Ralph C. d'Arge (1978), *Economics and the Environment: A Materials Balance Approach*, Washington, DC: Resources for the Future.
3. Cement is a powdery material made from four essential raw materials: aluminum, calcium, iron and silicon. Limestone is a major source of calcium (the main ingredient in cement).
4. Grecia Matos and Lorie Wagner (1998), "Consumption of Materials in the United States, 1900–1995," *Annual Review of Energy and the Environment* **23**: 107–22.
5. "Hotelling's Rule" is derived from a conceptual analysis published in Harold Hotelling (1931), "The Economics of Exhaustible Resources," *Journal of Political Economy* **39**: 137–75.
6. The minerals examined included: bauxite, coal, copper, gold, iron, lead, natural gas, nickel, petroleum, phosphate, silver, tin and zinc. See C.-Y. Cynthia Lin and Gernot Wagner (2007), "Steady-State Growth in a Hotelling Model of Resource Extraction," *Journal of Environmental Economics and Management* **54**: 68–83.
7. The minerals examined included: aluminum, coal, copper, lead, natural gas, nickel, petroleum (crude oil), silver, tin, and zinc. See Gerard Gaudet (2007), "Natural Resources Under the Rule of Hotelling," *Canadian Journal of Economics* **40** (4): 1033–59.
8. The minerals examined included: aluminum, coal, copper, gold, iron, lead, molybdenum, petroleum (crude oil), phosphorous, sulphur, and zinc. See William D. Nordhaus (1973), "The Allocation of Energy Resources," *Brookings Papers on Economic Activity* **3**: 529–70.
9. Harold J. Barnett and Chandler Morse (1963), *Scarcity and Growth: The Economics of Natural Resources Availability*, Baltimore, MD: Johns Hopkins University Press.
10. V. Kerry Smith (1979), *Scarcity and Growth Reconsidered*, Baltimore, MD: Johns Hopkins University Press.

Suggested reading: classic and contemporary

Ayres, R.U. (1999), "The Second Law, the Fourth Law, Recycling and Limits to Growth," *Ecological Economics* **29** (3): 473–83.
Daly, H.E. (1997), "Forum: Georgescu-Roegen versus Solow/Stiglitz," *Ecological Economics* **22** (3): 261–6.

Smith, V.K. and J.V. Krutilla (1984), "Economic Growth, Resource Availability, and Environmental Quality," *American Economic Review* **74** (2): 226–30.

Solow, R.M. (1974), "The Economics of Resources or the Resources of Economics," *American Economic Review* **64** (2): 1–14.

Stiglitz, J.E. (1979), "A Neoclassical Analysis of the Economics of Natural Resources," in *Scarcity and Growth Reconsidered*, ed. V.K. Smith, Baltimore, MD: Johns Hopkins University Press.

4 Natural resources, the environment, and policy: what is the public policy context for natural resource and environmental economics?

Like any intellectual undertaking, natural resource and environmental economics makes most of its progress when dealing with the little questions, the questions that are defined narrowly enough to allow a reasonable chance of finding answers. Yet we attempt to answer these small questions not only for their own sakes but also in the hope of casting some light on the big questions.

Many of the big questions for natural resource and environmental economists are the big questions for humankind. Questions involving decision-making include: What do we want, what do we have to work with, and how can we best use what we have to get what we want? What are our goals, and how can we most effectively mobilize our resources to achieve those goals? Questions involving efficiency include: How fast should we spend the world's bank account; that is, exhaust the world's stock of non-renewable resources? At what rate should the irreversible alteration of the environment and ecosystems proceed? At what rate should we restore and conserve ecosystems? Under what terms should present generations trade material goods and services for environmental amenities, and vice versa? What restraints should present generations voluntarily accept for the benefit of the future? Questions involving equity (or fairness) include: Is there a group (community, state, nation, society as whole) interest, and if so, how is it to be made known? By what authority and within what limits is the group interest to be imposed on individuals who see things differently? How are disagreements between and among groups and individuals resolved? Are some of the incentives that direct individual use of natural and environmental resources perverse, and if so, what can be done about it without violating individual rights? What should we do when someone is harmed by a group decision?

All questions in natural resource and environmental policy, whether big or small, broad and pervasive, or narrow and localized, are generally related to issues involving decision-making, efficiency, and/or equity.

Natural resource and environmental policy issues

The challenge to humankind is to manage the resources of the planet effectively so as to maximize the satisfaction derived from them. The challenge has a time dimension that is absolutely critical. If humankind were willing to accept the extinction or demise of civilization within a few generations, extraction of non-renewable resources such as crude oil and coal could proceed without restraint, and the harvest of renewable resources such as trees and fish could exceed equilibrium rates and thus bring about the demise of these resources. Wastes could be released into the geosphere, hydrosphere, and atmosphere at rates exceeding the capacity of these natural systems to assimilate them, causing irreversible environmental and ecosystem damage. Such a strategy would increase human consumption of material goods in the short run but would soon bring on a horrible end to civilization. On the other hand, a society that seeks the continuation of human progress would take a very different approach to natural resource and environmental management. Extraction of non-renewable resources would be viewed as a temporary expedient while techniques of utilizing renewable resources were perfected. The rates of harvesting renewable resources and releasing of wastes into the environment would be restrained to the levels consistent with the long-run maintenance of the biological system. The present population would be very reluctant to create toxic wastes that are almost indestructible.

Human society faces many specific challenges in the management of specific resources. Some examples may be helpful. Consider the land resource. Land is useful as substrate; that is, it supports plants and animals, watercourses, buildings, transportation arteries, and the like. It is useful as soil, which is a major component of ecosystems (our natural life-support systems). And it is useful as a store of value: it stores fossil fuels, precious metals, and other minerals. Within and among these broad categories the uses made of land influence other potential uses. Surface and open-cut (open-cast) mining drastically disturb the land surface and affect its suitability for agriculture, forestry, wildlife support, and residential and industrial use, as well as its aesthetic and ecosystem service values. Urban uses of land (buildings, transportation arteries, parklands, and so on) reduce the amount of land available for agriculture and open space. For obvious reasons, it is much less costly to convert land from agricultural to urban uses than vice versa. So, maintenance of land in agricultural and open-space uses is a decision that can be readily reversed, whereas conversion of such land to urban uses is a decision that can be reversed only at great expense. Intensive cropping now may exacerbate soil erosion and thus limit future agricultural production. Some kinds of land uses create nuisances that adversely affect other uses. Who wants to live next to a pig farm, an airport, a sawmill, or a pornographic movie house?

Consider the water resource. We use it directly for drinking and bathing. We use it in the heating, cooling, and cleaning of our homes. In industry, it is a component of manufactured goods, cools power plants, and supports commercial navigation. It supports fun and leisure in the form of recreational swimming, fishing, and boating. Households and industrial plants use water to dispose of wastes. Water, of course, makes plants grow so it is essential for agriculture, golf courses, and home lawns. Water or H_2O is also essential for ecosystem health and ecosystem services. There are potential conflicts within and among these uses. Intensive waste disposal use may result in the closing of a lake or beach for recreational swimming because of human health concerns. In addition, intensive waste disposal use may increase the costs of treatment of water to make it fit for many residential, commercial, and industrial uses. Using water for power plant cooling raises its temperature and may degrade ecosystem health and valuable ecosystem services such as fish harvest. In places like the American Southwest, the scarcity of water makes for vigorous competition among the various possible uses. The possibility of storing water in reservoirs introduces additional sources of conflict. Recreational and aesthetic uses of free-flowing streams are displaced, but still-water recreation opportunities are generated. Flood control and flow augmentation (to dilute pollutants during low-flow seasons) uses of reservoirs conflict with still-water recreation uses.

The air resource is useful for life-support, for visibility to facilitate movement and for aesthetic enjoyment, for transportation, for industrial processes, and for waste disposal.

Again, there are conflicts within and among these uses. For example, intensive waste disposal use restricts visibility and reduces the value of air for life-support.

We have scarcely begun to consider the complexity of the interactions among resource uses. Uses that directly affect one of the land, water, or air resources often influence the value that can be derived from the other resources. Urban, industrial, and transportation uses of land affect air quality. Impoundment of water in reservoirs inundates some land, and it may render other land more productive through irrigation, flood control, energy production, and navigation. Drainage of wetlands interferes with hydrological systems and may change flood patterns, groundwater systems, and ecological systems. Land disturbance for surface mining, building, road construction, or agriculture may influence water quality. The paving of land to increase its value for transportation also increases water run-off. Fertilizers and pesticides to increase the agricultural productivity of land may reduce the quality of water and modify ecological systems.

Resources are typically used in combination. Obviously, air transportation requires air, but also land as substrate for take-off, landing, and passenger movement to and from the plane, and land as a store of minerals to build and fuel the planes. Industrial processes typically use land as space and support and use minerals, water, and air in production and waste disposal. Studies have shown that land, water, and air (as sky), given that each has desirable aesthetic qualities, provide the greatest aesthetic satisfaction in combination. Agricultural production requires air, land, and water and will be adversely affected by the diminution of the quantity or quality of any of these resources.

In addition, although not the subject of this book, it is wise to recognize human resources. Human labor, knowledge, and technical capacity are employed to derive benefits from natural resource utilization. Modern societies invest heavily in the development of these human capacities, using human resources as complements to, and substitutes for, natural resources. Furthermore, given the dominance of human beings in the earth's ecosystems, the organizing, planning, and decision-making capacity of people as individuals and societies is crucial to human success in deriving satisfaction and ensuring the continuity of civilization.

All of these specific complementary and conflicting potential resource uses challenge humanity to use its organizational powers and to control its greed and selfishness in order to manage wisely the resources for the present and the future. After reading and studying this book, we hope that the reader develops a better understanding, of just what "manage wisely" means from a natural resource and environmental policy perspective.

Some common attributes of resource management problems
Most resource use, management, and conservation decision problems are perceived, and must be solved, in a complex context. Consider some of the attributes of that context:

1. The resources of immediate concern are components of highly complex systems. The earth's resource system is a vast, complex, dynamic, interactive system. Attempts to modify individual components of that system will result in changes elsewhere in the system. Yet human understanding of this system is very, very limited, and so the consequences of manipulating components of the system are not easy to predict. Often these consequences manifest themselves in unexpected ways and are observed some considerable time after the initial stimulus. Cause and effect are difficult to

link. The effects of new actions are difficult to predict; this is a major source of concern in a time of rapid technological progress. The language we use to describe these effects, including "spillovers," "side effects," and "unintended consequences," is an indication of our ignorance and naivety and our remarkably poor understanding of the systems concept in general and the resources system in particular.

2. Most alternative courses of action have consequences that we perceive from our limited base of knowledge as both beneficial and adverse. What is seen as beneficial to one individual may be seen as adverse by another.

3. Any decision will influence many people, whose well-being will be affected differently and whose power to participate in decision-making will vary widely. Thus, there are few resource-related decisions that are truly private, in the sense that all their impacts are confined to the individuals who voluntarily agreed upon the decisions.

4. In any society, resource-related decisions, whether initiated by private individuals and groups, or by public decision-making bodies, are made within a complex institutional structure that assigns legal rights and liabilities and thus establishes the structure of incentives. That institutional structure is itself dynamic, and though it typically has conservative mechanisms to promote its continuity, it also has adaptive mechanisms to help it adjust to emerging realities of scarcity and power. In the kinds of modern economies that allow significant economic freedom for the individual, resource-related decisions at the public level often involve changes in institutions, with a view to changing the incentives facing individuals and thus the decisions that individuals make.

Resource allocation policy problems are typically complex, as they concern complex physical and biological systems and must be solved within a complex social and institutional environment. Legitimate goals come into conflict, and individuals will balance their legitimate interests differently. The physical and biological systems present tradeoffs: if we decide to pursue goal A purposefully, we will incur losses with respect to goal B; to maintain a satisfactory condition with respect to goal B, we must forgo some of our potential success in the direction of goal A. What should we do? Even if we had full knowledge of the consequences of every possible action, the decision would not be easy. It would depend on our relative valuations: how much of A is worth how much of B? How much energy to encourage economic growth and permit material comfort is worth how much expense and how much risk of failure in nuclear waste disposal? In the likely event that different people will have different relative valuations, how will these be weighted to arrive at a decision for society? Given that we do not have full knowledge of the consequences of each action, not only relative valuations but also empirical estimates of the consequences, beneficial and adverse, will be different for different people.

The philosophical bases of policy
The idea of policy connotes decision and action by and for society. If an issue, problem or need can be resolved satisfactorily by people acting alone, or by a few individuals negotiating with one another, there is not a policy problem. But "society" is itself not a simple idea. Does society decide and act? Or are decisions and actions actually taken by individuals and coalitions of individuals who happen to be ascendant? The

implementation of policy requires the authority of the state. Usually someone is hurt by any policy initiative, and the physical power and moral authority of the state must be invoked in order to secure sacrifices from the injured parties for the good of others. The deeper philosophical issue, as it has customarily been expressed in Western societies since the Enlightenment, is the legitimacy of authority. On what bases and subject to what restrictions may the individual be open to harm imposed by the collective (that is, the state or the government)? Although this issue cannot be resolved here, it is useful to review some of the models of the relationship between citizens and government. These various models have philosophical roots that are centuries old, but they continue to exert great influence on the form of modern democratic governments and to shape the policy debates exercised by the participants therein.

The social contract
It is perhaps only a minor exaggeration to claim that today's major disagreements about the limits of governmental power to coerce individuals in the attempt to pursue the public good are essentially replays of the much earlier debates among social contract theorists. Today's clashes between individualists and defenders of "the public interest" are foreshadowed in the arguments of social contractarians John Locke and Jean Jacques Rousseau.[1]

Before introducing social contract theory, however, it is necessary to set the stage. For roughly 400 years before the birth of Christ and 1600 years thereafter, the Great Tradition of Greek philosophy dominated Western ideas about the relationship between government and citizens. Society was seen as the fundamental unit. That is, the individual alone does not and cannot amount to much. Rather, the individual is formed and shaped by society and derives opportunities for self-fulfillment from the institutions of society. The maintenance of these institutions is thus essential to order and stability, themselves high on the list of social goals. The sovereign (who in some versions was considered the earthly representative of the Deity) was seen as commanding the allegiance of society that, in turn, imposed duties on individuals. Whatever rights individuals enjoyed were derived from their attention to the duties that society demanded of them.

As England was emerging from feudalism, the old patterns of authority were breaking down, and the relationships among the Church, the monarchy, the aristocracy, and everyone else needed redefinition. Thomas Hobbes constructed a social theory rooted in individualism.[2] The individual, not society, was considered the fundamental entity, and the only truly fundamental right was that of the individual to preserve himself or herself and to choose the means of self-preservation. Rampant individualism, however, would lead to anarchy, an intolerable state in which the unbridled selfishness of each would render the lives of all insecure. Life would be "nasty, brutish and short." Individuals, because of a reasonable fear of anarchy, would choose to delegate some rights to authority (that is, a government), which would maintain order and take care of those essentials that individuals cannot independently provide. Thus, governmental authority is derived from individuals, who voluntarily delegate to it some rights that are fundamentally theirs.

As is obvious upon a little reflection, this model has some glaring holes. Once authority is transferred from individuals to government, what is to restrain government? What rights do individuals have to withdraw from a government they find unpleasant? Are there conditions under which it is permissible for individuals to rise up together and overthrow their government? Subsequent writers attempted to resolve these issues, in somewhat different ways. We consider three variants of social contract theory. Interestingly enough, the social contract model no longer enjoys the favor of political scientists (who consider the idea of social contract impossible and, what is more, non-essential), but these three variants of that model enjoy a continuing relevance to governmental institutions and political ideologies.

Rousseau and the general will   Rousseau's version of the social contract started with the premise that all persons are bound to the realization of equality, without which politics and justice would be contradictions in terms. Governments expressing the "general will" must legislate only laws addressed to the common good of society's members and extending the same rights to, and imposing the same duties on, each citizen.

It is assumed that a "general will" (or, in more modern terms, a public interest) exists and that in an environment of political equality, deliberative bodies are capable of identifying and interpreting it and establishing policies and programs to implement it. Under this view, there is no compelling need to minimize the size and power of government, so long as government serves the public interest. Government may seek to establish and promote conceptions of what is good for society.

Several developments in economics drew on and/or supplemented these ideas. The notion of market failure, originating with Alfred Marshall and A.C. Pigou, lent intellectual support to the idea that it was legitimate for government to second-guess market outcomes and to impose changes when market performance was found wanting. The social welfare function of Abram Bergson and Paul Samuelson, essential to the theory of maximum social well-being (see Chapter 8), can be viewed as a formalization of the "general will" idea.

Rousseau's theory was influential in establishing the forms of American government, with its emphasis on constitutional rule and the extension of the franchise. Its modern offspring, the public interest/market failure model, clearly influenced the course of American politics from the 1930s through the 1970s. Its basic premises are as follows:

- The political perfectibility of people. Once human beings are freed from essentially evil institutions and granted a genuine political equality, the influence of pure selfishness will wane, and the true public interest will be revealed in the political process.
- The basic problem concerning government is not so much to limit its size and scope as to ensure that it remains responsive to the public interest. To promote the public interest over the interests of a powerful but selfish few, some considerable regulation of individual activities for "public health, welfare, safety, and morals" may be justified. Programs to promote economic activity, to rectify market failure (that is, to internalize externalities and to provide public goods and merit goods), and to promote equality of economic opportunity may all be seen as enhancing the general welfare and thus within the purview of government.
- Continued vigilance and effort are necessary to ensure that government remains responsive to the public interest. A broad array of legislatures, committees, courts, tribunals, and an increasingly professional and planning-oriented civil service

are necessary to ensure the continued dominance of public interests over private interests in the political sphere.

- Given that the political sector will reveal the public interest, the administrative sector must adhere to an ethos that emphasizes the total submergence of the manager's personal objectives in favor of the politically revealed public interest and the objective, scientific facts of the situation. The managers are true professionals, neither self-interested nor politicized. They seek objective facts from researchers and educators, who are obliged to tell them all the facts and nothing but the facts. Thus armed, the managers allocate, invest, and regulate in the public interest.
- A large and important role remains for markets, but it is always legitimate for government to second-guess market behaviors and outcomes. The fine-tuning of market behaviors through taxation, public investment, and regulation is perfectly legitimate and often desirable.

Locke and individualism   John Locke, writing a little earlier than Rousseau, extended Hobbes's social contract model to provide for the overthrow of governments that lose their legitimacy. Because all fundamental rights reside initially with the individual, Locke reasoned, citizen sovereignty permitted and required the people to resist and overthrow a government that violated the public trust. Some commentators have seen in Locke's argument for the legitimate overthrow of misdirected governments a rationale for strict limits to the authority of any government. That is, individuals (even after the delegation of rights to government via the social contract) retain some basic rights, and a government invading or denying these rights would exceed its proper authority. Locke's social contract remains influential in the bills-of-rights emphasis in contemporary democratic theory and the voluntary exchange concept of economic freedom and justice.

Modern individualism as expressed by, for example, the political economist James Buchanan, emphasizes Pareto-safety (see Chapter 8) in economics and politics. No change that harms any individual can be considered an improvement. This criterion can be satisfied by voluntary trade in pervasive unregulated markets or by unanimous political choice. Actual compensation of those who might otherwise lose is an acceptable way to secure approval of political change, but a majority decision that imposes harm on minorities is not.

The basic premises of the individualistic model are as follows:

- Because society is merely a human artifact, all rights initially reside with the individual. To avoid anarchy, individuals would rationally delegate some rights to a central authority, that is, government.
- The citizens may legitimately resist and overthrow any government that violates the public trust, that is, acts beyond its authority legitimately derived from the people. Following overthrow, a new government must be installed.
- The rationale for the overthrow of governments that exceed their authority logically implies strict limits to the authority of any government. Individuals are guaranteed some fundamental rights and a government invading or denying these rights would exceed its rightful authority. Bills of rights are the keystone to a proper relationship between the individual and governmental authority.

- The basic behavioral premise is not the perfectibility of humankind but unquench-able human selfishness. Desirable institutions, therefore, are not those that appeal to behaviors quite alien to human nature but those that get the most social mileage from purely selfish behavior.
- The very concept of a public interest is greeted with deep suspicion.
- The idea of a social welfare function is explicitly rejected: if individuals were unani-mous about everything, it would not be needed, but in the absence of unanimity it would be coercive and hence intolerable.
- To the maximum extent feasible, the relationships among individuals and between the individual and government must be governed by the principle of Pareto-safety. Thus the individualistic tradition emphasizes voluntary exchange in the market and unanimity in the political sphere. The cornerstone of liberty is a set of com-plete, carefully specified, secure, enforceable, and transferable rights. The alloca-tion of resources and the distribution of rewards are optimized under a complete system of private property rights.
- The concept of market failure is greeted with considerable skepticism. In this respect, the research program initiated by the *Journal of Law and Economics* in the 1960s has enjoyed considerable success.[3] Market-like behaviors have been identified in many kinds of situations in which markets were previously thought not to exist. It has been established that externality is a fundamentally trivial concept: externality alone cannot persist; it can persist only when accompanied by non-exclusiveness and/or non-rivalry, but these latter two concepts are enough to explain the problem without recourse to the concept of externality. Comparative case studies have been completed, showing the superior performance of organiza-tional structures in which rights are well defined at the individual level.

Non-exclusiveness and non-rivalry (see Chapter 10) present persistent problems for the individualists, as does optimal taxation. The individualist solution to just about every problem is to assign exclusive property rights. However, there are cases in which the costs of exclusion are too high, or its ideological connotations too offensive to make this solution workable. In such cases, individualists tend to fight rear-guard actions, chal-lenging the notion of market failure itself. They argue that demonstrations of cases in which markets fail to optimize are simply not conclusive: the case for a government role can be based only on proof that government would do better. For non-rivalry problems (that is, public goods), some progress has been made in defining incentive-compatible mechanisms: devices that simultaneously determine the optimal amount of a non-rival good and optimal individual taxes. This approach is, of course, consistent with individu-alist concepts of optimal taxation derived from Knut Wicksell and Erik Lindahl.[4]

Bentham, utilitarianism, and the benefit–cost approach   Jeremy Bentham[5] popularized the idea that the basic human motivations were the pursuit of pleasure and the avoid-ance of pain. Goodness was identified via desires: what the individual wants is, for that reason, assumed to be good for that individual. When individuals differed about what was good, the option that promised the greatest good for the greatest number was to be socially preferred. This utilitarian criterion entailed obvious difficulties in cases in which a trivial good for each of many was opposed to a very great good for each of a few.

A solution to this problem was proposed much later by Nicholas Kaldor and John Hicks.[6] If those who would gain from a proposed change could compensate those who would lose, to the full extent of their perceived losses, the change would be acceptable. Note that this criterion differs from Pareto-safety in one crucial way: it requires only the possibility of compensation, whereas Pareto-safety requires that compensation actually be paid. Thus, the criterion became known as the potential Pareto-improvement. It boils down to the criterion that change is acceptable if the sum of money-valued gains (as judged by the gainers) exceeds the sum of money-valued losses (as judged by the losers). It is the basic criterion of benefit–cost analysis and states that change is acceptable when its benefits exceed its costs, regardless of the identity of gainers and losers. Obviously, it permits collective action that imposes harm on individuals and is indifferent as to whether the gainers are those already well off and the losers already badly off, or vice versa.

The potential Pareto-improvement, benefit–cost criterion is based on a particular utilitarian theory of the relationship between citizens and government. That theory has relatively few proponents if viewed as a general solution to the question of the legitimacy of authority. Nevertheless, there are several particular aspects of government activity in which it enjoys considerable support. The following ideas are derived directly from potential Pareto-improvement logic: public policy should generally encourage economic growth; policy initiatives (especially in the arenas of trade and commerce) should be evaluated in terms of benefits and costs; and public investments will be justified if they pass a formal benefit–cost test. Various laws and administrative regulations are in place, requiring benefit–cost analyses of particular kinds of policy initiatives.

Summary of philosophy and policy

The point of the above discussion on philosophy and policy is that when someone says something like, "Society must awaken to the dangers of inaction, determine its goals, and implement policies to attain them," a veritable mouthful has been said. Is society a meaningful concept, or are communities and nations composed only of individuals, each legitimately pursuing self-selected goals? Can collective goals be determined, or must individual self-interest always divide and conquer? Conversely, is individual freedom a dominant value, or must individuals always be subordinated to charlatans seeking self-aggrandizement while hiding behind pious appeals to the public interest? Can policies meaningfully be said to be in the public interest, or is policy merely the use of authority to pursue the private goals of individuals and coalitions?

These questions cannot be answered here (and we would be skeptical of anyone proposing definitive answers elsewhere). The purpose in raising them and briefly discussing their philosophical antecedents is to promote an informed but skeptical and questioning attitude toward the ideas of society, social goals, and public policy. In a book about natural resource and environmental policy, such questioning attitudes should be encouraged.

On the other hand, even our short discussion of some influential models of the philosophical bases of policy should be sufficient to dispel any notions that these questions have been little considered. Much high-quality thought has been invested in attempts to resolve them. The persistent philosophical problems that remain are evidence of the inherent difficulty of the questions.

The policy process

The philosophical models we introduced are normative. That is, they attempt to answer questions of legitimacy, justice, fairness, and freedom; in short, questions about how relationships ought to be between the individual and established authority. Each model is built on positive premises (fact-like statements about the way things are or seem to be). It is a fundamental law of logic, however, that normative conclusions cannot be derived from positive premises alone. To obtain conclusions about how things ought to be, normative premises must be introduced.

Now, consider a descriptive, or positive, model of the public policy decision process, that is, an attempt to understand how policy decisions are actually made. This particular model is not the conventional model (some elements of the conventional model emerged in the discussion of the public interest/market failure model of legitimacy). Instead it draws from relatively recent developments in the theory of public choice, which takes rent-seeking behavior seriously, and what some have called economic theories of politics. In common with most of mainstream economics, it starts with the premise that the elemental units of society (individuals or perhaps households) are atomistic and responsive to self-interest.

Consider a society of individuals seeking to satisfy a variety of diverse objectives by allocating their endowments according to maximizing principles. This leads to the diffuse model of the public policy decision process, the basic elements of which are:

- There are many arenas in which conflicts may be resolved. These include the legislature, the executive branch, the judiciary, and the marketplace.
- Individuals have diverse endowments (including income, wealth, property, professional reputations, personal standing in the community, native talent, acquired skills, and time) and seek to allocate these across the various arenas so as to maximize their own well-being. Different endowments are differentially effective in different arenas. Maximizing behavior includes both maximizing within the system and maximizing by attempting to change the system. Self-interested behavior includes coalition formation in those arenas in which collective modes of choice predominate.
- Even those who operate the various public decision institutions pursue their own self-interest. A basic problem for the design of any institution is that of establishing incentives that direct the efforts of personnel toward the institutional objectives.
- Public decisions are often not final. That is, they can often be reversed at some tolerable cost (notable exceptions, of course, include the irreversible destruction of natural systems). So those disappointed by a decision will often continue the battle, seeking its reversal in the same or different arenas.

This model yields a variety of implications. It encourages some skepticism about important aspects of the more normative models of government. In common with the individualistic model, it tends to undermine the notion of an identifiable public interest. On the other hand, its emphasis on the endogeneity of government tends to undermine the "government interference" rhetoric of individualists. Finally, it casts doubt on the traditional model of the proper relationship between the "decision-maker" and the scientific or technical "expert." Given the multiplicity of conflict resolution arenas, the open process in which agendas are set and conflicts are assigned among arenas, the lack of finality in many decisions, and the wide range of self-interested participants in the process, the notion of "the public policy decision-maker" loses its credibility.

This model, itself, makes few claims of optimality. Public interest theorists tend to see their worst fears of the free play of selfishness in government fulfilled in this model. Individualists find little comfort in a process in which selfish interests seek to form major-ity coalitions in order to use coercive institutions in ways beneficial to themselves. The individualistic scholar James Buchanan, for example, suggested the need for additional constitutional restraints on majority processes in government generally, and in taxation issues in particular.[7]

This diffuse model assigns a crucial role to information. Information is at once cog-nitive and suggestive: even the most innocuous "simple fact" when incorporated in a more general model of the relevant system and interpreted in the light of an individual goal structure suggests a course of action for someone. Information comes in various kinds and qualities. Information is generated and released into the system and analyzed, tested, and evaluated by those who receive it. It may be attacked by those who believe it to be inaccurate, but also by those who consider it destructive to their own objectives. Eventually, the information set which survives criticism influences the outcome of the public decision process. In sharp contrast with the public interest model, with its tech-nical experts providing objective facts on demand to the decision-maker who decides in the public interest, the diffuse model looks to open flows of information and unre-strained critical processes for essential safeguards in a governmental environment that is otherwise open to abuse.

The role of the economist

In the diffuse model of the public decision process, economists are among the many who generate and disseminate information. The population of generators and disseminators of policy-relevant information is diverse and includes the "interest groups" (those who stand personally and directly to gain or lose from specific policy decisions, have strong views about how things ought to be, and are willing to devote their own resources to promoting those views and organizing others for the same purpose); the professional advocates (lobbyists, lawyers, and others using acquired skills to promote and advocate the positions of the various interests); legislators, administrators, and those who staff the governmental institutions; journalists, reporters, and critics who staff the public information media; and scholars, academics, and researchers who are independent of the various interests and free to pursue the truth as they see it, according to the established ethics of scholarship and science.

People with training in economics may be found in each of these groups. Yet when we label someone an economist, we usually mean a professional scholar or researcher in economics. Even this group extends beyond the independent scholars to include at least some in the information media and on the staffs of government institutions. Yet for all of these, the role model is usually that of scholar and scientist; and that is the role model we shall consider. We must consider the role of the economist as one of many kinds of trained thinkers, analysts, and researchers who seek to bring information to bear on the policy process.

In principle, the scholars and scientists are distinguished from other participants in the policy process by: (1) expert knowledge, credentials, and established reputation in some discipline of study; and (2) adherence to the ethics of scholarship and science, which place truth above self-interest and attempt to establish and enforce protocols for the pursuit of truth. These ethics are quite demanding. The most logically sound methods of analysis and best obtainable data must be brought to bear on the question at hand. Analysis is pursued to its logical conclusion, even if that conclusion turns out to be incompatible with the analyst's personal inclinations. When possible, testable and refutable hypotheses are posed and tested rigorously with sound data in a logically consistent analytical framework. The scientist's reasoning, analytical framework, data, and conclusions are always exposed forthrightly to the examination and criticism of others. In these ways, scientific objectivity is actively sought.

There is a tradition that insists that scholars and scientists should deal only with the positive (the world of fact-like statements), to the exclusion of the normative. We interpret this tradition as having arisen from fears that a scholarly and scientific elite might, if it were not otherwise restrained, impose its normative beliefs on a gullible and defenseless public and/or its political leadership. That, obviously, is something to be avoided. But we believe the prominent role of criticism in both the concept of scientific objectivity and the diffuse public policy decision process provides substantial protection. Normative statements will be identified as such in the critical process, which accords no special respect to any particular normative statement merely because it was made by someone with scholarly or scientific credentials. Because society has these defenses, we see little harm in scholars and scientists venturing into the normative. It may not be the best use of their talents, and association with ill-thought-out normative viewpoints will do little to enhance the scientists' professional reputation. A society that maintains a strong tradition of criticism, however, will have little to fear from normative expressions, even from its scientists.

On the other hand, normative information has an essential role in society. If a society is to be more than simply a collection of individuals sharing nothing in common, it must have a system of goals and basic beliefs that command wide assent and respect. In a society that faces constant challenges from rapidly increasing technology and changing patterns of scarcity, problems of values and beliefs arise constantly and must be resolved if society is to progress without upheaval. Careful intellectual labor to establish coherent normative positions and to argue for their general adoption is essential to this process. Scholars and scientists have no monopoly on the talents or motivations to do this kind of work. Nevertheless, it would be a great and unnecessary sacrifice if an outmoded scientific ethic were to disqualify a portion of society's better intellects from contributing to the resolution of normative issues.

We have argued that there is no pressing social need to restrain the scholar and scientist from the normative area and, furthermore, that some genuine loss might ensue from such restraint. The distinction between positive and normative, however, remains useful. Although criticism is essential to quality control in both positive and normative arenas, the complete process of scientific objectivity, with its emphasis on the rigorous testing of refutable propositions, is amenable only to the positive.

The economist is a member of the scholarly and scientific community with specialized training in economics. We define economics as the study of choice in the face of scarcity. Without scarcity, the choices actually made are inconsequential. But given scarcity, every possible choice has its costs: action A will preclude action B, and the costs of action A are equal to the benefit that would have resulted from B if B had been chosen. With scarcity, every choice has consequences, and the individual who chooses well will achieve the highest possible satisfaction that his or her means permit. Societies that choose well will increase, over the long haul, the range of possible choices for their citizens.

Natural resource and environmental economics

Given the complexity of modern economic systems and the variety of problems they face, economists tend to specialize. Resource and environmental economists (REEs) are especially interested in the problems of maintaining and enhancing human existence in a world in which scarcity limits the availability of raw materials resources, the capacity of the environment to absorb wastes, and environmental amenities which uplift human experience. The problems that interest REEs are central and are intertwined with all other economic problems. And so REEs are broadly trained economists. They are aware of the macroeconomic implications of resource scarcity and environmental regulation. Nevertheless, for the most part, they tend to emphasize microeconomic theory and empirical methods.

Microeconomic theory is based on the analysis of the behavior of individuals as consumers, suppliers of labor, and entrepreneurs. For REEs, however, the analysis of individual decisions is seldom the ultimate goal. Rather, it is an intermediate step in the analysis of public policy issues that have consequences for productivity, environmental quality, and the distribution of income and opportunity at a more aggregate level. Thus, REEs use the more aggregate analyses offered by various developments and extensions of microeconomics: industry and sectoral analysis, general equilibrium analysis, and welfare economics.

Major concerns in natural resource and environmental economics are resource allocation in the present and the future, and the distributional outcomes of resource allocation decisions. How should a society allocate its resources now and in the future, and in what manner should the fruits of those resource allocation decisions be distributed among the members of a society? To raise these questions assumes there is something at stake. One does not question systems that are generally acknowledged as perfect. Thus, natural resource and environmental economics, by its very existence as a serious field of inquiry, raises questions about the effectiveness of existing market and institutional structures in allocating resources, in adjudicating among the claims of individuals in the present generation, and in adjudicating among the claims of present and future generations.

As its name implies, natural resource and environmental economics focuses on policy questions with respect to natural resources and the environment: land in its many dimensions (e.g., as soil; as an organizer of spatial relationships; as substrate for buildings, roads, and the like; and as store of mineral wealth), water, air, and ecosystems. Natural resource and environmental economics seeks to analyze problems in the allocation of these resources, to identify the causes of those problems, and to identify and examine alternative programs, policies, and projects being proposed as solutions. It focuses on the benefits and costs of alternative programs, policies, and projects, and the incidence of those benefits and costs including geographic incidence, incidence among economic sectors, incidence across socio-economic classes, and intertemporal incidence.

Natural resource and environmental economics approaches the analysis of these issues from a perspective that is typical of mainstream economics generally. It focuses on prices and costs, opportunity costs and the aggregate outcomes of individual choices, and the ways that alternative policies influence these things. The analytical perspective is individualistic at the outset. Preferences are treated as fundamental: what an individual wants is considered to be a serviceable indicator of what is good for the individual. Prices are treated as actually or potentially valid indicators of relative values (potentially when markets are incomplete or restricted in some way). As policy analysis proceeds, the realm of the normative is broached, and different perspectives emerge. Among microeconomists and REEs, the public interest/market failure approach, the utilitarian benefit–cost approach, and philosophical individualism are well represented. Regardless of personal differences in philosophies and preferences, REEs understand that although their contributions may be significant, their analyses, arguments, and conclusions will not be accepted uncritically out of respect for their authority. Whatever influence they ultimately enjoy will be determined by the ability of their work to withstand criticism.

Questions for discussion

1. What kinds of limits do you believe should be placed on the authority of government to control individual behavior in the public interest?
2. Explain why question 1 is basic to most natural resource and environmental policy issues.
3. "Economists have nothing to say, as economists, about values, whether of morality or art." What (if anything) does this statement mean? Do you agree or disagree with it?
4. "Natural resource and environmental economics, by its very existence as a serious field of inquiry, raises questions about the effectiveness of existing market and institutional structures in allocating resources, in adjudicating among the claims of individuals in the present generation, and in adjudicating among the claims of present and future generations." Does this mean that the natural resource and environmental economist is necessarily a radical? Radical in what respect(s)?

Notes

1. See Christopher Bertram (2004), *Rousseau and the Social Contract*, Florence, KY, USA and Milton Park, UK: Routledge, Taylor & Francis; E. Jonathan Lowe (1995), *Locke on Human Understanding*, Florence, KY, USA and Milton Park, UK: Routledge, Taylor & Francis.
2. See Glen Newey (2008), *Hobbes and Leviathan*, Florence, KY, USA and Milton Park, UK: Routledge, Taylor & Francis.
3. For example, see Ronald H. Coase (1960), "The Problem of Social Cost," *Journal of Law and Economics* **3** (1): 1–44; Carl J. Dahlman (1979), "The Problem of Externality," *Journal of Law and Economics* **22** (1): 141–62; Thomas W. Merrill (2002), "Introduction: The Demsetz Thesis and the Evolution of Property Rights," *Journal of Legal Studies* **31**: S331–S338.
4. See Richard A. Musgrave and Peggy B. Musgrave (1989), *Public Finance Theory and Practice: 5th Edition*, New York: McGraw-Hill.
5. See Paul Kelly (2009), *Bentham on Law and Morality*, Florence, KY, USA and Milton Park, UK: Routledge, Taylor & Francis.
6. Nicholas Kaldor (1939), "Welfare Propositions in Economics," *Economic Journal* **49**: 549–52; John R. Hicks (1939), "The Foundations of Welfare Economics," *Economic Journal* **49**: 696–712.
7. See James M. Buchanan and Gordon Tullock (1962), *The Calculus of Consent*, Ann Arbor, MI: University of Michigan Press.

Suggested reading: classic and contemporary

Randall, A. (1985), "Methodology, Ideology and the Economics of Policy: Why Resource Economists Disagree," *American Journal of Agricultural Economics* **67**: 1022–9.
Randall, A. and M.A. Taylor (2000), "Incentive-Based Solutions to Agricultural Environmental Problems: Recent Developments in Theory and Practice," *Journal of Agricultural and Applied Economics* **32** (2): 221–34.
Sabatier, P.A. (1991), "Toward Better Theories of the Policy Process," *Political Science and Politics* **24** (2): 147–56.

PART II

MICROECONOMIC THEORY FOUNDATIONS FOR PRODUCTION AND CONSUMPTION

5 Economic coordination and the price system: how does the market system work?

Economics is the study of economic systems. So its concerns, the variables on which it focuses, and its methodological approach are fashioned to a substantial extent by its vision of what economic systems are and how they work.

Economic coordination

What is an economy? There are many possible answers to this question, but one of the most serviceable is that an economy is a complex organizational system, a system for organizing the production of goods and services and their distribution among people. As such, it is inextricably linked with the environmental system (the atmosphere, lithosphere, hydrosphere, ecosystems, and ecosphere) and the social system (the system of rules, customs, traditions, organizations, and communications networks that guides, constrains, and channels the interactions among people). Clear boundaries defining what is and is not a part of the economic system do not exist. In fact, if that question is asked of many things, one by one, the answer that will emerge is that virtually everything either is a part of the economic system or is linked to the economic system in important ways.

An economy includes production sectors that extract or capture natural resources and combine them with capital (which is, in a sense, the savings from previous production) and labor, in processes that use knowledge and technology (the fruits of investment in people's own productive facilities) to produce goods and services.

It can be seen immediately that production processes are subject to the availability of natural resources, capital, and labor and to the technical characteristics of the production process. Furthermore, they are subject to the inexorable laws of physics, the first of which is that energy matter is neither created nor destroyed. So production is a process not of creation but of conversion. Useful production changes matter and energy into forms that meet some sort of demand by people for goods and services. Efficient production maximizes the increment in value that results from the production process. Useful and efficient production typically generates some wastes (that is, matter and energy of zero or negative value) along with its valuable outputs.

Consumption sectors are also included. People acting individually and sometimes collectively combine the outputs of the production sector (and, sometimes, natural resources directly) with their time, in processes that may use learned behaviors (consumption technologies), to obtain sustenance and satisfactions. Consumption processes are subject to the productivity of the society of which the individual is a member, the ability of the individual to command goods and services in competition with other individuals, and the laws of physics. Goods consumed do not disappear but are converted to other forms of energy matter, some of which are wastes.

So here is how an economy looks according to standard neoclassical economic theory. It includes production and consumption sectors, the former of which services the latter. The distinguishing feature of an economy is its coordination and organization function.

Production in a modern economy requires the coordination of individuals in technologically complex production units, and the functional coordination of input procurement, scheduling of interdependent production processes, sales, and investment for future production. More importantly, the derivation of sustenance and satisfactions through consumption must be coordinated with the production process. Those goods and services that are needed or desired should be produced, and those forms of energy matter that reduce rather than increase satisfaction must be avoided or rendered as harmless as possible. Inputs must be allocated to their highest-valued uses, and goods and services must be distributed to those who value them most. People who control raw materials, capital goods, labor, and technical abilities must be encouraged to devote them to production, and the total output of the production process must be distributed among competing consumers. Transportation, storage, and financial services must be supplied, unless production and consumption are to occur at exactly the same time and place. Any modern economy devotes a major proportion of its resources to these coordination functions.

Information on the relative values of all inputs, goods, and services must be generated and made widely available. A common measure of value must be established and used as currency to facilitate trade and permit the storage of purchasing power. In order to provide incentives for production and to ration goods and services among competing consumers, these value measures must be translated into income for producers and expenses facing consumers.

To make rationing devices work effectively and to provide incentives, a detailed system of rights must be established and enforced. These rights must define the conditions under which individuals have access to inputs, goods, services, and the environment, and the proper relationships among people. Who, and under what conditions, may do what to whom?

Given an adequate system of rights, the value of goods produced or services provided becomes the revenue of the producers and the value of the inputs used becomes their costs. The residual is profit, which permits them to purchase goods and services for consumption and to save for investment in future production. Here we have the rudiments of a simplified economic coordination system. The need of individuals for sustenance and their desire for additional consumption make income valuable to them and thus provide the incentives for production. If they can organize their production so as to be more effective in producing things that others value highly, then they can increase their consumption and save and invest for an even more prosperous future. Thus, the relative values that consumers place on different goods and services are reflected in production incentives. On the other hand, inputs, goods, and services that are scarce because of limited resource availability or costly production processes will be made available only at great expense. This in itself will limit the quantities demanded and ration the supply among those who have high incomes or who are willing to make great sacrifices, or both.

An economy, then, coordinates production and consumption, saving and investment, given resource scarcity, limited technology, the needs and desires of its citizens, and the system of rights.

How is coordination achieved?
Up to this point, everything that has been said is equally pertinent to an enterprise economy, a centrally planned economy, and a mixed economy in which central planning provides some goods and services and influences the incentives under which enterprise

sectors provide others. These different forms of economic organization differ in the ways the coordination function is performed. Because the coordination function always involves incentives and rewards, economies that differ in their coordination mechanisms most likely achieve different results in terms of what is produced, how much of it is produced, and who gets to consume it.

First, consider a pure enterprise economy. In such an economy, rights must be well specified, exclusive, enforceable, and transferable. Ownership of anything must guarantee the right to use it and to exclude others from using it. Ownership rights must be enforced, since a right that is not enforced is ineffective. There must be no restraints on the transfer of ownership rights. Individuals must be free to transfer ownership rights to others, and given this freedom, they will choose to do so whenever they are offered something of greater value in return. Who determines value? The parties to the exchange, or trade, determine value. Because trade is voluntary, it will take place only when both parties are satisfied that it is mutually beneficial; that is, when each is convinced that he or she will receive something of greater value (to himself or herself) than is given up. Exclusive rights facilitate trade by assuring individuals that they can use what they own, that they cannot use what they do not own, and that they can obtain desired things they do not own only by giving up less desired things that they own.

Because individuals are not arbitrarily restricted in their choice of trading partners, each is free to seek the most favorable terms of trade (that is, relative prices). Competition among buyers and sellers tends to result in the convergence of individual offers and asking prices and the establishment of relative prices that remain stable until there is some change in market conditions. Introduce a currency, money, as a medium of exchange and a store of value, and these relative prices become the money prices which we see on the "sticker price" of goods and services.

Given a complete system of ownership rights, price serves the coordination function for the enterprise economy. Prices provide the incentives for production, as income is determined by the price and the quantity of goods and services sold. Prices ration goods and services among consumers, as for each consumer, the sum of expenditures (prices multiplied by quantities) on all items of goods and services cannot exceed the budget. Because the prices for all goods and services are determined by supply-and-demand conditions, price movements provide an information system, signaling changes in scarcity and demand and providing incentives for producers and consumers to make adjustments to the new conditions.

Prices thus provide a feedback and self-correction mechanism in the market economy. A rise in the price of some commodity, reflecting increased relative scarcity, tends to encourage increased production and decreased consumption of that commodity, while simultaneously encouraging increased production and consumption of its substitutes, thus tending to correct the scarcity situation. Even for exhaustible resources, whose stocks are strictly limited, the price mechanism tends to correct scarcity problems by encouraging exploration and resource discovery, discouraging consumption, and encouraging conservation, recycling, and the production of substitutes.

Given that interest rates are prices of capital, the price system tends to stabilize the economy over time. Increases in interest rates, reflecting a shortage of capital, encourage saving while discouraging borrowing and delaying consumption, and thus generate more capital.

The price mechanism is the device that permits Adam Smith's famous invisible hand to perform its wondrous function, so that myriad decentralized decisions of individuals pursuing their own self-interest work in aggregate for the common good. Modern economists have proved that under certain quite demanding conditions, not necessarily bearing much similarity to the real world, the price system efficiently organizes the enterprise economy.

This is not to say that the price mechanism is entirely without costs and disadvantages: it is costly to operate. It works best with exclusive property rights and the widespread availability of information, but the establishment and enforcement of exclusive property rights and the provision of information are costly undertakings. The price mechanism works best when each buyer and seller operates on such a small scale that the decisions of anyone acting alone cannot influence price. Yet modern production processes often require such large-scale operations that individual firms have obvious opportunities to influence prices. Opportunities may exist for buyers or sellers to collude to influence price. Because the independent decisions that generate prices are made by individuals whose foresight is necessarily limited and imprecise, there is no assurance that prices are adequate guides for decisions with long-lived consequences.

The price mechanism can be a cruel disciplinarian. When production processes are subject to the vagaries of ephemeral weather patterns, as is the case with some agricultural products, violent price fluctuations may have a devastating impact on producers' incomes and consumer welfare. Changes in technology may sharply reduce the value of plant and equipment rendered obsolete, and the incomes of individuals whose skills are no longer so valuable.

There is a circularity between prices and incomes that is disconcerting to some who worry about whether the enterprise system is fair in the way it distributes income to individuals and groups. Prices help determine incomes, but prices themselves are in part determined by incomes. Effective demand is desire backed up by spending money. Thus in a price system, a rich person will tend to have more of an impact on relative prices and what goods and services are produced and sold as compared to a poor person. If incomes were more evenly distributed, it is predictable that relative prices would change. It should be noted that the rich may not always dominate a market. A large number of lower-income persons could have more of an impact on relative prices and what goods and services are produced than a smaller number of higher-income persons, since their aggregate demand would be higher.

Income is the reward for labor, skill, education, and training and also for the use of capital and resources owned. For the very rich, the greater portion of income comes from the latter sources. Although capital and resources must be rewarded in order to attract them to productive uses, the high incomes of their owners do not always seem fair to those who have little ownership or rights to capital and resources including natural resources. For these and other reasons, some societies have been reluctant to allow price, with a system of exclusive property rights, to function as the coordinating mechanism for their economies. Instead, centrally planned economic systems are operated.

Centralized planning agencies, dedicated (one hopes) to serving the best interests of the citizenry, are called on to carry out the economic coordination function. Resources and the capital stock may be owned by the collective (that is, the state) rather than the individual. In this way, the state attempts to avoid income inequality attributable to capital and resources. In addition, to the extent that the state takes a longer-term view of things than does the individual, the state seeks to avoid resource uses that sacrifice longer-term benefits for the sake of more immediate gains. Because there will be few, if any, very rich persons under such a system, resources will not be directed to producing playthings for the rich, but to satisfying the needs of the citizenry. Economic growth may be stimulated by encouraging saving and investment rather than immediate consumption. These are the ideal aims of some centrally planned socialist economies.

How are these broad social purposes to be translated into incentives encouraging individuals to offer their labor and invest in the development of their skills, and industrial managers to produce the things that are desired? The central planners typically establish a complex system of directives, production quotas, and rewards and penalties, backed up with continual exhortation that each individual do his or her best for the common good. These incentives will have varying degrees of effectiveness. However, the individual will respond most willingly when the course of action desired by the planners is also the one that increases his or her own welfare. Thus rewards must be related to skill, effort, and willingness to make desired adjustments, and so a degree of income inequality inevitably appears. How do the planners know which directives to issue and what production quotas to establish? They must have a massive amount of information about relative scarcities, relative values, and the relative efficiency of alternative production processes. This information must be gathered and analyzed in order to determine desired goals; then incentives must be established to achieve these goals. Notice that these are the functions that are performed by price in an enterprise economy. The coordination function in a planned economy is performed by a central agency using "shadow prices" (that is, prices that are imputed, not observed) to replace market-generated prices.

A mixed economy uses the price system to direct the activities of its enterprise sectors. However, the state retains the right to influence the patterns of production and consumption. The state may produce and distribute, outside the price system, certain goods that it believes are essential to the national security or of overwhelming social value. It may attempt to influence the behavior of its consumers and its enterprise production sectors by "fine-tuning" relative prices, directly or indirectly. It may do this in many ways: by taxation, subsidization, tariffs, import and export quotas, and public sector purchasing, all of which influence prices directly; and by regulation and modification of the system of property rights, which influence prices indirectly.

The mixed economy is, then, an attempt to take advantage of the inherent efficiency of the price system as a coordination mechanism, without entrusting all aspects of economic performance to the price system. Price retains major roles in creating incentives and distributing rewards, whereas public policy seeks to provide some minimal level of consumption for the least-effective income earners, so as to cushion the shock for those whose skills and resources are suddenly reduced in value by changes in market conditions, and to correct perceived resource misallocations that occur when the price mechanism fails to provide the "right" incentives. It is important to understand that the public sector role in the mixed economy involves substantial planning: collection and analysis of information, establishment of goals, and creation of incentives for achievement of these goals. Thus, public sector mismanagement and imperfect planning are quite possible. In a modern mixed economy, there is always room for sincere and vigorous debate as to whether the public sector is in general making things better or worse and whether particular public sector programs should be introduced, modified, or abandoned; and economists are, and should be, among the leaders in that debate.

The methodology of economics

The economics discipline is alive and vital. It has developed, with a good deal of sophistication and in substantial detail, an approach to its subject matter that is accepted by many of its practitioners. This mainstream approach, or methodology, serves both as an organizing framework for much of the research and scholarship undertaken by economists and as a focus for the continuing methodological debate and intellectual ferment within the economics profession.

The mainstream economists fall into several loose groupings. The middle ground is occupied by those who find the mainstream economic methodology useful, and even quite powerful, but who realize that it has some perplexing limitations, especially when applied to policy analyses. The reader who is not already familiar with these limitations will be acutely aware of them after studying Chapters 6–10. To one side of the middle, there is a group of free-market zealots who see the economic system in simple terms and who cannot understand why others fail to see what to them is obvious. They divide their time between proselytizing for free-market solutions among non-economists and attempting to keep the other groups of mainstream economists on the straight and narrow. To the other side of the middle, there is an ill-defined group of those who are quite uneasy about the limitations of mainstream economics in policy analysis and suspicious that the free-market zealots confuse methodology and ideology, but who are unable to develop a coherent alternative to the mainstream methodology. The best of these "free-market skeptics" are competent in their use of the mainstream methodology and their work is, if anything, improved by their awareness of its limitations; the worst of them offer a criticism that is less coherent than what they are criticizing. Outside the mainstream, there are Marxists, various kinds of more or less romantic socialists, and even a few anarchists.

Economics is not a monolith. The questions with which economics grapples are both important and interesting, and economics has attracted its share of intelligent and articulate individuals. We sincerely hope that sooner or later, some of our readers will be attracted to an in-depth study of, and perhaps active participation in, the philosophical and methodological debates that enliven economics. In the interim, however, a brief exposure to a simplified exposition of mainstream economic methodology must suffice.

The fundamental tool of mainstream economic methodology is abstraction. The economy is a complex system that interacts with other complex systems. The process of abstraction is an attempt to make the intractable tractable, by identifying and concentrating on crucial variables to the exclusion of less important variables. This process is absolutely essential. The person who says "everything depends on everything else" is in a sense correct, but he or she has neither advanced understanding nor provided useful information.

The economist constructs an abstract model, a simplified version of reality that strips away layer upon layer of detail while leaving basically intact the essential components of the system under study. Alternatively, the model may not replicate any actual components of the system: as long as it works as the essential components of the system work, it will suffice. Given that the model "works," simplicity is a positive virtue. If two models achieve similar results, the simpler will be preferred. Perhaps it is wise to expand on the phrase "achieve similar results." One test is prediction. The economist often evaluates models on the basis of how many different things they predict, under how wide a range of conditions, and the reliability of predictions.

In economic models, assumptions play a crucial role. For various purposes, economists make assumptions about: (1) human motivations; (2) the nature of the interrelationships among components of economic systems; and (3) the empirical magnitudes of important variables and parameters. In all three areas, assumptions may be used as substitutes for knowledge: to complete the system, it may be necessary to assume something about things that are unknown. In the first two areas, assumptions may also be used to simplify the model. Even when economists have considerable knowledge about a complex relationship, they may choose to substitute a simple set of assumptions for the more intricate reality that exists. The use of assumptions is an essential strategy in the economists' search for simplicity.

Without exception, mainstream economic models start with the assumption that decisions are made by rational individuals. "Rational" does not mean that a person decides and acts like a "normal" person. For that matter, "rational" is not a synonym for "sensible," as the latter term is popularly used. Rationality, in this context, means merely that the decision process is coherent and logically consistent. It is assumed that individuals are capable of ranking alternatives. For any pair of alternatives, the individual will prefer A to B (or vice versa) or will be indifferent as to A or B. Preferences are transitive; that is, if A is preferred to B and B is preferred to C, A must be preferred to C. Finally, the individual's preferences, given the constraints, will determine the choice.

In this framework, preferences are treated as data of the most fundamental kind. In mainstream economics, individual preferences are the ultimate source of economic value, not the opinions of political, cultural, and/or spiritual leaders about what is good and what is bad (although it is recognized that these opinions may influence individual preferences). The other body of data that is taken as fundamental is resource availability, limited by resource stocks and flows which, in turn, are constrained by ecosystem health and by the laws of physics governing the conversion of energy matter from one form to another and the entropic degradation of energy matter.

Technology, composed of the store of knowledge about ways to get things done, strictly limits (in a static time sense) people's capacity to use available resources to produce the things they value. Because people can and do influence technology over time by investing in its development and implementation, in economics it is not considered as fundamental as preferences and resource availability. At any given time, a society's technology and resource availability determine society's opportunity set, which is a set of all possible choices bounded by the constraints on the society. A society's cultural, religious, and political institutions further constrict that society's opportunity set, by defining some of the choices as unacceptable.

In a competitive process, the society's opportunity set is partitioned into individual opportunity sets. The individual's opportunity set is an array of the alternatives facing that individual, with prices or opportunity costs attached to each, and bounded by the constraints that impinge on the individual. Within his or her individual opportunity set, the rational individual makes choices on the basis of preferences. In a dynamic context, individual choices in one time period may influence the individual's opportunity set in later time periods, and in aggregate, individual choices will influence the society's opportunity set in later periods.

Now that the basic elements of a typical mainstream economic model have been identified, the model must be constructed. Model construction is an exercise in pure logic. The basic elements are organized into a logical system, which is activated by a set of motivational assumptions. If preferences and constraints together determine choice, the economist who can precisely define the constraints can make considerable progress in predicting choice by making some simple and manageable assumptions about preferences. The individual is assumed to prefer more to less, for all of those things that he or she positively values. But the incremental satisfaction obtained from each additional unit of a homogenous good diminishes. These motivational assumptions are basic to all mainstream economic models. For particular purposes, the economist may make some more specific assumptions including: (1) the consumer may or may not be concerned about the uncertainty with respect to future income; and (2) the producer may single-mindedly maximize profit in the present time period or may seek not only current profits but also leisure and the security that comes from long-term survival of the firm. Given a set of motivational assumptions, the economist's model becomes a precise and functional system, wherein changes in the magnitude of some variables lead inevitably to changes in other variables.

How is such a model used? First, it is used to predict. In theoretical exercises the actions of one hypothetical individual may be predicted, whereas in empirical work it is more common to predict the behavior of aggregates (for example, the actual and potential producers and consumers of a particular commodity and its substitutes). What is predicted? Most commonly, economists predict changes in behavior (that is, the decisions made) resulting from changes in the pattern of relative scarcity. Changes in income, production technology, and relative prices of goods and services all influence the pattern of relative scarcity confronting an individual. Changes in population, individual tastes and preferences in aggregate, technology, and the resource base influence the pattern of relative (and absolute) scarcity facing society as a whole.

How would one expect an individual to react to a personal income change, a change in the price of a valued commodity, an invention that increases his or her productive capacity, a change in the rate of taxation or a subsidy that benefits a competitor, the introduction of a new product on the market, or a law prohibiting trade in a commodity he or she does not produce but is accustomed to using? What would be the aggregate effect, in a given country, of a rise in the price of a commodity it exports, a rise in the price of an increasingly scarce exhaustible resource it imports, a technological improvement, the imposition of a new tax or an increase in the rate of an existing tax, an attempt to prohibit markets in a commodity desired by many, an income supplement for those who earn low incomes in the market or a program to provide certain commodities to low-income individuals at less than the market price? From prediction, it is a short step to policy analysis. In fact, the simplest form of policy analysis is prediction of the impacts of proposed policy change on relevant variables such as incomes, quantities supplied and demanded, and prices.

The policy analyst is primarily interested in examining the impacts of changes in institutions on opportunity sets and economic outcomes. Examples of such institutions include: laws, regulations, guidelines, and other policy pronouncements; taxes, administered prices, and other attempts to modify and direct the pattern of trade; and public invest-ments. Positive analyses are essential in order to predict the effects of changes in these kinds of institutions. In performing these kinds of analyses, economists typically use one or another variant of the mainstream economic model discussed above. However, when seeking to inform the process of institutional choice (that is, the policy-making process), economists find themselves increasingly confronted with normative questions: Which of the various policy alternatives is most desirable? The special difficulties that arise in considering normative problems are discussed at some length in Chapter 4.

Prices, demand, supply, and market equilibrium
Markets have a logic and a momentum of their own. Economists frequently insist that "there is no free lunch." Actually, we do not need economics to tell us that we can't get something for nothing – the laws of physics prove this point. But economics drives the lesson home, again and again. It is understandable that in times of persistently low product prices, farmers may feel strongly that prices should be supported above market levels, and many citizens may sympathize with them. Economics does not prove that such a strategy is impossible, but it does point out the impediments to a successful price support program including its costs in terms of valuable products sacrificed. If a society persists in attempting to achieve a price-support goal, economics can offer considerable insight into the least costly way of getting the job done.

It is equally understandable that in times of rising retail prices, citizens may feel strongly that price ceilings should be enforced. Attempts may be made to control prices in general, or specific prices such as those of gasoline or rental apartments. Economics can point out the impediments to successful programs, the resource and opportunity costs of implementing such programs, and the least costly method of implementing them with reasonable precision.

Casual and informed observers alike see increasingly acrimonious competition for water in arid lands (especially in places like the American Southwest, where there are sub-stantial rural and urban populations). They see environmental degradation and pollution. And they see some curious inconsistencies in the way that some natural amenities, such as access to outdoor recreation sites, are provided to and rationed among the public.

At first glance, these problems may not seem to have much to do with economics. After all, to the extent that these problems are resolved at all, they are resolved in the political arena. Yet economics has much to offer. It can explain why these problems are persistent, what forces work to exacerbate them, and how the incentives established in the political arena may be perverse and counterproductive. Economics, by identifying causes of these problems, points the way to their solution. If there are several possible solutions (as there usually are) economics can often identify good reasons to predict which particular solutions are likely to be most effective and/or less costly in terms of productive opportunities forgone.

Toward the end of this chapter, these problems and policy issues are again raised and the economic logic of markets is applied to defining and identifying causes and impedi-ments to solutions. Possible solutions, though not carefully analyzed, are suggested. In the interim, we shall review the economic theory of the consumer and the firm and establish the concepts of market equilibrium that are essential to economic analysts of economic, natural resource, and environmental problems.

Consumption and demand
The economic concept of consumption involves the transformation of goods, services, and amenities so as to provide satisfaction. What is consumed never disappears completely (to do so would violate the first law of thermodynamics). For example, when a person eats a meal, the food is transformed into energy and residual materials. In the case of food (and other goods called "rival goods"), one person's consumption strictly diminishes the amount available for others. But the concept of consumption is broad enough to include "non-rival goods," which have the characteristic that one person's use does not diminish the amount available for others. For example, when a person looks out upon a pleasing view, the services provided by the view are used to generate satisfaction, but the view is not changed for having been used in that way. Non-rival goods are discussed in Chapter 10, and so in the intervening chapters the analysis is confined to rival goods.

The consumer's problem is to maximize satisfaction by selecting from his or her opportunity set the most preferred attainable bundle of commodities (that is, goods, services, and amenities). If this problem is solved repeatedly, assuming different prices, individual demand curves can be generated for each kind of commodity. Then individual demand schedules can be aggregated across the relevant population to obtain market demand schedules. We next describe the steps in this process.

1. Specify utility function and indifference curves   The ideas of satisfaction and preferences are represented by *utility,* which is an *ordinal* concept. For the individual, the level of utility (U) enjoyed is some function, determined by individual preferences, of the amounts of commodities ($Z = Z_1, Z_2...Z_n$) consumed:

$$U = F(Z) \tag{5.1}$$

We could find all the possible combinations of the various goods that would yield some arbitrary utility level U'. These combinations could be expressed as an indifference surface. Working in two dimensions, the indifference curve I' is the locus of all combinations of Z_1 and Z_2 that together yield the utility level U'. The process can be repeated for higher utility levels, U' and U'', to obtain indifference curves, I'' and I'''. The slope of an indifference curve at any point is the rate of commodity substitution between Z_1 and Z_2 RCS_{Z_1, Z_2} at that point.

Indifference curves have several important properties: (1) they do not, and logically cannot, cross; (2) in the range of positive but diminishing marginal utility for both goods, indifference curves are negatively sloped and convex to the origin; (3) in any indifference map there are an infinite number of indifference curves, each representing one of the infinite number of possible utility levels – in economic diagrams, however, it is customary to show only a few representative curves; (4) indifference curves farther from the origin represent higher levels of utility. These properties facilitate the search for solutions to the consumer's maximizing problem.

2. Specify budget constraint   The opportunity set is defined as the array of alternatives that the individual faces, with the opportunity cost of each identified and bounded by the constraints that impinge on individual choice. In the simplest models, Z is the vector of

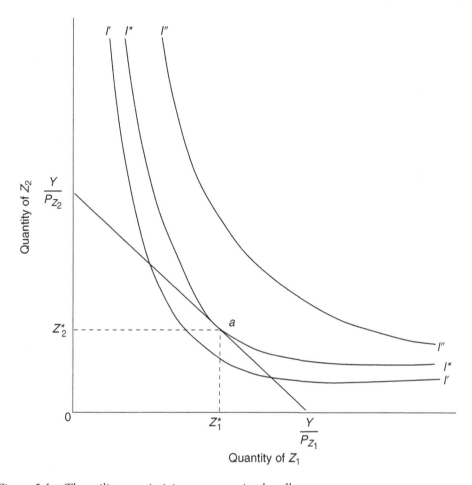

Figure 5.1   The utility-maximizing consumption bundle

alternatives; opportunity costs are represented by a vector of prices P_z; and the bound is represented by a budget constraint:

$$Y = \sum_{i=1}^{n} P_{z_i} \cdot Z_i \qquad (5.2)$$

where Y is the individual's total budget.

To treat prices (P_z) as parameters (as we have done), it is necessary to assume that the individual is a price taker: one individual's purchases are so small relative to the total quantities for sale that they do not affect prices. With this assumption, the budget constraint can be drawn (in two dimensions) as a straight line with the slope determined by the ratio of commodity prices and distance from the origin determined by the size of the budget (Figure 5.1).

3. Maximize utility subject to budget constraint   The individual's choice problem is solved by maximizing utility subject to the budget constraint. In a two-dimensional diagram (Figure 5.1), a geometric solution can be found by identifying the point of tangency between the budget constraint and a convex indifference curve ($I*$). Higher indifference curves are unattainable given the budget and prices assumed. Lower indifference curves are attainable, but less satisfactory. Note that no indifference curve lower than $I*$ is tangent to the budget constraint; lower indifference curves intersect it in two places.

This point of tangency identifies the utility-maximizing consumption bundle (Z_1^*, Z_2^*). At that point, the rate of commodity substitution is equal to the ratio of commodity prices:

$$RCS_{Z_1, Z_2} = \frac{P_{Z_1}}{P_{Z_2}} \tag{5.3}$$

This is the necessary condition for utility maximization. A sufficient condition (the condition that ensures a maximum rather than a minimum) is that the indifference curves be convex.

4. Derive individual demand curves   Now, allow the price of say Z_1, to vary while holding P_{Z_2} constant. For each possible value of P_{Z_1}, solve the individual's utility-maximizing problem. Note that income and substitution effects both occur. For example, as P_{Z_1} falls (Figure 5.2), the consumer's budget permits attainment of a higher utility level, just as an income increase would; in addition, the lower price of Z_1 relative to Z_2 results in some substitution toward Z_1. The points of tangency identified in this process define the quantities of Z_1 taken at various prices, assuming that the budget and the price of Z_2 remain unchanged. An ordinary demand curve for Z_1 is defined as:

$$Z_1^D = f(P_{Z_1} | P_{Z_2}, Y) \tag{5.4}$$

That is, the quantity of Z_1 demanded is a function of its price, given that P_{Z_2} and Y are held constant. Thus these points of tangency are points on the individual's demand curve for Z_1.

The assumptions that Y and P_{Z_2} are constant may be relaxed. If the budget is increased, more of Z_1 will be taken at each price, provided that Z_1 is a normal or superior good. The demand curve for Z_1 will shift to the right. Goods for which less is taken as income increases are called inferior goods. A change in the price of Z_2 may affect the demand for Z_1 in a variety of ways, depending on the relationship between Z_1 and Z_2. If Z_1 and Z_2 were close substitutes (for example, pork and beef), an increase in P_{Z_2} might lead the consumer to switch part of his or her consumption toward the relatively cheaper Z_1. The demand for Z_1 would thus shift to the right when P_{Z_2} increased and to the left when P_{Z_2} decreased. If Z_1 and Z_2 were complements (for example, bread and butter), an increase in P_{Z_2} would make both Z_1 and Z_2 less attractive to the consumer. Thus the demand for Z_1 would shift leftward when P_{Z_2} increased.

5. Aggregate individual demand to generate industry demand   The demand for the output of the whole industry producing Z_1 is determined by the horizontal summation of the individual demand curves: For any particular price of Z_1, sum the quantities taken by each consumer. That identifies one point on the demand curve for the output of the whole industry producing Z_1. Repeating the process for different prices yields a series of obser-

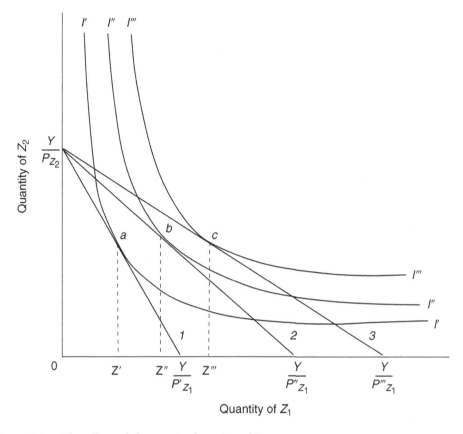

Figure 5.2   The effect of changes in the price of Z_1

vations from which the demand curve can be interpolated. The industry demand curve is flatter (more price elastic, as we shall see) as compared to the individual demand curves.

The industry demand for Z_1 may be responsive to many factors, including its own price, the prices of other goods, and income. The concept of elasticity is useful in quantifying this responsiveness. Elasticity of anything (say, A) with respect to anything else (say B) is defined as the proportional change in A resulting from a one-unit change in B, that is:

$$\frac{\Delta A}{\Delta B} \cdot \frac{B}{A} \tag{5.5}$$

where Δ indicates "the change in."

The price elasticity of demand,

$$\frac{\Delta Z_1}{\Delta P_{Z_1}} \cdot \frac{P_{Z_1}}{Z_1} \tag{5.6}$$

is almost always negative but relatively low in absolute value for necessities, though relatively high in absolute value for luxuries. The price elasticity of the demand for broad categories of goods is usually lower in absolute value than is that for specific commodities.

The cross-price elasticity of demand:

$$\frac{\Delta Z_j}{\Delta P_{Z_i}} \cdot \frac{P_{Z_i}}{Z_j} \quad i \neq j. \tag{5.7}$$

may be positive, zero, or negative. For good substitutes, the cross-price elasticity is positive, but it is negative for complements.

The income elasticity of demand:

$$\frac{\Delta Z_1}{\Delta Y} \cdot \frac{Y}{Z_1} \tag{5.8}$$

is positive for normal and superior goods and negative for inferior goods. The dividing line between normal and superior goods is placed at an income elasticity equal to 1 with superior goods having higher income elasticities.

Elasticities are of great interest in natural resource and environmental policy analysis. Debates about proposals to impose or increase excise taxes on petroleum fuels are much informed by estimates of own-price elasticity of demand. If demand is very inelastic, such taxes should be effective generators of revenue for government. If, on the other hand, demand is rather more elastic, excise taxes should be effective in encouraging conservation and discouraging imports of oil, but less effective in generating revenue. Experience since the oil shortages of the 1970s has shown that the demand for petroleum products is somewhat more elastic than had previously been suspected. Cross-price elasticities have been essential to projections and policy analyses that concern the substitution relationships among, for example, oil, natural gas, and coal.

Although there are few reliable estimates, there is much discussion of the income elasticity of demand for environmental quality amenities such as clean air and clean water. If the income elasticity of demand for such amenities is substantially greater than 1, as some have guessed that it is, we would predict that prosperous societies would spend a greater proportion of their total incomes on attaining environmental quality, whereas impoverished countries would spend a lower proportion of their total incomes for these kinds of amenities. Within a single country, a relatively high income elasticity of demand for environmental quality would suggest that these kinds of amenities are typically of greater concern to upper-income citizens than to lower-income citizens.

Some thoughtful observers believe that this kind of discussion is much too simplistic to be meaningful. It is likely that those things loosely grouped together as "environmental quality amenities" actually consist of a number of very different goods and services. The income elasticities of demand for such basic environmental quality services as sanitation, and air and water quality conducive to good health and normal life spans, are probably quite low. These things are likely viewed by most as "necessities of life." On the other hand, the income elasticity of demand for high levels of atmospheric visibility in remote wilderness areas may well be quite high.

Production and supply
Production, like consumption, is a process of transformation. In production, less valuable forms of materials and energy are transformed into forms more valuable to human beings. The laws of thermodynamics insist that in physical terms, energy matter can be neither created nor destroyed (the first law), although energy is transformed into less

available forms (the second law). Yet people are better off as a result of efficient production. Why? Because the end products are more directly useful to people than are the raw materials, enough so to more than compensate for the labor, plant, and management devoted to the exercise. This is the point missed by those who argue that the system of economic accounts should be replaced by, for example, energy accounts. When people are the ultimate users, not all calories are created equal!

The producing firm's problem is to maximize its owner's satisfaction by combining the resources at its command according to the laws of physics, so as to produce valuable outputs. Repeated solution of this problem, assuming different input and output prices allows the establishment of individual firms' demand schedules for inputs and supply schedules for outputs. Aggregation to obtain industry demand for inputs and supply of outputs is not so simple as it was for commodity demand schedules. Again, we shall review the steps in the process.

1. Specify production function and isoquants The transformation process is represented by the production function, which is a purely physical relationship between inputs and outputs. The physical effectiveness of this transformation process depends entirely on the technology of production. The production function for some commodity Z_i is a mathematical function of the inputs $X = (X_1, X_2, \ldots, X_m)$ used:

$$Z_1 = f(X) \tag{5.9}$$

The implementation of a different technology would shift the production function. Thus any production function can be thought of as a mathematical snapshot of a particular technology.

Moving to two dimensions, if $Z_1 = f(X_1, X_2)$ and X_1 and X_2 are both variable inputs, it is possible to set output at an arbitrary level Z_1 and draw the locus of all possible combinations of X_1 and X_2 that together produce exactly Z_1. This locus is called an isoquant. The isoquant map in production analysis is analogous to the indifference map in an analysis of consumer choice in all respects but one: each isoquant is associated with a specific cardinal quantity of output. The slope of an isoquant at any point is the rate of technical substitution of inputs (*RTS*).

2. Specify expansion path The efficient combination of inputs is identified by using an analysis similar to that for finding the utility-maximizing consumption bundle. If the firm is a price taker, the isocost line will be a straight line of slope equal to the ratio of input prices:

$$\frac{P_{X_1}}{P_{X_2}} \tag{5.10}$$

To solve the input combination problem, a constraint must be imposed. There are two obvious alternatives: (1) constrain the firm's expenditure on inputs in order to determine the output-maximizing combination of inputs given a cost constraint; or (2) constrain the quantity of output in order to determine the least-cost combination if inputs to produce a given output. Either way, the necessary condition for an efficient input combination is:

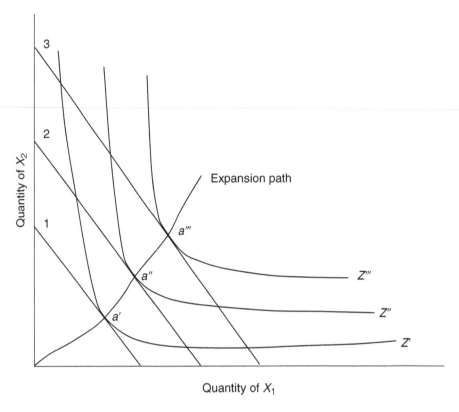

Figure 5.3   The expansion path

$$RTS_{X_1, X_2} = \frac{P_{X_1}}{P_{X_2}}$$ (5.11)

The sufficient condition is that the isoquants be convex to the origin or at least not concave. Convexity is the outcome when the marginal productivity of each input is positive but diminishing.

If the constraint (either one) is progressively relaxed to allow more expenditure on inputs and more output to be produced, the expansion path can be traced (Figure 5.3).

3. Specify profit function and cost curves   The firm owner's utility function may be expressed across several dimensions of the working environment: perhaps income and the accumulation of wealth, leisure, and status in the community, and the avoidance of extreme risks to current income and the capital assets represented by the firm. All of these motivations and more can be incorporated into production models. The simplest models, however, assume that the firm owner seeks to maximize profit (which provides income for current consumption and wealth-generating investment).

Profit, π, is defined as the difference between total revenue:

$$TR = \sum_{i=1}^{n} P_{Z_i} \cdot Z_i,$$

and total costs:

$$TC = \sum_{j=1}^{m} P_{X_j} \cdot X_j.$$ (5.12)

The total cost of producing a given commodity Z_i is itself a function of output:

$$TC = h(Z_i)$$ (5.13)

Because the production function expresses the relationship between the output of Z_i and the amounts of inputs (X) used, the total cost function is derived from the production function for Z_i and the input prices.

Depending on the length of the planning horizon, the levels of some inputs may not be under the effective control of the entrepreneur. It is too late to change the land and seed inputs when the planting season is long gone. Expenditures on these things are then fixed costs, whereas other inputs (fertilizer, pest control, harvesting, and post-harvest handling) remain subject to choice. Expenditures on these items remain variable costs. In thinking about next year's crop, however, the land and seed inputs may well be variable, although there is little real opportunity to increase farm size or invest in major capital improvements. In the very long run, these things too are subject to choice. The distinction between fixed and variable costs, and the notion that as the planning horizon lengthens more costs will be variable (until, finally there are no fixed costs from a very long-time perspective), are basic to the ideas of short-run and long-run costs. For a given state of technology, there is a single long-run cost curve from which can be derived a long-run average cost curve $(LRAC)$ and a long-run marginal cost curve $(LRMC)$. In the short run, however, different short-run cost curves are associated with different levels of fixed inputs. The relationships among three sets of short-run average cost curves $(SRAC)$ and marginal cost curves $(SRMC)$ and the long-run curves are shown in Figure 5.4.

4. Derive short-run and long-run supply curves   Now permit the price of output Z_i to vary. In the short run, the entrepreneur will cease production if $TR < TVC$, where TVC is total variable costs. Because for a price taker, P is average revenue, the individual supplies zero quantity when the price falls below the minimum average variable cost (AVC). At higher prices, the individual supplies output according to the rule $P_{Z_i} = MC_{Z_i}$. If P_{Z_i} exceeds ATC (average total costs), what economists call pure profits will be made in the short run. At prices between minimum ATC and AVC, production continues (at output levels set by the $P = MC$ rule), although the entrepreneur suffers a loss. Why? Because the loss, though real, is less than the fixed costs already incurred. Thus the loss from continued production is less than would be suffered if production ceased in the short run. The individual firm's short-run supply schedule is thus identical to the segment of its $SRMC$ curve that lies above the intersection of $SRMC$ and short-run AVC (Figure 5.5). In the long run, production will not continue in the face of persistent losses. The firm will dispose of its resources, including those fixed in the short run, as a loss-minimizing strategy.

In a long-run analysis, the distinction between AVC and ATC disappears (as, in the long run, all costs are variable). The firm's output decisions are still made according to the rule $P = MC$, and the firm's long-run supply curve is the segment of $LRMC$

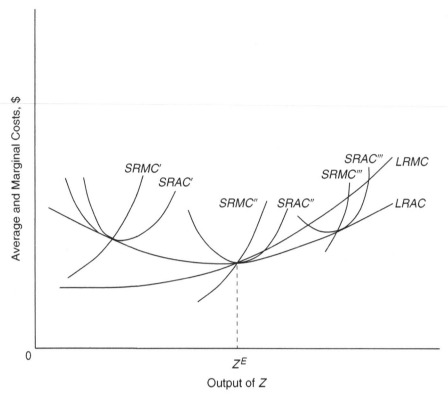

Figure 5.4   Average and marginal cost curves in the short and the long runs

above minimum *LRAC*. At prices above minimum *LRAC*, pure profits will be enjoyed. Assuming, however, that the firm's technology is available to current and potential competitors, these pure profits will attract new operations into the industry. Output will increase, and the unit price will be driven down toward minimum *LRAC*. Industry equilibrium occurs when $P = LRAC = LRMC$ and all firms are operating at the size associated with minimum *LRAC* (Figure 5.6). Pure profits disappear, but each firm earns the opportunity costs of the resources it controls.

5. Aggregate individual supply to generate industry supply   Aggregation of individual supply curves to generate on industry supply schedule, is not so simple as it was for demand curves. If the whole industry that produces Z_i is an insignificant demander of all the inputs it uses (that is, the industry is a price taker with respect to inputs), the horizontal summation of an individual firm's short-run supply curves would be adequate to generate the industry's short-run supply curve. But often the level of activity in a particular industry directly influences the demand for inputs and their price. If the price of inputs rises with output, that will tend to twist each firm's *MC* curve to the left, making the industry's supply curve steeper (less elastic) than the curve obtained by summing the *MC* schedules of price-taker firms.

In the long run there are two, somewhat counteractive, influences. As in the short run,

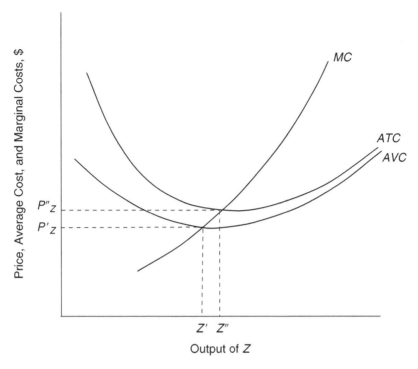

Figure 5.5   *Short-run supply is the segment of the marginal cost curve above its intersection with* AVC

the responsiveness of input prices to output changes would make the long-run supply less elastic. On the other hand, the potential entrance of firms in response to output price changes (and also of input-producing firms in response to higher input prices) tends to make the long-run supply more elastic. Really, the long-run supply is determined in general equilibrium, as the opportunity cost of any actual or potential firm's resources in the Z_i industry is determined by the market conditions (on the input and output sides) in all other industries. In practice, the industry's supply curves are usually estimated econometrically from observations of output prices and quantities, input prices, prices of products to which the firms could easily switch, and so forth. The industry's supply is thus modeled:

$$Z_i^S = f(P_{Z_i}, P_X, P_{\bar{Z}}, \ldots), \bar{Z} = \text{all } Z \text{ not } Z_i \tag{5.14}$$

This means that the industry supply of Z_i is determined by its own price, the price of inputs, the price of other commodities, and additional variables not specified here.

6. Find derived demand for inputs   An analysis of the producing firm also yields information about the demand for factors of production (called derived demands). The demands for raw materials are derived demands, and so this topic is of interest to resource and environmental economists.

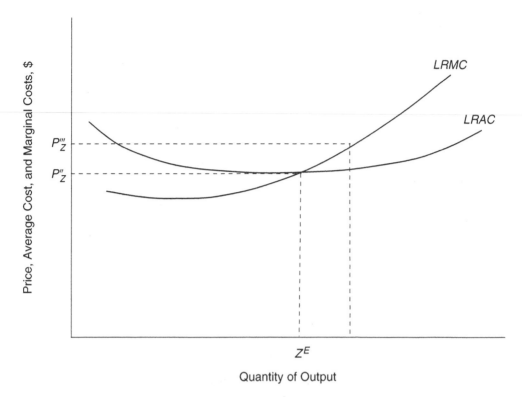

Figure 5.6   Long-run equilibrium price and output

Working with the production function, one may calculate the marginal productivity of each input:

$$MP_{X_j} = \frac{\Delta Z_i}{\Delta Xj} \qquad (5.15)$$

To determine efficient input use when prices P_{Z_i} and P_{X_j} are parametric, the value of marginal product of X_j is set equal to its price:

$$VMP_{X_j} = P_{Z_i}\left(\frac{\Delta Z_i}{\Delta Xj}\right) = P_{X_j} \qquad (5.16)$$

Thus for the individual firm facing parametric prices, the demand curve for an input is the *VMP* curve. In general form, the derived demand for X_j may be expressed as:

$$X_j^D = f(P_{X_j}, P_{Z_i}, P_{\overline{X}}, P_{\overline{Z}}), \ \overline{X} = \text{all } X \text{ not } X_j \qquad (5.17)$$

$$\overline{Z} = \text{all } Z \text{ not } Z_i$$

The derived demand for X_j is some function of the input's own price, product prices, and the prices of other inputs (which may be substitutes or complements in production). The particular function is derived from the firm's production function, which represents a particular technology. Shifts in technology, therefore, will shift the derived demand schedules for inputs.

7. Aggregate individual derived demand to generate industry derived demand If product prices remain parametric, the *industry derived demand curve* can be obtained by horizontally summing individual derived demands. The 'if' clause, however, is violated more often than not in the real world. If the price of X were to fall, all firms using that input would expand production. Assuming commodity demands to be less than perfectly elastic, the increased output would tend to shift commodity prices downward. This decrease in commodity prices would tend to shift input demand curves leftward. The aggregate effect of this sequence of adjustments is to make the derived demand curve for a factor of production steeper (more elastic) than it otherwise would be.

Demand, supply, and market equilibrium
We now consider the interaction of demand and supply, at the commodity or industry level, to determine equilibrium price. The demand curve for a commodity is a schedule relating the quantity of the commodity purchased to its price. Demand curves are expressed diagrammatically in price–quantity space (that is, in the positive quadrant of a diagram with price on the vertical axis and quantity on the horizontal axis) and typically slope downward to the right. As price rises, smaller quantities of the commodity are demanded.

The supply curve is a schedule relating the quantity of a commodity produced to its price and typically slopes upward to the right. As prices increase, making the commodity more attractive to producers, increased quantities are produced and find their way into the market. Because the supply curve and the demand curve are both expressed in price–quantity space, it seems useful to form a single diagram by superimposing the supply curve for a given commodity on the demand curve for the same commodity. In this way, a market diagram is formed.

The equilibrium price for the commodity Z in the market depicted in Figure 5.7 is P^e. At that price, Z^e units of Z are produced, and exactly that many units are purchased. As economists say, the market "clears." At the higher price P^h, the quantity of Z demanded is Z_d^h, and quantity supplied is Z_s^h, which is substantially larger. At the price P^h, a surplus of $Z_s^h - Z_d^h$ exists. Notice that when the amount Z_s^h is supplied on the market, the demand price for that quantity is not P^h, nor even P^e; it is lower than P^e. The excessive quantity of Z supplied as a result of the high price P^h provides a stimulus driving the price downward. As the price is driven downward, larger quantities are demanded. The market comes to equilibrium at the market-clearing price P^e. If, on the other hand, the price were P^l, lower than P^e, the quantity demanded would be Z_d^l and the quantity supplied would be Z_s^l. A *shortage* of $Z_d^l - Z_s^l$ would exist. That shortage would tend to drive the price upward and attract more Z production from suppliers. Eventually the market would reach equilibrium at the price P^e.

The market thus has a built-in, self-regulating tendency to reach equilibrium. Price serves to ration goods among consumers. Higher prices discourage consumption, and lower prices encourage it. Price, because it is directly reflected in the incomes of producers, provides incentives for production. Higher prices encourage increased production, and lower prices discourage it. Working on both the demand and the supply sides of the market, price directs the allocation of resources.

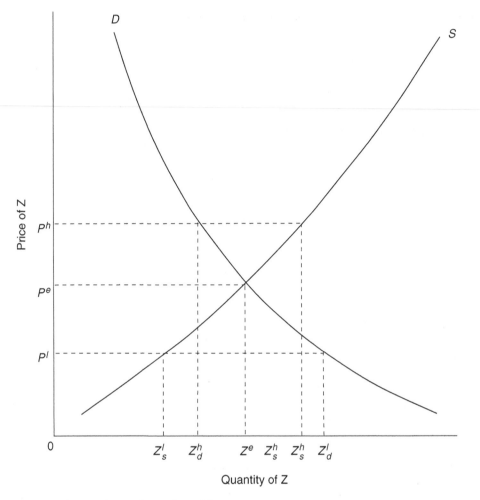

Figure 5.7   Demand, supply, and equilibrium price

The terms "surplus" and "shortage" refer to differences between the quantity demanded and the quantity supplied at particular prices. At a price higher than equilibrium, a surplus exists; at a price lower than equilibrium, a shortage exists. At the equilibrium price, the quantity supplied equals the quantity demanded, and the market clears. The market is a device which, when working well, eliminates shortages and surpluses. That does not mean that a system of markets guarantees utopia. The elimination of shortages does not mean that everybody has as much of every commodity as he or she would like. The elimination of surpluses does not mean that every producing firm receives the prices and revenues it would like. It simply means that markets through the 'invisible hand' move towards economic equilibrium by establishing the price at which quantity demanded equals quantity supplied, given consumers' utility functions, producers' production functions, and consumer's and producers' income and resource endowments.

Support prices and ceiling prices   Suppose that for reasons thought good, the government attempted to maintain the price of some commodity above equilibrium levels. Assume the commodity is wheat, and let P^h be the price that the government wants to maintain. What would be the result of such a policy? Figure 5.7 illustrates the answer. The quantity of wheat produced would exceed the quantity demanded at the price P^h, and a surplus would be generated. If left in the market, this surplus, as we have seen, would provide a powerful stimulus for a fall in wheat prices. But the government is committed to maintain the price of wheat at P^h. Clearly, the surplus must be removed from the market. The government can do this by purchasing it from farmers and keeping it out of the hands of consumers. Although the fundamental conditions remain the same, the government must repeat this activity each year. What can it do with its wheat purchases? It can store ever increasing quantities of wheat; it can deliberately destroy wheat; or it can give wheat (or sell it at very low prices) to consumers who cannot afford to buy wheat at P^h or even P^e. Alternatively, the government can attempt to limit the quantity supplied to the same amount as the quantity demanded at price P^h. It can do this by guaranteeing the price P^h and restricting production by acreage controls or marketing quotas. In fact, in the past 50 years, one or another variant of all of these policies has been tried in the United States from the 1930s up to when this book is being completed in 2010.

It is not impossible to support prices above their equilibrium level, and from time to time both private enterprise speculators and governments have performed useful functions by supporting prices during brief periods when prices would otherwise be unusually low. But to support the price of any commodity above its equilibrium level year after year is expensive and usually entails a waste of resources or government controls of production, or both.

In other circumstances, governments have attempted to place price ceilings on certain commodities so that the price may not exceed some level that is set below the equilibrium price. Return to Figure 5.7 and assume the commodity is rental housing. A government may simply pass a regulation that the price of rental housing (the monthly rent) must not exceed P^l. At the price P^l, the quantity of rental housing demanded exceeds the quantity supplied, and there is a shortage of rental housing. There are some consumers seeking rental housing who would be willing to pay a greater amount than the established price ceiling. The government would need to undertake an expensive effort to enforce the price-ceiling regulations, in order to stop people from obtaining rental housing by paying above-ceiling prices. In other words, a black market for rental housing could arise unless it is prevented by effective government monitoring and enforcement.

As time passes, the shortage of rental housing would remain, as the price ceiling would reduce the incentives for entrepreneurs to provide more rental housing. If rent ceilings were placed on some classes of housing but not on other classes, the housing market would be distorted as the production of rent-controlled types of housing lags, while the production of uncontrolled classifications of housing proceeds apace. Alternatively, the government could attempt to control the price of rental housing to renters at P^l, while paying some higher price to the owners of housing. In other words, it could offer rent subsidies that would enable the owners of rental housing to receive more than the renters were paying. Again, governments in various places have tried all these strategies. The point is not that it is impossible to control prices at some level below the equilibrium, but that to do so for an extended period of time involves coercion, wasted resources, or both.

Shifts in supply and demand   Earlier in this chapter, when the demand curve was first derived, we noted that any demand curve drawn on a two-dimensional diagram expresses the relationship between the price of a commodity and the quantity of that commodity demanded, assuming that income and the price of other commodities remain unchanged. Increases in income will most likely shift a demand curve outward, whereas decreases in income will shift it inward. Increases in the price of substitutes will most likely shift a demand curve out, whereas decreases in the price of substitutes will shift it in. Increases in the prices of complements will most likely shift a demand curve in, whereas decreases in the price of complements will shift it out.

The supply curve represented on a two-dimensional diagram is also a relationship between the price of a commodity and the quantity of that commodity (in this case, the quantity supplied). It is also subject to shifts if other important variables change. A decrease in the price of inputs will most likely shift a supply curve to the right by lowering the costs of producing the commodity supplied. Likewise, an increase in the price of inputs will most likely shift a supply curve to the left. The development and implementation of superior technology will change the production function so that more of the commodity can be produced with the same variable inputs thereby shifting the supply curve to the right.

In Figure 5.8, Panel a shows the result of demand shifts on equilibrium price and quantity. An inward demand shift decreases both price and quantity taken, whereas an outward demand shift increases both. But when holding demand constant, a leftward supply shift will increase the price and reduce the equilibrium quantity. A rightward supply shift will reduce the price and increase the equilibrium quantity (Panel b). It is always possible that both demand and supply may shift. For example, simultaneous rightward shifts in demand and supply will surely increase equilibrium quantity, but price may rise (Panel c) or fall (Panel d). The effect on price is not predictable without empirical estimates of the price elasticities of demand and supply.

Such simple analyses of the effects of changes in market conditions are examples of comparative static analysis. This kind of analysis compares the equilibriums achieved under different kinds of conditions, and is useful because it provides a simple and straightforward method of examining the outcomes to be expected if conditions were to change. It is called comparative static analysis because it compares static equilibriums under two or more sets of conditions, on the assumption that for each set of conditions all adjustments have been completed. It does not examine the process of adjustment.

This kind of comparative static analysis is used to analyze many different kinds of economic problems. The reader should practice this kind of analysis until it can be done easily. Think of examples of events that would result in a shift in one or both of the supply and demand curves, and analyze the effect on price and quantity. What is the effect on wages and employment opportunities for a category of skilled workers when a machine is invented that performs their task more effectively? What would be the effect on the price of lettuce of adverse climatic conditions during the growing season? If the regulation of airline passenger fares tends to keep them above equilibrium levels, what would be the effect of deregulation on airline fares and the number of passengers? Note that in the case of airline fares, some degree of deregulation has already taken place in many countries, allowing opportunities for the economist to analyze not just the thought

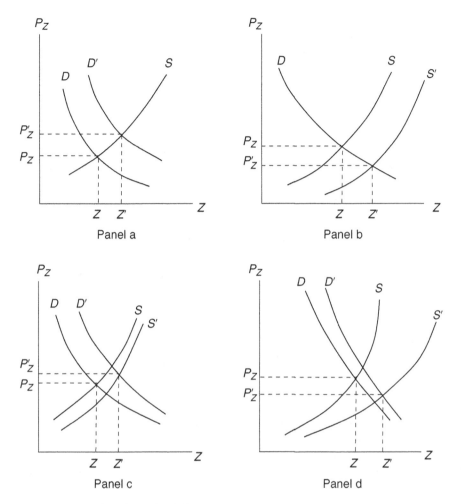

Figure 5.8   Demand and supply shifts

experiment (What if fares were deregulated?) but the actual experiment. What would be the effects of a health advisory on eating certain commercial fish species on the market price of that fish?

Market equilibrium analysis in natural resource and environmental economics
Often problems in natural resource and environmental economics involve incomplete markets, the absence of equilibrating prices, and/or complex dynamic equilibrium problems. These factors tend to complicate the analysis of these problems. Nevertheless, there are many problems in natural resource and environmental economics that can be analyzed fruitfully, if not completely, with simple demand, supply, and market equilibrium models. Below, we consider three such examples: irrigation water, pollution abatement, and outdoor recreation.

The market for irrigation water

In many parts of the world and in many periods of history, from ancient Babylon to the Murray River basin of Australia and the American Southwest in modern times, arid and semi-arid lands have been irrigated with the help of gigantic public works projects that store water, divert it, and deliver it to the irrigated lands. For our purposes here, the American Southwest of modern times makes an interesting example.

At any time, the supply of irrigation water in the American Southwest can be represented by a vertical line. Supply is completely inelastic; that is, it is unresponsive to changes in the price of irrigation water at any given time. The position of the vertical supply curve for irrigation water depends on a complex set of hydrological facts (rainfall, snowfall, run-off, river-system capacity, evaporation and seepage, and the like) and on the development and operation of public works projects that affect the capacity to store water and the uses that can be made of water once it is stored. Such a supply system is dearly unresponsive in the short run to changes in the demand price for water; hence the assumption of inelastic supply in the short run.

When the irrigation system in the Southwest was in its early stages of development, it was feasible to shift the supply line to the right, time and time again, by building new water storage and delivery systems. But there are some who argue that in the early twenty-first century, it is no longer possible to shift the supply curve systematically to the right by building more public works projects. The best dam sites have already been used, and the stored water is "recycled" over and over again in agricultural uses to the extent that agriculture, because of the salinity in the Colorado River water delivered to Mexico, has long been a source of diplomatic tension between the two neighboring countries. It is possible that building more dams in the Colorado River system would result in the delivery of less rather than more water, as additional dams would increase the rate of evaporation and seepage of water from the system. Because surface water appears to be completely utilized, and groundwater is being used at a rate faster than it can be naturally replenished, an argument can be made that the supply curve for irrigation water in the Southwest is more likely to shift to the left than to the right in the future. For these various reasons, an inelastic and non-shifting supply curve for irrigation water, even in the long run, is a serviceable analytic assumption.

The demand for water in the American Southwest can be divided into two broad categories: agricultural and urban. Because there are several rapidly growing cities in the Southwest and these cities rely for their water on the same river systems as does agriculture, and because residential and industrial uses of water are relatively high valued, urban demands are competing more and more directly with agricultural demand for water. Let D^u represent the demand for water in urban uses and D^a represent the demand for water in agricultural uses. The total demand for water, D^t, is simply the horizontal summation of D^u and D^a. If the price of water set not by a market but by the government is P, all demands at that price will be met, and there will be a small surplus of water. The quantity of water demanded, W_d^t, is less than the quantity supplied, W_s (Figure 5.9).

With the passage of time, however, the urban demand for water shifts to the right. The new urban demand curve is $D^{u'}$, the agricultural demand curve remains D^a, and the new total demand curve for water is $D^{t'}$. At the government-determined price, P, there is now a serious shortage of water. Quantity demanded, $W_d^{t'}$, exceeds quantity supplied, W_s (Figure 5.9). The price of P is no longer sufficient to ration the available water among the

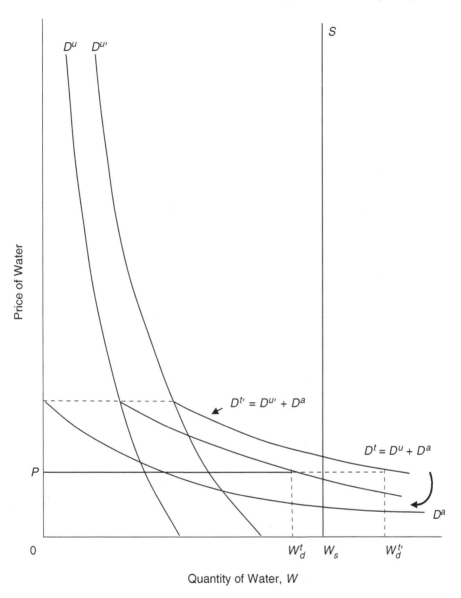

D^u $D^{u'}$

S

$D^{t'} = D^{u'} + D^a$

$D^t = D^u + D^a$

P

D^a

Price of Water

0   W_d^t W_s $W_d^{t'}$

Quantity of Water, W

Figure 5.9   Demand and supply of water

various users. Either the price must be permitted to rise, or some other rationing method must be found. When prices are set by government agencies, they no longer respond only to pressures of supply and demand; they respond also to political pressures. If the government is understandably reluctant to allow the price of water in agricultural uses to rise, some more elaborate method of rationing water among competing users must be found.

Suppose that the government reasons that urban users can afford to pay more for a

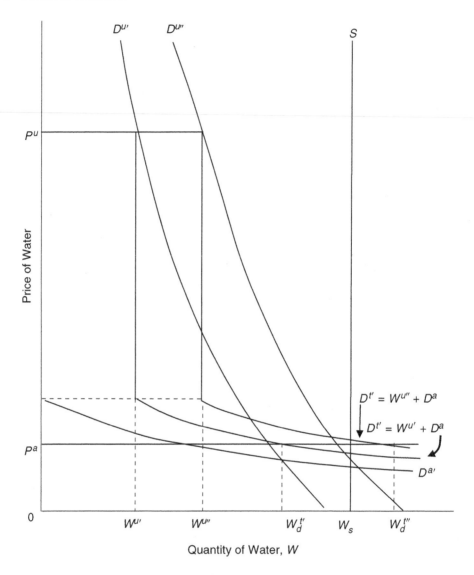

Figure 5.10   A two-price system for water

given quantity of water than agricultural users. It may then establish a dual price system, setting the price of urban water at P^u while maintaining the price of agricultural water at P^a. This effectively segregates the market for water. When urban users have siphoned off the quantity of water they demand, $W^{u'}$, at the price P^u, agricultural users may then satisfy their demands at the price P^a. Some surplus of water remains; W^r_d is now less than W_s (Figure 5.10). The dual price system for allocation of water has been effective in allocating the available water among competing users.

As still more time passes, the urban demand for water increases to $D^{u''}$. Suppose, again, that government agencies are understandably reluctant to raise the prices of water for either class of user. At P^u for urban users and P^a for agricultural users, not all demands can be satisfied, and so there is a severe shortage of water; W^r_d is greater than W_s (Figure 5.10).

Under political pressure from agricultural users, the government may choose to restrict the quantity of water available to urban users to the amount $W^{u'}_s$. Thus the water supply curve for urban users is arbitrarily placed at S^u. Then, $S^t - S^u$ becomes the supply of water available to agricultural users (that is, S^a). Notice that neither market is cleared. At P^u and S^u, there is a shortage of water for urban uses; that is, $W^{u'}_s$ is less than $W^{u'}_d$ (Figure 5.11). At P^a and S^a, there is a shortage of water for agricultural uses; that is, W^a_d (which is equal to $[W^{u'}_s + W^a_d] - W^{u'}_s$) is greater than $S^a = S^t - S^u$.

If it is a matter of government policy that neither P^u nor P^a be permitted to rise, non-price rationing devices must be found. The government may establish elaborate systems of water allotments. Each user may be permitted to divert some given quantity of water at the relevant price (P^u if an urban user, and P^a if an agricultural user). These allotments then become valuable, and a black market in water may arise. If the government is successful in preventing black markets, the only way in which their farmers could increase the use of water would be to purchase additional land that carries a water allotment of its own. Urban users would face a similar situation. So water allocation values tend to be included in the market price of real estate.

This analysis is quite instructive. It indicates what happens when demand continues to shift to the right, while supply is both vertical and non-shifting. It shows what happens when governments, for understandable political reasons, refuse to permit prices to rise to market-clearing levels. It shows what happens when government agencies attempt to segregate the market for a single commodity. And it provides a good starting point for anyone interested in understanding the complex politics of water in regions of the US and world where water for competing uses is becoming more scarce.

The market for pollution control
Pollution control is expensive. The act of polluting gives no pleasure to the polluter, and the resulting pollution is offensive to the receptor. It is perfectly reasonable to assume that polluters pollute only insofar as doing so is cost-saving to them. Thus pollution control, the act of reducing pollutant emissions, is expensive to the polluter. A polluting firm may reduce its emissions by reducing its total output of salable commodities or by increasing its use of pollution control inputs. A polluting consumer may decrease pollutant emissions by reducing participation in polluting activities or by purchasing emission-control devices (for example, for his or her automobile). For the polluting firm, pollution control is cost-increasing, and for the polluting consumer, pollution control is utility-decreasing. In both cases, the marginal sacrifices increase with more pollution abatement. Therefore, the supply curve for pollution abatement (the act of reducing polluting emissions) is positively sloped.

There is a demand for pollution abatement. Consumers obtain greater satisfaction from a pollution-free environment. Producing firms find that a clean environment reduces their cost of operation. For example, if clean water is delivered to the firm, the firm will no longer have to meet the expense of water treatments prior to using water in its production process. Clean air would reduce the firm's cost of maintenance of its plant, as the corrosive effects of air pollutants would be eliminated. So there is clearly

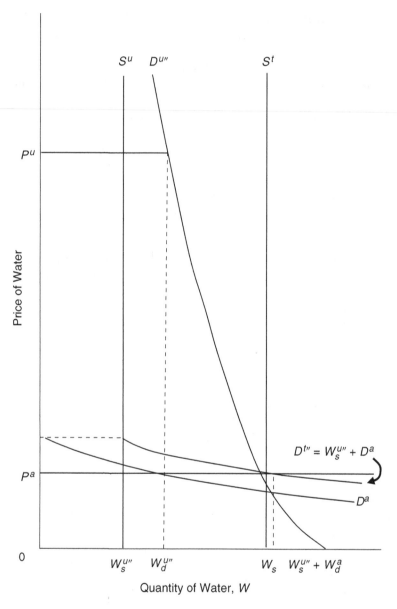

Figure 5.11   A two-price system for water, with rationing of water in urban uses

a demand for pollution abatement, and it is most likely a typical downward-sloping demand curve.

Yet it is difficult to observe operating markets for the control of many common types of pollutants. Market prices for pollution abatement go unobserved, and it does not seem likely that the equilibrium quantity of pollution abatement (Figure 5.12) is provided. Why? Figure 5.12 offers a significant hint. The demand curve for pollution abatement is

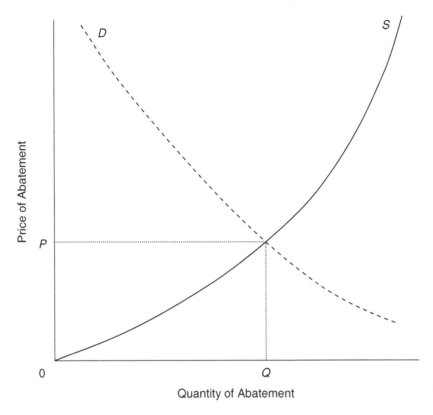

Figure 5.12   The market for pollution abatement

presented as a broken line. Markets in pollution abatement are poorly developed, especially on the demand side. For reasons that are discussed in detail in Chapter 10, it is difficult for the individual, acting as an individual, to purchase his or her preferred amount
of pollution abatement and to be assured of receiving exactly the amount purchased.
Thus, the broken demand curve for pollution abatement represents a true demand, but
an ineffective demand. The poorly developed market in pollution abatement does not
permit the demand curve to become effective.

Although supply and demand curves for pollution abatement clearly exist, and there
are good reasons to believe that these supply and demand curves are similar to the
supply and demand curves for many other commodities, the market for pollution abatement is ineffective. One does not observe the equilibrium price being generated nor the
equilibrium quantity of pollution abatement being provided. What can be done about
this situation? There are many possible solutions. All of them involve government activity in one way or another. The government may seek to establish the kinds of property
rights that would permit the broken demand curve of Figure 5.12 to become an effective
demand curve. For example, receptors of pollution may be granted property rights to
a clean environment, rights that they would forgo only if offered something they value
even more. Alternatively, government may attempt to establish the equilibrium price
for polluting emissions by taxation and charge that price to firms and individuals that

choose to emit pollutants. Or the government may take a different approach and impose restrictions on polluting emissions at the individual firm level. This strategy is commonly referred to as the use of emissions standards.

Each of these separate strategies has its difficulties and advantages (see Chapter 16). None of them seems to be perfect. The problems in the market for pollution abatement are typical of the problems that resource and environmental economists observe in any market in which property rights are ill-defined. Such ill-defined property rights may result either from societal preferences as implemented by government or from the physical nature of goods, like ambient air, that are non-rival and non-exclusive from the point of view of the individual.

The market for outdoor recreation
For many years, and in many countries, governments have set aside areas of land that are especially attractive from a scenic or ecosystem point of view and have made these available to visitors for their enjoyment. Because these lands are often viewed as part of the national heritage, it has often been a conscious governmental decision that markets in the enjoyment of this land should not be established. Ability to pay a market-established going price is not thought to be a suitable criterion for determining who should be allowed to enjoy the amenities of such lands.

Consider a national park, of limited size and with a limited recreation carrying capacity. To simplify the example, assume that camping is an essential part of the recreation experience, it is permitted only in designated areas, and that the number of campsites is strictly limited. Thus, the supply curve for campsites in this national park is strictly inelastic (that is, vertical) and non-shifting. Assume that the government has established a campsite fee at the level P. Demand for campsites may be represented by a typical downward-sloping demand curve. When demand is D', all of the demand effective at the price P is satisfied, and some unused campsites remain; that is, C_d' is less than C_s (Figure 5.13). With increasing affluence and ease of transportation, the demand for outdoor recreation in attractive sites increased rapidly for much of the late twentieth century. Over time, demand shifts to the right, and D'' becomes the demand curve for campsites. Now, in the most attractive destinations, there is a severe shortage of campsites at the going price; that is, C_d'' substantially exceeds C_s (Figure 5.13). If the government is reluctant to allow the camping fee to rise to the market-clearing price, some non-price rationing device must be found.

Typically, campsites are allocated on a first come, first served basis. People seeking campsites form queues, and if the queues are sufficiently long and are established sufficiently early in the day, prospective campers from distant places may choose to leave home very early in the morning or to arrive in the locality the previous night and sleep over in motels in order to establish a favorable position in the queue. Thus time and perhaps non-camping expenditures are substituted for camping fees as devices to ration a restricted number of campsites among a larger number of prospective campers. Those who are willing to invest more time than others are will satisfy their demand for a campsite. However, the agency that operates the national park is unable to collect this 'time in queue' and spend it. The policy of maintaining price at low levels and using time as a supplementary rationing device limits the budget of government agencies charged with the provision and operation of outdoor recreation areas. In some jurisdictions, non-price

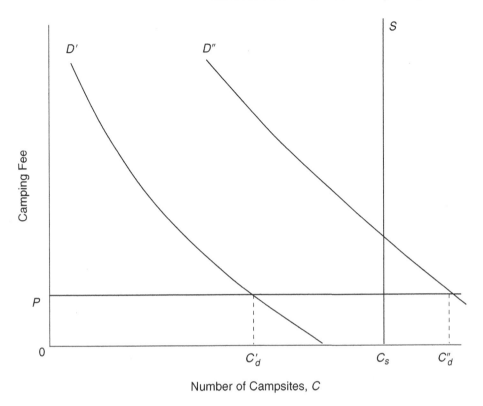

Figure 5.13   Growing demand in the market for outdoor recreation amenities

rationing is now performed through online reservations systems for campsites. This saves some wasted time in queue, and allocates the best campsites to the most far-sighted users, but it does little to augment revenue for the agencies charged with operating the parks.

It is often the case that the demand for outdoor recreation depends on the season. The supply of campsites is vertical and fixed year-round, but the demand for campsites in the middle of winter, D^w, is located far to the left. In winter there is a substantial surplus of campsites; that is, C_d^w is much less than C_s (Figure 5.14). In summer, the demand for campsites, D^s, shifts far to the right. At the going price, there is a severe shortage of campsites. In winter, the going price serves as a rationing device, although rationing is not needed. In summer, the going price is totally ineffective as a rationing device and must be supplemented with "time in queue."

It is possible that the agency operating the national park could increase both the number of users who are able to enjoy the park and its revenues by setting camping fees at zero during the winter and permitting them to rise to the market-clearing level during the summer. In the long run, such a strategy may be effective in shifting the supply curve of high-quality outdoor recreation sites to the right, as it would permit the agency to acquire a large enough budget gradually to purchase and develop additional high-quality recreation sites. But it would be a highly controversial strategy, as there are many who believe that access to high-quality outdoor recreation sites should not be restricted to

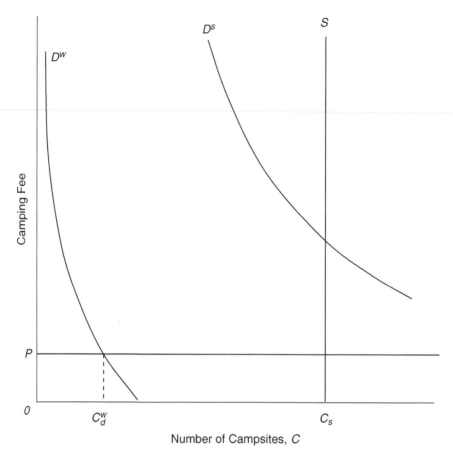

Figure 5.14   Seasonal variation in the market for outdoor recreational amenities

those who can afford to pay a market-determined user fee. Parenthetically, it should be noted that in the United States, there is a certain irony to this proposition. Many of the finest outdoor recreation sites in the United States are quite distant from major population centers. Access to those sites is in fact effectively restricted to those who can afford to pay – not the user fee, but the expense of traveling to get there.

Questions for discussion

1. Given the need to coordinate the production, consumption, and distribution of goods, services, and amenities, what role is played by rights in any economy?
2. Is there any reason to expect centrally planned economies to degrade the environment less than do enterprise economies?
3. There is a long-running debate in economics about how important it is that the assumptions of economic models approximate reality. What is your position on this debate?
4. If a malnourished person were given an income supplement exactly equal to the cost of enough additional food to permit him or her to achieve a specified nutritional standard, would you expect him or her to achieve the nutritional standard? If under these conditions, he or she did actually achieve the nutritional standard, what would that imply about the shape of his or her indifference curves?

5. What would you expect to be the sign and the approximate magnitude of each of the following elasticities:
   a. the income elasticity of demand for white-water canoeing?
   b. the price elasticity of demand for electricity?
   c. the demand elasticity of natural gas with respect to the price of oil?
6. In what way would you expect the availability of mass-transportation services to affect the price elasticity of demand for gasoline in metropolitan areas?
7. "Increases in production costs are always passed on entirely to the consumer." Under what conditions would this statement be true?
8. "The industry demand curve can be accurately derived by the horizontal summation of individual demand curves. However, the industry supply curve cannot be accurately derived by the horizontal summation of individual firm supply curves." Is this true? Why?
9. "If the price rises, demand will decrease." True or false?
10. Is it reasonable to conclude that price controls contributed for many years to the shortage of natural gas in the United States? Explain.
11. Because relatively little air pollution abatement is bought in unregulated markets, is it reasonable to conclude that there is little demand for it?
12. Because relatively few cassette tapes are bought in unregulated markets, is it reasonable to conclude that there is little demand for them?

Suggested reading: classic and contemporary

Friedman, M. (1953), "The Methodology of Positive Economics," in *Essays in Positive Economics*, ed. M. Friedman, Chicago, IL: University of Chicago Press.

Friedman, M. and R. Friedman (1990), *Free to Choose: A Personal Statement*, New York: A Harvest Book, Harcourt.

Galbraith, J.K. (1998), *The Affluent Society: 40th Anniversary Edition*, New York: Houghton Mifflin.

Stern, D.I., M.S. Common, and E.B. Barbier (1996), "Economic Growth and Environmental Degradation: The Environmental Kuznet's Curve and Sustainable Development," *World Development* **24** (7): 1151–60.

Swaney, J.A. (1985), "Economics, Ecology, and Entropy," *Journal of Economic Issues* **19** (4): 853–65.

Varian, H.R. (2005), *Intermediate Microeconomics: A Modern Approach*, New York: W.W. Norton & Company.

6 Economic efficiency: how does a healthy economy allocate natural resources to economic production and consumption?

By now, we have learned some things about markets, including: the conditions for individual utility and profit maximization; the conditions for efficient adjustment of individual consumption and production to given, market-generated prices; the process by which markets equilibrate supply and demand; and how markets generate prices. In Chapter 5, we discussed useful services to society provided by well-functioning markets, and how we use market logic to diagnose problems caused by poorly functioning markets. We also discussed impediments encountered when political jurisdictions attempt to override market forces.

Natural resource and environmental economics is, for the most part, concerned with the peculiar economic characteristics of resources and amenities and the impediments these characteristics impose on well-functioning markets, and with identifying and evaluating possible solutions to those problems. To perform these tasks, it is necessary to establish criteria by which to judge the current performance of resource and environmental markets and to evaluate alternative solutions. It is necessary to have a clear concept of what is good in order to identify what is not so good and what might be an improvement.

In this chapter and the next two chapters, we discuss criteria for judging the performance of an economy. The individual may well think highly of an economy that permits him or her to prosper, and poorly of one that does not. However, an economy is a creation of society and its laws. Its purpose is to provide the incentives that harness and coordinate individual creativity and to resolve conflicts that arise among individual aspirations. Its performance must be judged from a societal perspective. As we discussed in Chapter 4, however, there are no simple and sure ways to determine the proper relationships among individuals and between the individual and collective authority. There are competing philosophical schools of thought, but none has been able to prove its case so as to drive the others to defeat. Mainstream economics is itself a descendant of philosophy and, as such, addresses the social choice criterion problem with rigor and clarity. Nevertheless, the establishment of a universally accepted social choice criterion which has eluded philosophy also continues to elude economics.

In this chapter, we develop a rigorous concept of economic efficiency. Efficiency, in its own right, is a widely used criterion for economic performance. Furthermore, efficiency is a necessary component of many other, more complete social choice criteria that also consider distributional concerns. In this chapter, we examine the concept of efficiency in a static (or timeless) context. The concept of Pareto-efficiency is introduced, and necessary and sufficient conditions for Pareto-efficiency are derived. We show that under ideal conditions a competitive equilibrium is Pareto-efficient.

In Chapter 7, we introduce the idea of distinct time periods and consider how a concern for consequences at later times might affect current decisions. Conditions are established for intertemporal efficiency. Then in Chapter 8, the distribution of a society's economic product is introduced. Clearly, the maximum economic well-being for the whole society, if attainable, is what is desired, though this criterion has its analytical difficulties and ethical peculiarities. Accordingly, we examine the analytics and the ethics of maximum social well-being and some of the alternative choice and policy criteria that have been proposed. No criterion, it turns out, is without difficulties.

The static analytics of efficiency
One encounters many meanings for the term "efficiency," and many scientific disciplines have their own carefully defined concept of it. In this book, we shall confine the use of "efficiency" not just to economic efficiency but also to global efficiency, or Pareto-efficiency (named for the early twentieth-century philosopher and economist Vilfredo Pareto).[1] Pareto-efficiency involves efficiency in production, certainly, but also efficiency in consumption. Furthermore, for Pareto-efficiency, production and consumption must be efficiently coordinated so that what is produced depends not only on resource availability and technology but also on consumers' preferences.

The analyses of consumption and production (briefly reviewed in Chapter 5) show how individual decision-makers optimize by adjusting to the prices established in the economy at large. The following analyses are quite different. In the analyses of Chapter 5, we took preferences, production technology, and prices as given. Here we take preferences, production technology, and resource availability as given. Instead of asking how individuals adjust to given prices, we ask how prices emerge from individuals' independent decisions. We see how efficient resource allocation and commodity distribution depend on these prices.

Let us construct a simple model of a whole economy.[2] This economy consists of two individuals, whom we shall call 1 and 2; two commodities, which we shall call B and W (for bread and wine); and two inputs, which we shall call L and D (for labor and land). It may seem strange to develop a model of an economy that consists only of two persons, two commodities, and two resources, but there is a good reason for doing so: it permits us to use two-dimensional diagrams. Rest assured that all the results we can derive with our two-dimensional diagrams can also be derived for a much larger economy, in n dimensions, using vector calculus.

The production functions are:

$$B = h_b(L_b, D_b) \tag{6.1}$$

$$W = h_w(L_w, D_w) \tag{6.2}$$

where L_b = the amount of labor devoted to the production of bread, D_b = the amount of land devoted to the production of bread, and L_w and D_w are defined similarly for wine production. It is assumed that production technology remains constant throughout the analysis and that all units of each of B, W, L, and D are homogeneous in quality.

The utility functions are:

$$U_1 = f_1(B_1, W_1) \tag{6.3}$$

and:

$$U_2 = f_2(B_2, W_2) \tag{6.4}$$

where U_1 = the level of utility enjoyed by the consumer 1, B_1 = the amount of bread consumed by 1, W_1 = amount of wine consumed by 1, and U_2, B_2 and W_2 are similarly defined for consumer 2. The utility functions are assumed to remain unchanged during the course of the analysis; that is, the tastes and preferences of each individual are constant (fixed).

It is assumed that the marginal productivity of each input in the production of each output is positive but diminishing and that the marginal utility of each consumer from the use of each commodity is positive but diminishing. Thus, all isoquants derived from the production functions and all indifference curves derived from the utility functions are convex to the origin.

Efficiency in production
The production functions for bread and wine provide sufficient information to derive the isoquant maps for bread and wine (Figure 6.1). Isoquant maps alone, however, do not provide sufficient information to determine the conditions for efficiency in production. In analyses of the single firm in isolation, the economist can always use price information to construct a budget line. However, in the analysis of the efficient organization of the whole economy, price information must be derived, not assumed at the outset. How, then, can the production problem be solved? If we assume (quite reasonably, as this is an analysis of a whole economy) that resources are in fixed supply ($L_b + L_w = \bar{L}$ and $D_b + D_w = \bar{D}$), we can use this information to solve our problem. In Figure 6.1, we use the assumption of fixed resources to place bounds on both isoquant maps. Even if all labor were used to produce bread, there are limits to the amount of bread that can be produced. Quantities of bread that require more than the total supply of labor are simply infeasible, even if no wine at all is produced. Using this kind of logic, we can

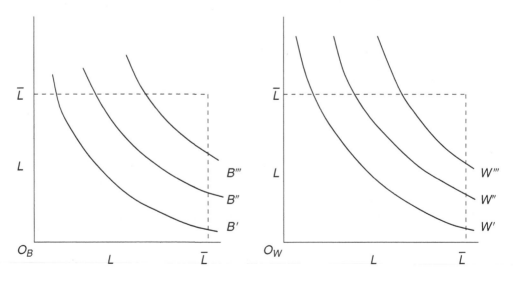

Figure 6.1   The isoquant maps, bounded by fixed resource supplies

place bounds on the isoquant maps. The broken lines in Figure 6.1 provide the boundary for the section of each isoquant map that is feasible, given strictly limited resource supplies.

Formation of the Edgeworth box   The feasible section of each isoquant map in Figure 6.1 is a rectangle, and because the dimensions of each of these rectangles were determined from the same information (that is, the total amount of labor and land available to the economy), each rectangle must be the same size as the other. This fact permits us to form the Edgeworth box.

Start with the bounded isoquant map for bread. Then take the isoquant map for wine and turn it over so that the origin for wine is now at the top right-hand corner, the amount of land used in the production of wine increases as one moves left along the land axis, and the amount of labor used in the production of wine increases as one moves down along the wine axis. The amount of wine produced increases as one moves down and to the left from the wine origin. Figure 6.2 shows the result of this maneuver. Now place the wine origin at the intersection of the broken lines on the bread isoquant map. This completes the formation of the Edgeworth box (Figure 6.3).

The Edgeworth box is a perfect rectangle. Its length is determined by total availability of land in the economy, and its height is determined by the total availability of labor. The production box we have just formed contains an infinite number of isoquants. As one moves away from the bread origin in the lower left-hand corner, one encounters isoquants representing increasing quantities of bread. As one moves away from the wine origin at the upper right-hand corner, one encounters isoquants representing increasing quantities of wine. Thus as one moves northeast inside the box, the production of bread increases as the production of wine decreases; as one moves southwest, the production of wine increases and the production of bread decreases.

Let us pause a moment to examine the analytic properties of the Edgeworth box (Figure 6.4). First, its exterior dimensions are uniquely determined by resource availability. Second, any point inside a production box is uniquely defined in terms of resource allocation and output. Consider point p, which is simply chosen at random and has no special significance. By drawing perpendicular lines horizontally and vertically from p, resource allocation (that is, L_b^p, L_w^p, D_b^p, and D_w^p) is uniquely defined.. Because the box contains infinite numbers of both bread and wine isoquants, there must be one of each type of isoquant passing through point p. Thus, the output of both bread and wine is also uniquely defined for any point in the Edgeworth box.

The production efficiency locus   At point p (in Figure 6.4), the bread isoquant, B^P, intersects the wine isoquant, W^P. Could there possibly be one or more resource allocations more efficient than that at point p? Consider first the bread isoquant, B^P, at point a. With the resource allocation represented by point a, it is possible to produce as much bread as at point p (B^P) and a greater quantity of wine ($W^{P'}$). Point a must therefore represent a more efficient resource allocation than does point p. Consider now the wine isoquant, W^P. At point c, it is possible to produce as much wine as at point p (W^P) and more bread ($B^{P'}$). Point c must represent a more efficient allocation of resources than does point p. Between points a and c, there is a series of points of tangency between bread and wine isoquants. At each of these points of tangency, there is more of both bread and wine

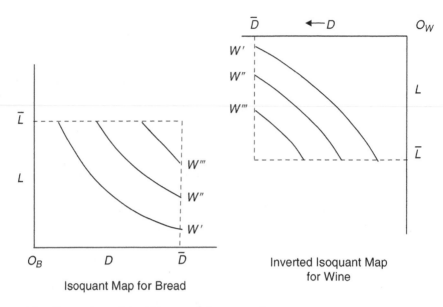

Figure 6.2   *Formation of the Edgeworth box: step 1*

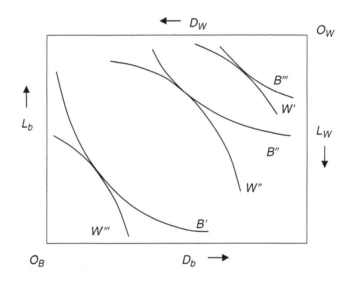

Figure 6.3   *Formation of the Edgeworth box: step 2*

produced than at point *p*. All these points must also represent more efficient resource allocations than does point *p*.

Segment *ac* must represent a locus of combinations of inputs, each of which is more efficient than is the input combination at point *p*. For any point inside the Edgeworth box, other than points at which there is a tangency between a bread isoquant and a wine isoquant, it is possible to find a similar line segment representing more efficient resource

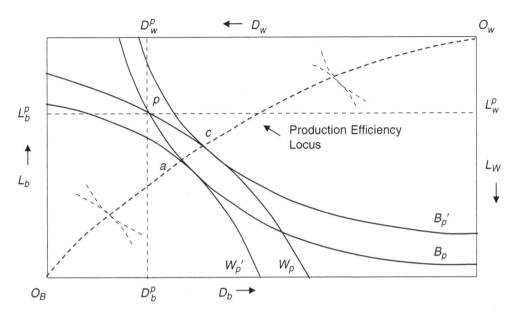

Figure 6.4 *The information content of a production Edgeworth box and the derivation of the production efficiency locus*

allocations. If the analysis with respect to point *p* were repeated for all other points inside the Edgeworth box, a curved line passing from the bread origin through points *a* and *c* to the wine origin would be found. This line is the locus of all of the points of tangency between bread and wine isoquants within the Edgeworth box. It is called the "production efficiency locus," which is defined as the locus of all possible combinations of land and labor that are efficient in the production of bread and wine. For any point off the production efficiency locus, a line segment joining more efficient resource allocations can be found on the production efficiency locus.

In our search for the efficient organization of our model economy, we have made substantial progress. We have eliminated every point off the production efficiency locus. But we still are left with an infinite number of points on the production efficiency locus, and any one of those could be the resource allocation that is consistent with global efficiency. So it is not possible to define a completely efficient economic organization by looking only at production.

The analysis thus far has taught us something important about production efficiency. It can be achieved only with resource allocations that lie on the production efficiency locus, and every point on the production efficiency locus has something in common. Because each is a point of tangency between a bread isoquant and a wine isoquant, the slope of the bread isoquant must be equal to the slope of the wine isoquant at that point. Thus, the rate of technical substitution (RTS) of the inputs must be equal in the production of each commodity, at every point on the production efficiency locus. That is:

$$(RTS_{D, L})_B = (RTS_{D, L})_W \qquad (6.5)$$

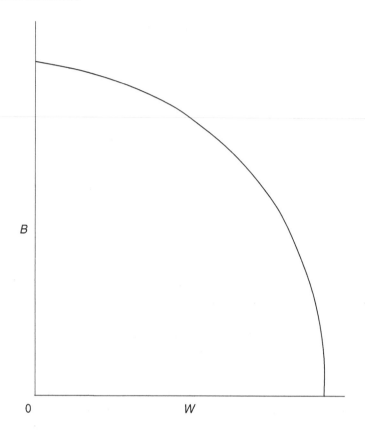

Figure 6.5   The efficient production possibilities curve

Efficiency in consumption

If there is no way to identify completely the conditions for economic efficiency by looking at production information alone, perhaps it would be helpful to use the information about tastes and preferences contained in the individual's utility functions. Construct a diagram whose axes are expressed in terms of the commodities, bread and wine. Because every point on the production efficiency locus is uniquely determined in terms of the quantities of bread and wine it represents, it ought to be possible to transfer the information contained in the production efficiency locus to the new diagram expressed in commodity space (that is, whose axes are defined in terms of quantities of the different commodities). For each point on the production efficiency locus, simply determine how much bread and how much wine that point represents, and then identify a point in commodity space representing exactly the same amount of bread and wine. When this process is completed for all points on the production efficiency locus, a unique efficient production possibilities curve, corresponding to the production efficiency locus, is derived (Figure 6.5).

The utility functions for the consumers, 1 and 2, provide enough information to permit the derivation of the indifference maps for those consumers (Figure 6.6). Note that the efficient production possibilities curve and both indifference maps are expressed in the

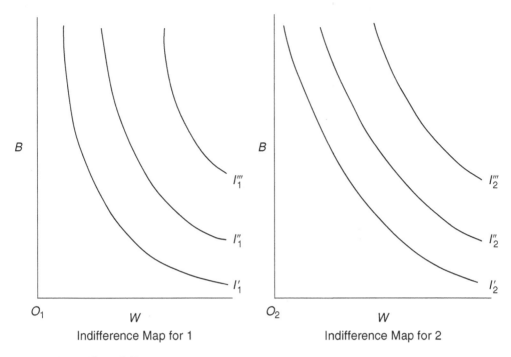

Figure 6.6   The indifference maps

same commodity axes. Let the origin of Figure 6.7 represent the origin for the production possibilities curve diagram and the origin for consumer 1's indifference map. Now, arbitrarily select point *d* on the production possibilities curve. Construct perpendicular lines to the bread and wine origins from point *d*. Point *d* now defines a product mix; at point *d* on the efficient production possibilities curve, B^d units of bread and W^d units of wine are produced. Remember that there is nothing special about point *d*; it merely permits us to ask a hypothetical question: If the model society chose to allocate its resources in such a way as to produce B^d units of bread and W^d units of wine, how would the consumers choose to distribute that bundle of commodities among themselves?

Notice that a rectangle, $O_1 B^d dW^d$, has been formed (Figure 6.7). The rectangle already contains individual 1's indifference map, with its origin at the point O_1. We can take individual 2's indifference map and turn it around, just as we did with the isoquant map for wine, and place its origin at the upper right-hand corner of that rectangle (that is, let $d = O_2$). By so doing, we have formed an Edgeworth box for consumption. The exterior dimensions of the consumption box are uniquely determined by the efficient production possibilities curve and the unique, but arbitrarily selected, point *d* on that curve. Thus the dimensions of the consumption box represent quantities of the commodities bread and wine.

The consumption box is literally full of indifference curves: indifference curves for individual 1, whose utility increases as one moves from the lower-left origin upward and to the right within the box; and indifference curves for individual 2, whose utility increases as one moves from the upper-right origin downward and to the left within the

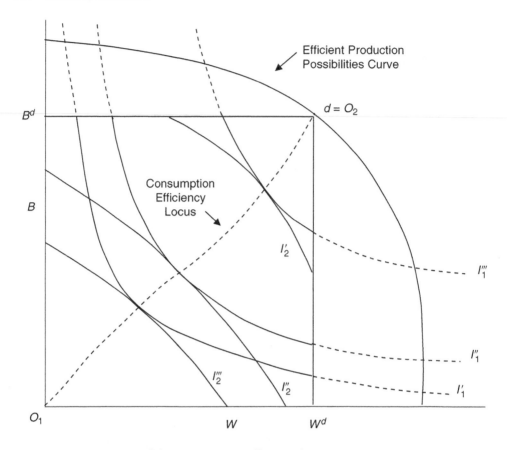

Figure 6.7   Derivation of the consumption efficiency locus

box. Any point within the consumption box is uniquely specified with respect to commodity distribution (B_1, B_2, W_1, and W_2) and the ordinal levels of utility enjoyed by 1 and
2. Using the same logic as we used to find the production efficiency locus, the "consumption efficiency locus" may be identified. It is a curved line from point O_1 to point $d = O_2$,
connecting all the points of tangency between indifference curves for individual 1 and
indifference curves for individual 2. The consumption efficiency locus is defined as the
locus of all distributions of commodities that are efficient in consumption. Points off the
consumption efficiency locus represent commodity distributions that cannot possibly be
consistent with global efficiency.

Notice that we have made further progress in our search for the efficient organization
of our model economy. For the product mix represented by point d, which we know is
efficient in production, all commodity distributions except those lying on the consumption efficiency locus have been eliminated as inefficient. But we are still left with an infinite
number of points along the consumption efficiency locus, each of which is a candidate for
selection as the efficient commodity distribution. Actually, as we shall see a little further
on, the situation is really worse. Point d on the efficient production possibilities curve
was selected quite arbitrarily, and any other point on that curve could have been selected

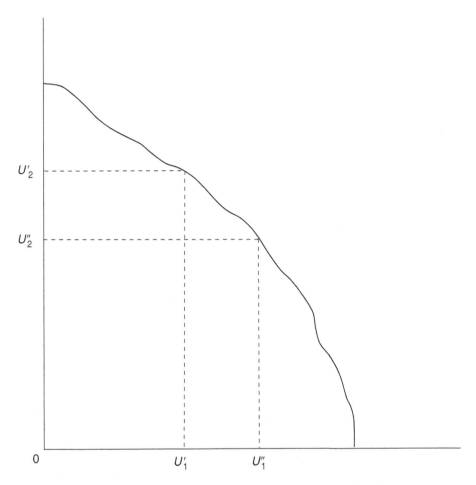

Figure 6.8   The utility possibilities curve, given the product mix B^d, W^d

with equal plausibility. For each other point on the production possibilities curve, a new consumption efficiency locus exists, unique to that point. But more on that later.

For any arbitrarily selected product mix on the efficient production possibilities curve, the consumption efficiency locus represents a locus of potentially efficient commodity distributions. The consumption efficiency locus is a locus of points of tangency between indifference curves, and at any point on it, the slope of the tangent to the indifference curve for consumer 1 must equal that for consumer 2. Thus the following condition must hold at any point on the consumption efficiency locus: the rate of commodity substitution (*RCS*) between bread and wine for consumer 1 must equal that for consumer 2. That is:

$$(RCS_{W, B})_1 = (RCS_{W, B})_2 \tag{6.6}$$

The utility possibilities curve   Construct a diagram, such as that in Figure 6.8, in which the axes are expressed in terms of the levels of utility enjoyed by the individuals 1 and 2.

Because utility is an ordinal rather than a cardinal concept (that is, differing alternatives can be ranked in terms of the relative amounts of utility they offer the individual, but it is not possible to say exactly how much utility each alternative provides), these utility axes must be expressed in ordinal rather than cardinal terms. Just as we took the production efficiency locus from its input space and mapped it into commodity space to derive the efficient production possibilities curve, we can take the consumption efficiency locus from its commodity space and map it into utility space to derive the utility possibilities curve.

Visual examination of Figure 6.8 clarifies a point that the more alert observer will have already deduced from Figure 6.7. Starting from some point off the consumption efficiency locus, it is always possible for two individuals to make a mutually beneficial trade; that is, they can make a trade that increases the utility of both or, at least, increases the utility of one without reducing the utility of the other. However, for any given product mix, once the individuals have traded to a point on the consumption efficiency locus, any further utility gains for one must come at the direct expense of a utility reduction for the other. In Figure 6.8, any movement along the utility possibilities curve (which is simply the consumption efficiency locus mapped between utility axes) involves a utility gain for one of the individuals at the direct expense of a utility loss for the other.

The grand utility frontier
Remember that point d on the efficient production possibilities curve was selected, in quite arbitrary fashion, in order to permit us to answer the question: What if the product mix were B^d, W^d. . .? Clearly, we have yet to find the most efficient product mix. We do this in an iterative fashion, repeating the analytical process for every other point on the efficient production possibilities curve; literally an infinite number of points. For each possible product mix represented by a point on the efficient production possibilities curve, a unique consumption efficiency locus can be found and can be mapped in utility space to derive a unique utility possibilities curve. When all possible points on the efficient production possibilities curve are considered, an infinite number of utility possibilities curves can be generated.

A representative sample of these utility possibilities curves is shown in Figure 6.9. Observe that the different utility possibilities curves intersect the U_1 and U_2 axes in different places, that many of the curves intersect one another, and that some curves lie wholly inside others. This last case occurs when one product mix dominates another.

Examine the outermost boundary of the feasible section of the utility possibilities diagram. Points that lie outside the outermost curve segment are infeasible, and points that lie inside the outermost curve segment are inefficient. However, the boundary itself is not a smooth and continuously differentiable curve, as is the efficient production possibilities curve. If one wants to move along the boundary, from the highest possible level of U_1 to the highest possible level of U_2, one does not move along a smooth curve but, instead, repeatedly switches from one utility possibility curve to another, always moving along the outermost curve segments. The path one would follow is a line joining the outermost segments of the various utility possibilities curves. This line, which is not a true curve, but a frontier or envelope curve, is known as the "grand utility frontier." By identifying the grand utility frontier, we have completed our search for Pareto-efficiency. We have eliminated all input combinations that do not lie on the

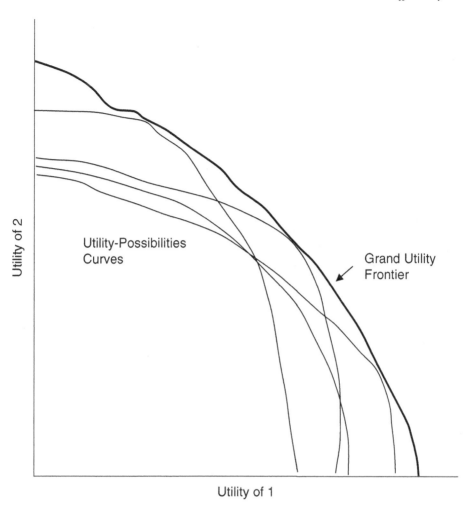

Figure 6.9   Utility possibilities curves and the grand utility frontier

production efficiency locus. We have eliminated all commodity distributions that do not lie on a consumption efficiency locus. Finally, we have eliminated all segments of consumption efficiency loci that do not lie on the grand utility frontier. Points inside the grand utility frontier are feasible but inefficient, and points outside the grand utility frontier are infeasible.

At any point on the grand utility frontier, the following proposition is true: it is impossible to reorganize the economy in such a way as to make one individual better off without simultaneously making another individual worse off. From any particular point on the grand utility frontier, movements in the feasible section of the northwest quadrant may make individual 2 better off but at the expense of individual 1, who will be made worse off (Figure 6.10). Movements in the feasible section of the southeast quadrant may make individual 1 better off, but at the expense of individual 2. Movements in the southwest quadrant are always feasible but will make both individuals worse off. Only movements in the northeast quadrant would make both individuals better off (or, on the boundaries of the northeast quadrant, would make one individual better off without making the other individual worse off). However, no movements in the northeast quadrant are feasible, given the resource availability, production technology, and utility functions we assumed at the outset.

Pareto-efficiency is defined as a situation in which everyone is so well off that it is impossible to make anybody better off without simultaneously making at least one person worse off. It is a situation in which all possibilities for voluntary trades, which would reallocate resources or redistribute commodities more efficiently, have been exhausted. There are no more opportunities for voluntary trade, and there are no more opportunities to improve the efficiency of the economic system. In a sense, Pareto-efficiency is a situation so efficient that it is impossible to reallocate resources or redistribute commodities in order to make things more efficient. Once Pareto-efficiency has been attained, all gains to individuals must come at the expense of other individuals.

All points on the grand utility frontier are, obviously, Pareto-efficient. Once again, there is an infinite number of such points. In our search for efficiency we have eliminated a multitude of input combinations that are inefficient, a multitude of commodity distributions that are inefficient, and a multitude of segments of utility possibilities curves that represented inefficient product mixes. We have made great progress. But we are still left with an infinite number of Pareto-efficient solutions arrayed along the grand utility frontier.

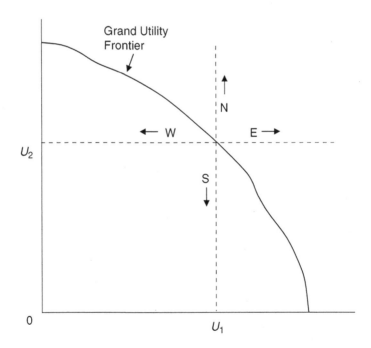

Figure 6.10   From any point on the grand utility frontier, it is impossible to reorganize the economy to make one individual better off without making another worse off

Necessary and sufficient conditions for Pareto-efficiency

Select, completely arbitrarily, any point *e* on the grand utility frontier (Figure 6.11). Point *e*, then, has the virtue of being an efficient organization of our model economy but has no special characteristics to distinguish it from other points on the grand utility frontier that also represent efficient organizations. So an examination of the economic characteristics of point *e* will enable us to draw some general conclusions about the nature of Pareto-efficiency.

Point *e* is on the grand utility frontier but also on one particular utility possibility curve (as the grand utility frontier is nothing more than an envelope of segments of utility possibilities curves). Take the utility possibility curve so identified, and return it to commodity space, from whence it originally came. Point *e'* in Figure 6.12 refers to the point on the consumption efficiency locus that corresponds to point *e* on the utility possibilities curve.

Note that the consumption efficiency locus with which we are now working is not just any consumption efficiency locus, but the specific consumption efficiency locus derived from the specific utility possibilities curve that touches the grand utility frontier at point *e*. Thus, the consumption efficiency locus runs from the point O_1 to the point *e''* on the

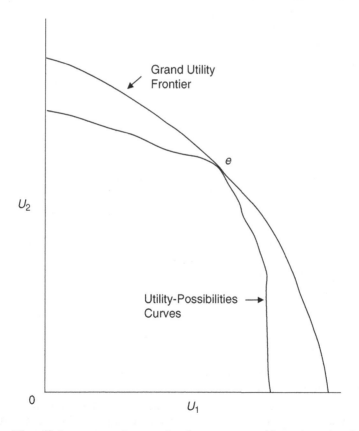

Figure 6.11   *The efficient economic organization represented by point* e *is arbitrarily selected for examination*

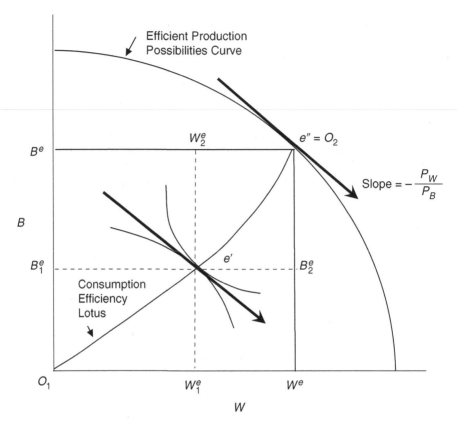

Figure 6.12   Efficient product mix, commodity distribution, and commodity price ratios

production possibilities curve. Construct a consumption box by drawing perpendicular lines from e'' to the bread and wine axes. Now, $e'' = O_2$, Point e'' defines the unique product mix. B^e and W^e, that is associated with the efficient point e. Point e' defines the unique distribution of commodities B_1^e, B_2^e, W_1^e, and W_2^e; associated with the efficient point e. Point e' is the point of tangency between a specific indifference curve for 1 and a specific indifference curve for 2. At point e' the slopes of those two indifference curves are equal. At that point, the slopes of the two indifference curves determine the marginal trading ratios of the two commodities, that is, the ratio of the prices of the commodities. Thus, at point e':

$$(RCS_{W,B})_1 = (RCS_{W,B})_2 = \frac{P_W}{P_B} \tag{6.7}$$

The rates of commodity substitution for both individuals are equal, and they are equal to the price ratio of both commodities.

It is also true that the slope of the tangent to the indifference curves for 1 and 2 at point e' is equal to the slope of the tangent to the production possibilities curve at e'' (note: in a two-dimensional, diagrammatic analysis, it is not possible to prove this contention. However, it is quite simple to provide a proof using differential calculus.) The slope of a

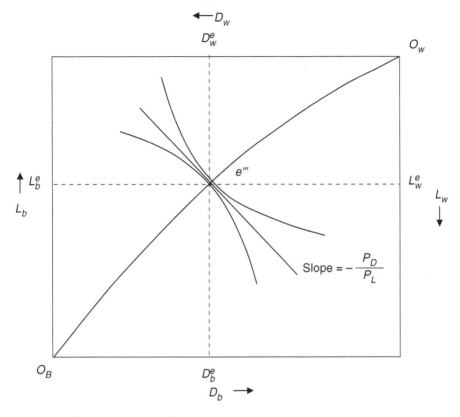

Figure 6.13   Efficient resource allocation and input price ratios

production possibilities curve at any point is equal to the rate of product transformation between the two commodities; that is, the marginal rate at which one commodity must be sacrificed in order to increase output of the other commodity, while technology and resource availability are held constant. Thus the rate of product transformation must be equal to the price ratio of the two commodities. That is:

$$(RPT_{W,B}) = \frac{P_W}{P_B} \tag{6.8}$$

Because the tangents at point e' and point e'' are of equal slope, we have:

$$(RCS_{W,B})_1 = (RCS_{W,B})_2 = (RPT_{W,B}) = \frac{P_W}{P_B} \tag{6.9}$$

The efficient production possibilities curve was derived at the outset from the production efficiency locus. Thus it is possible to map the efficient production possibilities curve back into input space, restoring the production efficiency locus and identifying the point e''' that corresponds to point e'' on the efficient production possibilities curve (Figure 6.13). Point e''' uniquely identifies the efficient resource allocation (L_b^e, L_w^e, D_b^e, and D_w^e) associated with point e on the grand utility frontier. A particular bread isoquant is tangent to some particular wine isoquant at point e''', and the absolute value of the slope of that tangent must be equal to the price ratio of the inputs. That is:

$$(RTS_{D,L})_B = (RTS_{D,L})_W = \frac{P_D}{P_L} \tag{6.10}$$

For the particular Pareto-efficient solution e, we have now uniquely defined the efficient resource allocation, product mix, and commodity distribution. We have also identified the efficient price ratios. If we had chosen to solve the same problem using differential calculus and if we assumed a specific supply of money in the economy, we could derive efficient prices for all commodities and all inputs, in money terms: P_L, P_D, P_B, and P_W.

Starting out with a set of production functions, a set of utility functions, and the information that resources are available in certain fixed quantities, and arbitrarily selecting a unique point on the grand utility frontier, we have derived answers to every question about the efficiency aspects of our model economy: How can resources be efficiently allocated to the production of commodities? What is the efficient mix of commodities to produce? What is the efficient distribution of commodities among consumers? What set of commodity prices is efficient? And what set of input prices is efficient?

Necessary conditions for Pareto-efficiency
There are three conditions necessary for Pareto-efficiency: efficient resource allocation, efficient product mix, and efficiency in consumption. The necessary linkage between production and consumption decisions is established by combining the conditions for an efficient product mix and efficiency in consumption.

Efficient resource allocation   The rate of technical substitution of any pair of inputs should be equal for all firms in the production of all commodities that use those inputs and should be equal to the ratio of the prices of the inputs:

$$(RTS_{D,L})_B = (RTS_{D,L})_W = \frac{P_D}{P_L} \tag{6.11}$$

for all firms.

Efficient product mix   The rate of product transformation of any two commodities should be equal for every producing firm and should be equal to the ratio of commodity prices:

$$(RPT_{W,B}) \text{ firm } 1 = (RPT_{W,B}) \text{ firm } 2 = \ldots = \frac{P_W}{P_B} \tag{6.12}$$

Efficiency in consumption   The rate of commodity substitution for any two commodities should be equal for each consumer and equal to the ratio of commodity prices:

$$(RCS_{W,B})_1 = (RCS_{W,B})_2 = \ldots = \frac{P_W}{P_B} \tag{6.13}$$

Coordination of production and consumption   By combining the second and third conditions, it is possible to derive the general condition that relates production and consumption. The rate of commodity substitution for any two goods should be equal for all consumers, and it should be equal to the rate of product transformation for the same two commodities for all firms, and both should be equal to the ratio of commodity prices:

$$(RCS_{W,B})_1 = \ldots = (RPT_{W,B})_1 = \ldots = \frac{P_W}{P_B} \qquad (6.14)$$

The sufficient condition for Pareto-efficiency
Given these necessary conditions for Pareto-efficiency, the sufficient condition is that all isoquants and indifference curves must be convex in the relevant ranges. Convex isoquants necessarily imply that the efficient production possibilities curve will be concave to the origin in the relevant range.

The necessary and sufficient conditions together guarantee Pareto-efficiency. With the necessary conditions alone satisfied, it is possible that we should suffer the embarrassment of minimizing what we wish to maximize. If the isoquants and indifference curves were concave to the origin, fulfillment of the necessary conditions would result in the achievement not of Pareto-efficiency but of the "Dostoevsky minimum" which is the situation in which everybody is so badly off that it would be impossible to make anybody worse off without making somebody else better off.

The non-uniqueness of efficient allocation, distribution and prices
All points on the grand utility frontier are Pareto-efficient. That means that it is possible, for any point on the grand utility frontier, to repeat the kind of analysis we have just performed for point *e*. For any point on the grand utility frontier, there will be a unique and efficient resource allocation, product mix, commodity distribution, and set of price ratios. However, the empirical magnitudes of each of these will most likely be different for any two points on the grand utility frontier. Figure 6.14 shows a commodity space diagram similar to that in Figure 6.12. The points *e'* and *e"* corresponding to point *e* on the grand utility frontier (Figure 6.11) are shown, as are points *f'* and *f"* corresponding to some different point, *f*, which could be specified on the grand utility frontier. Note that the product mix is different at *f"* from what it is at *e"*. Commodity distribution is different at *f'* from what it is at *e'*. Even the ratio of commodity prices, P_W/P_B, corresponding to point *f* on the grand utility frontier is different from that corresponding to point *e*. Since the points *f"* and *e"* on the efficient production possibilities curve map to the points *f'''* and *e'''* on the production efficiency locus, one can easily imagine that the ratios of input prices, P_L/P_D, would be different for the two different efficient solutions denoted by the points *f* and *e*. While the solutions denoted by the points *f* and *e* on the grand utility frontier are both Pareto-efficient, they imply different resource allocations, product mixes, commodity distributions and price ratios.

Efficiency, then, is not some unique point toward which society may direct its efforts. Rather, many efficient solutions are arrayed along the grand utility frontier, and each is different in resource allocation, commodity distribution, prices, and the distribution of well-being. Clearly, the question of optimal economic organization for society cannot be resolved by appeals to efficiency.

Pareto-efficiency and the market
Adam Smith's attribution of great and valuable powers to the "invisible hand" was surely based on the intuition that the independent decisions of myriad individuals in

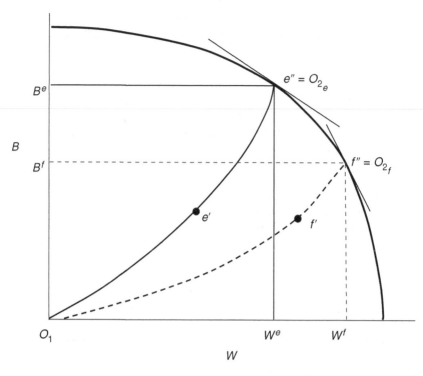

Figure 6.14   Different efficient solutions imply different product mixes, commodity distributions, and commodity price ratios

response to price signals are, in aggregate, efficient.[3] But the formal analytics of Pareto-efficiency were unavailable to him. In the 1950s, mathematical economists formally established that under ideal conditions a competitive equilibrium is Pareto-efficient.[4] A perfect, competitive market, given sufficient time for adjustment, would achieve Pareto-efficiency.

In the real world, the necessary conditions for Pareto-efficiency are likely to be more complex than those shown above because things like transportation costs and transaction costs (that is, the costs of negotiating and enforcing trades) may need to be included in the analysis. Transportation and transaction services are real and valuable. As long as the industries that provide these services are themselves competitive, the existence of such costs do not violate Pareto-efficiency. They do, however, complicate the necessary conditions; for example, accounting for transportation and transaction costs may result in prices faced by buyers deviating somewhat from those facing sellers.

An attractive feature of perfect, competitive markets is that their adjustment and equilibrating processes have a built-in tendency towards a Pareto-efficient solution. It is not true, however, that competitive markets offer the only hope of achieving efficiency. For example, it is possible theoretically for a centrally planned economy to be Pareto-efficient. To achieve this would require an elaborate and precise planning effort. Because freely adjusting prices are rejected out of hand in such economies, other devices must be found to monitor conditions of demand and supply, signal the needed adjustments in production and distribution, and provide the incentives ensuring that these adjustments will be made promptly. These tasks are not impossible without markets, just very difficult.

Deviations from Pareto-efficiency
With modern economic analysis, it can readily be shown that various departures from perfect market conditions result in violations of the necessary conditions for Pareto-efficiency. Examples of such departures include non-rivalry and non-exclusiveness (which are emphasized in Chapter 10), monopoly, and various governmental actions such as tariffs, subsidies, production and trade quotas, commodity rationing, price supports or ceilings, and most kinds of taxes, which along with any good they might do, tend to distort incentives: The necessary conditions for Pareto-efficiency may be used, in principle, for diagnostic and prescriptive purposes. Observation of price ratios that violate the necessary conditions permits diagnosis of inefficiency. If the goal is to restore efficiency, the prescription will usually be to eliminate the source of the distortion, or to introduce some corrective policy for re-establishing the efficient price ratios.

The theory of second best
Unfortunately, a problem arises when economists attempt to identify policies that would yield efficiency improvements. In a typical modern mixed economy, inefficiencies abound. However, it is both economically and politically infeasible to restructure the total economy in one massive upheaval and to establish the conditions for economic efficiency simultaneously in all sectors. Of practical necessity, economic policy must be undertaken in a piecemeal fashion. The impacts of particular laws, regulations, policies, or public investments are usually, for these practical reasons, studied one by one or in small groups called policy packages. The assumption beloved by economists, that all other things remain equal, is put to exhaustive use in these kinds of analyses.

Given that inefficiencies abound throughout the whole economy, does it make sense to undertake economic analyses and pursue policies aimed at encouraging efficiency in a particular sector or with respect to a particular policy or public investment? Common sense would seem to suggest that it does: that one must start somewhere, and it would surely be beneficial to establish the conditions for efficiency with respect to at least one previously inefficient circumstance within the economy. Unfortunately, the conclusion suggested by common sense is not valid as a general proposition, as demonstrated by R.G. Lipsey and K. Lancaster and their "general theory of second best."[5] This proposition may be stated in several ways, and it is useful to do so, as each of the various statements of the theory suggests a slightly different perspective on its application:

1. If there is introduced into a general equilibrium system a constraint that prevents the attainment of one of the conditions for Pareto-efficiency, the other conditions for Pareto-efficiency, although still attainable, will in general no longer be desirable.
2. Given that one of the conditions for Pareto-efficiency cannot be fulfilled, an optimal situation (in efficiency terms) can be achieved only by departing from all the other conditions for Pareto-efficiency.
3. There is no a priori way to judge various situations in which some of the conditions for Pareto-efficiency are fulfilled but others are not.

4.   It is not necessarily true that a situation in which more, but not all, of the conditions for Pareto-efficiency are fulfilled will be superior to one in which fewer are fulfilled.

The general theory of second best has been interpreted as proving that if Pareto-efficiency is unattainable, there will be no simple and generally sufficient conditions for improving efficiency (given fixed resources and unchanging technology and preferences). Thus a policy of seeking piecemeal improvements in efficiency would seem to be unreliable. The theory of second best would seem to suggest strongly that in practical situations in which many sources of inefficiency exist and all cannot be simultaneously eliminated, the economist's reliance on the necessary conditions for Pareto-efficiency as a guide to piecemeal policy is without foundation. But all is not lost.

The Lipsey–Lancaster proof of the general theory of second best relies on a simple mathematical analysis. O.A. Davis and A. Whinston re-examined that proof.[6] They discovered that if one makes an assumption about the relationships within the economy that is different from the assumption made by Lipsey and Lancaster, the theory of second best will no longer hold. Specifically, when the mathematical functions defining economic interaction are separable, an improvement toward efficiency may be achieved by applying the necessary conditions for Pareto-efficiency to one aspect of a generally inefficient economy. At first glance, the difference between the theory of Lipsey–Lancaster and that of Davis–Whinston appears to rest entirely on differences in assumptions about mathematical functional forms. What could that have to do with economics?

It turns out that the difference with respect to assumptions about functional forms is economically significant. In general, the mathematical functions describing interactions between economic sectors will be separable when all the interactions among those economic sectors are defined by efficient price ratios. Thus the necessary conditions for Pareto-efficiency may be introduced into one or more of the sectors whose interactions are defined by separable functions, without encountering the second-best problems raised by Lipsey and Lancaster.

In general, second-best problems will not be encountered when the sources of economic efficiency under analysis are of the following types: production indivisibilities, corner or boundary solutions, interdependent utility functions, and any situation in which one or a small group of individuals or firms fails to maximize utility or profits, as the case may be, for individual reasons. Introducing efficient input use, or efficient commodity distribution, into a sector will always result in an improvement in overall economic efficiency. On the other hand, second-best problems do occur when price ratios are distorted by monopoly, uncorrected externality, and non-optimal policies (for example, non-optimal tariffs or taxes).

There is a substantial category of economic problems to which the theory of second best is not relevant. However, the category of economic problems that do encounter the second-best situation is obviously also quite substantial. For this latter category of economic problems, exactly what constraints does the theory of second best place on the scrupulous economic policy analyst?

The theory of second best is expressed in non-quantitative terms.[7] It states simply that when the relevant conditions exist, it is inappropriate to insist that the necessary conditions for Pareto-efficiency be implemented in a piecemeal fashion. In these situations, scrupulous economic policy analysts cannot simply lean back in their armchairs and advise policy-makers to set the price ratios facing an inefficient sector equal to the relevant rates of substitution and transformation. "Armchair analyses" are not permissible.

Nevertheless, the theory of second best states only that (in the circumstances to which it applies) the optimal conditions will differ from the standard conditions for Pareto-efficiency, not that the optimal conditions do not exist or cannot be found. So it is always possible (in principle) to perform quantitative analyses to identify the conditions for an improvement in efficiency, case by case. When these conditions are found, they will surely deviate from the necessary conditions for Pareto-efficiency. Nevertheless, they will be conditions to improve the efficiency of the inefficient economy (or, in professional economic jargon, conditions for a second-best optimum). Armchair analysis is out, but even in the second-best situation, careful quantitative analyses can determine the conditions to improve efficiency.

Questions for discussion

1. Identify the ethical foundations of Pareto-efficiency. When made explicit, are they likely to command widespread assent?
2. What problems does non-uniqueness pose for the use of Pareto-efficiency concepts in prescribing policy?
3. Does the theory of second best leave the economist without a supportable basis for policy prescription, in a world in which inefficiency is pervasive?

Notes

1. The term "Pareto-efficiency," as used in this book, is synonymous with "Pareto-optimality" as used by many other authors. Here Pareto-efficiency is preferred, as the concept to which both terms refer is an efficiency concept; it is a social optimality concept only under some highly restrictive assumptions.
2. The following analysis is based on that presented in Francis M. Bator (1957), "The Simple Analytics of Welfare Maximization," *American Economic Review* **47** (March): 22–59.
3. Smith introduced the "invisible hand" concept in his 1776 *Wealth of Nations* book. See Adam Smith (Author) and Kathryn Sutherland (ed.) (2008), *An Inquiry into the Nature and Causes of the Wealth of Nations: A Selected Edition*, Oxford: Oxford Paperbacks, Oxford University Press.
4. For example, see Kenneth J. Arrow and Gerard Debreu (1954), "Existence of an Equilibrium for a Competitive Economy," *Econometrica* **22** (3): 265–90.
5. Richard G. Lipsey and R. Kelvin Lancaster (1956–57), "The General Theory of Second Best," *Review of Economic Studies* **24** (1): 11–33.
6. Otto A. Davis and Andrew B. Whinston (1965), "Welfare Economics and the Theory of Second Best," *Review of Economic Studies* **32** (January): 1–14.
7. Edward J. Mishan (1962), "Second Thoughts on Second Best," *Oxford Economic Papers* (New Series) **14** (October): 205–17.

Suggested reading: classic and contemporary

Bator, F.M. (1957), "The Simple Analysis of Welfare Maximization," *American Economic Review* **47** (March): 22–59.

Bishop, R.C. (1993), "Economic Efficiency, Sustainability and Biodiversity," *Ambio* **22** (2–3): 69–73.

Davis, O.A. and A.B. Whinston (1965), "Welfare Economics and the Theory of Second Best," *Review of Economic Studies* **32** (January): 1–14.

Griffin, R.C. (1995), "On the Meaning of Economic Efficiency in Policy Analysis," *Land Economics* **71** (1): 1–15.

Lipsey, R.G. and R.K. Lancaster (1956–57), "The General Theory of Second Best," *Review of Economic Studies* **24** (1): 11–33.

7 Intertemporal efficiency: how do we efficiently allocate natural resources over time?

Life goes on. Although nothing is certain, it behooves each of us to act today as though there will be a tomorrow. Each individual gains utility, to some degree, from present consumption, the expectation of future consumption, the accumulation of wealth, and the sense of having provided for one's heirs. On what principles does the individual base production and consumption decisions that influence opportunities in the present and the future? Under what conditions do the decisions of rational individuals ensure intertemporal efficiency for the whole economy? What are the economic roles played by financial markets and markets in capital assets?

Saving, borrowing, and investing

We start out by considering the saving, borrowing, and investment decisions of a single individual.

Time preference

Consider a single individual who must solve the problem of distributing his or her consumption activities across two time periods, which we will designate, with great imagination, period 1 and period 2. We will address only the issue of the person's total consumption in each period and will assume that the total consumption in each period can be defined by the size of the budget in each period – that is, Y_1 in period 1 and Y_2 in period 2.

First, assume that the individual receives an income of $\overline{Y}_1$ in period 1 and $\overline{Y}_2$ in period 2, so that $\overline{Y}_1 = \overline{Y}_2$. There is no way to transfer income from one period to another. Consider three different individuals, A, B, and C, from whose utility functions may be derived, respectively, the indifference curves I_a, I_b, and I_c. These indifference curves define the preferences of the three individuals as to the timing of their consumption activities. Because the individuals are unable to reallocate consumption across time periods, each of the three indifference curves passes through a common point that represents $\overline{Y}_1$ and $\overline{Y}_2$, the only feasible allocation of consumption across time (Figure 7.1).

If it were possible to reallocate consumption across the time periods, individuals B and C would do so. Consider the broken line WW, where $W = \overline{Y}_1 + \overline{Y}_2$. This is an intertemporal budget line. If the individual could transfer all of his or her consumption to period 1, the total consumption in that period would be W. Similarly, W could be consumed in period 2 if consumption in period 1 were zero. If it were possible to transfer consumption across time periods (that is, if the intertemporal budget line existed), individual B would transfer consumption from period 2 to period 1 so that her total consumption would be $Y_{1b}^* + Y_{2b}^*$, and she would achieve the higher indifference curve I_b^*. Individual B has a positive time preference; that is, she values immediate consumption more highly than consumption in later time periods. Individual C would transfer consumption from the immediate time period to the later time period, so that her total consumption would

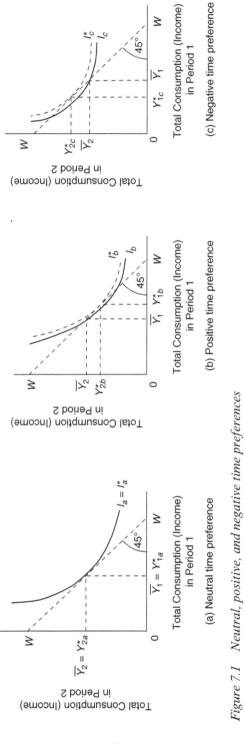

Figure 7.1   Neutral, positive, and negative time preferences

be $Y^*_{1c} + Y^*_{2c}$ and she would achieve the higher indifference curve I^*_c. Individual C has a negative time preference; she values consumption in a later time period more highly than immediate consumption. Individual A, who has a neutral time preference, would prefer the same total consumption in each time period. Because by assumption, the income in each period is equal, she would not choose to make any transfers across time periods.

Notice that these time preferences are all at the margin. In each case, we have drawn intertemporal indifference curves convex to the origin. This means that in each case we have assumed that the individuals strongly dis-prefer vastly unequal consumption across time periods.

Saving and borrowing

Now let *WW* be unbroken. That is, we now assume that the intertemporal budget line *WW* (designated intertemporal budget line 1 in Figures 7.2 a–b) actually exists. This line has a slope of -1. Individual A would choose to make no transfer of income across time periods (Figure 7.2a). On the other hand, individual B would transfer income from the second time period to the first. She would borrow a portion of her second period income in order to spend it in the first period. Her total consumption would be $Y^*_1{}' + Y^*_2{}'$ (Figure 7.2b).

The intertemporal budget line *WW*, of slope -1, assumes that income may be transferred across time periods on a one-for-one basis. In such a case, the individual with neutral time preference would equalize consumption in each period, and the individual with positive time preference would transfer consumption to the immediate time period.

College students, of all people, are aware that it is seldom possible to transfer consumption from the future to the present on a one-for-one basis. Customarily, future income undergoes some diminution when transferred to the present, whereas present income saved for the future tends to grow. In other words, the borrower pays interest, and the saver receives interest. The budget line *WW* assumes that the interest rate for both saving and borrowing is zero.

Now assume that the individual will receive incomes $\overline{Y}_1$ and $\overline{Y}_2$, in each time period; however, there is an option to save a portion of the income for period 1 and spend it, plus interest, in period 2. The individual could also borrow a portion of the period 2 income and spend it, less interest, in period 1. If we assume, unrealistically, that the interest rate, r, is equal for saving and for borrowing (that is, that the financial transactions costs are zero), the budget line 2 will become relevant. If all income, for both periods, were spent in period 1, $\overline{Y}_1 + \overline{Y}_2(1/1 + r)$ could be spent. If consumption in period 1 were zero, $\overline{Y}_2 + \overline{Y}_1(1 + r)$ could be spent in period 2. The slope of the intertemporal budget line 2 is $-(1 + r)$, where r is the interest rate. The higher is the interest rate, the steeper will be the intertemporal budget line. The existence of a positive interest rate is sufficient to induce individual A, who has a neutral time preference, to become a saver; her total consumption becomes $Y^*_1{}'' + Y^*_2{}''$. Individual B remains a borrower, but the positive rate of interest is sufficient to reduce the amount that she borrows.

Finally, consider the intertemporal budget line 3, which would be relevant if the individual were able to receive her total income for the two periods; that is, $\overline{Y}_1 + \overline{Y}_2 = W$ in the first period. The slope of budget line 3 is $-(1 + r)$, the same as the slope of budget line 2. Yet given a positive rate of interest, both individuals A and B are able to achieve higher total utility and greater total consumption in each time period under intertemporal budget line 3 than under intertemporal budget line 2. The present value of $\overline{Y}_1 + \overline{Y}_2 = W$, received in period 1, is greater than the present value of an income stream consisting of $\overline{Y}_1$ in period 1 and $\overline{Y}_2$ in period 2.

The foregoing analyses make several important points. First, individuals have preferences as to the timing of consumption: they may have a positive, negative, or neutral time preference. second, the existence of capital markets which permit intertemporal transfers of consumption increases, or at least does not decrease, utility. Third, positive rates of interest tend to encourage saving and discourage borrowing. The individual consumer will determine his or her preferred rate of saving or borrowing by identifying the point of tangency between his or her intertemporal indifference curve and intertemporal budget line. The necessary condition for intertemporal efficiency in consumption is:

$$RCS_{Y_1,Y_2} = \frac{P_{Y_1}}{P_{Y_2}} = \frac{1+r}{1} = 1 + r \tag{7.1}$$

where 1 and 2 are consecutive time periods.

Observe that the efficiency conditions for intertemporal consumption are simply a special case of the conditions established in Chapter 6; the rate of commodity substitution (RCS) is equated with the relevant price ratio. Note that current consumption is the more expensive, because one must either borrow against future income or forgo interest earnings. Thus if the price of consumption in period 2 is 1, the price of period 1 consumption will be $1 + r$.

The fourth point is that when interest rates are positive, the present value of $\$W$ in time period 1 is greater than is the present value of the income stream $\$w_1 + \$w_2 + \ldots + \$w_n$, where 1, 2,. . ., n represent successive time periods and $w_1 + w_2 + \ldots + w_n = W$.

Investing and borrowing

The above analyses have been confined to the decision problem of a consumer who may transfer income among time periods using capital markets. Now, we consider an individual who has no market opportunities for the intertemporal transfer of capital but who has productive opportunities. That is, he may take part of his income, $\overline{Y}_1$, in period 1, and invest it in productive opportunities. Given the concave intertemporal production possibilities curve, P_2P_1, he would choose to invest the amount $\overline{Y}_1 - Y_1$ in the first period, which would permit his consumption to increase by $Y_2 - \overline{Y}_2$ in period 2. By taking advantage of this productive opportunity, he would be able to move from the indifference curve $\overline{I}$ to the higher indifference curve I (Figure 7.3). The efficiency condition for investment, for an individual who faces only productive opportunities, is:

$$RCS_{Y_1,Y_2} = RPT_{Y_1,Y_2} \tag{7.2}$$

Now consider an individual who enjoys both market and productive opportunities for intertemporal transfer. She invests $\overline{Y}_1 - Y_1^i$ (an even greater amount than $\overline{Y}_1 - Y_1$) in year 1. This raises her potential income in year 2 to Y_2^i. Her efficiency condition for investment is:

$$RPT_{Y_1,Y_2} = 1 + r \tag{7.3}$$

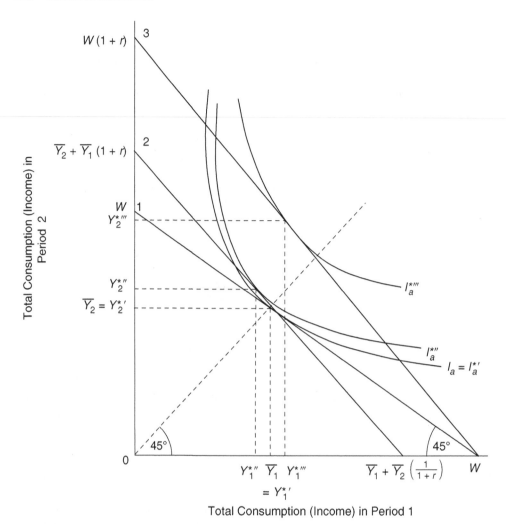

Figure 7.2a   Intertemporal consumption decisions for a consumer with neutral time preference

Having a positive time preference, she prefers a relatively higher consumption in period 1. Using the market opportunities available to her, she borrows the amount $Y_1^* - Y_1^i$, thus achieving the level of consumption Y_1^* in year 1 and Y_2^* in year 2 (Figure 7.3). Her efficiency condition for borrowing is:

$$RCS_{Y_1, Y_2} = 1 + r \tag{7.4}$$

By using both the productive opportunities and the market opportunities available to her, she is able to attain the indifference curve I^*, which is the highest feasible indifference curve. The intertemporal efficiency condition for an individual facing both productive and market opportunities is:

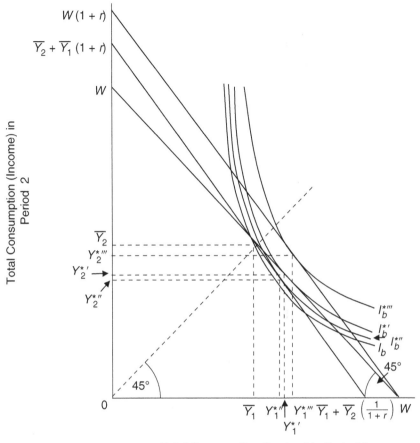

Figure 7.2b Intertemporal consumption decisions for a consumer with positive time preference

$$RCS_{Y_1,Y_2} = RPT_{Y_1,Y_2} = 1 + r \qquad (7.5)$$

Market equilibrium, interest rates, and aggregate investment

As we saw in Chapter 5, individual demand schedules (for any commodity) may be generated from individual indifference maps by examining the quantity taken of one commodity as its price changes. Market-demand schedules may be found by horizontally summing individual demands. The two-period indifference map used to derive intertemporal efficiency conditions for an individual facing a given interest rate can also be used to derive the demand and supply of the next-period consumption, Y_1. If the current price of current consumption, Y_0, is indexed at 1, the current price of Y_1 will be $1/(1 + r)$.

The supply of funds for next-period consumption (S_1) is the sum of the endowed supply $\overline{Y}_1$ and S_1^p, the supply from productive opportunities (Figure 7.4a). The price

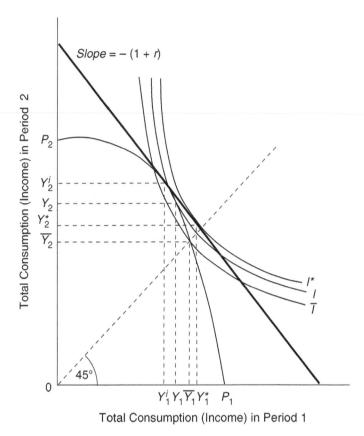

Figure 7.3   Investment and borrowing: the intertemporal decision of an individual with productive and market opportunities

of next-period consumption (hence the interest rate r^*) and its equilibrium quantity Y_1^* are determined by the intersection of D_1 and S_1. The contribution of productive opportunities to next-period consumption, Y_1^P, is determined by the intersection of S_1^P and the equilibrium price of next-period consumption, $1/(1 + r)$. Obviously, $Y_1^* = \overline{Y}_1 + Y_1^P$.

Turning to current consumption (Figure 7.4b), we see that the current supply of funds from production opportunities, S_0^P, is negative at the equilibrium next-period price (opportunity cost) of current consumption, $1 + r^*$. It is more common, however, to speak not of a negative supply of funds from production but of a positive demand for investment funds. The demand for investment funds, D_0^I, is the mirror image of the supply of funds from production. The supply of investment funds, S_0^S, is the endowment, $\overline{Y}_0$, plus the (negative) mirror image, S_0^D, of the demand for current consumption (Figure 7.5a). At equilibrium, the opportunity cost of current consumption is $1 + r^*$, and $Y_0^I = Y_0^S$ is saved and invested. Note that current consumption is $Y_0^* = \overline{Y}_0 - Y_0^I$, and thus $Y_0^I = Y_0^S = -Y_0^P$, where the last-mentioned quantity is found in Figure 7.4b.

The perpetuity model deals with the trade-off between current consumption and a

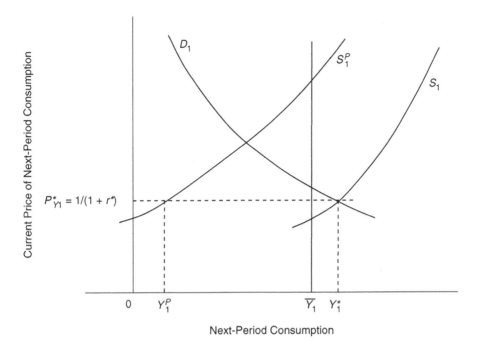

(a) Demand for next-period consumption, Y_1, and supply from endowments and productive opportunities

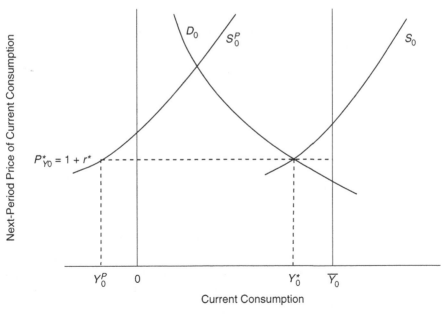

(b) Demand and supply of funds for current consumption

Figure 7.4 Market equilibrium in the two-period model

perpetual future income flow (that is, a sequence of annual consumption, the same amount in each period, extending from year 1 to infinity). In this model, the relevant price is the interest rate, r, and investment and savings are treated as committed in perpetuity. Thus, we have a market diagram (Figure 7.5b) that shows the equilibrium rate of interest, r^*, determined by the intersection of the demand for investment and the supply of savings.

The demand for investment funds is determined by the marginal efficiency of investment, *MEI*. The supply of savings is determined by the rate of time preference, *RTP*. Starting with the two-period model, we are able to derive the equilibrium conditions for the market in investment and savings (Figure 7.5a). These conditions can be interpreted in a perpetuity model (Figure 7.5b) as yielding the familiar equilibrium condition for investment and saving:

$$MEI = RTP = r^* \tag{7.6}$$

This market diagram is useful, as is any other market diagram, for predicting the effects of various disturbances. We consider two simple examples. First, a ceiling on interest rates would reduce savings and increase the demand for investment funds, most likely prompting credit rationing. Second, a capital-intensive technological improvement is likely to shift *MEI* to the right, increasing interest rates, savings, and investment.

Money, the price level, and interest rates
Regard money as a simple counting device that has no purpose other than to facilitate trade by reducing transaction costs. Money, then, is worth what one can buy with it. If the quantity of money were to increase without any change in the available quantities of all goods, services, and resources, money incomes and the money prices of all goods, services, and resources would rise proportionally: that is, the price of any item, i, initially P_1, would increase to aP_1. The rate of price increase, a is called the rate of inflation.

If a is positive, the "money rate of interest" will be greater than the real rate of interest. With continuous compounding:

$$r^m = a + r \tag{7.7}$$

where r^m = money rate of interest, a = the anticipated inflation rate for the term of the loan, and r = real rate of interest. Observed interest rates thus reflect both the real interest rate and the anticipated rate of monetary inflation.

Wealth, capital, and asset markets
Assume an anticipated stream of revenue, $p(t)$, where t ($t = 0, 1, 2, \ldots, T$) indicates time in years. The present value of this revenue stream may be calculated using a procedure called discounting. To account for the positive time preference and the opportunity costs of capital, future revenues are discounted at the rate of compound interest. The present value of $p(t)$ is given by the formula:

$$PV[p(t)] = p_0 + \frac{p_1}{1 + r} + \frac{p_2}{(1 + r)^2} + \ldots + \frac{p_T}{(1 + r)^T} = \sum_{t=0}^{T} \frac{p_t}{(1 + r)^t} \tag{7.8}$$

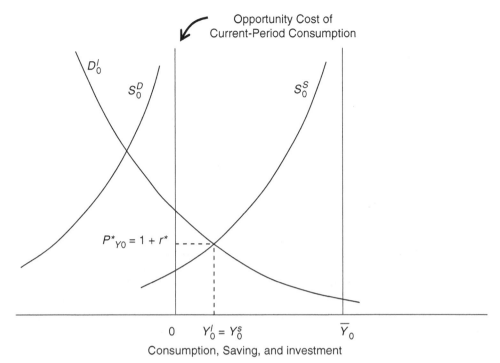

(a) Demand and supply of investment funds in a two period model

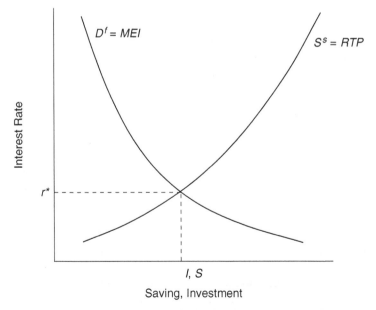

(b) Saving, investment, and the interest rate in a perpetuity model

Figure 7.5 Equilibrium saving, investment, and interest rate

An enforceable claim to such a stream of revenue, $p(t)$, is a form of wealth. In the initial period, the wealth represented by $p(t)$ is its present value:

$$W[p(t)] = PV[p(t)] \tag{7.9}$$

Perhaps the revenue stream is produced by a capital good or asset. A capital good is a physical object existing in the present but providing a source of income or consumption opportunities in the future. Capital goods are thus intermediate goods valuable not for their own sakes but only insofar as they represent the potential of generating consumption goods. If we use Y_0 to denote the current period's consumption, the relationship among wealth, consumption, and capital (K) will be defined by:

$$W_0 = Y_0 + K_0 \tag{7.10}$$

Note that Y_0 and K_0 are not individually fixed but are subject to the above equality constraint. The process of investment involves diverting some of Y_0 to K_0; the process of disinvestment involves transforming some of K_0 into Y_0. For the individual investor who presumably wishes to maximize the present value of his or her current and future consumption possibilities, the optimal investment package is that package P^* which maximizes wealth W_0, where:

$$W_0^{P^*} = \sum_{t=0}^{T} \frac{p_t}{(1 + r)^t} = Y_0 + K_0^{P^*} \tag{7.11}$$

An additional project should be included in the investment package if it would increase W^P. The marginal condition for investment states that the value of capital formed by an incremental investment should be just equal to the present value of consumption sacrificed. This is equivalent to the previously stated efficiency condition:

$$RPT_{Y_1, Y_2} = 1 + r = RCS_{Y_1, Y_2} \tag{7.12}$$

for the two-period case.

Markets in assets
Consider, as above, some package of investments P that yield a stream of revenue $p(t)$ in times $t = 0, \ldots, T$. How many years is T? That is, how long is the investor's time horizon? Is T the investor's expected date of retirement, his or her last year of life expectancy, the life expectancies of his or her immediate heirs, or some distant time reflecting the investor's concern for the well-being of future generations and the continuity of society? If there are well-developed markets in the assets represented by P, the answer may well be "none of the above."

There is some concern as to whether private farmers have sufficient incentives to conserve the productivity of the soil. Sometimes it is claimed that because farmers are mortal, whereas the land can be productive "forever," farmers might rationally permit soil productivity to decline faster than society would prefer. Consider an Iowa farmer, 57 years of age, with plans to retire and move to Arizona at 65. Has he any reason to care about the productivity of his farm beyond $t = 8$? From society's perspective, the present value of that farm, F, is:

$$W_0^F = \sum_{t=0}^{\infty} \frac{p_t}{(1 + r)^t} \tag{7.13}$$

But for a farmer eight years from retirement, perhaps the present value of its earning potential is only:

$$W_0^{F8} = \sum_{t=0}^{8} \frac{p_t}{(1 + r)^t} \tag{7.14}$$

Perhaps he has no reason to care about the productivity of the farm after he has moved on.

But this is not the whole story. The future productivity of the land determines its value as an asset. If there are well-functioning markets in land as a capital asset, the price that the farmer will receive for his land when he retires will reflect its future productivity. That is:

$$W_0^F = \sum_{t=0}^{s} \frac{p_t}{(1 + r)^t} + K_s^F \equiv \sum_{t=0}^{s} \frac{p_t}{(1 + r)^t} + \sum_{t=s+1}^{\infty} \frac{p_t}{(1 + r)^t}$$

$$\equiv \sum_{t=0}^{\infty} \frac{p_t}{(1 + r)^t} \tag{7.15}$$

where $t = 0, \ldots, s, \ldots, \infty$, and s is the time period in which the farm is sold.

For the farmer in this example, K_8^F is maximized when $\sum_{t=9}^{\infty} (p_t)/((1 + r)^t)$ is maximized; that is, when the present value of revenues after the farm has been sold is maximized. The farmer planning to retire presumably seeks to maximize W_0^F. To do so, his perspective must include the productivity of the asset both before and after he sells it. He must behave as though his time horizon were infinite.

It is clear that asset markets offer enough incentives for an owner with a short personal time horizon to make plans consistent with a much longer-term perspective. With well-functioning asset markets, which allow an owner to transfer the remaining revenue potential of an asset at any time and receive its present value, the relevant time horizon is unrelated to the owner's personal situation and determined instead by the potential productive life of the asset itself.

The above analysis shows it is generally wrong to argue that individual landowners will behave shortsightedly when conserving the productivity of their soil. If there is a "soil conservation problem," it does not arise from disparities between individual time horizons and that of society. Asset markets take care of that problem.[1] Efficient asset markets serve to arbitrate among claims to current and future income and consumption, thus encouraging efficient levels of conservation, saving, and investment. Just as ideal competitive markets perform Pareto-efficiently in the static environment, so ideal asset markets provide intertemporal Pareto-efficiency.

Questions for discussion

1. Under what conditions could a rational individual be simultaneously:
   a. an investor and a borrower?
   b. a saver and a borrower?

2. In the history of the US economy, sometimes there are periods when the observed interest rates for borrowers are lower than the actual rate of inflation. How could this happen?
3. Explain how well-functioning asset markets effectively extend an individual's investment time horizon beyond his or her own expected lifespan.

Note

1. We have not, however, proved conclusively that there really is no soil conservation problem, for two reasons. First, it may be true that capital markets in general discount the distant future too much. That is, the market-determined r may be "too high," or higher than the social discount rate (see Chapters 12 and 19). If this is true, then the soil conservation problem might be real. However, it would not be a special problem but, rather, one manifestation of a general problem that also results in insufficient capital accumulation and a too-rapid depletion of exhaustible resources. Second, if there really is a soil conservation problem, it will most likely arise from the lack of information concerning the effects of current cultivation practices on future productivity. It may be that farmers are unaware of the damage they are doing to the soil until it is too late. A related problem does appear to be real. Eroded soil enters streams as suspended sediment, silting up the streambeds and polluting the water. It seems that there are no satisfactory markets to take care of this soil erosion-related problem.

Suggested reading: classical and contemporary

Arrow, K.J., W.R. Cline, K.-G. Maler, M. Munasinghe, R. Squitieri, and J.E. Stiglitz (1996), "Intertemporal Equity, Discounting and Economic Efficiency," in *Climate Change 1995: Economic and Social Dimensions of Climate Change – Contribution of Working Group III to the Second Assessment Report of the Intergovernmental Panel on Climate Change*, ed. J.P. Bruce and E.F. Haites, Cambridge: Cambridge University Press.

Browning, M. and T.F. Crossley (2001), "The Life-Cycle Model of Consumption and Saving," *Journal of Economic Perspectives* 15 (3): 3–22.

Hirschleifer, J. (1970), *Investment, Interest and Capital*, Englewood Cliffs, NJ: Prentice-Hall.

Solow, R.M. (1986), "On the Intergenerational Allocation of Natural Resources," *Scandinavian Journal of Economics* 88 (1): 141–9.

PART III

ECONOMIC THEORY AND INSTITUTIONS FOR PUBLIC POLICY

8 Criteria for economic policy: how do we tell a good natural resource and environmental policy from a bad one?

When economists evaluate natural resource and environmental policy, economic efficiency is often a dominant concern. This concern is expected since all economists tend to agree that efficiency is a "good thing." However, economic efficiency by itself is an insufficient criterion for economic policy. First, society might recognize other "good things;" that is, other legitimate goals instead of or in addition to economic efficiency. Second, efficiency itself is not unique. There are, in principle, an infinite number of efficient solutions, each associated with a different distribution of the social product (see Chapter 6). Agreement that efficiency is a goal for society would not resolve the philosophical questions about the legitimacy of authority and the relationship between government and citizens (see Chapter 4). If an efficiency-improving policy would injure some individuals, is that policy to be judged as justified by its efficiency properties, or illegitimate because it injures some people? If an efficiency-improving policy fails to alleviate the misery of the worst-off members of society, will its failure in that respect make it illegitimate? In this chapter, we directly confront the criterion problem in terms compatible with the general equilibrium efficiency analysis of Chapter 6 and the philosophical discussion of Chapter 4.

Maximum social well-being

A lofty and desirable state for any society is maximum social well-being, a condition in which society is as well off as it can possibly be, given its resource base, its productive technology, and the tastes and preferences of its members. These givens, if you remember, are exactly those that defined the grand utility frontier (see Chapter 6). Every point on that frontier is efficient in the sense that no feasible reorganization starting from that point could make one person better off without hurting another. Points inside the frontier are wasteful, because reorganizations that could simultaneously benefit all persons remain unexploited.

So the search for maximum social well-being must start on the grand utility frontier. The question is, On what basis can society choose one from among the efficient solutions on the grand utility frontier? Consider the function $W = w(U_1, U_2)$, where W = social well-being. This has been called the social welfare function (SWF), or the Samuelson–Bergson social welfare function (after two famous economists of the twentieth century).[1] W is expressed as a function of U_1 and U_2, that is, the levels of utility enjoyed by the individuals 1 and 2. The existence of such a function assumes that there is some way to develop a consensus across society as to how utility should be distributed among individuals and that this function can express such a consensus. The SWF is the societal analogue of the individual utility function. Just as an indifference map can be derived from an individual utility function, so a social indifference map can be derived from a social welfare function.

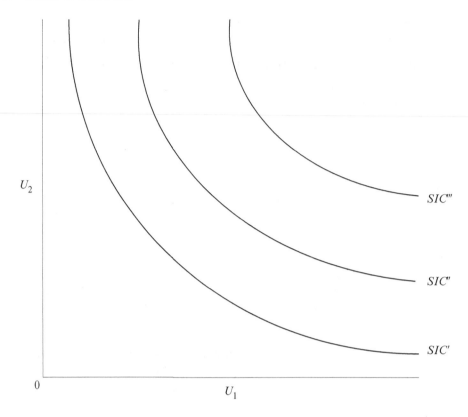

Figure 8.1   The social indifference map

A social indifference curve is the locus of all possible combinations of utility levels for the individuals 1 and 2 that would result in the same level of social well-being. The social indifference map is expressed in utility axes. The social indifference map shown in Figure 8.1 indicates that the society whose preferences it represents has a definite but relatively weak preference for the equality of well-being among its members: its best-off member would have to become better off at a rapid rate in order to compensate for a relatively small diminution of the well-being of its worst-off member. A stronger preference for equality would be indicated by a much sharper curvature of convex social indifference curves (*SICs*).

Remember that the grand utility frontier was also expressed in utility space. It is possible, as in Figure 8.2, to superimpose the social indifference map on the grand utility frontier. The point of tangency at which the highest feasible social indifference curve just touches the grand utility frontier from above is the "bliss point," the point of maximum social well-being. The bliss point is Pareto-efficient, as it is on the grand utility frontier. Of all the Pareto-efficient points on the grand utility frontier, it is most preferred, as it permits the highest possible level of maximum social well-being.

Necessary conditions for maximum social well-being
The necessary conditions for maximum social well-being are: (1) Pareto-efficiency; (2) tangency between the grand utility frontier and the social indifference curve.

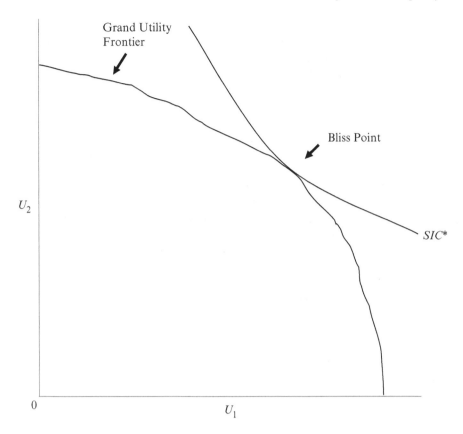

Figure 8.2   The maximization of social well-being

Sufficient condition for maximum social well-being
A sufficient condition for maximum social well-being is that a unique, true tangency exists between the grand utility frontier and a social indifference curve. Pareto-efficiency implies that the grand utility frontier, although not necessarily smooth, will be generally concave to the origin. The social indifference curve is a smooth curve, but there is no reason that it must be convex to the origin. Convexity implies that society wants to avoid the extreme deprivation of any of its members. However, there may be societies that simply do not feel that way. Thus it is possible for a social indifference curve to be concave. The sufficient condition will be satisfied if the social indifference curve and the grand utility frontier (GUF) are of such shapes that the SIC is tangent to the GUF from above at one, and only one point.

   The social indifference curve and the social welfare function can exist only under some rather strong assumptions about the society's ability to achieve a consensus as to how economic well-being ought to be distributed among its members. Therefore, it is wise to note that the sufficient condition for maximum social well-being requires that the social welfare function exists.

The existence of the social welfare function
The social welfare function (SWF) is a mathematical relationship precisely expressing the societal preference as to how economic well-being (or, if you will, utility) should be distributed among the individual members of society. How could such a societal preference be established? Some (many?) individuals may have developed personal philosophies about how the rewards of economic activity should be distributed, though these personal philosophies are likely to vary widely from one individual to another. Furthermore, even those individuals who have developed personal philosophies about distribution in general are likely to take a less detached approach to impending events that threaten to make themselves worse off while making others better off. For these reasons, we cannot expect the SWF to emerge from unanimous agreement among citizens.

Perhaps a dictator could specify the SWF for society. This solution would be unsatisfactory to all persons who adhere to even a minimal set of precepts about individual dignity. It is also unrealistic, as the single dictator would have no capacity to enforce their chosen social welfare function on everyone else. (Real-world "dictators" are not individuals making decisions unconstrained by the wishes of others; typically, they rule with the express support of one or more powerful factions and the tacit consent of the "silent majority." Dictators who lose these bases of support tend to enjoy brief regimes followed by long exiles or, for the less fortunate, violent deaths).

Because we cannot expect the SWF to emerge from unanimous consent and we would not accept (as either ethical or practicable) an SWF imposed by a dictator, we must search for ways in which the consensus implicit in the social welfare function concept could be established more or less democratically. Although various kinds of political and governmental institutions are in varying degrees effective in adjudicating among the claims of competing individuals, coalitions, and philosophies, nothing that can be identified as a social welfare function seems to emerge from the process.

If a social scientist, armed with carefully designed questionnaires and a well-tested attitude-measuring scale, were to bypass the political process and seek to estimate the SWF from surveys of citizens, it is unlikely that they would be successful. First, they would need to collect and analyze a truly horrendous quantity of data. But that is a relatively minor problem. The major problem would be that in order to force the conflicting observations from individuals into the form of the SWF, the social scientist would need to invent a whole set of rules for making the various trade-offs. But this would solve the problem only by circumventing it; the analytical process assumes in advance the SWF it sets out to find.

Kenneth Arrow, a Nobel laureate in economics, developed an interesting, rigorous, mathematical proof of a proposition that some interpret as showing that the SWF cannot exist in a democratic society.[2] Arrow set out to find what he calls a "constitution," a social decision rule that always yields a consistent answer when applied to any problem. Any constitution acceptable to a democracy should, Arrow reasoned, meet several conditions: (1) it must be consistent with individual rationality; (2) individual rationality must be translated into collective rationality (for example, if any one of a set of possible alternatives were to rise in the ranking of one individual without falling in the ranking of any other individual, it should rise or at least should not fall, in the social ranking); (3) neither individual nor collective preference orderings should be influenced by alternatives that are irrelevant (that is, that are not elements of the opportunity set from which selections must be made); (4) the social preference ordering should not be imposed from outside the society; and (5) no individual should be a dictator (a dictator is defined as one whose preference ordering is always the social preference ordering, regardless of the preferences of everyone else).

Arrow was able to show, using a simple analysis in which three individuals, 1, 2, and 3, ranked three alternatives, A, B, and C, that a democratic majority voting process is unable to yield a decision rule that never violates any of the five conditions. Suppose individuals have the following preference orderings (in which the preferred alternative is stated first and the least preferred last):

- individual 1: A, B, C.
- individual 2: B, C, A.
- individual 3: C, A, B.

Given the above preferences, simple majority voting would yield the following result: A is preferred to B by a two-to-one majority; B is preferred to C by a similar majority; and C is preferred to A by a similar majority. This yields a social preference ordering of A B C A, which clearly violates the conditions of rationality. If A is preferred to B and B is preferred to C, how could C possibly be preferred to A?

Arrow's theorem, the "impossibility theorem," is controversial on two general sets of grounds. First, some have questioned the idea of a constitution. Perhaps it is possible for a society to reach a workable consensus about the meaning of social well-being without that consensus meeting the strict criteria for a constitution. The economist Paul Samuelson (of the Samuelson–Bergson SWF) insists that Arrow's constitution is a logical construct quite different from the SWF.[3] Second, many have questioned the conditions that Arrow required. Is it necessary that a reasonable social decision rule meet every one of those conditions? Although there has been many years of debate on that question, it must be noted that new and more sophisticated versions of Arrow's theorem have been developed, each dropping one of Arrow's conditions.

Many analysts have focused on the voting process itself, considering different kinds of voting processes in order to identify those that may avoid Arrow's paradox.[4] Some have demonstrated that with many alternatives to rank and many individuals voting, Arrow's paradox occurs very infrequently. Others have shown that when almost everyone conceives the alternatives in roughly the same way on some objective scale (for example, height in feet or cost in dollars), even though individuals may have very different preferences among the alternatives, Arrow's paradox will not be observed. Other theoretical analyses have shown that various voting strategies commonly observed in the real world of political and committee decision processes (for example, vote trading and voting strategies based on game-theoretic principles) may successfully avoid the Arrow paradox.

Although the Arrow theorem and the multitude of more specialized impossibility theorems that have been more recently developed[5] are impressive exercises in logic, it is not clear that these kinds of theorems conclusively prove that an SWF cannot exist. Nevertheless, although scholars may argue about the possible existence of a SWF, there is literally no one who can make a serious and plausible claim to know precisely the SWF for any society. Even though the SWF is a useful device for developing the theoretical principle of maximum social well-being, economists are simply unable to use the SWF in making quantitative analyses of practical economic problems.

Criteria for economic policy
In the absence, for all practical purposes, of a precisely specified social welfare function, what can practicing natural resource and environmental economists say for sure about the social desirability of various alternative policies? Some things, as we have seen, are known about economic efficiency. But the grand utility frontier presents an infinite number of Pareto-efficient solutions, each with different distributional consequences. Efficiency alone provides no guidance to how a society may rationally choose among these alternatives.

Because the present generation of economic analysts lacks the necessary social preference information to implement the maximum social well-being criterion, and the theoretical analyses along the line initiated by Kenneth Arrow cast serious doubt that social welfare function information will ever be available, it is appropriate to examine policy criteria that do not depend on the SWF notion. As we examine the potential criteria by which to judge policy alternatives, we shall be especially concerned with what is required or permitted with respect to economic efficiency and economic injury. Economic injury is defined as a reduction in individual utility as a direct or indirect result of a public policy decision. Our definition of economic injury is thus quite similar to the popular notion of a "windfall loss."

In the analyses that follow, the grand utility frontier is expressed in income axes rather than utility axes. This procedure is helpful as it permits a discussion more relevant to the real world in which income, not utility, is measured. There is some justification for replacing utility axes with income axes, as utility is believed to be positively correlated with income. However, as any good economist knows, it is not a strictly legitimate procedure: utility is ordinal and not subject to interpersonal evaluation, whereas income is cardinal and may be summed across individuals.

Economic efficiency as a criterion
Economic efficiency alone may be used as a criterion by which to judge alternative economic policies and public sector activities. Some economists, impressed with the logical and empirical difficulties inherent in the social welfare function concept, insist economists are qualified by their professional training to speak of efficiency and to use efficiency as a policy criterion, but to go no further. This point of view regards economists as professionally trained to identify policies that would eliminate waste but as having no professional qualifications permitting them to choose among alternative efficient solutions, each of which has different distributional consequences.

Consider Figure 8.3. Point *a*, lying inside the grand utility frontier, is economically inefficient. Points *b*, *c*, and *d* all are on the grand utility frontier and thus all are economically efficient. An economist using efficiency as the sole criterion would find that policies moving the economy to points *b*, *c*, and *d* all represent improvements over point *a* and all are equally desirable. Examine the northeast quadrant with its origin at point *a*. This quadrant contains all possible situations in which at least one party is made better off and no party is made worse off compared to the initial starting point *a*. Thus, of our three efficient solutions, *b*, *c*, and *d*, only *c* is a solution in which neither party is injured.

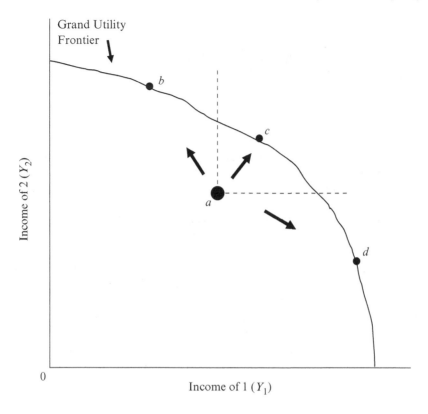

Figure 8.3   Efficiency as the criterion

Starting at *a*, a policy that resulted in the efficient solution *b* would result in economic injury to 1, and a policy resulting in *d* would result in economic injury to 2. Economic efficiency alone is a criterion that eliminates inefficient (that is, wasteful) solutions, but it does not distinguish between policies that result in economic injury for some and policies resulting in economic injury for no one. Under this criterion, whoever gains or loses is irrelevant.

Constant proportional shares
Consider a criterion that defines as an improvement any solution resulting in a greater income for someone, as long as everybody's income increases proportionally. Under this criterion, everyone must benefit from a policy change, and each must benefit in strict proportion to his or her initial income. In Figure 8.4, there are three inefficient starting points, *a*, *b*, and *c*, all of which lie within the grand utility frontier. If we draw a series of rays from the origin passing through each of points *a*, *b*, and *c*, and continue the rays out to the grand utility frontier, we define points *a'*, *b'*, and *c'* all of which are Pareto-efficient. Starting at *a*, for example, any point on the line segment *aa'* represents an improvement, and *a'* represents the optimum policy.

Under the constant proportional shares criterion, a movement toward efficiency is necessary for a proposed policy to be considered an improvement, and an optimal policy

---

APPLICATION: EXAMPLE OF USING ECONOMIC EFFICIENCY TO EVALUATE NATURAL RESOURCE AND ENVIRONMENTAL POLICY AND MANAGEMENT

Federal, state, and local government agencies that manage water resources are often faced with decisions that will reallocate water to different uses and parties. In Figure 8.3, suppose that Individual 1 is a farmer and Individual 2 is a real-estate developer. Both individuals need access to water to support their businesses and incomes. In many parts of the United States, water is scarce to the point that it must be rationed between Individual 1 and Individual 2 according to some set of water rights and institutions (e.g., water withdrawal permits). Assume that under the current system of water rights and institutions, Individuals 1 and 2 find themselves at the economically inefficient point *a* in Figure 8.3. Using economic efficiency as the evaluation criteria, a change in water rights or institutions that moved Individuals 1 and 2 to points *b*, *c*, and *d* would be considered improvements, even though both are made better-off only by the move to *c*. Thus, for example, a reallocation of water permits from the farmer to the real-estate developer that harms the farmer (move to point *b*) is allowed as would be a reallocation of permits from the real-estate developer to the farmer that harms the developer (move to point *d*). All that is required in either case is that efficiency be achieved by the reallocation of water permits.

---

is Pareto-efficient. However, from any starting point, only one point on the grand utility frontier is acceptable, and all other efficient solutions are eliminated. There can be no real injury: that is, no one can be made worse off. In addition, there can be no relative injury: no one can be made worse off relative to anybody else.

Notice, however, that at point *a*, 1 had a low income relative to 2, and at situation *c*, 2 had a low income relative to 1. At *a'*, individual 1's income has not improved relative to that of individual 2; similarly, at *c'*, individual 2's income has shown no relative improvement compared with 1's. The constant proportional shares criterion does not permit those who were badly off at the outset to become relatively better off as a result of new policies. Real or relative redistributions of income are prohibited. It may be argued that individuals who suffered a low income, say at point *a*, did so as a result of some past economic injury. That line of argument suggests that the constant proportional shares criterion permits no new relative economic injury while embedding and reinforcing past patterns of relative economic injury.

It is not common to find serious proposals that the constant proportional shares criterion should be rigidly implemented throughout a whole economy. But from time to time one does see arguments that it should be partially implemented. For example, labor unions sometimes argue for wage increases on the grounds that such increases are necessary to maintain a historical relationship between labor income and total income. Similarly, one occasionally encounters proposals saying that those on institutionally determined incomes, for example social security recipients, should have their incomes maintained at some constant fraction of gross domestic product (GDP). Public serv-

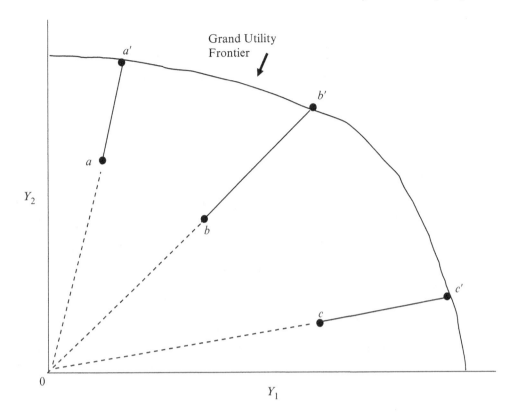

Figure 8.4   Constant proportional shares

ants such as public school teachers, police officers and firefighters often point out that their salaries do not tend to keep up with inflation, thus reducing their real income and purchasing power over time. All these arguments amount to proposals in support of applying the constant proportional shares concept, at least in certain circumstances, as a benchmark by which to judge the "fairness" of institutionally determined incomes.

Pareto-safety
The criterion of Pareto-safety defines as an improvement (that is, a Pareto-improvement) any change that would increase the income of at least one person and reduce nobody's income. The northeast quadrant of Figure 8.5 defines the Pareto-safety region as starting at point *a*. A policy resulting in a movement to any point in the northeast quadrant would be considered an improvement; a policy resulting in a movement to any point on the segment *a′ a″* of the grand utility frontier, which lies within the northeast quadrant, would be considered an optimal policy. There is no acceptable basis for judgment among points that lie on that grand utility frontier segment as to which point is "best."

A policy is judged to be an improvement if it results in a northeasterly move toward the grand utility frontier. Optimal policies require that efficiency be achieved. However, policies that result in moves from the inefficient point *a* to the efficient points *b* and *c* would not be considered improvements, much less optimal. No new real economic injury

---

APPLICATION: EXAMPLE OF USING CONSTANT PROPORTIONAL SHARES TO EVALUATE NATURAL RESOURCE AND ENVIRONMENTAL POLICY AND MANAGEMENT

Let us return again to the water allocation example we used previously to illustrate economic efficiency as the evaluation criteria, except this time we use constant proportional shares to evaluate policy and management changes. Suppose under the current set of water rights and institutions, the farmer (Individual 1) and real-estate developer (Individual 2) find themselves at point *a* in Figure 8.4. Under constant proportional shares, a reallocation, say of water permits, cannot make the farmer or developer worse off in terms of both real and relative economic injury. Thus, any reallocation of water permits between the farmer and real-estate developer would have to move both individuals along the line between point *a* and point *a'*. For both individuals to be as well off as they could be, the reallocation of permits would eventually need to lead the farmer and real-estate developer to point *a'* where economic efficiency is achieved. Note, however, that economic efficiency is necessary only for a maximum improvement, not for any improvement (any policy or management action that resulted in a move from point *a* to a point somewhere between point *a* and point *a'* would be considered an improvement).

---

is permitted. But relative economic injury is permissible: it is not essential that every individual in a society maintains his or her proportional share of income, only that no one actually loses real income. Pareto-safety permits relative redistribution of income as the total income of society grows, but no redistribution so great that any party actually receives less income. To this extent, the criterion of Pareto-safety at least partly embeds and reinforces past patterns of economic injury.

Pareto-safety, as a policy rule, would protect individuals from being made worse off by actions imposed on them by government. It would not, however, protect them from the dynamic consequences of the choices freely made by themselves and others in the market. That is, individuals would not be protected from market-generated changes in relative scarcity and technology that might leave them worse off. To offer such protection would be to undermine the incentives to adjust to new realities which are among the prime virtues of the market as an institution.

The Pareto-safety criterion has solid roots not only in welfare economics, but also in social contract philosophy. It is a fundamental precept of Locke's individualistic version of the social contract in which all rights reside with individuals. From the Lockean perspective, government acquires only those rights delegated by individuals. There are some concerns (public safety, for example) that can be attended only by a governmental authority with coercive power. However, to Locke, these are special cases. For a broad range of more typical cases, Pareto-safety is satisfied by voluntary exchange (who would willingly enter a trade that would leave oneself worse off?). In politics, it is satisfied by a unanimity decision rule.

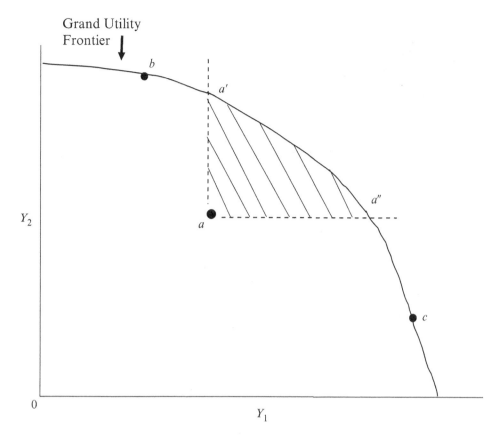

Figure 8.5 Pareto-safety

Maximum social well-being

There is surely no need at this point for a reminder of the difficulties inherent in the idea of a social welfare function. Nevertheless, it is interesting and instructive to evaluate maximum social well-being (MSW) as a policy criterion, asking what it requires and permits with respect to economic efficiency and injury. The social indifference map, superimposed on the grand utility frontier (Figure 8.6), is presented using broken lines to reinforce the logical doubts and empirical uncertainties that surround the notion of a social welfare function. From point *a*, any situation lying above the *SIC* passing through point *a* would be considered an improvement. The optimal situation would be at the point of tangency between the grand utility frontier and the highest feasible social indifference curve – that is, the bliss point.

Notice that the *SIC* passing through point *a* intersects the grand utility frontier at two points. The segment of the grand utility frontier bounded by those two points of intersection defines the set of efficient solutions that would be regarded as improvements, starting from point *a*. No efficient solution lying outside that segment would be considered an improvement. Not only that, but moves from the efficient points *b* and *c* to the inefficient point *a* would be considered improvements. Movements toward efficiency are

APPLICATION: EXAMPLE OF USING PARETO-SAFETY TO EVALUATE NATURAL RESOURCE AND ENVIRONMENTAL POLICY AND MANAGEMENT

Federal, state, and local government agencies that manage public forests are often faced with trying to accommodate people who want to use a public forest for competing uses; for example, wildlife hunting (a consumptive use), and wildlife observation, say birdwatching (a non-consumptive use). In Figure 8.5, assume that Individual 1 is a hunter and Individual 2 is a birdwatcher. Assume also that Y_1 represents the total benefits to Individual 1 of hunting in the forest expressed in dollar terms, and Y_2 represents the total benefits to Individual 2 of birdwatching in the forest expressed in dollar terms (we will discuss in later chapters how economists value recreation in dollar terms). Suppose that under the current management plan for the forest, the hunter and birdwatcher find themselves at point *a* in Figure 8.5. Under Pareto-safety, a new forest management plan cannot make the hunter or birdwatcher absolutely worse off (e.g., no new real economic injury is allowed). Thus, only new management plans that moved the hunter and birdwatcher into the hatched area in Figure 8.5 (including the borders) would be considered management improvements.

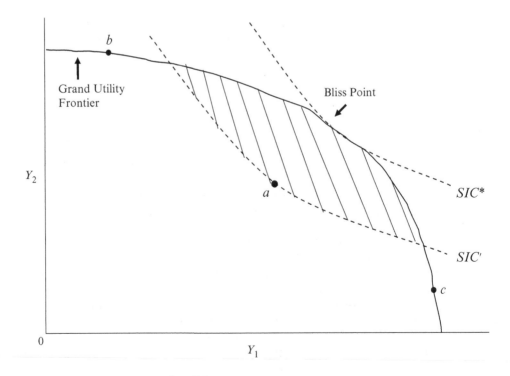

Figure 8.6   Maximum social well-being

not necessarily welfare improvements, nor do moves away from efficiency necessarily decrease welfare.

The criterion of maximum social well-being permits real economic injury, but within limits. Those limits are defined by the shape of the social indifference curve itself. In general, economic injury to individuals is permitted as long as there is a social consensus that the outcome represents an improvement in social well-being.

The maximum social well-being criterion has had somewhat of a checkered career in economics, being introduced via the Samuelson–Bergson social welfare function but subjected to attack by many who use the Arrow impossibility theorem as a weapon against it. A vocal group of individualistic economists reject MSW without appeal to the Arrow theorem. They say that even if the SWF could be shown to exist in Arrow's sense, they would reject its use on ethical grounds: it necessarily involves the coercion of the individual by the collective.

The idea of MSW has obvious philosophical connections with Rousseau's version of the social contract. A social welfare function would, it seems to us, necessarily provide a mathematical formalization of the concept of the "general will" or the "public interest." The tolerance of MSW for individual injury as long as social well-being is served in the process is entirely compatible with Rousseau's belief that there is no compelling need to limit the scope and authority of government so long as it remains responsible to the general will. In practical politics, it is common to encounter arguments favoring programs that redistribute income, wealth, and opportunity and that direct resource allocation via regulation, taxation, or public investment, on the grounds that such programs serve the public interest.

Maximum value of social product

One special form of the social indifference curve is a straight line, extending to both axes, of slope −1. Such a social indifference curve provides that each dollar of income be weighted equally, regardless of to whom it accrues. The value of society's output is to be calculated without distributional weights and a policy that results in the maximum value of social product (MVSP) is preferred. Starting from point a, the set of possible improvements is defined by a line of slope −1 passing through point a; all points above that line are considered improvements, according to the criterion of MVSP (Figure 8.7). The optimum solution, a', is determined by the tangency of the grand utility frontier with the highest feasible line of slope −1.

Under this criterion, an improvement need not necessarily represent a movement toward efficiency. From either b or c, a move to a away from efficiency would be an improvement. But the optimal solution must be efficient. Economic injury is permissible as long as the sum of the dollars gained by the gainers exceeds the sum of the dollars lost by the losers. Thus the criterion of maximum value of social product is totally neutral with regard to income redistribution. Income redistribution is never required for its own sake, and policies that happen to redistribute income are never prohibited so long as the total dollars gained by the beneficiaries exceed the total dollars lost by the losers.

In economic theory, the conceptual basis of MVSP has been developed in detail in such topical areas as national income accounting, welfare indices, consumers' and producers' surplus, and benefit–cost analysis. The MVSP criterion is one way to implement Jeremy Bentham's utilitarian criterion, "the greatest good for the greatest number."

APPLICATION: EXAMPLE OF USING MAXIMUM SOCIAL WELL-BEING TO EVALUATE NATURAL RESOURCE AND ENVIRONMENTAL POLICY AND MANAGEMENT

Suppose in Figure 8.6 that Individual 2 lives upstream on a river from Individual 1 and both use the river water to support their incomes; let's say Individual 2 is a manufacturer and Individual 1 is a recreation outfitter (e.g., fishing and rafting). Assume that the manufacturer is currently emitting a level of pollutants into the river that is negatively impacting the outfitter's fishing and rafting business. This initial situation places Individuals 1 and 2 at point *a* in Figure 8.6. Point *a* is not only economically inefficient, but may be viewed by society as unfair or unjust according to the social preferences defined by some social welfare function. Given social preferences represented by the social indifference curves (*SICs*) in Figure 8.6, society would like to move Individual 1 and 2 to the bliss point where social well-being is maximized. This particular move makes both individuals better off and may be accomplished, say, by subsidizing the manufacturer to reduce pollution. Note, however, that this criteria does not require everyone to be made better off. For example, suppose the starting point is point *b* instead of point *a*. A move from point *b* to the bliss point would make Individual 1 better off and Individual 2 worse off. This move might be accomplished, for example, by some form of regulation or taxation on the manufacturer that would reduce pollution emissions, making the recreation outfitter better off and the manufacturer worse off (since we assume the regulation or taxation would reduce the manufacturer's income). As long as social well-being is increasing, real and relative economic injury are allowed.

Thus it has firm roots in utilitarian philosophy. It is not true, however, that utilitarian criteria are necessarily of the MVSP type; there are other approaches within the utilitarian framework.

In modern mixed economies, no one seriously suggests that the criterion of maximum value of social product should be applied, pervasively and without exception, to all policy decisions. But this criterion is widely applied to certain classes of decisions. For example, the benefit–cost criterion, that the benefits to whomsoever they accrue should exceed the costs, is synonymous with the criterion of maximum value of social product. The idea that the best economic policy is the one that maximizes the rate of economic growth, or growth in gross domestic product (GDP), is related to the criterion of maximum value of social product in the following way: GDP is a highly unsatisfactory measure of a nation's economic productivity; however, if GDP were an adequate measure of the value of social product, the criterion of maximum value of social product would be a criterion of maximum GDP.

Composite criteria
The normative criteria for natural resource and environmental policy discussed so far in this chapter are single criteria. None seems entirely satisfactory. Objections to some are raised on ethical and philosophical grounds, and objections to others are based on

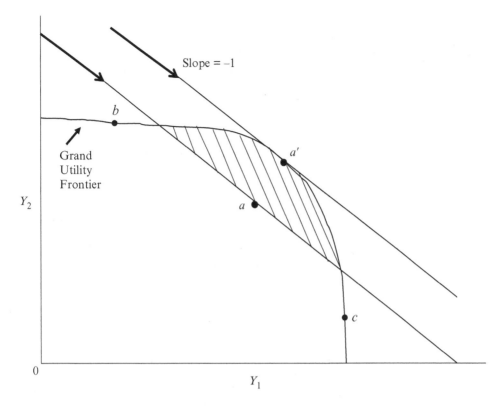

Figure 8.7   Maximum value of social product

pragmatic grounds; and, it seems, most of these criteria are vulnerable to objections on both kinds of grounds. There are, of course, other single criteria that could be, and have been, seriously proposed.

The reasonable objections to the various single criteria have led some thinkers to propose the use of multiple or composite criteria. For example, some have proposed the criterion of maximum value of social product, with the proviso that no policy that would make the poor worse off is acceptable. This kind of criterion could be described as maximum value of social product, subject to Pareto-safety for the poor but not for the rich. It is possible to generate other composite criteria.

For example, consider the following criteria to be implemented simultaneously: (1) policies that reduce the value of social product are unacceptable; (2) the income of the well-off individual, 2, should not be increased; (3) permissible redistribution will not proceed past the point of equality (that is, individual 1 will not be permitted to become richer than individual 2); and (4) the optimal policy will be that policy which, though satisfying conditions (1)–(3), results in the maximum attainable value of social product. As Figure 8.8 demonstrates, it is possible with a composite criterion such as this to define a zone of policy improvements and an optimal policy. The optimal policy, which would move the economy to point *a'*, is an efficient policy. Permissible economic injury is defined by the conditions that make up the composite criterion.

APPLICATION: EXAMPLE OF USING MAXIMUM VALUE OF
SOCIAL PRODUCT TO EVALUATE NATURAL RESOURCE
AND ENVIRONMENTAL POLICY AND MANAGEMENT

Suppose a federal government agency is managing a public land area that
could be used for mining and/or recreation development and we are measuring social product by GDP. Mining development (e.g., oil, natural gas, coal)
contributes to GDP by the total value of the mining products generated from
the public land. Recreation development (e.g., skiing, hiking, biking, camping)
contributes to GDP by the value of expenditures on recreational activities supported by the public land. In Figure 8.7, assume that Individual 1 is a recreation
developer and Individual 2 is a mining developer. The straight lines in Figure
8.7 represent different levels of GDP. Suppose that under the current management plan, Individual 1 and Individual 2 are at the economically inefficient point
a in Figure 8.7. In order to maximumize social product (measured by GDP), a
change in the management plan would need to move Individuals 1 and 2 to
point *a'* indicating an increase in both mining and recreational development on
the public land (making both individuals better off). Note that this need not be
the case. For example, if the starting point happened to be point *b*, maximizing
social product would result in more recreation development and less mining
development (making Individual 2 worse off). If the starting point happened to
point *c*, maximizing social product would result in more mining development
and less recreation development (making Individual 1 worse off). Real and relative economic injury are allowed as long as social product (e.g., the sum of the
value of mining products and recreation expenditures) is increasing.

---

*A note on the Kaldor–Hicks criterion, the compensation tests, and the "potential Pareto-
improvement"*

In the late 1930s, economists Nicholas Kaldor and John Hicks, feeling that the only reasonable objection to the Pareto-improvement criterion was that few policy actions could
satisfy it, proposed compensation tests.[6] For example, starting with policy situation A,
if it were possible to introduce policy A' so that those who gained could afford to compensate the losers and have some gains remaining, the change from A to A' would be a
potential Pareto-improvement. The idea was that the possibility of compensation would
expand the set of policy actions that could result in Pareto-improvements.

   Just what kind of criterion would be established by using this kind of compensation
test? The answer depends entirely on whether or not the compensation was actually paid.
If the compensation must be paid, the compensation test criterion would reduce to an
actual Pareto-improvement, albeit with compensation. If the compensation need not be
paid, the compensation test criterion would require only that the sum of the gains (in
dollar terms), to whomsoever they were to accrue, exceeded the sum of the losses. In this
case, the potential Pareto-improvement criterion would be identical to the maximum
value of social product criterion.

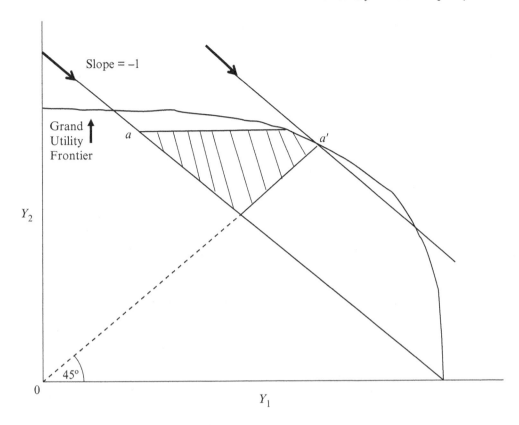

Figure 8.8   A composite criterion

Constitutional processes

The various policy criteria described above provide two general philosophical approaches to defining what is "good" for society. Specifically, most of the criteria discussed – economic efficiency, maximum social well-being, and maximum value of social product – attempt to define good outcomes. It is the consequences of policy which are judged good or bad. The case for the Pareto-safety criterion, on the other hand, is not that it yields outcomes that are independently judged good, but that it yields outcomes the involved parties voluntarily accept. What is claimed to be good about Pareto-safety is that it is a good process for making public decisions. If the process is good, the argument goes, whatever emerges from that process must also be good. Although the other criteria considered offer competing ways to judge the consequences of policy (good policies are those with good consequences), Pareto-safety judges the decision process (good policies are those resulting from good processes).

The problem with Pareto-safety is that many who accept the concept that "whatever emerges from good processes is good" cannot really accept Pareto-safety as a good process. The difficulty has already been highlighted. Pareto-safety has the desirable property that change must be universally agreeable, but it fails to address the issue of "change from what?" If the status quo is unjust, the beneficiaries of that injustice can always block any change to redress the injustice. This major ethical difficulty with Pareto-safety has stimulated a search for alternative principles by which to define good decision processes.

The Rawlsian constitution

The philosopher John Rawls defined justice and fairness (both synonyms for the social good, in his lexicon) as whatever emerges from just processes.[7] Because there can be no assurance that any existing status quo is just, his chief project was to define a process whereby a just starting point, or constitution, may be identified. Then, and only then, does it make sense to talk about just processes for change.

The constitution itself must be just, and clearly, it could be judged to be just if everyone agreed to it at the outset. Such agreement is unlikely among an ordinary population composed of people who have vested interests to protect. Furthermore, if the population were defined as those currently of mature age, the preferences of the young and unborn might be systematically ignored or devalued. This concern is obvious to economists and policy-makers with an intertemporal perspective.

But imagine that individuals could withdraw behind a veil of ignorance in which they each knew, in Rawls's felicitous phrase, everything in general but nothing in particular. That is, they know everything about how the world works and its fundamental limitations, but they do not know their own positions in the world. Not knowing what position each will hold after the constitution is settled, each is more likely to consider the welfare of all strata of society when voting on the constitution. The constitution, itself assuredly just, would govern all public decisions thereafter.

The notion of the veil of ignorance constitutional process is Rawls's major contribution. But he could not resist speculation as to the kind of constitution a population may agree upon. If, for example, all citizens were extremely risk averse, then all would be most concerned with minimizing the misery of the worst-off persons in society (for fear that once the veil of ignorance were lifted, they would find themselves members of that group). This would provide a motivation for an egalitarian constitution. But an inequality of rewards is necessary to encourage saving, investment, risk-taking, the development of superior talents, and hard work. So there is likely to be some degree of inequality that would raise the total social product so much that even the poorest person would be better off than under a strictly egalitarian rule. The extremely risk-averse population would choose a constitution permitting just enough inequality to maximize the well-being of the worst-off citizen. This distributional rule has become known as "Rawls's maximin principle." Nevertheless Rawls developed it as an example of how a population might choose, not an ethical statement as to what should be chosen.

Buchanan's constitutional/contractarian process

James M. Buchanan had long supported Pareto-safety as a social decision rule, but he eventually came to appreciate that Pareto-safety is just only if the status quo it protects is just.[8] He adopted the Rawlsian veil of ignorance process as a way out of this dilemma. If the status quo were itself chosen in a Rawlsian manner, there could be no objection to subsequent adherence to a Pareto-safety rule. Thus Buchanan proposed a two-stage decision process. In the initial constitutional stage, a population would establish a just starting point under veil of ignorance procedures. In the second stage (lasting for all time thereafter), the Pareto-safety rule would reject any change that did not enjoy the support of all involved parties.

The search for just, fair, and equitable decision processes is an interesting departure. In some ways it represents a return toward the individualism of an earlier time and a step away from the maximum social well-being and maximum value of social product approaches with their connotations of the expert planners identifying what is best for society and continually adjusting things in that direction. For this reason, perhaps, we find the constitutional processes approach appealing. For practical reasons (for example, the real-world impracticability of the veil of ignorance process), this approach is unlikely to generate applicable policy criteria. It could, however, change the way we think about "the criterion problem" and the normative bases of public decisions more generally.

What can the economist do?

In this chapter, necessary and sufficient conditions have been defined for maximum social well-being. Nevertheless, this chapter must have been disillusioning to the neophyte economist who had hoped to use economic analyses to solve all the world's problems.

The social welfare function, which is essential to the derivation of the conditions for maximum social well-being, is unknown; and even more damaging, impressive arguments have been made that a social welfare function satisfying a number of axioms of logic and reasonable conditions for democratic choice processes cannot exist. So economists cannot define the conditions that would generate the best of all possible worlds, except in an entirely abstract formulation. This ought not to be surprising, nor ought it to be considered evidence of intellectual weakness on the part of economists. Several millennia of intense intellectual activity by theologians and philosophers have failed to generate societal consent on the same basic question: How shall society determine what is good and what is evil? It is surely unfair to expect economics (which made its debut as a branch of moral philosophy) to answer definitively these questions in its brief, 200-year, history. In addition, any attempt by economists to define what is good or bad for all of society would be met with considerable objections from a number of ethical perspectives.

In the absence of a social welfare function, economists have considered a number of other criteria by which policy proposals may be judged as good or bad. All these criteria identify economic efficiency as one necessary condition for an optimum. However, some do and some do not require a movement toward efficiency in order for a proposed policy to be considered an improvement. Each of the proposed policy criteria encounters serious ethical questions, and each makes a different judgment about the relative priority of the individual vis-à-vis "the public." Ironically, efficiency as a criterion provides no protection at all for the individual, but the protection of the individual is dominant under Pareto-safety (ironically, we say, because it is fairly common in casual discussion to treat these two criteria as synonymous). The remaining criteria define the societal goal differently and place different limits on acceptable economic injury to individuals.

Those that accept economic injury, subject only to the restriction that aggregate social well-being or the value of social product must be increased, are criticized by some because of the economic injury they permit. Other criteria, such as constant proportional shares which permits no real or relative economic injury, and Pareto-safety which permits no real economic injury, are criticized by others with equal sincerity on the grounds that in any economy with a long and dynamic history, past patterns of economic injury would be suddenly embedded, reinforced, and carried forward into the future.

In this chapter, we have learned something about the economic and ethical implications of various criteria for economic policy, but we have not solved the criterion problem. The argument that economists are not equipped by their professional discipline to solve this problem and that therefore it should be left to the "decision-maker" is not helpful, as it fails to face up to the question of the legitimacy of the decision-maker's power. Similarly, the argument that the solution of the criterion problem should be left to the political process is not helpful, as there is no assurance that the political process itself is perfect.

Harking back to Chapter 4, we offer the following heuristic conclusions:

1. The economist is equipped to help establish the basic parameters of any economic issue and to perform analyses to determine the relationships among the variables therein.
2. Given that political leadership may choose to identify some of these variables as "targets" and some as "instruments," the economist is equipped to develop tools and data to implement politically determined objectives.
3. Items 1 and 2 are certainly useful things to do, but they do not exhaust the list of tasks the economist may usefully perform. Clarification of ethical, normative, and goal-related issues is a demanding intellectual activity and one of great value to humanity. It is absurd to argue that intellectual activity should be confined to the realm of fact-like statements. Attempts to distinguish between science and other intellectual pursuits by saying that science deals only with facts have failed. "Final solutions" to value-related questions will not likely be forthcoming, but their clarification is essential to a civilized society.
4. Although we are not enamored of the role of economists as advocates, we see little harm (and perhaps some good) to society from economists advocating criteria for policy decisions. The harm is minimized because the critical process is sufficiently well developed to prevent a misguided or megalomaniacal economist from misleading the public for too long. The possibility of good arises because coherent and effective advocacy may well help clarify goals.
5. The scientific status of "economic efficiency" is simply not strong enough to support the fairly widespread notion that economists should confine their policy pronouncements to matters of efficiency. The normative content of the efficiency concept should be obvious to all who have read this far. Moreover, the non-uniqueness of efficiency makes it impossible in practice to promote efficiency without "taking sides." The applied economist identifying (or advocating) an efficiency-improving policy initiative is drawing attention to (or promoting) one among a myriad of such possibilities. They all differ not so much in their efficiency properties as in their allocative and distributional consequences. To focus on a particular efficiency-improving proposal is thus to spotlight a particular allocative and distributional prospect.

Questions for discussion

1. "Economists can identify inefficiency and point out the way to make the situation efficient. Beyond that their professional expertise is exhausted." Evaluate this statement.
2. "The pursuit of maximum value of social product, without reference to Pareto-safety, would leave citizens at the mercy of their government." Discuss.
3. "There is no public interest, but there is a 'public interest' interest." Explain and evaluate this statement.
4. How do constitutional processes resolve some of the problems inherent in various proposed criteria for economic policy? What are their limitations?
5. Global climate change policies are controversial for many reasons including economic efficiency and equity (e.g., economic injury concerns). What criteria would you recommend for evaluating whether a particular global climate change policy is "good" for society? Why?

Notes

1. See Abram Bergson (1938), "A Reformulation of Certain Aspects of Welfare Economics," *Quarterly Journal of Economics* **52**: 311–34; Paul A. Samuelson (1948), *Foundations of Economic Analysis*, Cambridge, MA: Harvard University Press.
2. See Kenneth J. Arrow (1951), *Social Choice and Individual Values*, New York: Wiley.
3. See Paul A. Samuelson (1967), "Arrow's Mathematical Politics," in *Human Values and Economic Policy*, ed. Sidney Hook, New York: New York University Press, Pt I, C.
4. Duncan Black (1948), "On the Rationale of Group Decision Making," *Journal of Political Economics* **56** (February): 23–34; Duncan Black (1958), *The Theory of Committees and Elections*, Cambridge: Cambridge University Press; James M. Buchanan and Gordon Tullock (1962), *The Calculus of Consent*, Ann Arbor: University of Michigan Press; James S. Coleman (1966), "The Possibility of a Social Welfare Function," *American Economic Review* **56** (December): 1105–22; James S. Coleman (1970), "Political Money," *American Political Science Review* **64** (December): 1074–87; Gordon Tullock (1959), "Problems of Majority Voting," *Journal of Political Economics* **67** (December): 571–9; Gordon Tullock (1967), "The General Irrelevance of the General Impossibility Theorem," *Quarterly Journal of Economics* **81** (May): 256–70; Gordon Tullock (1970), "A Simple Algebraic Logrolling Model," *American Economic Review* **60** (June): 419–26; Gordon Tullock and Colin D. Campbell (1970), "Computer Simulation of a Small Voting System," *Economic Journal* **80** (March): 97–104.
5. See, for example, Jerry S. Kelly (1978), *Arrow Impossibility Theorems*, New York: Academic Press.
6. John R. Hicks (1939), "The Foundations of Welfare Economics," *Economic Journal* **49**: 696–712; Nicholas Kaldor (1939), "Welfare Propositions in Economics," *Economic Journal* **49**: 549–52.
7. See John Rawls (1971), *A Theory of Justice*, Cambridge, MA: Harvard University Press.
8. See James M. Buchanan (1977), *Freedom in Constitutional Contract*, College Station, TX: Texas A&M University Press.

Suggested reading: classic and contemporary

Arrow, K.J. (1967), "Public and Private Values," in *Human Values and Economic Policy*, ed. S. Hook, Pt I, New York: New York University Press.
Arrow, K., W. Cline, K.-G. Maler, M. Munasinghe, R. Squitieri, and J. Stiglitz (1996), "Intertemporal Equity, Discounting, and Economic Efficiency," in *Economic and Social Dimensions of Climate Change*, ed. J. Bruce, L. Hoesung, and E. Haites, Cambridge: Cambridge University Press.
Baumol, W.J. (1965), *Welfare Economics and the Theory of the State*, 2nd edn, Cambridge, MA: Harvard University Press.
Boadway, R. (1974), "The Welfare Foundations of Cost–Benefit Analysis," *Economic Journal* **84** (December): 926–39.
Chipman, J.S. and J.C. Moore (1978, "The New Welfare Economics: 1939–1974," *International Economic Review* **19** (3): 547–84.
Dolan, P. (1998), "The Measurement of Individual Utility and Social Welfare," *Journal of Health Economics* **17** (1): 39–52.
Johansson, P.-O. (1991), *An Introduction to Modern Welfare Economics*, Cambridge: Cambridge University Press.
Just, R.E., D.L. Hueth, and A. Schmitz (2004), "Pareto Optimality and the Pareto Condition," in *The Welfare Economics of Public Policy: A Practical Approach to Project and Policy Evaluation*, ed. R.E. Just, D.L. Hueth, and A. Schmitz, Cheltenham, UK and Northampton, MA, USA: Edward Elgar.

Mitchell, W.C. (1989), "The Calculus of Consent: Enduring Contributions to Public Choice and Political Science," *Public Choice* **60** (3): 201–10.
Mueller, D.C. (1976), "Survey on Public Choice," *Journal of Economic Literature* **14** (June): 395–433.
Suzumura, K. (1999), "Paretian Welfare Judgements and Bergsonian Social Choice," *Economic Journal* **109** (April): 204–21.

9 Rules of the game: how do they influence efficiency and equity and how can we get them right?

We have defined the necessary and sufficient conditions for Pareto-efficiency. The question that now faces us is: What kinds of economic organization are conducive to the achievement of efficiency?

Conceptually, it is possible for a directed economy in a totalitarian state to achieve Pareto-efficiency. To do so, the director of the economy would need to set all of the price ratios equal to the relevant rates of substitution and transformation. That is, the director would establish an efficient set of incentives for production and an efficient set of price ratios (or some equally effective indicators of the terms of trade) to ration goods among consumers and to encourage efficient commodity substitution in the face of changes in relative scarcity. To establish these efficient signals, or "shadow prices," the economic director would need to gather and accurately process a massive amount of economic information. The enormity of the information-gathering and computation tasks has led most economists to suspect that the achievement of Pareto-efficiency in a directed economy, although conceptually possible, is most unlikely to happen. In practice these difficulties, along with a penchant for permitting political goals and considerations to interfere with economic planning, have led to obvious inefficiencies and economic dislocations in most directed economies.

On the other hand, it is not merely conceivable that a free-enterprise competitive economy may achieve Pareto-efficiency. The price system provides a built-in mechanism that tends to move the economy in the direction of efficiency. Using a highly abstract theoretical model in a static analysis, it has been shown that an ideal competitive economy tends to reach equilibrium and that the competitive equilibrium is Pareto-efficient.[1] But an efficient decentralized economy requires the support of an institutional structure to enforce contracts and secure expectations.

Ideally, transactions are secured by complete contracts; contracts that fully specify the rights and duties of the parties for every possible future state of the world. However, because it would be prohibitively expensive to write enforceable complete contracts, contracts in the real world are usually incomplete. When a dispute arises and the case falls into a gap in the contract, the parties must engage in bargaining or the courts must step in and fill in the gap. It is easy to imagine the chaos that would ensue if each contract was incomplete and one-of-a-kind, and the courts had to resolve all disputes without much guidance in the way of laws and precedent.

The remainder of this chapter will explore the institutional conditions under which a competitive economy may achieve Pareto-efficiency and the implications of different institutional structures for both efficiency and the distribution of economic well-being.

Use without rules: a parable
Imagine, for a moment, a society in which it was illegal to interfere with, or in any way impede the activities of, any person attempting to take any automobile for his or her own

use. This would certainly be a radical change in the laws with which we are familiar. Not only would automobile theft be legal, but the term itself would have no meaning. How would such a law affect the production, use, and exchange of automobiles?

Anyone in need of transportation would simply take the nearest convenient automobile, drive it to his or her destination, and abandon it there. When the time came to return, the person would simply take the same automobile, or another, and drive it home or to wherever else he or she wanted to go. For a brief period after a law like this had been established, things would probably work fairly well. Because most people who go somewhere eventually return, we would expect that automobiles, in general, would tend to be located where they are needed. A person in need of transportation would, therefore, most likely find an abandoned automobile nearby.

But as time passed, one would expect to see some major changes in the patterns of production, maintenance, and use of automobiles. People would continue to purchase gasoline for automobiles, but they would soon learn to put only enough fuel for the planned trip in the fuel tank. Automobiles with some fuel remaining in the tank would be the first to be taken by others in need of transportation. One could predict a sudden increase in the demand for portable gasoline containers, as anyone planning a trip away would be wise to bring sufficient gasoline to make it back (in a different automobile) at least as far as the first gas station.

Quite soon, we would begin to notice deterioration in the quality of the society's automobile stock. No one would pay to have major maintenance or repairs performed on an automobile he or she had recently picked up and expected to abandon soon. Given this decline in the quality of the automobile stock, prudent persons would carry toolkits along with their portable fuel containers, so that if the need arose, they could perform minor repairs en route.

The automobile stock would age quite rapidly, as no one would have any incentive to purchase a new automobile. Automobile manufacturers would go out of business, suffering major capital losses and causing a sudden increase in the supply of workers on the labor market. These outcomes could be avoided only if the government decided, on the grounds that an "automobile emergency" existed, to use tax revenues to purchase new automobiles that would be strategically placed around population centers. But for the purposes of this little parable, assume that government chose to forgo that alternative. In addition to the effects on the market in new automobiles, one would also expect used-car dealers, automobile auctions, and manufacturers of all but the least expensive replacement parts to go out of business.

In a relatively brief period of time following the introduction of laws that abolished the concept of automobile theft, the automobile markets with which we are familiar would completely disappear, along with the industries that manufacture, exchange, and service automobiles. There seems no question that the society would be worse off, as automobile transportation (which we must assume to be strongly desired, as it is purchased in large quantities when effective and unrestricted markets exist) would soon be effectively removed from individual opportunity sets.

Many configurations of rules are conceivable
Clearly, use without rules leads to disaster. But many configurations of rules are conceivable, and many of the possible configurations would improve things relative to a free-

for-all. Rules that specify and enforce individual ownership and use of automobiles are of course possible, but the options do not end there. Rules have long allowed employers to maintain fleets for use by their employees, finance companies to lend money to individuals for purchasing autos, leasing companies to enter into long-term contracts with individuals who wish to use but not own the vehicles, and rental car companies to maintain fleets for short-term rentals. More recently, car-sharing firms (e.g. Zipcars) have emerged, offering very short-term pick-up here, drop-off there rentals from lots of street-side locations in some major US cities and college campuses. Paris and other European cities have developed similar arrangements for very short-term bicycle rentals. Genuine common property arrangements are relatively rare for automobiles, but employer-owned car pools and rental car operations have some common property elements in that operators are motivated to provide good care for the vehicles by a sense of shared obligation as well as fear of penalty for egregious breaches.

All of the arrangements mentioned above are effective to a considerable degree. It might be claimed that only individual ownership is strictly efficient, but that efficiency claim is true only in a quite limited sense. With individual ownership of automobiles, we still have closely related inefficiencies in the provision of roads and highways, the market for fuels, the control of automobile emissions, and the provision of safety, among others. That is, while individual ownership may be secured by property rights the contract between owners, drivers, passengers, fellow road-users, and society at large remains incomplete in many important aspects.

In pursuit of perfection

Complete contracts
Ideally, all transactions are secured by contracts that are complete – contracts that fully specify the rights and duties of the parties for every possible future state of the world – and fully enforced. An economy characterized by complete contracts would achieve Pareto-efficiency. But it is prohibitively expensive to write complete contracts, so contracts in the real world are usually incomplete. Government must stand ready to resolve disputes arising from incomplete contracts, and it usually relies on law and precedent for guidance and direction. In an idealized competitive economy – no participant has market power, all have full information, and trade is consummated and enforced frictionessly – an ideal system of property rights would assure Pareto-efficiency by providing an efficient default to fill the gaps in incomplete contracts.

Property rights: basic concepts
A competitive economy relies on prices as signals to direct independent producers and consumers to behave individually in such a way that the aggregate outcome of their independent endeavors is efficient. To achieve this result, the competitive economy relies on free and unrestrained trade. The necessary conditions for Pareto-efficiency are, in fact, marginal conditions for efficient trade. Pareto-efficiency is achieved when all potential gains from trade in all sectors of a (perfect) economy are exhausted. The institutional conditions that encourage the achievement of efficiency in competitive economies are, thus, institutional conditions that facilitate trade. Key among those institutions are property rights: property rights specify both the proper relationships

among people with respect to the use of things and the penalties for violating those proper relationships.

Ownership   One rather simple legal change, the abolition of the concept of automobile theft, would be sufficient to reduce automobile markets to a free-for-all in a relatively brief time. This legal change is simple, yet quite radical. It would effectively abolish the concept of ownership.

Ownership is a legal device that assigns the right to use. In a market economy based on the concept of private property, payment results in ownership. Ownership carries with it the right to use, subject to various possible restrictions. The least restrictive kind of ownership is exclusive ownership, which carries with it the right to use and to determine who, if anyone else, may use and under what conditions. Exclusive ownership is the legal antonym of *res nullius*, a Latin term meaning literally "nobody's property." Our imaginary law that would abolish the concept of automobile theft would effectively reduce ownership rights in automobiles to the *res nullius* situation.

Ownership is an essential precondition for trade. Who in their right mind would pay for something without assurance that they could use it? Or conversely, who in their right mind would pay to use something when they could not be stopped from using it free of charge?

Specification of rights   Individuals independently exercising their various ownership rights may often come into conflict. My pig farm may reduce the satisfaction you enjoy from your home in an expensive new subdivision. Your neighbor's failure to maintain his property in good condition may also reduce the satisfaction you derive from your home. Some more distant individual or entity may reduce the utility of everyone in the neighborhood by expelling pollutants through a smokestack into the atmosphere.

To resolve these conflicts, it is not sufficient merely to declare that exclusive ownership exists. It is also necessary to specify the rights that accompany ownership. When different owners conflict, whose rights predominate? When owners and non-owners conflict, what rights are assigned to the property owner simply because he or she owns property and what rights are assigned to the non-owner simply because he or she is an individual human being? Clearly, restrictions must accompany ownership rights. If anyone could use anything they owned in any way they pleased, utter chaos would ensue.

In order that exclusive property rights may achieve their fullest effectiveness, thus permitting the resolution of conflicts among owners and between owners and non-owners by trade, property rights must be completely specified. The rights that accompany ownership must be specified, along with the restrictions applying to owners and the corresponding rights of non-owners.

Transferability   If trade is to be effective in allocating resources and resolving conflicts, rights must be transferable. An individual who desires to acquire a specific right must be permitted to make an offer to some other individual who already owns that right. An individual who is willing to relinquish an owned right, in exchange for some consideration of greater value, must have the right to sell. In that way, rights can gravitate to their highest-valued uses. Restrictions on the transfer of rights (as opposed to restrictions on use, necessary for the complete specification of rights) are sources of inefficiency. Such restrictions erect barriers to the achievement of equality between price ratios and the relevant rates of substitution and transformation.

Because the complete specification of rights entails the specification of a variety of different kinds of rights associated with a particular thing (that is, a particular piece of property), complete transferability of rights requires that the different types of rights associated with ownership of a particular thing should be transferable independently of one another. For example, the cause of efficiency is served when the government-created right to market, say, tobacco may be transferred independently of the ownership rights pertaining to land. Furthermore, efficiency is served when the rights pertaining to landownership may be subdivided in many ways, and the subdivided rights transferred. This process permits leasing, renting, sharecropping, easements, and rights of way, all of which work to make land utilization more efficient than it would be if ownership rights were undivided. For example, it may be more efficient for a utility company to purchase an easement to run a transmission line across someone's farm, rather than purchasing the whole farm in fee-simple title or abandoning the plan.

To the uninitiated, the idea of trade in rights may sound a little strange. One tends to think of trade as the physical transfer of things; that is, property objects. Yet the fundamental characteristic of trade is the transfer of rights rather than the physical transfer and removal of things. When one "buys" land, one does not pick up that piece of land and carry it home. Rather, one acquires certain specified rights to use that land. Even in the case of a small item purchased from a department store, the fundamental characteristic of trade is not physical removal but the transfer of the right to remove and use. Removal alone can be accomplished by shoplifting, but shoplifting is considered not a transfer of ownership rights but a violation of them.

Enforcement   Incentives most certainly exist for violating the rights pertaining to the ownership and transfer of property. To steal is cheaper than to buy, if the thief is assured that apprehension and penalty are unlikely. Pollution is an inexpensive method of waste disposal, if the polluter is assured that the rights of others (owners and non-owners) will not be enforced.

To be effective, a system of rights must be enforceable and effectively enforced. An unenforced right is effectively no right at all. Returning momentarily to the automobile example, the unsatisfactory results in the automobile market are attributed to the abandonment of exclusive ownership rights in automobiles and their replacement with a free-for-all. However, exactly the same results would occur if, instead, exclusive ownership rights to automobiles remained on the books but enforcement broke down entirely.

Effective enforcement is the discovery of violations, the apprehension of violators, and the imposition of appropriate penalties. The complete specification of rights should include the specification of penalties for their violation. Then perfect enforcement guarantees that those penalties will be imposed in the event of a violation. To be effective, the specified penalties should be sufficiently large that they exceed the benefits anyone could hope to obtain from violating them. If enforcement is imperfect, as it must always be in the real world, the expected value of penalties (that is, the amount of the penalty multiplied by the probability that it will actually be imposed) must exceed any possible gains a violator could hope to obtain.

Property rights and economic efficiency

In an economy that is otherwise conducive to efficiency (that is, it does not include monopolies, non-rivalry in consumption, or continually declining cost curves), non-attenuated property rights ensure Pareto-efficiency.[2] A set of non-attenuated property rights is:

1. Completely specified, so that it can serve as a perfect system of information about the rights that accompany ownership, the restrictions on those rights, and the penalties for their violation.
2. Exclusive, so that all rewards and penalties resulting from an action accrue directly to the individual empowered to take action (that is, the owner).
3. Transferable, so that rights may gravitate to their highest-value use.
4. Enforceable and completely enforced. An unenforced right is no right at all.

The alert reader will notice something a little strange about this definition of non-attenuated rights. Whereas the efficiency conditions for economic activity require that any production or consumption activity be pursued until its marginal benefits are equal to its marginal costs, the definition of non-attenuated rights suggests that the specification, transfer, and enforcement of rights should be carried to the point of perfection. However, specification, transfer, and enforcement are all costly activities, and the pursuit of perfection in these activities may result in prohibitive costs. These costs have been called transaction costs.

These costs are not wasted money but are expended in exchange for valuable transactions services. In a modern economy, the transactions industry is quite massive. It includes sales personnel and their support staffs back at the front or head office, agents of all kinds, attorneys, the police and judicial systems, and the large and growing private sector enforcement system, which includes everyone from the mundane nightwatchman to the glamorous "private eye." If one thinks about it, one will conclude that almost everyone who wears business dress to work and a good many others are employed in the transactions industry. It is clearly no minor industry, and transactions cost are clearly no trivial expense.

Accordingly, the definition of non-attenuated property rights provided above is clearly an ideal and is correct only if transactions services are costless. In a more realistic economic model, efficiency can be approached if, in addition to all the other necessary and sufficient conditions, the investment in specification, transfer, and enforcement of property rights proceeds to the point at which the marginal conditions for efficiency are satisfied.

Property rights and the non-uniqueness of Pareto-efficiency

Recall the grand utility frontier which is the locus of all attainable Pareto-efficient solutions to the general economic problem (Chapter 6). Each Pareto-efficient solution is associated with a different distribution of utility or, loosely, income. Conversely, the Pareto-efficient solution is unique only if the distribution of income is first specified. In the simple two-dimensional formulations used in Chapters 6 and 8, income was used as a surrogate for the multifaceted concept of economic well-being. One significant facet of economic well-being is the rights the individual enjoys: both the rights associated with property objects and other kinds of rights.

To say that for efficiency, property rights must be non-attenuated does not in itself tell us everything we need to know about property rights. One can conceive of many different sets of rights with respect to a particular kind of property object, all of which are exclusive, transferable, and enforced, but each of which is specified differently from the others. The polluter may have unrestricted access to the environment for use in waste disposal, or the receptor may have the right to insist that polluting emissions be restricted to zero. Alternatively, it is possible to consider intermediate specifications: for example, the polluter may release x tons of effluent annually, whereas the receptor is entitled to insist that no more than x tons be released.

It is conceivable that non-attenuated rights with either extreme specification, or any one of the multitude of possible intermediate specifications, could be established. Any of these possible specifications of non-attenuated rights would lead to efficiency, but the efficient solution would be different for each different specification of rights. The idea that efficiency is non-unique and that a unique efficient solution can be defined only by prior specification of the distribution of income (see Chapters 6 and 8) may now be extended. Efficiency is non-unique, and a unique Pareto-efficient solution may be identified only by prior specification of the distribution of income, wealth, and legal rights, which include property rights.

In the 1980s and 1990s a "property rights movement" arose and gained some traction in politics and the courts. Its agenda had little to do with efficiency, which may be advanced by strengthening contracts and clarifying property rights, but everything to do with distribution. It focused on using legislation and especially the courts to transfer rights and thus wealth to owners of real property.

Conservative reinforcement   Each different specification of non-attenuated property rights gives rise to a different Pareto-efficient solution. Each different Pareto-efficient solution involves different resource allocation, commodity distribution, and price ratios (Chapter 6). So prices themselves are functions of property rights. More specifically, the prices that are efficient under one specific non-attenuated specification of property rights would be inefficient under a different specification of property rights.

The interrelationship between property rights and prices has an important implication for the empirical economic analysis of the impacts of alternative specifications of rights. If the output generated under (non-attenuated) property-right specification A were valued according to its own efficient prices, it would be found to be an efficient bundle of output. Similarly, if the output generated under property-right specification B were evaluated according to its own efficient prices, it would be found to be efficient. However, if the output generated under property-right specification A were valued according to the prices that would be efficient under specification B, and vice versa, both bundles of output would be found to be inefficient. The same general idea remains true when, as is usually the case, neither property-right specification A nor B is perfectly non-attenuated. To value the output generated under specification A using prices relevant to specification B, and vice versa, would introduce a downward bias into the resulting estimates of the value of social product.

Unfortunately, this problem arises more often than not in empirical research that attempts to predict the economic outcome of potential changes in the specification of property rights. Both the output under the existing specification of rights and the output under the proposed specification are valued using existing, observed prices. Yet those prices themselves were generated under the existing structure of property rights. This analytical practice necessarily introduces a bias into the analysis, and the bias is necessarily in favor of the existing specification of property rights. This bias has been called conservative reinforcement, because it tends to validate the existing situation.[3] The proposed specification of rights is clearly handicapped by any evaluation procedure that values the output generated under both the existing and the proposed structure of rights according to prices pertinent to the existing structure. Whenever customary techniques of empirical economic analysis are used to predict the economic impacts of institutional change, the danger exists that conservative reinforcement may be introduced into the evaluation process.

Contracts, rules, rights, and institutions

Incomplete contracts and property rights
The ideal set of rules involves complete contracts defaulting, in the event of some incompleteness in contracts, to a system of non-attenuated property rights. In the real world, because specification, transfer and enforcement are costly and hence imperfect, incompleteness is pervasive. So, due to transactions cost, contracts are incomplete and are backed up imperfectly by property rights that are attenuated. Incomplete contracts remain, and are likely to induce problems including asymmetric information, adverse selection, and moral hazard. Whereas the property rights literature of the 1960s and 1970s was rather unified and prone to sweeping generalizations, today's literature on the same general subject matter is much more diverse and goes by a variety of names including contract theory, mechanism design, asymmetric information theory, and the new property rights approach. Problems are specified and diagnosed in more precise detail, and solutions can be quite specific rather than broad and sweeping.

Problems of pervasive incompleteness
In the real world, complete contracts and non-attenuated property rights serve as unattainable ideals. Because specification, contracting, and enforcement are expensive, contracts remain incomplete and are backed up imperfectly by property rights that are attenuated.[4] Some common problems and issues related to pervasive incompleteness in contracts and property rights are discussed below.

Asymmetric information   At least one party to a transaction has relevant information unavailable to the other(s). Consequences of asymmetric information may include adverse selection and moral hazard. Some asymmetric information models are also useful in situations where at least one party can enforce, or effectively penalize breaches of, certain parts of an agreement whereas the other(s) cannot.

Adverse selection   The ignorant party lacks information while negotiating an agreed understanding of or contract to the transaction. When an insurance company cannot effectively discriminate against people who pose a high risk of insured losses (it lacks the necessary information, or it is constrained from discriminating), insured pools are likely to over-represent high-risk people. This drives up the insurance premium, encouraging low-risk people to flock to any provider who finds a way to cherry-pick the applicants.

Low-quality vehicles ("lemons") are likely to be over-represented in the used car pool because buyers, lacking information that would help them discriminate, are inclined to assume that any used car is probably of low quality. Owners, dissatisfied with the price offered, are likely to hold onto high-quality used vehicles which, of course, makes the skeptical buyers' expectations self-fulfilling.

Moral hazard   The ignorant party lacks information about performance of the agreed-upon transaction or lacks the ability to penalize underperformance. In such circumstances, underperformance is likely to become the norm. Bailouts of lenders who find themselves holding too many non-performing loans may encourage others to engage in risky lending behavior. The concept that some lenders are too big to be allowed to fail makes sense in one way, because their failure would undermine confidence in financial markets. Yet it sets up the expectation of bailouts, which systematically increases the prevalence of high-reward but risky loans.

Moral hazard may apply to agricultural conservation programs if farm-level implementation of conservation practices, or better yet conservation performance, is hard for the conservation agencies to monitor. Farmers stinting on conservation effort would undermine the performance of the programs and the willingness of the public to fund them.

Crop insurance pays farmers in years when the insured yield is not attained. Such programs must be carefully designed to avoid adverse selection (the insured pool may over-represent farmers who ordinarily get relatively low yields) and moral hazard (once insurance has been obtained, farmers may be tempted to stint on effort and practices favorable for high yields).

Mechanism design   Principal–agent theory and mechanism design offer insights about how to make the best of these situations. The goal is to design incentive-compatible mechanisms, so that agents have incentives to align their performance with the principal's objectives. A process is said to be incentive compatible if all of the participants fare best when they truthfully reveal any private information sought by the mechanism. A simple incentive-compatible mechanism is a sealed-bid second-price auction, where the highest bidder gets the item but pays only the price offered by the second-highest bidder – that way, all bidders have an incentive to reveal their true willingness to pay. Some incentive-compatible mechanisms are much more complicated.

While pervasive incompleteness appears to be problematic in a number of ways, all may not be lost. Two very different kinds of empirical observation, painstaking social anthropology[5] and the laboratory experiments of contracts researchers,[6] point toward similar conclusions: common property arrangements often substitute conventions for provisions that would (in an ideal world) complete the contract, and may be surprisingly effective and resilient in a variety of social and political environments. Thus, the employment of effective common property arrangements implies that incompleteness of contracts is not necessarily a slippery slope to free-for-all disaster. Nevertheless, details matter, and there may be ways short of completing the contract to improve system performance.

Institutions
The discussion of property rights to this point has emphasized efficiency aspects. We have seen that any specification of property rights, as long as rights are non-attenuated,

may lead to the attainment of an efficient solution. Yet different specifications of rights will lead to efficient solutions that differ, perhaps quite radically, in the resultant distribution of economic well-being.

This kind of discussion is valid and serves a useful purpose in the discussion of economic policy. On the one hand, it suggests that if Pareto-efficiency alone is all that is desired, the role of government in economic affairs may be largely confined to the specification of a non-attenuated set of property rights. On the other hand, it suggests that a government which seeks the attainment of economic efficiency and certain specific goals with respect to the distribution of economic well-being may seek to specify non-attenuated property rights while manipulating the specification of those rights in order to achieve its distributional goals. Nevertheless, this kind of discussion in itself can be quite misleading, as it fails to recognize the role of property rights within the total institutional structure, and the role of institutions, broadly conceived, in a dynamic society.

Institutions are the "going concerns" (to use a phrase made famous by the late John R. Commons[7]) that order the relationships among individuals in society. Institutions include laws, constitutions (which have been called "laws about making laws"), traditions, generally accepted moral and ethical precepts, and "customary and accepted ways of doing things." The market, as idealized by economic theorists or as implemented in the practice of commerce, is itself an institution. Institutions of one kind or another direct, control, restrain, or at least influence almost every activity and interpersonal relationship in a complex modern society. Time and time again, anthropologists have marveled at the complexity of the elaborate institutional structures that exist in technologically unsophisticated societies. The alternative to a complex institutional structure, it seems, is anarchy.

Institutions restrict individual freedom by limiting the harm an individual can impose on others. By the same token, institutions enhance the freedom of individuals by ensuring them of protection from the harm that others may do them. Institutions define the "rules of the game" and, by so doing, help define the structure of incentives facing individuals. Institutions also work to ensure their own continuity, through the conscious and unconscious shaping of the thought patterns and ethical systems of each new generation.

In the long run, social change is inevitable. Patterns of scarcity change; technological progress changes the opportunities confronting individual and societies; and demands change as populations grow or decline and individual tastes and preferences are modified. In this broad process of change, institutions play a crucial but delicate role. They must accommodate change, but they must restrict the rate of change and preclude changes thought to be thoroughly undesirable. Orderly social and economic interaction requires an environment of considerable stability. Life and comfort are precarious when all things are negotiable. Thus the institutional structure must resist change, placing barriers in the way of all change so that only those proposals for change that have substantial support can be implemented. On the other hand, institutional structures that are entirely rigid are eventually doomed. When the pressures for change become massive, the alternative to peaceful change is bloody revolution.

The institutional structure is inextricably intertwined with the moral and ethical system of society. Institutions that are consistent with the moral and ethical values of the society in which they exist will be relatively easy to enforce: compliance will be substantially voluntary. On the other hand, institutions that are at variance with the society's value system will experience little voluntary compliance and may be enforced only with substantial effort. Even with regard to the relationship between institutions and value systems, we encounter the inevitable tension between adaptability and stability. Institutions shape, and are shaped by, moral and ethical value systems.

Property rights are just one facet of a total institutional framework. This places significant restrictions on the manipulation of property rights for social and economic policy purposes. Although any specification of non-attenuated property rights may lead to efficiency, many possible specifications will be at variance with the moral and ethical value systems of society. These specifications are simply not realistic policy options. Furthermore all societies have chosen, for their own unfathomable reasons, to classify some things as simply inappropriate to exclusive ownership and unrestricted trade. Thus, the establishment of a completely non-attenuated set of property rights, essential to the achievement of Pareto-efficiency, is itself at variance with the moral and ethical value system of any society.

For this reason, the wise and pragmatic resource and environmental economist will recognize the limits to what can be attained through manipulation of property rights and the specification of non-attenuated property rights. There will be some problems for which workable, if not Pareto-efficient, solutions may best be achieved with some other kind of institutional structure. It is helpful to realize that non-attenuated property rights and *res nullius* are not the only two possible structures of rights. Instead, they represent the extremes on a continuum of possible structures. In many societies, and for many different problems, some variation of *res communis* (property held in common), often with elaborate rules relating individual contributions to individual rewards, provides a workable, if not Pareto-efficient, institutional framework that has the distinct advantage of being compatible with the social value system.[8]

Questions for discussion

1. "Everybody's property is nobody's property." Evaluate this statement.
2. "The air pollution problem could be solved by simply specifying exclusive rights to air." Do you agree?
3. As this book is being completed in 2010, no nation, corporation or person has established private property rights to the natural resources of the moon orbiting planet Earth. Do you expect this situation to change in the future? Why or why not?
4. "To say that for efficiency, property rights must be non-attenuated does not in itself tell us everything we need to know about property rights." Explain and expand on this statement.
5. Suppose an official person knocks on the door of your apartment or house and said she is collecting information on the value to you of cleaning up your tap water which recently has shown a cloudy color because of sediment (dirt) in the water pipes. Specifically, her question to you is, "What is the most your water bill could increase per month in order for the sediments problem to be solved and your tap water to run clear?" What incentives do you have for stating an amount that is either higher or lower than your true willingness to pay? What type of mechanism (way of collecting information or asking questions) may help provide incentives for you and others to reveal your true maximum willingness to pay for clean, clear tap water?
6. Give an example of "moral hazard" and discuss what might be done to deal with this problem. Are complete contracts a possible solution? How about common property arrangements?
7. "Institutions must accommodate change while restricting the rate of change." Does this seemingly contradictory statement make sense?

Notes

1. Kenneth J. Arrow (1951), "An Extension of the Basic Theorems of Classical Welfare Economics," in *Proceedings of the Second Berkeley Symposium on Mathematical Statistics and Probability*, ed. Jerzy Neyman, Berkeley and Los Angeles, CA: University of California Press, pp. 507–32.

2. See Steven Cheung (1970), "The Structure of a Contract and the Theory of a Non-Exclusive Resource," *Journal of Law and Economics* **13**: 49–70.
3. See Warren J. Samuels (1972), "Welfare Economics, Power and Property," in *Perspectives of Property*, ed. Gene L. Wanderlich and W.L. Gibson, Jr, University Park, PA: Pennsylvania State University, Pts I–III.
4. For more detail and discussion, see G.A. Akerlof (1970), "The Market for 'Lemons': Quality Uncertainty and the Market Mechanism," *Quarterly Journal of Economics* **84** (3): 488–500; E. Maskin and T. Sjostrom (2002), "Implementation Theory," in *Handbook of Social Choice and Welfare I*, ed. K. Arrow, A. Sen, and K. Suzumura, Amsterdam: Elsevier; J.E. Stiglitz (1987), "Principal and Agent," *The New Palgrave: A Dictionary of Economics* **3**: 966–71.
5. For example, see Elinor Ostrom (1990), *Governing the Commons: The Evolution of Institutions for Collective Action*, Cambridge: Cambridge University Press.
6. See Vernon L. Smith (1994), "Economics in the Laboratory," *Journal of Economic Perspectives* **8** (1): 113–31.
7. John R. Commons (1924), *Legal Foundations of Capitalism*, Madison, WI: University of Wisconsin Press.
8. See Siegfried von Ciriacy-Wantrup and Richard C. Bishop (1975), "Common Property as a Concept in Natural Resources Policy," *Natural Resources Journal* **15**: 713–29.

Suggested reading: classic and contemporary

Akerlof, G.A. (1970), "The Market for 'Lemons': Quality Uncertainty and the Market Mechanism," *Quarterly Journal of Economics* **84** (3): 488–500.

Cheung, S. (1970), "The Structure of a Contract and the Theory of a Non-exclusive Resource," *Journal of Law and Economics* **13**: 49–70.

Ciriacy-Wantrup, S. von and R.C. Bishop (1975), "Common Property as a Concept in Natural Resources Policy," *Natural Resources Journal* **15**: 713–29.

Furubotn, E. and S. Pejovich (1972), "Property Rights and Economic Theory: A Survey of Recent Literature," *Journal of Economic Literature* **10**: 1137–62.

Maskin, E. and T. Sjostrom (2002), "Implementation Theory," in *Handbook of Social Choice and Welfare I*, ed. K. Arrow, A. Sen, and K. Suzumura, Amsterdam: Elsevier.

Smith, V.H. and B.K. Goodwin (1996), "Crop Insurance, Moral Hazard and Agricultural Chemical Use," *American Journal of Agricultural Economics* **78** (2): 428–38.

Stiglitz, J.E. (1987), "Principal and Agent," *The New Palgrave: A Dictionary of Economics* **3**: 966–71.

10 Market failure and inefficiency: what could cause an undesirable market allocation of resources?

The economic arena is one of conflict. Given that resources are scarce, production possibilities are limited by technology, and individuals are both selfish and insatiable, how could it be anything else? Chapters 5–7 develop a view of markets as incredibly effective devices for conflict resolution. If the structure of rights is hospitable to the fullest development of markets (that is, is non-attenuated), markets will establish prices that offer incentives for production, generate personal incomes, ration commodities among consumers, and provide a continuous flow of information about relative scarcity. In this way, markets allocate resources and distribute commodities, without the need for external direction, in a manner that ensures globally efficient outcomes from the independent decisions of self-motivated individuals. The market derives its effectiveness from contracts that approach the ideal of completeness and property rights that approach the ideal of non-attenuation, and performs its functions through the instrumentality of efficient relative prices.

As is well known, not all individuals and societies see markets in such a favorable light. Many are frankly alarmed by the instabilities, myopia, and perceived waste and distributive injustice generated by uncontrolled markets.[1] Some counsel the abandonment of the market mechanism and its replacement with other conflict-resolution institutions, which are typically promoted as "more humane."

This chapter is not addressed to these primarily ethical concerns. Instead, we focus on and accept the fundamental efficacy of markets as devices to direct the allocation of resources. This chapter undertakes a much more limited inquiry: to explore the existence and nature of what has been called "market failure" or, more charitably, "market imperfection." It will be seen that there are circumstances in which the outcomes of free markets are inefficient. These circumstances typically involve incomplete contracts, deficiencies in property rights, and/or peculiarities in the physical nature of the goods involved. These problems are manifested in inefficient prices that send the wrong signals and provide the wrong incentives.

In this chapter, economic analyses are developed that are especially relevant to many natural resource and environmental problems. Analyses of non-rivalry and non-exclusiveness are pertinent to many problems in natural resource allocation: for example, the management of fish and wildlife populations, the maintenance of the scenic beauty of outdoor environments and the diversity of natural environments, the management of public lands, the exploitation of oil and groundwater pools, and the provision of natural resource services and environmental amenities by public sector agencies. In these contexts, the economic analyses of providing services, pricing, and rationing among users help identify possible solutions to the inefficiencies and waste that arise. The analyses of congestible goods and "natural monopoly" are pertinent to the provision of outdoor recreation facilities, roads and bridges, and public utilities (for example, water, telephone service, electricity, and natural gas).

In considering conflicts of the "nuisance" type in which the actions of one party, such as a polluter, cause annoyance to others – for example, users of air and water – the puzzling concept of externality arises. Here we examine externality and consider what is necessary for it to arise and persist. It turns out that those externality problems that are persistent – such as air and water pollution and some kinds of neighborhood disamenities – also involve non-rivalry and/or non-exclusiveness.

The logic of economics is helpful in understanding why imperfections in the markets for these goods, services, and amenities occur and in predicting the consequences of these imperfections. It is helpful also in suggesting possible solutions and in predicting the responses of individuals and firms to those solutions, if implemented. In that way, alternatives can be evaluated with a degree of reliability before implementation. In some cases, there is no entirely satisfactory solution, but even in these cases, economic logic can help us understand why no perfect solution exists and can help us identify the most effective of the various available imperfect solutions.

Non-exclusive goods and resources

There are a number of different goods, services, amenities, and resources that are non-exclusive. Non-exclusiveness undermines property rights and results in inefficiency. Without exclusion, it is impossible to collect a price for use. Under such circumstances, price serves neither to ration the good or resource among users nor to provide revenue for the production of the good or the maintenance and conservation of the resource. The typical allocative results of non-exclusiveness are the underprovision of a good, service, or amenity relative to the efficient level of provision; excessive levels of discommodities and disamenities relative to the efficient level; overexploitation of a resource relative to the efficient level of exploitation; and underinvestment in the management, conservation, and productive capacity of a resource.

The solution to the problems engendered by non-exclusiveness is obvious, especially in a society that values individual initiative. Ideally, exclusive non-attenuated property rights could be established and enforced. Then the entirely self-motivated actions of independent individuals will be sufficient to ensure efficient outcomes. Many societies in many places have specified exclusive property rights with respect to some previously non-exclusive goods and resources. For example, the abuses that result from the non-exclusive use of grazing land were halted in many societies by the establishment of private property in land.

Nevertheless, some goods and some resources remain non-exclusive, even in those societies that place the highest value on private property and individual enterprise. Why? There are two broad classes of reasons. The first major reason is cultural and political. All societies identify some goods, services, amenities, and resources that, it is thought, ought to be beyond the reach of commerce. There are many different ways of expressing this idea: "The best things in life are free;" "Some things ought not to be bought and sold but should be considered everyone's birthright;" and "Some things are too important to be left to the market." Different cultures have entirely different notions as to which goods, amenities, and resources ought to be immune from market influences, and some societies place many more items in that category than do others. In the United States, unique natural areas and wonders such as the Grand Canyon, wild rivers, and historical sites are often protected and managed as "non-exclusive" resources for these types of cultural and political considerations.

The second major reason that some goods and resources are non-exclusive lies not in the arenas of culture, tradition, and politics but in the basic characteristics of the goods and resources themselves. Why are there oyster farms but no swordfish farms (at least as this book is being completed in 2010)? Oysters are sedentary and grow to maturity while attached to a particular rock. Thus societies that choose to define exclusive property rights in oyster beds have little difficulty in so doing. Oyster beds can be clearly and easily delineated, and the oysters will remain in place. Exclusive property rights in oysters, once established, are easily secured and enforced. Thus, oysters can effectively be produced in efficient, private-sector operations similar to farming on dry land. On the other hand, swordfish is a highly mobile species of ocean fish. It is very difficult to delineate and enforce exclusive property rights to particular swordfish, or alternatively to individual small tracts of ocean and then confine particular swordfish to specific tracts.

Thus, ownership of swordfish is currently established not throughout the life cycle as in typical livestock farming and some types of fish farming,[2] but at the point of capture by the fisherman. More generally, there are many goods and resources that, because of their physical characteristics, are not well adapted to the specification of exclusive property rights therein. The costs of specifying, securing, and enforcing exclusive rights in such goods and resources exceed any benefits that may be gained.[3]

In the case of goods and resources for which exclusion is infeasible, the economist's advice that efficiency can be achieved through the establishment of non-attenuated property rights is not helpful. A number of important natural resources and environmental amenities fall into this category. These include ambient air; water in streams, lakes, and the ocean; migratory species of wildlife; and species that have little commercial value. They also include fish in international ocean waters and in lakes and streams too large for individual private ownership, and oil, natural gas, and groundwater pools that lie beneath lands owned by many different individuals. There are also disamenities and negatively valued resources for which effective exclusion is infeasible. These include pest populations, disease-causing organisms for which there is no known method for obtaining immunity, and pollutants carried by ambient air or non-exclusive hydrological systems.

When exclusion is feasible, the specification of exclusive property rights is a political decision. But when exclusive property rights are infeasible, the range of political choice is more limited. The totally non-exclusive, *res nullius*, situation has some undesirable properties from the perspective of economic efficiency. Often, however, a society has options within the set of *res communis* kinds of rights – rules that specify who shall have access to the good or resource, and under what conditions, may be established and enforced. Hunters and anglers may be subject to licensing requirements, restrictions on the hunting and angling seasons, bag limits, and the methods that may be used for hunting and angling. The farmer drawing from a groundwater pool may be subject to restrictions on the capacity of the pump, the days on which it operates and the number of hours it operates on a given day, or the total quantity of water withdrawn in a given time period.

In some cases, rules of access emerge from the social dynamics of a small group of deeply involved persons with common interests, rather than from action by the central government. These informal rules of access may not be enforceable in courts of law but are nevertheless effectively enforced by the group itself. Consider, for example, the elaborate informal demarcation of territory that exists among lobstermen in the Canadian Maritimes.

Res communis rules of access do not have all of the efficient characteristics of non-attentuated property rights. But they may provide a system of workable rights when exclusion is infeasible. There is a wide variety of possible specifications of these kinds of rules of access within the realm of *res communis*. Consider, for example, an ocean fishery. With the increasing demand for seafood and improved fishing technology, open access to the fishery has resulted in overfishing. Fish are harvested at a rate that threatens the biological capacity of the fish population to replenish itself. The current level of fish harvests cannot be sustained indefinitely. This problem is typical of those encountered when property rights are non-exclusive. Yet the establishment of non-exclusive property rights in an ocean fishery, particularly in international waters, would be prohibitively expensive. What can be done?

There is a substantial demand for seafood. The fishery represents a renewable resource that ought not to be allowed to deteriorate through mismanagement. A fishing industry has been established for many years, and the resources invested in that industry (fishing boats and equipment, and fishing skills) are not especially mobile. For these various reasons, it seems that something should be done to preserve and perpetuate the fishery. In addition, there is the problem of overinvestment in inputs used for the capture of fish. It seems that too many fishermen are pursuing too few fish and that each is investing in innovative technological equipment to make themself more effective in the chase for an ever-diminishing stock of fish.

In a management situation such as described above, various types of rules of access could be used. Before implementation, the relative efficiencies of alternative rules should be considered. To implement any government-imposed access rules, an agency with authority over the fishery would have to be established. The agency could choose to limit the fishing season. Surely, with fewer days of fishing permitted, the reproductive stock of fish could be maintained. But this approach would be relatively ineffective in maintaining the reproductive stock, although it would likely have a perverse effect on the problem of overinvestment in fishing inputs. With a restricted fishing season, fishermen would compete with one another to purchase and use the biggest and fastest fishing boats and the most effective technology to locate and capture fish. Another approach would be to restrict entry into the occupation of fishing. This would likely be done by licensing fishermen and granting licenses only to those who are presently occupied as fishermen and to their heirs. Although such a licensing strategy would create valuable property rights for fishermen (that is, their licenses, which would acquire a capital value), it would do little to conserve the fishery.

The agency may choose to restrict other kinds of fishing inputs. It may limit the size of fishing boats or their capacity to store and refrigerate fish, or it may restrict or prohibit the use of particularly effective devices for locating or capturing fish. These kinds of input restrictions would be relatively ineffective in conserving the fishery, as astute fishermen would soon substitute other kinds of inputs for the restricted kinds. This process of input substitution, however, would result in an inefficient investment of resources in fishing.

The agency could try a different approach. It could establish marketing quotas for fish and distribute those quotas among fishermen. Fish caught in excess of the marketing quota could not be sold. Each fisherman, once their marketing quota was established by the agency, would be free to determine the least-cost combination of inputs (capital, technology, labor, and time) to produce their given quota of fish. If the fish-marketing quotas were transferable (that is, could be sold to other fishermen), the process of dynamic adjustment in the fishing industry would be encouraged. More productive fishermen could expand their operations, and technologically advanced firms could enter the industry. Exiting fishing firms would enjoy additional capital liquidity when they sold their fish-marketing quotas to entering or expanding firms.

This example illustrates some general principles pertaining to the relative efficiency of various kinds of access rules. If the problem is overexploitation of a resource, the preferred solution will involve the direct restriction of the rate of exploitation (for example, the rate at which fish are captured and marketed), rather than the restriction of various inputs used in the process of exploitation. When restrictive rules are necessary, efficiency will be served if the rights created by those rules are transferable. Finally, it should be reiterated that even the more efficient kinds of *res communis* access rules will not result in the attainment of Pareto-efficiency. But when exclusion is infeasible, intelligently devised access rules may result in workable, second-best solutions that sustain productivity in the long run, discourage waste of inputs, and permit firms in the industry to earn reasonable and sustainable incomes.

Non-rivalry in consumption

Consider a good that, once produced, is available to all consumers without rivalry. The total quantity of the good is determined in the production process, but it is not necessary to divide the total output of the good among the various consumers. Each effectively has access to the total quantity of the good. Consumption by one individual does not reduce the amount remaining for other consumers. But most goods are not like that. The bread and wine of Chapter 6 were rival in consumption. Individual 1 was able to consume exactly the total production of each good minus the amount consumed by individual 2.

There are some goods, services, and amenities, however, which are non-rival in consumption. And many of these are important to natural resource and environmental policy. If ambient air of a given quality is provided, each of us may breathe that air and use it as a visual medium without effectively reducing the amount of it available for others. If one of the authors of this book is at an attractive scene alone, the scenic beauty available to him will not be diminished by 50 percent when he is joined by another observer. If one of the authors obtains utility from the simple knowledge that a previously endangered species somewhere in the world is flourishing, the utility he gains will not be diminished if others also gain utility from similar knowledge.

Non-rivalry is, clearly, a physical attribute of the affected good itself. It is not simply the result of an institutional choice, as non-exclusiveness may be. Non-rival goods differ from rival goods as follows: an ordinary rival good, Z_R, must be distributed among consumers $j = 1, \ldots, m$ so as to satisfy the constraint:

$$Z_R = \sum_{j=1}^{m} Z_{R_j} \qquad (10.1)$$

Individual consumption is additive, and the total amount consumed cannot exceed the amount available. For a non-rival good, Z_N, the total amount may be enjoyed by an individual j; that is:

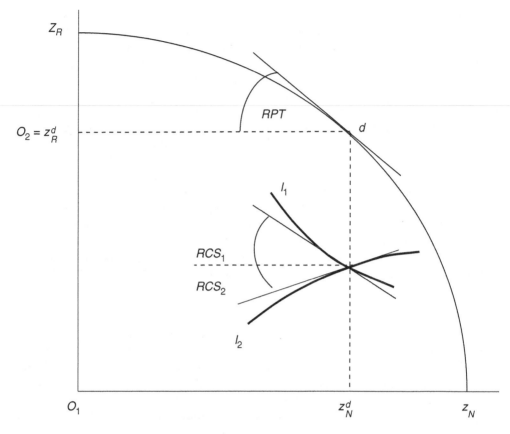

Figure 10.1   Efficient product mix and commodity distribution in an economy with rival and non-rival goods

$$Z_N = Z_{Nj} \tag{10.2}$$

but there is no meaningful sense in which the amount taken by j diminishes the amount available for anyone else. That is:

$$Z_N - Z_{Nj} = Z_N \tag{10.3}$$

The mathematics looks a little strange, but that is how it is with non-rival goods. The analysis of goods like that would surely differ from the analysis of ordinary rival goods.

Remember Figure 6.12, which showed how an efficiently produced but arbitrarily chosen package of bread and wine would be distributed among two consumers. For an economy consisting of the two goods, Z_R and Z_N (where Z_N is non-rival), Figure 10.1 provides the relevant analysis. The production efficiency locus is unchanged in concept: inputs must be allocated across Z_R and Z_N, and Z_N can be produced in any quantity between zero and the amount that would be produced if all inputs were directed toward producing Z_N. The product mix d is, as in the rival-goods case, chosen arbitrarily. The problem of distributing commodities among the consumers is, however, different when one is a non-rival commodity.

Because all of Z_N^d is available to each consumer without rivalry, there is no need to worry about dividing it among consumers. The only problem is to distribute Z_R^d. So the origin for consumer 2 is placed not at point d but at Z_R^d. The consumption efficiency locus is the line dZ_N^d. We know this because each consumer will take all of Z_N^d, whereas Z_R^d must be divided among them so that $Z_R^d = Z_{R_1}^d + Z_{R_2}^d$. Notice that the consumption efficiency locus is not a locus of tangencies between indifference curves. It is clearly not true that RCS_{Z_R, Z_N} should be the same for each individual or that it should equal RPT_{Z_R, Z_N} as was the case in a pure rival-goods economy.

Instead, the rate of product transformation must be equal to the sum of the individual consumers' rates of commodity substitution. For two consumers:

$$(RCS_{Z_R, Z_N})_1 + (RCS_{Z_R, Z_N})_2 = RPT_{Z_R, Z_N} \tag{10.4}$$

More generally, the summary necessary condition for Pareto-efficiency is:

$$\sum_{j=1}^{m} RCS_{Z_R, Z_N} = RPT_{Z_R, Z_N} \tag{10.5}$$

That is, the non-rival good will be provided in optimal quantity only if the aggregate marginal valuation that all consumers place on it (in terms of rival goods) is equal to the opportunity cost (in terms of rival goods) of the marginal unit of the non-rival good produced.

Supply and "demand" for non-rival goods

Instead of evaluating Z_N in terms of some particular rival commodity Z_R, we could evaluate it in terms of the dollar numeraire. The total (dollar) value that an individual obtains from Z_N is a function of the quantity provided. The total value curves of three individuals are illustrated in Figure 10.2. The total value curve typically passes through the origin, as the zero level of provision would have zero value. Assuming positive but diminishing marginal utility for Z_N, the total value (TV) curve would have a positive but decreasing slope. To determine the total value to all actual and potential users of a non-rival good, individual values are summed vertically. Thus the aggregate total value curve for the non-rival good in a society consisting of three persons is derived by the vertical summation of the three individual total value curves (Figure 10.2).

To focus on the marginal value of increments in the level of provision of a non-rival good, it is possible to derive individual marginal value curves by taking the first derivative of the individual total value curves. Individual marginal value curves may be summed vertically so as to derive the aggregate marginal value curve. The efficient level of provision of a good, the level at which the sum of the individual marginal valuations is exactly equal to the marginal cost of an increment in the level of provision, is determined by the intersection of the aggregate marginal value curve with the marginal cost curve (Figure 10.3). When MV_j indicates individual j's marginal valuation of Z_N, the condition for determining the efficient quantity is:

$$\sum_{j=1}^{m} MV_j = MC \tag{10.6}$$

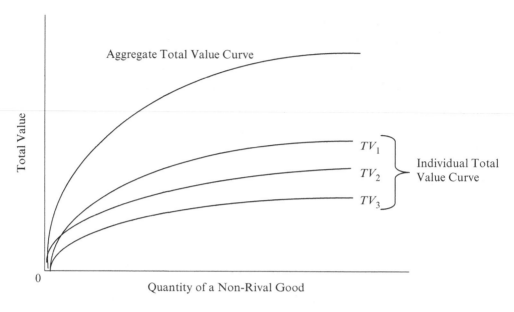

Figure 10.2   Individual and aggregate total value of a non-rival good

The relationship between the aggregate marginal value and the marginal cost for a non-rival good is analogous to the demand–supply relationship for a rival good. The analogy, though perfect on the supply side, is incomplete on the demand side. For rival goods, one needs to know the quantity taken at various parametric prices. For non-rival goods, the relationship is inversed: one needs to know the marginal valuations of various quantities. For industry demand, the quantities of rival goods taken are summed across individuals; this aggregation process is called horizontal summation. For non-rival goods, the aggregate marginal value is determined by summing individual valuations; this process is called vertical summation. Finally, for rival goods, the demand–supply intersection defines the market price relevant to each consumer. For non-rival goods, the analogous intersection identifies an aggregate marginal valuation equal to the marginal cost, but nothing analogous to a market price. As illustrated (Figure 10.3), individual marginal values at the efficient quantity are, in general, different for each individual.

Pricing and rationing non-rival goods
Is it possible to establish a pricing system for a non-rival good that would result in efficient production and rationing among consumers through voluntary means? Pareto-efficiency in the market for non-rival goods would require among other things that each individual pay a marginal price equal to their marginal valuation of the good:

$$MV_j = P_j \text{ for all } j = 1, \ldots, m \tag{10.7}$$

But as we have seen, marginal valuations differ across individuals. That, of course, implies that prices must be personalized. Each consumer should face a personal price satisfying the above condition. In the jargon of economics, perfect price discrimination

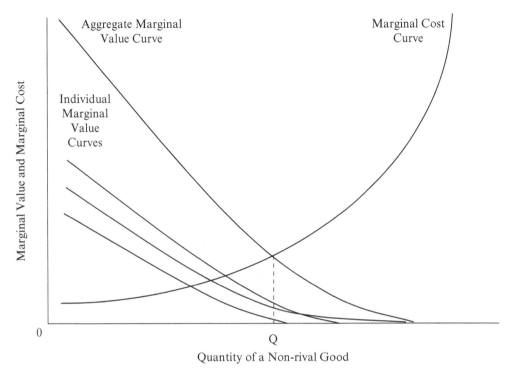

Figure 10.3   The efficient level of provision of a non-rival good

is necessary. The difficulty arises in ensuring accurate revelation. If only the individual knows for sure what their personal valuation is, how can others (for example, the supplier) know that the individual is not cheating by stating something less than the true MV_j? If the consumer had to pay the amount they voluntarily stated and if they had reason to expect or hope the payments of others might be sufficient to ensure that enough of the non-rival good were produced, the temptation to understate MV_j would be obvious. In the extreme, j may insist that $MV_j = 0$. If others paid enough to provide the good, j could use it for free; hence the term "free-rider effect." To eliminate strategic behaviors, it would be necessary to exclude all who do not pay their personal MV_j. This is a much more demanding type of exclusion than is required for efficient trade in rival goods, in which it is necessary only to exclude those who do not pay the going price applicable to all.

Experimental research has shown that extreme free-rider behavior is by no means universal in many situations.[4] Nevertheless, the possibility that various kinds of strategic behavior might distort voluntary markets in non-rival goods is a legitimate worry. In the absence of technologies to read people's minds and verify their MV, economists have focused on complex incentive mechanisms (often packages of direct and side taxes) that would make any other strategy more costly to the individual than truth telling would be. Although progress has been made on theoretical models and incentive-compatible empirical mechanisms for valuing non-rival goods,[5] there is still a long way to go before incentive-compatible mechanisms are routinely used to achieve Pareto-efficiency in markets for non-rival goods.

Considering the difficulties with perfect price discrimination, is there any alternative to the complete abandonment of pricing for non-rival goods (presumably leaving their provision to the tender mercies of the public sector and voluntary philanthropy)? If ordinary exclusion such that those who do not pay the going price are effectively prohibited from using the good is feasible, non-discriminatory pricing strategies may be pursued. Is there any non-discriminatory pricing system that will result in the efficient production and rationing among consumers of a non-rival good? Consider the marginal cost of adding an additional consumer for an indivisible good once it has been produced. Because consumption is non-rival, the marginal cost of adding an additional consumer is zero. Thus, it would be inefficient to exclude any consumer whose money value for the good is any positive amount. Prices greater than the smallest conceivable positive amount would inefficiently exclude consumers.

The revenue available to the producer of a non-rival good is the price collected from each user summed over all users. If the efficient price to consumers is some infinitesimally small positive amount, it is likely that the total revenue to the producer will be insufficient to permit them to recoup the costs of producing the good. Thus, very low positive prices will most likely fail to collect sufficient revenue to cover the costs of providing the good, and higher positive prices will inefficiently exclude potential consumers whose valuation of the good is positive but low. There is no non-discriminatory pricing system that will permit the achievement of Pareto-efficiency in the private sector production of non-rival goods.

Under certain circumstances where it is possible to exclude users who do not pay, a private sector producer of a non-rival good may be able to collect sufficient revenue to create the incentive to produce the good. If there is open entry into the industry of producing that good, competition among producers may drive down the price until the total costs of production are equal to the total revenue and no pure profits exist. But such a solution is inefficient because consumers with positive but low valuations of the good are excluded. However, it may well be a second-best solution that permits the private sector to provide the good and ration it among consumers without recourse to price discrimination and without excessive profits. Unfortunately, open entry into the business of producing a non-rival good is often an unrealistic assumption. In such circumstances, price regulation often replaces open entry as the device to ensure that the producer does not enjoy excessive profits. As is well known, such regulation meets with varying degrees of success but is seldom completely satisfactory.

Non-rival goods may, of course, be provided by the public sector. The public sector may choose to finance the provision of these goods out of general revenues and make them available to all consumers. Alternatively, under conditions where it is possible to exclude those who do not pay, the public sector may choose to charge a non-discriminatory price for the enjoyment of a non-rival good. Under this latter approach, the public sector has the option of setting the price so that the revenues it receives will recover the exact cost of providing the good or some higher or lower revenue level.

A note on public and private goods

Much of the literature in welfare economics, public finance, and resource economics addresses something called "public goods." In this book that term has been avoided because the public good is a concept that, because of inconsistent definition, has caused confusion. In his classic article, Paul A. Samuelson defined a public good in exactly the same way as we defined non-rival goods in this chapter.[6] A public good is a good that is consumed without rivalry. However, Samuelson's paper and much of the subsequent literature implied that public goods are non-exclusive in addition to being non-rival in consumption.

We find it useful to conceptualize non-rivalry in consumption and non-exclusiveness as distinct phenomena that may or may not be observed together. Therefore, we do not use the term "public good." Instead, we identify four categories of goods: rival, exclusive goods; rival, non-exclusive goods; non rival, exclusive goods; and non-rival, non-exclusive goods. Each of these four categories of goods has its distinguishing characteristics with respect to the possibility that the good may be provided by markets and the possibility that its provision may be Pareto-efficient.

Rival, exclusive goods

Rival, exclusive goods is the category (termed "private goods" by those who use the term "public goods" to describe non-rival goods) that includes bread and wine, the efficient production, distribution, and consumption of which were examined in Chapter 6. Such goods may be provided by markets, and given perfect markets, Pareto-efficiency in their provision may be achieved.

Rival, non-exclusive goods

Because it is impossible to collect payments for the provision of rival, non-exclusive goods, they cannot be offered in private markets. Such goods may be provided by private philanthropy (but usually in suboptimal quantities) or by the public sector, which would finance them from general revenues. If it were physically and economically feasible, exclusion could be introduced into the market for such goods. Then the public sector could offer such goods and charge a fee for their use and enjoyment. Alternatively, the private sector could provide these kinds of goods. If exclusive and non-attenuated property rights were specified and enforced, the private sector could then offer these kinds of goods in a Pareto-efficient manner. Fish caught for consumption in international ocean waters is an example of a rival, non-exclusive good.

Non-rival, exclusive goods

Non-rival, exclusive goods can be provided by either the public sector, which could choose to charge a fee for their use and enjoyment, or the private sector. Second-best solutions may be achieved, but the non-rivalry precludes the attainment of Pareto-efficiency in the absence of perfectly discriminatory pricing. Viewing flowers in a private garden which charges an entry fee is an example of a non-rival, exclusive good, assuming congestion is not a problem.

Non-rival, non-exclusive goods

Non-rival, non-exclusive goods may be provided only by private philanthropy (usually in suboptimal quantities) or by the public sector, which would finance their provision from general revenues. If exclusion were physically and economically feasible and politically acceptable, exclusive rights could be specified, and the goods could be provided through the market or by the public sector on the basis of user charges. If this occurred,

Pareto-efficiency would be impossible, but second-best solutions may be attainable. Ambient air and scenic views in public parks are examples of non-rival, non-exclusive goods, assuming free access and that congestion is not a problem.

Congestible goods
There is a class of goods that behave like non-rival goods within a certain range as the number of users increases from zero to some positive number that could be quite large. Over this range, additional consumers may be added without any rivalry. Eventually, however, the congestion of users sets in, and the addition of more users reduces the utility of all users. For a given level of provision of a congestible good, the marginal cost of adding additional users is zero until congestion sets in; as users are added beyond this range, however, the marginal cost of adding additional users begins to rise. Eventually, the marginal cost of adding additional users approaches infinity as an absolute capacity constraint is reached (Figure 10.4). Any good that can be enjoyed by many individuals but is subject to a capacity constraint, and for which the fixed cost of provision far exceeds the marginal cost of adding additional users until the capacity constraint is approached, has the characteristics of a congestible good.

Congestible goods include roads, bridges, pipelines, and transmission lines, and almost anything that is provided to the public within walls – for example, restaurant services, concerts, and spectator sports. Many natural and environmental amenities have the characteristics of congestible goods – for example, campgrounds, swimming pools,

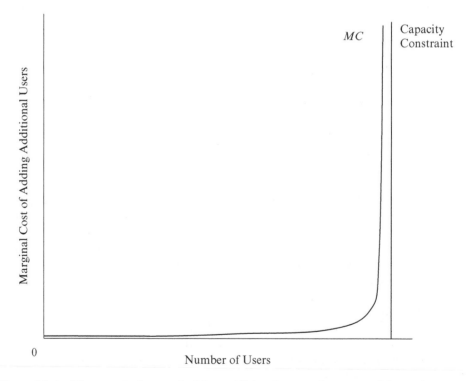

Figure 10.4   The marginal cost of adding additional users of a congestible good

golf courses, downhill ski areas, hiking trails, hunt areas, and fishing and boating sites. Telephone, cellular phone and Internet services are also examples of congestible goods.

The basic economic questions with respect to congestible goods are: (1) How should the capacity constraint be determined; that is, how large should the facility be? and (2) How should access to the congestible good be rationed among individuals? Economists O.A. Davis and A. Whinston addressed these questions.[7] They considered an economy with one rival and one congestible good, and solved the following problem: Maximize the sum of the money value of the individuals' utility, subject to: (1) a constraint on available resources; (2) the production functions for the rival and congestible goods; (3) a constraint that no more of the rival good can be consumed than is available in each time period; and (4) a constraint that no more of the congestible good can be consumed than is available in the first time period.

The solution of this problem permits the following conclusions: (1) production and consumption of the rival good can satisfy all the necessary and sufficient conditions for Pareto-efficiency; (2) Pareto-efficiency in the provision of the congestible good is impossible without resorting to perfectly discriminatory pricing; (3) a workable second-best solution for providing and pricing a congestible good assumes individuals consume the congestible good in each time period so that the money value of their marginal utility is equal to P_t, which is the shadow price of access to the congestible good in the time period t; and, if the net revenue from the congestible good is to be maximized, the capacity should be chosen in the initial period so that:

$$\sum_{t=0}^{T} \frac{p_t}{(1 + r)^t} \cdot X_t = MC \qquad (10.8)$$

where there are T total time periods, r = the rate of discount per unit of t, $X_t = 1$ if the marginal unit of capacity (that is, the last seat in a concert hall) is occupied in time t, and $X_t = 0$ if not, and MC = the marginal costs of increments in the capacity of the congestible good in the initial time period.

All of this implies the following. If the demand for a congestible good is variable over time, but the supply is fixed by a decision in the initial time period, the most appropriate access fee, p_t, may be zero in periods of light use. However, the capacity of the congestible good should not be so large that the capacity constraint is never binding. If the cost of provision of the congestible good is to be covered by revenue raised from access fees, p_t must be greater than zero in some time periods. If the access fee is to serve as a rationing device, p_t should be set equal to the marginal cost of adding an additional user during periods of great demand and heavy congestion. Furthermore, if the access fee is to ration the congestible good, when demand is variable across time periods, p_t should be published in advance for each time period so that users may choose not only how often but also at what times to use the congestible good. This time-variable pricing according to congestion, for example, is the idea behind charging lower and higher lift ticket prices at downhill ski areas during periods of low and high congestion, respectively.

If there is no mechanism for excluding those who do not pay, it is impossible to use time-variable prices to ration demand and generate the revenue with which to provide a congestible good. In such cases, the congestible good is provided by the public sector using general revenues, by private philanthropy, or not at all. The only effective rationing device is the crowding itself: the disutility from congestion is sufficient to discourage some potential users.

Even when exclusion and thus the use of access fees to ration the congestible good are feasible, public agencies may choose to provide congestible goods by using general revenues and setting p_t equal to zero or to some amount much lower than the market would bear during periods of high demand. For example, green fees at a public golf course will typically be lower as compared to a private country club golf course on a Saturday, Sunday or holiday. The typical result of such a policy is that time in queue and tolerance of inconvenience as rationing devices are partly or totally substituted for price.

When price is used to ration congestible goods and to generate revenues for their provision, one or another variation of the pricing strategy wherein p_t varies across time periods is often observed. Public transportation facilities may offer reduced charges during off-peak hours. The authorities that operate toll roads and bridges could, if they chose, follow a similar policy. However, it seems that they rarely do. In many parts of the world, publicly or privately owned electric utilities offer time-variable charges. Vacation resorts often offer off-season rates. Another example of time-variable charges for congestible goods is provided by landline telephone companies (or utilities) in many countries, whose tolls for long distance calls vary substantially according to the day of the week and the time of day. More recently, the advent and widespread use of cellular phones is reducing the demand for long-distance phone calls made via landlines, but time-variable charges have not disappeared. In many cellphone contracts, included weekday use is limited (and contracts with more included weekday minutes are more expensive) and relatively high rates are charged for additional minutes, but unlimited night and weekend use is allowed without additional charges.

Monopoly

Resource and environmental economists tend to focus their analyses of inefficiency on non-exclusiveness, non-rivalry, congestible goods, and externality (see below). However, it is wise to remember that the classical source of inefficiency is the absence of competition that is manifested, in its most extreme form, by monopoly. And monopoly is of concern to the resource and environmental economist. It is always possible that a monopolist may gain control of the stock of an important resource. For example, nations controlling substantial proportions of the earth's reservoirs of particular resources, especially petroleum, have formed cartels that have acted in a monopolistic manner.

The simple textbook analysis of monopoly proceeds as follows. Assume that an industry, consisting of one monopolistic firm, has constant marginal and average costs, at the level $MC = AC = R$. The demand curve for its product is DD'. Under perfect competition, the industry would produce an output of Z'', and that output would be priced at $R = MC$. However, the marginal revenue curve of the monopolist is DM. Setting marginal revenue equal to marginal cost, the monopolist selects the level of output Z', which he sells not at the price R but at the price P, which is the demand price for Z' units of output (Figure 10.5).

The monopolist restricts output at the level Z' and enjoys an excess profit equal to $PBAR$. The area $BCZ''Z'$ approximates the value of demands that would have been served by a competitive industry but are not served by the monopolist. It would cost $ACZ''Z'$ to serve those demands. Thus the triangle BCA is an approximate estimate

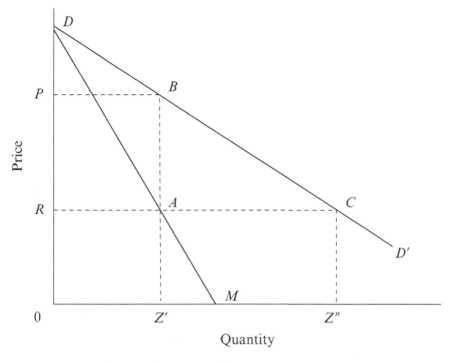

Figure 10.5 Price and output for a monopolist

of the economic loss that results from the monopolization of the industry. Under the assumptions of this analysis, monopoly is most certainly a source of inefficiency.

Natural monopolies and congestible goods
Specialists in public finance have long argued that there is a class of services that, in the normal course of events, are offered at a given place by only one firm or agency. The services have a strong spatial dimension. Often, they must be provided at the customer's place of business or residence, and the distribution system is capital-intensive. For some given capacity of the distribution system, the average cost of providing service declines as the output increases, until the capacity limit is reached. Thus for a service region, the costs of providing service are minimized when only one firm offers it. Such firms are called natural monopolies. Examples include landline telephone services; water, electric, and gas utilities; and railroads. Typically these services are provided by public agencies or firms franchised and regulated by the state, which obviously has a strong interest in the pricing and rationing of such services. In the case of franchised private firms, the state usually interprets its role as guardian of the public interest to ensure that these firms do not use their regional monopoly status to generate excessive revenues and profits or to restrict unduly the quantity and quality of services provided. Public regulatory agencies or commissions are often assigned to regulate these firms' schedules of charges (usually to limit profits to some acceptable rate of return on investment), services provided, and, sometimes, planned capital investments (to ensure that the customers are not burdened

with increased charges attributable to overexpansion of the firms' capacity). Such regulation may be effective in varying degrees but is seldom entirely successful.

The alert reader will have noticed that the kinds of enterprises cited above as natural monopolies provide services that had previously been identified as congestible goods. It happens that the theories of natural monopoly and congestible goods developed from different roots. But it is now obvious that these theories address the same set of problems. The distinguishing feature of natural monopolies, capital-intensive delivery systems of fixed capacity and the decreasing marginal (and average) costs of additional service until capacity is approached, is also typical of congestible goods. The case of declining long-run marginal (and average) costs for natural monopolies is discussed in more detail in Chapter 18 dealing with water demand and supply.

Natural monopolies are by no means impregnable in the long run as new technologies are introduced, allowing quite different technologies to compete effectively. Examples include cellular telephone service, which has gained market share versus landlines in long-distance telephone service; satellite television service, which competes with cable; and private package delivery services that compete effectively with the US Postal Service. To celebrate the US bicentennial in 1976, the American Telephone and Telegraph Company published advertisements proclaiming that its monopoly on long-distance telephone service was as American as apple pie. How much that picture has changed in little more than a generation!

Externality

Now we come to the most widely discussed source of market failure, externality. Externalities can have beneficial or adverse effects, but it is the latter case, external diseconomies, that seems to draw the most attention. External diseconomy refers to situations in which one party creates an annoyance for others and does not take any account of that annoyance. Clearly, if that kind of thing were pervasive, it would have disastrous effects on resource allocation and social cohesion as the population of unmollified victims of others' thoughtlessness proliferated. But it is not clear how and why such behavior would persist: surely the offended parties would find ways to make the actor consider the costs that his or her actions imposed on them. Obviously, the only way to understand the nature of externality and what if anything should be done about it, is to analyze the concept.

An externality[8] is said to exist whenever:

$$U_j = [X_{1j}, X_{2j}, \ldots, X_{nj}f(X_{mk})], j \neq k \tag{10.9}$$

where X_i ($i = 1, 2, \ldots, n, m$) refer to activities, and j and k refer to individuals. That is, an externality is said to exist whenever the welfare of some individual j is affected by those activities under their control and also by the effect, $f(X_{mk})$, of an activity, X_{mk}, that is under the control of somebody else, k. Externality is obviously a broad concept, referring to any situation in which the utility of one individual is influenced by an activity under the control of another. If one thinks about it a little, it will become apparent that almost any activity involves externality. Clearly, if externality is to be an analytically useful concept, it must be defined more precisely.

A relevant externality exists whenever the affected party, j, has a desire to induce the acting party, k, to modify their behavior with respect to the activity X_{mk}. An externality becomes relevant whenever the affected party is not indifferent to it. Thus the class of activities that may be called relevant externalities remains huge. For example, any activity that changes prices and thus forces an individual to adjust his or her consumption bundle could be called a relevant externality to that individual. But the ability of markets to adjust prices to reflect the changing relative scarcity does not cause inefficiency; instead, it is useful precisely because it permits efficiency. A concept of externality that focuses on inefficient externalities is necessary.

A Pareto-relevant externality exists when it is possible to modify the activity, X_{mk}, in such a way so as to make the affected party, j, better off without making the acting party, k, worse off. When a Pareto-relevant externality exists, there is the unrealized potential for a Pareto-improvement. Thus Pareto-relevant externalities can exist only when the economy is not Pareto-efficient. Finally, we have a definition of externality that focuses on externalities that result in inefficiency. From now on we shall, unless it is explicitly stated otherwise, use the term externality to mean Pareto-relevant externality.

It is useful to distinguish between two types of externality. An external diseconomy exists when the affected party, j, is made worse off by activity X_{mk} and has a desire to induce the acting party, k, to reduce the level of that activity. The external diseconomy will be Pareto-relevant if it is possible to reduce the level of the activity X_{mk}, in such a way so as to make at least one party better off but to make no one worse off.

An external economy is an externality in which the affected party, j, is made better off by the activity X_{mk} and therefore has a desire to induce the acting party, k, to increase his or her level of that activity. A Pareto-relevant external economy exists when it is possible to increase the level of the activity, X_{mk}, in such a way so as to make at least one party better off but to make no one worse off.

Examples of problems often analyzed as external diseconomies include polluting emissions and effluents from industrial processes, non-point pollution from construction sites and farming operations, polluting emissions from consumption activities (for example, automobile exhaust emissions and tobacco smoke), and any activity that imposes noise, ugliness, or other offensive impacts on affected parties.

It is often argued that external economies occur when, for example, one firm invents a new product or an improved production process, which is then available to other firms to use free of charge; when one firm provides specialized job training for its employees, who are then free to enter the employment of other firms who did not bear the expense of job training; when individuals who have themselves immunized against a contagious disease not only protect themselves but also protect others by reducing the probability of an epidemic; when individuals, by investing in their own education, also contribute to the creation of a more civilized society, which benefits everyone; and when an individual who invests in the beautification of his or her own property raises the value of neighboring property and provides pleasure for passers-by.

As indicated, these situations are often analyzed as externalities. But we should point out now that other approaches to their analysis are often available. For example, non-rivalry and/or non-exclusiveness concepts may permit insightful analyses. Furthermore, to list these examples of situations that have been called externalities is not to make any claim that they are, in general, Pareto-relevant. Inefficiency must be demonstrated in each case, not merely assumed because spillovers appear to exist. For example, the external economy related to job training provided by private firms does not seem to be a significant source of inefficiency or inequity. Labor economists have found that the trained workers, who gain from acquiring skills that they can sell to the highest bidder, actually bear most of the costs of their training by accepting lower wages during their formal training and early in their careers.

Externality, markets, and prices

Consider a simple Pareto-relevant external diseconomy in consumption. The utility of the individual j is affected by a vector of activities under his or her control, $X_{1j}, \ldots, X_{nj}$, and also by the activity X_{mk} which is not under his or her control. Because it is an external diseconomy, the individual's marginal utility for increments in X_{mk} is negative.

The individual's budget constraint is:

$$Y_j - \sum_1^n p_i X_{ij} = 0 \qquad \begin{array}{l} i = 1, \ldots, n \\ i \neq m \end{array} \qquad (10.10)$$

where Y_j = the income of j and P_i = price of X_i. Because j is unable to influence the level of the activity X_{mk}, that activity does not appear in his budget constraint, and so the price to him of $f(X_{mk})$ is effectively zero.

If the individual j maximizes his utility subject to his budget constraint, the first-order conditions for a maximum will be that the RCS between any two consumption activities is equal to the ratio of the prices of those activities. For any pair of activities in X_{1j}, $\ldots$, X_{nj}, this condition causes no problem: the marginal utility from each of these consumption activities is positive, as is the price of each activity. However, a problem arises with respect to the RCS between any activity, X_{ij}, and the external diseconomy, $f(X_{mk})$. Because the marginal utility from X_{ij} is positive and marginal utility from $f(X_{mk})$ is negative and because the price, p_i, is positive, the condition for efficiency in consumption,

$$RCS_{X_{ij}, f(X_{mk})} = \frac{p_i}{p_{f(X_{mk})}} \qquad (10.11)$$

can be satisfied only if the price of $f(X_{mk})$ facing the individual j is negative. However, that price is zero. Thus the efficiency condition is violated. Pareto-relevant externalities are simply manifestations of inefficient pricing. Efficiency can be achieved when a Pareto-relevant externality exists only if the correct price, or shadow price, is placed on the externality (negative for a diseconomy or positive for an economy).

If the price of the externality, $f(X_{mk})$ were not zero but, rather, an efficient negative price, that price would influence the behavior of both the affected party and the acting party. The affected party would have an incentive to tolerate the activity, X_{mk}, as her income (that is, the budget that she has available to purchase other goods and services) would rise as the level of the activity, X_{mk}, increases. The acting party would have an incentive to reduce the level of the activity, X_{mk}, as her income would fall as the level of the external diseconomy, $f(X_{mk})$, rises. Observe that these price incentives are simply the opposite of the incentives that positive prices introduce into the markets for typical commodities: positive prices induce the consumer to economize on his or her purchases and the producer to supply the commodity. Thus the efficient negative price for an external diseconomy results in the treatment of that diseconomy as if it were a simple discommodity (that is, anything that provides negative utility for the consumer, who would be willing to pay positive amounts to get rid of it). Conversely, the efficient positive price for an external economy would result in its being treated just like any other commodity. Clearly, if a complete set of markets existed, including markets in external effects which are just as real as are any other discommodities or commodities, prices for external effects would emerge. Pareto-relevant externalities are symptomatic of incomplete markets, which in an enterprise-oriented society suggests incomplete property rights.

Externality and property rights
We have seen that a Pareto-relevant external diseconomy is an inefficient situation that can be remedied if an efficient negative price is placed on the externality. For a simple externality involving only two parties, the requirement of a negative price could be satisfied in either of two ways. The acting party could pay compensation to the affected party, the amount of compensation increasing as the level of the external diseconomy increases. Alternatively, the affected party could bribe the acting party to reduce the level of the external diseconomy. A positive price for reductions in the level of the external diseconomy is equivalent to a negative price for the external diseconomy itself.

Under what circumstances might one expect to find acting parties offering to pay compensation to affected parties? The right to create external diseconomies may be valuable to the acting parties. If that right is not otherwise available to them, the acting parties may offer to buy it. Thus, when the affected parties are entitled to insist that uncompensated external diseconomies be reduced to zero, the acting parties may have an incentive to offer compensation in exchange for permission to create some positive level of diseconomy. Similarly, an affected party would bribe the acting party to reduce the level of external diseconomy, only if: (1) he has no right to force the acting party to desist; (2) at the margin, he is willing to pay for a reduction in the diseconomy; and (3) he is assured that by paying the bribe, he is actually buying a guarantee of relief from the external diseconomy.

Given that the external diseconomy imposes disutility on the affected party and that a reduction in the level of the external diseconomy would impose disutility on the acting party, a well-specified set of property rights is all that is needed to encourage trade between the involved parties, thus establishing an efficient negative price for the external diseconomy. But who will offer a payment to whom? The party disadvantaged by the specification of rights is the one who will offer payment.

The Coasian market solution   Consider a simple Pareto-relevant external diseconomy involving two parties, one acting and one affected, in a legal environment of non-attenuated rights. Assume that transaction costs are zero and that there are no income effects. Under these rather idealized circumstances, we now examine the market for abatement of the external diseconomy.

Figure 10.6 is a typical market-equilibrium diagram, adapted for use in analyzing the market for abatement of external diseconomies. Because external diseconomies are "bads," generating negative utility, the abatement thereof is a "good," generating positive utility. That is, abatement has the desirable result of reducing an undesirable effect. Thus abatement cannot proceed beyond the initial level of the external diseconomy. Therefore, the market diagram is bounded on the right by a vertical line intersecting the

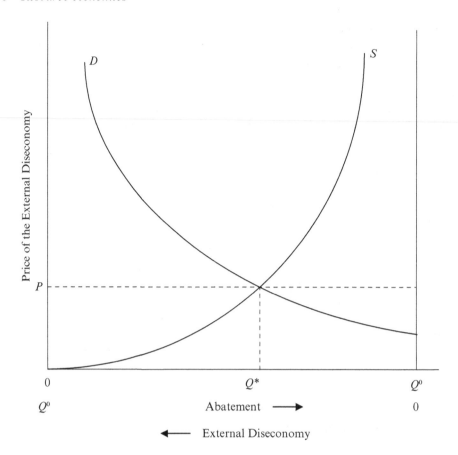

Figure 10.6   *The Coasian market solution, assuming zero transaction costs and zero
income effects*

horizontal axis at the point of complete abatement – that is, the point at which there is
zero external diseconomy remaining. The horizontal axis may be read in two ways: from
the left to the right, starting at zero abatement and ending at a level of abatement equal
to the initial level of external diseconomy, Q^0; or from the right to the left, starting at zero
external diseconomy and ending at the initial level of the external diseconomy, Q^0.

The affected party has a demand for abatement. If he is a consumer, the demand curve
will reflect the money value of the marginal utility obtainable from abatement; if a producer, the demand curve will reflect the value of the marginal damages to the production
process that would be avoided by abatement. It is reasonable to assume that the demand
curve for abatement will slope downward and to the right. The acting party has a supply
curve for abatement. If she is a producer, the supply curve will reflect the incremental
production expenses necessary to provide increasing levels of abatement; if a consumer,
the supply curve will reflect the incremental expense of providing abatement and/or the
marginal disutility to the acting party of reducing the level of a pleasurable consumption
activity in order to abate the external diseconomies it creates. Because the initial level
of the external diseconomy, Q^0, is exactly the equilibrium amount when the external

diseconomy is unpriced, it is reasonable to expect the supply curve for abatement to pass through the origin and to slope upward to the right.

Consider, first, what would happen under a non-attenuated full liability rule, L^f. Such a rule specifies that on appeal from affected parties, the authorities will enforce a requirement that external diseconomies be limited to zero. This kind of rule is completely specified, enforced, and transferable. Transferability is achieved through the requirement that the affected party's right to relief from external diseconomies be enforced only on appeal by the affected party. The authorities would permit the creation of external diseconomies in the absence of such an appeal, thereby providing incentives for trade.

Imagine the following scenario. Upon perceiving the presence of an external diseconomy, the affected party notifies the acting party that he intends to appeal to the authorities for enforcement of the L^f rule. Because the L^f rule would surely be enforced on appeal, resulting in complete abatement at substantial cost to the acting party, the acting party offers compensation in the hope of inducing the affected party to accept some positive level of external diseconomy. For any given level of external diseconomy, the acting party would be willing to offer compensation as great as her supply price for abatement, but no greater. The affected party would be willing to accept compensation as low as his demand price for abatement, but no lower. Given the usual perfect-market assumptions, an equilibrium would be reached in which the amount of abatement provided is Q^*; the amount of external diseconomy remaining is $(Q^0 - Q^*)$; and an amount of compensation equal to $P(Q^0 - Q^*)$ is paid by the acting party to the affected party. Note that for amounts of abatement exceeding Q^*, the unit compensation received by the affected party exceeds his demand price for abatement. Thus he is willing to enter into an agreement under which less than complete abatement is provided. Similarly, the acting party is willing to abate units of externality up to and including Q^*, since for those units her cost of abatement is less than the compensation the acting party would demand. Under the L^f rule, Q^* is the efficient level of abatement. The marginal costs of providing more abatement exceed the marginal benefits, whereas the marginal costs of providing less abatement are exceeded by the marginal benefits.

Notice that the efficient abatement of an external diseconomy does not, in general, result in its complete elimination. Some external diseconomy remains. The efficient level of abatement eliminates all Pareto-relevant external diseconomy. The external diseconomy remaining is simply not Pareto-relevant. It would be impossible to modify further the externality in such a way as to make at least one party better off without making another party worse off.

Now consider the non-attenuated zero liability rule, L^z. Such a rule states that affected parties have no right to relief from external diseconomies unless they choose to purchase such a right. If the right were purchased, it would be enforced on appeal to the authorities. In the absence of trade between the involved parties, the level of external diseconomy would be Q^0 and zero abatement would be provided. The affected party, having no right of relief from the external diseconomy, must tolerate it or bribe the acting party to reduce the level of external diseconomy. The affected party is able to offer bribes as high as his demand price for abatement, but no higher. The acting party is willing to accept bribes as low as her supply price for abatement, but no lower. Given the usual perfect-market assumptions, an agreement will be reached wherein the level of abatement provided is Q^*; the amount of externality remaining is $(Q^0 - Q^*)$; and a total bribe equal to $P \cdot Q^*$

is paid to the acting party. This market outcome is efficient and results in the elimination of all Pareto-relevant externality.

Given non-attenuated property rights, trade between the parties involved in an externality situation will eliminate Pareto-relevant externalities and result in an efficient situation. Under the assumptions of this simple example, the allocation of resources is independent of the particular rights specified. The L^f rule results in the same equilibrium level of abatement as does the L^z rule. Only the distribution of income is influenced by the specification of rights. Under L^f, a payment is made by the acting party to the affected party; under L^z, payment is made by the affected party to the acting party. L^f and L^z are, of course, merely the end points on a continuum of possible specifications of property rights with respect to external diseconomies. It is possible to conceive of intermediate liability rules, which would permit the acting parties to create some limited amount of external diseconomy, while enforcing that limit in the event that an affected party should appeal to the authorities on the grounds that the limit has been exceeded.

The above analysis demonstrates the Coase theorem, which had its origins in the writings of R.H. Coase.[9] That theorem states that given non-attenuated property rights, trade among involved parties will eliminate Pareto-relevant externalities, resulting in an efficient solution. Furthermore, the final allocation of resources will be invariant to the initial specification of property rights.

The Coasian analysis has made a number of important contributions to the understanding of externality and, more generally, of the functioning of markets. It suggests that market phenomena may be more pervasive than was generally recognized and that market behavior is likely to occur whenever gains from trade exist, even in arenas customarily considered to be outside the market. It has elucidated the concept of property rights and has led economists to analyze trade in rights rather than in objects. Since the development of the Coase theorem, economists have been much more careful than they once were about using terms such as "market failure" and recommending governmental regulation of market activity as the solution to perceived inefficiency.

On the other hand, some economists have misused the Coase theorem to conclude falsely that establishing a transferable liability law, any transferable liability law, is all that governments need do in situations of perceived inefficiency and that the particular specification of the liability law chosen is unimportant.[10] This kind of logic has led some to argue, in a caricature of the Coasian analysis, that there is no need for explicit policies to handle the problem of, say, air pollution. This argument states that in the absence of any explicit policy, the L^z law exists and ensures that the efficient amount of air pollution, but no more, will be created. More generally, some have used the Coase theorem to argue that whatever exists must be good because if it were not good at the outset, subsequent trade would have made it good. These kinds of arguments are generally invalid because they simply take the Coase theorem too far. The result shown in Figure 10.6, in which the final resource allocation was not influenced by the initial assignment of liability, is not generally valid. Things are more complicated in the real world.[11]

In the analysis depicted by Figure 10.6, the allocation of resources was not influenced by the specification of property rights, but the resultant distribution of income is so influenced. Under the L^f law, the acting party pays compensation to the affected party, and under the L^z law, the affected party pays bribes to the acting party. Thus, the specification of property rights influences the budget constraints of the involved parties. Compared

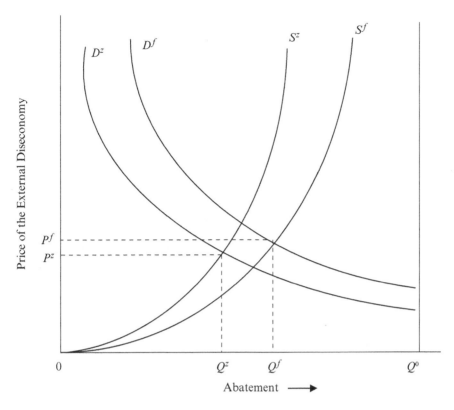

Figure 10.7   The Coasian market solution: the effect of non-zero income effects

with the situation under an L^z law, the budget constraint of the affected party under an L^f law is larger, and the budget constraint of the acting party is smaller. If the demand and supply of abatement of external diseconomies are influenced by the budget constraints of the demander and supplier, income effects will be observed and will be sufficient to shift the demand and supply curves for abatement. The demand curve D^f, for abatement under the L^f law lies to the right of the demand curve, D^z, for abatement under the L^z law. The supply curve, S^f, under the L^f law lies to the right of the supply curve, S^z, under the L^z law (Figure 10.7). The result, in general, of non-zero income effects is that the efficient quantity of abatement under the L^f law is greater than is the efficient quantity of abatement under the L^z law. The equilibrium bribe or compensation price of abatement under the L^f law may be higher or lower than under the L^z, depending on the relative magnitudes of the income elasticities of demand and supply for abatement. This finding with respect to quantity of abatement is quite general. Under an L^f law the efficient quantity of abatement will be as great as or greater than the quantity of abatement provided under the L^z law; if income effects are positive, the quantity of abatement under the L^f law will be greater.

The Coase theorem pertains to the solution of externality problems through trade, and trade commonly involves positive transaction costs. The effect of positive transaction costs is to reduce the effective value of any offer of payment. The amount paid is equal to

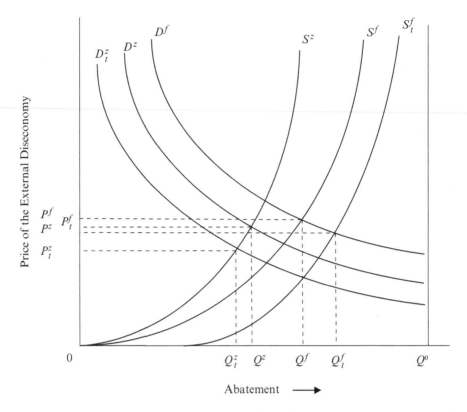

Figure 10.8   The Coasian market solution: the effect of positive transaction costs and non-zero income effects

the amount received minus the transaction costs. The effect of transaction costs are illustrated in Figure 10.8. Under the L^z law, the effective demand for abatement is reduced to D_t^z. Under the L^f law, transactions costs make abatement cheaper (relative to negotiating to compensate receptors); thus the effective supply of abatement is S_t^f. The effect of positive transactions costs is to increase the divergence between the equilibrium quantity of abatement provided under L^z and under L^f with $Q_t^z < Q^z \le Q^f < Q_t^f$.

There is a simple method of checking on the logic of the analysis used in Figure 10.8. If the transaction costs (that is, the costs of consummating trade) were larger than the potential gains from that trade, no trade would occur. If no trade occurred, the equilibrium resource allocation would be exactly that allocation initially specified by the structure of the property rights. Under the L^f law, the affected party has a right to total abatement; when transaction costs are so high as to prohibit trade, total abatement will be the result. Under the L^z law the acting party has a right to pollute as they please; when transaction costs are prohibitive, zero abatement will be the result.

In the real world, the assumption of positive income effects is more realistic than is the assumption of zero income effects, and the assumption of positive transaction costs is more realistic than is the assumption of zero transaction costs. Under the more realistic assumptions, the efficient quantity of abatement depends on the specification of property rights. More generally, the first part of the Coase theorem (that an efficient solution will be achieved) remains valid, but the second part (that resource allocation is invariant to the specification of rights, provided that the rights are non-attenuated) does not. This conclusion ought not to surprise those who have read Chapter 9. It is a general conclusion that within the universe of non-attenuated property rights, the efficient solution varies with the specification of property rights. In general, the efficient quantity of abatement of an external diseconomy will be greater under a specification of property rights that protects the affected parties and less under a specification that protects the acting parties.

It is also interesting to observe that the specification of rights determines which externalities are Pareto-relevant. With positive income effects and transaction costs, any externality lying to the right of Q_t^z is Pareto-irrelevant under L^z, whereas under L^f any externality lying to the right Q_t^f is Pareto-irrelevant. Thus the externalities that are considered Pareto-relevant are determined by the property rights with respect to externality.

The persistence of externality   When property rights are non-attenuated and transaction costs are low, the Coasian analysis shows that externality problems will be resolved through voluntary exchange. Under these conditions, Pareto-relevant externality cannot persist. It may arise when some annoyance is introduced into a previously stable system, but it cannot persist. The fact that Pareto-relevant externality cannot persist does not ensure that the annoyance will go away. As we have seen, usually some positive amount of it remains even when efficiency has been restored to the system. Furthermore, when transaction costs are very high, the equilibrium solution is to leave the annoyance unchanged.

We must ask ourselves what circumstances would lead to such prohibitive transaction costs. Various trade barriers, perhaps, and monopolistic restrictions to competition in the transactions industry itself could have that effect. But in a market-oriented society, these are (one hopes) exceptional cases. More typically, exorbitant transaction costs are attributable to breakdowns in property rights or the physical attributes of the good to be traded (the annoyance and reductions therein) – that is, to non-exclusiveness and non-rivalry. The persistent cases of inefficient externality are those that involve non-exclusiveness and/or non-rivalry. In these cases, the pursuit of gains from trade does not ensure the restoration of efficiency, because the preconditions for efficient trade are absent. The interesting thing is that the concept of externality is not essential to this analysis; what is essential is the non-exclusiveness and/or non-rivalry. Externality, then, is nothing special. An inefficient situation can only persist if non-exclusiveness and/or non-rivalry are present as well.

This theoretical finding with respect to the persistence of externality accords with ordinary experience. Annoyances between two (or just a few) parties do not become matters for public policy. Well-established legal concepts, such as nuisance, are adequate to take care of the problem by providing a basis for negotiated agreements or, failing that, swift judicial resolution of the conflict. The annoyances that become public policy issues are those that involve, for example, air and water quality, neighborhood amenities, outdoor recreational and wildlife resources, and threats to the genetic capital stock. The conflict inherent in the notion of externality is not decisive in determining whether a "spillover" will become a policy issue. What is decisive is whether the "spillover" involves non-exclusive and/or non-rival goods and resources. For those annoyances that spill over into the public arena of non-exclusiveness and non-rivalry, the Coase theorem is entirely irrelevant. It is a theorem pertaining to the allocation of ordinary rival goods in a legal environment of non-attenuated property rights. As such, it does not ensure that those environmental problems that attract the public attention can be resolved through trade.

With respect to both kinds of goods, ordinary rival goods and the non-exclusive and/or non-rival type, conflicts may arise when some annoyance is introduced. Private law, with its concepts of nuisance, trespass, and the like, is a solid basis for systematically resolving conflicts concerning rival goods. But private law is oriented toward property interests and does not have a concept, analogous to nuisance, to deal with invasions of non-exclusive (that is, unowned) media like the air, water, or neighborhood ambience. We think it would be a good idea to extend private law concepts to such problems. But the customary solutions to these problems involve public law concepts such as regulation via the police power or the direction of resource allocation through the power to tax.

Pollution and similar problems: jointness in production and consumption
Pollution and similar problems are, as we have seen, best explained as degradations of non-rival and/or non-exclusive resources such as ambient air and water. The public sector provision of non-rival and/or non-exclusive amenities is always an option. But in environmental quality cases, the seemingly direct route of the public sector producing a cleaner environment is seldom the preferred one. Instead, the control of pollution, the cause of disamenity, is sought.

Pollution is generated jointly with desired production or consumption activities. These desired activities are usually subject to well-specified property rights and price structures, but their joint products (e.g., air and water pollution) are neither desired nor well incorporated into markets. Pollution control strategies involving public sector activism may take a variety of routes.

Polluting emissions may be taxed in order to place a negative price on the (otherwise unpriced) disamenity. This strategy, recommended by the early twentieth-century economist A.C. Pigou, is often called Pigouvian taxation.[12] In more recent years, other economic incentives in the form of pollution credit trading have been advocated. Governments may choose to regulate the quantity of emissions via emissions standards. Alternatively, the joint-product nature of pollution may suggest attempts to influence the related production or consumption activity. If the joint products (e.g., goods and pollution) are produced in strictly fixed proportions, government could control pollution through economic incentives or regulating the marketed output. If the output mix can be varied, government may subsidize directly or through economic incentives or require by regulation the use of inputs that would reduce the proportion of pollution generated in the course of the desired activity. As it turns out, all of these approaches have been attempted in various jurisdictions. The economics of these approaches is discussed in Chapter 16 dealing with polluting emissions control.

Concluding comments
Many problems in environmental quality, preservation of natural environments, neighborhood amenities, provision of aesthetic and recreational resources, transportation,

public utilities, and collectively provided services can be attributed to various kinds of market imperfections. However, "market failure" has given rise to a confused and sometimes misleading literature. To conclude this chapter, let us address two issues and state our position on each.

Market failure and government failure
Contemporary critics have argued that the market failure analysis of economists such as Pigou incorporated into the "new" welfare economics of Kaldor, Hicks, and Samuelson rationalizes the paternalistic, democratic state; the "welfare state," if you will. The idea is that analyses of market failure always seem to find inefficiency and to suggest government-imposed solutions. As a half-century of research efforts, encouraged for example by the *Journal of Law and Economics*, has made clear, market failure is not always what it seems. In some cases, market failure is diagnosed only because the analyst has failed to observe the costs of operating a market. The absence of a market is not always market failure. Some markets are just not worth the cost. In other cases, government (through distorting taxes, subsidies, regulations, or restraint of trade) is the cause of the problem, and less rather than more government might be the most direct solution. More generally, government (which is always subject to the attempts of myriad special interests to manipulate it) has its own problems. To demonstrate that markets perform poorly in some areas is not tantamount to showing that government would do better.

Imperfect markets are real and cause real problems in the natural resource and environmental economy. One must, however, be constantly wary of the insinuation that market failure itself justifies governmental intervention. It must be shown, not merely assumed, that the government would do better.

The semantics and analytics of market failure
As various passages in this chapter have suggested, the semantics of market failure have become confused in the literature. It is true that semantics can sometimes be trivial, but more often than not, we fear, sloppy semantics is symptomatic of sloppy concepts and analyses.

Several market failure concepts are often found in the literature: common property resources, public goods, natural monopoly, and externality. They all have their problems. The analysis associated with "common property resources" is usually an analysis of *res nullius* (that is, non-exclusiveness), not *res communis* (that is, property held in common). Analyses of "public goods" focus sometimes on the aspect of non-rivalry and sometimes on the free-rider effect, which is clearly a symptom of non-exclusiveness. But which of these phenomena makes a public good public? Some analyses emphasize non-rivalry, others focus on non-exclusiveness, and still others insist that both problems must be present together. The non-pure case of public goods (called congestible goods in this chapter) has been recognized with an analysis suspiciously like that for natural monopoly. Finally, the concept of externality has been shown in the Coasian analysis to have little power: externality alone will not persist but will spontaneously disappear as the involved parties seek the available gains from trade. Externality is a persistent source of inefficiency only when accompanied by non-exclusiveness and/or non-rivalry, and it is the non-exclusiveness and non-rivalry that are crucial to the analysis. We believe that the semantics and analytics of market imperfection would be much improved by more informed use and perhaps even abolishing the four terms discussed above (common property resources, public goods, natural monopoly, and externality). What is valid and analytically helpful in these terms is captured in the concepts of non-exclusiveness, non-rivalry, and congestible goods. Moreover, these latter concepts avoid the confusions that plague the former terms.

Questions for discussion

1. "We observe in the real world actions that are taken not because the benefits from the action exceed the total costs but because the actor finds it possible to impose some or all the costs on others." List the various types of such actions, identifying in each case the circumstances that permit the actor to impose some of the costs on other people.
2. Given that ambient air is non-rival and non-exclusive, how might the demand curve for air pollution abatement be estimated?
3. Is it conceivable that there could be too little pollution? Explain.
4. "The Coase theorem proves that government has no business getting involved in pollution control regulations." Evaluate this statement.
5. "If government insists on regulating, then surely it should regulate performance rather than inputs." Do you agree? Explain. With your discussion as background, evaluate the economic efficiency of programs that:
   a. mandate the use of scrubbers on coal-burning, electricity-generating plants in order to control air pollution;
   b. restrict the design of fishing nets in order to maintain the fish resource.
6. Simple, partial equilibrium analyses tell us that: (a) a monopolist inefficiently restricts output; and (b) a polluter inefficiently expands output. What can we say about the level of output of a polluting monopolist? Is the case of a polluting monopolist an application of the theory of second best?

Notes

1. See, for example, Richard H. Day (1978), "Adaptive Economics and Natural Resources Policy," *American Journal of Agricultural Economics* **60** (May): 276–83.
2. For example, farming of catfish and tilapia in private freshwater ponds and salmon farming in saltwater pens located in open ocean areas.
3. We are not saying that commercial fish farms for swordfish will never develop. Indeed, private fish farming enterprises continue to develop in perhaps unexpected and unforeseen ways (e.g., recent developments in private tuna fish farms and ranches). With respect to many natural resources over history, we have seen that when economic incentives change and become high enough, private markets develop. In the case of swordfish, new, cost-saving technology for deep-sea fish farming, reasonable input prices (e.g., reasonable prices for fuel and labor), and high final product prices may result in the establishment of a profitable deep-sea swordfish farming industry sometime in the future.
4. For example, see Yan Chen and Charles Plott (1966), "The Groves–Ledyard Mechanism: An Experimental Study of Institutional Design," *Journal of Public Economics* **59**: 335–64.
5. For example, see Richard T. Carson and Theodore Groves (2007), "Incentive and Informational Properties of Preference Questions," *Environmental and Resource Economics* **37** (1): 181–210; Ronald G. Cummings, Steven Elliott, Elenn W. Harrison, and James Murphy (1997), "Are Hypothetical Referenda Incentive Compatible?," *Journal of Political Economy* **105** (3): 609–21; Vernon L. Smith (1980), "Experiments with a Decentralized Mechanism for Public Goods Decisions," *American Economic Review* **70**: 584–99.
6. Paul Samuelson (1954), "The Pure Theory of Public Expenditure," *Review of Economics and Statistics* **36**: 387–9.
7. Otto A. Davis and Andrew B. Whinston (1967), "On the Distinction between Private and Public Goods," *American Economic Review* **57** (May): 360–73.
8. The definitions that follow are those of James M. Buchanan and W. Craig Stubblebine (1962), "Externality," *Economica* **29**: 371–84.
9. Ronald Coase (1960), "The Problem of Social Cost," *Journal of Law and Economics* **3**: 1–44.
10. See, for example, Harold Demsetz (1964), "The Exchange and Enforcement of Property Rights," *Journal of Law and Economics* **7**: 11–26.
11. The following analysis is based on Alan Randall (1972), "Market Solutions to Externality Problems: Theory and Practice," *American Journal of Agricultural Economics* **54** (May): 175–83.
12. Arthur C. Pigou (1940), *The Economics of Welfare*, London: Macmillan.

Suggested reading: classic and contemporary

Bator, F.M. (1958), "The Anatomy of Market Failure," *Quarterly Journal of Economics* **72** (3): 351–79.

Baumol, W.J. (1972), "On the Taxation and Control of Externalities," *American Economic Review* **62**: 307–22.

Buchanan, J.M. and W.C. Stubblebine (1962), "Externality," *Economica* **29** (116): 371–84.

Chen, Y. and C. Plott (1996), "The Groves–Ledyard Mechanism: An Experimental Study of Institutional Design," *Journal of Public Economics* **59**: 335–64.

Christy, F.T., Jr (1975), "Property Rights in the World Ocean," *Natural Resources Journal* **15**: 695–712.

Coase, R. (1960), "The Problem of Social Cost," *Journal of Law and Economics* **3**: 1–44.

Cropper, M.L. and W.E. Oates (1992), "Environmental Economics: A Survey," *Journal of Economic Literature* **30**: 675–740.

Dahlman, C.J. (1979), "The Problem of Externality," *Journal of Law and Economics* **22** (1): 141–62.

Davis, O.A. and A.B. Whinston (1967), "On the Distinction between Private and Public Goods," *American Economic Review* **57** (May): 360–73.

Groves, T. and J. Ledyard (1977), "Optimal Allocation of Public Goods: A Solution to the Free Rider Problem," *Econometrica* **45** (4): 783–809.

Haddock, D.D. (2004), "When are Environmental Amenities Policy-Relevant?," *Natural Resources Journal* **44** (Spring): 383–424.

Head, J.G. (1976), "Mixed Goods in Samuelson Geometry," *Public Finance* **31**: 313–37.

Randall, A. (1972), "Market Solution to Externality Problems: Theory and Practice," *American Journal of Agricultural Economics* **54** (May): 175–83.

Randall, A. (1983), "The Problem of Market Failure," *Natural Resources Journal* **23**: 131–48.

Samuelson, P. (1954), "The Pure Theory of Public Expenditure," *Review of Economics and Statistics* **36**: 387–9.

Samuelson, P. (1955), "A Diagrammatic Exposition of a Theory of Public Expenditure," *Review of Economics and Statistics* **37**: 350–56.

11 Institutional framework: what is the social and legal context for natural resource and environmental decisions and policy?

The theoretical analyses of the previous chapters have made clear, time and time again, the crucial role of institutions in shaping individual opportunity sets and the outcomes of economic interaction. Non-attenuated property rights were found to be essential, in principle, if the independent economic activities of individuals were to result, in aggregate, in economic efficiency. The particular specification of property rights was found to influence resource allocation, commodity distribution and consumption, the prices at which trade takes place, and the incomes of individuals. Regulatory and public finance institutions were found to enable the collective management of non-rival and non-exclusive resources. In the case of those goods which are non-exclusive because of prohibitive exclusion costs, public sector economic activity offers the only means for efficient provision. Price regulation was seen to be a commonly used, if not especially effective, method of discouraging the generation of "pure profits" in those industries which enjoy monopoly power. Taxation policy will be seen (in Chapters 15 and 17) to provide a means whereby a degree of collective control can be exercised when private decisions lead to intertemporal resource misallocation (under- or overexploitation). In these ways, the role of institutions in influencing economic outcomes in an economic system that relies principally on individual action motivated by individual interests was recognized.

Although the role of public institutions was thus recognized, institutions themselves were presented in a rather abstract form. Thus, we have not yet presented a comprehensive picture of the role of government and other collective institutions in a modern mixed economy or of the complex framework within institutional decisions influencing the utilization of particular resources. The purpose of this chapter is to provide the rudiments of such a picture.

Interactions among private and public sectors

A modern mixed economy allows individuals acting independently and in pursuit of their own self-interest to have major roles in making economic decisions. However, not all economic outcomes are entrusted to the private markets and interactions between independent individuals. Although individuals influence economic outcomes through the allocation of their budgets, they also seek a different kind of influence through the use of their political and legal endowments: the rights to vote; to speak and write in order to persuade others; to work in political parties, interest groups, and issue-oriented organizations; and to litigate. The very same individuals pursue their self-interest through economic, political, and legal means. Thus there is a significant role for government in economic activity, and individuals seek to use both the market and the government to pursue their private goals. Individuals who sense that their comparative advantage lies in the political and/or legal arenas seek to expand the economic influence of government, whereas those whose comparative advantage is in the market seek to maximize the economic role of markets. Regardless of which group is in the ascendancy in a particular country at a particular time, the interactions between government and the market are pervasive.

Given that individuals seek to use both the market and the government to achieve their ends, the terms "government interference" and "government intervention," in common usage among certain groups of economists, appear remarkably naive. Government is best viewed as endogenous to (that is, springing from within) the social system, rather than as some external agent that "interferes" or "intervenes."

A useful way to approach the issue of private–public sector interactions is to first consider the minimal state (that is, the most confined role for the political-legal sector that is compatible with economic productivity and social harmony), and then consider the forces that may lead the political-legal sector to grow beyond the minimal state.

The minimal state
In a system seeking to maximize the scope for private initiative while providing the basis for political stability and socio-cultural continuity, what is the most confined role for collective political-legal activity which is compatible with economic productivity and social cohesion? In order to consider this question, it is helpful to introduce the term "the state" to denote the whole range of political-legal institutions and activities that a society collectively establishes and undertakes in order to achieve those ends it believes are not best served by purely private initiative. The question then is: What are the roles and functions that must be undertaken by the minimal state?

The minimal state must establish and enforce rights, preferably non-attenuated rights, defining the relationships among individuals with respect to one another, their government, and their property objects (human rights, civil rights, and property rights). Without a comprehensive system of rights, interpersonal relationships would be insecure, and conflicts would tend to be adjudicated by force (plunder and war) rather than through trade.

In order to establish such a system of rights, it is necessary for the state to: (1) undertake legislation to specify rights; (2) engage in policing and enforcement to enforce the rights specified; (3) operate a judicial system to resolve conflicts among individuals, between individuals and the police, between individuals and the legislature, and between legislation and "higher" (for example, constitutional) law; and (4) conduct military defense to protect the rights of individuals within the society when these are threatened by alien threats.

The minimal state must "do something about" situations in which exclusive rights are infeasible and a natural monopoly exists. Without state action, non-exclusive resources would be abused and overexploited, and non-exclusive goods, services, and amenities would be seriously underprovided. These situations would soon become intolerable to the society. For example, consider "natural monopoly" which arises in industries that face continually declining marginal (and average) cost curves and, therefore, tend to result in spatial monopoly (the establishment of a single firm to provide services to a given region). If entirely uncontrolled, "natural monopoly" leads to excessive profits (which may be tolerable to the society) and territorial wars among predatory firms seeking to expand their spatial monopolies (which would surely be intolerable). The call to "do something" would lead the state to take one or more of the following actions: (1) some kind of regulation of access to non-exclusive resources or some kind of taxation policies to influence the pattern of their exploitation; (2) some form of state economic activity either to provide non-exclusive goods, services, and amenities or to subsidize their provision by the private sector; and/or 3) some form of state licensing, franchising, and/or regulation of spatial monopoly. In order to perform these services, the state would need to procure materials and services and to collect the revenues with which to pay for them.

To permit the coordination of state activities, an administrative structure within the state (that is, a bureaucracy) would need to be established. Thus even the minimal state exerts substantial influence on the patterns and outcomes of private economic activity. Through procurement and revenue collection, the minimal state influences the demand for goods and services, their prices, and the incomes of those who provide them. By establishing and enforcing rights, the state influences resource allocation, commodity distribution, prices, and the distribution of income and wealth. The undertaking of legislative, policing, judicial, military, licensing, franchising, taxation policy, and regulatory activities by the minimal state establishes the state as both a modifier of economic activity and an economic force in its own right. The ways in which it chooses to carry out its role as an economic unit will influence, directly or indirectly, all other economic units in the society.

Beyond the minimal state
The economic influences of even the minimal state are, in themselves, quite pervasive. In addition, they provide the seeds for the growth of the state as an economic, political, and legal institution. Because the state establishes and enforces interpersonal rights, it will attract the attention of all those citizens who have a personal interest in the particular kinds of rights specified, all those who have a personal interest in the degrees of severity and selectivity of enforcement, and all those who pursue legislative, law-enforcement, legal, judicial, and military careers. Thus, we see the growth of the bureaucracy and the establishment of public employee interest groups and private lobbies designed to influence the pattern and direction of state activity.

The obvious need for some state activity in regulation, direction through tax policy, or direct provision of goods and services arising from the prohibitive costs of exclusion with respect to certain goods and resources and from the existence of spatial monopoly, sows the seeds of a more pervasive government influence on private activity. If non-exclusive goods and resources and spatial monopoly are sufficient rationale for direct government activity or government influence through regulatory and taxation policy, surely externalities, non-rivalry, monopoly in general, and the need to provide "merit goods" (those goods that are thought to be socially desirable in quantities larger than are purchased in the market) will be equally good reasons for activist governmental policy. Thus we find governments in modern mixed economies regulating land use, public health and safety, and environmental quality; providing education, public health services, flood control, irrigation water, drainage, outdoor recreation, ballet, opera, literature and the fine arts; protecting cultural, historical, and natural monuments and treasures; controlling the prices charged by monopolies, oligopolies, and cartels; or regulating mergers among firms, with a view to limiting the formation of firms which may eventually attain monopolistic or oligopolistic positions in their particular markets. More recently, the government has stepped (or been pulled) into the market to rescue private companies from bankruptcy and/or shepherd them through bankruptcy.

The need to procure materials and services enables the state to use its procurement policies to encourage the economic progress of particular industries, particular regions of the country, or particular, identifiable groups of citizens. The need to collect revenue gives the state the opportunity to use taxation policy to discourage economic activities it dislikes and encourage those it likes, and to redistribute income and wealth among its various citizens. Thus we see excise taxes, sales taxes, property taxes, taxes on imports and exports, user taxes, taxes on luxury items, and progressive income taxes, all of which are intended to influence economic outcomes as well as to collect revenues.

As individuals and interest groups perceive the state's actual and potential economic importance, they will invest in influencing the state according to the same decision criteria used to determine their private sector investments. Thus, although there are forces encouraging the growth of the state and its expansion into new areas of activity, there are also forces seeking to restrain the growth of the state, to discourage its expansion into different kinds of activities, and to encourage an actual retrenchment in total state activity. Furthermore, the above simple dichotomy is complicated by a legion of economic interests asking that government send money but otherwise keep its hands off their business. The political and legal battles that almost always arise when the state enters a new economic arena are battles between those individuals who expect the proposed state activity to make them better off and those who expect it to make them worse off.

Loci of decision-making within the state

Our discussion may have left the impression that the state is a monolith. Nothing could be further from the truth. At the most atomistic level, the state is composed of every individual who votes, pays taxes, contributes to political causes, pleads their case before the judiciary, speaks up at a town hall or county commissioners' meeting, petitions administrative agencies, or is employed in any state function. In this sense, almost every individual plays a role in the state, and each makes individual decisions as to how he or she shall play that role.

At a more functional level of analysis, the state may be seen as consisting of many different units, each having different kinds of responsibilities, each exercising different kinds of authority, and each having jurisdiction over different subpopulations of society, defined in terms of geographic, occupational, industry, or interest group constituencies. These different organizational units of the state may find themselves in conflict with each other. In addition, although each unit may be able to establish rules and incentives to encourage a common purpose among its employees and constituencies, each individual employee, constituent, or client pursues his or her own self-interest within that structure of incentives and seeks to modify that structure of incentives to make it more to his or her liking. Given this view of the structure of the state, it is important and meaningful to explore the loci of economic decision-making power, not only between the private sector and the state, but also within the state. To begin this inquiry, it is useful to consider both the functional and the jurisdictional division of powers within the state. What kinds of things may each unit of the state undertake, and over what regional jurisdiction may each unit exercise its powers?

The division of state functions
It is common to divide the state's functions into three categories: legislative, administrative, and judicial. These are the famous "three branches of government" under the "separation of powers" doctrine that is basic to the republican democracy practiced in the United States. In parliamentary democracies, it is also necessary to take care of these three fundamental activities of government. However, under that form of government, the legislative and administrative functions are more nearly merged through the devices of party responsibility and the selection of cabinet ministers (heads of administrative departments) from among legislators of the majority party or coalition. Although it is useful to talk about the state's legislative, administrative, and judicial functions, there are different undertakings within each of these broad functions, considerable interaction among the three functions, and a number of activities of the state that are not conveniently categorized in any one of these three functions. Some examples from the United States should help clarify these points.

Legislation seems to be a straightforward function: the making of laws. However, there is much interaction among units of government in the field of legislation. The constitution restricts the items and activities that may be legislated, and the judiciary interprets the constitution. With the ever-increasing economic, social, and technological complexity of society and the state itself, legislatures find it impossible to write laws with enough precision and detail to permit their direct implementation. So legislation more and more takes the form of enabling legislation. The legislature, in effect, states in fairly general terms those things it wants to see achieved with respect to a particular problem situation. It assigns to some administrative agency the duty of carrying out its wishes. The first task of the administrative agency is to draft, submit to public review and comment, and eventually promulgate detailed regulations for implementing the legislation. Thus to a significant extent, administrative agencies legislate. The regulations promulgated by administrative agencies are then subject to judicial review to determine whether they fulfill the legislative mandate without exceeding the authority granted to the agency under the legislation. The legislature may summon members of the agency's staff to appear before it in legislative hearings to explain and defend the agency's performance in implementing the legislation.

The workaday function of the judiciary is to dispose of criminal trials and civil litigation, thus enforcing the system of rights specified by the legislature. However, the judiciary gains the greatest public notice when it adjudicates disputes regarding the scope and functions of the state itself; decides the constitutionality of legislation, regulations, or administrative action, and reviews regulations and administrative actions intended to implement laws passed by legislatures.

The primary role of the administration is to implement the laws passed by the legislature, subject to judicial review. In this role, the administration is sufficiently complex. There are agencies to collect revenues, spend revenues, oversee budgetary matters, and prevent financial shenanigans within other government agencies and to apprehend the perpetrators thereof. There are agencies to encourage production, control pollution, enforce product safety and industrial safety regulations, and combat inflation. Agencies exist to encourage the exploitation of resources, conserve resources, provide services through the public sector, and encourage the vigor of the private sector. Above all, there are agencies to coordinate the relationships among agencies, adjudicate disputes between agencies, and enforce the law as it pertains to other agencies. In addition, the administration plays a significant part in legislation, by proposing legislation, by approving or vetoing (subject to possible legislative override) bills passed by the legislature, and by appointing the members of the judiciary who review legislation.

In addition, there are many state activities that do not fit easily into the legislative, administrative, or judicial categories. There are quasi-independent, but wholly government-owned, corporations such as the US Postal Service and the Tennessee Valley Authority. There are undertakings that combine private sector and government initiative, such as the synthetic fuels program. There are all kinds of boards and commissions to which citizens are appointed as members, to decide such things as what uses shall be permitted of particular tracts of land, which beauticians shall be licensed to provide services for fee, and what rates for service will be charged to the customers of electric utilities.

Jurisdiction

Over what populations do the state's various units have jurisdiction? There are some governmental units whose jurisdictions are determined by occupational or interest group categories. But the jurisdiction of governmental units is most commonly determined by geographic boundaries. The broadest subdivisions of jurisdiction are national versus local or, in those countries with federal systems of government, federal, state, or local. Because each citizen, consumer, and firm is simultaneously a constituent of a locality, a state, and a country, it is necessary to assign the functions of government systematically among the various geographically based jurisdictions.

In the United States, the states are the primary units of government, holding all those powers not specifically assigned to the federal government. The federal government, however, has been adept at expanding its effective jurisdiction in a number of ways. Various parts of the federal constitution constrain the states from undertaking certain actions, and the federal courts have from time to time interpreted the constitution to favor the rights of the federal government vis-à-vis the states. The federal right to supervise interstate trade has provided, under judicial interpretation, an excuse for the federal government to regulate, if it so chooses, just about anything that crosses state boundaries. More creatively, the federal government has learned to use its substantial financial clout to regulate indirectly many of those things it has no constitutional right to regulate directly. The federal government is, far and away, the major collector of revenues, a substantial proportion of which it returns to the states. More and more, the federal government mandates specific actions on the part of the states in order for them to qualify for federal financial assistance. In that way, the federal government effectively regulates many activities whose regulation is constitutionally the responsibility of the individual states.

In the United States, individual states exercise police power (the power to regulate), and they are expected to provide most of the services that citizens expect from their government (except for such obviously national undertakings as national defense). Local governments (that is, city and county governments) are literally creatures of state government. They are established by state government; their geographic boundaries are determined by state government; and the powers they exercise are granted to them by state government and could be revoked if the state government so choses. States typically delegate to local governments the provision of many kinds of services that are conveniently provided at the local level (such as public schools and municipal water), and many regulatory functions, such as planning and zoning, building codes, and health and safety regulations. In recent years, however, the states have been more inclined to specify the performance expected of local governments, under the threat of revoking the powers delegated to local governments.

The federal–state–local trichotomy is insufficient to categorize fully the geographic boundaries of jurisdiction of governmental units. There are many interstate and multi-state governmental units: for example, interstate river commissions and agreements. Within states, there are various regional governmental units spanning several local jurisdictions: for example, regional planning districts, soil and water conservancy districts, public utilities districts, and river basin commissions. This brief listing is enough to suggest that many of these regional (that is, multilocality) units are established at the initiative of the federal government, rather than state governments.

Economic decision-making and the law
Any system of laws defines the rights of people with respect to one another and with respect to their government. In any society with established procedures and traditions and in which citizens have definite expectations concerning the broad configuration of laws, there are some basic and durable legal constructs. These constructs form the building blocks of the system of rights. The process of institutionalizing and implementing policy is, for the most part, a process of using these constructs in ways that are more or less creative, rather than the more revolutionary process of creating and establishing whole new legal constructs.

Given that certain basic legal constructs form the building blocks of both individual rights and public policy instruments with respect to natural and environmental resources, the study of resource and environmental policy cannot proceed in a legal vacuum. In this section, a small number of basic legal constructs and concepts are introduced and explained, rather imprecisely, in lay language. The discussion proceeds in terms of the laws of the United States, but because much of American law had its origins in English tradition, and especially English common law, many of these legal concepts will be applicable, with fairly minor modifications, to other countries whose legal traditions are based on English law.

Private law concepts of property
The private law property concept that corresponds most closely to the abstract notion of ownership is fee-simple title. Property is "owned," and the owner may use it in any way they see fit, subject only to any existing deed restrictions (see below) and to the other provisions of private and public law (which may restrict the rights of the owner). Owners may dispose of their property in any way they see fit including transferring it to another person or parties through voluntary exchange, by making a gift, or by willing it to their heirs.

The rights of fee-simple titleholders may be limited by deed restrictions, which are private agreements voluntarily entered into. These may include contracts or estates in land. Contracts are personal agreements and therefore, in the case of land, do not "run with the land." The beneficiary of a contract is left without protection in the event that the grantor sells the land. Estates in land "run with the land." The beneficiary remains the dominant party, even if the grantor transfers the land to another. Deed restrictions are generally enforceable by the courts, upon complaint by a plaintiff, who must be a party to the agreement. There are some limits to the kinds of deed restrictions that will be enforced by the courts. For example, if a deed restriction has been consistently violated over time, the courts will usually refuse to enforce it. Deed restrictions that violate other, dominant provisions of private or public law are not enforceable. For example, racially discriminatory deed restrictions are not enforceable.

Easements provide an arrangement whereby the property owner sells some of the rights in that property to another party, the beneficiary, who becomes the dominant party with respect to those rights. Easements are estates in land and "run with the land" in perpetuity. An easement can be removed only if the dominant party voluntarily transfers it to the property owner. In the case of positive easements, the dominant party buys the right to do something with another's property. Examples of rights transferred as positive easements include the right to travel across another's land in order to gain access to one's own lands, the right to construct utility lines or a canal across another's land in order to provide service to one's own land; and the right of access for hunting, fishing, or recreational uses. In the case of negative easements, the dominant party buys from the owner his or her right to do something, thereby foreclosing some of the owner's options. Negative easements may foreclose an owner's right to convert land into some different use or to degrade the land's aesthetic qualities.

Private property rights are subject to, and therefore protected by, the laws of nuisance, trespass, and the like. These laws define the rights of owners inconvenienced by the actions of others. They are enforceable, under private law, in civil litigation. These laws offer property owners some protection against annoyances imposed on them by others. But this protection has been continually eroded since the onset of the industrial revolution by courts failing to enforce them in cases in which, in the judgment of the court, enforcement would preclude or impede economic progress. The laws of nuisance, trespass, and so on provide no protection for a damaged party who cannot identify the party responsible for the damage and cannot demonstrate that the damage is creating an economic loss. These laws have been notoriously inadequate in dealing with the degradation of non-exclusive resources (e.g., ambient air, or water in streams, lakes, or the ocean).

Standing to sue
The concept of standing to sue is pertinent to both private and public law. Litigation under private or public law will be dismissed by the courts if it is ruled that the plaintiff has no standing to sue. Under private law, in order to obtain standing, a plaintiff must usually establish that they have a significant economic interest in the protection sought from the courts. This economic interest is usually established through property ownership. Thus parties offended by degradation of non-exclusive resources have generally been unable to obtain standing to sue under private law. Public laws customarily specify who, and under what conditions, has standing to sue. Different public laws may define standing quite differently.

Public law
The fundamental concepts of public law that define the tools available to governments for use as instruments in implementing natural resource and environmental policy are the power of eminent domain, the police power, and the power to tax.

Eminent domain   Eminent domain is the power of the "sovereign" (originally, under English common law, the king of England) to take property legally for the public purpose. The power of eminent domain is vested in the federal and state governments, and the latter may delegate it to local governments. Governments may choose to extend the power of eminent domain to certain quasi-public and even privately owned units: for example, urban renewal commissions and investor-owned utilities.

Because condemnation involves the appropriation of property objects, just compensation must be paid. More than 150 years ago, the US Supreme Court defined just compensation as the fair market value; that is, the price that would be agreed upon by a willing buyer and a willing seller. Note that this is not Pareto-safe compensation: the power of eminent domain is invoked only when the seller is unwilling. Just compensation is usually determined in negotiations between the unit exercising the power of eminent domain and the property owner, but the courts stand ready to determine just compensation in the absence of an out-of-court compensation settlement. If an out-of-court settlement is made, an interested party may sue the governmental unit, claiming that it has exceeded its authority by paying excessive compensation, provided he or she obtains standing. For this kind of suit, standing may pose a problem. However, in many states, a taxpayer has standing.

The power of eminent domain, vested in the sovereign, is not unlimited. Condemnation must be "for the public purpose." Gradually, the courts have expanded the definition of the public purpose. For example, after much litigation, urban renewal was accepted as a public purpose.

The police power   The police power is the power of government to regulate the behavior of citizens in order to protect the public's health, welfare, safety, and morals. The police power is vested in state government, which may delegate it to local governments. In America, the federal government does not enjoy police power. However, the federal government, which customarily collects more taxes than it directly spends, returns considerable funds to state and local governments in the form of various kinds of grants, which can result in de facto police power by establishing regulations and denying funds to states that do not enact and enforce regulations consistent with federal regulations.

Because the police power is the power to regulate behavior, rather than to appropriate property objects, compensation is not required. This is clearly a legalistic, rather than an economic, distinction since regulation can reduce the value of property objects by restricting the uses that can be made of them.

The police power is not unlimited. The Fifth and Fourteenth Amendments to the US Constitution guarantee equal protection under the law and protect property against "taking without due process." If police power regulation substantially reduces the value of property objects and leaves the property owner with essentially no way to derive economic benefits from their property, the courts may declare it an unconstitutional taking of property. Almost every time a governmental unit invokes a new form of regulation under the police power, a spate of litigation involving the "takings" issue follows. Although individual cases show varied results, overall American courts have tended to favor governmental units (e.g., the "public interest") over private individuals and parties (e.g., the "private interest") in cases where government use of police power to control annoyances arising from the use of natural and environmental resources is challenged.

Police power regulation takes many forms, several of which provide tools for governments in implementing natural resource and environmental policy. These include land-use zoning, building codes, health and safety codes, subdivision controls, air and water quality regulations, and surface-mining and reclamation regulations. Police power regulations may be enforced under both criminal law and civil law. In the latter case, the solution is often an "equitable remedy;" for example, the violator is ordered to cease the offending behavior or, in the case of zoning and building regulations, to remove the offending structure. Police power regulations are often implemented by specially constituted boards and commissions, whose members are appointed by governments. These boards and commissions are responsible to some governmental unit, but often they exercise substantial discretion. For example, they may grant variances and special exceptions to the regulations.

The economics of police power regulation   Police power regulation provides a mechanism whereby citizens, exercising political power through governmental units, may seek to control the uses by owners of their property without bearing the expense of just compensation under the power of eminent domain. It is therefore not surprising that police power is a preferred tool of governments and that property owners often attempt to defend their pre-existing rights against a proposed expansion of the police power. Controversial examples in the US include government restrictions on ocean beach front land development, and government programs limiting extraction of minerals on certain classes of public lands. In both of these cases, the "taking" issue arises. Landowners may claim that beach protection programs leave them with no economically feasible use of their land.[1] When mineral rights are privately owned, mineral owners may claim that regulations restricting or forbidding mineral extraction on public lands leave them with no economically feasible use of their mineral resources.

Although it is clear that police power gives government a relatively inexpensive method of controlling the uses of privately owned property, it is equally clear that the use of police power may substantially influence the income and wealth of property owners. In some cases, economic injustice may be perceived, such as when a newly imposed regulation "wipes out" a property owner's prospects of income and wealth. In other cases, a change in a police power regulation may provide "windfall gains" for property owners. This may often be the case when land-use zoning regulations are changed in the face of growing demand for land in more intensive uses to permit a previously prohibited commercial use of land. Thus, planning and zoning commissions, for example, have substantial powers to confer economic benefits ("givings") and losses ("takings") upon individuals. The public must be constantly alert to arbitrary and capricious uses of land-use authority and to attempts by prospective beneficiaries to offer inducements that are illegal or of dubious morality to authorities in order to change land-use regulations in ways that would confer windfall gains to the beneficiary.

The power to tax
The power to tax is the power to raise revenues for the purposes of government. Although it is clear that taxation gives government a tool to influence the economic incentives facing individuals and thus implement allocative and distributional policy, the primary constitutional purpose of taxation is to raise revenues rather than to provide a

policy tool. The power to tax is vested in federal and state governments, and the latter may delegate that power to local governments. New taxes may be introduced, and the rates of taxation may be increased without compensation.

The power to tax is not unlimited. The Fifth and Fourteenth Amendments to the US Constitution guarantee equal protection under the law. Thus people must be treated equally under taxation law unless there is a basis for classification, in which cases with similar circumstances must be treated alike. The equal-protection clauses may limit the power of governments to use taxation as a policy tool. In addition, constitutional prohibitions on interference with interstate trade limit the use of taxation by a state as a policy tool (for example, taxes which give the citizens of one state some protection against annoyances created in another state).

Rates of taxation must be determined by legislative bodies. It is unlawful for a legislature to permit administrative discretion in the establishment of tax rates. Therefore, a legislature cannot, for example, establish a system of effluent taxes, leaving the precise definition of effluent tax schedules to an administrative agency. It has been speculated that this may in part explain the obvious American preference for the use of the police power, rather than the power to tax, as a policy tool to control external diseconomies. A legislature may pass enabling legislation for police power regulation, assigning to an administrative agency the task of specifying and adopting precise regulations. But a legislature may not use the power to tax in an analogous fashion. Because the constraints on the labor force and expertise that face legislative bodies are much more severe than those facing administrative bodies, it is understandable that legislatures seem to prefer the regulatory route, whereby programs enabled by legislatures may be "fleshed out" by administrative agencies.

The economics of taxation   It is clear to anyone with a rudimentary understanding of microeconomic theory that the power to tax involves the power to modify prices, thus reallocating resources and redistributing income and wealth. A whole subdiscipline of economics, public finance, has been developed to analyze the economics of taxation. In natural resource and environmental economics, many theoretical analyses have been devised demonstrating that for some particular resource or environmental problem, the modification of incentives via taxation is more effective, or less likely to result in inefficiency, than is regulation (see Chapter 16). But constitutional restrictions on the power to tax, which include the equal-protection clauses and the provisions that prohibit legislatures from assigning to administrative agencies the task of determining taxation rates, make taxation a rather blunt policy tool.

Summary and perspective
Our discussion in this chapter is intended to flesh out a little the previous and somewhat abstract concept of institutions. In addition, it is intended to make, directly or by way of illustration, the following major points. Government activities and undertakings have a pervasive influence on private activity in the "minimal state" as well as under the kinds of governments found in modern mixed economies. Furthermore, there is no clear and absolute distinction between government and the economy. Government activity influences economic interaction. More fundamentally, each individual is simultaneously an individual, a member of some kind of economic unit, and a constituent of many govern-

mental units. Each has endowments that are useful in the market and endowments that are useful in the political-legal arena, and he or she uses both kinds of endowments to further his or her own interests. Thus, individuals seek to use government, just as they seek to use the market, to further their own objectives.

Government is also not a monolith. It is divided into many different units, along both functional and jurisdictional lines, and the interactions among these units are complex. It is unreasonable to expect that government will always act consistently and cohesively, as if with a single will. Government, though it exists to resolve conflicts, is itself an arena of conflict. Different units of government exist for different purposes, are authorized to use different mechanisms in order to achieve their objectives, and receive support from different segments of the citizenry and the private sector. Individual economic actors and the markets resulting from their interaction are influenced substantially by the incentives that emerge from "government" (the political-legal arena), and it is the outcome of the conflict between individuals and government units, and among government units themselves, that determines those incentives.

Conflicts over natural resource and environmental issues do not emerge and are not resolved in a legal vacuum. It is therefore important for the serious student of natural resource and environmental economics to understand the basics of the law and legal system. In this chapter we have provided some of the more important basic legal concepts that natural resource and environmental economists may encounter in their professional and personal lives. Along with the growth of the natural resource and environmental economics profession over the past several decades, the field of environmental law has also expanded. Thus, natural resource and environmental economists may find themselves rubbing shoulders with environmental lawyers (and ecologists, and others) in the pursuit of natural resource and environmental conflict resolution.

Questions for discussion

1. *Webster's Dictionary* defines anarchy as: "a Utopian society having no government and made up of individuals who enjoy complete freedom." Compare and contrast anarchy with "the minimal state:" Is anarchy feasible? If so, would that contradict the idea of "the minimal state?"
2. "Rules simultaneously restrict the individual and liberate him." What does this statement mean? Does it offer an important insight, or is it merely internally contradictory?
3. Some have argued that in democracies, the public sector always tends to grow relative to the private sector. Using the concepts presented in this chapter, construct an argument that would reach this conclusion. Then evaluate your argument.
4. In the United States, some have complained about "the increasing tendency of the judiciary and the bureaucracy to legislate." Assuming that this tendency exists, is it desirable? Is it inevitable?
5. Some writers have conceptualized the rights pertaining to, say, land as "a bundle of sticks." By this, they mean that the rights are not monolithic but, instead, consist of many different kinds of rights that may be severed and assigned separately or in various combinations. Does this analogy make sense? Support your conclusion with examples.
6. "Just compensation under eminent domain is not Pareto-safe compensation." Carefully develop this argument.
7. Under eminent domain, just compensation prevents a total loss of economic value. However, such "wipeouts" may result from police power regulations or changes in taxation policy. Does this give economists any reason to conclude, along with Dickens,[2] that "the law is an ass, an idiot?" Explain.
8. It has been observed that the rationale for effluent taxes was developed largely in the United States; yet they have been implemented more often in Western Europe than in this country. How could this be? Might the US constitution's restrictions on taxation be a contributing factor?

Notes

1. For further discussion of these cases, see Marie K. Truesdell, John C. Bergstrom, and Jeffrey H. Dorfman (2006), "Regulatory Takings and the Diminution of Value: An Empirical Analysis of Takings and Givings," *Journal of Agricultural and Applied Economics* **38** (3): 585–95.
2. Charles Dickens, *Oliver Twist*, Chapter 10.

Suggested reading: classic and contemporary

Aghion, P. and P. Bolton (2003), "Incomplete Social Contracts," *Journal of the European Economic Association* **1** (1): 38–67.

Brennan, G. and J.M. Buchanan (1980), *The Power to Tax: Analytical Foundations of a Federal Constitution*, Cambridge, UK: Cambridge University Press.

Breton, A. and A. Scott (1978), *The Economic Constitution of Federal States*, Toronto: University of Toronto Press.

Buchanan, J.M. and G. Tullock (1962), *The Calculus of Consent*, Ann Arbor, MI: University of Michigan Press.

Commons, J.R. (1936), "Institutional Economics," *American Economic Review* **26** (1): 237–49.

Janda, K., J.M. Berry, and J. Goldman (2008), *The Challenge of Democracy: Government in America*, 9th edn, Boston, MA: Houghton Mifflin.

Miceli, T.J. and K. Segerson (1994), "Regulatory Takings: When Should Compensation Be Paid?," *Journal of Legal Studies* **23**: 749–76.

Michelman, F.L. (1967), "Property, Utility, and Fairness: Comments on the Ethical Foundation of 'Just Compensation' Law," *Harvard Law Review* **80**: 1165–258.

Pogodzinski, J.M. and T.R. Sass (1990), "The Economic Theory of Zoning: A Critical Review," *Land Economics* **66** (3): 294–314.

Reich, C.A. (1963), "The New Property," *Yale Law Journal* **73**: 733–87.

Runge, C.F., M.T. Duclos, J.S. Adams, B. Goodwin, J.A. Martin, R.D. Squires, and A.E. Ingerson (2000), "Public Sector Contributions to Private Land Value," in *Property and Values: Alternatives to Public and Private Ownership*, ed. C. Geisler and G. Daneker, Washington, DC and Covelo, CA: Island Press.

Williamson, O.E. (2000), "The New Institutional Economics: Taking Stock, Looking Ahead," *Journal of Economic Literature* **38** (3): 595–613.

Wunderlich, G.L. and W.L. Gibson, Jr (1972), *Perspectives of Property*, University Park, PA: Pennsylvania State University Press.

PART IV

MEASURING AND COMPARING BENEFITS AND COSTS OF NATURAL RESOURCE AND ENVIRONMENTAL POLICY AND PROJECTS

12 Benefit–cost analysis: how do we determine if the benefits of a resource policy outweigh the costs?

For federal water projects in which public funds are invested to provide a stream of public and private benefits, the United States has required formal economic evaluation since passage of the Federal Water Resources Planning Act of 1965.[1] This evaluation is to take the form of benefit–cost analysis (BCA) and is to be performed in accordance with a set of guidelines that have been refined over the years. The resulting analysis and its supporting plans, specifications, and data are congressional documents. As a precondition for project authorization, benefit–cost calculations must be performed and displayed and must demonstrate that the projected benefits from implementation of the proposed project exceed the projected costs. Clearly, the purpose of these requirements is to provide a filter that would systematically eliminate, prior to consideration in the political domain, those projects deleterious to national economic development.

Although BCA is always an evaluative tool, there is no inherent reason that it should be used as a filter. On the one hand, it could be more than a mere filter. A large and often sophisticated literature explores, develops, and sometimes promotes the use of BCA in ranking projects and determining optimal project size. The goal is the optimal package of optimally sized projects, all from the perspective of economic efficiency. To our knowledge, no political jurisdiction has ever mandated that public works programs or regulatory policy packages be assembled in strict obedience to that criterion. However, many agencies use BCA as a more or less strict ranking device for internal planning.

On the other hand, BCA can be used as less than a filter. In the last several decades, there has been a growing public recognition that many different kinds of governmental projects and programs dealing with natural and environmental resources involve some public or private economic sacrifice in order to obtain some public or private benefits. In other words, the decisions concerning a broad array of resource and environmental management programs have been recognized as economic decisions. This public awareness has extended to the Congress and to the administrative agencies, which now require economic analyses along benefit–cost lines as a routine part of the planning process for an array of natural resource and environmental policy decisions. In these applications, benefit–cost analysis takes its place as one of a considerable number and variety of planning and evaluative tools. There are no requirements that the benefits of a project or program must be found to exceed the costs as a precondition for its implementation.

In other cases, BCAs may be performed by researchers in academic organizations, research foundations, or "public interest" lobbies. The findings of these efforts, though having no "official" status, may be influential if they are disseminated so as to attract attention in professional or political circles or the news media. Their influence, however, is always as one of many different information inputs into a diffuse public decision-making process. Though failure to make a positive contribution to national economic development does not boost a proposal's chances, neither is it (nor should it be, according to this role model) the death knell for a proposal that serves other worthwhile goals.

Regardless of whether BCA is used as a filter, a ranking device, or a contribution to an informal and multidimensional information system, it carries some imperative or suggestive force. So the parties with a stake in the success or failure of a proposal are interested in the outcome of its BCA. These quality control problems can be resolved if: (1) there are clearly specified principles for empirical BCA based on sound economic theory; and (2) BCA documents are routinely opened to public scrutiny, so that the criticism can expose any deviations from proper theory and practice. There is little that the authors of a book such as this can do about the second of these conditions, beyond endorsing it wholeheartedly. It is possible, however, to attend to the first, by explaining the guidelines for BCA according to basic economic principles.

The theory of BCA: a test for potential Pareto-improvements

A major conceptual principle is that BCA is a test for potential Pareto-improvements (PPI). All else follows logically from this principle. A potential Pareto-improvement (PPI) (see Chapter 8) is a change that could make, after compensation, at least one person better off and no one worse off. In other words, if there were sufficient gains to compensate all losers to the extent of their self-evaluated losses and still have some gains remaining, the change would be judged a PPI. Clearly, the PPI criterion is identical to the maximum value of social product criterion (see Chapter 8). If the sum of gains exceeds the sum of losses, the change is a PPI and will pass the Maximum Value of Social Product (MVSP) test for improvements.

Several maintained assumptions follow from the principle of BCA as an empirical test for PPIs. At the individual level, the beneficial and adverse effects of an undertaking (that is, gains and losses) are evaluated according to the principle of consumer sovereignty. What the individual wants is, *ipso facto*, regarded as good for the individual. Individual valuations, as we already know, are determined by individual preferences and endowments, including the individual's rights. For valuation, the PPI presupposes a particular set of rights: the individual has a right to the status quo and can veto any undesired change thereof; thus valuation occurs under a Pareto-safety rule.

The collective decision, however, is not Pareto-safe. Rather, the criterion sums individual gains and losses "to whomsoever they accrue." This aggregation rule, as was made clear in Chapter 8, is a special kind of social welfare function. It is indifferent regarding distribution, treating dollar gains (losses) as equally valuable (undesirable), regardless of the circumstances of the individual concerned. Efficiency is a necessary condition for an optimum, according to both the maximum value of social product criterion and Pareto-safety. Because the PPI values individual gains and losses as though Pareto-safety were in effect, an improvement according to the PPI is (at least potentially) an efficiency improvement.

For these reasons, BCA is often called a test for efficiency, and with some justification. In the real world, however, inefficiency is the norm, and the reasonable objective for public projects and policies is to make improvements rather than to attain an optimum. Thus, there are two caveats that should be kept in mind. First, if compensation is not systematically paid (as it usually is not), there is no assurance that a PPI will improve efficiency. Second, in a world of pervasive inefficiency, the theory of second best (see Chapter 6) is likely to be relevant to valuation and pricing in BCA. Prices that seem efficient in partial equilibrium analyses may not necessarily offer incentives that would optimize a pervasively inefficient system.

The typical program or project: non-marginal changes in a complex environment

The first law of thermodynamics applies to programs and projects, too, as they cannot create something from nothing. Rather, at some expense, they transform an existing environment into a modified environment. It is helpful to think through this process.

Recalling the discussion of natural capital (N) and ecosystem goods and services (E) in Chapter 2, consider a vector of ecosystem goods and services $\underline{E} = (E_1, \ldots, E_k, \ldots, E_m)$ valued by people, generated from the complex physical supply of natural capital in a region. The ecosystem goods and services are likely to be diverse: for example, water, timber, and wildlife; aesthetic services, including atmospheric visibility; landscape amenities; recreation opportunities; waste disposal and treatment services; storm protection and flood control. Many of these goods and services are likely to be non-marketed. The supply of each of these services in any time period, t, is a function of the attributes, $\underline{A} = (a_1, \ldots, a_r, \ldots, a_s)$ of the natural capital which are uniquely determined by geological, hydrological, atmospheric, and ecological relationships:

$$E_{1t} = f_1(\underline{A}_t)$$
$$\vdots \qquad \vdots \tag{12.1}$$
$$E_{mt} = f_m(\underline{A}_t)$$

People enter the system as modifiers of natural capital. They may do this directly, for example by reassigning land to other uses, diverting water, removing vegetation, or disturbing soil for mining. They may also modify the natural capital as a side-effect (expected or unexpected) of some other decision, for example disturbing land elsewhere for cultivation or mining or deposition of wastes in water upstream. For each kind of natural capital attribute:

$$a_{1t} = g_1(\underline{F}_t, \underline{X}_t)$$
$$\vdots \qquad \vdots \tag{12.2}$$
$$a_{st} = g_s(\underline{F}_t, \underline{X}_t)$$

where $\underline{F}$ is a vector of ecosystem structure and functions, for example, chemicals and chemical cycles and geological, hydrological, atmospheric, and ecological processes, and $\underline{X}$ is a vector of human-controlled inputs and activities, including harvesting effort.

Both $\underline{F}$ and $\underline{X}$ are subject to scarcity, and the attribute production functions are determined by the laws that govern natural systems and by technology. The production system for ecosystem goods and services is now complete remembering that the level of demand for some kinds of goods and services, E_k, influences the level of $\underline{X}$ and interactions between $\underline{X}$ and $\underline{F}$ are possible and likely. For example, the attempt to enjoy high levels of waste assimilation services involves high levels of pollution inputs, which may modify certain chemical cycles which are part of $\underline{F}$, in a particular ecosystem.

Now consider the value of ecosystem goods and services (presented in a slightly different, but analogous form in Chapter 2). Each individual, j, enjoys utility in each time period, t:

$$U_{jt} = U_{jt}[\underline{E}_{jt}^a, \underline{Z}_{jt}^b(\underline{E}_{jt}^b), \underline{Z}_{jt}^a] \tag{12.3}$$

where Z is a vector of valued goods and services not directly generated from natural capital, N. For example, Z includes things bought at the local shopping center. The ecosystem good and service vector E is composed of E^a, which are enjoyed directly, and E^b which are inputs into the production of Z^b. Finally, Z^a are those Z that are produced independently of E. This formulation permits both direct and derived demand for ecosystem goods and services.

Individual valuation of the vector of ecosystem goods and services, $V_{jt}(E_{jt})$, according to the PPI criterion is discussed in detail later in this chapter. For now, let us just say that PPI-consistent individual demand curves for E_{jt} can be found by minimizing expenditures subject to the constraint that utility be maintained at the initial level. From these demand curves, $V_{jt}(E_{jt})$ can be calculated.

The capital value of natural capital N is obtained by summing the net values of goods and service flows, discounted at the rate r across time periods and individuals:

$$PV(N) = \sum_t \sum_j V_{jt}(E_{jt})/(1 + r)^t \qquad (12.4)$$

Thus, natural capital acquires economic value to the extent that the goods and services it provides are valued by people. Those good and services are determined by natural capital attributes (e.g., quantity and quality of surface and groundwater in an area or region), which are themselves determined ecosystem structure and functions (e.g., chemical cycles) and by the activities of people. If ecosystem structure and functions were to be disturbed, say by changes in the X vector of human-controlled inputs, natural capital attributes could change, changing the E vector of the goods and services it provides and its capital value.

Consider a project Δ, which would change X to X^Δ, thus converting natural capital, N, to some "with project" state, N^Δ, at some conversion cost, $C^\Delta = \Sigma_t C_t^\Delta/(1 + r)^t$. The proposed project would replace the "without project" stream of services, E, with some "with project" stream, E^Δ. The net present value of such a project is:

$$PV(\Delta) = PV[(N^\Delta - C^\Delta) - N] = \frac{\Sigma_t[V_t(E_t^\Delta) - C_t^\Delta - V_t(E_t)]}{(1 + r)^t} \qquad (12.5)$$

where $V_t(E_t^\Delta) = \Sigma_j V_{jt}(E_{jt}^\Delta)$ and $V(E_t) = \Sigma_j V_{jt}(E_{jt}^\Delta)$. If $PV(\Delta)$ is greater than zero, the project will be a potential Pareto-improvement and will therefore pass the benefit–cost filter.

Perhaps it would be helpful to summarize the message of this section into six succinct statements:

1. An existing environment can be viewed as a natural capital asset, producing services that people value.
2. A proposed project or program is a proposal to modify that environment at some cost, changing the services it produces.
3. BCA compares (a) the value of the "with project" environment, minus the costs of transforming the environment into that state, with (b) being the value of the "without project" environment. If (a) exceeds (b), the project will be judged a PPI and pass the filter.

4. For BCA, value information about the environments, N and N^Δ, and the goods and services, E and E^Δ, is equally useful, because the asset-pricing model (see Chapter 7 and equation 12.5) specifies the relationship between asset values and the value of service flows.
5. Valuation according to the PPI principle will result in the proposal's passing the filter if, and only if, those who prefer E^Δ are willing to pay enough to buy it (or, equivalently, its time stream of services) from those who prefer E. The actual purchase, and the Pareto-safe compensation for losers that it implies, is not required.
6. The complex relationships among ecosystem structure and functions, human-controlled inputs, natural capital attributes, and the ecosystem goods and services provided (see equations 12.1 and 12.2) must be understood and quantified if the results of BCA are to be complete and reliable.

If valuation proceeds via the goods and services route (see point 4), the BCA practitioner must rely on specialists in many other scientific disciplines to elaborate and quantify the relationships in equations 12.1 and 12.2.

If the asset-pricing route is taken directly (and that assumes non-attenuated property rights to environmental assets), the asset markets will reflect the true value of environments only insofar as the market participants comprehend the relationships summarized in equations 12.1 and 12.2. But when dealing with complex environments, this is an unreasonable assumption. We are continually learning about newly discovered but important environmental relationships.

BCA valuation concepts
As the asset-pricing model (e.g., see equation 12.5) makes clear, the value of a project depends on two things: the net value of services it produces in each time period, and the rate at which future benefits and costs are discounted. For valuing services, the principles of efficient valuation (or, in the simplest cases, pricing) are relevant. The discount rate is itself a price (see Chapter 7): the price paid to use funds before they would otherwise be available, or received for delaying the use of funds. The same principles of efficiency that apply to valuation of benefit and cost items also pertain to selecting the appropriate discount rate.

The discount rate
The principles of efficiency do not distinguish between public and private enterprise. Thus the discount rate is determined according to the principle that the value of capital formed by public investment should just equal, at the margin, the value of private capital and consumption sacrificed. Efficiency in both the private and public sectors would equate the discount rate with the market rate of interest, the marginal efficiency of investment, and the marginal rate of time preference. In practice, however, the discount rate applied to public investments may diverge from the market rate of interest, usually on the low side. Some argue that this divergence is inefficient and occurs only because the government can raise at least a portion of its capital coercively (e.g., by taxation or through control of the money supply) which shields it from market realities. Thus, it is argued, the government may choose on the basis of artificially low discount rates reducing the wealth of society. Others make a different argument. Markets are best adapted

to investments with relatively short life expectancies (anything from overnight to, say, 30 years). This results, it is claimed, in market rates of interest that are higher and so discount the future more than is appropriate for a farsighted government. The debate about the discount rate has important consequences for the results of BCA. Higher discount rates, *ceteris paribus*, will result in fewer proposals passing a BCA filter and higher rankings for proposals that would generate substantial benefits in early years, whereas the major costs would come later.

For public investments that are comparable to the general run of private investments – that is, projects that are small relative to the size of the economy and have time horizons numbered in years rather than centuries – there seems little justification to use discount rates lower than the efficient market rate. Diverting funds from the private sector to the public sector to achieve a rate of return lower than the real *r*, is clearly an inefficient undertaking and, in any competent evaluation, must be identified as such. There may be good reasons to undertake an inefficient public sector investment, but the inefficiency of such an investment should be recognized. It serves no useful purpose to bias the efficiency evaluation of such a project, through manipulation of the social discount rate to make the inefficient appear efficient.

To conclude that for typical public investments the social discount rate should be set equal to:

$$MEI = RTP = r \qquad (12.6)$$

does not resolve the empirical problem. At any time there is not one, but many observable market interest rates, and to add to the confusion, these rates fluctuate over time.

The observed interest rate reflects four different economic parameters: (1) *r*; (2) transaction costs in the financial sector, which result in the borrowers paying higher rates than the savers receive; (3) anticipated inflation; and (4) the lender's risk, which reflects the possibility that for various reasons the borrower might not repay the principle and the accrued interest. It is no simple task to infer the true value of *r* from the observed interest rates. Nevertheless, we shall now attempt to resolve some of the relevant issues.

Public investments are not risk free, and the public sector is not exempt from transactions costs. In these respects, public investments are much like the loans made by large banks to favored corporations. The risk premium and transactions costs inherent in the bank's prime interest rate is appropriate to public investments.

In principle, money interest rates (*m*) are adjusted for anticipated inflation (*a*), so that $m = r + a$. However, anticipated inflation can be forecast only imperfectly (recently experienced inflation offers clues, but no more), and in times of uncertainty about future inflation, *m* tends to be adjusted upward to reflect both the expected *a* and the uncertainty attached to *a* and thus to *m* in future periods. Because it is *m* (not *r*) that is observable, the task is to infer *r* from observations of *m*. Historically, estimated real interest rates (money interest rates minus current, not anticipated, inflation rates) have fluctuated widely.

Interest rates cannot be equal for savers and borrowers in a world in which transaction costs are positive. The monetary interest rate for savers, m^s, must be less than that for borrowers, m^b, by an amount equal to transactions costs, *t*: that is, $m^b = m^s - t$. The distortionary influence of personal and corporate taxes is considerable: a saver is rewarded with m^s minus taxes; a borrower needs to earn at least m^b to make it worthwhile to invest borrowed funds; and a corporation will need to obtain a return better than m^s plus corporate taxes on stockholders' capital if it is to compete for savings and thus attract stockholders. These various complications take a good deal of unraveling, and any answer, it seems, will attract debate.

The use of a real discount rate, as opposed to m, corrects for inflation. Consistency requires that all other prices used in BCA should likewise be corrected for inflation. Beneficial and adverse effects throughout the (multiyear) planning period should be valued in constant dollars at the prices prevailing when the BCA is performed.

All of the above is based on investment theory and therefore assumes that public undertakings are generically similar to private investments generating ordinary income and typically reaching maturity in one generation or less. Events that will occur several generations hence will have only a slight influence on present values, even at relatively low (positive) discount rates. Yet it is not satisfying to conclude that a drastic ecological disturbance several generations from now should have only minor influence on decisions made today. Economists have reached something approaching consensus that discount rates applied to these kinds of very long-run concerns should be as low as possible, and in any event no higher than the rate of growth of the overall economy (see Chapter 19).

Valuing beneficial and adverse effects
Where the proposed undertaking will use only small quantities of inputs and provide only small quantities of outputs relative to the total quantities of inputs and outputs in their respective markets, the appropriate measure of value is the quantity change multiplied by the efficient unit price. Efficient marginal prices are defined as those that satisfy the marginal conditions for Pareto-efficiency (see Chapter 6). When quantity changes are only marginal and observed prices may reasonably be assumed to be efficient, valuation provides few problems for BCA. But the BCA practitioner will often encounter situations in which quantity changes are non-marginal and efficient prices (or any prices at all) are unobservable.

Next we present a general framework for the valuation of changes in the level of provision of goods, services, and amenities that is applicable to marginal and non-marginal quantity changes and to the valuation of priced and unpriced goods. Consistent with our earlier observation that projects and programs typically introduce non-marginal changes in resource use and the product mix, we move quickly from the valuation of marginal changes to economic surplus and the valuation of non-marginal changes. Then, consistent with the principle that BCA is a test for PPIs, we derive the Hicksian compensating measures of economic surplus. Finally, we derive a general framework for valuation that is consistent with the Hicksian compensating measures of economic surplus but also yields the marginal result: value equals unit efficient price multiplied by the quantity change as a special case.

First, consider the value of the output of a single small firm in a competitive industry. The unit price of output is determined by the intersection of the demand and supply curves for the industry's output, D_I and S_I, respectively. The demand curve for the output of a single firm, D_i, is then a horizontal line intersecting the price axis at the equilibrium price, P, for the industry's output. The output of the individual firm, Q_i, is

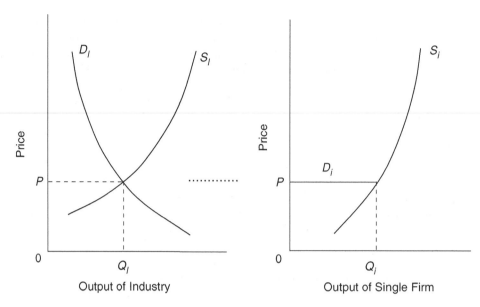

Figure 12.1 Industry demand, supply, price, and quantity; and the price and quantity of output for a competitive firm

determined by the intersection of $P = D_i$ and the firm's supply curve, S_i. The total value, V, of the firm's output is given by:

$$V \equiv TR = P \cdot Q_i \qquad (12.7)$$

That is, the value of the firm's output is equal to the firm's total revenue (TR), which is equal to the quantity of output multiplied by the competitive unit price of that output (Figure 12.1).

Now consider a large-scale project that permits a non-marginal increase in industry supply, from S_I to S'_I, by increasing the availability of some factor of production (for example, irrigation water). The total revenue, TR, from this incremental output is equal to $Q'_I - Q_I$ multiplied by P', the new lower equilibrium price of the industry's output; that is:

$$TR = P'(Q'_I - Q_I) \qquad (12.8)$$

The consumers benefit from the project in two ways: they enjoy an increase in total output from Q_I to Q'_I and a decrease in the unit price from P to P'. The producers gain in one way (by expanding output) but lose in another (by receiving a lower price per unit).

Marshallian economic surplus   The consumers' gain is approximated by the area $PABP'$ (Figure 12.2). This is the increase in the Marshallian *consumers' surplus*. It is composed of two parts: $PACP'$, which represents the value of the price reduction for the initial quantity Q_I; and ABC, which is the area above the new price line, below the demand

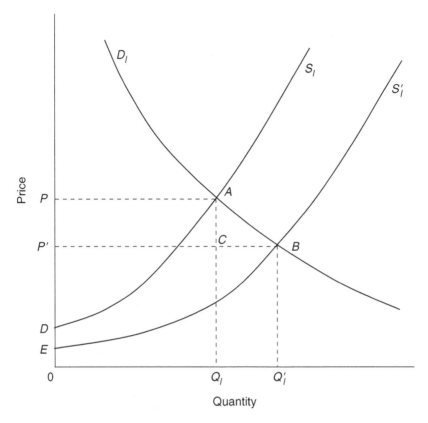

Figure 12.2 *Non-marginal shift in supply as a result of implementing a proposed project: price and quantity effects and the change in economics surplus*

curve, and between the old and new quantities. ABC approximates the value to consumers of the quantity increment in excess of its price.

The area below a supply curve approximates the total costs of producing the goods. Therefore, the area above the supply curve but below the price line approximates the producers' surplus; that is, the return to fixed resources or economic rent. When the quantity was Q_I', the producers' surplus was PAD. With the output expanded to Q_I, the producers' surplus becomes $P'BE$. The *change in economic surplus* resulting from the output increase is approximated by the algebraic sum of gains and losses to consumers and producers, that is, by $PABP' - PAD + P'BE$. The net change in economic surplus is thus approximately $DABE$.

Now consider a project that increases the availability of some unpriced good from Q_I to Q_I'. To determine the benefits to the consumers of that project, we conceptualize it as one that shifts the (perfectly inelastic) supply curve from S_I to S_I' (Figure 12.3). The benefits (that is, the increase in the consumers' surplus) are approximated by Q_IABQ_I', the area below the demand curve and bounded by the "with project" and "without project" quantities.

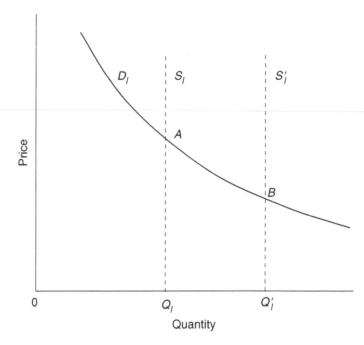

Figure 12.3   A non-marginal increase in supply: the change in Marshallian surplus

Hicksian economic surplus   In our discussion of economic surplus, the verb "to approximate" was used often enough to raise suspicions among the observant. Now we must address the issue of exact economic surplus. Because consumers' surplus and producers' surplus are analytically similar concepts,[2] we will work with consumers' surplus. (The same ideas can be applied to producers' surplus.) The theoretically correct version of consumers' surplus is not the Marshallian version but the Hicksian version. Hicksian consumers' surplus theory recognizes two concepts of consumers' surplus: a compensating version and an equivalent version. The compensating version defines the value of a change in output as the amount of compensation, paid or received, that would return consumers to their initial welfare position after the change. The equivalent version defines the value of a change in output as the amount of compensation, paid or received, that would bring consumers to their subsequent welfare position if the change did not occur.

The relationships between the alternative Hicksian measures of consumers' surplus and the Marshallian measure are shown in Figure 12.4. The ordinary, or Marshallian, demand curve, D_I, is reproduced from Figure 12.3, and again, Marshallian consumers' surplus is $Q_I A B Q_I'$. In addition, there are two Hicksian income-compensated demand curves, D_I^H and D_I^H.

Income-compensated demand curves show the quantities taken at various prices if income were adjusted at each price so as to maintain a constant level of utility. Compare them with ordinary demand curves. First, they are generally steeper, because at lower prices some income is removed so the consumer does not enjoy a welfare gain from the lower price. With no welfare gain, he or she will not purchase as much as would a con-

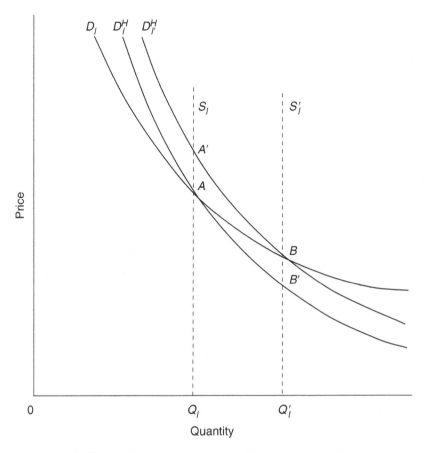

Figure 12.4   Marshallian and Hicksian concepts of consumer's surplus

sumer whose income were not continually adjusted to eliminate utility changes. Second, there are two of them. Why? If there is to be income compensation, some specific utility level must be maintained. One could compensate to the initial utility level, generating the demand curve D_I^H passing through point A. The compensating measure of consumer's surplus is thus $Q_I A B' Q_I'$. Alternatively, one could compensate to the subsequent utility level, generating demand curve $D_{I'}^H$ passing through point B. The equivalent measure of consumers' surplus is $Q_I A' B Q_I'$.

Note that for an increment in a valued commodity, the compensating measure is smaller than the equivalent measure. If we were evaluating a decrement in a valued commodity, so that Q_I' (Figure 12.4) were the initial state, the measures would be reversed, and the compensating measure of welfare loss would be larger (in absolute value) than the equivalent measure.

For many goods, services, and amenities commanding a modest fraction of a consumer's budget, the differences between compensating and equivalent measures are trivial, and the Marshallian measure is an acceptable approximation of the Hicksian measure.[3] However, for commodities that are vitally important (an extreme example is

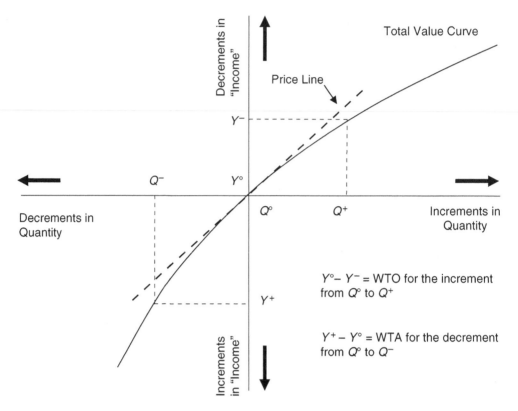

Figure 12.5   The total value curve for an individual consumer

the avoidance of one's own untimely death), the compensating and equivalent measures diverge substantially.

Note that the compensating measures of value are the amount that the consumer is willing to pay (WTP) for an increment and willing to accept as compensation (WTA) for a decrement. These are logically equivalent in a market situation to the buyer's best offer and the seller's reservation price. These, of course, are Pareto-safe prices. Therefore, the PPI criterion requires that beneficial and adverse effects be valued by the Hicksian compensating measures of economic surplus.

A general model for valuing increments and decrements in output[4]
The total value curve (Figure 12.5) is consistent with the Hicksian compensating measures of value. In a four-quadrant diagram, the origin is placed at the consumer's initial position (which is consistent with the definition of the Hicksian compensating measure of value, which uses the consumer's initial welfare level as the reference). As one moves to the right of the origin, the quantity of output, Q, provided increases; as one moves to the left of the origin, the quantity provided decreases. As one moves up from the origin, the consumer's "income," Y (or more precisely the value of all other goods and services he or she enjoys), decreases; as one moves down from the origin, this "income" increases. The total value curve is continuous on both sides of the origin. On the right side, it lies in the northeast quadrant,

indicating that the consumer is willing to pay positive amounts of money (that is, to permit his or her "income" to decrease) in order to obtain increments in quantity. To the left of the origin, the total value curve lies in the southwest quadrant, indicating that the consumer is willing to accept positive amounts of money (that is, to enjoy an increment in "income") concurrently with a decrease in quantity. The total value curve is, therefore, an indifference curve between "income" and the quantities of a particular good, service, or amenity, passing through the origin of a diagram in which the horizontal axis represents quantity in increasing amounts and the vertical axis represents "income" in decreasing amounts.

Given an empirical estimate of the total value curve, the total value to an individual of increments or decrements (which may be non-marginal) in the quantity provided of a good, service, or amenity (which may be unpriced) can be estimated in a form consistent with the potential Pareto-improvement criterion. For any proposed change in output, individual total values may be aggregated across the relevant population. The total value curve provides a general framework for the valuation of increments and decrements in the quantities of goods, services, or amenities that would be provided as a result of a project's implementation. There remains, however, a special case that is of interest. Consider a very small change in the quantity of a good provided in a very large competitive market. For such a good, the price line may be presented as a straight line. Because for such a good the consumer will be in equilibrium at the outset, the price line will be tangent to the total value curve (an indifference curve, remember) at the origin (Figure 12.5).

In a particular case, the valuation of increments and decrements in output attributable to the implementation of a proposed project may be performed with reference to the price line rather than to the total value curve. This special case occurs when the proposed project would result in small changes in quantity relative to the total quantities exchanged in competitive markets with very low transaction costs. For a real-world example, the price line will provide a serviceable basis for the valuation of the increment in the output of grain that would result from the implementation of a project affecting a small local region. Grain markets are organized on a worldwide scale, and transaction costs in those markets are relatively small per unit of grain exchanged. Thus, $P(Q'_I - Q_I)$ is an indicator of the value of increments or decrements in grain resulting from the implementation of such a project.

BCA in practice

Empirical BCA is almost always performed as a case study: the BCA of a particular proposal or a group of alternative proposals for dealing with the same problem or opportunity. Each case is different, and almost any case will test the ingenuity of the analyst. Practical BCA is part economics, part accounting, and part good old-fashioned detective work. The evidence is seldom all available in a state readily adaptable to BCA, and often some crucial pieces of information are best known to the parties that have a direct interest in the outcome of the analysis. Nevertheless, the relatively few and straightforward theoretical principles developed in the first part of the chapter can be distilled into guidelines for handling most every practical problem arising in BCA. The exception, of course, is the lack of essential data. We now address these practical issues.

The choice of a criterion

There is a venerable tradition among textbook writers[5] of making a big deal about the choice of a benefit–cost criterion. Should it be net present value (NPV), the benefit–cost ratio (BCR), or the internal rate of return (IRR)? Our answer is that there's not much to choose between them. But first, let us examine each of the proposed criteria.

Net present value   A project's NPV is defined as:

$$\text{NPV}(\Delta) = \sum_{t=0}^{T} \frac{B_t - C_t}{(1 + r)^t} \qquad (12.9)$$

where $B_t = $ the benefits accruing in year t, $C_t = $ the costs accruing in year t, and $T = $ the last year in which the project influences the productivity of its environment.

For a filter, the criterion is that any project with NPV > 0 is acceptable. For any given constraint on capital available in year zero, the optimal package of projects is the one with the maximum NPV > 0. If one desires to rank projects in order of priority when capital is limited, NPV cannot be used in any way that is both simple and correct. Ranking projects according to the magnitude of NPV would be misleading, as NPV provides no direct information about the capital requirements of projects. If project A has slightly larger NPV but much larger initial capital requirements than does project B, it is by no means certain that A should have higher priority than should B in a capital-constrained decision environment.

Benefit–cost ratio   The simplest BC ratio (BCR) is:

$$\text{BCR} = \frac{\displaystyle\sum_{t=0}^{T} B_t/(1 + r)^t}{\displaystyle\sum_{t=0}^{T} C_t/(1 + r)^t} \qquad (12.10).$$

The filter criterion is that acceptable projects have BCR > 1 For any given constraint on capital available in year zero, the optimal package of projects is the one with the highest BCR > 1 for the whole package. For ranking projects in a capital-constrained environment, a ranking by magnitude of the BCR is never strictly valid because the BCR is a ratio of average benefits to average costs, and as every good economist knows, optimizing is done at the margin.

As is well known, a benefit is a negative cost, and vice versa. To calculate NPV this provides no problem: after discounting, the whole analysis boils down to addition and subtraction. With the BCR, exactly the same data are used, but an extra operation, division, is performed. This has led some authors[6] to wonder in print whether some categories of costs are best subtracted from the numerator or added to the denominator. If some costs are borne by entrepreneurs (for example, the costs of inputs in farming) and others by the public (reservoir construction), perhaps the appropriate ratio is $(B - C_{\text{private}})/C_{\text{public}}$. If capital costs are distinguishable from operating costs and the latter are paid directly from operating revenue, one could argue that capital is really the scarce factor. So why not define the ratio as:

$$\frac{B - C_{\text{operating}}}{C_{\text{capital}}}$$

These choices among the ways to specify the BC ratio will not affect the outcomes of the filter and optimal package decisions. They may change the relative rankings of projects by the BCR, but as we have argued, the BCR is never a strictly valid way to rank projects, anyway.

Internal rate of return   The internal rate of return is the discount rate,ρ, at which NPV is zero:

$$0 = \sum_{t=0}^{T} \frac{B_t - C_t}{(1 + \rho)^t} \tag{12.11}$$

For a filter, those projects with $\rho > r$ are acceptable. With a limited budget, the optimal package of projects is the one that has the largest $\rho > r$ for the whole package. For ranking projects in a capital-constrained environment, the magnitude of ρ, the average internal rate of return, is not a strictly valid criterion.

Which criterion?   As indicated at the outset, there is not much to choose. NPV, BCR, and IRR would agree in every case as to whether a particular proposal passes the filter. All criteria would select the same optimal package in a capital-constrained environment. None provides a strictly valid ranking of projects. All of these criteria deal with total and/ or average, not marginal, costs and benefits. As we have seen, this poses problems for ranking projects. The reason is that they are "bottom-line" criteria, attempting to summarize a multitude of information in a single number. This same characteristic causes difficulties in selecting the optimal size of projects. Ideally, one would like to select the optimal package of optimally sized projects. Optimal sizing requires equating the NPV, BCR, or IRR for the marginal increment in project size across all candidate projects.

These problems can be solved by backing off the bottom line and using the information that went into it to perform marginal analyses consistent with microeconomic principles. In the computer age, there are operations research techniques and computational algorithms that can select an optimal package of optimally sized projects. Even the difficulties posed by discrete project sizes (e.g. only one project can be built at a particular site, and because of engineering considerations, only a few alternative sizes are feasible) can be circumvented with methods such as mixed integer programming.

A final comment   Although NPV, BCR, and IRR all do much the same thing, IRR seems to generate more controversy than the other two. First, the calculation of ρ is quite cumbersome but in the age of inexpensive but powerful calculators and microcomputers, this is not a convincing objection. Second, when the time path of costs and benefits crosses over several time periods (e.g., periods when benefits are greater than costs are interspersed with periods when benefits are less than costs) ρ may not be unique, which is probably a much more serious objection to IRR. Third, professionals in project evaluation in developing countries tend to prefer IRR because the bottom-line result can be calculated without making an overt choice of r. The real rate of interest may be difficult to determine and/or politically sensitive in developing countries' economies.

We do not find this third argument convincing. It is necessary to decide on the value of r in order to conduct the filter test, $\rho > r$. If there are good reasons (which sometimes there are) to proceed with proposals that fail the filter test rigorously applied, is it really harder to explain a favorable decision when $\rho < r$ than when NPV < 0 or BCR <1?

Because we believe that the first and third arguments regarding IRR can be discounted but that the second cannot, we favor the use of NPV or BCR. To choose between them is merely to decide whether NPV > 0 contains more or less information than does BCR >1. What do you think?

Identifying and quantifying beneficial and adverse impacts

BCA must proceed according to the logic of equations 12.1–12.5. First, the baseline conditions must be identified and quantified in terms of equations 12.1 and 12.2. The relationships between human-controlled inputs, X, and the flow of environment or ecosystem goods and services, E, must be established. Then these same items must be projected through the year T with the project and without the project. The question is: In what ways will the proposal, if implemented, change the productivity and input use of the affected environmental asset?

These tasks, establishing baseline conditions and projecting the future with and without the project, do not necessarily require economic expertise. Often the tools of other disciplines and the specialized knowledge of their practitioners are essential. Economists are trained to think in systems terms and to be ever-conscious of second-, third-, and nth-round effects of disturbances. This frame of mind is helpful in these tasks, but it is not the exclusive property of specialists in economics.

The specialized work of economists is in the empirical application of equations 12.3–12.5, economic valuation and implementation of the criteria. In that sense, it is said that the economist lives high on the information food chain. He or she gathers and metabolizes information that is often generated by others. Nevertheless, the economist must always be alert to gaps in the information provided and to inappropriate information.

Now we address some specific issues arising at the baseline and projections stage.

Project life

Beneficial and adverse effects are projected through the year T, after which the project is treated as having no further impact. How many years away is T? From the natural sciences perspective, it should be the last year that the project has an impact. But this is not known with certainty. One should be wary of overoptimistic projections of T. There have been cases of dams with projected T of 50 or 100 years that required extensive and unscheduled repairs and reinforcements before year 25 and reservoirs that accumulated enough silt to halve the storage capacity by year 10. From the economic perspective, costs and benefits in later years are heavily discounted: $(1 + .06)^{50}$ is quite a large denominator, after all. This reduces, but does not eliminate, the inaccuracy induced by overoptimistic projections of T.

Salvage values and decommissioning costs

There are many kinds of projects, especially capital-intensive structural projects, that don't just disappear at the end of year T. If the project has a positive salvage value at the end of its effective life, that value should be included in the BCA calculations. Salvage values may well be negative. What does one do with a nuclear power plant that has outlived its usefulness? One does not just padlock the front gate and walk away. The costs of decommissioning a nuclear power plant so that it poses minimal danger are substantial. What about an aged reservoir? One cannot just walk off and leave the hulk of an obsolete dam littering the riverbed and a stream altered by the denudation of its banks and silt accumulation in its bed without imposing a further time stream of adverse impacts. When the salvage value of an exhausted project is negative, that too should be included in the BCA calculations.

Technological change

When projecting the time stream of inputs and services with and without the project, the issue of technological change arises. There is a general expectation of continued technological progress, but there are few credible predictions of when specific developments will occur and what industries they will affect. Under these conditions, it is usually best to assume that technological progress will affect all sectors equally, which has the same arithmetic effect on the outcome of BCA as assuming that there will be no technological change at all. Thus unless one has convincing evidence of unequal effects of future technology, it is best to make projections assuming no technological change.

Categories of services

In identifying baseline conditions and making projections, the most important consideration is to avoid unnecessarily restricting the scope of the inquiry. Those who tend to make the mistake of equating the economic with the commercial may be insensitive to significant impacts on important environmental services that are not directly reflected in the markets. It is useful to consider three categories of services: user services, options, and existence services.

User services arise when some element of the environment (natural capital) is combined with other commodities in order to create satisfaction. For most kinds of proposals, user services generate the bulk of the value. Consider some examples. Trees are combined with harvest equipment and labor, transportation, milling, and carpentry and then with other structural materials, furniture, and people's time so as to produce housing services that satisfy people. Forests provide lumber that helps provide housing services. This is a user service that leaves a detailed trail of use and value information in the records of commerce.

A forest environment (including trees and many other plant and animal species) is combined with transportation, food and lodging, specialized clothing and equipment, and people's time to produce recreational experiences that satisfy people. This is a user service whose value cannot be directly observed in the markets. Nevertheless, visitation records show evidence of use, and information from the transportation, lodging, and like markets may show considerable indirect evidence of value. For still other kinds of user services such as transcontinental air passengers viewing Rocky Mountain wilderness areas, direct evidence of use and value is difficult to find.

The point is that a wide variety of user services may be provided by projects and programs. Although some pass directly through commercial channels and leave a trail of evidence useful in BCA, others do not but may nevertheless be major sources of benefits and costs. Consider a program to improve air quality. Perhaps most of its beneficial impacts including improved health, aesthetic experiences, and so forth, are user services that leave only indirect evidence of use and value in the records of commerce.

When there is reason to wonder whether some desired facility or service will be available for use in future years, rational persons may be willing to purchase an option that would ensure its future availability. Trade in options is common in the land, commodities, stock, and financial markets. The same types of motivations that result in buying these options may well exist with respect to treasured environmental resources but, in these cases, would not be expressed in observable markets. Economists agree that option services and demands are real and perhaps substantial for certain unique environmental resources such as the Grand Canyon in the southwestern US. But there is debate about whether the value of an option is greater or less than the expected value of future use, and some disagreement about how best to measure the benefits and costs associated with options.

Existence services arise when just knowing that something continues to exist is a source of utility or pleasure, even for those who have no expectation of ever using it. Obvious cases pertain to endangered species and inaccessible wilderness areas: many more people care about the preservation of these things than can expect to see them or otherwise use them directly. Because existence services by definition arise without use, direct evidence of the demand for existence services and their values is not obtainable from commercial records.

In principle, the existence of almost anything may be valued. It is reasonable to expect, however, that the contribution of existence services to benefits and costs will be greater in total for those items that are highly appreciated and have few substitutes, and greater at the margin for these items whose existence is scarce. Existence services are likely to be important to BCA of projects and policies affecting threatened or endangered ecosystems, environment, species, and the like.

Use, option and existence services generate different types of active and passive use values which are discussed in more detail in the next chapter. Many of these values may be observed and measured. Theory and techniques for quantifying these values in monetary terms are also discussed in the next chapter.

Increased economic activity in the project region
A project or program that concentrates resources and assigns them to a defined region often induces increased economic activity in that region. This is a major reason for the strong local support often accorded to proposed projects. Project construction may bring additional workers into the project region, increasing the demand for goods and services provided by local businesses. When a part of the local labor force is unemployed or underemployed, project construction may create an effective demand for that labor. Some project inputs, other than labor, may be purchased locally. Following construction, operation of the project may increase local economic activity. A labor force will be employed for project operation and maintenance. For example, the irrigation water, flood protection, and outdoor recreation facilities provided by a water resource project may expand the opportunities open to local businesses, provide employment for the local labor force, and attract new businesses and workers into the project region.

The proper handling of increased regional economic activity in BCA has long been a subject of controversy. Local advocates and their allies in the public agencies often argue that the increased regional economic activity induced by a project should count as a beneficial effect, and thus its value should be used to bolster the benefits side of the BCA ledger. BCA is a test for PPIs on a national scale. Though induced economic activity may well benefit a project region, there is seldom a significant net gain to the nation from this source. Given that resources, including labor, are mobile, it is reasonable to assume that the activity induced in the project region was attracted from elsewhere in the nation. Losses elsewhere approximately cancel the induced gains in the project region.

There may be policy objectives served by inducing increased economic activity in a particular region. Perhaps the region has special economic problems or needs that make it an appropriate focus for a nationally financed regional development effort. The approach of the US Water Resources Council (WRC) is an appropriate response to such concerns. The WRC established a system of multiple accounts for project evaluation. The BCA criterion is applied at the national level in the National Economic Development (NED) account, and induced regional economic activity is not included. There are other accounts, however, that are not subject to a BCA test but offer useful information about project impacts. One such account is entitled Regional Economic Development (RED), and it documents the projected contribution of a proposal to regional economic activity.

Assessing priced and unpriced changes
As the general model for valuing changes in output (Figure 12.5) makes clear, a precise valuation of benefit and cost items requires an accurate estimation of the Hicksian compensating measures of economic surplus. If the quantity changes are small relative to the size of the market and the markets are efficient, the unit prices will be accurate value indicators. If the quantity changes are larger but the markets remain efficient, the standard demand and supply information will often be sufficient to allow estimation of the Hicksian compensation values for changes in production and input use.

Price changes during the life of the project
Just as services flows and input use (see equations 12.1 and 12.2) must be projected through the project life, with and without the project, so must their values. Obviously, the prediction of prices is hazardous when T is 50 or 100 years into the future. How should future price changes be handled? This question has two aspects. First, changes in the general price level are eventually reflected in money interest rates. The procedure of using a real interest rate, which corrects for general inflation, and valuing all future goods and services as constant (deflated) prices is both simple and logically consistent. Second, the relative prices of various services and inputs will surely change during the life of a long-term public investment. Yet there is often little basis for predicting relative price changes. Unless the analyst has strong evidence to the contrary, it is best to use current prices, a practice that assumes no changes in future relative prices.[7]

Now we consider the approaches to be taken when for various reasons, market observations do not yield complete and accurate value information.

Price distortions
When market prices diverge from efficient prices because of tariffs, quotas, trade barriers, subsidies, regulation, price controls or other distortions, it is the task of the benefit–cost analyst to estimate efficient prices and, if necessary, the demand and supply schedules that reflect underlying conditions rather than distortions imposed on the market. Estimated efficient prices are often called "shadow prices."

Administered prices

For some kinds of environmental services including, but not confined to, many outdoor recreation services, prices are established politically or administratively without regard to market conditions. If the administered prices are rigid, there will be no price variation necessary for estimating demand schedules. If the prices are set so low that the quantity demanded often exceeds the quantity supplied, as frequently happens with government camping grounds in peak vacation periods, not even one point on the demand curve can be observed.

Unpriced goods and services

There are many kinds of environmental services which are not directly priced because of non-exclusiveness (sometimes combined with non-rivalry). These include ambient air and water quality, scenery, ecological diversity, and the preservation of species. Important categories of user services, most options, and all existence services are unpriced.

For goods and services that are administratively priced or not priced at all, the BCA practitioner must estimate the appropriate Hicksian compensating measures of value. For many such goods, markets may provide considerable indirect information. The analyst's task is to extract and interpret this information, a task that often requires considerable insight and ingenuity.

Markets in travel services may reveal information about the value placed on recreation sites. And markets in housing may reveal information about the value placed on local and regional variations in air and water quality. Finally, the labor market may reveal information about the value of amenities and on-the-job health and safety conditions.

There are other cases in which markets generate relatively little information, even the most indirect kinds. Little can be learned from markets about the value of pure existence services or the benefits of nature study, for example. In many other cases, the conditions necessary for indirectly extracting value information from related markets are just not present.

Since the 1970s, economists have moved in the past three decades to refine two kinds of valuation methods: those that analyze related markets in order to make inferences about the value of environmental services and those that seek to induce citizens to report reliably the value they place on environmental services. Both approaches have their difficulties, strengths, and weaknesses. They are introduced and briefly discussed in Chapter 13.

Concluding comments

BCA can become a complex and even arcane pursuit. Scholars and practitioners have their own preferred approaches to various problems, many of them too specialized to rate a mention in a brief general introduction such as presented in this chapter. Many presume to advise others, and there is a modest industry of proposing, analyzing, and rebutting purported solutions to various conceptual and pragmatic difficulties in BCA.

We do not mean to make light of the problems that arise in BCA. There are enough difficulties to challenge the finest theoretical and applied analyst. There are more than enough opportunities for those with strong preferences about the outcome of proposals, supporters and opponents, to interpret BCA procedures in ways that make it more likely that the end result will be consistent with their preferences.

Nevertheless, we do want to reiterate a fundamental point. If one relentlessly follows the logic of two simple propositions, the correct solutions to all the conceptual problems of BCA will emerge, and considerable progress is possible in resolving even the more intractable empirical problems. These propositions are:

1. Projects or policies never create something out of nothing. Rather, they modify an existing environment at some cost, changing its flow of services and its derived demand for inputs.
2. Benefit–cost analysis is a test for potential Pareto-improvements.

Questions for discussion

1. In an imaginary economy that has achieved a Pareto-efficient competitive equilibrium, what is the highest conceivable benefit–cost ratio for a proposed project? Explain.
2. Some have argued that the discount rate used in evaluating public sector investments should be lower than the real opportunity cost of capital in the private sector. Evaluate this argument.
3. Compare and contrast the maximum present value, the benefit–cost ratio, and the internal rate of return as criteria for public investment decisions. Is there really much at stake in choosing among these criteria?
4. In some situations, the value of project inputs or outputs may be determined by multiplying quantity by price; in other situations, the appropriate measure of value is the aggregate change in the consumers' surplus. For each of the following items, which is the appropriate approach to valuation?
    a. A relatively small increase in the output of wheat.
    b. Protection from an environmental hazard, such as major flooding, thereby improving the health and safety of a target human population.
    c. Elimination of the last free-flowing trout stream in a geographic region of considerable size.
    d. Cement for construction.
    e. Hydropower.
    f. An exotic specialty crop.
5. Suppose that in a particular region irrigated farm acres produce relatively low-valued commodities (for example, wheat, hay, pasture). Some economists have recommended that in the benefit–cost analysis of all proposed irrigation projects in the region, agricultural benefits should be calculated as though low-valued crops would be produced, regardless of what crops would actually be produced at the proposed project site. Develop the economic logic underlying this recommendation.
6. Some have argued that when evaluating proposed projects that would provide food in developing countries in which malnutrition is prevalent, food should be valued not at its actual price but at the price that would prevail if everyone could afford to avoid malnutrition. Can you accept this argument? Why or why not?
7. List the benefit and cost items you would consider in a benefit–cost analysis of a proposed program to regulate the disposal of nuclear wastes. How would you attempt to estimate the value of the benefits and costs associated with these items?
8. Consider a proposed project that would increase the wages of a low-income population. In a net benefit–cost analysis, is it appropriate to count as benefits both the total value of the project's output and the savings in public assistance (e.g., food stamps) expenditures that would result from the increase in earnings of low-income persons?

Notes

1. In the US, the origins of formal benefit–cost analysis of water resource projects can be traced back to the Federal Flood Control Act of 1936.
2. Edward J. Mishan, "What is Producers' Surplus?," *American Economic Review* **58** (1968): 1269–82.
3. For approximation methods, see Robert D. Willig (1976), "Consumer's Surplus without Apology," *American Economic Review* **66**: 587–97; Alan Randall and John R. Stoll (1980), "Consumer's Surplus in Commodity Space," *American Economic Review* **70**: 449–55. General methods for calculating exact Hicksian compensation and equivalent measures of welfare change from observable ordinary demand information are reported by Jerry A. Hausman (1981), "Exact Consumer's Surplus and Deadweight Loss," *American Economic Review* **71**: 662–76; V. Kerry Smith and George Van Houtven (2004), "Recovering Hicksian Consumer Surplus within a Collective Model: Hausman's Method for the Household," *Environmental and*

Resource Economics **28**: 153–67; Yrjo O. Vartia (1983), "Efficient Methods of Measuring Welfare Change and Compensated Income in Terms of Ordinary Demand Functions," *Econometrica* **51**: 79–98.

4. This model is developed and applied in David S. Brookshire, Alan Randall, and John R. Stoll (1980), "Valuing Increments and Decrements in Natural Resource Service Flows," *American Journal of Agricultural Economics* **62**: 478–88.
5. For example, Peter G. Sassone and William A. Schaffer (1978), *Cost–Benefit Analysis: A Handbook*, New York: Academic Press.
6. For example, Otto Eckstein (1958), *Water Resources Development: The Economics of Project Evaluation*, Cambridge, MA: Harvard University Press.
7. The argument for assuming different trends in future prices is presented and applied in Anthony C. Fisher, John V. Krutilla, and Charles J. Cicchetti (1972), "The Economics of Environmental Preservation: A Theoretical and Empirical Analysis," *American Economic Review* **62**: 605–19.

Suggested reading: classic and contemporary

Ackerman, F. and L. Heinzerling (2002), "Pricing the Priceless: Cost–Benefit Analysis of Environmental Protection," *University of Pennsylvania Law Review* **150** (5): 1553–84.
Arrow, K.J., M.L. Cropper, G.C. Eads, R.W. Hahn, L.B. Lave, R.G. Noll, P.R. Portney, and M. Russell (1996), "Is There a Role for Benefit–Cost Analysis in Environmental, Health, and Safety Regulation?," *Science* **272**: 221–2.
Boardman, A.E., D.H. Greenberg, A.R. Vining, and D.L. Weimer (2005), *Cost–Benefit Analysis: Concepts and Practice*, 3rd edn, Englewood Cliffs, NJ: Prentice Hall.
Eckstein, O. (1958), *Water Resources Development: The Economics of Project Evaluation*, Cambridge, MA: Harvard University Press.
Gramlich, E.M. (1990), *A Guide to Benefit–Cost Analysis*, 2nd edn, Englewood Cliffs, NJ: Prentice Hall.
Mishan, E.J. and E. Quah (2007), *Cost–Benefit Analysis*, 5th edn, Florence, KY, USA and Milton Park, UK: Routledge Taylor & Francis.
Peterson, G.L. and A. Randall (eds) (1984), *Valuation of Wildland Resource Benefits*, Boulder, CO: Westview Press.
Sassone, P.G. and W.A. Schaffer (1978), *Cost–Benefit Analysis: A Handbook*, New York: Academic Press.

13 Measuring economic values: how do we account for all relevant benefits and costs in natural resource and environmental decisions?

When the relationships between human-controlled inputs and the production of environmental or ecosystem goods and services (see Chapter 12, equations 12.1 and 12.2) are well specified and all beneficial and adverse effects are efficiently priced in infinitely large markets, benefit–cost analysis (BCA) is a straightforward task. To determine each item's contribution to benefits or costs, the quantity change (positive or negative) attributable to the project is multiplied by its efficient unit price. Many discussions of BCA are addressed, explicitly or implicitly, to this kind of situation. Nevertheless, these simple cases are quite rare among proposals dealing with natural resources and environmental quality. In this chapter, we consider strategies for measuring economic values and implementing BCA in the difficult cases.

Often markets cannot be treated as infinitely large relative to the impacts of proposed projects or programs. Rather, the proposed undertaking is large enough to influence significantly the prices of some goods and services. Beneficial and adverse effects are frequently non-marginal, inframarginal, or lumpy. These problems are addressed in some detail in Chapter 12, in which a model is developed that shows the conceptually correct treatment of non-marginal quantity changes and establishes the theoretical link between marginal and non-marginal valuation.

Total economic value

Fully informed policy decision-making requires measurement of the total economic value of natural resource and environmental goods and services. This total economic value can be divided into two broad categories: active use value and passive use value.

Active use value

Active use value (AUV) is the value of the utility derived from actively using goods or services derived from natural resources or the environment. Active AUV can be subdivided based on whether activities which generate value occur on or off site, and whether these activities are consumptive or non-consumptive. Suppose that the "site" we are interested in from a policy perspective is a freshwater reservoir such as those managed by the US Army Corps of Engineers in the eastern US and by the US Bureau of Reclamation in the western US. On-site, consumptive AUV would be derived from consumptive activities which occur at the reservoir such as commercial and recreational fishing. On-site, non-consumptive AUV would be derived from non-consumptive activities which occur at the reservoir or lake such as wildlife observation. Off-site, consumptive AUV would be derived from consuming natural resource and environmental goods and services at an off-site location; for example, drinking water provided by the reservoir at one's home residence. Off-site, non-consumptive AUV would be derived from non-consumptive activities which directly use natural resource and environmental goods and services provided by the reservoir at an off-site location; for example, swimming in a downstream river fed by the reservoir or using electricity at a business or home which was generated by a hydropower plant at the reservoir.[1]

Passive use value

Passive use value (PUV) is the value of the utility derived from passively using a resource. Suppose that people have preferences about states of the world. Then a state of the world in which the resource is intact and thriving may generate PUV. This category of value always occurs off-site and is always non-consumptive because use is passive, not active. Suppose again that we are interested in goods and services provided by a freshwater reservoir. Aesthetic PUV would be derived from off-site sensory activities or experiences such as viewing someone else's photographs of the lake or listening to audio tapes or CDs of lake sounds (e.g., calls of birds that live in the lake habitat). Vicarious PUV would be derived from imagining the lake-related experiences of other human and non-human agents. One type of vicarious PUV is bequest value, which for example would be the value a person places on knowing that the lake and the goods and services it provides will be preserved for other people to enjoy (actively or passively) within the same generation or across generations. Existence value would be derived, for example, from the satisfaction a person receives from merely thinking about natural resources (such as threatened or endangered fish species) existing in the lake ecosystem for their own sake. Because passive use values can be experienced by people without actually coming in contact with a natural resource (for example, traveling to a river to go fishing), these values may potentially be aggregated over very large numbers of people resulting in relatively high aggregate passive use values, especially for unique natural resources.[2] Note that in the case of a freshwater reservoir, there may have been substantial PUV for preserving the reservoir site as a free-flowing stream – in a BCA of the reservoir project, the total economic value perspective would consider PUVs both with and without the reservoir project.

Origin and nature of non-market commodities

Many natural resource and environmental goods and services are traded in economic markets with market prices. For example, commercial fishing results in food products which are sold in wholesale and retail food markets (including restaurants) at current market prices. Thus, some components of total economic value are in the nature of market commodities and the value of these commodities can be measured using market prices. In general, market prices are most feasible and appropriate to use when measuring total economic value components associated with goods and services which are rival and exclusive, e.g., private goods such as tilapia or trout bought at the local supermarket for consumption at home. However, many components of total economic value are in the nature of non-market commodities defined as goods and services which for some reason or another escape market provision and pricing.

Why do some goods and services escape market exchange? What is the nature of such goods and services? These questions are addressed briefly in this section. The failure of markets to account adequately for certain economic goods is largely dependent on the degree of rivalry in consumption and exclusiveness in provision. Market failure arises when goods display elements of non-rivalry in consumption and/or non-exclusiveness in provision (see Chapter 10).

Certain natural resource and environmental goods and services provide examples of rival, non-exclusive goods. For example, because of extremely high transaction costs associated with establishing private property rights, ocean game fish (e.g., king mackerel) are available to sport fishermen to catch and consume on a non-exclusionary basis. However, after a certain point on the biological growth curve, consumption of fish by one party reduces the quantity of fish available to any other party. Hence, ocean game fish are generally rival in consumption, and non-exclusive in provision.

Because of non-exclusion, ocean game fish escape adequate consideration by unfettered markets, giving rise to externalities. An externality is defined broadly as an interdependence between economic agents for which a market does not exist.[3] In the case of game fish, the externalities are generally in the form of external costs. Specifically, when fishing by one party reduces game fish populations, costs are imposed on other parties. These costs, however, are not accounted for in the market. The end result is excessive sport fishing effort.

Consider next the case of commodities which are non-rival in consumption and exclusive in provision. A good is non-rival in consumption if consumption by one party does not reduce the quantity of the good available to any other party. Certain natural resource and environmental goods and services also provide examples of non-rival, exclusive commodities. For example, people receive aesthetic services from viewing certain natural scenery. In some cases, it may be possible to establish private property rights to the natural scenery and exclude people from viewing it if they do not pay an admission price (e.g., cave formations).

The characteristic of non-rivalry, however, presents a conceptual problem. When goods are non-rival in consumption, more than one person can obtain satisfaction from the good without reducing the satisfaction obtained from the good by any other person. Thus, it is actually economically inefficient to exclude people from consuming the good.[4] However, as pointed out previously, if exclusion is not permitted, there is little incentive for private producers to provide the service.

Thus, in order to provide non-rival, exclusive goods in economically efficient quantities, some other means of provision may be needed. The government provides a number of non-rival, and potentially exclusive goods. The aesthetic services provided by scenic views found in public parks are a case in point. Often, the government provides these services at no charge or at a very low price, as called for by economic efficiency concerns.

Finally, consider the case of goods which are both non-rival in consumption and non-exclusive in provision. Once again, certain natural resource and environmental goods and services provide examples of non-rival, non-exclusive goods. For example, consider scenic views provided by agricultural land. These scenic views are generally open to general public "consumption" on a non-exclusionary basis. Moreover, consumption exhibits elements of non-rivalry. That is, all consumers receive the same quantity of scenic views since consumption of views by one person does not reduce the quantity of views available to anyone else. Because of the characteristics of non-rivalry and non-exclusion, scenic views provided by agricultural land escape adequate consideration by private land markets. One result of this lack of consideration is the emergence of externalities. In this case, the externalities are in the form of external benefits which accrue to the general public from private agricultural land.[5]

The characteristics of non-rivalry and non-exclusion also give rise to various "public goods" which are not traded in markets. Examples include various services provided by national environmental quality. For instance, most individuals feel a clean, unpolluted environment enhances their overall "quality of life." This quality-of-life service is generally non-rival in consumption and non-exclusive in provision. Because of these characteristics, the quality-of-life service provided by national environmental quality will be underprovided by private markets. Bequest and existence values associated with preservation of unique natural environments (e.g., the Grand Canyon in Arizona) and threatened and endangered wildlife species (e.g., Arctic polar bears) are also examples of non-rival, non-exclusive goods and services which will generally be underprovided by private markets. In these cases of underprovision, non-rival, non-exclusive goods and services are generally provided by the government or philanthropy at no charge to beneficiaries.

In summary, a number a factors may contribute to the existence of non-market goods in the economy. Some of these factors are related to the characteristics of non-rivalry and non-exclusiveness. Other reasons for the existence of non-market goods, however, can be found. For example, goods may escape market exchange because of society's desire to reallocate resources in order to achieve "higher social goals" such as equity and fairness.[6] Meeting such goals may require that provision of certain commodity service flows be removed from the marketplace and replaced by government provision.

Whenever goods are not exchanged in markets, market prices for these goods do not exist. However, the lack of a market price does not necessarily indicate that the goods have a zero economic value. Indeed, service flows for non-market commodities may often constitute a large portion of the total economic value of a good. Thus, proper management and allocation of resources often require quantification of the value of these services using non-market valuation techniques.

Valuation in the absence of direct markets

As discussed above, for many components of total economic value, there are no direct markets to reveal efficient marginal prices which we need to estimate demand schedules. For these cases, methods for non-market valuation have been developed. Here we introduce some of the better known among these methods.

Each of the mainstream methods of non-market valuation has its theoretical framework: a logical structure that identifies and validates the potential of the method while delimiting its domain of application. The theoretical frameworks for the various methods are developed to different degrees and in different directions. Nevertheless, they all share one basic concept. Non-market goods and services are represented in the utility function in the same way as other goods and services, and were it not for conditions such as non-rivalry, non-exclusiveness, or a political decision to provide and ration them independently of the market which distinguish them from ordinary goods, they would be traded and valued in the same manner as market goods and services.

Introducing some non-market commodity, Q, there are two ways to express the utility function. First:

$$U = U(Q, Y) \tag{13.1}$$

where Y is the "numeraire" or the value of all goods and services other than Q. Equation 13.1 is the formulation implicit in the general value model (see Chapter 12, especially Figure 12.5 and the related text). Second, we may write the alternative form:

$$U = U(Q, \underline{Z}) \qquad (13.2)$$

where $\underline{Z}$ is a vector of ordinary market goods. An equivalent formulation is:

$$U = U(\underline{P}, Q, M) \qquad (13.3)$$

where $\underline{P}$ is a vector of prices of $\underline{Z}$ and M is money income.

These two ways to express the utility function suggest two different avenues for estimating the value of Q and thus the benefits (costs) of increments (decrements) in Q. One avenue related to the first formulation of the utility function (equation 13.1) is to ask people in a survey or experimental setting to evaluate trade-offs between Q and Y using stated preference techniques. Alternatively, one may use the second formulation (equations 13.2 and 13.3) to extract indirectly information about the value of Q from observations of markets in $\underline{Z}$ using revealed preference techniques. In either case, the overall conceptual goal of non-market valuation is to estimate one or more of the following welfare change measures: willingness to pay (WTP) for an increase in Q; willingness to pay (WTP) to prevent a decrease in Q; willingness to accept compensation (WTA) for a decrease in Q; or willingness-to-accept compensation (WTA) to forego an increase in Q. These four welfare change measures, illustrated by Figure 12.5, are measures of Hicksian consumer's surplus and represent the theoretically preferred measures of changes in welfare or well-being resulting from changes in Q.[7]

Stated preference non-market valuation techniques
Stated preference techniques use responses to valuation questions posed to people in a survey or experimental setting to measure WTP or WTA for changes in non-market commodities as illustrated by the total value curve in Figure 12.5. The total value curve is an indifference curve which shows trade-offs an individual is willing to make between changes in a non-market commodity and changes in income. For an individual initially enjoying Q^0 and Y^0, the total value curve indicates WTP for an increase in Q and WTA for a decrease in Q as follows:

$$U(Q^0, Y^0) = U(Q^-, Y^+) = U(Q^+, Y^-)$$

$$= U(Q^-, \overline{Y} + WTA) = U(Q^+, Y - WTP) \qquad (13.4)$$

Contingent valuation method
If we could observe indifference curves, measuring WTP or WTA using a total value curve would be a rather straightforward task. However, because indifference curves are not ordinarily observable, we need some other way of observing consumer behavior with respect to trade-offs between Q and Y. One approach for making these observations, termed the contingent valuation method (CVM), involves the creation of a hypothetical or experimental market or referendum in which survey respondents or experimental

subjects reveal relevant points on their indifference surfaces. In the hypothetical or experimental market or referendum, the level of Q is varied; and the values stated by participants for changes in Q are recorded and treated as contingent values; that is, the stated values are interpreted as values for various levels of Q contingent on the existence of the posited market or referendum.

There are several steps in any CVM study, and several alternative approaches may be available for each step. Data collection may proceed via surveys (mail, telephone, face-to-face, Internet, or some combination thereof) or in various experimental formats (perhaps using computer laboratories). Issues of defining the relevant user population and sampling must be resolved.

Instruments for data collection (often, but not necessarily, questionnaires) will typically contain a CVM module and other modules for collecting related information helpful to the analysis (for example, attitudes, historical and prospective patterns of Q-related activities, and sociodemographic information). Although the general principles of instrument design apply to all modules, the CVM module needs some specific discussion here.

The CVM module must accomplish the following purposes:

1. Establish the baseline conditions with respect to the physical availability of Q and the institutions that regulate citizens' access to and use of Q.
2. Define and describe the change in Q that would result from the proposed project or policy.

For items 1 and 2 a considerable variety of devices may be used. Verbal and quantitative descriptions and visual displays, including photographs, sketches, diagrams, graphs, and charts, are frequently used. More exotic communication devices that use the senses of taste and smell have been used occasionally. The purpose of these multimedia communications is to help sharpen and standardize participants' perceptions of baseline and with-policy conditions. Note that the data collection method may limit the choice of communications media: for example, telephone surveys are confined to spoken communication.

3. Establish the context of contingent choice. The participants may, hypothetically, obtain the increment (decrement) in the commodity Q by paying (receiving) some stated amount through some specified institutional channels. Payment may be a daily access fee, an annual fee for access, an additional tax, or whatever. Some studies have stated: "Implementation of the proposal will cost your household x annually via higher taxes and prices." If Q is a non-rival and/or non-exclusive good or service, the institutional channels for payment should be appropriate to these kinds of goods or services.
4. Obtain statements of the participants' maximum WTP (minimum WTA) or, alternatively, their acceptance or rejection of one or more (ΔQ, payment) pairs.

Statistical analysis is required for several purposes:

1. To estimate aggregate WTP (WTA) for ΔQ over the affected population or, more ambitiously, to estimate the aggregate total value curve for Q.
2. To statistically relate individual WTP (WTA) to policy or project-related site char-

acteristics and participant characteristics. These relationships are helpful in generalizing the results of a particular CVM case study to other similar situations.

3. To conduct tests for internal consistency within the CVM data set and consistency among the results of several related valuation exercises (often using different valuation methods). These tests are useful in validating the CVM exercise or diagnosing any problems it may have.

Statistical analysis of CVM responses is closely tied to the particular bid elicitation method implemented in the CVM instrument or model. For example, if the bid elicitation method is an open-ended valuation question such as: "What is the most you would be willing to pay for a 25 percent increase in Q? \$_____ (fill in the blank)," the researcher directly observes individual statements of maximum WTP for a sample of people participating in a CVM survey. Measures of central tendency (e.g., mean or median) WTP can then be estimated using simple average equations or by estimating a bid function using regression analysis with stated WTP (the answer to the open-ended question) as the dependent variable and changes in Q and other appropriate explanatory variables (e.g., income and other sociodemographic variables) as independent variables. The estimated bid function can then be used, for example, to predict mean WTP for the sample.

Suppose the bid elicitation method is a closed-ended valuation question such as: "Would you vote for a referendum in your town which if passed would increase Q by 25 percent at a cost to you and your household of \$50 per household per year? _____ Yes _____ No (check one)." In the case of a closed-ended question, the researcher does not directly observe WTP, rather he or she observes "yes" or "no" responses to paying a given amount of money (posted price) for Q. Alternative conceptual models and statistical techniques have been developed for estimating measures of central tendency (e.g., mean or median WTP) from closed-ended CVM responses. The reader is referred to several excellent sources of information for the specific conceptual and statistical details including "how to" steps and instructions.[8]

The validity question   Before leaving the subject of CVM, it is appropriate to consider the validity of these methods. First, the WTP and WTA observations generated by CVM are well adapted to welfare change measurement and, thus, BCA. As the general valuation model demonstrates, they can be interpreted directly as observations of the appropriate compensating values of economic surplus. This is a major advantage of CVM, an advantage not often shared by alternative methods. On the other hand, questions are often raised about the quality of CVM-generated value data. In particular, some economists argue that responses may be susceptible to strategic manipulation by participants since markets and referendums are contingent (or hypothetical) rather than "real" (e.g., people don't actually hand over money).

To make a general statement, the quality of the value data depends on the characteristics of the contingent market or referendum. Thus it is best if the contingent market or referendum has the following characteristics:

- It is designed to conform to the basic theory of valuation for BCA.
- The market is specified and described in sufficient detail to allow communication of its salient dimensions: What status quo rights do individuals have? What

rights will be (hypothetically) transferred if a trade can be agreed upon? It is best if realism and relevance are served at this stage by specifying institutions that are familiar and recognized as functional, at least in principle. However, extraneous concerns – for example, about taxation policy or utility rate regulation – should not be introduced in the attempt to promote realism.

- The good or service, Q, must be defined, and the offered increment or threatened decrement therein must be specified.
- It must encourage the accurate revelation of individual valuations (e.g., be "incentive-compatible").

After many years of experience with CVM dating back to the 1970s, it seems to us that the really interesting issues still concern this last item. There are two concerns often raised: individuals may behave strategically, misreporting their "true" valuations in order to influence the outcome of the research, and individuals may treat the whole exercise as hypothetical or inconsequential and thus devote little effort to the introspection that is necessary to discover their "true" value of Q. Let us consider these issues in some detail.[9]

Assume that an individual, an experimental subject or survey respondent, believes that the results of the valuation exercise will influence policy. It is not essential to believe that it will be decisive; influential is enough. Assume also that the individual perceives that she is a member of a sample of citizens participating in the exercise. Does she "take it seriously"? It is reasonable to assume she will take it at least as seriously as she does voting in elections or participating in a political poll (where, again, her influence is magnified because she is a member of a sample chosen to represent a larger population).

Now assume that formulating ("figuring out") her WTP or WTA for specified changes in Q (or, even more difficult, specifying her total value curve) is not so simple a task that it can be accomplished instantaneously and costlessly. The choices offered in the contingent market or referendum will seldom be familiar and routine, even with the best research design. There will be a positive relationship between the effort she invests in value formulation and the precision of the value at which she arrives. If the value formulation task is difficult and/or the individual limits the effort she invests therein, she may solve the value formulation problem incompletely or imprecisely.

This discussion places in perspective the difference between contingent markets or referendums and "real" markets or referendums. First, the goods or services offered in contingent markets are not always familiar, and individuals may not associate these particular goods with trading possibilities. Unfamiliar goods are often introduced in "real" markets and referendums. So this distinction between "real" and contingent markets and referendums is, if anything, a matter of degree. Second, the penalty for a wrong decision may be substantial in "real" markets: your money is gone, and you are left with some purchase that has disappointed you. There is, however, a penalty for a wrong decision in a contingent market or referendum: one's opportunity to influence policy is wasted or misused. Again, the distinction between "real" and contingent markets and referendums is, if anything, a matter of degree.

If value formulation is imperfect in contingent markets and referendums, the formulated values will include some error. Can we identify the direction of that error? It turns out that if valuation is performed in the Hicksian compensating framework (that is, WTP for increments in Q and WTA for decrements), imperfect value formulation will lead to an understatement of WTP and an overstatement of WTA. The directional effect of incomplete value formulation is to understate the value of gains and overstate the value of losses. This kind of error has a conservative influence on BCA.

Now assume that the individual is not above strategic behavior, which we define as reporting something other than one's formulated value in order to influence the results of the exercise in one's favor. Some participants will reject this kind of behavior on moral grounds, and others may realize that finding an optimal strategy is itself a resource-consuming activity and so decide to forgo strategic behavior. Nevertheless, it is prudent to consider what kind of effect any participants who do choose to act strategically might have on the reported contingent valuation results.

To identify the optimal strategies for our participants, we must first specify the incentives that they face. Assume that the individual will gain positive utility from both Q and Z. In other words, she likes Q and does not like taxes or payments that would reduce her disposable income. The key issue, then, is how her participation in the exercise is likely to influence: (1) the chances that a policy to increase Q will be implemented; and (2) her disposable income if the policy is enacted. One can model a variety of alternative contingent markets in order to examine how their structure will affect these things. Here we outline some of these models for WTP; the arguments are analogous for WTA, in which the effects are usually similar but of opposite sign.

We can dispose quickly of two rather obvious cases:

1. The government will provide the increment in Q without regard to the outcome of the benefit–cost analysis. The researcher will collect the stated WTP from each participant at the end of the exercise. However, Q is non-exclusive, and the participants will enjoy the increment in Q regardless of their reported (and paid) WTP. Strategizing respondents would report zero or very low values for WTP.
2. The government will provide the increment in Q if, and only if, the estimated benefits for the affected population exceed the costs. The researcher never collects the stated WTP, and nor does anyone else. The participants are forever immune from bearing any of the costs. Strategizing respondents would state high values for WTP in order to increase the probability of implementing the policy.

These cases can be immediately dismissed, as they are false representations of the policy environment. Case 1 is of some interest in experimental economics as the case most likely to elicit free-rider behavior. But it is not common policy practice to implement proposals independently of benefits and costs and to finance them through contributions determined by self-reported WTP. Case 2 has some appeal on the surface, as in BCA practice the researcher seldom collects WTP. But a deeper analysis suggests that the participants realize that if the exercise is to affect policy, they will eventually pay, one way or another, for the increments in Q. The assumption that the participants are forever immune from contributing toward the costs of policy is untenable.

More relevant models of the incentives influencing behavior in contingent markets include the following cases:

3. The proposal will be implemented if the estimated benefits exceed the costs, and citizens will pay in proportion to the stated WTP.
4. The proposal will be implemented if the estimated benefits exceed the costs, and citizens will pay their per capita share of the costs.
5. The proposal will be implemented if a majority of citizens approves it, given that each will pay their per capita share of the costs.

In each case, the participant who likes Q but dislikes bearing additional expenses must devise a strategy designed to increase the expectation that the policy is implemented but, ceteris paribus, to reduce the expected cost they will bear.

The optimal reporting strategies corresponding to cases 3–5 are:

3. Report WTP equal to or less than one's formulated WTP. The optimal reporting strategy is related to sample size. Generally it is best to report a WTP approaching one's formulated WTP if one believes that the sample is small; with very large samples, the tendency toward free-riding is stronger.
4. If one suspects one's formulated WTP is quite different from that of other citizens, exaggerate the difference so as to shift the sample mean reported WTP nearer to one's formulated WTP. If one believes that one's WTP is a little higher than the mean, report a value still higher; likewise, if one's WTP is likely to be lower than the mean, report a value still lower.
5. No strategy is individually preferable to telling the truth. If the stated per-capita cost is lower than one's WTP, it is best to report approval but if one's WTP is lower than the stated cost, it is best to report disapproval.

What effect would these individually optimal strategies have on the estimated benefits of increasing the level of Q? In case 3, there would be a tendency to underestimate benefits. In case 4, the variance of individual WTP would be increased, widening the confidence interval around the estimated benefits. If the reported WTP is limited to a minimum of zero but has no upper limit, the mean reported WTP might be biased upward. However, there are statistical methods for dealing with this problem. If these methods are used, the total estimated benefits would not be affected by the reporting strategies. In case 5, there is no reporting bias.

Observe that case 5 departs a little from the idea of a contingent market, and so it is better described as a contingent policy referendum. But that is no cause for the BCA analyst to be concerned. As we have seen, it is immune to strategic manipulations: truth-telling is the individually preferred strategy. Furthermore, the referendum question, "Would you approve or disapprove a program to provide ΔQ if it cost your household $\$x$ annually?" requires only that the participant determine whether their WTP for ΔQ would be less than or greater than $\$x$. For all but the near indifferent, this requires only a much simplified value formulation task.

This conceptual analysis of the participant's likely behavior in a contingent valuation exercise has several implications, and these implications seem to have been corroborated in empirical applications. First, although the incentives for careful decision-making and the truthful reporting of valuations are not as strong as they are in private goods markets, they are by no means absent in contingent valuation exercises. This suggests that carefully designed contingent valuation studies will collect a substantial body of serviceable value data, perhaps along with a minority of less reliable observations.

Second, for a fairly wide range of contingent market designs, we can be confident that any biases introduced in formulating and/or reporting WTP will have the effect of understating it. This applies to contingent markets or referendums based on Hicksian value measures applying appropriate statistical analysis.

Third, contingent valuation formats come in considerable variety, and their performance characteristics will differ in ways that are, to some extent, predictable. Thus the quality of contingent value data can be improved with careful attention to the contingent market or referendum design. Using the Hicksian value measures and referendum formats, as in case 5, are obvious ways to minimize bias in the estimated benefits while ensuring that any remaining bias is toward understatement.

Choice experiments
During the 2000s, a broad class of stated preference techniques falling under the broad category of "choice experiments" have gained popularity. In a choice experiment (CE), either in a survey or laboratory setting, CE participants are presented with alternative Q "packages" with different levels of multiple "attributes" and asked to choose between two packages or rank two or more packages in order of preference. For example, suppose the Q of interest is a new public park. Attributes of the new park may include total acreage, water acreage, miles of hiking trails, developed campsites, picnic pavilions and the entry fee. A typical choice experiment may present participants with the following packages and choices:

BOX 13.1 PUBLIC PARK ATTRIBUTES AND ATTRIBUTE LEVELS

Attributes	Attribute Levels	
	Park Plan A	Park Plan B
1. Total Acreage	500	350
2. Water Acreage	75	120
3. Miles of Hiking Trails	100	50
4. Developed Campsites	40	40
5. Picnic Pavilions	3	6
6. Entry Fee	$5	$10

Please indicate your preference between Park Plan A and Park Plan B (check one)

_____ I prefer Park Plan A
_____ I prefer Park Plan B
_____ I prefer neither plan (that is, I prefer no new park)

Thus, in the above CE question, the participant is asked to indicate a choice between three alternatives: Park Plan A, Park Plan B, or no new park.

In a full-scale choice experiment, many different pairwise comparisons of park plans would be presented to a sample of people – for example, residents of a county where the new park is proposed to be built. In the different pairwise comparisons, the levels of attributes of Park Plan A and Park Plan B are varied according to an optimal experimental design. The resulting data set therefore shows survey respondents' or laboratory subjects' selections of Park Plan A, Park Plan B or no new park under alternative assumptions about the level of park attributes including the entry fee. These data can then be statistically analyzed to derive the marginal implicit price or marginal WTP for each park attribute. For example, after statistical analysis the results may show that the marginal implicit price or marginal WTP for hiking trails is $1.50. We interpret this number as implying that county residents are willing to pay $1.50 for each additional mile of hiking trails added to a new park. Thus, a particular strength and application of choice experiments is estimating the marginal or incremental value of multiple attributes to the total value of some Q package. Recent research has shown the consistency between Hicksian welfare measures and the above CE formulation where participants are given the choice to maintain the status quo.[10]

Choice experiments have been applied to measure the marginal or incremental value of a variety of Q package attributes including attributes of farmland protection programs (e.g., type of farmland protected), hunting and fishing experiences (e.g., catch rates), and pollution control programs (e.g., types of pollutants controlled). There now exists a large body of literature describing conceptual models and empirical estimation techniques for various CE formats. We refer the interested reader to this literature for more detailed information on choice experiments including application steps and instructions.[11]

Revealed preference non-market valuation techniques
The idea has long been abroad that various non-marketed goods and amenities may have substitutes and/or complements that are routinely exchanged and priced. In such cases, the markets in these substitutes and complements could (one presumes) generate a good deal of implicit information about the demand for related non-market goods if only one knew how to isolate and interpret that information. This insight has been the impetus for development of a broad class of related methods for non-market valuation generally termed "revealed preference techniques." This terminology stems from the observation that people reveal their preferences and values for Q through their purchases of related substitutes or complements.

The general theoretical basis for revealed preference techniques is explained by first expressing a consumer's utility function in the form:

$$U = U(Q, \underline{Z})$$
(13.5)

Maximizing utility subject to the budget constraint $\underline{P}\underline{Z} = M$ creates a set of Marshallian demands for the individual Z_i in $\underline{Z}$:

$$Z_i = Z_i(\underline{P}, Q, M)$$
(13.6)

If the utility function is nonseparable in Q and Z meaning that $U(Q, Z) \neq U_q(Q) + U_z(Z)$, the amount of Q provided will influence the ordinary demand (that is, the price-quantity relationship) for Z_i. By estimating the demand for Z_i given various levels of Q, it should in principle be possible to describe a demand schedule for Q. Then the Marshallian economic surplus associated with a change in Q can be calculated. Given estimates of the Marshallian surplus, the theoretically correct Hicksian measures of value can be approximated or calculated exactly. Unfortunately, analytical difficulties preclude prescribing a general operational procedure for generating a demand schedule for Q from demands for z_i conditioned on various levels of Q. But methods have been developed for two special cases which enjoyed fairly broad application; the travel cost method and hedonic price method.

The travel cost method and hedonic price method are based on the concept of weak complementarity. Weak complementarity occurs if, when the quantity of Z_i demanded in Equation (13.6) is zero, the marginal utility of Q in equation (13.5) also is zero. For example, the travel cost method is typically used to value the quantity and quality of outdoor recreation. In this method, demand curves for recreation visits (or trips) are estimated using travel expenditures as a proxy for the price of visits to recreation sites. The weak complementarity assumption is that when the visit (Z_i) is not made to a recreation site (e.g., the trip is not taken), the marginal utility of the destination site quality (Q) is zero. A typical application of the hedonic price method is to value environmental amenities (e.g., air quality, water quality) of residential real estate. In this method, implicit prices for environmental amenities are derived from differential payments people make for residential real estate with different levels of environmental amenities. The weak complementarity assumption is that if one does not purchase real estate in a certain neighborhood (Z_i), one does not care about the level of environmental amenities (Q) in the neighborhood. If Q and Z_i are weak complements, when Q increases, the demand for Z_i will shift outward. The Marshallian surplus from an increment in Q, from Q' to Q'', is measured as the area between the two demand schedules $Z_i(\underline{P}, Q', M)$ and $Z_i(\underline{P}, Q'', M)$.

Travel cost method

In order to enjoy the amenities provided by many outdoor recreation sites, it is necessary first to travel to the site, then to provide for one's subsistence at the site, and finally to return home. This observation led economist Harold Hotelling to suggest that the value of the amenities provided by outdoor recreation sites may be inferred from observation of the market for travel and subsistence purchased by users of the site. As implemented by Marion Clawson and Jack L. Knetch and refined by them and a host of others,[12] the travel cost method (TCM) of inferring the demand for recreation sites is implemented following the major approaches described below.

Zonal TCM The original means for implementing the TCM dating back to Clawson and Knetch is referred to as the zonal travel cost method. In this approach, the total use of the recreation site is objectively measured, usually in number of visits, using vehicle recorders, camper registration records, and the like. A random sample of users is then surveyed. A considerable variety of information may be collected, but the emphasis is always on obtaining reliable information about the visitor's place of permanent residence, the distance traveled to get to the site, and the expenses (e.g., for transportation, food, lodging, and any use or access fees) resulting from the visit. The information from the survey sample is then statistically analyzed and aggregated over the total population of the site's users by zone of origin (e.g., county of origin). A relationship between the distance traveled from the zone of origin and the expense of the trip is estimated statistically.

By comparing survey data on the zone of residence for visitors and census data describing the populations of origin zones, a statistical relationship between the cost of visiting the site and the proportion of those individuals facing that cost who choose to visit the site (e.g., visit per capita) is estimated. This relationship is a kind of demand curve, as it relates travel costs (a surrogate for price) to usage of the site (an indicator of quantities demanded). This estimated relationship is then transformed, using the assumption that potential visitors would respond to an increase in access fees for using the site in the same way that they would respond to an increase in travel costs to get there, into a demand curve relating the price of using the site to the quantity of use demanded. This relationship is then used to estimate the value of services offered by the recreation site.

Individual TCM   Although the zonal TCM is still applied today, the most common modern means of applying the travel cost method is the individual travel cost method. The individual TCM, which is argued to be more consistent with standard neoclassical demand theory, uses individual recreation site visitors as the unit of observation rather than origin zone populations as in the zonal TCM. A stylized individual TCM recreation demand equation may be specified as:

$$TRIPS_i^j = f(COST_i^j, SUBSTITUTE_i^j, INCOME_i, H_i) \tag{13.7}$$

where $TRIPS_i^j$ = annual trips by individual i to site j, $SUBSTITUTE_i^j$ = substitutes for site j available to individual i, $INCOME_i$ = personal or household income for individual i, and H_i = non-income personal or household characteristics of individual i (e.g., age, household size,).

To estimate equation (13.7), a survey is typically taken of site j visitors in which visitors are asked to report their total annual visits or trips to site j, their travel expenditures to and from the site, their on-site expenditures, their travel time to and from the site, additional sites they use as substitutes for site j, their origin (e.g., permanent residence), their personal or household income and other personal or household characteristics. Using appropriate statistical techniques for the type of data collected, equation (13.7) is then estimated which provides an estimated demand function for site access.[13] This demand function for a typical user is illustrated by the curve labeled D' in Figure 13.1. Once this demand function has been estimated, we can estimate Marshallian consumer's surplus for site access. For example, in Figure 13.1, the "choke price" for the typical user (cost per trip where the typical user stops coming to the site) is given by C^* and the travel cost currently faced by the typical user is assumed to $\overline{C}$. At this cost, the typical user will make $\overline{T}$ trips to the sites (say per year). Total consumers surplus for the typical user is the area below the demand function and above current travel costs illustrated in Figure 13.1 by the triangular area $\overline{C}, C^*, a$. Using duality theory, we may also be able to estimate Hicksian welfare measures from the estimated recreation demand function.

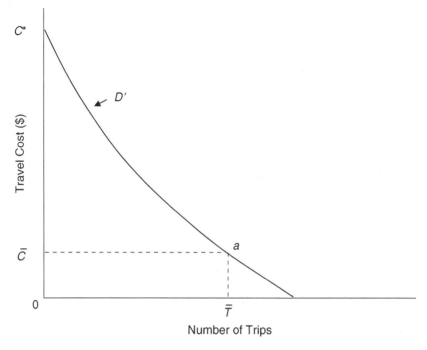

Figure 13.1   Travel cost method (TCM) demand function

A variation of the individual TCM which provides an alternative method for dealing with substitute sites is the random utility model (RUM) TCM. The RUM-TCM conceptualizes the recreation site choice decision in a decision-tree framework. In the first stage of the decision-tree, for example, a person may decide to take a recreation trip for a particular activity; e.g., she decides: "I am going trout fishing today." In the next stage of the decision process, she may choose which specific site to go trout fishing from her trout fishing site choice set (e.g., all the trout fishing sites she is willing and able to choose from). For example, she decides: "I am going to Site A today, rather than Sites B, C, D or E." The next day she may again decide to go trout fishing, but choose to go to Site D rather than Sites A, B, C, or E.

To estimate a RUM-TCM demand equation, the researcher, for example, collects data on the choices individuals make as to where to go trout fishing and the characteristics of those sites such as distance from a visitor's home and site quality (e.g., recreation facilities, water quality, catch rates). Using appropriate statistical techniques, a model is estimated from which the marginal implicit price or marginal value for site characteristics can be derived; for example, the model may show that visitors are willing to pay $3 more for each additional trout caught at a site (hence, $3 is the marginal implicit price or value). The estimated RUM-TCM model can also be applied to calculate changes in Marshallian consumer's surplus resulting from non-marginal changes in site characteristics (e.g., WTP for a non-marginal change in catch rate). It may then be possible using duality theory to derive Hicksian exact welfare measures from the Marshallian consumer's surplus measures.[14]

The travel-cost method of estimating the value of outdoor recreation services has been widely applied by researchers and is accepted for use in official benefit–cost analyses of federal water resources projects. However, there are some unresolved difficulties in the use of the technique and some limitations on its applicability. A major unresolved difficulty concerns the time cost of travel. Because the traveler invests both time and income in order to enjoy the services provided by a recreation site, their expenses alone will underestimate the total sacrifice made in order to use the site and, therefore (it is reasonably assumed), of their willingness to pay to use it. Unfortunately, because travel costs and travel time are highly correlated with each other, it has proved difficult to obtain reliable statistical estimates that separate the influences of travel time and travel costs on the use of the site. Solutions that simply add to the travel cost a "time cost" equal to travel time multiplied by a (usually small) fraction of the visitor's hourly wage are not entirely satisfactory.

The applicability of the travel-cost method is limited by the assumption that all expenditures during the trip may be regarded as paid specifically for using the site. This assumption is violated when the trip itself is a source of utility and when the trip entails visits to many different sites. The assumption that travel expenditures are an indicator of willingness to pay to use a site is violated when travel expenses themselves are small and presumably an insignificant portion of the total sacrifices made by site users. This problem limits the use of the travel-cost method for valuing services provided by recreation sites in or near large urban areas.

With respect to interpreting and measuring travel costs for use in estimating travel-cost method demand models, there is a more vexing fundamental difficulty pointed out by Randall.[15] It is not possible, in general, for researchers objectively to observe and measure travel costs, for two reasons. First, individual recreators' travel costs are inherently subjective (the opportunity cost of leisure time is a good example) and endogenous (e.g. they reflect household decisions that may have been influenced by recreational preferences, such as where to live and what kind of motor vehicle to own). Therefore, important components of the true travel costs are unobservable to researchers. Second, in the absence of fully observable travel costs, researchers make subjective decisions about the protocol used for estimating travel costs from what data can be observed (e.g., decisions about what proportion of time costs should be included when estimating travel costs). If travel costs are in fact subjective, welfare estimates derived from these costs will also be subjective and sensitive to the personal judgments and decisions of individual recreators and researchers alike.

Hedonic price method

The hedonic price method (HPM) focuses on deriving underlying implicit prices for non-market commodities from observable market data. Assume that Z_i can be defined by a vector of characteristics, $C_i = (c_{i1}, \ldots, c_{iq}, \ldots, c_{in})$, and that a purchaser, j, can vary c_i by choosing a particular unit, Z_{ij}. In other words, Z_i is not an ordinary homogenous good but a class of goods like "house," "automobile," or "vacation trip," and so different members of the class may possess different packages of characteristics. As the individual selects (say) a particular house or car, the amount of residential air quality or automobile safety they obtain is determined by that decision and, presumably, influences their choice. For any unit of Z_i, say Z_{ij}, its price $p_{z_{ij}}$ is:

$$p_{z_{ij}} = p_{z_i}(c_{ij1}, \ldots, c_{ijq}, \ldots, c_{ijn}) \tag{13.8}$$

where $p_{z_i}(\cdot)$ is the hedonic price function for Z_i. If the hedonic price equation can be estimated from observations of the prices $p_{z_{ij}}$ and characteristics c_{ij} of different Z_{ij}, then the expected price of any particular unit of Z_i can be calculated, given knowledge of its characteristics. The implicit price of c_{iq}, the amount Q enjoyed along with Z_i, can be found by differentiation:

$$p_{i_{iq}} = \frac{dp_{z_i}(\cdot)}{d_{c_{iq}}} \tag{13.9}$$

The implicit or hedonic price given by equation (13.9) may be interpreted as the value of Q, consumed as a characteristic of Z_i, at the margin. Below we describe two common approaches for estimating implicit (hedonic) price functions and prices.

The property value method[16] It is reasonable to assume that some kinds of natural resource and environmental amenities are enjoyed in a complementary manner with residential land. Thus observations of markets in residential land have been used to value the amenities provided by beachfront, lakeside, and riverside environments. In large metropolitan areas, where the quality of ambient air varies within the metropolis, observations of the demand for residential land have been used to infer the value of increments in air quality. Below the application of the land value method for valuing increments in air quality is briefly discussed.

A large metropolitan area is divided into well-defined subregions, typically census tracts (so that many of the kinds of data to be used in the analysis are available from census information). Data on the actual sales of residential land in each of the subregions are usually obtained from local government authorities that record real-estate transactions. Observations of ambient air quality (recorded by federal, state, and/or local environmental quality authorities) are arrayed by subregion. A detailed list of all other variables that may be expected to influence the sale price of residential land is made, and observations of these variables are obtained (from census and other information) by subregion. Relevant variables typically include indicators of the quality of residential structures on the land (e.g., number of rooms, total square feet of floor space, and the proportion of homes that provide amenities like central heating, air conditioning, and adequate plumbing); the distance from shopping centers, places of work, and the like; indicators of neighborhood quality (e.g., the density of housing, the proportion of land in the neighborhood devoted to parks, and the like); and the demographic characteristics of the neighborhood (e.g., per capita income, the mix of ethnic groups, and the crime rate).

A statistical relationship, in which the sale price of residential land is explained by ambient air quality and other variables such as those just enumerated, is hypothesized and estimated. When the researcher is satisfied that a reliable and statistically valid relationship has been estimated, attention is then focused on the regression coefficient for the air quality variable. If that coefficient is statistically significant, the researcher concludes that there does exist a relationship between ambient air quality and the market value of the residential land. If the (significant) coefficient has a positive sign, residents will be willing to pay more for land located in areas that enjoy relatively clean air.

Then, performing whatever mathematical manipulations are required by the particular form of the statistical equation estimated, the researcher uses the significant positive coefficient of the air quality variable to estimate quantitatively the increment in the sale price of residential land that may be attributed to a one-unit increment in the quality of the ambient air. This increment in sale price is the present value of the time stream of benefits from the increment in air quality. By a simple calculation, the annual benefits per household from a one-unit increment in air quality may be calculated, and the total annual benefits for an improvement in regional air quality may be calculated by aggregating over the number of households in the region.

For benefit–cost analysis, we are often interested in estimating the welfare impacts of non-marginal changes in Q. For example, suppose a proposed air pollution control program is expected to increase "excellent" air quality days in a metropolitan area from Q' (say, 150) days a year to Q'' (say, 200) days a year. One method for estimating the benefits of this plus 50 "excellent" air quality days is first to estimate an implicit or hedonic price function from property value data as described above. The next step is to calculate an inverse ordinary demand function or marginal WTP function for "excellent" air quality days from the implicit price function (corresponding to equation 13.8) for "excellent" air quality days. Once we have derived the marginal WTP function, illustrated by the curve labeled *MWTP'* in Figure 13.2, we then integrate under this demand function from Q' (150) to Q'' (200) "excellent" air quality days. This integral, illustrated by the area Q', Q'', b, a in Figure 13.2, is an estimate of the change in Marshallian consumers surplus associated with the plus 50 "excellent" air quality days.

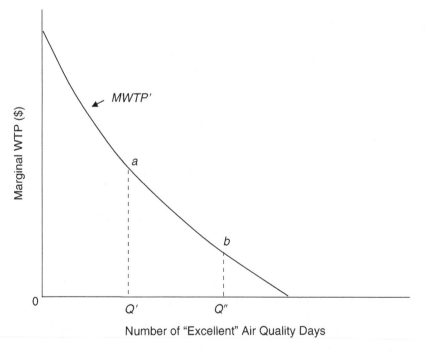

Figure 13.2   Inverse demand function for "excellent" air quality days

Employing duality theory, Hicksian welfare measures can then be estimated from the ordinary demand function. Details on the theory and techniques for implementing the hedonic price method including deriving welfare measures can be found in several good references.[17]

The property value method has been used in many research studies. It encounters some statistical difficulties, as there is no foolproof way for the analyst to be sure that the most reliable possible statistical relationship has been estimated. The method encounters some conceptual difficulties:[18] (1) it is not clear that because some residents are willing to pay a certain premium in order to enjoy a one-unit improvement in air quality relative to that obtained by other residents, all residents would be willing to pay the same premium for a one-unit improvement in air quality above their own homes; and (2) because residents typically spend a substantial portion of their time outside the home, one would expect that their willingness to pay for improved ambient air in the vicinity of the home may underestimate their willingness to pay for improved ambient air in the total metropolitan environment.

A relatively new approach to using property value and characteristic data to estimate environmental quality in metropolitan areas is the use of spatial general equilibrium models. In these models, the effects of environmental quality (e.g., air quality) on household location decisions are modeled in a general equilibrium framework, rather than the partial equilibrium framework used for traditional hedonic property value models. By exploiting the quantitative relationships revealed in the model between household location decisions and environmental quality, the economic value of spatially delineated environmental quality can be estimated.[19]

The wage rate method   Many policy decisions dealing with environmental quality, hazardous and toxic wastes, product safety, and workplace safety involve choices regarding the appropriate economic sacrifice in order to improve human health and safety. Thus, the benefit–cost analyst frequently encounters the need for estimates of the economic value of increments in human health and safety. Courts frequently confront a similar economic problem when they are required to determine the appropriate compensation for death or injury.

Some courts and some policy-makers have been willing to consider evidence of the present value of expected earnings forgone as a result of injury or premature death. However, this kind of evidence of the economic value of human health and safety is unsatisfactory because it places no value on the lives of the unemployed, retired persons, and homemakers, and values the lives of others in strict proportion to the market valuation of their labor. This method is based on the ethical supposition that human beings live to work and have no worth beyond that of the labor they would provide in the course of a normal lifespan.

An approach that seems more acceptable in its ethical implication is based on the idea that life and health are the fundamental sources of utility for the individual. Thus it asks not how much the labor market is willing to pay for an individual's services, but how much that individual is willing to accept in return for a decrement in life expectancy.

The wage premium required to induce a worker to accept employment in a hazardous occupation may be interpreted as evidence of a willingness to accept compensation for decrements in his or her own expectancy of health, safety, and longevity. A classic wage rate study was conducted by Thaler and Rosen. In their study, the authors obtained records from insurance companies which enabled them to estimate the probability of mortality on the job for different kinds of occupations.[20] For workers in each of these occupations, they determined the wage rates and the variables (e.g., education, occupational training, and demographic characteristics) that may influence the job opportunities available to each worker. Using statistical techniques similar to those used in applying the property value method, they estimated the wage premium required to attract a worker into an occupation that would increase their probability of mortality in one year by 0.001. This technique provides a fairly reasonable method of estimating an individual's Hicksian compensating value for marginal changes in expected health and safety and is thus useful in many kinds of policy analyses. But because the mortality expectancies associated with the various occupations ranged from roughly 0.003 to 0.007, the Thaler–Rosen analysis does not provide an acceptable basis for estimating the present value of a person's life.[21]

Over the past several decades, the basic approach pioneered by Thaler and Rosen has been extended to develop various measures of the "value of a statistical life" or VSL. A VSL is defined as the mean value expressed in monetary terms of avoiding one statistical death, say by reducing the risk of mortality from exposure to toxic pollutants. The US Environmental Protection Agency uses VSL estimates to quantify the economic benefits of mortality risk reductions when comparing the benefits and costs of environmental rules and regulations. Recent analyses of hedonic wage rate studies suggest a range of VSL estimates from about $1 million to $10 million.[22] An inappropriate interpretation of these dollar values, however, would be to say: "Joe Brown's life as an individual human being is worth $5 million." The value of an individual human being's life as a mother, father, son, daughter, friend, and so on is one of those intangible things in life we cannot put a price on. An appropriate interpretation of a VSL estimate of $5 million is that it represents the mean statistical value of reducing the risk of mortality in a population by one person.

Another application of hedonic wage rate models has been to develop quality-of-life estimates for different geographical places. For example, Blomquist, Berger and Hoehn combined hedonic wage rate and residential property value models to estimate quality of life in US urban areas, and then applied their estimates to rank US urban areas in term of quality of life.[23] The basic idea behind their model is that people make trade-offs between income and urban amenities (and disamenities) such as pleasant weather, high-quality schools, pollution, and crime, and these trade-offs show up in differential wage levels and residential property prices across communities. Statistical (econometric) models can then be used to estimate the relationships between wages (income), property prices, and urban amenities. The statistical results can be interpreted as compensating wage differentials (the extra wage a marginal mobile resident would have to be paid to live and work in County X). The quality-of-life rankings are inverse to the compensating wage differentials – households would accept lower wages to move to high-amenity counties, and vice versa.

A comparison of stated and revealed preference approaches

There is a tendency in the literature to treat stated and revealed preference approaches as rival research programs. This tendency is evidenced by the surveys of valuation methods,[24] which introduce both kinds of methods and address the relative strengths and weaknesses of each, and by the empirical literature[25] directly comparing the results obtained using a representative of each class of methods.

The notion of rival research programs is, however, of only limited validity. True, there is a domain of valuation problems to which both classes of methods are applicable. This domain is characterized by the following conditions: (1) the subject of valuation is an amenity, Q, that is weakly complementary to a set of market goods (or, alternatively, the level of Q is one characteristic of a set of market goods; and (2) there is a historical record of market transactions that supply observations of Q over the full range of policy interest. Within this domain, revealed and stated preference approaches each enjoy advantages that the other cannot claim. For example, valuations generated by stated preference techniques can be directly interpreted as Hicksian consumer's surplus measures. Valuations generated by revealed preference techniques can only be directly interpreted as Marshallian consumer's surplus measures. In this respect, stated preference methods are preferred to revealed preference methods since Hicksian consumer's surplus measures are the theoretically appropriate welfare measures for benefit–cost analysis. It is true that it may be possible to derive the theoretically appropriate Hicksian consumer's surplus measures from Marshallian consumer's surplus measures, but this transformation requires various more or less benign assumptions and contrived mathematical manipulations. On the other hand, revealed preference techniques use observations generated by actual transactions, whereas the transactions that generate stated preference data are non-binding because they are contingent on circumstances defined by "if . . ." statements. For this domain of valuation problems, stated and revealed preference techniques may be treated as rivals, if one wishes, or as complementary approaches that permit some independent replication of results.

In every case, the reported applications of these various methods include some kind of evidence of the undertaking's success. Plausible value estimates are obtained and, for example, estimates may be replicated within or across studies, or it may be demonstrated that (some of) the variation in individual valuations is explained by estimated economic relationships with robust coefficients of the expected sign. The body of such evidence is impressive. There seems little doubt that in appropriate applications, CVM, CE, TCM, and HPM, to name only the more common methods, can cast considerable light on the economic value of natural resource and environmental goods and services.

But the "crucial experiment," testing a refutable hypothesis to the effect that estimated values are or are not equal to the real values, is seldom permitted. In this situation, demonstrations showing that different non-market valuation techniques generate consistent results indicate supportive, but not conclusive, evidence of reliability. Various researchers have attempted such comparisons with considerable success.[26]

There is another domain of valuation problems for which the revealed preference techniques offer no operational alternatives to stated preference techniques. This second domain includes cases in which: (1) no markets suitable for revealed preference analysis exist; (2) the range of experienced levels of Q is not inclusive of all policy options; or (3) new information (about, say, environmental hazards to health) is not reflected in a data set of market transactions adequate for statistical analysis. For this domain of valuation problems, stated preference techniques currently stand as the only viable options. Note that case 1, where there are no markets suitable for stated preference analysis, applies to some categories of on-site amenity use and perhaps also to most situations involving off-site (e.g., vicarious) uses, option values and passive use values.

Hybrid revealed–stated preference models

In the above section we have portrayed revealed and stated preference methods as alternative methods or tools for valuing non-market goods and services. It is possible, however, to combine these two methods or tools into hybrid revealed–stated preference valuation approaches. One of the most common hybrid approaches is to combine revealed and stated travel behavior data to estimate a hybrid travel cost model for valuing recreation quantity and quality. For example, suppose we are interested in estimating anglers' responses to changes in fish catch. We may conduct a survey that collects revealed preference data on anglers' actual number of fishing trips to a site and actual catch rates at the site. In the survey we may also collect stated preference data by asking anglers to state how many trips they would take to the site at different hypothetical catch rates. We can then combine these revealed and preference data to estimate a hybrid travel cost model showing the relationships between an angler's actual and intended trips (or contingent trips) to the site and the angler's actual and hypothetical catch rates at the site.[27] A number of previous studies provide more theoretical background on and empirical examples of hybrid revealed–stated preference approaches including recreational and environmental quality applications.[28]

Benefit transfer

In certain policy and management situations, there may not be enough money and/or time to collect the primary data needed to implement any of the revealed and stated preference non-market valuation techniques discussed above. In such situations, benefit transfer may provide an alternative for estimating the value of changes in non-marketed goods and services. Benefit transfer involves using "off the shelf" secondary data collected to meet a particular valuation objective to estimate economic value changes at "study sites" to estimate the value of non-marketed commodity changes at some "policy site." There are two general approaches to benefit transfer: value transfer and function transfer. Types of value transfer include single-point estimate transfer, measure of central tendency transfer, and administratively approved unit value transfer. Types of function transfer include benefit–demand function transfer and meta-analysis function transfer.[29]

Under the value transfer approach, typically a single point estimate of the mean or median value for a non-marketed good or service at a study site (or perhaps an average across several study sites) is transferred to the policy site. For example, in the US State of Georgia, the US Army Corps of Engineers manages several large reservoirs including Hartwell Reservoir, Lanier Reservoir, Thurmond Reservoir and West Point Reservoir. Suppose a new reservoir management policy at Thurmond Reservoir is expected to increase recreational fishing days and there is a need to estimate the economic value of this change. Suppose further that non-market valuation studies have already been conducted at Hartwell, Lanier, and West Point reservoirs which showed that value of a fishing day to be $38 per day at Hartwell Reservoir, $27 per day at Lanier Reservoir and $10 per day at West Point Reservoir. Benefit transfer would involve using these "study site" values of a fishing day to estimate the value of a fishing day at Thurmond Reservoir rather than conducting a new primary data study at Thurmond.

Hartwell Reservoir and Thurmond Reservoir are in the Savannah River water-shed along the Georgia–South Carolina border and Lanier Reservoir and West Point Reservoir are in the Chattahoochee River watershed along the Georgia–Alabama border. Thus, we may choose to use the Hartwell Reservoir estimate of $38 per day as an estimate of the value of a fishing day at Thurmond Reservoir since these two reservoirs are in the same watershed. However, if fishing experiences and user populations are judged not too different between the Savannah River and Chattahoochee River watersheds, we may approximate the value of a fishing day at Thurmond Reservoir by using the average of fishing day values from Hartwell, Lanier and West Point, which equals $25. The US Army Corps of Engineers has official procedures for value transfer termed the "unit day method" which allow for adjustments to be made to study site values to reflect conditions better (e.g., site quality) at the policy site.[30] As part of the US Renewable Resources Planning Act national assessment of the demand and supply situation for natural resources, the United States Department of Agriculture (USDA) Forest Service also provides suggested procedures and estimated study values for applying the value transfer approach when using benefit transfer to estimate recreation values for US National Forest policy and planning.[31]

Most economists would agree that the function transfer approach should be superior to the value transfer approach since it provides a theoretical and statistically based means for adjusting study site values for transfer to a policy site. In this approach, statistical estimation of a theoretically-based benefit–demand function or meta-analysis function provides a value estimator model of the general form:

$$VALUE_j^i = (ATTRIBUTES_j^i, USERPOP_j^i, INSTITUTIONS_j^i) \qquad (13.10)$$

where, $VALUE_j^i$ = value of non-marketed good or service j at policy site i, $ATTRIBUTES_j^i$ = attributes of policy site i impacting the quantity or quality of non-marketed good or service j provided at the policy site, $USERPOP_j^i$ = characteristics of the user population for non-marketed good or service j at policy site i, $INSTITUTIONS_j^i$ = institutions at policy site i including property rights and other rules and regulations impacting the quantity or quality of non-marketed good or service j provided at the policy site.

Referring back to our example of US Army Corps of Engineers reservoirs in the State of Georgia, a linear version of a value estimator model might be specified as:

$$FISHDAYVALUE = \alpha + \beta_1 FISHCATCH + \beta_2 INCOME + \beta_3 CATCHLIMIT \qquad (13.11)$$

where, $FISHDAYVALUE$ = the value of a fishing day at Thurmond Reservoir, $FISHCATCH$ = average fish catch per day at Thurmond Reservoir, $INCOME$ = average income of Thurmond Reservoir anglers, $CATCHLIMIT$ = catch limit per day at Thurmond Reservoir, α = estimated intercept (constant term), and β_1, β_2 and β_3 are estimated coefficients on the explanatory variables. Equation (13.11) could be estimated by combining data for, say, all reservoirs in the state of Georgia and perhaps also in surrounding states, and then estimating a benefit–demand model.[32] Given the existence of enough previous studies, it may also be possible to estimate equation (13.11) using meta-analysis. Meta-analysis would involve combining estimates of fishing day values from previous studies with observations of determinants of fishing day values from these previous studies (including methods of valuation) to estimate the parameters in equation (13.11).[33]

Once we have estimated equation (13.11), the value of a fishing day at Thurmond Reservoir can be calculated by plugging in values for *FISHCATCH*, *INCOME*, and *CATCHLIMIT* to the right-hand side of the equation and solving for the left-hand-side variable. The result represents the predicted value of a fishing day at Thurmond Reservoir which we would use as our estimate of the value of a fishing day at this reservoir. An advantage of using an estimate value estimator model such as equation (13.11) for benefit transfer is that value estimates can be adjusted in the future as conditions change (for example, as fish catch changes at a reservoir due to environmental changes, user income changes due to changes in the national or state economy, or institutions change due to new laws and legislation).

Strategies under incomplete value information
The general conceptual model for BCA (see Chapter 12, equations 12.1–12.5) is simple enough in principle and serves as a useful guide for organizing one's thinking. But at every step, the path from concept to empirical application is enormously complex. Merely to identify the elements of E, the vector of ecosystem goods and services provided by natural capital, may be an overwhelming task. Those elements that are inputs into the organized production of marketable commodities (e.g., timber products, livestock grazing, and minerals) may be fairly well defined and routinely recorded. For publicly owned recreation sites, management agencies now routinely record recreational visits to national parks, national forests, and public reservoirs and beaches. However, a few recent studies have found that for some kinds of relatively scarce environmental resources, the values generated through visits to recreation sites are swamped by the values accruing to a larger population who in some way appreciates the environment without actually visiting it. That is, existence services to non-visitors are in some environments considerably larger than are recreation visitor services. Yet existence services themselves have a somewhat nebulous character, and recent attempts to define such services have produced less than impressive results. Environmental services, such as ecosystem diversity and the integrity of hydrological systems, may be recognized in principle but tend to escape precise definition and quantification. Furthermore, in the context of exponentially growing scientific and technical knowledge, there is the possibility that currently unrecognized services will acquire significant value in the future.

If the mere identification and measurement of environmental or ecosystem goods and services are difficult tasks, the specification of the production system for these goods and services (see equations 12.1 and 12.2) is considerably more challenging. Yet it is a crucial step in the evaluation of policy alternatives. Policy alternatives are implemented via the deliberate manipulation of the X vector of human-controlled inputs. Again, more is known about the production systems for commercial services and recreation visitor days than about those for less well-defined kinds of ecosystem goods and services.

Observe that the identification of ecosystem goods and services and the estimation of the technical relationships governing their production are tasks for ecologists, physical scientists, and the like, rather than economists. Economists do not measure these things but use measurements made by others. In that sense, economists live high on the information food chain. Although others have sometimes placed economists on the defensive by criticizing the reliability and precision of non-market benefit estimation methods, economists are wont to retort that many estimates of underlying (e.g., ecological) relationships are even less precise.

Moving now to the demand system for environmental services (see equations 12.3 and 12.4), we find once again that the availability of information is much greater, and its cost is much lower, for some kinds of services as compared to others. Markets offer considerable information about the demand for those services traded commercially. Nevertheless, there may be difficulties in BCA in cases where prices are determined administratively rather than in competitive markets. There is now a considerable reservoir of empirical information about the demand for recreation services, but much of the emphasis has been on estimating the value of visits or days at a specific site under narrowly defined partial equilibrium conditions. Relationships among substitute sites are less well understood; general equilibrium demand systems have seldom been attempted; and off-site values (e.g., option value, quasi-option value, and passive use value) have received empirical consideration in only a few previous studies. In general, value estimation is technically more demanding at the conceptual and empirical levels for those goods that are neither divisible nor traded in large, competitive markets.

Having taken a closer look at the general conceptual model for BCA, it must be concluded that many of its elements are poorly specified and elusive in measurement and that many crucial production and demand relationships are unknown. Furthermore, it seems certain that more and better information is available with respect to the kinds of services that customarily enter commerce and those that are now routinely recorded by management agencies. Not only is the necessary information matrix incomplete; it is systematically more complete with respect to the kinds of things that come to the attention of, say, accountants rather than things concerning, say, ecologists. Although all aspects of BCA are susceptible to incomplete and inaccurate empirical analysis, the information base for evaluating marketed good and services is inherently richer and less costly to assemble than is that for non-marketed goods and services.

If the information base for BCA is not merely incomplete but more complete with respect to some kinds of goods and services than are other kinds, there will be a threat of systematic bias. Such a bias may distort the outcome of public decisions and, in extreme cases, may negate the information value of BCA. In such a context, it is imperative that efforts be channeled toward redressing imbalances in the information base for applied BCA.

Formal BCA reduces a large amount of information that varies in kind and quality to a single number such as a net present value or a benefit–cost ratio. Goods and services for which no value data are available are treated as making zero contributions to benefits, costs, and net present value, unless care and effort are expended specifically to correct such misinterpretation. Next we consider several strategies for BCA in limited information situations.

Valuation of non-marketed goods and services
As we have seen, there has been substantial progress in developing, refining, and validating techniques for the valuation of non-marketed goods and services. The absence of

value information revealed in organized markets is no longer a good reason to exclude non-marketed benefit and cost items from formal BCA.

It has been argued that given the inherently richer database for the valuation of marketed goods, efforts should be specifically channeled toward the economic valuation of non-marketed goods and services. But there are some limits on the amounts of talent and funding that can reasonably be directed to such a project. In addition, the prospects for success are better for some categories of goods and services than for others, and in problem cases, the difficulty is as likely to lie in the absence of physical and biological data as in the failure to develop appropriate economic valuation methods. It must be expected that economic value data, comparable to that available for commercially marketed goods and services, will remain unavailable for some non-marketed goods and services which nevertheless are important considerations when selecting appropriate natural resource and environmental policies. In such cases, all obtainable information should be documented. This implies in some cases the careful assembly and display of information that falls short of conveying dollar value numbers.

Documentation of positive value
It is often possible to show that natural resource and environmental goods and services are being provided and have a positive value. For example, recent research indicates that the general public places a high priority on protecting wilderness areas, not because they would like to visit a wilderness area, but because they believe it is important to protect broad ecosystem services (such as air and water quality) supported by healthy ecosystems.[34] Given the current state of the art with respect to ecosystem service valuation, it is not always possible to take the next step: to estimate benefits in dollar terms. Nevertheless, careful documentation that (for example) wilderness values are real and positive helps counter the erroneous implication that those things that cannot be reliably valued in dollar terms are without value.

Documentation of positive production
As a last resort, it may be possible to show that certain kinds of environmental goods and services are being provided in positive quantities. For example, scientists can measure the amount of carbon sequestered by a tropical forest in Brazil or a stand of timber in a southeastern US pine plantation. This kind of information also helps correct the tendency to ignore those things that cannot be incorporated in a single benefit cost or net present value. In general, the analyst's operating rule should be to value in economic terms those goods and services that can be valued; failing that, to show that observable behavior necessarily implies a positive valuation for particular services; and failing even that, to show that the production of environmental goods and services is positive. All of these various kinds of evidence have their place in the final display of results from BCA.

Sensitivity analysis
When technical coefficients and value estimates are uncertain, sensitivity analysis is appropriate. Benefit and cost estimates are based on the "best" estimates of coefficients and prices, but the possible range of values of these parameters is recognized. The arithmetic is reiterated, using the end points of this range and perhaps several interme-

diate values. The purpose is to determine whether the final conclusions are sensitive to assumptions about technical and price parameters for particular natural resource and environmental goods and services. When uncertainty is unequally distributed across the vector of goods and services, particular attention should be addressed to sensitivity analysis where the uncertainty is the greatest. Clearly, the BCA exercise will be inconclusive if sensitivity analysis demonstrates that the benefits of the proposed change exceed its costs under some plausible technical and price assumptions but not under others.

Inverse sensitivity analysis
There may be natural resource and environmental goods and services recognized as significant but for which it is impossible to make plausible estimates of crucial technical or value coefficients. In such cases, inverse sensitivity analysis should be used. Rather than determining how alternative estimates affect benefit–cost outcomes, inverse sensitivity analysis asks, "How large would an unquantified benefit or cost item need to be in order to reverse the conclusion of a BCA omitting that item?" Inverse sensitivity analysis is a useful indicator of the robustness of BCA conclusions in cases in which particular benefit and/or cost items are admittedly unquantifiable.

Alternatives to benefit–cost analysis
In response to complaints that there are cases in which an approximately accurate estimation of both benefits and costs is impossible, alternative and less complete formulations have been developed. Two of the better known are cost-effectiveness analysis and risk–benefit analysis.

Cost-effectiveness analysis   Cost-effectiveness analysis seeks to identify the least-cost way in which to achieve a given objective, without asking whether there is any economic justification for achieving that objective. Obviously, cost-effectiveness analysis is most appropriately applied in cases where there is overwhelming support for project objectives, and thus the real question is not whether the objective should be fulfilled but how it may be fulfilled least expensively. Unfortunately, the cost-effectiveness format is also used, by default as it were, in cases where there is no clear consensus about how best to measure program benefits. If benefits may be quantified, but not in economic terms, though costs are economically quantifiable, the cost-effectiveness criterion provides guidance as to the least-cost method of obtaining the specified benefits.

If several candidate projects or programs would achieve exactly the same benefits that can be quantified in non-monetary terms (e.g. number of human lives saved by a disease control program), cost-effectiveness analysis requires merely that the costs of the alternative projects or programs be arrayed. Strict application of the cost-effectiveness criterion would require selection of the alternative with the lowest total cost. Unfortunately, alternatives with different costs also often promise different arrays of benefits. When different alternatives offer homogeneous benefits, but in different quantities, a cost-effectiveness ratio (that is, cost per unit of output) may be calculated. Such a ratio gives information about the average costs per unit of output of the alternative projects or programs, but does not give enough information to determine the economic efficiency of the various alternatives. When, as is often the case, alternative projects and programs promise to provide qualitatively different outputs, even the cost-effectiveness ratio (with all of its obvious inadequacies) is no longer meaningful.

Risk–benefit analysis   With the recent and growing awareness of the risks in creating nearly indestructible toxic and hazardous wastes, the use of risk–benefit analysis has been growing. The underlying concept is that economic progress often entails the acceptance of some degree of risk to environmental quality or human health and safety. A trade-off between risk and economic productivity is thus explicitly recognized. Risk–benefit analysis arrays the economic benefits from various project and program alternatives alongside quantitative estimates of the risks involved. In its most complete form, risk–benefit analysis compares expected project benefits with the expected economic value of potential environmental or human hazards. However, the latter are often unmeasurable in economic terms, and reliable estimates of the probabilities of various catastrophes or hazards of specified magnitudes are unavailable. In these cases, risk–benefit analysis remains incomplete. Furthermore, it should immediately be obvious that even a complete risk–benefit analysis is only a partial guide to economic decision-making.

Questions for discussion

1.   Global climate change could benefit some people while resulting in costs on others. For example, some farmers may be able to produce more crops at a lower cost (because of more favorable temperatures and rainfall) while other farmers may only be able to produce less at a higher cost (because of less favorable temperatures and rainfall). In what other ways might some people gain and some people lose from global climate change, and how would you go about identifying and measuring these benefits and costs?
2.   Economists (e.g., Thaler and Rosen) claim to have developed a serviceable method of estimating the willingness of workers to pay for reductions in work-related mortality and morbidity. Can you think of a suitable methodology estimating the WTP of retired persons for an increment in life expectancy?
3.   A major concern of skeptics of the fledgling research program in contingent valuation in the 1970s can be summarized by the statement: "Ask a hypothetical question and you'll get a hypothetical answer." Would you expect a similar reaction to CVM to be prevalent among resource economists today? Why or why not?
4.   Can you think of one (or, better yet, several) techniques that could be used to determine the aggregate value to your class of the reference materials placed on reserve at the library for this course? Design a research project in which the technique(s) could be implemented.

Notes

1.   John C. Bergstrom and John B. Loomis (1999), "Economic Dimensions of Ecosystem Management," in *Integrating Social Sciences with Ecosystem Management*, ed. H. Ken Cordell and John C. Bergstrom, Champaign, IL: Sagamore Publishing Co.
2.   Bergstrom and Loomis, "Economic Dimensions," op. cit.
3.   Ronald C. Griffin and John R. Stoll (1984), "Evolutionary Processes in Soil Conservation Policy," *Land Economics* **60**: 30–39.
4.   William J. Baumol and Wallace E. Oates (1988), *The Theory of Environmental Policy: Second Edition*, Cambridge: Cambridge University Press, Chapter 3 ("Externalities: Definition Significant Types, and Optimal-Pricing Conditions").
5.   John C. Bergstrom, B.L. Dillman, and John R. Stoll (1985), "Public Environmental Amenity Benefits of Private Land: The Case of Prime Agricultural Land," *Southern Journal of Agricultural Economics* **17**: 139–49.
6.   Griffin and Stoll, "Evolutionary Processes," op. cit.
7.   See Alan Randall and John R. Stoll (1980), "Consumer's Surplus in Commodity Space," *American Economic Review* **70**: 449–55; A. Myrick Freeman III (2003), *The Measurement of Environmental and Resource Values: Second Edition*, Washington, DC: Resources for the Future; Richard E. Just, Darrell L. Hueth, and Andrew Schmitz (2004), *The Welfare Economics of Public Policy: A Practical Approach to Project and Policy Evaluation*, Cheltenham, UK and Northampton, MA, USA: Edward Elgar.

8. For example, see Ian J. Bateman and Ken G. Willis (eds) (1999), *Valuing Environmental Preferences: Theory and Practice of the Contingent Valuation Method in the US, EU and Developing Countries*, Oxford: Oxford University Press; Timothy C. Habb and Kenneth E. McConnell (2002), *Valuing Environmental and Natural Resources: The Econometrics of Non-market Valuation*, Cheltenham, UK and Northampton, MA, USA: Edward Elgar; Patricia A. Champ, Kevin J. Boyle, and Thomas C. Brown (eds) (2003), *A Primer on Non-market Valuation*, Dordrecht: Kluwer Academic Publishers.

9. The following passages summarize the argument developed in John P. Hoehn and Alan Randall (1987), "A Satisfactory Benefit Cost Indicator from Contingent Valuation," *Journal of Environmental Economics and Management* **14** (3): 226–47.

10. Brian Roe, Kevin J. Boyle, and Mario F. Teisl (1996), "Using Conjoint Analysis to Derive Estimates of Compensating Variation," *Journal of Environmental Economics and Management* **31** (2): 145–59.

11. For example, see Champ et al., *Primer on Non-market Valuation*, op. cit.; Habb and McConnell, *Valuing Environmental and Natural Resources*, op. cit.

12. See Marion Clawson and Jack L. Knetch (1965), *Economics of Outdoor Recreation*, Baltimore, MD: Johns Hopkins University Press; Champ et al., *Primer on Non-market Valuation*, op. cit.; Freeman, *Measurement of Environmental and Resource Values*, op. cit.

13. See Habb and McConnell, *Valuing Environmental and Natural Resources*, op. cit.

14. See Champ et al., *Primer on Non-market Valuation*, op. cit.; Habb and McConnell, *Valuing Environmental and Natural Resources*, op. cit.

15. Alan Randall (1994), "A Difficulty with the Travel Cost Method," *Land Economics* **70** (1): 88–96.

16. See A. Myrick Freeman III (1974), "On Estimating Air Pollution Control Benefits from Land Value Studies," *Journal of Environmental Economics and Management* **1**: 74–83.

17. See Champ et al., *Primer on Non-market Valuation*, op. cit.; Freeman, *Measurement of Environmental and Resource Values*, op. cit.; Habb and McConnell, *Valuing Environmental and Natural Resources*, op. cit.

18. For a more sophisticated discussion of the conceptual difficulties encountered in using the property value method, see Karl-Goran Maler (1974), *Environmental Economics*, Baltimore, MD: Johns Hopkins University Press, pp. 178–99.

19. For more discussion of this approach, see Holder Sieg, V. Kerry Smith, H. Spencer Banzhaf, and Randall P. Walsh (2004), "Estimating the General Equilibrium Benefits of Large Changes in Spatially Delineated Public Goods," *International Economic Review* **45** (4): 1047–77; V. Kerry Smith, Holder Sieg, H. Spencer Banzhaf, and Randall P. Walsh (2004), "General Equilibrium Benefits for Environmental Improvements: Projected Ozone Reductions Under EPA's Prospective Analysis for the Los Angeles Air Basin," *Journal of Environmental Economics and Management* **47** (3): 559–84.

20. Richard H. Thaler and Sherwin Rosen (1976), "The Value of Saving a Life: A Market Estimate," in *Household Production and Consumption*, ed. Nestor Terleckyj, New York: Columbia University Press.

21. Thaler and Rosen claim, however, that their method does offer an acceptable basis for estimating the combined willingness of 1000 workers to pay to prevent one additional work-related death.

22. Janusz R. Mrozek and Laura O. Taylor (2002), "What Determines the Value of Life? A Meta-Analysis," *Journal of Policy Analysis and Management* **21** (2): 253–70; Kip W. Viscusi and Joseph E. Aldy (2003), "The Value of a Statistical Life: A Critical Review of Market Estimates Throughout the World," *Journal of Risk and Uncertainty* **27** (1): 5–76.

23. Glenn C. Blomquist, Mark C. Berger, and John P. Hoehn (1988), "New Estimates of Quality of Life in Urban Areas," *American Economic Review* **78** (1): 89–107. For more recent studies on this topic, see Patrick Bayer, Nathaniel Keohane, and Christopher Timmins (2009), "Migration and Hedonic Valuation: The Case of Air Quality," *Journal of Environmental Economics and Management* **58**: 1–14; Matthew E. Kahn (1995), "A Revealed Preference Approach to Ranking City Quality of Life," *Journal of Urban Economics* **38**: 221–35.

24. See, for example, Freeman, *Measurement of Environmental and Resource Values*, op. cit.

25. See, for example, David S. Brookshire, Mark A. Thayer, William D. Schulze, and Ralph C. d'Arge (1982), "Valuing Public Goods: A Comparison of Survey and Hedonic Approaches," *American Economic Review* **72**: 165–77; Richard Carson, Nicholas Flores, Kerry Martin, and Jennifer Wright (1996), "Contingent Valuation and Revealed Preferences Methodologies: Comparing the Estimates for Quasi-Public Goods," *Land Economics* **72**: 80–89.

26. Richard C. Bishop and Thomas A. Heberlein (1979), "Measuring Values of Extra-Market Goods: Are Indirect Measures Biased?," *American Journal of Agricultural Economics* **61**: 926–30; Brookshire et al., "Valuing Public Goods," op. cit.; Fredrik Carlsson and Peter Martinsson (2001), "Do Hypothetical and Actual Marginal Willingness to Pay Differ in Choice Experiments? Application to the Valuation of the Environment," *Journal of Environmental Economics and Management* **41** (2): 179–92; Jack L. Knetch and Robert K. Davis (1966), "Comparisons of Methods for Recreation Evaluation," in *Water Research*, ed.

Allen V. Kneese and Stephen C. Smith, Baltimore, MD: Johns Hopkins University Press, 1966); John A. List and Craig A. Gallet (2001), "What Experimental Protocol Influence Disparities Between Actual and Hypothetical Stated Values?," *Environmental and Resource Economics* **20**: 241–54.

27. For an empirical example of applying a hybrid approach to estimate the relationship between fishing trips and fish catch rates, see John C. Bergstrom, Jeffrey H. Dorfman, and John B. Loomis (2004), "Estuary Management and Recreational Fishing Benefits," *Coastal Management* **32**: 417–32.

28. See, for example, Wiktor Adamowicz, Jordan Louviere, and Michael Williams (1994), "Combining Revealed and Stated Preference Methods for Valuing Environmental Amenities," *Journal of Environmental Economics and Management* **26**: 271–92; Trudy A. Cameron (1882), "Combining Contingent Valuation and Travel Cost Data for the Valuation of Non-market Goods," *Land Economics* **68**: 302–17; Dietrich Earnhart (2001), "Combining Revealed and Stated Preference Methods to Value Environmental Amenities at Residential Locations," *Land Economics* **77** (1): 12–29; Ju-Chin Huang, Timothy C. Haab, and John C. Whitehead (1997), "Willingness to Pay for Quality Improvements: Should Revealed and Stated Preference Data Be Combined?," *Journal of Environmental Economics and Management* **34** (3): 240–55.

29. For more background on benefits transfer methods, see Randall S. Rosenberger and John B. Loomis (2001), "Benefit Transfer of Outdoor Recreation Use Values: A Technical Document Supporting the Forest Service Strategic Plan (2000 revision)," Gen. Tech. Rep. RMRS-GTR-72, Fort Collins, CO: US Department of Agriculture, Forest Service, Rocky Mountain Research Station.

30. See US Water Resources Council (1983), *Economic and Environmental Principles and Guidelines for Water and Related Land Resources Implementation Studies* (March), Appendix 3 to Section VIII (NED Benefit Evaluation Procedures: Recreation).

31. See Rosenberger and Loomis, "Benefit Transfer of Outdoor Recreation Use Values," op. cit.

32. For an actual example, see John Loomis, Brian Roach, Frank Ward, and Richard Ready (1995), "Testing Transferability of Recreation Demand Models Across Regions: A Study of Corps of Engineer Reservoirs," *Water Resources Research* **31** (3): 721–30.

33. For more detail and citations to empirical examples, see John C. Bergstrom and Laura O. Taylor (2006), "Using Meta-Analysis for Benefits Transfer: Theory and Practice," *Ecological Economics* **60**: 351–60.

34. Cassandra Y. Johnson, J.M. Bowker, H. Ken Cordell, and John C. Bergstrom (2004), "Wilderness Values in America: Does Immigrant Status or Ethnicity Matter?," *Society and Natural Resources* **17**: 611–28.

Suggested reading: classic and contemporary

Bergstrom, J.C., J.R. Stoll, and A. Randall (1989), "Information Effects in Contingent Markets," *American Journal of Agricultural Economics* **71** (3): 685–91.

Blomquist, G.C., M.C. Berger, and J.P. Hoehn (1988), "New Estimates of Quality of Life in Urban Areas," *American Economic Review* **78**: 89–107.

Boyle, K.J. and J.C. Bergstrom (1992), "Benefit Transfer Studies: Myths, Pragmatism and Idealism," *Water Resources Research* **29** (3): 657–63.

Cameron, T.A. (1988), "A New Paradigm for Valuing Non-Market Goods Using Referendum Data: Maximum Likelihood Estimation by Censored Logistic Regression," *Journal of Environmental Economics and Management* **15**: 355–79.

Hanemann, W.M. (1984), "Welfare Evaluation in Contingent Valuation Experiments with Discrete Responses," *American Journal of Agricultural Economics* **66**: 332–41.

Loomis, J.B., and R.G. Walsh (1997), *Recreation Economic Decisions: Comparing Benefits and Costs*, State College, PA: Venture Publishing.

McConnell, K.E., I. Strand, and L. Blake-Hedges (1995), "Random Utility Models of Recreational Fishing: Catching Fish Using a Poisson Process," *Marine Resource Economics* **10**: 247–61.

PART V

OPTIMAL MANAGEMENT OF NON-RENEWABLE AND RENEWABLE RESOURCES

14 Exhaustible, non-renewable resources: what is the optimal use and management of non-renewable resources over time?

It is characteristic of intertemporal resource allocation problems that decisions made now help determine, favorably or adversely, opportunities in the future. In making current decisions, it behooves us to consider future opportunity costs. Furthermore, intertemporal allocation decisions for natural resources and environmental services are not made in isolation from other decisions with long-term implications. Markets in natural resources are directly linked to financial markets and markets in capital assets. All of this suggests the obvious: intertemporal resource allocation decisions to exploit now or to conserve for later, are investment decisions and can be analyzed with investment theory models (see Chapter 7), appropriately specified.

Optimal depletion of an endowment

Start with the simplest possible case, the individually optimal depletion of an endowment. Consider a shipwreck survivor floating in the middle of the ocean in a life raft well stocked with fresh water, but all food was lost in the shipwreck except for a bag of cookies. The survivor believes she has enough food in the form of a bag of cookies to survive for seven days after which the raft will drift into known commercial shipping lanes where she expects to be rescued. The food supply (bag of cookies) in the raft at the beginning of the first day is given by S_0 with $S_0 > \Sigma_{t=1}^{T} N_t$, where N_t is the minimum nutritional requirement for period t and $T = 7$: that is, her food endowment is more than enough to provide minimal subsistence until rescue if rationed carefully. Her decision problem is to maximize the present value of utility from a stream of consumption $C = \Sigma_{t=1}^{T} C_t$ subject to the constraint $S_0 = \Sigma_{t=1}^{T} C_t$. This constraint requires that cumulative consumption exactly equal the initial stock; thus the cookies neither spoil nor multiply while awaiting consumption, and the survivor is expected to exhaust the stock by the time of her rescue. At what rate does she eat the cookies? Does she simply divide the initial stock by the number of time periods and eat S_0/T cookies in each period (we might call this the "everything I need to know I learned in kindergarten" solution)?

Using an iterative two-period model (Figure 14.1a), the initial opportunity set is bounded by a straight line (S_0S_0) of slope -1, which can be interpreted as the intertemporal production possibilities curve. First-period consumption, C_1, and the stock, $S_1 = S_0 - C_1$, carried forward are determined by the tangency of S_0S_0 and an intertemporal indifference curve. For the second period, the opportunity set is bounded by the line S_1S_1, and the consumption, C_2, is determined by tangency. This process is repeated for each time period, and a time path of consumption is identified.

With a positive time preference, the consumer chooses a smoothly decreasing time path of consumption (Figure 14.1b). Her decision rule is:

$$RCS_{C_t, C_{t+1}} = RPT_{C_t, C_{t+1}} = 1 \tag{14.1}$$

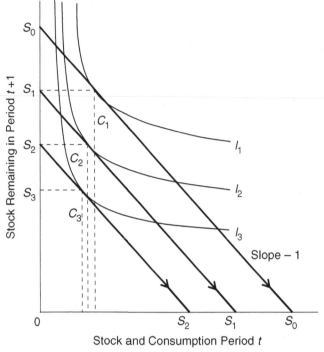

(a) Determination of each period's consumption

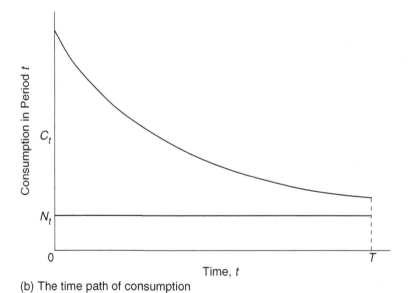

(b) The time path of consumption

Figure 14.1   Optimal depletion of an endowment

where $t = 1, 2, \ldots, T - 1$.

Now suppose that there are weevils, that got in to the life raft from the ship, so that the cookies left uneaten will deteriorate. The constraint is now $S_0 = \Sigma_{t=1}^{T} C_t(1 - d)^t$, where $0 \le d \le 1$ is the "deterioration factor." The intertemporal production possibilities line now has a slope of $-(1 - d)$. The intertemporal decision rule becomes:

$$RCS_{C_t', C_{t+1}'} = RPT_{C_t', C_{t+1}'} = \frac{(1 - d)^{t+1}}{(1 - d)^t} = 1 - d \qquad (14.2)$$

where $t = 1, 2, \ldots, T - 1$. The first-period consumption is lower than for the case in which there is no spoilage, but nevertheless consumption is reduced to a proportionally greater extent in later time periods (Figure 14.2). Weevils do two things: they diminish the consumer's wealth, thus reducing consumption in every period, and they reduce the productivity of conservation and hence the rewards for restraint, and so the chosen consumption path is tilted toward the present.

Now consider a third case. Instead of cookies, suppose that the survivor has edible algae, so that the uneaten portion grows exponentially. The constraint becomes $S_0 = \Sigma_{t=1}^{T} C_t(1 + g)^t$, where $0 \le g \le 1$ is the growth rate of the algae. The survivor now has a productive opportunity not merely to conserve but also, in a sense, to invest. Her decision rule is now:

$$RCS_{C_t'', C_{t+1}''} = RPT_{C_t'', C_{t+1}''} = \frac{(1 + g)^{t+1}}{(1 + g)^t} = 1 + g \qquad (14.3)$$

where $t = 1, 2 \ldots, T - 1$. With g positive, consumption is increased in the initial time period, but even more so in later periods (Figure 14.2). The potential for growth of the unused stock increases the consumer's wealth, raising consumption in each period, and tilts the consumption path toward later time periods. The higher the growth rate, g, the more pronounced this effect will be. If g exceeds the survivor's rate of time preference (a circumstance not illustrated in Figure 14.2), consumption in the final period will exceed that in period 1, and the time path of consumption will have a positive slope.

The answer to our initial question of whether or not the survivor eats S_0/T cookies in each period is that it all depends on her time preference. The answer would be "yes" only in the special case where $-d$ or g is equal to the survivor's rate of time preference. If the time preference is positive and positive growth cannot occur, there is no possibility that S_0/T cookies will be eaten in each period. However, it is by no means obvious that pure time preference is, or should be, positive in the case of optimal depletion of an endowment. In Chapter 19, we argue that utility-discounting makes little sense, and that discounting is motivated by the productivity of capital and the concomitant reward for saving and investment. In the cookie-eating case, productivity of capital is zero or negative unless $g > 0$. To solve the cookie-eating problem, the "everything I need to know I learned in kindergarten" solution might be a good starting point, after all.

The concept of user cost

These same results, and some additional ones, can be obtained with an alternative model focusing on the concept of user cost. Our survivor faces no production costs in the usual sense: the cookies are just lying there in the sack ready for the taking, and the biological processes of the algae proceed without any inputs from the survivor.

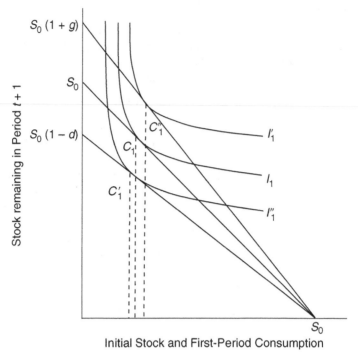

(a) First-period consumption

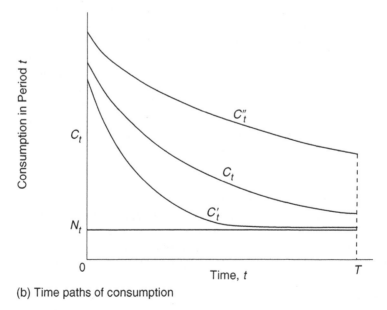

(b) Time paths of consumption

Figure 14.2   Optimal depletion with spoilage, C′$_t$, and growth, C″$_t$, of the unused stock

Nevertheless, the fact of scarcity itself imposes costs in the intertemporal setting. Consumption in period 1 comes at the expense of satisfaction forgone in later periods. The user cost of the first-period consumption is defined as the value of that forgone satisfaction. If user cost can be quantified, the two-period depletion model can be solved in a simple one-period diagram: optimal first-period consumption is determined by the intersection of period 1 demand and marginal user cost. Because second-period demand is adequately reflected in the user cost schedule, the first-period solution is optimal in the intertemporal sense.

To derive the marginal user cost (MUC) schedule, it is necessary to use a four-quadrant diagram that considers the demand in each period and the intertemporal production possibilities (Figure 14.3). Contemporaneous demand is the same in period 1 (northeast quadrant) and period 2 (southwest quadrant), but period 2's demand is discounted to reflect a positive marginal time preference in this particular example: note that we argue in Chapter 19 that neutral time preference may be appropriate in the pure consumption case, where a positive discount rate would imply utility discounting. Intertemporal production possibilities are described in the southeast quadrant: in Figure 14.3, the unused stock neither grows nor deteriorates, and the intertemporal production possibilities are described by a straight line, $S_0 S_1$, of slope 1. Now we are ready to find MUC.

First, draw a horizontal dotted line from the intercept of D_2 and the Q_2 axis to $S_0 S_1$, and then draw a vertical line to find point a on the Q_1 axis. If the first-period consumption is equal to or less than a, the marginal user cost will be zero because the unused stock will remain large enough to satisfy all second-period demands. The first-period use of a or less imposes no user costs. Now consider the user cost that would be imposed if all first-period demands were satisfied. Draw a dotted vertical line down from the intercept of D_1 with the Q_1 axis to $S_0 S_1$, and then complete a rectangle by taking the line horizontally to D_2, vertically to the 45° line in the northwest quadrant and horizontally to the northeast quadrant. The northeast corner of this dotted rectangle is point b, a point on MUC. Because D_1 and D_2 are linear, MUC will also be linear and can be identified as the line segment ab. MUC has a positive slope, indicating that the greater is the first-period consumption, the greater will be the user costs.

Now that we know the MUC schedule, we can find the optimal first-period consumption, C_1, by the intersection of D_1 and MUC. Given C_1 and $S_0 S_1$, it is simple to find C_2, the optimal second-period consumption. How do the possibilities of deterioration and growth in storage affect MUC? In Figure 14.4, we consider three production possibilities: $S_0 S_1$; $S_0 S_1'$; and $S_0 S_1''$, where $S_1' = S_0 (1 - d)$ and $S_1'' = S_0 (1 + g)$. Notice that MUC becomes positive (that is, scarcity sets in) earliest when the uneaten cookies deteriorate (MUC') and latest when the uneaten algae grow (MUC''). To look at it another way, the survivor is wealthiest when she possesses algae capable of producing yet more food if uneaten.

However MUC'' is much steeper than MUC'. Once scarcity is at hand, the marginal sacrifice from further consumption in the first period increases rapidly; such consumption subtracts not only from the initial stock but also from the regenerative capacity of that stock. MUC' is of lesser slope because the opportunity cost of early consumption is somewhat mitigated by the deterioration that would take place if cookies were saved for later. Examining C_1 and C_2, C_1' and C_2', and C_1'' and C_2'', we see the consumption time paths of Figure 14.2b emerging.

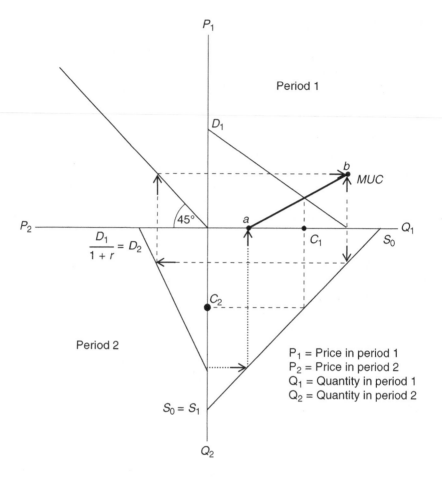

Figure 14.3   A two-period, user-cost model of optimal depletion

Because the northeast quadrant is an ordinary "demand and supply" model for period 1, the equilibrium shadow prices for food in period 1 (P_1, P_1', and P_1'') can be determined under each of the three intertemporal production regimes. Note that these are shadow prices, not market prices, as there are no markets in which the prisoner can make intertemporal trades. In each case, the positive price does not reflect ordinary production costs (they are zero) but, rather, user costs. These shadow prices represent the charge against current consumption that would lead to the optimal pattern of intertemporal consumption under each regime.

In summary, the optimal depletion of an endowment that will be exhausted by time T depends on only three things: (1) the individual's first-period demand; (2) her rate of time preference; and (3) the user cost. The user cost reflects future demands and the production possibilities pertaining to the unused portion of the endowment (does it shrink, grow, or just sit there as time passes?). Intertemporal use decisions for natural resources depend on these things, too, but other considerations also enter the picture. Resources, once extracted or harvested, may be sold and the proceeds invested in

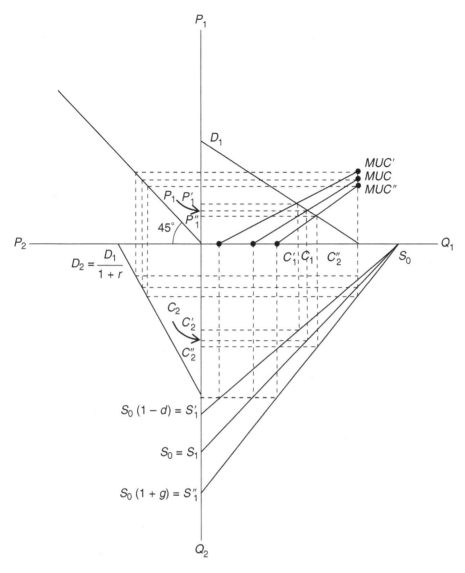

Figure 14.4   *User cost and optimal depletion with deterioration and growth of the unused stock*

capital markets, which introduces a positive opportunity cost of capital even in the case of neutral time preference. The remaining unused resources (e.g., a mineral deposit that cannot grow and deteriorates insignificantly when left unused or a stand of timber that will grow for some years and deteriorate thereafter if left unharvested) may be sold in asset markets. These market opportunities expand the resource owner's options beyond those of the prisoner and, at the same time, provide a mechanism by which the equilibrating forces of the marketplace are brought to bear on resource extraction and harvesting decisions.

Extraction of non-renewable resources

At the outset, consider a mineral deposit of finite quantity, S_0, and homogeneous quality. Extraction itself is costly, but homogeneous quality implies that the marginal extraction cost (MEC) is constant. The deposit can be converted to raw materials, H_t, subject to the constraint $S_0 = \Sigma_{t=1}^{T} H_t$, given that unmined stocks neither spoil nor grow. The MUC schedule can be derived (as in Figure 14.3) using the intertemporal production possibilities line of slope -1. The marginal cost of first-period extraction (MC) is the sum of MEC_1 and MUC_1. Optimal first-period resource use is thus H_1^*, and its market price should be p_1^* (Figure 14.5). Optimal first-period extraction occurs when:

$$p_1^* = MEC_1 + MUC_1 \tag{14.4}$$

Note that the unit cost of extraction is MEC and cost would be just recompensed if raw materials sold at the unit price $\hat{p}_1$. The difference between these prices, $p_1^* - \hat{p}_1$ is the unit resource rent and is equal to MUC. If the resource deposit is subject to non-attenuated property rights, the rent will be a payment to the owner of the deposit that serves to bring the future opportunity costs of current extraction to bear on the extraction decision.

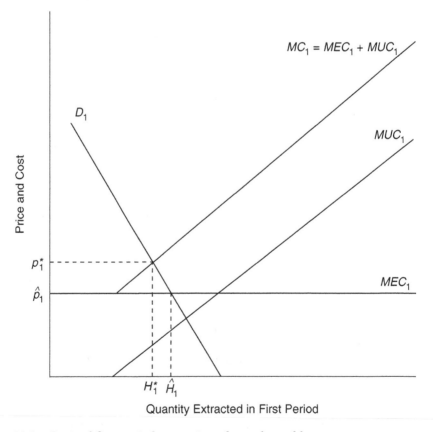

Figure 14.5   Optimal first-period extraction of an exhaustible resource

Given that resource deposits can be owned and traded, they will acquire a capital value. At any time t, the mineral deposit is valued in the asset market at the discounted value of the net rents from the future extraction and sale of raw materials. That is:

$$K_t = \sum_{\tau=t+1}^{T} \frac{(p^*_\tau - \hat{p}_\tau)H_\tau}{(1 + r)^\tau} \tag{14.5}$$

where $t = 0, 1, \ldots, T$.

Perfect asset markets reflect the net present value of future mineral extraction. The rents received by the resource owner are not pure profits, but the opportunity costs of holding the mineral deposit rather than doing whichever is most profitable of the following alternatives: extracting it all in the first period or selling the deposit in the assets market.

Intertemporal equilibrium in resource markets

If extracted now and converted into H_1, a unit of S will yield to the mine owner a royalty of $(p^*_1 - \hat{p}_1)$. However, a royalty could be earned from that same unit of S if it were extracted at any other time $t = 2, \ldots, T$. How does the mine owner decide when to extract the resources she owns?

The resource owner converts wealth (minerals in the ground) to current income by extracting and selling raw materials. Her decision problem is similar to any other investment decision problem. She may invest in conserving the minerals in the ground, liquidate the deposit and invest it in financial securities that yield interest at the rate r, liquidate some portion of either the deposit or the financial securities to pay for current consumption, or borrow for current consumption while conserving the mineral deposit.

If she expects $(p^*_t - \hat{p}_t)$ to be the same in each period t, she should extract the whole deposit in the first period and invest the proceeds in financial securities whose value, after all, will grow at the rate of compound interest. If she expects $(p^*_t - \hat{p}_t)$ to grow at some rate higher than r, it will pay to leave all reserves untouched, borrowing if necessary for current consumption. Her attainable wealth (that is, the present value of the revenue stream) is:

$$PV(S_0) = \sum_{\tau=0}^{t} \frac{(p^*_\tau - \hat{p}_\tau)H_{\tau+K^0_t}}{(1 + r)^\tau} \tag{14.6}$$

where:

$$K^0_t = \sum_{\tau=t+1}^{T} \frac{(p^*_\tau - \hat{p}_\tau)H_\tau}{(1 + r)^\tau} \tag{14.7}$$

is the asset value at time 0 of the deposit if sold at any time t. Notice that unless:

$$p^*_0 - p_0 = \frac{p^*_1 - \hat{p}_1}{1 + r} = \ldots = \frac{p^*_T - \hat{p}_T}{(1 + r)^T} \tag{14.8}$$

(that is, the present value of unit royalties is constant across time periods), she will extract the entire deposit in the single period when the PV of unit royalties is the highest.

What will she do if the present value of unit royalties is constant across time periods? She will be indifferent as to the rate of extraction. If she and all other owners of resource deposits are indifferent as to when they extract and sell the raw materials, how can users be assured of an orderly flow of raw materials to market? Very small adjustments in p^* are enough to encourage supply in any period. Thus, the price mechanism ensures a continuing aggregate flow of raw materials into a competitive market, even though each individual supplier is almost indifferent to the timing of the extraction.

A further explanation of the relatively orderly flow of mineral raw materials to market is based on the observation that, in many minerals industries, mining is a capital-intensive activity. Capital investment determines the scale of mining operation. Once the scale has been decided, *MEC* is constant over only a relatively narrow range of output. In response to a price increase, output expands only modestly in the short run; a short-run price decrease reduces output only a little as long as the price remains above the marginal extraction cost.

In order that the present value of unit royalties be constant across time periods, the undiscounted royalties must grow at the rate of interest:

$$d(p^* - \hat{p})_t/dt = r \cdot (p^* - \hat{p})_t, \text{ or } dMUC_t/dt = r \cdot MUC_t \qquad (14.9)$$

This condition determines the optimal stock to carry forward.

What happens to the price of raw materials over time? The following relationship must hold:

$$p_t^* = MEC_t + MUC_1(1 + r)^t \qquad (14.10)$$

Does this mean that raw material prices must rise with time? Under the assumptions of this simple model, it does, unless the temporal rise in *MUC* is offset by decreases in *MEC*. This could happen if technological advances reduced extraction costs as time passes. For the special case in which extraction costs are negligible (the cookies, again), the price must rise at the rate of interest.

What about the time path of extraction at the industry (aggregate) level? In the simplest case, in which demand and *MEC* are constant across time periods, aggregate extraction declines smoothly with time. In the real world, in which demand changes with time and *MEC* may decrease (with improvements in extraction technology) or increase (if deposits are non-homogeneous and the best deposits are extracted first) with time, the time path of extraction may be quite complicated.

Are raw materials markets stable?

How do raw materials markets react to price shocks? Do stabilizing or destabilizing tendencies predominate? If the price of raw materials fell, *ceteris paribus*, and this led resource owners to expect still lower prices and royalties in the future, would they not be tempted to increase extraction rates immediately? This response would flood the market with minerals and lead to still further price decreases.

If the price of raw materials rose, leading resource owners to raise their estimates of future prices, would they not be tempted to delay extraction in order to benefit from the higher future price? If so, this would exacerbate the shortage, sending prices still higher. Such responses, increasing extractions rates in the face of a price decrease, and decreasing extraction when prices rise, would be destabilizing to the raw materials markets.

However, this analysis is too simple to be trusted. The resource owner seeks to maximize wealth, that is, the present value of earnings from the deposit, which is a capital asset. With well-functioning asset markets, the capital value of the remaining deposit at time t, K_t, adjusts instantly to any change in expectations concerning future royalties. Asset values adjust from K_t to K_t, with the owner expecting to earn $r \cdot K_t$ (that is, a rate of return equal to the interest rate), given the new royalty expectation. With instant adjustment in asset values, resource owners again will become willing to supply raw materials in each period. Thus, asset markets tend to dampen any instability in the rate of extraction.

Extraction with recycling and exploration

Recycling processes permit discarded resource products to compete with stocks as sources of new raw materials. The stock accounting identity is:

$$S_t = S_0 - \sum_{\tau=1}^{t} (H_\tau - C_\tau) \tag{14.11}$$

where C is the amount recycled. The optimal current-period consumption of raw materials occurs when the following condition is satisfied:

$$p_t^* = MEC_t + MUC_t = MCC_t + MUCS_t \tag{14.12}$$

where MCC is the marginal recycling cost and $MUCS$ is the marginal user cost, or price, of recyclable scrap. Given that the user of raw materials is indifferent as to whether they are refined from scrap or newly extracted minerals, the cost of recycled raw materials bounds the price of "new" raw materials and thus determines the royalty, MUC. Note also that scrap is scarce, because $C_t \leq \sum_{\tau=0}^{t-1} (H_\tau - C_\tau)$; that is, the amount available for recycling is limited to the cumulative amount extracted and not yet recycled. Thus scrap acquires a positive user cost or price, $MUCS$. Rents, MUC, grow at the rate of interest:

$$dMUC_t/dt = r * MUC_t \tag{14.13}$$

but a technological innovation that reduced MCC_t would lead to a reduction in unit royalties and a downward adjustment in the asset value of reserves.

Exploration

Consider a situation in which there is at any time t a known reserve, $\hat{S}_t$ and the possibility of increasing the known reserve in future periods through exploration, a costly process. The stock accounting relationship is:

$$\hat{S}_t = \hat{S}_0 - \sum_{\tau=1}^{t} (H_\tau - R_\tau) \tag{14.14}$$

where R_τ is the quantity of resources discovered in period τ.

Exploration generates two products, newly discovered resource stocks and information that may reduce the effort required for further discoveries. It remains true that optimal current-period extraction occurs when the following condition is satisfied:

$$p_t^* = MEC_t + MUC_t \tag{14.15}$$

However, MUC_t is now related directly to the economics of discovery:

$$MUC_t = MHC_t - IV_t \tag{14.16}$$

where MHC is the marginal replacement cost of stocks and IV is the value of information from exploration. Exploration and discovery have transformed the exhaustible resources problem into one of optimal replacement. It also remains true that:

$$dMUC_t/dt = r \cdot MUC_t \tag{14.17}$$

that is, resource rents must grow at the rate of interest. Technological advances in exploration would have the effect of reducing MHC_t and thus MUC_t, driving down p_t^* and increasing H_t^*. Intertemporal equilibrium would be restored, again, via adjustments in the asset values of existing reserves.

A cautionary note is in order. It is true analytically that exploration transforms the exhaustible resources problem into one of optimal replacement. Nevertheless, we cannot conclude that exploration eliminates the fear of running out of resources. In a finite world, we would expect the costs of resource discovery to rise as the quantity awaiting discovery diminishes, that is, as the limits are approached.

Institutions, policies, and the extraction of non-renewable resources: some comparative static results

Institutions and policies that are under the control of society may influence the costs of discovery, extraction, and resource use and, hence, raw materials prices and the rate of resource extraction. Here we consider some of the more obvious possibilities, emphasizing near-term future effects.

Property rights

The preceding analyses assume non-attenuated property rights. When one stops to think of property rights, it becomes clear that a considerable array of rights is involved. Pertinent are rights to known mineral deposits, exploration sites, information generated by exploration, and environmental effects of resource extraction and use. We shall consider these one by one.

Mineral deposits   If mineral deposits were subject to a *res nullius* situation (see Chapter 10), only the extraction costs would be considered by mine operators. User costs would be real to society, but the *res nullius* situation would not permit royalties or rents to rise above zero. With competitive extraction, price would equilibrate at $\hat{p} = MEC$ (Figure 14.5). Because $\hat{p} < p^*$ with negative-sloped demand, the rate of extraction $\hat{H}$ would be greater than H^*. With rents equal to zero, exploration effort and new discoveries would be limited to zero. Recycling may be positive if $MCC < MEC$, but at price $\hat{p}$, the quantity recycled would be less then the amount optimal at p^*.

Exploration sites   The results obtained in the previous section assume that firms may acquire exclusive rights to explore designated territories under arrangements that would grant the explorer ownership rights to discovered resources. Consider, instead, a situation in which *res nullius* applied to exploration sites but the resources found were captured by their discoverers ("finders keepers"). One would predict excessive and duplicative exploration activity as firms rush to convert undiscovered minerals to privately owned resources. One would expect increased discovery to reduce the asset value of existing reserves. Lower rents would reduce the price of raw materials, increasing the quantity demanded and reducing the quantity recycled. Extraction would be accelerated.

Information from exploration Exploration generates not only resource discoveries but also valuable information that tends to reduce the cost of further discoveries. Together, secure exclusive tenure to exploration sites and exclusive and transferable rights to information generated in exploration would result in efficient exploration. One aspect of this efficient situation would be the emergence of efficient trade in information. With secure tenure to sites, firms that produce information from exploration would have nothing to gain by withholding information from others who would be willing to pay for it.

If information were not exclusive, explorers (that is, the information producers) could not reap its value to others. Being rewarded with less than the full value of what is produced by exploration, they would underinvest therein. What would make exploration information non-exclusive? Most likely the cost of exclusion. Exploration activity and subsequent extraction are often highly visible (and advances have been rapid in technologies that enable interested parties to maintain observation and surveillance of others' activities). So it may be prohibitively costly for an exploring firm to stop others from observing its activities and making valid inferences about what was learned.

The preceding analysis considers non-exclusiveness of information in the context of exclusive property rights to exploration sites. On the other hand, non-exclusive exploration sites would inefficiently inflate the value of information as knowledge permits capture, and capture is the method by which ownership of reserves is established. Explorers would jealously guard information and withhold it from everyone else. To the extent that they succeed, duplicative exploration effort would result.

Environmental damage from extraction If environmental damage is a non-exclusive joint product of the extraction process, the mine operator will face an extraction cost, $M\widetilde{E}C$, that is less than the true social *MEC*. This would lower the firm's marginal cost of supply and thus reduce, in the first round, the competitive price of raw materials. In symbols, $M\widetilde{E}C < MEC$ results in $\tilde{p} < p^*$ and $\widetilde{H} > H^*$. This increased extraction would raise resource rents, so that $M\widetilde{U}C > MUC$, which would induce increased exploration and raise $\tilde{p}$ somewhat in a second-round effect. Nevertheless, $\tilde{p}$ would come to rest at a level below p^*, and recycling would be reduced.

Environmental damage from using raw materials Consider a situation in which the burning of coal causes non-exclusive environmental damage. The product (say, electricity) then sells at an inefficiently low price and in inefficiently large quantities. The derived demand for coal shifts rightward, so that $\tilde{p} > p^*$. As a result, $\widetilde{H} > H^*$, $M\widetilde{U}C > MUC$, and exploration effort is greater than it would be otherwise. Recycling is not relevant to the coal example. But in the general case, recycling would be encouraged by the higher price of raw materials.

Economic policies

Here we consider the effect of interest rates, which are influenced by general economic policies, and also some specific tax and subsidy policies directed toward the exhaustible resources sector.

Higher "real" interest rates   The real rate of interest, r, is a key variable in the economics of exhaustible resources. In the US, fiscal and monetary policies can exert considerable influence on "real"[1] interest rates. So it is interesting and policy-relevant to inquire about the effects of higher interest rates on the exhaustible resources sector. Because:

$$dMUC/dt = r * MUC_t \tag{14.18}$$

higher r requires a more rapid growth rate of resource rents that, with an unchanged demand and *MEC*, drives down current rents and the asset values of reserves. The current price of raw materials falls, increasing the rate of extraction and decreasing exploration and recycling. The faster rate at which MUC grows may eventually reverse these effects in later years.

Property taxes   A property tax on unmined minerals gives the owner an incentive to lower the tax bill by reducing the reserve carried. Thus, a property tax increases the rate of extraction, which lowers the price of raw materials and drives down the rents accruing to the owners. Exploration and recycling activity also are reduced.

Severance taxes   A severance tax is paid on each unit extracted and can thus be expressed as a vertical shift in *MEC*. The price of raw materials is increased, and extraction and MUC are reduced. Exploration is reduced, but recycling would tend to increase.

Depletion allowances   Depletion allowances are negative severance taxes and can be analyzed as such.

A complication: non-homogeneous resources and stock effects

If stocks are non-homogeneous, it follows that some will be more valuable than others, in that they are of higher quality or more accessibly located. For these more attractive reserves, the *MEC* of a unit of raw materials is lower. It makes sense that the more attractive stocks would be exploited first and that the extraction costs would increase as the remaining stock diminished. This stock effect (when non-zero) must be incorporated in the condition that determines the optimal stock to carry forward. When the stock is non-homogeneous:

$$dMUC/dt + SE = r * MUC_t \tag{14.19}$$

where the stock effect, $SE = MEC(\partial^R t)/(\partial^S t)$, is the reduction in future extraction costs from holding the marginal unit of stock. Positive stock effects reduce the equilibrium growth rate of rents. This condition is a generalization of the condition $dMUC/dt = r * MUC_t$, which applies in the specific case of homogeneous reserves.

Rents as a scarcity indicator

The time path of rents is, in principle, the preferred scarcity indicator for non-renewable resources. In the simplest case of a homogeneous, finite reserve of known size, rents grow at the rate of interest reflecting increasing scarcity as extraction continues through time. But this regular and predictable behavior of rents does not apply to more complicated resource systems and systems subject to shock. The behavior of rents effectively reflects emerging conditions in the non-renewable resources sector, as the following examples demonstrate.

Nonhomogeneous resources and increasing extraction costs create the stock effect, which allows for the slower growth of rents, thus reflecting the declining quality of reserves that remain as time passes. If the (changing) demand for raw materials were to shift rightward, p^* and H^* would increase. The demand curve would intersect MC at a higher level, reflecting the increased MUC and hence the higher resource rents. The increased scarcity that resulted from increased demand would lead to an increase in rents.

If the demand for raw materials became more elastic, for example, because of the greater availability of substitutes, $p^*(t)$ would rise more slowly over time. With no change in MEC, the residual, $MUC(t)$ would be reduced and would grow more slowly. The greater availability of substitutes alleviates scarcity, and this is correctly reflected in lower and slower-growing rents.

An innovation in extraction methods would reduce MEC and p^*, thus increasing H^*. Demand would intersect MC farther to the right. MC would be reduced, but not as much as the reduction in MEC. MUC and, hence, rents would increase, as the innovation would effectively make reserves scarcer and more valuable.

A reduction in recycling costs would, under competitive conditions, reduce p^* and H^*, thus reducing resource rents. Interestingly enough, with limited scrap available for recycling, the rent value of scrap ($MUCS$) would increase.

A reduction in costs of discovery would drive down rents because, by $MUC = MHT + IV$, resource rents would be limited to the net costs of replacing the reserves. Again, the behavior of rents would reflect changes in the scarcity.

As these examples demonstrate, the behavior of rents over time reflects the changing economic conditions in the exhaustible resources sector. Rents reflect MUC which, by definition, is the future opportunity cost incurred as a result of current use. Rising resource rents indicate that reserves are becoming scarcer in the full economic sense of the term. Events that introduce good substitutes for raw materials or cost-saving innovations in resource discovery would alleviate scarcity, which would be reflection in the behavior rents. Nevertheless, resource rents have some serious limitations as scarcity indicators. Complete markets in raw materials, reserves, exploration territory, and risk hedging (with non-attenuated property rights in each) are necessary in order for rents to provide accurate scarcity signals. Existing markets may be in some ways incomplete and imperfect.

Another, practical difficulty arises for those who observe the behavior of rents in order to learn about scarcity. Rents are seldom observed and recorded in routinely collected data. Being a residual that accrues to the owner of reserves, rental payments are often internal to the integrated mining firm. Even when interfirm payments are made, they are seldom public information.

Questions for discussion

1. There was a time when the United States simultaneously pursued the following policies with respect to oil: the amount of oil permitted to be imported was restricted by quotas, and an oil-depletion allowance was applicable to domestic production. What effects would you expect this combination of policies to have had on the consumption of oil, the domestic production of oil, and the rate of discovery of new domestic reserves?
2. In a market economy, what are the economic limits to recycling?
3. In this chapter, the economics of recycling was discussed in terms of non-renewable resources. Can you develop an economic analysis of recycling paper products?
4. Economic models of mineral exploration typically treat the quantity of new discoveries as a function of current exploration effort and the quantity of past discoveries. Does that make sense in a world in which total stocks (known and undiscovered) must be finite?
5. A wine lover has a given cellar capacity, a budget constraint, and a utility function that includes preferences with respect to the quantity and quality of wine he consumes. The quality of wine at the time of consumption is a function of initial quality and time spent aging in the cellar. He wants to optimize the initial quality of wine purchased and the time that each bottle is aged, subject to a constraint that his total consumption equal Q in each period. Which, if any, of the intertemporal resource allocation decision models presented in this chapter is adaptable for solving his problem? How should it be adapted?

Note

1. The real interest rate is defined as the nominal interest rate minus the anticipated rate of inflation. Since anticipations are difficult to observe, so is the real interest rate. One proxy that is often used is the apparent "real" interest rate, defined as the nominal interest rate minus the current observed rate of inflation.

Suggested reading: classic and contemporary

Cairns, R.D. (1990), "The Economics of Exploration for Non-Renewable Resources," *Journal of Economic Surveys* **4** (4): 361–95.

Gaudet, G. (2007), "Natural Resource Economics Under the Rule of Hotelling," *Canadian Journal of Agricultural Economics* **40** (4): 1033–59.

Heal, G.M. (1993), "The Optimal Use of Exhaustible Resources," in *Handbook of Natural Resource and Energy Economics*, Vol. 3, ed. A.V. Kneese and S.L. Sweeney, Amsterdam: Elsevier B.V.

Hotelling, H. (1931), "The Economics of Exhaustible Resources," *Journal of Political Economy* **29** (April): 137–75.

Howe, C.W. (1979), *Natural Resource Economics: Issues, Analysis, and Policy*, New York: Wiley.

Solow, R.M. (1974), "The Economics of Resources or the Resources of Economics," *American Economic Review* **64** (May): 1–14.

15 Renewable resources: what is the optimal use and management of renewable resources over time?

Renewable resources have some capability of regeneration or renewal over a relatively short period of time; for example, days or months or a few years. Some resources are renewable because they are living organisms and their populations can be regenerated or renewed through biological reproduction supported by the ecosystem processes and functions discussed in Chapter 2. Other resources, primarily solar radiation and wind, are renewable because of the ultimate source of these resources in the sun which burns continually (and is expected to continue burning for a very, very long period of time).

Biotic resources: general background

Biotic (living) resources differ from non-renewable resources in that they are capable of growing and reproducing over time. The stock-accounting identity for biotic resources is analogous to that for exhaustible resources with exploration discussed previously. It is:

$$\hat{S}_t = \hat{S}_0 - \sum_{\tau=1}^{t} (H_\tau - R_\tau) \tag{15.1}$$

where H is the amount harvested or exhausted and R is the amount renewed or replaced through growth or net recruitment, as the case may be. Although the analysis of exhaustible, non-renewable resources with exploration prepares us to consider biotic resource use and management, there are additional complications we must consider.

First, growth and recruitment are governed by complex biotic and ecological relationships: extinction thresholds, sigmoid growth curves, carrying capacities, and the like. When attempting to specify these relationships, the economist becomes a user of information generated by natural scientists. Second, the issues of property rights and the costs of exclusion are paramount. When property rights are non-attenuated (as may in principle occur when crops, forest products, and livestock are produced on privately owned land), biotic resources may be managed much as inorganic inputs are typically managed in production processes. If on the other hand, the establishment of exclusive property rights in biotic resources is infeasible (e.g., in the case of ocean fisheries), biotic resources must be unmanaged: management throughout the life cycle is impossible. A degree of control over the long-run productivity of this kind of biotic resource is attainable only by manipulating the rate of harvest.

Forest resources

Again, we seek to establish the two basic conditions for efficient resource allocation: (1) the static condition, which determines the price of resource products in any period; and (2) the intertemporal condition, which determines the optimal stock to carry forward. The static condition is the now familiar:

$$p_t = MEC_t + MUC_t \tag{15.2}$$

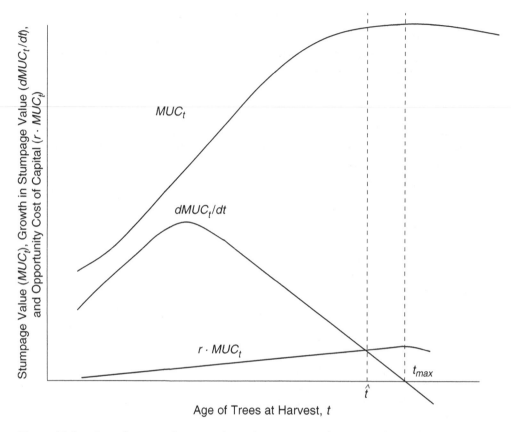

Figure 15.1   Age of trees at harvest: the right answer to the wrong question

and may be illustrated by a diagram analogous to that of Figure 14.5. Note that in forestry circles, MUC goes by a specialized name: "stumpage value," or the price that a logging operator would pay for the right to harvest a stand of timber.

The age of trees at harvest: the right answer to the wrong question
The stock-accounting identity is the now familiar:

$$S_t = S_0 - \sum_{\tau=1}^{t} (H_\tau - R_\tau) \tag{15.3}$$

where R is the addition to the stock from growth. Holding the area of land constant, growth is a non-linear function of S_t. That is, growth depends on the age and size of the trees, but it is not a straight-line relationship. Sigmoid growth curves are commonly assumed, in which growth is slow when the trees are very small, increases rapidly as the trees get larger, slows down as they approach maturity, and eventually becomes negative with senescence and decay. This pattern of growth is illustrated (in stumpage-value terms) by the curves labeled MUC_t and $dMUC_t/dt$ (Figures 15.1 and 15.2).

Consider the decision problem of the owner of a newly planted stand of trees, who

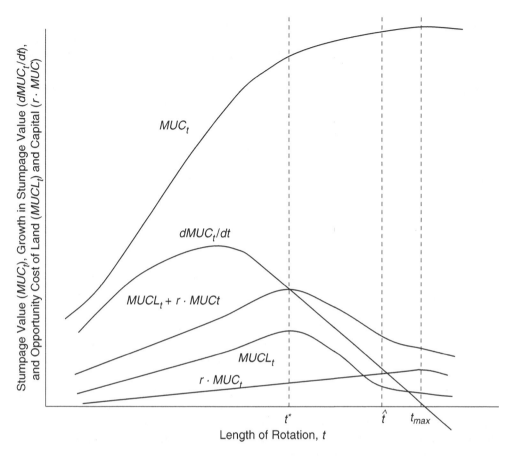

Figure 15.2   Forest management: the optimal rotation

seeks to determine the optimal time to harvest them. Assume that he wants only to maximize the present value of the current stand of trees. At any time he can harvest the trees and realize a net return of MUC_t, which if invested in the financial markets will generate a revenue stream $r \cdot MUC(t)$. Clearly, he will allow the trees to stand as long as their growth in stumpage value, $dMUC_t/dt$, exceeds $r \cdot MUC_t$. Thus the present value of the stand of trees is maximized when they are harvested at age $\hat{t}$ (Figure 15.1). At that time:

$$dMUC_t/dt = r \cdot MUC_t \qquad (15.4)$$

The optimal rotation
It is unlikely that an individual would be concerned about the present value of future revenue from a stand of trees, but not the land on which they are growing. That being the case, the landowner would seek to maximize not the present value of a particular stand of trees but, rather, the present value of an indefinitely long stream of revenue from the land. The landowner's problem is to identify the optimal rotation: the optimal age of trees at harvest, assuming that the land will be replanted.

In the optimal rotation problem, the operator is concerned (as usual) with the opportunity cost of capital. However, a sigmoid growth pattern of trees introduces an additional opportunity cost. A tract of land can be carrying only one stand of trees at any time. If it is carrying an aging stand of slow-growing trees (for example, as t approaches $\hat{t}$), it could instead be carrying a younger stand of trees that grow in stumpage value more rapidly. This difference in the annual net value of productivity is the opportunity cost of using the land to support the older stand.

Define the opportunity cost of land, $MUCL_t$, as the annual value of land rent (net of planting costs) when the rotation is t years long. Then the opportunity costs of carrying an existing stand include both the opportunity cost of capital, $r \cdot MUC_t$, and that of land, $MUCL_t$. The optimal length of rotation is t^* years, which is shorter than $\hat{t}$ (Figure 15.2). With a rotation t^* years long:

$$dMUC_t/dt = r \cdot MUC_t + MUCL_t \qquad (15.5)$$

Note that the opportunity to replant and enjoy a period of rapid growth induces the landowner to enter an indefinite rotation sequence in which the age of trees at harvest, t^*, is less than $\hat{t}$, the optimal age at harvest when there is no opportunity to replant.

Sensitivity of the optimal rotation
The optimal rotation is sensitive to changes in economic conditions, institutions, and policy decisions. Let us consider how these things affect the length of the optimal rotation.

Price of lumber   An increase in the price of lumber would increase MUC_t, $dMUC_t/dt$, $r \cdot MUC_t$, and $MUCL_t$. Thus the effect of a lumber price increase on optimal rotation is indeterminate in general and must be solved numerically for particular examples. Notice that the relative effect of a lumber price increase on $r \cdot MUC_t$ depends on the size of r. Examining Figure 15.2, we conjecture that for very low values of r, the optimal rotation may lengthen, whereas for very high values of r, it may be shortened.

Rate of interest   An increase in the rate of interest, r would raise $r \cdot MUC_t$, tending to reduce the length of the optimal rotation.

Cost of harvesting   A cost-reducing innovation in timber harvesting would reduce MEC_t. With a downward-sloping demand, the amount harvested in the current period would increase, thus increasing MUC_t and hence $dMUC_t/dt$, $r \cdot MUC_t$, and $MUCL_t$. As in the case of a lumber price increase, the effect on optimal rotation is generally indeterminate: the higher r is, the more likely it is that the optimal rotation will be reduced.

Distance from the sawmill   Marginal harvesting costs, MEC_t, increase with distance from the mill, so that the stumpage value of more distant stands is lower. Thus increasing the distance from the mill reduces $dMUC_t/dt$, $r \cdot MUC_t$, and $MUCL_t$ with a generally indeterminate effect on the optimal rotation.

Non-exclusiveness of trees   If trees are non-exclusive while standing and become the exclusive property of the individual who harvests them, the stumpage value will fall to zero, and the price will be equal to the marginal extraction cost. The harvest will increase in the early periods (but may well fall in later periods as good stands of timber become scarce). Because there is no reward for replanting, the issue of optimal rotation is moot. Notice that this arrangement is grossly inefficient. While the stumpage value is zero, MUC is real and positive and is increased by the accelerated rate of harvest. Imagine that a public agency granted exclusive rights to harvest standing timber at a time of the logging operator's choosing, but that the rights to the subsequent use of the land revert to the agency upon harvest. This arrangement would lengthen the rotation from t^* to $\hat{t}$ years (Figure 15.2).

Severance tax   A severance tax would increase MEC_t, thus reducing MUC_t. Again, the effect on optimal rotation is generally indeterminate.

A property tax on standing timber   The owner's property tax bill can be reduced by reducing the stumpage value of standing timber, averaged over the rotation. This requires that the rotation length be reduced.

Optimal rotation and the quantity of timber harvested
The impacts on rotation length of changes in lumber prices, harvesting costs, and severance taxes are generally indeterminate. However, these things have clear impacts on the total quantity of timber harvested and brought to market in any period. A lumber price increase will clearly increase the harvest, and an increase in harvesting costs or severance taxes will clearly reduce the harvest. If these effects on the quantity harvested are clear but those on rotation length are indeterminate, what is going on?

Timber stands vary in quality and accessibility. Thus, there are two possible responses to, say, an increase in harvesting costs. The harvest in any period will be reduced, but this may be accomplished by lengthening the rotation or abandoning marginal stands of timber. Although the effects on optimal rotation may be generally indeterminate, it is clear that an increase in harvesting costs (or severance taxes or a fall in the price of lumber) would lead to the abandonment of some marginal timber lands.

Increasing the distance from the mill has, as we have seen, a generally indeterminate effect on the rotation length. However, it is clear that for a given price of lumber, there will be some distance beyond which timber stands are of no economic value and therefore will be abandoned by entrepreneurs.

A non-exclusive biotoc resource: the ocean fishery
Now consider a non-exclusive resource like an ocean fishery, in which it is infeasible to establish exclusive property rights to individual fish. For this reason, the ocean fishery cannot be privately managed as can the forest on privately owned land. In the case of the forest, the landowner controlled the number of trees per acre of land, the time of planting, and the time of harvest, thus effectively controlling the forest throughout its life cycle. In the case of the non-exclusive ocean fishery, however, only the rate of harvest can be controlled. Controlling the rate of harvest in a non-exclusive ocean fishery is not as simple as controlling the rate of harvest in a privately owned forest: because no single private individual controls access to the ocean fishery, the rate of harvest must be controlled through the use of policy tools implemented at the institutional level.

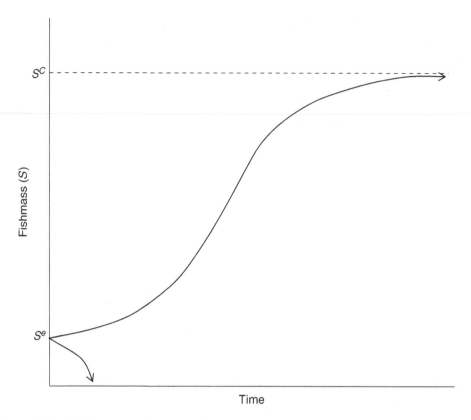

Figure 15.3   Fishmass as a function of time

A static analysis

Assume that the fishery is circumscribed in space and bounded in terms of the ecological variables such as total nutrients, water temperature, and the like which determine its ability to support fish. Then there will be a maximum fishmass, S^c, that it can support. S^c is the carrying capacity of the fishery. Perhaps there is some minimum fishmass, S^e, below which recruitment (that is, net growth in the fishmass) is negative until the fishery is extirpated (exhausted). S^e is the extinction threshold for the fishery. For $S > S^e$, growth is sigmoid until the fishmass approaches its Malthusian limit, S^c (Figure 15.3).

Recruitment is the new fish population increment resulting from births, deaths, and changes in the size of the fish. If we express recruitment, R, as a function of fishmass, S (Figure 15.4), we can see that recruitment is negative below S^e and zero at S^e. For $S^e < S < S^c$, recruitment is positive and reaches a maximum level R^m when the fishmass is S^m. If harvest (H) were set at the level $H^m = R^m$, the fishery would produce its maximum sustainable yield or harvest. There are two levels of fishmass, S^2 and S^3, which will sustain any lower level of harvest, for example, H'.

To sustain the harvest level H', should we maintain the fishmass at S^2 or S^3? The answer depends on what is costly. If it is necessary to feed the fish and the amount of costly feed they consume increases with the fishmass, then the manager will seek to

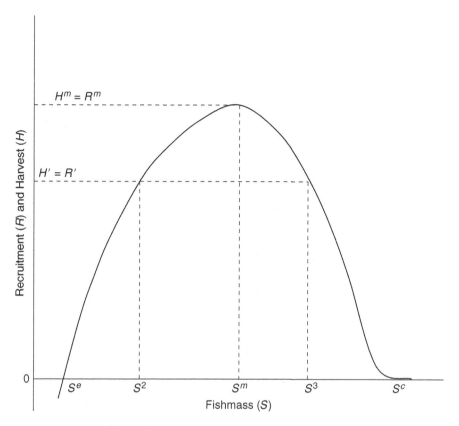

Figure 15.4   Sustainable yields

maintain the fishmass at S^2. In a non-exclusive ocean fishery, however, that is not the problem. Inputs are applied only at harvest time. Harvest requires effort, which we define as E, an index of inputs with unit price w. For any level of H, E decreases as S increases. Therefore, if the harvesting effort is the important cost item, the manager will prefer to harvest H' from the greater fishmass, S^3.

From a zero level when E is zero, H increases with E until H^m is attained. A further effort will reduce H by reducing S. For very large levels of E, H will be zero as the fishery is "fished out" (Figure 15.5). The total cost of effort, $w \cdot E$, is a linear function of E. If the access to the fishery is non-exclusive, the level of effort E^b will be attracted to the fishery, the rent will be zero and the price of fish will be $p = MEC$ where $MEC = \partial R/\partial E$. E^b can be thought of as the "break-even" level of fishing effort.

But if the manager can control E, the efficient E^* at which the rent from the fishery is maximized should be chosen. The price of fish will be:

$$p = MEC + MUC \qquad (15.6)$$

and the fishmass will be maintained at the level S^* consistent with E^*, rather than S^b consistent with E^b. Not surprisingly, $S^* > S^b$. The efficient level of harvest, H^*, may be

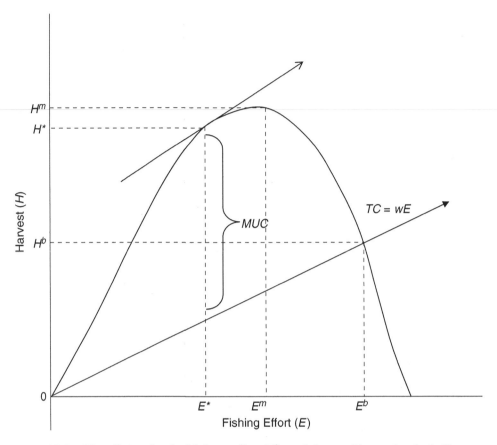

Figure 15.5   The efficient level of fishing effort, E*, *and the equilibrium level of effort under open access,* E^b

larger or smaller than H^m, depending on the shape of the $H = f(E)$ curve and the unit cost of effort, w. Observe also that the maximum sustainable yield, H^m, will be efficient if, and only if, the fishing effort is costless.

Intertemporal equilibrium
The stock-accounting identity is the familiar:

$$S_t = S_0 - \sum_{\tau=1}^{t} (H_\tau - R_\tau) \tag{15.7}$$

However:

$$R_\tau = h(S_\tau) \tag{15.8}$$

and

$$H_\tau = f(S_\tau, E_\tau) \tag{15.9}$$

These latter relationships introduce additional complexity in the second basic condition, which determines the optimal stock to carry forward. When we define:

$$\frac{dR_t}{dS_t}MUC_t \tag{15.10}$$

as the "stock effect on recruitment" and

$$MEC_t\frac{\partial^H t}{\partial^S t} \tag{15.11}$$

as the "stock effect on effort per unit catch," the second basic condition is:

$$dMUC_t/dt + MEC_t\frac{\partial H_t}{\partial S_t} = \left(r - \frac{dR_t}{dS_t}\right)MUC_t \tag{15.12}$$

Thus, if the interest rate is high relative to stock effects, rents to the fishery should grow over time. However, relatively high stock effects could lead to an intertemporal equilibrium with increasing stocks and falling rents. This phenomenon, if it occurred, would be confined to the phase in which stocks were relatively low and growing fast (Figure 15.3) and recruitment were increasing (Figure 15.4).

Is it possible that the efficient intertemporal equilibrium solution would call for the exhaustion (extirpation) of the fishery? This and related questions can be answered with an optimal control model, in which H (or E) is the control variable. The main problem is to choose the level of H_t (or E_t) in each period, so as to maximize the net present value of fishery services (the difference between pH_t and wE_t discounted and summed across an infinite number of time periods), subject to the relationships specified at the start of this subsection. Optimal control models are mathematically complex, and neither the setting up of such models nor their solution is within the scope of this book. But we next shall discuss some characteristics of the kinds of solutions that may be derived from optimal control models of fishery.

1. In order to achieve a bounded steady-state solution, r must be greater than dR_t / dS_t for some values of S_t. It is also necessary that for some values of S_t, $dR_t / dS_t > r$; otherwise, if dR_t / dS_t is never greater than r, the present value of the fishery will be maximized by deliberately exploiting it in such a way as to bring about its extirpation as soon as possible. If the productivity of the fishery is too low for all levels of S_t, exhausting it will be preferable to maintaining it.
2. Depending on the empirical specification of $R_t = h(S_t)$ and $H_t = f(S_t, E_t)$, p, w, and r, the steady-state solution (if attainable) may involve either a greater or a lesser fishmass than existed in the initial time period. If any of the relevant empirical facts were to change from one time period to another, the pre-change steady-state solution would no longer be appropriate, and the system would move toward a new steady-state solution (if attainable).
3. Assuming that a steady-state solution is attainable, it may be institutionally implemented as follows: (a) the amount of fish caught, H_t may be directly controlled in each time period, preferably through the use of marketable rights to sell fish; or (b) if the fishing effort, E, is to be the control variable, it may be controlled in each

time period by the imposition of two taxes, a tax on the fish caught and a tax on the capital inputs into the fishing effort.

4. Given the wide range over which the relevant prices, fishmass production functions, costs of E, and interest rates may vary in the real world, there is no a priori assurance that a steady-state (that is, a stable sustained yield) solution will be attainable for each fishery. Other outcomes, each possible, include solutions that lead to the extirpation of the fishery, solutions in which fishing activity is unprofitable and the fishing industry eventually goes out of business, solutions in which the production of fish caught is cyclical and fluctuates across time periods, and solutions that involve multiple equilibria, as opposed to a unique and stable equilibrium.

Policies to control harvest or effort in the non-exclusive fishery
The public agency charged with managing a non-exclusive fishery seeks to manipulate H_t, the amount of fish harvested. It may do this indirectly, by manipulating E, an index of the total effort, or (more likely) some particular input(s) into the fishing. A more direct approach is to control, via marketing quotas, the amount of fish sold. Several variations of these approaches were discussed in some detail in Chapter 10. Two general principles emerge:

1. The more direct the relationship is between the policy instrument and its target, the better will be the prospects for an efficient policy. The nets' mesh size or the length of the fishing season are only tenuously related to the harvest; they are rather poor policy instruments. The amount of fish sold is much more closely related to harvest and is thus a better policy instrument.
2. The characteristics of non-attenuated property rights tend to promote efficiency. Thus, well-specified, exclusive, and transferable marketing quotas are policy instruments with desirable efficiency characteristics.

Solar radiation, wind, and biofuels
In recent years there has been much interest in tapping the energy for human use provided by renewable resources including solar radiation, wind, and biofuels. As discussed in Chapter 2, there is a one-way flow of solar radiation from the sun to the planet Earth. This solar radiation can be used directly to heat buildings and for natural lighting through passive solar technology; for example, large south-facing windows that collect heat from solar radiation during the winter when the sun is lower in the sky. Active solar technology, for example, converts solar radiation from the sun to electrical energy using solar cell and panel technology. The one-way flow of solar radiation from the sun also causes the blowing of wind in the earth's atmosphere. Wind may be used to turn the blades of a windmill providing energy to water pumps (e.g, the use of windmills on farms to pump water from underground aquifers for watering livestock). Wind may also be used to turn the blades of a windmill connected to an electricity generator for converting wind energy to electrical energy. The electrical energy generated from solar radiation or wind can be immediately used or stored for later use in batteries. Solar radiation and wind are renewable resources in the sense that more of these resources are provided each day (with variations in intensity) so long as the one-way flow of solar radiation from the sun to the planet Earth continues.

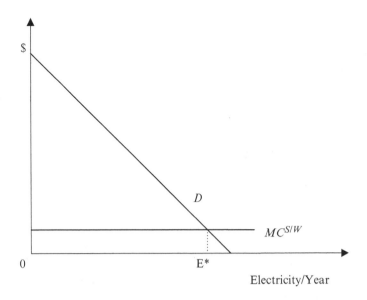

Figure 15.6   Electricity consumption with low marginal costs

The economics of solar radiation and wind use is unusual because once the infra-structure costs of passive solar, active solar, or windmill technology have been incurred, the marginal costs (e.g., price) of additional units of solar or wind energy are very low if not zero. Figure 15.6 depicts a household's or firm's demand curve for electricity on an annual basis. Suppose that this household or firm has invested in active solar and/ or windmill technology capable of meeting its annual electricity demand. Given that the household or firm has incurred the necessary active solar or windmill power infra-structure costs (which are now sunk), we assume the marginal cost (or price) to the household or firm of additional units of electricity is very low and flat as illustrated by the curve labeled $MC^{S/W}$ shown in Figure 15.6. Following the equimarginal principle, the household or firm will consume electricity up to point where demand (marginal benefits) equals marginal costs (price) at E*.

The ability to consume essentially as much electricity as one wants at a very low price is a strong economic incentive for households and firms to invest in active solar and/or windmill power technology. These technology investments, however, can be quite expen-sive. Thus, the household or firm needs to decide if it "makes sense" to incur these high costs or continue to obtain electricity from traditional sources (e.g., non-renewable, fossil fuel-dependent sources). Assuming that the marginal cost (price) of electricity obtained from active solar or windmill power sources is lower than electricity obtained from tradi-tional sources, this decision involves comparing the flow of energy cost savings over time to the initial capital costs of the active solar or windmill technology (see Chapter 7 for more background and discussion on capital investment theory).

Let the price of electricity obtained from traditional, say non-renewable, sources in year t be denoted by P_t^N, and the price (or marginal cost) of electricity obtained from active solar or windmill power technology in year t be denoted by $P_t^{S/W} = MC_t^{S/W}$. Thus, cost savings per unit of electricity in year t ($ECSU_t$) is equal to $ECSU_t = P_t^N - P_t^{S/W}$.

Total annual costs savings in year t $(ECST_t)$ are equal to $ECST_t = E_t \cdot ECSU_t$ where E_t is the total units of electricity consumed by the household or firm in year t. The discounted value of the annual flow of cost savings incurred by switching to active solar or windmill power is given by:

$$\sum_{t=1}^{T^*} \frac{(E_t \cdot ECSU_t)}{(1 + r)^t} \tag{15.13}$$

where T^* is the household's or firm's time horizon which is usually equal to the life expectancy of the capital equipment – say 20 years. Next, let the up-front capital costs of active solar or windmill power technology be denoted by $CapitalCost_{S/W}$. If the expression in equation (15.13) is greater than $CapitalCost_{S/W}$, it would make economic sense for the household or firm to invest in active solar or wind power technology. If the expression in equation (15.13) is less than $CapitalCost_{S/W}$, then the household or firm would lose money by investing in solar or windmill technology and should not invest (unless the household or firm has some overriding non-economic reason for wanting to switch to solar or wind power). If the expression in equation (15.13) is equal to $CapitalCost_{S/W}$, then the household or firm should be indifferent between investing and not investing from an economic perspective.

Biofuels refers to different types of fuels derived from plants and other organic matter including plant and animal by-products. Because these fuels are derived from plants and animals which are renewable resources, these fuels are also renewable. Plants and organic matter may be burned in power plants to generate electricity or refined to produce ethanol which is then mixed with gasoline to burn in cars, trucks, and other internal-combustion-powered vehicles. Corn is one of the primary crops grown and harvested in the US and other nations to produce ethanol. Biodiesel fuel derived from vegetable oil or animal fat may be burned in cars, trucks, and other diesel engines either by itself alone or blended with petrodiesel.

The economics of biofuels is a rather complicated story of the market forces of demand and supply, discussed in Chapter 5, and government intervention discussed in several places throughout this book (e.g., see Chapters 10 and 11). Most economists agree that, at this point in time, production and consumption of biofuels at a large scale would not be possible without substantial government subsidies. The efficiency and equity of biofuels (see Chapters 6, 7, and 8 for a discussion of these terms) is a subject of much current debate. Whenever government intervention impacts input or output prices, economists are concerned about the effects of these artificial price changes on economic efficiency. In general, unless the government is very good at setting efficient prices through policy tools, economic inefficiency in some form is the result of input or output price changes imposed by government intervention (e.g., prices are "too high" or "too low" as compared to the efficient price). In recent years, public policies promoting ethanol production have been criticized in some circles as being "unfair" to the poor, particularly in developing countries, because these policies drive up the price of food derived from corn and other biofuel feedstocks.[1]

Questions for discussion

1. In some uses, mineral products may be substitutes for forest products. How might the optimal mineral extraction and optimal timber harvest models be integrated in order to analyze this situation?

2. Explain how increased demand for timber products for use as biomass in energy production may impact the optimal timber rotation.
3. What principles could be used for resource allocation in an agency such as the US Forest Service, which manages land producing timber, range for grazing, outdoor recreation facilities, and habitats for rare and endangered species?
4. Under what conditions, if any, would it be the preferred policy to permit the local exhaustion of a biotic resource?
5. Under what conditions, if any, would it be the preferred policy to permit the extinction of a species?
6. We have seen some of the difficulties that arise in attempting to optimize the long-term management of a fishery, in which a single resource manager (or management institution) controls the fishing inputs or the rate of fish harvest. What problems might arise in the long-term management of fish resources in international waters? How might these problems be overcome?
7. Discuss the long-term potential and prospects for solar, wind, and biofuel-based energy production and consumption to replace fossil fuel-based energy production and consumption from economic, environmental, and ethical perspectives.

Note

1. For more detailed discussion on the economics of biofuels and the efficiency and equity of biofuel policies and programs, see Harry De Gorter and David R. Just (2009), "The Welfare Economics of a Biofuel Tax Credit and the Interaction Effects with Price Contingent Farm Subsidies," *American Journal of Agricultural Economics* 91 (2): 477–88; Organisation for Economic Co-operation and Development (OECD) (2006), "Agricultural Market Impacts of Future Growth in the Production of Biofuels," *OECD Papers* 6 (1): 1–57; Uwe A. Schneider and Bruce A. McCarl (2004), "Economic Potential of Biomass Based Fuels for Greenhouse Gas Emission Mitigation," *Environmental and Resource Economics* 24 (4): 1573–02; David J. Tenenbaum (2008), "Food vs. Fuel: Diversion of Crops Could Cause More Hunger," *Environmental Health Perspectives* 116 (6): A254–7.

Suggested reading: classic and contemporary

Anderson, L.G. (1986), *The Economics of Fisheries Management*, Baltimore, MD: Johns Hopkins University Press.

Anderson, L.G. and D.R. Lee (1986), "Optimal Governing Instrument, Operation Level, and Enforcement in Natural Resource Regulation: The Case of the Fishery," *American Journal of Agricultural Economics* 68 (3): 678–90.

Benitez, L.E., P.C. Bemitez, and G.C. van Kooten (2007), "The Economics of Wind Power with Energy Storage," *Energy Economics* 30 (4): 1973–89.

Bowes, M.D. and J.V. Krutilla (1985), "Multiple Use Management of Public Forestlands," in *Handbook of Natural Resource and Energy Economics*, Vol. 2, ed. A.V. Kneese and J.L. Sweeney, Amsterdam: Elsevier B.V.

Copes, P. (1986), "A Critical Review of the Individual Quota as a Device in Fisheries Management," *Land Economics* 62: 278–91.

Gordon, H.S. (1954), "The Economic Theory of Common Property Resource: The Fishery," *Journal of Political Economy* 62: 124–43.

Grafton, R.Q., L.K. Sandal, and S.I. Steinshamn (2000), "How to Improve the Management of Renewable Resources: The Case of Canada's Northern Cod Fishery," *American Journal of Agricultural Economics* 82 (3): 570–80.

Howe, C.W. (1979), *Natural Resource Economics: Issues, Analysis, and Policy*, New York: Wiley.

Munro, G.R. and A.D. Scott (1985), "The Economics of Fisheries Management," in *Handbook of Natural Resource and Energy Economics*, Vol. 2, ed. A.V. Kneese and J.L. Sweeney, Amsterdam: Elsevier B.V.

Pimentel, D., G. Rodrigues, T. Wang, R. Abrams, K. Goldberg, H. Staeckner, E. Ma, L. Brueckner, L. Trovato, D. Chow, U. Govindarajulu, and S. Boerke (1994), "Renewable Energy: Economic and Environmental Issues," *Bioscience* 44 (8): 536–47.

Sumaila, U.R. and A. Charles (2002), "Economic Models of Marine Protected Areas: An Introduction," *Natural Resource Modeling* 15 (3): 261–72.

Tsur, Y. and A. Zemel (2000), "Long-Term Perspective on the Development of Solar Energy," *Solar Energy* 68 (5): 379–92.

Wilen, J.E. (2000), "Renewable Resource Economics and Policy: What Differences Have We Made?," *Journal of Environmental Economics and Policy* 39: 306–27.

PART VI

THE ECONOMICS OF AIR, LAND, AND WATER RESOURCE USE AND POLICY

16 The control of polluting emissions: how can we protect the environment and people from air pollution?

Air pollution existed even in pre-industrial times, when it typically resulted from the combustion of biological materials. Smoke from the burning of wood frequently polluted the air above urban centers, and grass and forest fires made air pollution a transitory phenomenon in even the most rural environments. Following the industrial revolution, the combustion of fossil fuels and the by-products from the manufacture and use of chemicals added greatly to the quantity and multiplied the variety of pollutants in the air. Rural regions such as the Ohio River valley now have significant air pollution problems, as they are invaded by airborne pollutants generated in the cities and also generate significant air pollutants locally from automobiles, local industries, and large installations such as coal-burning electric generators that are with increasing frequency being located in rural regions.

Air pollution is ugly, causing discoloration and reducing atmospheric visibility. It is costly; for example, when airborne corrosive materials increase maintenance costs and accelerate the deterioration of buildings, industrial plant, and equipment. Some kinds of pollutants diminish the productivity of biological resources, as they, for example, retard plant growth on farms and in forests. There is substantial medical and statistical evidence that increasing levels of air pollution are positively related to human morbidity and mortality[1] (people get sick and die). All of this suggests that air pollution is most definitely a discommodity.

The economic theory of pollution and its control

Because, insofar as is known, nobody goes around polluting the air for the sheer joy of it, it is reasonable to surmise that air pollution occurs because it is an inexpensive way for the producer of waste materials to dispose of them. Because the ambient air is both non-rival and non-exclusive (see Chapter 10), it is unlikely that anyone disposing of wastes into the air would personally suffer all the costs of the resulting air pollution damage. It is tempting to define air pollution as an external diseconomy, and many analysts do just that. However, as we have seen (Chapter 10), externality is a rather weak concept that offers no analytical results beyond those that emerge from analyses of non-exclusiveness and non-rivalry.

The resource allocation and pricing effects of pollution

Air pollution is produced jointly with a production or consumption activity that is otherwise desirable and often, but not always, occurs in response to market incentives. Consider the production of electricity using coal-burning steam generators, a process that results in air pollution. The pollution is produced jointly with the electricity, but the commodity is marketed and the discommodity is not. Under these conditions, the price of electricity is P_e and the market equilibrium quantity of electricity is Q_e (Figure 16.1).

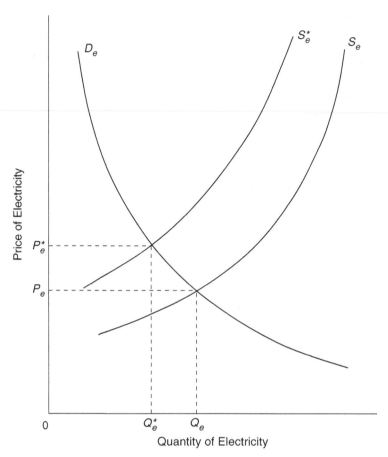

Figure 16.1   Allocation and pricing effects of unpriced pollution

Now assume that the correct negative price was placed on the air pollution, restoring the situation to efficiency. This would increase the costs borne by the generator operator (or more correctly, the operator of the integrated electricity and air pollution enterprise). The supply curve for electricity would shift to the left (S_e^*), reducing the equilibrium quantity of electricity to Q_e^* and increasing its price to P_e^*. The important point is that Q_e^* and P_e^* are the efficient quantity and price of electricity. When residual discommodities are produced jointly with some other activity and released into the collective goods environment without charge to their producer, too much of the other activity (electricity production, in this example) takes place, and its market price is too low. The same result occurs when the joint activity is a consumption activity, for example, driving automobiles for pleasure. If the resulting air pollution is unpriced, too much driving will take place, and the price to the driver will be too low. The market failure resulting from non-exclusiveness and/or non-rivalry permits the acting party (the generator operator or the automobile driver) to impose some of the integral costs of the activity on the general public. Bearing only a part of the total costs of the joint activity, the acting party will choose to do more than the efficient amount of it.

Solutions to the pollution problem

Economic theory offers three basic approaches to the problem of air pollution due to residuals from production or consumption activities. Tax subsidy approaches attempt to restore efficiency by manipulating the price of residuals. Regulatory approaches directly or indirectly attack the quantity of residuals released. "Cap-and-trade" programs use government authority to establish the total quantity of residuals, but use markets to allocate residuals production among the various potential polluters. In each of these approaches, government plays a major role. The Coasian notion of spontaneous markets in the rights to annoy and to be protected from annoyance (see Chapter 10) does not transfer well to collective goods (or collective "bads" in the case of pollution).

Tax-subsidy solutions   The tax or subsidy approach, associated with the economist A.C. Pigou, uses the central authority of government to establish the price (if all goes well, an efficient price) of residuals. A negative price would be placed by a public agency on the residuals. This would be achieved in either of two ways. Taxes could be levied on the acting party in direct proportion to the residuals released. Alternatively, the baseline level of emissions could be established (usually the equilibrium amount when their price is zero), and the agency could subsidize the acting party for reductions in residuals.

Consider a simple case of a pollution tax. A straight-line tax is levied on polluting emissions. That is, the same tax is levied on each unit of emissions, regardless of the level of total emissions. The equilibrium quantity of emissions is determined by the intersection of the tax line and the supply curve for abatement (Figure 16.2).

Note that the demand curve for abatement is presented as a broken line. This is done for two reasons: (1) because the demand curve is ineffective and the tax line is effective; and (2) because with inadequate property rights, the demand curve cannot be observed but must be estimated.

A government agency whose prime goal is economic efficiency will use all the information and expertise at its command to attempt to set the tax so that the tax line passes through the intersection of the supply curve and the demand curve. In Figure 16.2, the tax line crosses the supply curve for abatement at a point slightly lower than the intersection between supply and demand, with the result that the equilibrium level of abatement is slightly less than the level indicated by the intersection of supply and demand. The tax line was deliberately drawn so that it failed to pass through the exact point of intersection between supply and demand. This is intended to emphasize that government agencies, facing both conceptual and empirical difficulties, are unlikely to achieve a perfectly efficient tax rate. However, it is not significant that the tax line intersects the supply curve at a point below the intersection of supply and demand; it could just as easily have intersected the supply curve at some point above the supply-demand intersection.

Given the emissions tax rate suggested in Figure 16.2, the equilibrium level of abatement is Q^*, and a total tax equal to the tax rate multiplied by $(Q^0 - Q^*)$ is collected. The total resource cost of obtaining abatement is the area below that segment of the supply curve for abatement that lies between zero and Q^*. The total expense imposed on the industry by the pollution tax program is equal to the total resource cost plus the total tax collected.

This kind of Pigovian tax solution uses the power of government to institutionalize a negative price for a non-exclusive discommodity. But it leaves substantial discretion to

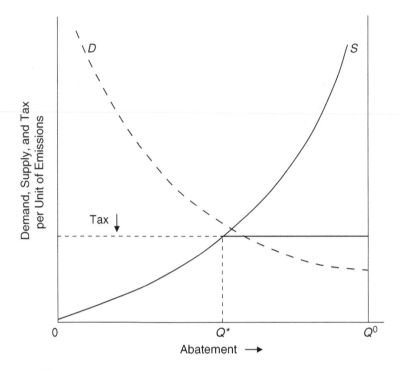

Figure 16.2   The Pigovian tax solution

the private sector. Each polluting firm or consumer is free to determine how best to minimize the cost imposed. Each may determine and implement the least-cost method of pollution abatement, and each may choose how much abatement to provide, subject always to the constraint that taxes must be paid for unabated pollution. These taxes provide a continuing incentive for improved abatement performance; for example, through the implementation of cost-reducing abatement technology.

In the real world, there have been relatively few instances when governments have implemented the rather straightforward Pigovian solution illustrated in Figure 16.2, though variants of the tax subsidy idea have been tried in various places. Unfortunately, not all tax subsidy variants have the desirable economic characteristics of the Pigovian solution. For example, policies that subsidize the use of particular pollution-control devices, directly or through special tax deductions or investment credits, are considerably less efficient. By identifying particular pollution-abatement inputs for favored tax subsidy treatment, the market in abatement inputs is distorted, and the innovation of substitute inputs that are not similarly favored is discouraged.

Regulation   An alternative approach is to regulate directly the quantity of pollution that is permitted. For each polluting firm and consumer, a government agency would determine the maximum permissible amount of pollution. In the case of air pollution, this kind of regulation is called an emissions standard; for water pollution, it is an effluent standard. The standard may be represented by a vertical line, as in Figure 16.3. The

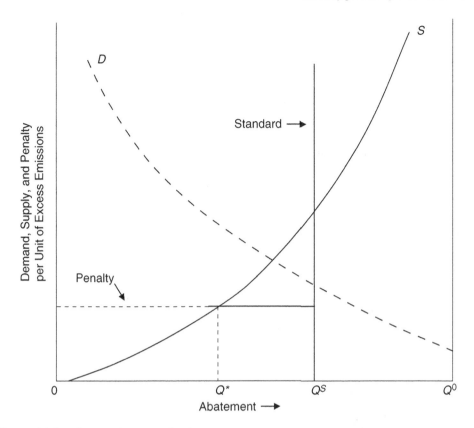

Figure 16.3   An emissions standard

standard indicates that the level of abatement Q^s must be provided, or the polluter will be considered in violation. Notice that there is no incentive for abatement beyond that required by the standard. The amount of pollution $Q^0 - Q^s$ is permitted without charge or penalty. This is a crucial difference between a regulatory solution and the Pigovian emissions tax; in the case of the tax, all unabated emissions are taxed. On the other hand, with a regulatory approach, there is no incentive for abatement beyond that required by the standard.

Is there any assurance that polluters will comply with the standard? If there is no penalty for failing to comply, it is unreasonable to expect compliance. If penalties are prescribed but not enforced, it is equally unreasonable to expect compliance. Thus, the equilibrium level of compliance cannot be determined without considering the expected penalties for failing to comply. Penalties may take various forms: lump-sum fines; fines for each day the standard is violated; fines per unit of emissions beyond those permitted under the standard; or perhaps jail terms for the violators. In Figure 16.3, a straight-line fine per unit of excess emissions is assumed. This kind of penalty is analytically interesting, although it does not appear to be commonly used by regulatory agencies.

The polluter will abate to the point at which the expected penalty line intersects their supply curve for abatement if that point lies to the left of the standard, or will comply with the standard if the intersection of the expected penalty line and the supply curve lies to the right of the standard. Figure 16.3 shows the most interesting case. The polluter provides abatement to Q^*, pays expected penalties equal to the expected per-unit penalty multiplied by $Q^s - Q^*$, and enjoys the privilege of $Q^0 - Q^s$ emissions without penalty.

In Figure 16.3, the standard is drawn slightly to the right of the intersection of the supply curve for abatement with the broken demand curve for abatement; the expected penalty line is drawn to intersect the supply curve for abatement at a point to the left of the standard; and the equilibrium outcome includes some abatement, the payment of some penalties for emissions, and the emission of some pollutants without penalty. Although this is the most interesting case, there is no reason to expect it to be typical. On the other hand, conceptual and empirical difficulties make it unlikely that a regulatory agency could succeed in setting a standard exactly equal to the efficient level of abatement. The setting of the penalty is not conceptually difficult: it simply needs to be so high and so well enforced that all polluters will prefer to comply with the standard. But government agencies have experienced substantial political pressures militating against such effective penalties.

Again it must be noted that in the real world, different regulatory approaches have been tried. In particular, approaches that regulate not total emissions but the use of particular pollution control inputs are likely to introduce inefficiencies and distortions in the market for pollution control inputs while discouraging innovations in the kinds of pollution control inputs that are not required by regulation.

Emissions taxes or standards – which approach is less costly?   It is interesting to consider which of the governmental approaches, emissions taxes or standards, provides a given level of abatement at the lowest resource cost. Consider an industry that emits a particular kind of pollutant. For simplicity, the industry will be represented by three firms, which have the supply curves for abatement S_1, S_2, and S_3. Given a straight-line emissions tax, as shown in Figure 16.4, the tax line intersects the supply curve S_1 at point A, and supply curve S_2 at B, and the supply curve S_3 at C. The standard line intersects the supply curve S_1, at point D, S_2 at point B, and S_3 at point E. To permit a simple diagrammatic analysis, the supply curves for abatement and the tax and standard lines are drawn so that:

$$Q_1 + Q_2 + Q_3 = 3Q_2 \tag{16.1}$$

and

$$Q_3 - Q_2 = Q_2 - Q_1 \tag{16.2}$$

Thus the industry offers the same total amount of abatement under the standard and the tax. For each firm, under each institutional alternative, the total resource cost of offering abatement is the area under the supply curve of abatement between zero and the level of abatement provided.

The total resource cost of abatement under the emissions tax is subtracted from the cost under the emissions standard as follows:

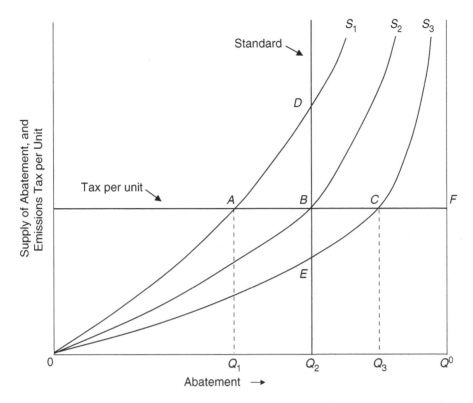

Figure 16.4 *The resource cost of abatement: a comparison of emissions taxes and*
standards

$$\text{Standard: } 0DQ_2 + 0BQ_2 + 0EQ_2$$
$$\text{Minus tax: } 0AQ_1 + 0BQ_2 + 0CQ_3$$
$$= DQ_2Q_1A + 0 - CQ_3Q_2E \qquad (16.3)$$

Because $DQ_2Q_1A > CQ_3Q_2E$, the total resource cost under the emissions tax is less
than the total resource cost under the emissions standard, for the same total quantity of
abatement. Why would this be? The reason is that the emissions tax encourages the most
efficient supplier of abatement, whose supply curve is S_3, to do the lion's share of the
abating. The least efficient abater, whose supply curve is S_1, does the least abating.

Although the resource costs of achieving a given level of total abatement are lower
with emissions taxes than with emissions standards, we observe that the representatives
of polluting industries typically lobby in favor of emissions standards rather than taxes.
The reason for this preference is obvious. Under emissions taxes, polluters not only meet
the cost of providing their equilibrium level of abatement but also pay the tax on unabated emissions, which amounts to the rectangle AFQ^0Q_1 for firm 1, BFQ^0Q_2 for firm
2, and CFQ^0Q_3 for firm 3. These taxes represent an additional expense to polluters. But
they may be viewed as compensation to the receptors of pollution for the pollution that
remains, and receptors may thus consider the taxes perfectly fair.

The analysis in Figure 16.4 demonstrates that under conditions of static technology, emissions taxes achieve a given level of total abatement at a lower resource cost than do emissions standards. Remember that emissions taxes have the additional advantage of offering continuing incentives for innovations in pollution abatement, which would reduce both the remaining emissions and the pollution-associated costs faced by the polluters.

Cap-and-trade programs   For many years (e.g., see J.H. Dales[2]), economists have advocated using markets and market incentives to achieve pollution control goals at minimum cost. Dales suggested markets in pollution permits, quotas, or certificates; that is, legal instruments permitting the owner to emit pollution up to a specified maximum amount. The currently favored form of pollution trading is called "cap-and-trade." In a cap-and-trade program, the pollution control agency determines the total permissible emissions of a given pollutant in a geographic region – this is the "cap." If the agency used an efficiency criterion and had sufficient information at its disposal, it would decide to permit total emissions of $Q_e = Q^0 - Q_a$ (Figure 16.5a). In the case of air pollution, the permissible total emissions would be determined after consideration of the supply curve for abatement (reductions in emissions), the demand for ambient air quality, and the physical relationship between emissions and ambient air quality.

Under one version of cap-and-trade, pollution permits permitting the exact quantity of total emissions, Q_e, that would result in the attainment of the desired ambient air quality would be printed and auctioned to polluters. Each polluter would be permitted to emit pollutants for which they had purchased permits but would face prohibitive penalties for excess emissions. The demand curve for permits, which is the mirror image of the industry's supply curve for abatement, intersects with the government-determined vertical supply line for pollution permits (Figure 16.5b), determining the price of pollution-emission permits, P_e. The individual polluter responds to the pollution permit program as though it were equivalent to a program of straight-line emissions taxes. He or she provides the level of abatement determined by the intersection of the price line for permits with his or her own supply curve for abatement (Figure 16.5c).

The pollution permit program illustrated in Figures 16.5b and 16.5c has certain advantages that it derives from its use of economic incentives. The initial permit auction serves both to allocate emissions permits (that is, the right to pollute) to the highest-cost abaters and to generate income for the public sector in much the same way as an emissions tax does. This income may be viewed as compensation to the general public for the pollution emitted. In addition, the pollution permits would be freely transferable at any time – this is the "trade" component of cap-and-trade programs. This trade component encourages innovation in pollution abatement, because innovators are rewarded by income from the sale of permits no longer needed. Furthermore, industrial growth could be accommodated as new polluters purchased unneeded permits from established polluters in the region. This would encourage efficient pollution abatement for both new and established polluters. In the United States, the most successful ongoing cap-and-trade program is the one established by the US Environmental Protection Agency for SO_2 emissions from coal-fired electricity power plants (see discussion below for more details).

An alternative version of cap-and-trade would assign caps (maximum permissible emissions) to individual firms – this version has proven more acceptable politically because it relieves polluters of the burden of buying permits at the outset. Low-cost abaters could

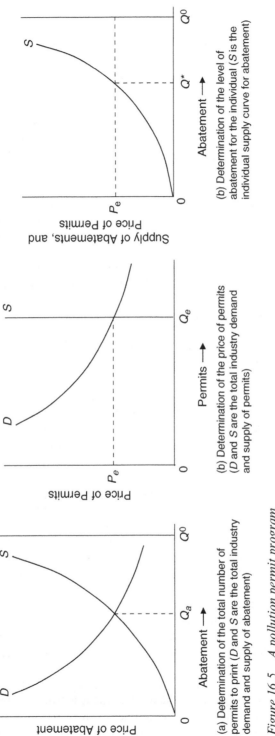

Figure 16.5 A pollution permit program

315

earn pollution reduction credits (PRCs) by demonstrating emissions consistently below their assigned caps, and these PRCs could be sold to higher-cost abaters. Again, aggregate abatement costs are minimized by markets that equalize marginal abatement costs across firms, and assign the lion's share of abatement to lower-cost abaters.

Analysis of cap-and-trade programs is useful, as it draws attention to certain important problems that were glossed over in the discussion of emissions taxes and standards. In implementing a program of taxes or standards, it is necessary for the agency first to establish an ambient air quality standard and then to determine the total emissions per unit time that would result in attainment of the ambient air standard in a given region. If the agency chooses to establish an emissions tax, it must have information concerning the aggregate supply curve for the abatement of each pollutant. Without that information, it cannot be reasonably sure that the tax it establishes will achieve the ambient environmental quality standards. If emissions standards are to be used, it is necessary first to determine the relationship between emissions and ambient environmental quality and then to establish an individual emissions standard for each polluter. In a dynamic economy, in which polluters are free to move into and out of the region, individual emissions standards must be adjusted from time to time to ensure that the aggregate emissions of all polluters do not violate the ambient environmental quality standards.

Some additional considerations in the choice of instrument

Uncertainty and the choice between price and quantity controls   In a certain world, the same (perhaps optimal) level of abatement could be achieved by a pollution tax or a control on the quantity of emissions. However, if compliance costs were uncertain, a pollution tax would effectively fix the marginal cost of compliance, leaving the level of compliance uncertain. On the other hand, quantity controls, in the form of standards or tradable permits, would fix the level of compliance but result in uncertain marginal costs. This fundamental difference in the face of cost uncertainty leads to different welfare outcomes for the two policy instruments.[3]

A double dividend?   Even if a pollution tax and a quantity control (a standard, or tradable permits) were otherwise equivalent, we might perhaps prefer the tax for fiscal reasons. Specifically, because government must raise revenues and most revenue-raising mechanisms distort economic incentives, a pollution tax might be argued to do not one but two good things: help clean up the environment, and reduce government reliance on distorting taxes. However, economists have argued that this "double dividend" is, at least in part, a matter of wishful thinking. The argument is that, yes, a pollution tax would restore efficiency in the polluting sector and reduce emissions, and reduce reliance on distorting taxes, but it would also introduce an inefficient excise tax on the commodity produced in the polluting process (say, electricity). Excise taxes, too, are distorting, and it has been argued that workers facing such a tax would demand higher wages, imposing additional costs on the economy.[4]

All three effects – the direct gain from internalizing the pollution externality, the gain from reducing reliance on distorting taxes, and the loss from an excise tax on, say, electricity – are valid considerations. The double dividend question (do the welfare gains from a pollution tax exceed the benefits from abatement?) is harder to answer. Among other things, it depends on whether pollution abatement is a local or a global public good. In the case of a local tax to produce a global public good (e.g. greenhouse gas reduction), the excise tax on electricity is a source of local welfare loss and thus threatens the double dividend. The result of a local tax to produce a local public good is different. Because the direct gain from pollution control is a net benefit, workers would on balance be attracted to, not repelled from, the region that imposed the tax. In that case, the prospects for a double dividend are more promising.

Note that the double dividend question is an important consideration in the choice between pollution taxes and cap-and-trade schemes. Pollution taxes are more likely to generate double dividends. Nevertheless, cap-and-trade schemes seem more politically acceptable in many jurisdictions, presumably because polluting industries regard them as less onerous.

A concluding comment on the economic theory of pollution control
The preceding analyses, though instructive, are highly simplistic. They are for the most part static, whereas the real world is dynamic. They tend to gloss over the massive informational problems that exist, especially with respect to air and water pollution given our ignorance of basic environmental processes, and the vagaries of climatic and hydrological conditions.

The analyses of governmental solutions – for example, emissions taxes, standards, and pollution certificates – ignored the important issue of transaction costs. Yet common sense and casual observation tell us that the transaction costs borne by individuals, firms, and government agencies will be substantial. Transaction costs will be incurred in establishing specific policies, implementing those policies, and enforcing them. The analyses tended to gloss over the issue of enforcement. How can government effectively monitor the emissions of individual polluters to ensure that each is abiding by the terms of the program (be it a pollution tax, a standard, or a cap-and-trade program)? If the agency must rely on emissions data provided by the polluters themselves, can it create and implement incentives for honest reporting?

Policies of the 1970s: "the environmental decade"[5]
Given the non-rival and non-exclusive characteristics of ambient air, pure Coasian market solutions have seldom been effective in reducing the inefficiently large amounts of air pollution. It is relatively easy to demonstrate conceptually that policies that work through the price system, such as emissions taxes, provide a given level of air pollution abatement at a lower resource cost than do regulatory approaches such as emission standards. Nevertheless, state and federal air pollution control policies in the United States have emphasized various regulatory approaches. This is consistent with US political traditions, in which regulatory approaches are customarily selected in preference to approaches that rely on modifying price incentives, and is also consistent with the observation (see Chapter 11), that the US Constitution simply makes it easier for legislators to pursue policy objectives via the police power rather than the power to tax.

Since the 1970s, air pollution control policies have been pursued in the United States through a complex regulatory approach in which the federal government has taken the lead, in spite of the constitutional provisions that vest the police power in the states (see Chapter 11). A complex web of federal and state enabling legislation, regulations, and enforcement has been established. Different provisions were applied to different pollutants, different locations, and different emissions sources. It would be inappropriate and impracticable to describe them in detail here. Rather, we shall discuss in general terms some of the more significant aspects of this regulatory approach.

Many of the environmental pollution policies in force today in the US have their origins in the 1970s. Riding a wave of increased public concern over environmental pollution problems, the US Environmental Protection Agency (EPA) was established in December 1970 and the US Congress began to pass a number of important environmental legislation and programs. The 1970 amendments to the US Clean Air Act directed the US EPA to determine standards for ambient air quality that would protect human health. These were designated the primary standards and were to be drawn up rapidly. Secondary standards, more stringent than the primary standards and designed to protect property and the public welfare, were established to be implemented on more flexible time schedules. In those areas that had historically suffered substantial pollution from industrial and mobile sources, the primary standards represented the immediate air quality target. In areas that had historically enjoyed high levels of air quality, the EPA was instructed to achieve "prevention of significant deterioration" (PSD) of air quality. After a spate of litigation, in which it was determined that PSD meant pretty much what it said, the 1977 Clean Air Act amendments required that in certain pristine areas, atmospheric visibility had to be protected.

Thus, the operative ambient air quality standard varied across regions, ranging from the primary standards in heavily populated and industrialized regions, through the secondary standards in many areas, to standards that would maintain atmospheric visibility above certain remote and pristine lands, mostly in the western states. Federal legislation required that the states establish and implement air quality standards at least as stringent as the federal standards. Ironically, the US Supreme Court ruled that states may not enforce standards more stringent than the applicable federal standard when a federal source of emissions is involved.

For point sources, the 1970 Clean Air Act amendments directed the Environmental Protection Agency to require that new point sources use the "best adequately demonstrated control technology" (BACT). Concern with benefits and costs was not explicit in this criterion (although careful definition of "adequately demonstrated" may implicitly imply economic considerations). In order to meet ambient air quality standards, the 1970 Clean Air Act empowered the US EPA to require polluters to retrofit emissions control devices. The US EPA was also empowered by the Act to deny permits for new polluting installations if granting such permits would result in ambient air quality standards violations. These amendments put the EPA into the business of regulating the use of emissions control inputs, rather than emissions control performance. Regulating emissions control inputs represented a major challenge to the US EPA since this approach requires a detailed study of control technology and, in the case of very large point sources, may also involve the regulatory agency becoming involved in the design of individual installations.

For mobile sources, the 1970 amendments actually specified the permissible emissions standards for automobiles. These standards applied to new cars; the control of emissions from old cars remained a matter for the states to do something, or nothing, about. Automobile emissions standards were defined in terms of grams of various pollutants per mile driven. By 1975, new cars could emit only about 5 percent of the typical pre-1967 emissions of hydrocarbons and carbon monoxide, and by 1976, new cars were to meet a similar standard for nitrogen oxides. By the late 1970s, it became clear that to meet these standards would mean very expensive control devices and fuel costs. A series of delays was granted, and the mobile source standards were modified several times. The 1970 amendments also authorized the establishment of national emissions standards for toxic pollutants which applied to small firms (e.g., local dry cleaners) and large firms (e.g., regional oil refineries) alike.

The 1970 amendments permitted a bewildering array of federal and state regulations, in the event that fitting emissions control devices proved insufficient to satisfy the ambient air quality standards. These included land use controls, transportation controls, and the shutdown of major polluters. Taken seriously, these provisions would have amounted to an unprecedented mandate for joint federal–state efforts to regulate public and private life.

Any approach to air pollution control must have considerable flexibility. Because the relationship between emissions and ambient air quality varies with the weather, so that a level of emissions that is acceptable at most times leads to extreme deterioration of ambient air quality during temperature inversions, provisions are needed for extraordinary emissions controls during extraordinary weather conditions. The 1970s' regulatory structure had provisions for such extraordinary controls, including permitting agencies to require that major polluting installations cease operations during extreme weather conditions.

An economic critique of 1970s' policies

The standard economic critique of the policies of "the environmental decade" attacks both goals and methods. With respect to goals, economists complained that policies essentially took no account of benefits and costs, in total or at the margin. The 1970 clean water legislation, with its target of zero discharge into the nation's waterways by 1984, is an extreme example. Nevertheless, there are plenty of examples of "economically unrealistic" and inflexible goals in the air pollution laws and regulations. With respect to methods, economists offered their standard generic argument that pollution taxes offer several advantages, including resource cost savings over regulatory approaches, and a detailed critique of the particular modes of regulation that were implemented.

The regulatory approach applied to point sources is especially prone to inefficiency, as it regulates emissions control inputs rather than emissions control performance. This approach encounters severe difficulties in accommodating growth, because a continuing increase in the number of installations, each achieving the same percentage of reduction in emissions by using the same BACT, will eventually result in violating the ambient standards.

The BACT approach, which required the use of particular inputs, discouraged independent innovation in emissions control and effectively prohibited the use of substitute control inputs. For example, electric utilities, if emissions were regulated on the basis of tons per kilowatt hour of electricity produced, could satisfy the standards by burning low-sulfur coal or by installing scrubbers and burning higher-sulfur coal. The BACT approach, combined with emissions-control targets expressed not in tons per unit of product but in percentage reduction of uncontrolled emissions, limits the possibility of substituting low-sulfur coal for scrubbers. In effect, this kind of regulation penalizes the use of higher-cost low-sulfur coal. Not surprisingly, it gained most of its political support from those states that have predominantly high-sulfur coal reserves.

Emissions control regulations, of course, must be backed up with effective enforcement. The most effective enforcement establishes penalties (and the probability that the penalty will actually be imposed) sufficiently high that the benefits a polluter may expect from violation are much lower than the costs. However, this approach has been considered politically unacceptable. After the detection of a violation, the usual enforcement approach is negotiation and persuasion, although regulations often prescribe or at least permit monetary penalties for violation. The most significant powers of the enforcers derive from their persistence, from the threat of negative publicity and resulting damage to the corporate image of a major industrial polluter, and from the threat that monetary penalties may actually be imposed. Major industrial violators are not without bargaining power, as they may plausibly claim that strict enforcement would drive them out of business or force them to relocate, thus lowering regional employment and income. It is not uncommon for the workforce, if organized, to join management in these kinds of arguments. A common outcome of this process of negotiation and persuasion is the issuance of a variance. If the enforcement agency accepts the argument that the polluter is making a good-faith effort to comply but has been impeded by circumstances beyond their control, a variance may be granted permitting emissions beyond the standard for some period of time, at the end of which the variance will expire and the standard will be enforced.

The 1970s' approach to mobile source emissions, and especially to automobile emissions, has been roundly criticized. It applied to new cars but not to used cars. The EPA tested representative specimens of each make and model of new car. Periodic testing of the existing automobile stock was left to the states, if they so chose; and most did not so choose.

Manufacturers were required to provide 50 000-mile warranties for emissions control systems. But there were some disincentives for owners to maintain these systems. Systems that do not use catalytic converters tend to reduce gasoline mileage and engine performance. The temptation to disconnect such systems remained strong, in spite of prescribed penalties which were seldom administered when there was no provision for periodic emissions testing. Systems that did use catalytic converters required unleaded gasoline, which was more expensive and often less readily available than was regular gasoline. It was easy to fill one's fuel tank with regular, and it was necessary to do it only a few times in order to render the catalytic converter ineffective.

The 1970s' approach to automobile emissions control required expensive emissions control equipment on all new cars but did almost nothing to require continuing and effective control of emissions. An advantage of the regulatory approach to automobile emissions, compared with the BACT approach to point sources, was that automobile manufacturers were free to choose their preferred control technology, provided that their test cars passed the emissions test.

On the other hand, the automobile emissions control program, unlike the point sources program, took no account of regional differences in air quality. Permissible emissions per mile driven were the same for all regions (except California, and the California rules were instituted at state, not federal, initiative). It is easy to identify both inefficiency and inequity in a system that requires the same emissions control devices on cars used in crowded metropolitan areas and those used in remote rural regions.

Another limitation of the 1970s' approach is that the process for setting ambient air quality standards did not strictly require consideration of benefits and costs. Rather, the process for setting ambient air quality standards focused on balancing various legislative, regulatory and perhaps even judicial interests. To an economist, ignoring the benefits and costs of air quality standards would be like a consumer purchasing a new car without looking under the hood or considering the price – which is not what a prudent person would do unless he or she has money to burn.

The economists' critique can be summarized. The air pollution control policies of the 1970s were inefficient in that they did not stipulate that most of the abating be done by the least-cost abaters. They led to interregional distortions and were not well adapted to a dynamic economy. The use of negotiation and persuasion as primary enforcement tools weakened the effectiveness of the regulations. To the extent that the regulations did require the use of particular pollution abatement inputs, they introduced inefficiencies by discouraging emissions reducing substitutions of inputs and innovations in pollution control technology. Emissions standards also did not encourage abatement beyond the standard, and made no provision for compensating receptors for the pollution that remained. Finally, it was not strictly necessary to consider benefits and costs when setting air quality standards.[6]

If most economists had their way, environmental pollution control programs would rely primarily on incentives that operate by modifying prices, rather than on regulatory requirements. Thus, their approach is aimed at taking maximum advantage from the efficiency of, say, emissions taxes relative to emissions standards. If economists were in charge, ambient air quality standards would be established, following benefit–cost analysis based on technical parameters established through careful research. Technical research would establish the relationships among emissions, ambient air quality, and the level of each of the various kinds of damage that results. Benefit–cost analysis would compare, in total and at the margin, the benefits from abatement (that is, the value of the damages that would be avoided by abatement) with the costs of achieving abatement. Ambient air quality standards would be established at the level where marginal benefits of additional abatement were equal to marginal costs. Of course, benefit–cost analysis is not quite so simple as it sounds: major difficulties are introduced by the general ignorance about the long-run consequences of various pollutants and by the need to place economic values on reductions in human morbidity and mortality.

Following the establishment of ambient air quality standards, most economists would recommend pollution taxes or pollution markets – either way, a price on pollution would be established. Here, we outline a program of emissions taxes. A system of per-unit emissions taxes would be determined for each category of pollutants. In order to set the appropriate emissions tax, it is first necessary to estimate the supply curve for the abatement of each category of pollutants. Using this estimated relationship, the level of per-unit tax that would result in the total amount of emissions consistent with the ambient air quality standard would be estimated. That per-unit emissions tax would be levied on all emissions sources, a process that requires emissions monitoring and an agency to collect the emission tax continuously, just as the US Internal Revenue Service continuously collects other kinds of taxes. Ambient air quality monitoring would continue. If errors in estimating the economic relationships discussed above resulted in imperfect consistency between the ambient air quality standard and the achieved ambient air quality (as most economists admit would be quite likely), the level of per-unit emissions taxes could be varied iteratively until the appropriate tax was determined by trial-and-error adjustment. To those who objected that this process of iterative adjustment would generate uncertainty, some economists in cavalier manner would respond that it is the proper role of the economic decision-maker to respond to uncertainty. Most economists would recommend that the ambient air quality standard and the level of emissions taxes should be permitted to vary across regions in response to regional differences in the level of polluting activities, atmospheric conditions, and the demand for clean air.

Following a period in which much of the economic literature suggested that emissions taxes alone would constitute an entirely sufficient air pollution control policy, economists came to realize the importance of transient weather conditions to the relationship between emissions and ambient air quality.[7] A level of emissions that is tolerable under most weather conditions results in unacceptable ambient air quality during temperature inversions. Thus later and more sophisticated economic analyses have recommended that a generally applied system of emissions taxes be backed up with emissions standards (up to and including total prohibitions when necessary) to be invoked during periods of extreme weather conditions.

Although many economists have been fairly satisfied with the above recommendations for improving pollution control in the case of stationary sources, such as factories, they have recognized that mobile sources, such as automobiles, present special problems in the establishment and enforcement of emissions tax systems. Although automobiles in aggregate are major polluters, each individual automobile is a relatively minor polluter and there are millions of them. The continuous monitoring of individual automobiles would be prohibitively expensive. In addition, automobiles, being designed for transportation, occasionally move across regional boundaries, even if they are most commonly used within the vicinity of the operator's residence. Thus, a policy pertaining to regional differentials in emissions taxes poses particular problems in the case of mobile sources. Nevertheless, some economists have argued that a viable system of emissions charges for mobile sources is feasible.[8]

It has been suggested that automobiles in the US should be tested for emissions at regular intervals, perhaps annually or semi-annually. After testing, each automobile would be issued a sticker that would indicate its emissions class. The emissions classes would be based on emissions per gallon of fuel used under "normal" driving conditions. The nation would be divided into regions on the basis of the average cost of damages per unit of automobile emissions. For an automobile in a given emissions class, because total emissions are closely correlated with the quantity of fuel used, the emissions taxes could be collected at the fuel pump. The tax would be based on the quantity of fuel purchased, the emissions class of the automobile, and the air quality region in which the fuel pump is located.

Such a system would entail only a moderate increase in the bureaucratic hassles that confront the gasoline retailer. Fuel pumps that automatically included the tax in the customer's bill could readily be designed. In addition, this system would have several significant advantages. Individual owners would choose their basic automobiles, the emissions controls devices to be fitted (as factory-fitted options), their maintenance programs, and their driving habits, in the same general way that they make other economic decisions. As a result, a given level of abatement would be achieved at the lowest opportunity cost. There would be incentives for maintaining emissions control devices, for continuously improving emissions control technology, and for retrofitting in the event that a highly effective and inexpensive emissions control device were developed. Finally, automobiles customarily operated in remote rural environments where air pollution does not present significant problems would no longer be required to have the same emissions control equipment as would those customarily operated in regions that have serious air pollution problems. This would eliminate a major source of inefficiency and inequity in current policy with respect to pollution from automobiles.

The cost and effectiveness of the 1970s' policies
For all the major categories of air pollutants except one, there were significant reductions in national emissions from 1970 to 1980. Particulate emissions decreased by 46 percent, sulfur dioxide (SO_2) by 17 percent, volatile organic compounds (VOCs) by 10 percent, and carbon monoxide (CO) by 9 percent. But there was a small (less than 1 percent) increase in national nitrogen oxides (NOx) emissions.[9]

It is noteworthy that each of the major emissions source categories closely paralleled the national total emissions trends. Clearly, no major source of air pollution emissions was able to escape the burden of emissions reduction. Throughout the 1970s, mobile sources and stationary sources bore approximately equal shares of the costs of air pollution abatement expenditures. In the early 1980s, however, the expenditures for mobile source abatement continued to accelerate, whereas those for stationary sources declined a little. In 1980, stationary source emissions exceeded those from mobile sources in four of the five categories, but mobile sources emitted far more carbon monoxide. From these crude observations, it is not possible to judge whether the distribution of air pollution control expenditures has been guided more by equity considerations than by considerations of efficiency.

Data on the costs of air pollution control are quite complete and (since the Clean Air Act amendments of 1977) must be reported regularly to the US Congress. Benefit estimation has proved to be much more difficult, because many important benefit categories are concerned with non-marketed, non-exclusive, non-rival goods and amenities. Since the 1970s, the US Environmental Protection Agency has sponsored innovative research designed to measure the economic benefits of pollution control. Despite successes in estimating the benefits of controlling particular pollutants in particular circumstances,[10] complete and reliable national aggregate benefit estimates for air pollution control remain elusive. Consequently, whether or not the total national benefits from air pollution control have exceeded the costs over time is still an open question. There is even less evidence to indicate the relationship between marginal costs and benefits for abating particular pollutants from particular sources in particular regions. Thus, we simply do not know much about the efficiency of air pollution control policy at the margin.

Policies of the 1980s: a turn towards market incentives
In 1981, the Council on Environmental Quality appointed by the incoming Reagan administration reviewed the policies and accomplishments of "the environmental decade." Though applauding the successes of the 1970s, the council was quite critical of

the policies of that era. Its major complaints concerned the inflexibility of prescriptive regulation and the minor role that economic incentives had played in environmental policy. The council announced for the 1980s three major goals for US domestic policy (a fourth goal concerned global cooperation):[11]

1. Balancing the costs and benefits of environmental controls.
2. Allowing market incentives to work in environmental policy.
3. Decentralizing government responsibilities for environmental improvement.

A brief review of US environmental policy through the 1980s suggests that the progress toward accomplishing these goals was noticeable but modest. With respect to stationary sources, the major innovation was expansion of emissions trading, a policy actually initiated in the late 1970s. There are three categories of emissions trading: "bubbles," an arrangement by which emissions from several neighboring outlets (not necessarily owned by the same firm) can be combined and treated for regulatory purposes as a single source; "banks," an arrangement by which emissions credits can be stockpiled for subsequent trading; and "offsets," which allow new polluting installations to enter a region where ambient air quality is already as bad as permissible, as long as they can obtain agreements from existing installations to reduce their emissions by an amount that exceeds the emissions from the new installation. Together, these policies added considerable flexibility to stationary source air pollution control.

Although pollution control procedures for stationary sources became a bit more flexible in the 1980s, various factors combined to have the opposite effect with respect to mobile sources. Permissible carbon monoxide emissions dropped dramatically between 1979 and 1981, and automobile fuel-economy standards became much more stringent throughout the early 1980s. These two regulatory influences together effectively allowed automobile manufacturers no choice, and since the 1983 model year, catalytic converters and computer-measured fuel-injection systems became standard throughout the industry. In effect, it is almost as though the BACT strategy had been applied to mobile sources.

In the early 1980s, the US EPA moved to require states failing to attain the ozone standard to establish mandatory inspection and maintenance programs for automobiles. This program was directed at one of the much-remarked-upon weaknesses of the mobile sources program – the failure to encourage the maintenance and upgrading of pollution controls on in-service vehicles. By the mid-1980s, mandatory inspection and maintenance programs applied to all or part of 32 states.

The increased concern with benefits and costs did not appear to have resulted in much relaxation of environmental standards in the 1980s, as some people may have hoped or feared. On the other hand, stringent new policies for the removal of lead from gasoline were announced in 1985, largely as a result of an EPA-sponsored benefit–cost analysis that demonstrated overwhelming benefits from reducing lead emissions. In the 1980s, a substantial degree of control was achieved for the five major categories of pollutants which enabled the US EPA to turn its attention toward other air pollution problems, for example hazardous and toxic gases, long-distance transportation of sulfur and nitrogen oxides that results in "acid precipitation," and indoor air pollution.

The downward national emission trends observed in the 1970s for sulfur dioxide (SO_2), volatile organic compounds (VOCs) and carbon monoxide (CO) continued in the 1980s.

From 1980 to 1990, SO_2 emissions decreased by 10 percent, VOC emissions decreased by 23 percent and CO emissions decreased by 17 percent. In the 1980s, the trend in national nitrogen oxides (NOx) emissions turned downward with emissions decreasing 6 percent from 1980 to 1990. The trend in national particulate emissions turned sharply upward in the 1980s with almost a 300 percent increase in emissions from 1980 to 1990.[12]

Policies of the 1990s: establishing the viability of market trading
In the 1990s, emission allowance trading as a means for controlling stationary source (point source) air pollution became more firmly established. The US Clean Air Act Amendments of 1990 set SO_2 reduction goals to be met over the decade for the primary reason of curbing acid rain problems. Thus, these reduction goals and the means for achieving these goals, including emission allowance trading, has since become known as the Acid Rain Program administered by the US EPA.

SO_2 emitters subject to the 1990 Clean Air Act Amendments were primarily composed of coal-fired electricity power plants. States having the highest number of power plants subject to the Amendments included Georgia, Illinois, Indiana, Kentucky, Missouri, Ohio, Pennsylvania, Tennessee, and West Virginia. Thus, the east coast and midwestern regions of the US were most affected by the Acid Rain Program. These regions also were experiencing major acid rain problems.

The centerpiece of the Acid Rain Program is an SO_2 emission allowance "cap-and-trade" system. Under this system, the 1990 Clean Air Act Amendments set an overall "cap" on SO_2 emissions and then allocated SO_2 emission allowances to power plants. After receiving emission allowances, power plants were allowed to trade allowances (or permits) at "market" prices; that is, prices set by the interaction of willing buyers and sellers of allowances. This system allowed more efficient power plants to sell excess allowances to less efficient power plants. This system also provides incentives for a less efficient power plant to invest in pollution control technology so that it too may be able to obtain and sell excess allowances, or at least not need to purchase allowances to meet pollution standards. However, each power plant has the flexibility to pursue the least-cost means of meeting pollution standards (e.g., investing in pollution control technology or purchasing emission allowances). The flexibility to pursue least-cost means of pollution control while meeting SO_2 reduction goals was seen as one of the major advantages of the emission allowance trading system.

By all accounts, the SO_2 emission allowance trading program got off to a shaky start in the early 1990s, primarily because of suspicion and uncertainty over whether or not such a market-based incentive system would really work. However, by 1995, early nervousness over the program seemed to have been overcome and trades started to steadily increase throughout the rest of the decade as shown in Figure 16.6. In just about every category including the establishment of a well-functioning emission allowance trading market, pollution control cost savings, pollution reduction and public acceptance, the SO_2 trading program in the 1990s was declared a success.[13] From 1990 to 2000, national SO_2 emissions reduced by almost 30 percent, putting a major dent in the nation's acid rain problems.

With respect to mobile sources of air pollution, the US Clean Air Act Amendments of 1990 implemented a comprehensive approach to control of emissions from cars, trucks, buses, and "non-road equipment" (recreational vehicles, lawn and garden equipment, and so on). These mobile sources are major contributors to emissions of carbon

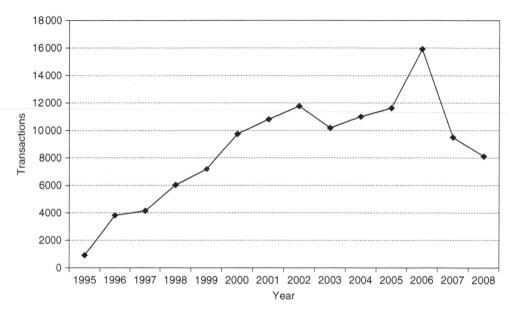

Source: US Environmental Protection Agency.

Figure 16.6   US SO$_2$ emission allowance transactions

monoxide (CO), nitrogen oxides (NOx) and volatile organic compounds (VOCs). Air pollution problems from mobile sources increased in the 1990s because of rapid economic growth and population growth resulting in more total and per capita driving miles. Also, in the late 1980s the "minivan" was invented which soon became the vehicle of choice for many American families growing up in the burgeoning suburbs. Also, throughout the 1990s, the popularity of sport utility vehicles (SUVs) and pickup trucks as personal vehicles rapidly increased. By the year 2000, minivans, SUVs, and pickup trucks (collectively termed "light-duty trucks") accounted for about 50 percent of the new passenger car sales. Because of their relatively large engines and overall bulk, a light-duty van or truck likely consumes more gasoline per mile and may pollute up to three to five times more than a typical sedan-type passenger car.

The mobile source provisions in the 1990 Clean Air Act Amendments are more along the lines of prescriptive regulation. On the input side, the 1990 Act requires petroleum refineries to produce cleaner fuels and automobile manufacturers to produce cars with "cleaner-burning" engines. In addition to passenger cars, the 1990 Act emission regulations cover diesel trucks, buses, and "non-road equipment." Certain regions of the US with air pollution problems (e.g., large urban metropolitan areas) are also required to adopt and run passenger vehicle inspection and maintenance programs. The 1990 Amendments also issued regulations to help reduce emissions associated with vehicles refueling at service stations (e.g., special fuel pumps which help reduce emission of vapors when consumers are pumping fuel).

The emission of toxic pollutants such as lead has been a major air pollution policy concern in the US. Excessive lead has very adverse health effects on people including damage to the brain, nervous system, and organs including the heart. Children are especially at risk to brain and nervous system disorders caused by excessive exposure to lead. Responding to the risks posed by lead poisoning, the US EPA began phasing out leaded gasoline in the 1970s with stronger restrictions in the 1980s followed by complete ban in 1996. As a result of these aggressive actions, national lead emissions fell by 900 percent from 1980 to 2000.

Since passage of the 1990 Clean Air Act Amendments, drivers may have noticed more stickers on gasoline pumps stating something like, "may contain up to 10% ethanol." The Act included provisions encouraging the development of alternatives to gasoline and diesel for powering vehicles including ethanol, natural gas, propane, methanol, electricity, and biodiesel. With respect to air pollution, alternative fuels may be cleaner burning as compared to gasoline and diesel resulting in reduced toxic emissions. Other proffered advantages of alternative fuels is the ability to produce these fuels domestically (thereby reducing US dependence on imported oil) from renewable materials such as wood, waste paper, grasses, vegetable oils, and corn (e.g., in the case of ethanol and biodiesel). In order to promote alternative fuels, the 1990 Amendments required EPA to establish a national renewable fuel program with the goal of increasing the production and consumption of "blended fuels" which mix renewable fuels with gasoline and diesel.

A relatively new approach to air pollution control implemented in the 1990 Clean Air Act Amendments involves regional planning and development "conformity" provisions. Under these provisions, federally funded transportation projects must be consistent with state air quality goals, not cause new air pollution problems, make existing air pollution problems worse, or delay attainment of air quality standards. From a broader planning perspective, regions with persistent air quality problems are required to develop long-term plans to manage urban growth and transportation to mitigate air pollution problems.[14]

Policy developments in the 2000s
In the short history of air pollution control regulation presented above, we saw that in the United States air pollution regulation started out in the 1970s following prescriptive approaches for the most part. In the 1980s, market-based incentive approaches for reducing pollution emissions were debated and initiated. Market-based incentive approaches for stationary-source pollution became more firmly established in the 1990s with the SO_2 emission allowance "cap-and-trade" market under the US EPA Acid Rain Program serving as the "poster child" and major success story. In the 2000s, the SO_2 market under the Acid Rain Program became a "mature" and well-functioning market with a relatively stable volume of transactions as shown in Figure 16.6.

Throughout much of the 2000s, the trend in America towards bigger vehicles being driven more miles per capita continued. In the late 2000s, the US EPA estimated that motor vehicles accounted for about one-half of each of the following pollutants in the United States: smog-forming volatile organic compounds (VOCs), NOx, and toxic air pollutants in the United States. Also, the US EPA estimated that by the late 2000s, motor vehicles, including non-road vehicles, accounted for about 75 percent of national carbon monoxide emissions. To meet the challenge of reducing and controlling these emissions, the US EPA has continued the prescriptive regulations contained in the 1990 Clean Air Act Amendments discussed above and expanded these regulations to cover the large number of minivans, SUVs, and other "light-duty trucks" that Americans gravitated towards in the 1990s and 2000s. As this book is being written in the late 2000s, the US has just gone through a period of rapidly increasing gasoline prices which now has many Americans looking towards purchasing smaller, more fuel-efficient vehicles including gasoline and electric-powered hybrid vehicles. There is currently much discussion among government officials, automobile manufacturers, and consumers about shifting towards 100 percent electricity-powered vehicles. By the time this book is published and read by some student out in the world, that student may be driving one of these electric vehicles.

With respect to environmental quality concerns, the big story in the 2000s is global climate change. The United Nations Intergovernmental Panel on Climate Change (IPCC) released its assessment on global climate change in 2007 which provided scientific evidence of a recent global warming trend. This report along with earlier climate change studies caused much concern among scientists, politicians and the general public about the need to "do something" about global warming. As discussed in Chapter 2, a contributing factor to global warming is the "greenhouse effect" wherein increased levels of CO_2 and other "greenhouse gases" in the atmosphere trap heat in the earth's environment for longer periods of time. Thus, a major focus of policy debate in the US and world in the 2000s was how best to reduce emissions of CO_2 and other "greenhouse gases."

Largely as a result of the Kyoto Treaty and Protocol which took effect in 2005, cap-and-trade carbon markets emerged in the 2000s as a major instrument for reducing global CO_2. Under the Kyoto Protocol, participating nations agreed to a national cap on CO_2 emissions which could in part be met by purchasing carbon credits from a willing seller. For example, farmers in Brazil may earn carbon credits by planting trees on their land. These farmers could then sell these credits to an electric power company in Japan who needs the credits to offset increased CO_2 emissions from a new power plant expansion project. The US is currently not a participant in the Kyoto protocol carbon markets. However, other carbon markets are developing in the US and other nations outside of the Kyoto protocol. For example, the Chicago Climate Exchange (CCX) was launched in the US in 2004 as a voluntary carbon credit market operating much in the same way as the Kyoto Protocol carbon market. By 2007, the CCX had gone global with members from Australia, Brazil, Canada, Chile, China, Costa Rica, India, New Zealand, and the US. Other regional carbon markets are emerging in the US as well. For example, as this book is being written, a mandatory regional cap-and-trade carbon market termed the Regional Greenhouse Gas Initiative is being established in the northeastern region of the US. At this point in time, mandatory and voluntary carbon markets are still in the experimental and developmental stages. Time will tell whether cap-and-trade carbon markets turn out to be another long-term success story akin to the US cap-and-trade SO_2 market.

Questions for discussion

1. How best can the economist counter the following arguments:
   a. "Emissions taxes provide a license to pollute."
   b. "Emissions taxes sell out the environment to polluters."
   c. "If emissions taxes were imposed, industrial polluters would not reduce their emissions but would merely pass on the taxes to the consumer."
2. Evaluate the contention that emissions taxes are undesirable because they would make the country's products less competitive in international trade.

3. Do you think individual states should be free to determine air pollution control policies without supervision by the national government? Why or why not?
4. If emissions taxes were imposed, what should be done with the revenues thus collected?
5. How do you explain the apparent reluctance of enforcement authorities to impose substantial penalties on large industrial firms found in violation of emissions standards?
6. Should the role of emissions trading be expanded still further? How might that be accomplished?

Notes

1. Lester B. Lave and Eugene P. Seskin (1977), *Air Pollution and Human Health*, Baltimore, MD: Johns Hopkins University Press.
2. John H. Dales (1968), *Pollution, Property and Prices*, Toronto: University of Toronto Press.
3. See Martin L. Weitzman (1974), "Prices vs. Quantities," *Review of Economic Studies* **41**: 477–91.
4. See Lawrence H. Goulder (1994), *Environmental Taxation and the "Double Dividend": A Reader's Guide*, Cambridge, MA: National Bureau of Economic Research; A. Lans Bovenberg (1999), "Green Tax Reform and the Double Dividend: An Updated Reader's Guide," *International Tax and Public Finance* **6**: 421–43.
5. The sobriquet "the environmental decade" was assigned in Council on Environmental Quality (1981), *Environmental Quality*, Washington, DC: US Government Printing Office.
6. The lack of strict consideration of benefits and costs when setting air quality standards continues to the present time. For example, in a 2001 ruling, the US Supreme Court sided with the US Environmental Protection Agency on the Agency's interpretation that the Clean Air Act does not require consideration of costs when setting national ambient air quality standards.
7. See William J. Baumol and Wallace Oates (1975), *The Theory of Environmental Policy*, Englewood Cliffs, NJ: Prentice-Hall, Chapter 11.
8. A. Myrick Freeman III (1982), *Air and Water Pollution Control: A Benefit–Cost Assessment*, New York: Wiley.
9. Source: US Environmental Protection Agency, "National Emissions Inventory (NEI) Air Pollutant Emissions Trends Data," http://www.epa.gov/ttnchie1/trends/.
10. For example, see Jane V. Hall, Arthur M. Winer, Michael T. Kelinman, Frederick W. Lurmann, Victor Brajer, and Steven D. Colome (1992), "Valuing the Benefits of Clean Air," *Science* **255** (5046): 812–17; Alan J. Krupnick and Paul R. Portney (1991), "Controlling Urban Air Pollution: A Benefit–Cost Assessment," *Science* **252** (5005): 522–8; Bart Ostro and Lauraine Chestnut (1998), "Assessing the Health Benefits of Reducing Particulate Matter Air Pollution in the United States," *Environmental Research* **76** (2): 94–106; V. Kerry Smith and Ju-Chin Huang (1995), Can Markets Value Air Quality? A Meta-Analysis of Hedonic Property Values Studies," *Journal of Political Economy* **103** (1): 209–27.
11. Council on Environmental Quality (1981), *Environmental Quality*, Washington, DC: US Government Printing Office.
12. Source: US Environmental Protection Agency, "National Emissions Inventory (NEI) Air Pollutant Emissions Trends Data," ttp://www.epa.gov/ttnchie1/trends/.
13. Bonnie G. Colby (2000), "Cap-and-Trade Policy Challenges: A Tale of Three Markets," *Land Economics* **76** (4): 638–58; Reimund Schwarze and Peter Zapfel (2000), "Sulfur Allowance Trading and the Regional Clean Air Incentives Market: A Comparative Design Analysis of Two Major Cap-and-Trade Permit Programs?," *Environmental and Resource Economics* **17**: 279–98.
14. Much of the discussion in this section of mobile air pollution control under the 1990 Clean Air Act Amendments is summarized from the US Environmental Protection Agency (2007), "The Plain English Guide to the Clean Air Act," Publication Number EPA-456/K-07-001, Washington, DC: US Environmental Protection Agency, Office of Air Quality Planning and Standards, April.

Suggested reading: classic and contemporary

Baumol, W.J. and W.E. Oates (1975), *The Theory of Environmental Policy*, Englewood Cliffs, NJ: Prentice-Hall.
Bohm, P. and C.S. Russell (1985), "Comparative Analysis of Alternative Policy Instruments," in *Handbook of Natural Resource and Energy Economics*, ed. A.V. Kneese and J.L. Sweeney, Amsterdam: North-Holland.
Christiansen, G.B. and T.H. Tietenberg (1985), "Distributional and Macroeconomic Aspects of Environmental Policy," in *Handbook of Natural Resource and Energy Economics*, ed. A.V. Kneese and J.L. Sweeney, Amsterdam: North-Holland.
Palmer, K., W.E. Oates, and P.R. Portney, (1995), "Tightening Environmental Standards: The Benefit–Cost or the No-Cost Paradigm?," *Journal of Economic Perspectives* **9** (4): 119–32.
White, L.J. (1982), *The Regulation of Air Pollution Emissions from Motor Vehicles*, Washington, DC: American Enterprise Institute.

17 The economics of land: how do land markets work and how do we manage land use?

Land is a major factor of production, an important consumption good, a popular vehicle for wealth-holding, and highly acceptable collateral for securing loans. As would be expected, markets in land are highly developed, sophisticated, and well integrated into financial markets.

Land uses influence neighborhood characteristics, air and water quality, and the diversity and integrity of ecosystems. Thus, land uses determine the levels of a wide variety of non-exclusive and collectively consumed amenities. As might be expected, there is considerable support for various policies to influence land use in the interest of broad segments of the public by manipulating incentives and constraints facing landowners. Policies regulating and taxing various land uses are complex and politically sensitive.

Land rents

The simplest model to explain the value of land as a capital asset (see Chapter 7) focuses on the present value of the stream of future earnings (rents) from land. The market price of land P_t^h in year t is determined as follows:

$$P_t^h = \sum_{\tau=t+1}^{\infty} \frac{p_\tau^h}{(1+r)^\tau} \tag{17.1}$$

where p_τ^h is the land rent for the τth period. Though it is true that more complex models include additional factors, the stream of land rents remains a major determinant of land asset prices. So let us commence by attempting to explain land rents.

Farmland rents I: fertility and rent

Early in the nineteenth century, David Ricardo attempted to explain land rents and land-use patterns as resulting from differences in the fertility of land. Here we consider a modern economic analysis in the Ricardian tradition.

Assume a regional society with land available in effectively unlimited quantities. However, there is a range of land qualities, with land of the highest qualities being scarce. Express land quality in a single dimension F, $0 < F < \infty$, where larger values for F indicate higher soil fertility. Consider the crop, z_i, with the production function:

$$Z_i = a_i f(L, h, F) \tag{17.2}$$

where L is labor, h is land, and a_i is a proportionality factor for crop z_i. Output per acre, $\mathbf{Z}_i = z_i/h$, is thus:

$$\mathbf{Z}_i = a_i f(\mathbf{L}, F) \tag{17.3}$$

where $\mathbf{L} = L/h$ and the marginal productivities of $\mathbf{L}$ and F are positive and diminishing.

Where p_{z_i} is the unit price of output and w the price of labor, per-acre profits, Π, can be expressed as:

$$\Pi = p_{z_i} a_i f(\mathbf{L}, F) - w\mathbf{L} - p^h(F).$$

At equilibrium, profits (Π) are driven to zero, but land rents per acre, $p^h(F)$, may be positive. For any given levels of p_{z_i}, w, and production technology, there will be some minimal level of fertility, F_{min}, at which $p_{z_i} a_i f(\mathbf{L}, F_{min}) = w\mathbf{L}$ and $p^h(F_{min}) = 0$. Land of fertility F_{min} earns no rent, and all land of lesser fertility is abandoned. Land with $F > F_{min}$ earns positive rents that increase with F.

If, for example, p_{z_i} were to increase, *ceteris paribus*, a new $F'_{min} < F_{min}$ would emerge. The product price increase would allow the cultivation of some previously submarginal land, and for land with $F > F'_{min}$, $p^{h'}(F) > p^h(F)$; that is, rents would increase. Thus, Ricardian analysis provides a theory of land rent, but, it is less successful in generating a theory of land use.

First, in the most general analysis, it is unclear whether or not the most fertile land would attract larger $\mathbf{L}$, labor per acre. One may have expected $\mathbf{L}$ to increase with F, but that is not a general result. Second, consider alternative crops z_i and z_j, with $a_i \neq a_j$. How is land allocated to these crops? If the economy is open to trade, with product prices determined in a world market, the region will be a monoculture. Every cultivated acre will be devoted to the same crop, which is the most profitable crop for any $F \geq F_{min}$. If the economy is closed to trade, product prices will adjust until $p_{z_i}/p_{z_j} = a_j/a_i$ and farmers everywhere are indifferent as to which crop is grown on which land as long as $F \geq F_{min}$. A simple Ricardian theory cannot explain which enterprises are located where.[1]

Farmland rents II: location and rents
Contemporaneously with Ricardo (but, as far as we know, without any mutual contact) J.H. von Thunen was developing a theory of land rents based on the organizing principle of distance from some crucial location. Thunen imagined a large city in the midst of a featureless, fertile plain of uniform soil quality. Far from the city and in every direction, an impenetrable wilderness separates this isolated region from the rest of the world. Thunen's question was: How will the distance from the city influence the location of different farming enterprises, the intensity of the land use, and the rents that accrue to the land?

Farms occupy space, and so no two farms can be on the same land. Thus, along any ray emanating from the city, one farm must be at a greater distance from the city as compared to another farm. If some essential activity (for example, marketing) takes place in the city and the distance imposes a cost, well-defined patterns of land use and rents can be predicted. What follows is a modern analysis in the Thunen tradition.

Neither distance (D) nor soil fertility (which is assumed to be homogeneous) influences production. Thus for a single crop, z_i:

$$Z_i = a_i f(\mathbf{L}) \qquad (17.4)$$

However, distance directly influences profits:

$$\Pi_i = (p_{z_i} - s_{z_i}D)a_i f(\mathbf{L}) - w\mathbf{L} - p^h(D) \tag{17.5}$$

where s is the ton-mile transportation cost. At the zero profit equilibrium, land rent is equal to revenue net of transportation costs minus labor cost:

$$p^h(D) = (p_{z_i} - s_{z_i}D)a_i f(\mathbf{L}) - w\mathbf{L} \tag{17.6}$$

Optimizing labor use per acre,[2] it is found that labor use diminishes with distance, reaching zero at:

$$D_{\max} = \frac{p_{zi}}{s_{z_i}} \tag{17.7}$$

Land at $D_{\max}$ and beyond is (obviously) abandoned. The output per acre also declines with distance and reaches zero at $D_{\max}$. Furthermore, land rent is zero when $\mathbf{L} = z_i = 0$ at $D_{\max}$. Land rent is positive and diminishes as D increases for $D < D_{\max}$. If the product price were to increase, *ceteris paribus*, a new $D'_{\max} > D_{\max}$ would be determined; some previously submarginal land would be brought into production. Output, labor intensity, and land rents would increase at locations nearer to the city than $D'_{\max}$.

Now we introduce alternative crops. For simplicity, consider two crops, z_1 and z_2. Optimizing labor use per acre, we obtain:

$$(p_{z_1} - s_{z_1}D)a_1 \frac{\partial f(\mathbf{L}_1)}{\partial \mathbf{L}} = w = (p_{z_2} - s_{z_2}D)a_2 \frac{\partial f(\mathbf{L}_2)}{\mathbf{L}} \tag{17.8}$$

where $\partial f(\mathbf{L}_i)/\partial \mathbf{L}$ is the marginal physical product of labor devoted to z_i. Given the closed economy of the isolated region, output prices will adjust so as to ensure that both crops are produced. What can we say about the location of production?

Assume that output is measured in weight units, $s_{z_1} = s_{z_2}$ and $a_1 > a_2$. Thus, for a given $\mathbf{L}$, more weight of z_i is produced per acre, and its transportation cost per acre is thus higher. When D approaches zero, $(p_{z_1} - s_{z_1}D)a_1 > (p_{z_2} - s_{z_2}D)a_2$ and z_1 is produced. As D increases, $s_{z_1}Da_1$ increases faster than does $s_{z_2}Da_2$, and thus the per-acre revenue net of transportation costs falls faster for crop z_1. Eventually, D becomes so large that $(p_{z_1} - s_{z_1}D)a_1 < (p_{z_2} - s_{z_2}D)a_2$ and z_2 is produced.

The alternative enterprises are located according to distance, with a sharp boundary at some distance D_1 where:

$$(p_{z_1} - s_{z_1}D_1)a_1 = (p_{z_2} - s_{z_2}D_1)a_2 \tag{17.9}$$

The commodity with the greater transportation cost per acre is produced monoculturally in a distance zone defined by $0 < D \le D_1$, and there is a monoculture of the less weighty commodity in the zone $D_1 \le D \le D_{\max}$.

This result is illustrated in Figure 17.1, where the net rent per acre, $p_1^h(D)$, is a function of the distance from the city. Where $a_1 > a_2$, the rent function $p_1^h(D)$ is steeper than $p_2^h(D)$. At any distance, the enterprise with the highest net rent is chosen. Thus, z_1 is produced in the zone $0 \le D \le D_1$, and z_2 is produced in the zone $D_1 \le D \le D_{\max}$. Within each zone, rents decline smoothly with distance.

Rents are equal at the zone boundary, where the rent curves intersect. Thus with

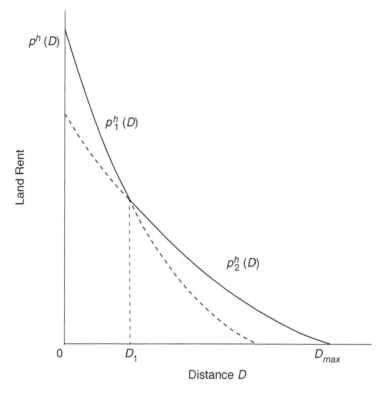

Figure 17.1   Rent functions and optimal locations for Crops 1 and 2

multiple enterprises, the land rent curve is continuous but kinked at the zone boundaries. On the other hand, the labor use per acre declines smoothly with increasing distance, within and across zone boundaries. Note that these results are depicted (Figure 17.1) in linear space. If we had used two-dimensional space, the linear distance zones would appear as a series of rings concentric at the market city.

It is interesting to note that the Thunen approach produces more interesting results than does the Ricardian approach. Both approaches create a theory of differential land rents, with lower rents for less attractive land (less fertile, for Ricardo; and farther from the central market, for Thunen). Rents are zero for the least attractive land in use, and all even less attractive land (e.g. land with negative rents) is abandoned.

Beyond this, more definitive analytical results emanate from the Thunen model (in which D imposes a cost and thus enters the profit function) than from the Ricardian model (in which F enters the production function). The Thunen models offer a theory of labor intensity and the location of alternative production enterprises, but Ricardian models do not.

Urban land rents: Thunen goes to town
Thunen's organizing principle of distance-imposed costs can be transferred readily to the urban scene. For the simplest case, consider a city with a single central business district

(CBD) where each household "sells" labor. Each consumer-worker chooses a residential location by maximizing a utility function.

$$U(D) = U[h(D), z(D)] \qquad (17.10)$$

in which the level of satisfaction increases with the amounts of residential land (h) and other goods (z) consumed. The budget constraint is:

$$y - p^h(D)h(D) - p_z z(D) - s(D) = 0 \qquad (17.11)$$

where y is income, and s, the cost of commuting, increases with D. Note that land rents are a cost to the consumer-worker but represent income to the landlord. With a given income and costly commuting, $y - s(D)$ diminishes as D increases.

Consider two alternative locations, $D_2 > D_1$. With $y, p_z, s(D_1)$, and $s(D_2)$ held constant, what land rents would make the consumer-worker indifferent between living at D_1 or D_2? Taking the indifference curve ($U = U^0$), $y - s(D_1)/p_z$, and $y - s(D_2)/p_z$ as given, we identify the tangency points A and B (Figure 17.2). The consumer-worker is indifferent between the consumption bundles $[h(D_1), z(D_1)]$ and $[h(D_2), z(D_2)]$, where $h(D_2) > h(D_1)$ and $z(D_2) < z(D_1)$. Land rents $p^h(D_1)$ and $p^h(D_2)$ would make him or her indifferent between locating at either D_1 or D_2. By inspection, we see that $p^h(D_1)/p_z > p^h(D_2)/p_z$ and thus $p^h(D_1) > p^h(D_2)$.

To summarize, the consumer-worker is willing to pay a higher rent per unit for land nearer the CBD and is indifferent between either a smaller residential lot close to the CBD or a larger lot farther out. The individual bid-rent function defined as the set of prices for land at various distances that would keep the individual indifferent between alternative places of residence, is of negative slope (Figure 17.3). Imagine that all consumers were identical in income and preferences and that moving one's residence was costless. Each landlord (a local monopolist owning a parcel of land located uniquely at some specific distance D_j) tries to anticipate correctly the bid-rent function and charge exactly the indifference rent for location D_j. A landlord charging more would have vacancies, whereas one charging less would be besieged with would-be occupants.

With identical consumers and costless residential mobility, this bidding process will reach a static equilibrium in which the individual bid-rent function (Figure 17.3) becomes the rent gradient for the whole city. All consumer-workers will be indifferent as to where they live in the city, and each will achieve the same utility level.

For a little more realism, imagine that there are K classes of consumers, with individuals identical within classes but different across them. Then the rent gradient would be the envelope of the different bid-rent functions. Consumers in class i would bid more for land in a particular zone, Z_i, but would be outbid by others elsewhere. A pattern would emerge of distinct but internally homogeneous neighborhoods arrayed according to distance from the CBD. The residential city is bounded at D_A, where the agricultural rent function, p_A^h, intersects the bid-rent function of the kth (that is, the last) class of city dwellers (Figure 17.4).

Is there any basis for predicting what kinds of people would live in the various urban distance zones? Assume that their preferences are identical but that the classes have different incomes and that residential land is a non-inferior good. Then at any zone boundary, the inner commuter will have a lower income than will the outer commuter.

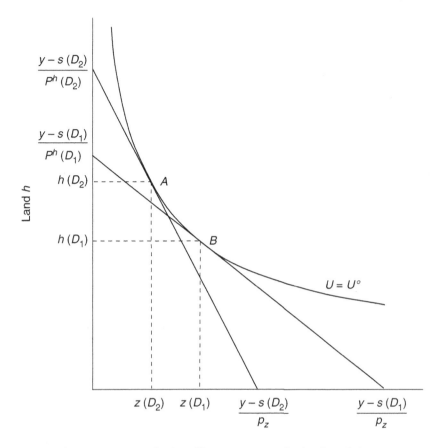

Figure 17.2   The consumer-worker's willingness to pay for land, and the consumption bundle of land and goods at distances D$_1$ and D$_2$

Generalizing this result, the neighborhood zones will be arrayed with income and lot size increasing with distance. Lower-income households will live on small lots near the CBD and upper-income households on larger suburban lots.

This simple model in the Thunen tradition yields some strong results regarding rent and land use. Land rents decline and lot sizes increase until there is a sharp boundary between urban and agricultural land uses. If incomes vary but preferences do not, occupant incomes will increase with distance and lot size.

More detailed models of urban land use and rents can, of course, be constructed. But the gain in descriptive reality is often accompanied by an offsetting loss of generality. If we allow preferences to vary among classes of consumer-workers, the neat pattern we just predicted could become unraveled.

More interesting, consider what happens if commuting takes time as well as money. If higher-income people also have a higher opportunity cost of time (for example, because their wage rate is higher), their total commuting costs at any distance will exceed those for the lower-income workers. The income pattern of distance-zone occupancy becomes, in general, unclear. For some, commuting costs may dominate the tendency to increase

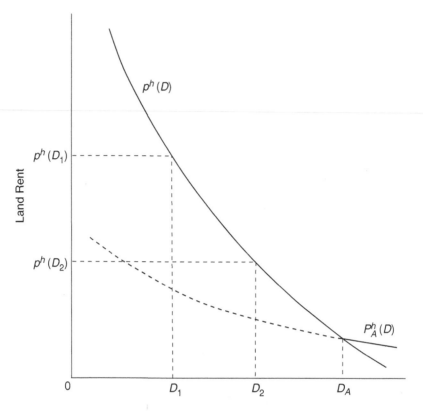

Figure 17.3   The bid-rent functions for urban workers and agricultural uses

land consumption. These people would congregate not in a district of large estates on the city's edge but in a district of fine townhouses near the CBD.

Other considerations may be introduced such as multiple places of employment (the CBD, the docks, a manufacturing district, suburban shopping centers), topographical features (harbors, rivers, hills), differences in the age and quality of housing (in addition to differences in lot size), differences in neighborhood amenities (schools, parks, cultural facilities, crime protection), which are helpful in specifying empirical models for particular applications but, again, produce few unexpected general results.

Land prices, economic conditions, and capital gains
The models of land use and land rents we introduced focus on differential rents: how and why different parcels of land earn different rents. Plugging rents back into the asset-pricing model, we can explain why different parcels of land sell for different prices.

In this section, we examine the relationships among land prices, land rents, financial markets, and macroeconomic conditions. Here we are concerned with how land prices react to changes in interest and inflation rates, changes in real rents, and impending changes in land use. The role of expectations becomes paramount: in the asset-pricing model, the known rents of the fleeting present are small compared with the stream of future rents that can only be anticipated.

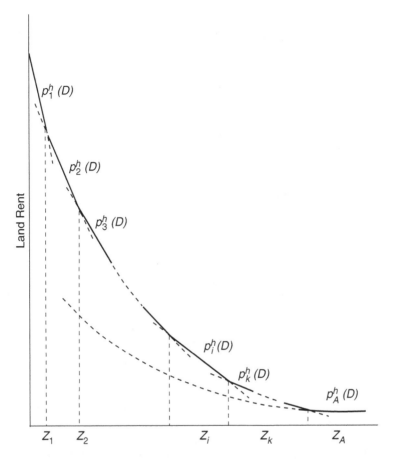

Figure 17.4   The rent gradient and distance zones (Z_i) for a city with K classes of consumer-workers surrounded by farmland

Rational markets and normal returns to landownership
The total return to the landowner includes a stream of rents during the term of owner-ship and a capital gain (or loss) at the time of resale. Where the values of all parameters dated $t = 1, \ldots, \infty$ are expected (as opposed to known for sure), a risk-neutral buyer expecting to hold a parcel of land for T years would be willing to pay:

$$p_0^h = \sum_{t=1}^{T} \frac{p_t^h}{(1 + r)^{t}} \ldots + \ldots \frac{P_T^h}{(1 + r)^T} \tag{17.12}$$

to buy it. A wealth-maximizing seller having the same expectations as the buyer would accept no less than P_0^h. Thus the net present value of the opportunity to purchase land would tend toward zero:

$$NPV = 0 = \sum_{t=1}^{T} \frac{p_t^h}{(1 + r)^{t}} \ldots + \ldots \frac{P_T^h}{(1 + r)^{t}} - P_0^h \tag{17.13}$$

In other words, the expected internal rate of return from landownership would tend toward r, the market rate of interest. A land purchase would be anticipated to yield a normal return.

The "rational markets hypothesis" posits that current asset prices reflect all current market information. This hypothesis suggests strongly that it is not possible to use market information to enjoy above-normal returns from ownership of land (or other assets). Planned above-normal returns are available only to the clairvoyant. Others can only gamble for above-normal returns, betting that their own expectations are more accurate than those that motivate the market.

Some time later, expectations regarding future rents or interest rates could change (in a way unanticipated at $t = 0$). Land prices would adjust so as to restore an anticipated normal return from ownership, given the new expectations. This adjustment would generate one-shot windfall gains (or losses) for those who already owned land. Favorable changes could, therefore, mean above-normal returns for those established landowners. Prospective entrants could not participate, however, because land prices would (almost instantly) reflect the new expectations.

In summary, our approach to the analysis of land prices is founded on the proposition that although *ex post* above (or below) normal returns to landownership are entirely possible, *ex ante* returns are normal.

Asset market adjustments to real price and interest rate changes
We interpret $p^h(t)$ as the anticipated time stream of future rents; that is, residuals from total revenue after other costs have been paid. Changes in anticipated technology and real prices for products and factors change $p^h(t)$. Real interest rates are also subject to change: although it is mathematically convenient to fix r throughout the term of the analysis, reality is better described by a time stream of anticipated rates, $r(t)$.

As is clear from an inspection of the asset-pricing formula, a change to more optimistic expectations (for example, regarding higher product prices or lower interest rates) would increase asset prices, whereas a change toward pessimism would have the opposite effect. The experience of the United States in the 1980s, when farmland prices fell dramatically after policy redirections that led to higher real interest rates and reduced the demand for US farm-product exports, confirms the predictions of the asset-pricing model.

Inflation
Assume that the general price level is expected to increase at the rate $a > 0$ and that the prices paid and received by farmers are expected to inflate at the same rate. How will this anticipated inflation affect farmland prices?

To answer this question, it is convenient to switch from the familiar discrete-time analysis to a continuous-time analysis. Whereas the price of land at $t = 0$ is expressed in discrete time as:

$$P_0^h = \sum_{t=1}^{\infty} \frac{p_t^h}{(1 + r)^t} \tag{17.14}$$

the analogous expression in continuous time is:

$$P_0^h = \int_0^{\infty} e^{-rt}[p^h(t)]dt \tag{17.15}$$

Note $r \neq r$; r is the interest rate that, with continuous compounding, is equivalent to r. An advantage of the continuous-time formulation is that it yields a simple capitalization formula for the price of the land asset when $p^h(t) = p_0^h$

$$P_0^h = \int_0^\infty e^{-rt}[p^h(t)]dt = \frac{p_0^h}{r} \tag{17.16}$$

for any value of t.

Now define NP_0^h as the nominal price of land at $t = 0$. If real rents are expected to be unchanged with time, $p_0^h = p_t^h$ for any value of t, nominal land rents will grow with inflation so that $np_t^h = p_0^h e^{at}$. Under these conditions:

$$NP_0^h = \int_0^\infty e^{-[r+a-a]t} p_0^h dt = P_0^h \tag{17.17}$$

The effects of anticipated inflation on interest rates and the growth in nominal rents are mutually canceling. Anticipated future inflation does not change the price of land at the outset. But with the passage of time, $NP^h(t)$ and $P^h(t)$ diverge: $NP_t^h = P_0^h e^{at}$, and $P_t^h = P_0^h$. Nominal land rents inflate at the rate of inflation. Thus, landownership is a perfect hedge against fully anticipated inflation.

Anticipated capital gains
Can a landowner plan to enjoy anticipated (as opposed to windfall) capital gains from holding land assets? The short answer is "yes," but he or she must pay for them at the outset. Assume that real rents are expected to grow at the rate g, that is, $p_t^h = P_0^h e^{gt}$. The price of farmland will also grow over time at the rate g:

$$P_t^h = \int_0^\infty e^{-rt} p_0^h e^{gt} dt = P_0^h e^{gt} \tag{17.18}$$

Thus, holding land will result in anticipated capital gains, though anticipated above-normal returns are not involved. Land prices at the outset will adjust to reflect the expectation of growing rents and capital gains:

$$P_0^h = \int_0^\infty e^{-rt}(p_0^h e^{gt})dt = \frac{P_0^h}{r-g} \tag{17.19}$$

The larger is g, the higher the price of land will be at the outset. The buyer pays at the outset (via a higher purchase price) for the anticipated capital gains.

Land-use changes
For any plot of land there will be several possible uses, each offering some given rent. Thunen theories predict that land will be assigned to the highest market value of these uses and that the rents available from lower-rent uses will not influence land use or rents received.

Imagine a plot of farmland generating a current rent p_{a0}^h which is expected to grow at the rate g_a. The current rent for the same land in urban use is $p_{u0}^h < p_{a0}^h$, but urban rents are expected to grow at the rate $g_u > g_a$. It is predictable that at some time t^*, this plot will be converted from agricultural to urban uses (Figure 17.5). The time path of rents is

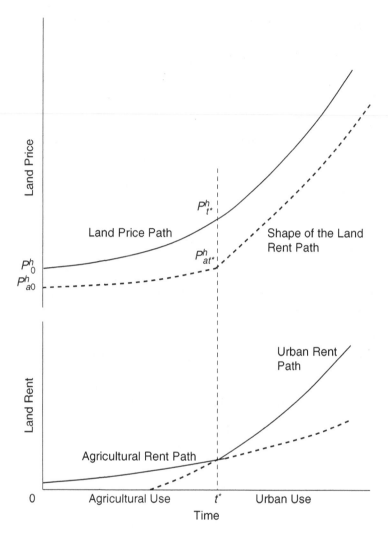

Figure 17.5   Changes in land use: the behavior of land rents and prices when land use changes

kinked at t^*, with rents growing at the rate g_a before t^* and g_u thereafter. At t^* agricultural and urban rents are equal: $p_{at}^h{}^* = p_{ut}^h{}^*$.

With this pattern of expected rent growth and land-use change, what can we predict about the time path of land prices? After t^*, we know that land prices will grow at the rate g_u. But what will happen before t^*? If there had been no urban prospects, the price of land at t^* would have been $P_{at}^h{}^* = p_{at}^h{}^*/r - g_a$. However, with the switch to urban uses, $P_t^{h*} = p_{ut}^h{}^*/r - g_u$. Given that $p_{at}^h{}^* = p_{ut}^h{}^*$ and $g_u > g_a$, it is obvious that $P_t^{h*} > P_{at}^h{}^*$. By t^* the price of the land has achieved a level well above its agricultural value, but correctly anticipating its value in urban uses.

The eventual conversion to urban use affects land prices at the outset. With only agricultural prospects, p_{a0}^h is the present value of a rent stream growing at rate g_a. But with conversion at t^*, P_0^h is the present value of a rent stream growing at g_a until t^*, and the higher rate g_u thereafter. The future land-use conversion prospect is reflected in farmland prices from the outset. Again, a buyer of land in anticipation of conversion would be faced with a price that would allow only a normal return on the investment. The time path of land prices is not shaped like the kinked time path of rents (Figure 17.5). Instead, it rises smoothly from an initial growth rate slightly higher than g_a to the growth rate g_u at t^* and thereafter.

Institutional rigidities

As is well known, institutional rigidities may impede the smooth adjustment of markets, including markets in land assets. Of special interest here are rigidities in capital markets and institutions concerning land-use conversion.

Capital markets   Any public policies or programs which intervene into capital markets and hinder the normal market adjustment of interest rates and the flow of capital available to real-estate developers and consumers may result in artificial changes in land and real-estate prices. For example, in the United States, a variety of institutions resulted in the availability of relatively "easy credit" extended to real-estate developers and homeowners throughout the 1990s and early 2000s which resulted in an unprecedented and unsustainable run-up in land prices, especially residential land. This land price "bubble" eventually popped in the mid-2000s, triggering a major recession in the world economy as the creative but opaque securitized mortgage instruments that started showing up on the balance sheets of banks and financial institutions around the world lost value suddenly.

Land use conversion restrictions   Institutional devices such as zoning and green-belt regulations are expressions of public interest in the non-exclusive services and disservices that are produced jointly with various land uses. Without passing any judgment on the general merits of such institutions, it should be observed that they do impede (or subsidize) and redirect land use conversion. With such institutions in place, land markets will be motivated by the current information concerning them. Land prices will tend to adjust to levels that yield anticipated normal returns given market expectations (including expectations regarding institutional behavior).

But these institutions also increase the possibility that some individuals may be able to obtain information before it is generally known in the market. Also, some individuals may have more power or influence as compared to others, say, to obtain a favorable zoning change after purchase. Therefore, these institutions increase the opportunities of above-normal profits for persons with special access to information and/or special influence on institutional decisions.

Land-use policy tools

Institutional devices to influence and direct land use are provided by private law, the law of eminent domain, the police power, and the power to tax, used separately and in various combinations.

Private law

Private law provides for the establishment and security of property rights and thus facilitates the resolution of land-use conflicts through the market. Private law provides devices whereby individuals operating independently, and groups operating collectively, may pursue their goals with respect to land use.

Deed restrictions   Deed restrictions offer a private-law device for the control of non-exclusive disamenities through the elimination of incompatible land uses. A developer acquires a relatively large tract of land with the intention of subdividing it into suburban, or sometimes rural, residential units. In order to increase the attractiveness of these units to prospective purchasers, the developer establishes a series of deed restrictions. These restrictions limit the choices a purchaser may make with respect to the use of the land. However, the purchaser cheerfully accepts these limitations, assured that neighboring tracts of land will not be used in ways incompatible with his or her own intended land use. Prospective purchasers shop around among various subdivisions, attempting to find a subdivision offering the preferred set of deed restrictions, subject to the purchaser's budget constraint. Developers carefully evaluate the market potential of their land prior to subdivision and seek to establish the set of deed restrictions that will maximize their profits from the development.

In residential subdivisions, deed restrictions typically limit or eliminate industrial, commercial, and agricultural land uses. Deed restrictions may establish minimum lot size, minimum setback from roads and streams, and minimum size of the houses eventually built and the construction materials used. Some deed restrictions are remarkably detailed – for example, requiring particular modes of landscaping, prohibiting outdoor clotheslines, banning mobile homes or temporary structures during the construction period, banning disabled automobiles, and/or limiting the number of automobiles and recreational vehicles that may be parked on each lot outside an enclosed garage. People who live in "mini-farm" subdivisions may be subject to minimum lot size restrictions, minimum setback from the road, minimum house size, restrictions on construction materials, and restrictions that eliminate industrial and commercial land uses while limiting agricultural land uses to "no hogs, no chickens, and a maximum of one head of livestock per acre." In times past, deed restrictions banning certain racial and ethnic groups from particular subdivisions were routine, but these kinds of deed restrictions are no longer permissible or enforceable.

Deed restrictions are an effective mechanism for the elimination of incompatible land uses within subdivisions. They have the advantage that they are non-coercive, in that the developer may, within broad limits, select the kind of deed restrictions to impose, and the buyer may choose among alternative subdivisions with different sets of deed restrictions. However, deed restrictions are generally ineffective in controlling disamenities that cross subdivision boundaries. Because individual subdivisions tend to be small relative to whole communities or metropolitan areas, deed restrictions may effectively control incompatible uses within subdivision boundaries but are usually ineffective as tools for implementing broader land-use policy on a community, metropolitan, or regional basis.

Easements and fee simple title purchase   When a public or governmental institution has a strong desire to maintain a particular land use on a particular tract of land, it may seek to purchase an easement or to purchase the land in fee-simple title. It may seek to purchase riparian lands, low-lying and flood-prone lands, and lands that provide high-class natural environments or habitats, with the specific intention of foreclosing industrial, commercial, or residential development. Alternatively, a public institution or governmental unit may seek to purchase an easement from the landowner, which would permit him or her to continue current and similar land uses, while foreclosing the right to convert the land to more intensive industrial, commercial, or residential uses. On the outskirts of certain large metropolitan areas, governmental units have purchased scenic easements that foreclose the landowner's option for intensive development, while permitting and encouraging the continued use of the land in working farms or, perhaps, aesthetically pleasing "green" uses such as golf courses.

The purchase of easements or of land in fee-simple title is an effective way in which the public may assert and secure a right to preserve land for aesthetically pleasing uses or to foreclose developments thought to be undesirable. The main factor discouraging more widespread use of this tool is its expense. Public institutions and governmental units, with their limited budgets, are likely to avoid the purchase of easements or land in fee-simple title if they can achieve their land-use objectives with equal or similar effectiveness by using the police power or the power to tax. In instances in which the governmental unit is willing to pay the fair market price for easements or for title to land, the owner, sensing their strategic position, may hold out, demanding a price that exceeds the fair market value of the land. In this instance, the governmental unit (subject to restrictions discussed in Chapter 11) may invoke its power of eminent domain and thus purchase the land at fair market value.

In recent years, "purchase of conservation easements" or PACE programs have become a very popular means for state and local governments and private land trusts (often working together) to preserve agricultural land and environmentally sensitive land (e.g., land that provides important environmental and ecosystem goods and services). The federal government also supports PACE programs for agricultural lands through the federal Farm and Ranch Lands Protection Program which provides matching funds to state and local governments for purchasing conservation easements to keep productive farm and ranchlands in agricultural uses. This program is administered by the US Department of Agriculture (USDA) Natural Resources Conservation Service. According to the Land Trust Alliance, total acres conserved in the US by local and state land trusts using conservation easements was about 6.2 million acres in 2005, up from just about 2.5 million acres in 2000.

The police power
State governments may use police power directly or, by delegation, may permit local governments to use police power in order to regulate the use of land to protect the public health, welfare, safety, and morals. The police power has permitted land-use zoning, subdivision controls, building codes, and a variety of specialized restrictions, such as those that eliminate taverns in the immediate vicinity of churches and that confine sexually oriented businesses to designated locations. In addition, police power permits the regulation of public utilities and thus provides a legal basis for the use of public utility regulation to eliminate some of the public finance problems that encourage urban sprawl.

Land use zoning　Land-use zoning has been used with varying degrees of effectiveness, in one governmental unit or another, to attack each of the perceived land-use problems discussed above: nuisance spillovers and incompatible uses; urban sprawl; the perceived need to preserve historic districts and green space; and the perceived need to maintain the biological productivity of land. In the United States, zoning is most commonly implemented by local government units. The zoning powers enjoyed by local governments units vary, however, from state to state. In many states, different local government units have responded differently to the delegation of zoning authority: some use all of the authority delegated, whereas others steadfastly refuse to use all of the powers at their disposal.

Zoning may seek to eliminate incompatible uses by designating particular zones for particular types of uses. A typical zoning scheme establishes agriculture as the highest and best land use, with single-family residences as the next highest use, and, in any particular zone, permits higher but not lower uses. Thus, residences are permitted in industrial zones, but not vice versa.

A comprehensive program of land-use zoning is most effective when based on a comprehensive land-use plan. In this way, the pattern of land use can be made compatible with transportation facilities, utilities, drainage and flood protection, and the provision of schools and similar public sector services.

Zoning is usually carried out by elected local government bodies or by zoning boards or commissions whose members are appointed by elected government bodies. Zoning authorities are empowered to zone land at the outset, to grant specific variances and exceptions from an existing zoning arrangement, and to rezone land in order to permit more intensive uses of land that had been previously reserved for less intensive uses.

Initial zoning, by permitting intensive uses on some land but not on other land, confers the potential for large capital gains on some landowners but not others. Individual applicants may have much to gain financially from granting a variance or exception to an existing zoning provision. When land is rezoned to permit more intensive use, in order to accommodate future growth in the community, some favored individuals will enjoy "windfall gains," but others will not. These circumstances place immense burdens on members of zoning boards and commissions. They are subjected to intense pressures from competing private interests and public interest groups. Because of the large profit potentials at stake, it is not unknown for zoning board members to be tempted with bribes or other inducements that are illegal or of dubious morality. This is only to be expected, as zoning boards are empowered to redefine the rights that pertain to property and to create, maintain, and on occasion modify an artificial scarcity of land that is available for various purposes. Thus, zoning regulations raise the windfalls and wipeouts and takings issues (discussed in Chapter 11).

Let us now consider the effectiveness of zoning in achieving its various goals. In general, of course, the effectiveness of zoning regulations depends on the quality of the planning efforts on which they are based, on the willingness of zoning boards to make difficult decisions for the long-term benefit of the community at large, and on the integrity of zoning board or commission members. Beyond that, there are some more specific things that can be said. Zoning can be relatively effective in controlling or eliminating incompatible uses. It can be effective in directing development away from flood plains, steep and unstable slopes, and natural or built environments deemed worthy of preservation. Over time, as cities grow, zoning may be less effective in protecting residential landowners from the disamenities associated with more intensive development. It may be impossible to resist pressures to permit multi-family dwellings in areas previously reserved for single-family residences, or to permit commercial developments along residential streets that have become major traffic arteries.

Zoning has been even less effective in preserving agricultural land and limiting urban sprawl. There is powerful pressure to rezone agricultural land for residential uses as a metropolitan area grows. Ironically, agricultural zoning, which often requires that 5 or perhaps 10 acres must be owned before construction of one single-family dwelling is permitted, seems to have accelerated the subdivision of large and productive farms into "baby farms." A fairly accurate general statement is that although zoning may be effective in directing urban growth, it is typically ineffective in limiting or restraining such growth.

Subdivision controls   To control urban sprawl and to limit the inequities resulting from average-cost pricing of services provided by local governments and public utilities, many jurisdictions have initiated subdivision controls. A proposed subdivision must be approved by the cognizant authority. Evidence must be presented that the subdivision is "needed" and therefore does not represent a wasteful use of land. However, these provisions are quite easily satisfied, because the mere fact that a developer seeks to undertake subdivision is evidence that a demand for the proposed housing exists.

A more significant influence of subdivision controls is derived from provisions requiring that the developer bear the initial capital costs of providing at least some services to the subdivision. Typically, the developer may be required to provide roads within the subdivision and (perhaps) roads linking the subdivision to major traffic arteries, drainage for the subdivision, a domestic water system, and a system for the collection and treatment of sewage. In principle, these kinds of provisions are conducive to both economic efficiency and equity in land use, as the price of homes in new subdivisions reflects, at least in part, the costs of providing services and utilities to fringe areas of the metropolitan area.

In application, subdivision controls have exhibited two weaknesses. Firstly, they seldom specify that developers must bear the initial capital costs of all relevant services and utilities. Although many jurisdictions require developers to build internal roads, fewer require them to build roads from the subdivision to major traffic arteries, and few may require them to bear the costs of widening and upgrading major traffic arteries if that should prove necessary. Although many subdivision controls require the provision of water and sewer services, very few require the provision of electric transmission lines, natural gas pipelines, or schools. Under average-cost pricing, residents of established neighborhoods bear a substantial portion of the costs of extending these services to new subdivisions. Subdivision controls have perhaps been more successful in requiring that developers set aside open space and parkland but less successful in requiring that the parkland be adequately landscaped and developed for recreational purposes. Secondly, quality control with respect to the facilities provided by developers has often been inadequate. After a specified period of time, or after a specified portion of the lots in the subdivision have been sold, the service and utility facilities provided by developers typically are sold to a corporation (which may be a cooperative of subdivision residents) or revert to the local government jurisdiction. Under these conditions, it is rational for developers to plan and construct these facilities with only a short time horizon in mind. Thus, one observes subdivision roads that soon deteriorate and sewage treatment plants that soon become significant sources of pollution. Eventually, the public sector may often be obligated to correct the situation at considerable expense. In this way, the effectiveness of subdivision controls is often reduced, and their purposes are subverted.

Building codes   Building codes are, for the most part, regulations aimed at protecting health and safety. As such, they protect the consumers, who may often lack the expertise to protect themselves. On the other hand, these codes may increase construction costs and retard innovations in construction techniques.

Building codes may exert some relatively minor influence on land use, by eliminating some structures that would be aesthetically inferior or would deteriorate rapidly and by requirements such as those that specify a minimum distance of buildings from property boundaries and utility lines.

Public utility regulation   Public utilities, which typically enjoy a monopoly within their service areas, are regulated with respect to the services they provide and their charges for those services. Utility regulation commissions could, if they chose, eliminate some of the public finance problems that encourage urban sprawl, by restructuring rate schedules to impose the costs of providing services to new developments on residences and businesses in those developments. However, and perhaps unfortunately, the various state regulatory commissions have been mostly unwilling to take this route.

Taxation

State and local jurisdictions typically tax property in order to raise revenues. But as we have already seen, the power to tax is the power to modify prices and thus to modify economic incentives. It is frequently suggested, therefore, that property taxation strategy should be a tool to implement land-use policy.

Property taxation strategies are most commonly implemented at the urban–rural fringe, with the intention of restricting urban sprawl and delaying the premature conversion of land from agricultural uses. A common strategy is "use-value taxation," wherein property is taxed on the basis of its value in its current use, rather than on its market value which may reflect the value of the land in an alternative and more intensive use. It is clear that use-value taxation, by reducing the taxes paid on land in agricultural uses, represents a subsidy for farmers. However, our purpose here is to examine its effectiveness as a tool for land-use policy.

It is often argued that market-value taxation imposes an unbearable cost on farmers near the urban–rural fringe, making farming unprofitable and thus accelerating the conversion of land from agricultural uses. Though this may be true, it is only a part of the story. To believe that use-value taxation alone will be sufficient to prevent the premature conversion of farmland, it is necessary to believe that farmers are entirely aware of the costs they actually bear but entirely oblivious of opportunity costs. If the market value of land substantially exceeds its use value in agriculture, those farmers who respond to economic incentives are likely to find irresistible the inducements to sell their land to a buyer with non-agricultural uses in mind, regardless of use-value property taxation provisions. Furthermore, experience has shown that use-value taxation often serves merely to provide an unnecessary subsidy to speculators and land developers, who purchase farmland near the urban–rural fringe and leave it unused or in low-intensity agricultural uses while awaiting the optimal time for its conversion to urban uses.

In the political arena, property taxation policy has, for the reasons suggested above, become a battleground between those who are most concerned that use-value taxation remain a subsidy for farmers, speculators, and land developers and those who would prefer that it became a more effective tool for land-use policy. The latter usually take the approach that use-value taxation should be available only to those landowners who are bona fide farmers and who intend that their land remain in agricultural use for a considerable time period. In various jurisdictions, several mechanisms have been implemented in an attempt to satisfy these objectives.

Rollback provisions require that in the event that agricultural land is converted to urban uses, the difference between the market-value taxes and the use-value taxes and the interest on that difference be collected for the previous several years. Various jurisdictions specify different periods for the collection of "back taxes"; periods of three, five, and ten, years are among the more common. Rollback provisions serve to correct partially the apparent inequities that occur when landowners enjoy the benefits of use-value taxation while preparing to convert the land to urban uses. However, the total back taxes plus interest are likely to be an insignificant sum when compared with the capital gains to be enjoyed from land conversion. Accordingly, rollback provisions offer only a limited disincentive for premature land conversion.

Some jurisdictions have attempted to formalize the informal understanding between landowners and their state or local governments expressed in rollback provisions, by establishing procedures whereby use-value taxation may be enjoyed only by landowners who enter into formal agreements to forgo land conversion for a period of, say, ten years. Violation of this kind of agreement usually invokes rollback provisions and additional penalties. Such arrangements have had limited effectiveness. When such agreements are voluntarily entered into by individual landowners and their governments, the landowners most likely to be tempted by the profits from premature land conversion are those least likely to enter into such agreements. In addition, should conversion prospects improve markedly during the ten-year period, the rollback provisions and penalties are seldom great enough to discourage conversion.

These kinds of agreements are in some ways analogous to the purchase by local governments of easements that foreclose development. Local government, by voluntarily limiting the amount of taxes it collects on the land, in a sense is purchasing the right to foreclose development inexpensively and on "time payment." Although this represents a cheap way to buy such a right, the right so obtained is much less valuable than is an easement foreclosing development. Under an easement, the beneficiary (that is, local government) is and remains the dominant party. But under this kind of agreement, developments (of the type intended to be foreclosed) may proceed without penalty at the end of the agreement period or with only a relatively insignificant penalty while the agreement is in effect.

Some heavily urbanized states, anxious to preserve the rural character of their remaining agricultural regions, have experimented with agricultural districts.[3] These offer property tax benefits, and sometimes other inducements, to landowners to keep their land in agricultural uses. They differ from the typical "use-value taxation with rollback provision" arrangement in that they are not agreements between the government and rural landowners one by one, but require a collective agreement among the landowners who wish to be included in an agricultural district. The primary advantage claimed for agricultural districts is that they offer each landowner assurance that the district will retain its agricultural character into the distant future and thus encourage continued investment to maintain and increase the agricultural productivity of the land (an encouragement entirely absent when a rural landowner expects that the surrounding land, and perhaps also their land, is a candidate for conversion to urban uses).

Summary: the effectiveness of traditional police power and taxation policies in forestalling premature and undesirable land-use conversion
We have seen that subdivision controls and public utility regulations are usually insufficient to offset the incentives for premature conversion of rural land that are inherent in the customary modes of financing local government services and public utilities. Furthermore, use-value taxation, even with rollback provisions, seems insufficient to cancel out the incentives for premature development. Zoning may be helpful in directing urban development away from specific, unsuitable lands, but it has not been especially effective in discouraging urban sprawl. Also, because of the immense effects that specific applications of zoning regulations may have on individual fortunes, there is continuing concern that zoning tends to treat landowners inequitably and to offer sometimes irresistible temptations to corrupt zoning authorities.

Some innovative suggestions for land-use policy
There have been a number of suggestions for land-use policy that use some of the principles of economics. Next, we briefly discuss two of these.

The auctioning of zoning changes
The economist Marion Clawson argued along the following lines.[4] The community has made increasingly valuable the right to use land in intensive urban uses, as it is community growth that creates the demand for land in such uses and the community activity of zoning that creates the valuable right so to use land. Developers who wish to convert land to more intensive uses find the right to do so valuable and would be willing to pay for that right in a market if they could no longer obtain it through the political process.

Accordingly, Clawson proposed that zoning authorities, after deciding which lands should be subject to zoning changes and variances, should auction the rights so created to the highest bidder. Implementation of such a proposal would have the following effects. Because of the relaxed restrictions on the operation of the price mechanism, markets in land would tend to become more efficient, spatially and intertemporally. Land would be more likely to gravitate to its highest-valued use. The activity of land speculation would become less profitable, because the economic surplus that arises from changes in rights pertaining to land use would flow in large part to the local government that conducts the auction and collects the sums of money bid. In this way, some of the obvious inequities that result from zoning would be eliminated, along with most of the incentives for corruption on the part of zoning authorities.

This proposal is yet to be implemented in any jurisdiction, perhaps because it is contrary to some deeply embedded political traditions, and perhaps because land speculators and developers form an unusually effective lobby that prefers business as usual to the Clawson proposal.

Transfer of development rights

The proposal for transferable development rights (TDRs) is aimed at accommodating pressures for more intensive development that arise from population growth and economic progress while providing for the preservation of natural or built environments deemed worthy of preservation, and at the same time eliminating the inequitable treatment of owners of different tracts of land. Ordinary zoning to prevent development in floodplains, agricultural areas, and areas of historical or architectural significance is often resisted by landowners in those areas, because it would foreclose their prospects for profit from land-use conversion while enhancing the profit prospects of landowners in other areas. Independent observers may also see inequity in such an arrangement. The TDR proposal is aimed at eliminating this inequity and thus increasing the political acceptability of proposals to preserve the character of areas deemed worthy of preservation.

The TDR proposal is best conceptualized as a version of zoning, but one that increases the scope for market behaviors. In the simplest case, the zoning authority divides its jurisdiction into two zones: a zone in which intensive land development is to be concentrated (called the development zone, DZ) and a zone in which the current land use is to be continued (called the transfer zone, TZ). Transferable development rights would be created and distributed among landowners in both zones. The basis for the initial distribution of TDRs is a matter of some contention, but a possible solution is that each landowner would receive one TDR for each $X assessed valuation of land he or she owns in either zone. A schedule relating the required number of TDRs to the intensity of proposed individual developments in the DZ would be established by the zoning authorities.

In order to receive approval of a development proposal, a developer would need to own both land in the DZ and the requisite number of TDRs. Thus, a market in TDRs would be established, and as development proceeded in the DZ, it would soon become necessary to purchase TDRs from landowners in the transfer zone. In this way, landowners in the TZ would be able to share in the profits from development without endangering the benefits that the public at large obtained from the preservation of TZ land in its current use. The expense of purchasing TDRs would discourage premature development in the DZ and would tend to limit the profits obtained by DZ landowners from conversion to more intensive land uses. Thus, the TDR proposal would enable a community to enjoy many of the benefits from zoning, while eliminating the windfalls and wipeouts and takings problems commonly associated with zoning.

In the United States, initial implementation of TDR programs was associated with the preservation of historic districts and of beachfront environments, but it appears to have the potential for more widespread implementation in communities that would like to control the pattern and direction of intensive development. The success of TDR programs in the US, however, is open to debate. According to Walls and McConnell, who conducted a recent assessment of TDR programs in the US for Resources for the Future, although over 140 localities throughout the US have TDR programs on the books, "only a handful have been successful at establishing a working market and in preserving land."

As part of their assessment, Walls and McConnell examined TDR programs and offer insight and what seems to work and not work with respect to the design and implementation of these programs.[5]

Questions for discussion

1. Ricardo's analysis of land was an essential ingredient in Malthus's dismal theory of population. Can you explain the link?
2. Why did the concept of distance from markets turn out to be more useful than the concept of land fertility in developing theories of the location of economic activity?
3. It has been said that just beyond the fringes of growing cities, farmers are speculators and speculators are farmers. Does economic theory support this proposition? Explain.
4. In the early and mid-1980s, the prices of US farmland fell sharply after an earlier period of price increases. Historical data on sales of land suggest that sales tend to increase when land prices are rising and decrease when they are falling. Is this observation consistent with the theory introduced in this chapter?
5. Are you in favor of spending federal, state and local funds to purchase conservations easements from private landowners to protect agricultural land and environmentally sensitive land? Why or why not?

Notes

1. If several dimensions of soil fertility were recognized, along with different fertility requirements for different crops, enterprise locations may be determined. However, these kinds of adjustments to the Ricardian model have an ad hoc flavor and produce no unexpected results.
2. For a demonstration of this exercise, see Alan Randall and Emory N. Castle (1985), "Land Resources and Land Markets," in Allen V. Kneese and James B. Sweeney (eds), *Handbook of Natural Resource and Energy Economics: Volume II*, Amsterdam: Elsevier.
3. See Howard E. Conklin and William G. Lesher (1977), "Farm-Value Assessment as a Means for Reducing Premature and Excessive Agricultural Disinvestment in Urban Fringes," *American Journal of Agricultural Economics* **59**: 755–9; Howard E. Conklin and William R. Bryant (1974), "Agricultural Districts: A Compromise Approach to Agricultural Preservation," *American Journal of Agricultural Economics* **56**: 607–13.
4. Marion Clawson (1967), "Why Not Sell Zoning and Rezoning? (Legally, That Is)," *Land Use Controls* **1**: 29–30.
5. Margaret Walls and Virginia McConnell (2007), "Transfer of Development Rights in US Communities: Evaluating Program Design, Implementation and Outcomes," Washington, DC: Resources for the Future, September.

Suggested reading: classic and contemporary

Alonso, W. (1964), *Location and Land Use: Toward a General Theory of Land Rent*, Cambridge, MA: Harvard University Press.

Bergstrom, J.C. and R.C. Ready (2009), "What Have We Learned from Over 20 Years of Farmland Amenity Valuation Research in North America?," *Review of Agricultural Economics* **31** (1): 21–49.

Diamond, D.B. and G.S. Tolley (eds) (1982), *The Economics of Urban Amenities*, New York: Academic Press.

Goetz, S.J., J.S. Shortle, and J.C. Bergstrom (eds) (2005), *Land Use Problems and Conflicts: Causes, Consequences and Solutions*, London and New York: Routledge.

Melichar, E. (1979), "Capital Gains versus Current Income in the Farming Sector," *American Journal of Agricultural Economics* **61**: 1085–92.

Messer, K.D. (2007), "Transferable Development Rights Programs: An Economic Framework for Success," *Journal of Conservation Planning* **3**: 47–56.

Morrisette, P.M. (2001), "Conservation Easements and the Public Good: Preserving the Environment on Private Lands," *Natural Resources Journal* **41**: 373–426.

Plantinga, A.J. and D.J. Miller (2001), "Agricultural Land Values and the Value of Rights to Future Land Development," *Land Economics* **77** (1): 56–67.

18 The economics of water: how is water valued and allocated?

Water is a complex natural resource. In some cases it looks like a rival, exclusive private good. In other cases it looks like a non-rival, non-exclusive public good. In reality, water has both private and public good characteristics which presents difficult economic, environmental, and social issues related to its use, valuation, and management. Concerns and conflicts over water seem to be increasing all over the world. Water is, after all, essential to life. Suppose you became lost in a desert without food or water supplies. Although you may survive in the desert for up to a month without food intake, the average person would survive only about three days without freshwater intake. Of course, the birds and the bees and flowers and trees also need water to survive. In addition to sustaining life, water is used by people in agriculture, manufacturing, transportation, and recreation. Water also is home to a multitude of fish, shellfish, mammal, insect, and plant species. Someday maybe even people will live underwater in self-contained, artificial ecospheres.[1] It is clear that the use, management, and valuation of water will be one of the most pressing policy issues in the twenty-first century and beyond. In this chapter, we provide a discussion of water allocation and pricing, the scarcity value of water, and the role of federal water projects in helping to meet water needs in the United States.

Major water uses in the US listed by the US Geological Survey include public water supply, private domestic water supply, irrigation, livestock, aquaculture, industrial, mining, and thermoelectric power. Total fresh and saline water withdrawals were estimated at 408 000 million gallons per day in 2000 (approximately 80 percent from surface water supplies and 20 percent from groundwater supplies). Of the 408 000 million gallons per day total withdrawal estimate, about 47 percent is withdrawn for thermoelectric power generation, about 34 percent is withdrawn for irrigation, about 11 percent is withdrawn for public water supply, about 4.6 percent is withdrawn for industrial use, about 0.4 percent is withdrawn for livestock use, and private domestic water supply, mining, and aquaculture account for about 1 percent each of total withdrawals (Table 18.1).

Public water supply

About 85 percent of the US population is served by public water supply; 63 percent of public water supply is withdrawn from surface water and 37 percent comes from groundwater. In the US, local government municipalities (e.g., cities, counties, townships) are the primary providers of public water supply. Thus, public water supply is often referred to as municipal water supply. In most cities, towns, and counties in the US, the major demanders of municipal water supplies are residential households. For example, residential water use accounts for almost 60 percent of total water provided to customers by the City of Atlanta Water Bureau. An individual household's demand for water is determined in general by the following equation:

$$D_w^{r_i} = f(P_w^{r_i}, I^{r_i}, S^{r_i}, T^{r_i}) \tag{18.1}$$

Table 18.1   Estimated water withdrawals by major water use in the US, 2000 (million gallons per day)

Source	Fresh Water	Saline Water	Total
Public Supply	43 300	0	43 300
Domestic Private	3 590	0	3 590
Irrigation	137 000	0	137 000
Livestock	1 760	0	1 760
Aquaculture	3 700	0	3 700
Industrial	18 500	1 280	19 780
Mining	2 010	1 490	3 500
Thermoelectric Power	136 000	59 500	195 500
Total	345 000	62 300	408 000

Source: Susan S. Hutson, Nancy L. Barber, Joan F. Kenny, Kristin S. Linsey, Deborah S. Lumia, and Molly A. Maupin (2004–05), "Estimated Use of Water in the United States in 2000," USGS Circular 1268, Denver, CO: US Geological Survey, Information Services (released March 2004, revised April 2004, May 2004, February 2005).

where $D_w^{r_i}$ = residential demand for water by household i, $P_w^{r_i}$ = price or cost of water to residential household i, I^{r_i} = income of residential household i, S^{r_i} = size of residential household i, and T^{r_i} = tastes of preferences of residential household i.[2] The summation of individual residential water demand functions across all household in a city, town or county provides the aggregate residential water demand function for the city, town or county illustrated by D_w^R in Figure 18.1.

City, town, or county municipal water suppliers generally charge customers for water use. How do these municipalities determine what to charge for water customers and what is the quantity demanded? Municipal water suppliers tend to fall under the category of natural monopoly. A natural monopoly does not mean a monopoly that deals exclusively with natural resources. In the context of the term "natural monopoly," "natural" refers to the fact that characteristics of the industry naturally lead toward monopoly being the most efficient means for providing the good or service. Thus, natural monopoly may apply to many different types of goods and services, some natural resource dependent and some not. Examples of natural resource dependant industries with natural monopoly characteristics include water, natural gas, and electricity utilities. Examples of industries with natural monopoly characteristics which are not natural resource dependent include landline telephone companies and cable television and Internet providers.

From a theoretical perspective, the defining characteristic of a natural monopoly is declining average and marginal costs of production throughout the relevant range of production, as illustrated by the long-run average and marginal cost curves labeled *AC* and *MC* respectively in Figure 18.1. In the case of a public water utility, a declining average cost curve means that as more households are connected to the public water supply, the average costs of providing water to each household decreases; that is, there are increasing returns to scale in production. Think about what this looks like for a county water utility. In order to build a public water supply and delivery system, the county must first secure a source of water by constructing a county reservoir, installing

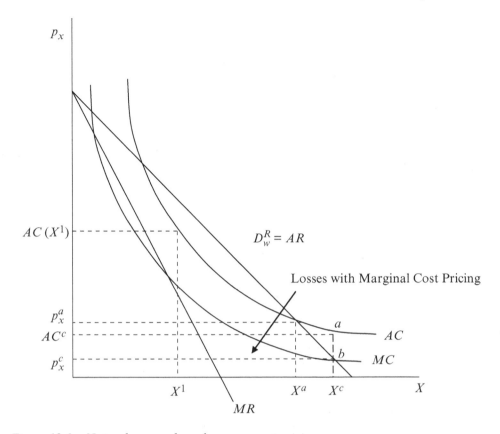

Figure 18.1 Natural monopoly and average cost pricing

intake pipes to existing rivers or lakes, and/or drilling wells into groundwater supplies. In order to meet federal and state drinking water quality standards, the county will most likely also need to build a water treatment plant which removes harmful chemicals and adds beneficial chemicals (e.g., fluoride) before the water is delivered to households. The county must then construct a pressurized water delivery system composed of water tower and pipes running underground to neighborhoods and business districts.

Designing, constructing, operating, and maintaining a county water utility is extremely expensive. Suppose the county goes ahead and incurs these costs and at first serves a relatively small number of household and businesses, say X^1 in Figure 18.1. At X^1 the average costs of production (total costs divided by gallons of water delivered) will be quite high. As more and more households and businesses connect to the public water supply, the average costs of production (average cost of a gallon of water delivered) decreases. This occurs because once the city has built the public water system, it is relatively inexpensive to add more customers. Also, as the county grows in population, it is much cheaper to add new households and businesses to the existing water system than to build a new water system which would compete with the existing one (imagine the costs of replicating the existing water system – for example, two sets of water delivery pipes running throughout the county). The characteristic of declining average costs in the relevant range of production is why economists, engineers, and government officials agree that it is generally more efficient and better for there to be only one provider of water to a community.

OK, so if there is to be only one utility providing water to a community which in our example above is a county, how much water should the county utility provide and how much should it charge? In Figure 18.1, assume the curve labeled $D^R_w = AR$ represents the demand curve (and the county water utility's average revenue curve) for water in the county. The curve labeled MR represents the county water utility's marginal revenue curve for water provision which lies below its average revenue curve (which, as presented in Chapter 10, is generally the case for monopolies). In the case of a natural monopoly (increasing returns to scale industry) the ever-decreasing average (and marginal costs) of production within the relevant range of production means that the firm's long-run marginal cost curve labeled MC in Figure 18.1 will always fall below the firm's average cost curve.

As discussed in Chapter 5, in a competitive market firm-level output is set where demand equals marginal cost (X^c gallons per year in Figure 18.1) and the economically efficient price is where price equals marginal cost. Notice, however, that if the county water utility provides X^c gallons of water to customers and charges a price (water rate) of $P^c_X = MC$, total revenues ($P^c_X \times X^c$) will not be enough to cover total costs ($AC^c \times X^c$) meaning that the utility will be operating at a loss equal to the rectangle AC^c, a, b, P^c_x. Thus, if the utility practiced marginal cost pricing, the loss or deficit would need to be made up by lump-sum subsidies.

Since the policy of most local governments is for water utility revenue to at least cover water utility costs, most water utilities in the US practice some form of average cost pricing rather than marginal cost pricing (even though economic efficiency analysis call for marginal cost pricing). Thus, for example, in Figure 18.1 the county water utility may attempt to set water delivery output at X^a gallons per year and charge a price of P^a_x per gallon so that total revenue just covers total costs. In reality, the water rate may be set a bit higher than P^a_x to allow for some minimal return on investment (which may be set aside, for example, to fund future water system expansions). Such pricing strategies are inherently second-best rather than efficient, because some demand with willingness to pay greater than MC remains unserved. Declining block pricing, where each customer is charged a higher price for the first, say, 10 000 gallons of use and a lower price per gallon for use beyond that threshold, is sometimes used as an approximate solution to the second-best problem.

There is an important caveat to the above analysis. With growing demand, the AC of urban water provision does not decline forever – eventually, new water sources have to be tapped and new storage and delivery systems constructed, and the capital costs will be substantial. AC declines with growing water use until system capacity is reached, but at that point AC increases abruptly as capacity is expanded in lumpy fashion. Some jurisdictions have discovered that AC after expansion is even higher than it was when the original facility was opened – that could happen if, for example, expanded capacity could be provided only by developing inferior reservoir sites. Declining block pricing has been losing favor, because it encourages low-value use of water, thereby increasing the growth rate of demand and hastening the time when water utilities are obliged to undertake expensive capacity expansions.

Irrigation

As shown in Table 18.1, irrigation of agricultural crops accounts for about 34 percent of all daily water withdrawals from surface and groundwater in the US Because irrigation places such large demands on water withdrawals, conflicts with other water demanders including other industries and cities are major public policy issues in many parts of the US including most of the western US and lately the southeastern US because of rapid population growth combined with prolonged drought. The demand for irrigation water, as in other industries, is a derived demand – so called because the demand for water is derived from the demand for the commodity being produced. Consider a neoclassical production function for some agricultural commodity, Q, say corn:

$$Q = f(W, Z) \tag{18.2}$$

where Q represents the production of corn measured in bushels, W represents water input measured in gallons or acre feet and Z represents a vector of all other inputs. In a competitive market for corn, the farmer's profit maximization problem is given by:

$$\max \Pi = [P_C \times f(W, Z)] - P_W W - P_Z Z \tag{18.3}$$

where P_C = market price of corn per bushel, P_W = price (or cost) of water per gallon or per acre foot, and P_Z = vector of prices of all other inputs. Given this profit maximization problem, the farmer's derived demand for water in the production of corn is given by:

$$\frac{\partial \Pi}{\partial W} = P_C \frac{\partial f}{\partial W} - P_W \tag{18.4}$$

The above equation makes it clear that the derived demand for water is a function of the price of corn, the price or cost of water, and the technical relationship between the water input and corn production (e.g., how much more corn is produced when more water is applied to the crop). Thus, we can represent the derived demand for irrigation water generally as:

$$D_W = f(P_Q, P_W | T) \tag{18.5}$$

where D_W is the demand for irrigation water in the production of Q, P_Q is the market price of Q, P_W is the price (or cost) of irrigation water, and T is fixed production technology. A farmer's derived demand curve for water (W) is illustrated in Figure 18.2 by the downward-sloping curve labeled D_W. What is the price or cost of irrigation to a farmer and the quantity demanded? Suppose, as is typically the case in eastern US states, that once a farmer has installed an irrigation system, the price or cost of irrigation water is primarily composed of the cost of pumping water from the ground or surface water and distributing this water to crops. Let this price be denoted by P_p in Figure 18.2. According to the equimarginal principle of continually balancing marginal benefits and marginal costs to achieve economic efficiency, a farmer will continue to pump and distribute water to crops until $MB_p = P_p$ at point a on D_W. At this point, the quantity demanded of water for this particular farmer is equal to W^*.

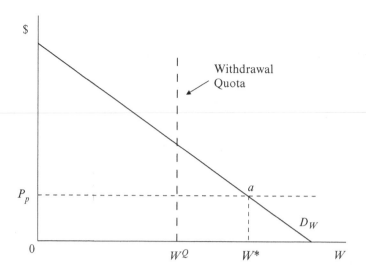

Figure 18.2   Private single-user irrigation pumping cost and use

In many areas of the US, farmers are required to hold an irrigation pumping permit which sets a limit or quota on how much water the farmer can withdraw from a surface or groundwater source. The withdrawal quota is illustrated in Figure 18.2 by the vertical heavy-dashed line which sets the limit or quota on the farmer's water withdrawals at W^Q. In Figure 18.2, the withdrawal quota has been set by the administrative authority below the farmer's optimal private withdrawal rate of W^*. It is also possible for the administrative authority to set the withdrawal quota above the farmers optimal rate (e.g., to the right of W^* in Figure 18.2). In this case, the farmer would possess excess withdrawal rights which he or she could use in the future (say, if pumping costs decreased).

What is the price and quantity demanded of water in regions where water is sold? One such place is the Central Valley of the State of California in the US. The Central Valley Water Authority manages a huge federally subsidized water system which sells irrigation water to farmers in California. Theoretically, if operating as a natural monopoly with decreasing costs, the Central Valley Water Authority should price irrigation water according to the average cost pricing principle discussed above for public residential water supplies. However, research suggests that while the Central Valley Water Project may once have been experiencing decreasing costs, this has not been the case since the 1980s.[3] This situation is illustrated in Figure 18.3 where an increase in demand for water from the Central Valley Water Project from D_w^1 to D_w^2 over time is shown to move the project into the portion of its long-run average cost curve where average costs are increasing. It can be argued that, at this point, marginal cost pricing is appropriate (to reflect the marginal cost additional use imposes on the system) whereas when demand was at D_w^1 average cost pricing would be appropriate (to provide revenue sufficient to cover costs) – but, again, we are in the second-best realm. Clearly, there is a theoretical argument that the Central Valley Water Authority should now be charging a price to farmers for irrigation water, P_w^*, which is equal to the marginal cost of water provision. However, instead of practicing marginal (or average) cost pricing, the Central Water Authority

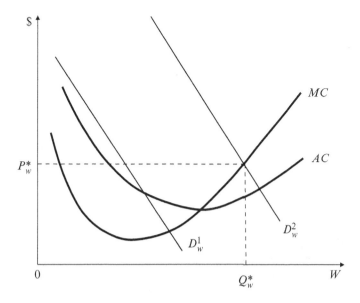

Figure 18.3   Increasing costs over time and marginal cost pricing

sets irrigation water prices administratively according to various non-economic criteria including a farmer's ability to pay.[4]

Other major water uses
Other water uses listed in Table 18.1 including private domestic water supply, livestock watering, aquaculture, industrial, and mining share the characteristic of private, rather than public provision. For example, private domestic water supply involves residential households providing their own drinking water through private groundwater wells. Farmers and ranchers also water their livestock using private groundwater wells, private ponds, and/or pumping from other surface water bodies at their own expense. Freshwater aquaculture operations utilize their own private ponds and lakes. Industrial and mining operations also provide for their own water needs using private groundwater wells or pumping from surface water bodies at their own expense.

In the case of private domestic water supply, the demand for water by an individual residential household is determined by equation 18.1, just as in the case of public water supply. The primary difference is the price or cost of water. For example, once an individual household has paid for the installation of a private groundwater well and delivery system (e.g., plumbing into and throughout the house), the marginal price or cost of water to the household is negligible. Thus, economic theory predicts that households in this situation will continue to use water until the marginal benefits fall to zero or near zero. Farmers and ranchers watering their livestock, aquaculture operations, industrial operations, and mining operations all have a derived demand for water which is calculated in the same manner as described for crop irrigation above. Once these users have installed wells, pumps, delivery and distribution systems, the marginal costs of water use are also relatively small. Thus, economic theory predicts these users will continue to demand and use water until the marginal benefits are relatively small – this basically boils down to using as much water as you want.

As shown in Table 18.1, thermoelectric power plants are the largest users of water in the US, drawing water from both freshwater sources such as rivers and lakes and saltwater sources such as bays and estuaries. In thermoelectric power plants, the burning of fossil fuels or nuclear reactions are used to heat and turn liquid water into steam. The steam then turns turbines generating electricity. Water is also used to cool the power-generating equipment in the power plant. In the process of cooling the power-generating equipment, the water heats up and must be cooled before it is returned to rivers, lakes, bays, or estuaries. There are two major environmental concerns related to the use of water by thermoelectric power plants. On the water intake side, there is concern over entrainment and impingement. Entrainment refers to fish eggs and larvae taken into the power plant cooling system as water is withdrawn from a river, lake, bay, or estuary. Impingement refers to mortality of mature fish and shellfish as they are trapped against screens protecting water intake pumps. On the water discharge side, the concern is over thermal pollution, which refers to the return of water to rivers, lakes, bays, or estuaries of a higher temperature compared to the intake water temperature. Many aquatic plant and animal species are sensitive to changes in water temperature and can be damaged by abrupt changes in water temperature such as would occur if superheated water from thermoelectric power plants was discharged directly into rivers, lakes, bays, or estuaries.

As a result of these environmental concerns, Section 316(a) of the 1972 amendments to the Federal Water Pollution Control Act (PL 92-500) requires thermoelectric power plants to provide for a reduction in the temperature of cooling water before it is returned to the environment. This temperature reduction is commonly accomplished through the use of large cooling towers where the superheated water sits and cools to an acceptable temperature before being discharged. The cooling towers also allow a portion of the superheated water to be discharged into the atmosphere through evaporation (which is another potential environmental concern). Section 316(b) of the 1972 Water Pollution Control Act amendments require power plants to employ "best technology available" (BTA) to minimize adverse environmental impact associated with entrainment and impingement.

As in the case of other industrial uses, the thermoelectric power industry has a derived demand for water which is driven by the price and demand for electricity. As the price of electricity increases and/or the demand for electricity increases (e.g., the demand curve for electricity shifts out), the derived demand for water use in thermoelectric power plants will increase (and vice versa). After a power company has paid the costs of constructing a thermoelectric power plant including equipment required to meet environmental regulations, the marginal cost of withdrawing water is relatively low. Economic theory predicts that a power plant will continue to withdraw and use water until the marginal benefits to the plant of doing so equal the marginal costs to the plant. Thus, since the marginal costs of water withdrawal and use to the power plant are relatively low, it is not surprising from an economic standpoint that thermoelectric power plants withdraw such large quantities of water from rivers, lakes, bays, and estuaries in the US.

Scarcity value and water markets

In the above discussion of water uses in the US, we have seen that the equimarginal principle governs all types of water uses including residential, commercial, and industrial;

that is, people or firms use water until marginal benefits are equal to marginal costs. Many economists argue that in most cases the price residential, commercial, and industrial water users pay for water is too low because it does not reflect the scarcity value of water. The scarcity value of a gallon or acre-foot of water is the true marginal value to society of that gallon or acre-foot of water. This true marginal value captures all benefits to society of water which are recognized by people and reflected in their preferences, including drinking water benefits, recreational benefits, environmental benefits, and production and provision of commercial and industrial goods and services.

Let the true marginal value of water to society be denoted by MSV_w. To meet economic efficiency in the use and allocation of water, economic theory states that the following condition must hold:

$$P_w = MSV_w = MSC_w \tag{18.6}$$

where P_w = price of water to customers and MSC_w = marginal cost to society of water provision. Let's see if this condition is met in the case of any of the above major uses of water. First of all, whenever average cost pricing is used, such as in the decreasing-cost industry cases discussed above, equation 18.6 above cannot hold by definition since the price of water to customers is pegged to average cost rather than marginal cost. What about the private water system cases discussed above such as private domestic water supply and agricultural irrigation in the eastern US? After these water users have paid for installation of their own water system, they pay a relatively low marginal price or cost for water (essentially the costs to them of pumping and distributing water throughout a residential house or agricultural crop field). This relatively low marginal price or cost of water is highly unlikely to reflect other societal values of water other than benefits to the private water system owner. As discussed above, water prices to customers are often set administratively, such as in the case of the Central Valley Water Authority in California. If water system administrators have accurate estimates of the marginal societal value of water and marginal costs of water provision, it is possible they could set the price of water $P_w = MSV_w = MSC_w$. However, the likelihood of administrators having access to such detailed estimates of the societal benefits and costs of water is remote.

The failure of other water pricing mechanism to achieve economic efficiency is a primary reason why economists argue in favor of using water markets to price and allocate scarce water supplies. As discussed in Chapters 9 and 10, non-attenuated property rights are necessary in principle for markets to work efficiently. Thus, in order to establish a water market, the first step is to establish legally a serviceable system of property rights to ground and surface water supplies. Once these water rights are established, a governing body such as a water authority needs to be put in charge of monitoring and enforcing water rights and the transfer of these rights from one party to another through market trade and transactions. Enforcement may require calling in higher legal authorities via the court system. For example, the State of Colorado in the US has a system of state water courts with an appointed water judge and water referee who adjudicate water rights and disputes throughout the state. In other states, especially in the eastern US, water rights and disputes are adjudicated through the regular local, state, and federal court systems (e.g., there is no special water court system . . . yet).

Once the legal and administrative means are in place, water markets function conceptually just like any other market. Water is bought and sold (e.g., traded) as a commodity with a going market price which is set by the interaction of market demand and supply. A simplistic water market is illustrated in Figure 18.4. The aggregate (market) water demand and supply curves are shown in panel (c) reproduced in both the top right and bottom left of the figure. The aggregate water supply curve is the horizontal summation of individual water supply curves shown in panels (a) and (b). The aggregate water demand curve is the horizontal summation of individual water demand curves shown in panels (d) and (e). Through market trade and transactions (e.g., bargaining) between water demander and suppliers, a going market price for water is established denoted by P_w^* in Figure 18.4. At this going market price, the aggregate quantity demanded of water is equal to the aggregate quantity supplied of water at Q_w^*. Thus, in the water market illustrated in Figure 18.4, at a particular place and time, P_w^* and Q_w^* are the "market clearing" or equilibrium price and quantity of water provided. At this equilibrium point, water supplier 1 provides $Q_{w,s}^1$ gallons or acre-feet of water to the market as shown in panel (a) and water supplier 2 provides $Q_{w,s}^2$ gallons or acre-feet of water to market as shown in panel (b). The horizontal summation of water supply implies $Q_w^* = Q_{w,s}^1 + Q_{w,s}^2$. On the demand side, at the market equilibrium point in panel (c), water demander or customer 1 purchases and receives $Q_{w,d}^1$ gallons or acre-feet of water and water demander or customer 2 purchases and receives $Q_{w,d}^2$ gallons or acre-feet of water. The horizontal summation of water demand implies $Q_w^* = Q_{w,d}^1 + Q_{w,d}^2$. Thus, in a properly functioning water market, the aggregate quantity of water demanded by customers at the going market price is equal to the aggregate quantity of water provided by suppliers at that price; e.g., $Q_{w,d}^1 + Q_{w,d}^2 = Q_{w,s}^1 + Q_{w,s}^2$.

An immediately apparent advantage of a water market is that it provides a decentralized mechanism for allocating scarce water supplies to water demanders or customers. The allocation mechanism is the price of water which is set by market forces of supply and demand. A disadvantage of water markets is that allocation of water to customers is based not only on willingness to pay, but also ability to pay. Since not all people or businesses have equal ability to pay, water markets may be viewed as an unequitable or unfair water allocation mechanism. Another advantage of water markets are the incentives that are provided for people and firms to become private water suppliers and thereby help to meet water demands and needs in a community or region. A disadvantage is that people and firms will not necessarily step up to become private water suppliers for a variety of reasons including insufficient profitability (e.g., more profitable alternative enterprises exist) and risk and uncertainty (e.g., ground- and surface water quantity and/or quality is uncertain).

One of the strongest arguments in favor of water markets from an economic perspective is their ability to account for the scarcity value of water and achieve economic efficiency. Recall from the scarcity value discussion earlier in this section that economic efficiency in water markets would require $P_w^* = MSV_w = MSC_w$, where P_w^* is the market-clearing or equilibrium price of water. Assuming that water demanders or customers are acting as rational utility maximizers and the water market is open to all water demanders or customers (e.g., residential, recreational, commercial, and industrial demanders or customers), then social preferences will be captured in the price of water with the end result of $P_w^* = MSV_w$. That is, the marginal value society places on water will be equal to the going market market price of water. Assuming that water suppliers are acting as rational profit maximizers and the water market is open to all potential water suppliers (e.g., all individuals and firms who own water rights), then opportunity costs of alternative water uses will be captured in the price of water with the end result of $P_w^* = MSC_w$. Thus, in a properly functioning water market, equation 18.6 will hold, implying that the price of water accurately reflects the scarcity value of water and economic efficiency is achieved. The reader should note, however, that economic efficiency may not necessarily be the overriding policy goal when it comes to water use and allocation, and refer back to Chapter 8 for further theoretical insight. In the US, existing water markets are found primarily in western states.[5]

Federal water projects
As discussed above, in the United States water is often allocated and priced by local government agencies or water authorities and in some cases by water markets (primarily in the western US). In the US, the federal government also plays a large role in water allocation and management as evidenced by large federal water projects managed by the US Army Corps of Engineers and Tennessee Valley Authority in the eastern US and by the US Bureau of Reclamation in the western US. Why is there such a large direct federal government investment in water projects in the US and what do these projects look like?

The problem
River basins in the US are large units typically encompassing many individuals and firms and frequently crossing local and state jurisdictional boundaries. Ownership of water in river systems is vested in the public sector as a public trust. State governments establish and enforce water rights, which assign to individuals the right to withdraw and use water for various purposes. When major rivers cross state boundaries, states may subordinate a part of their authority, with respect to granting water rights to individuals, to an interstate river compact or commission. The federal government has jurisdiction over all navigable waters.

River systems are unpredictable in that flooding or periods of drought may occur. In addition, massive modifications to river systems (e.g, the building and maintenance of dams, flood control structures, or navigation locks) may render river systems more effective in providing services to individuals and communities. Given the massive size of river systems, the massive capital requirements for large-scale river system modifications, the tradition of homesteading and the family farm (which has resulted in the division of river basin lands into many small, independently owned tracts), and the vesting of ownership rights to rivers in the public sector, large-scale river modification projects must be carried out by the public sector, and usually by the federal government, or not at all.

From project building to project management
For many years now, the federal government has financed, constructed, and operated major structural projects concerned with water resources. Since the 1930s, programs to develop and manage "water and related land resources" have become institutionalized. One or more of the federal water-resources agencies is active in every major river basin in the United States. In many of these river basins, federal water-resources agencies operate a system of dams and reservoirs which were built for multiple designated public

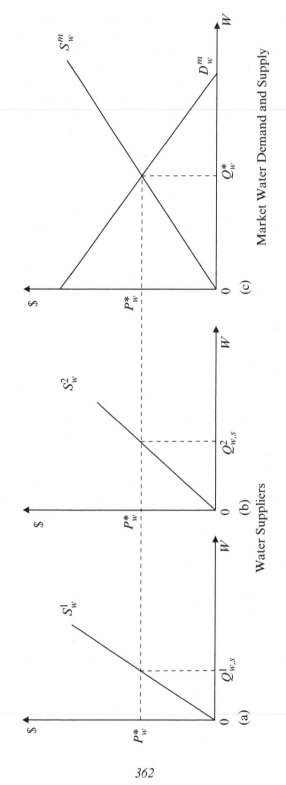

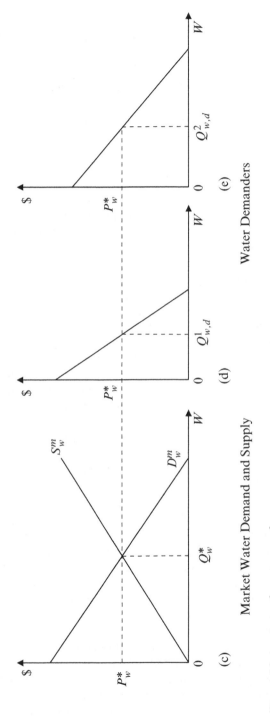

Market Water Demand and Supply

Water Demanders

Figure 18.4   A simple water market

363

purposes including hydropower, flood control, and commercial navigation. In more recent years, recreation, drinking water and "environmental flows" have been added to the list of federal dam and reservoir project purposes. The term "environmental flows" refers to downstream water flows necessary for sustaining fish and wildlife habitat and populations.

Beginning in the late 1930s during Franklin D. Roosevelt's Great Depression-era "New Deal" social works programs, the US embarked on an aggressive federal dam and reservoir building program that lasted about 40 years. During this time period, water projects consisting of huge dams and entire systems of dams and reservoirs were built in river basins throughout the US including projects operated by the Tennessee Valley Authority on the Tennessee River and its tributaries in the American South; projects operated by the US Bureau of Reclamation on the Colorado River in the American West; and dams and reservoirs operated by the US Army Corps of Engineers throughout the nation.

What drove the aggressive program of water project development in the US, especially dam and reservoir construction, in the several decades during and following the Great Depression? One driver was the Great Depression itself and the desire by the federal government to stimulate the economy by putting people to work on public works projects. In addition to directly putting money into people's pockets, the federal government saw dam and reservoir projects as stimulating long-term economic growth by providing "cheap" hydroelectric power and preventing floods and costly flood damage. The entrance of the US into World War II in the 1940s added national defense as a critical driver of additional hydroelectric dam project building to help provide increasing demands for electric power needed to support the war effort. After World War II, the era of "big water project development" continued in the US for a couple of more decades primarily for economic development reasons, including agricultural irrigation and drinking water in the arid American West and power generation, commercial navigation and flood control in all US regions.

Increased concern during the 1970s' "environmental decade" over the environmental impacts of big water projects was a major factor leading to the sharp decrease in new projects of this type in the US since the 1970s. In particular, federal environmental protection policies implemented in the 1970s including the National Environmental Protection Act (NEPA) and the Endangered Species Act increased the costs of new water projects and gave opponents effective tools for blocking new projects.[6] So, in the twenty-first century, federal water resources agencies are pretty much out of the business of building new, big reservoir projects.[7] These agencies, however, still play a huge role in operating those reservoir projects that have already been constructed, making crucial water resource allocation decisions, constructing new projects other than big dams and reservoirs, and maintaining an active program of river basin planning. In this institutional environment, citizens of the river basins, and especially those with a particular economic interest in water resources, have intense motivation to pressure the federal government to operate water projects in their best interest.

Given these expectations and past patterns of institutional behavior, in a river basin that has already enjoyed substantial federal investment in water projects, citizen pressure develops to allocate more water from existing projects to meet their needs and wants, and perhaps for additional water project investment. Perhaps population growth and increasing economic activity have led to increasing demands for irrigation water; water for residential, commercial, and industrial uses; additional flood protection; river-flow augmentation to reduce the concentration of pollutants in the river; minimum river flows to protect threatened or endangered fish or shellfish, or water-based outdoor recreational activities. Severe floods or drought as recently witnessed in the midwestern US (floods), southwestern US (droughts), and southeastern US (floods and droughts) have intensified local interests in federal water resource project management and policies.

The initial sentiment in favor of changing water allocations from existing projects or initiating new projects is likely to come from those groups that have been traditional supporters of water resources programs and from similarly placed groups which have not yet enjoyed the benefits of federally funded water projects and which feel that it is now their turn. These groups most likely already enjoy close relationships with the local and regional staff of the federal water resources agency most active in their river basin. So it is relatively easy for the private interests which would benefit most from changing management of existing water projects or initiating new projects to make their desires known to the local and regional staff of the federal agency most likely to lend staff resources, political influence, and power within the administration to change management of existing projects or fund new projects.

Even before support for existing project management changes or new projects begins to appear among private individuals and interest groups, it is likely that the cognizant federal water resources agency (which, for brevity, we shall simply call the Agency) will already have contemplated existing project management changes or new projects, under the guise of its continual planning process. Thus, at the time of initial discussions concerning the proposed management change or new project between the Agency and its potential clientele, neither party is entirely unprepared. The parties are generally familiar with each other's goals, perceived needs, and operating procedures, and each party is likely to have done some advance planning.

The Agency, sensing a degree of local support for a management change or new project, which would advance the Agency's internal goals of security, longevity, and increasing size, moves its planning effort into high gear, and focuses it on the planning of one or a small number of specific project or policy changes or initiatives designed to meet the felt needs of its clientele groups. At this stage, there is considerable interaction between the Agency and its traditional clientele groups but usually considerably less interaction between the Agency and the regional general public at large. The outcome of this process of planning and interaction with clientele groups is often the proposal by the Agency's local or regional office of a specific existing project management change or new project (hereafter called the Project or Policy Proposal).

It would be quite rare these days for the Project or Policy Proposal to include new big reservoir projects. However, it is still common for the Agency to propose large projects to facilitate navigation, and smaller-scale new reservoir projects. In recent decades, for example, outdoor recreation and environmental flows have become important public purposes and uses of federal water resource projects. Thus, for example, the Agency may propose a new construction project for recreational facilities on an existing federal reservoir or along a navigable river over which the federal government has jurisdiction. The Agency may also propose a new management policy that would result in a non-marginal reallocation of water from one public purpose and use (e.g., hydropower) to another (e.g., recreation).

The federal role

The Agency's local or regional office prepares detailed plans for the Project or Policy Proposal and detailed documentation and justification of the Proposal. This documentation finds its first use in the efforts of the local or regional office to persuade its national leadership to support the Proposal. In the case of new water projects, since passage of the Flood Control Act of 1936, Congress may authorize flood-control projects only if it is first demonstrated that the benefits to whomsoever they accrue will exceed the costs. This requirement has since been extended to all new federal water resources projects. A benefit–cost analysis of the project must be performed, and it must demonstrate that the new project will have a benefit–cost ratio in excess of 1.

The benefit–cost analysis is performed by the Agency, which places the Agency in the anomalous position of evaluating a project it has proposed and would implement if approved. The benefit–cost analysis is performed in accordance with guidelines set by the Agency and other institutions.[8] In performing the benefit–cost analysis, the Agency is expected to seek input from all other federal and state agencies and other identifiable groups that may be expected to have information or expertise relevant to the Project. The Office of Management and Budget, a federal executive watchdog agency, may examine the benefit–cost analysis. Another federal agency (for example, the Economic Research Service of the US Department of Agriculture, US Environmental Protection Agency, or the US Fish and Wildlife Service) may also be assigned to examine the benefit–cost analysis and its supporting documents. Eventually, the Agency submits to Congress a request for authorization of the new project, along with appropriate supporting documentation (including the mandated benefit–cost analysis).

In the event that the benefit–cost analysis indicates that the expected benefits from the new project would fail to exceed its costs, it is pointless even to submit a request for congressional authorization. This requirement, coupled with the arrangement whereby the agency who performs the benefit–cost analysis is the same one that proposed the project and would implement it if authorized and funded, seems to provide a built-in incentive for optimistic benefit–cost analysis.

The request for authorization of the new project is assigned, along with many other similar requests, to a congressional subcommittee, which then holds legislative hearings. Agency staff, representatives of other federal and state agencies that may have pertinent information, and interested members of the public may testify. At this point, significant local opposition may be heard, perhaps for the first time. Assume, so that our narrative may continue, that Congress authorizes the new project. At this point, project opponents have no recourse to the judiciary: project authorization is considered a congressional decision, and the benefit–cost analysis is considered a congressional document. Thus neither the authorization decision nor the documentation that is a prerequisite for that decision may be reviewed by the courts.

The National Environmental Policy Act (NEPA) requires that an environmental impact assessment (EIA) of the new project must be performed and an environmental impact statement (EIS) must be prepared and submitted.[9] NEPA may also require that an EIA and EIS be conducted before major changes in the operation of existing projects are implemented. The EIA is to consider and evaluate all the potential effects that construction and operation of the new project or change in the operation of an existing project would have on the environmental and quality of life in the affected region, and the EIS is to report the findings of this assessment. The Agency has detailed guidelines for the performance of the EIA and the preparation of the EIS.[10]

An important component of the EIA–EIS process is the requirement that the Agency, which is necessarily a proponent of the Project or Policy Proposal, prepare and present public information concerning both the beneficial and the adverse effects that the Proposal may be expected to have. In addition, the elaborate requirements for public comment and public hearings provide a forum for opponents of the Proposal. Thus, the EIS process may be important in catalyzing opposition to proposals whose potential effects include some that may be considered adverse by various segments of the public (often, groups that are not among the Agency's traditional clientele groups and thus played little or no part in the interactions leading to the original Proposal). The effects of opposition thus catalyzed may be felt at several points in the continuing institutional processes through which the Proposal must pass if it is to be implemented. Opponents, by using NEPA to challenge legally the details of how the Agency implemented the EIA–EIS process in a particular case, may be able to delay or derail the proposed project.

Congressional authorization of a new project does not end Congress's involvement. For example, construction of a new project must also be funded. In fact, if no funds are allocated to the approved project for several consecutive years, project authorization will lapse (however, a continuing trickle of funds for planning is enough to keep a proposal on life support). Water projects are funded under the public works sections of the federal budget, following subcommittee hearings, subcommittee approval, approval of the Congress, and presidential assent of the budget. The subcommittee hearings concerning funding provide another forum in which project proponents and opponents make their respective cases for and against project funding.

Assume that Congress allocates funds to construct a new project or significantly change the operation of an existing project. But these funds cannot be spent until the EIA–EIS requirements under NEPA have been satisfied. In addition, several other administrative and judicial hurdles remain. The Agency may have to obtain a permit from the US Army Corps of Engineers, which has jurisdiction over all navigable US waters. Depending on the Project or Policy Proposal's specifications, permits may need to be obtained from other agencies. In order to implement the Proposal, it may be necessary to condemn, under the power of eminent domain, land or other resources owned by private individuals. The condemnation process may lead to litigation. If it is found that the new project or change in operation of an existing project may destroy the significant habitat of an endangered species, litigation under the US Endangered Species Act may result in a permanent injunction against the Proposal's implementation or a court order that the Proposal be modified in such a way that the significant habitat will not be destroyed.

So far in this section we have restricted our discussion to public water projects such as federal dams and reservoirs operated by federal agencies such as the US Army Corps of Engineers, US Bureau of Reclamation, and Tennessee Valley Authority. However, throughout the US there are many private dams and reservoirs owned and operated by private power companies. The primary purpose of these dams and reservoirs is hydroelectric power generation, which provides revenue to the power company through sales to electricity customers. Most of these dams and reservoirs are also operated to provide recreational opportunities which may also provide revenue to the power company through real-estate sales, real-estate leases, and recreation access fees.

Most private power company dam and reservoir projects must obtain and operate under a federal license issued by the Federal Energy Regulatory Commission (FERC). These licenses are valid for a specific number of years (e.g., 40 years) after which the company must apply for a new project license. As part of the FERC relicensing process, the power company may be required to conduct environmental, social and economic assessments (akin to the NEPA EIA) of the project and its future operations. The relicensing process may also require various degrees of public comment and involvement (akin to the NEPA EIS). The purpose of the environmental, social, and economic assessments and public comments and involvement is to provide FERC with information and input which the agency may use to stipulate the terms of the new license. The terms of the new license typically attempt to achieve a balance between the private purposes and uses of the project (e.g., power generation, recreation from private lakeside residences) and the public purposes and of the project (e.g., wildlife habitat, recreation from public access areas).

An interesting development is the growth of dam removal and river restoration activities in recent years. Old dams, many of them privately owned, that have outlived their usefulness due to siltation that reduces storage capacity, or perhaps due to their small capacity that renders them inefficient vis-à-vis today's technology, are removed and the free-flowing character of the streams is restored. Interestingly, the net benefits of dam removal are often positive,[11] even though the net benefits of the dams may well have been positive when they were first built. As time passes and technology changes, free-flowing streams become more scarce, and preferences toward the environment change, it may be the case that a particular dam and reservoir may no longer be the most efficient use of a given stream bed and its surrounding riparian land.

The role of state government
In the case of federal water-resources projects, the role of state government is limited but not insignificant. Under many water resources programs, state governments are required to share certain categories of project costs. In the case of projects intended to offer certain services to state and/or local governments (e.g., residential, commercial, and industrial water for delivery through municipal water systems), it is required that state governments enter into firm contractual agreements concerning these services. In addition, many but not all federal water resources agencies maintain a firm tradition that they will not implement new projects that are opposed by the government of the state in which the proposed project is located. Thus, state governments have several means for expressing support or opposition to a proposed federal water resources project during the decision-making process. Individuals and groups who feel strongly in favor of or in opposition to the project will attempt to influence the role that state government plays in this process.

Many existing federal water projects composed of a system of dams and reservoirs in a river basin cross state lines. For example, the US Army Corps of Engineers operates a system of federal dams and reservoirs on the Chattahoochee River which forms the border between the US states of Georgia and Alabama. In addition, the waters of the Chattahoochee River eventually flow into Apalachicola Bay in Florida. Thus, Alabama, Georgia, and Florida all have a stake in how the US Army Corps of Engineers manages this system.

As a result of rapid population growth in Alabama, Georgia, and Florida in the 1980s and 1990s, and prolonged drought in the southeastern US during this same time period, competition between the three states for scarce Chattahoochee River water has blown up into a tri-state "water war." At the top of the Chattahoochee River basin system of dams and reservoirs is found the Buford Dam and Lanier Reservoir Project. This project was constructed in the 1950s for the original primary purposes of hydropower, flood control, and navigation. Recreation, wildlife habitat, and drinking water supply have also become important uses of Lanier Reservoir over the years.

Metropolitan Atlanta has been withdrawing water from Lanier Reservoir for municipal drinking water for many years and the reservoir is now metro Atlanta's primary source of drinking water. The reservoir shoreline has also been heavily developed for recreation including private lake residences, commercial marinas, and public parks and boat ramps. People in the state of Georgia who use Lanier Reservoir for outdoor recreation and drinking water obviously want the US Army Corps of Engineers to keep as much water in the reservoir as possible. However, there are of course trade-offs and again "no such thing as a free lunch!" Keeping more water in the reservoir may impede downstream benefits of Chattahoochee River water to Alabama and Florida, especially during times of drought. Thus, it is no surprise that Alabama and Florida generally oppose reservoir management actions which would keep more water in the reservoir at the expense of their citizens' uses of Chattahoochee River water for economic development, recreation, and environmental purposes.

Since the 1990s, Georgia, Florida, and Alabama have been engaging in legal and administrative battles over the allocation of Chattahoochee River water in a classic struggle involving federal, state, and local interests. Although the federal government through the US Army Corps of Engineers controls the system of dams and reservoir on the Chattahoochee River as can basically do what it wants (within legal bounds), the states do play a role in how the system is managed. For example, the governors and congressional delegations of each of the three states over the years have tried various ways of putting pressure on the US Army Corps of Engineers to change management of the system in ways favoring their home state's interests. The federal government, in turn, has encouraged the three states to get together and come up with a mutually agreed-upon plan or compact for managing the system and allocating scarce water supplies. As this book is being completed in 2010, these efforts have failed to resolve the long-standing tri-state "water war."

Recently, the "water war" dispute has been litigated in federal court where most state disputes over water and water rights seem to end up. In July 2009 a federal judge ruled in favor of Alabama and Florida, which argued that metro Atlanta, Georgia was illegally withdrawing municipal drinking water from Lanier Reservoir. The judge ruled that metro Atlanta's massive withdrawals are illegal and inconsistent with the original congressionally designated purposes of the Buford Dam and Lanier Reservoir Project. The judge allowed Georgia three years to get congressional approval for a change in the designated purposes of the Project or else cease all municipal drinking water withdrawals except for two relatively small cities in the northern metro Atlanta area that were originally allowed to use Lanier Reservoir for municipal drinking water supplies. Such draconian action would cause severe drinking water supply problems for metro Atlanta – thus, we can be sure that the Georgia congressional delegation backed by the Georgia Governor will be working overtime trying to change the official designated purposes of the Buford Dam and Lanier Reservoir Project. We can also be sure that the Alabama and Florida congressional delegations backed by the governors of these states will be working equally hard to protect their home states' interests.

Citizen roles

The complex institutional procedures through which new federal water resources projects are proposed and built, and changes in the operation of existing federal projects are proposed and carried out, provide citizen access at many different points to federal and state governments and to the legislative, administrative, and judicial processes. Legislation implemented in the 1970s, especially the National Environmental Policy Act and the 1973 amendments to the Endangered Species Act, has expanded the opportunities for citizen input into administrative processes and for citizen suits. The net impact of this legislation has been to broaden the avenues available to project opponents, relative to those for project proponents.

Throughout this discussion of the institutional arrangements through which water resource projects are implemented, reference to citizen roles has consistently been made in terms of "traditional clientele groups," "project components," and "project opponents." These groups, it was implicitly assumed, are for the most part centered in the project region and therefore most likely to experience directly the beneficial and adverse impacts of the Project or Policy Proposal, if implemented.

There is a much larger group of citizens, the taxpayers of the United States, who have an interest in the Project or Policy Proposal: most of them can expect to contribute to the Proposal's costs but not to enjoy its benefits directly. However, this group is large and diffuse, and the contribution of each individual toward the Proposal's costs is likely to be very small. Thus, there is a sense in which sound decision-making with respect to the Proposal is a non-exclusive good for the general taxpayer, who would gain little direct and exclusive benefit from active participation in the decision-making process. On the other hand, the beneficial and adverse impacts on citizens in the project region may be strictly exclusive or, at least, shared among a group much smaller than the group of nationwide taxpayers.

If this is a reasonable statement concerning individuals, it will be reflected in the behavior of their congressional representatives. The implementation of a water resources Project or Policy Proposal that enjoys local support in a congressperson's district will be a non-exclusive good for the remaining members of the US House of Representatives. For these reasons, it is widely believed that the existing institutional arrangements for the implementation of water project proposals, whose impacts are localized but whose costs are shared throughout the nation, result in an inefficiently large aggregate investment, not only of capital but also of environmental resources, in such projects.

The growing awareness of this phenomenon may be responsible for the apparent increase in the vigor and effectiveness of groups seeking to influence how existing federal water projects are managed and whether or not new projects are approved. In addition, it is possible that as time passes and the more desirable water project and policy proposals are implemented, the menu of remaining proposals awaiting authorization and implementation will become less attractive. For example, after extensive dam building in any region of the US or world, dam building must necessarily become a declining industry as the marginal dam on the marginal tributary of the marginal river moves closer and closer to authorization.

In some cases the costs of a new water project or a change in the operation of an existing project may impose considerable costs on a relatively small group, whereas the benefits are spread over a relatively larger group. In this case, those people bearing the costs have much incentive to devote time, effort, and money to change the water project or policy proposal in their favor. For example, as discussed above, if the congressionally designated uses of the Buford Dam and Lanier Reservoir Project are not changed in the next three years, the metro Atlanta region in the State of Georgia stands to lose its major source of drinking water which will impose considerable costs on metro Atlanta businesses and citizens. Benefits of reducing metro Atlanta water withdrawals from Lanier Reservoir will be spread out over a relatively larger group of people, some in Georgia, but mostly in the states of Alabama and Florida and the US nation as a whole (for example, wildlife habitat benefits which accrue to the nation as a whole). Because of the looming social and economic costs associated with losing access to Lanier Reservoir for drinking water supplies, metro Atlanta businesses and citizens can be expected to be heavily involved in the effort to lobby and influence Congress to change the designated purposes of the Buford Dam and Lanier Reservoir Project.

Questions for discussion

1. Under what conditions would "average cost pricing" and "marginal cost pricing" of water be appropriate?
2. Do you think water markets are a good way of pricing and allocating water? Why or why not?
3. Do you think that environmental regulations with respect to "impingement and entrainment" place unnecessary financial burdens on utility companies which operate thermoelectric power plants? Why or why not?
4. Would you support a proposal to create a separate agency to make economics evaluations of proposed federal water projects? Why or why not?
5. Would you expect the proposal in Question 4 to be warmly received in Congress? Why or why not?
6. How much water do you think the metropolitan Atlanta area should be allowed to withdraw from Lanier Reservoir for drinking water? Be specific in your answer about withdrawal amounts and justify your answer from economic, environmental, and ethical perspectives.

Notes

1. Does living underwater sound far-fetched? Maybe not considering that in 2007 marine biologist Lloyd Godson lived for two weeks underwater in what has been deemed the first self-sufficient, self-sustaining underwater human habitat. This experiment in underwater living was sponsored by Australian Geographic.
2. A comprehensive review of studies which have estimated empirical water demand functions for residential households is provided by Fernando Arbues, Maria Angeles Garcia-Valinas, and Roberto Martinez-Espineira (2003), "Estimation of Residential Water Demand: A State-of-the-Art Review," *Journal of Socio-Economics* **32**: 81–102.
3. Yvonee Levy (1982), "Pricing Federal Irrigation Water: A California Case Study," *Federal Reserve Bank of San Francisco Economic Review* Spring: 35–55.
4. Levy, "Pricing Federal Irrigation Water," op. cit.
5. For a thorough review of water markets in the western US, see Thomas C. Brown (2006), "Trends in Water Market Activity and Price in the Western United States," *Water Resources Research* **42**, W09402.

6.   A classic example is the case of the Tellico Dam and Reservoir Project which was proposed by the Tennessee Valley Authority for the Little Tennessee River in the American South. Opponents successfully used the National Environmental Policy Act (NEPA), the Endangered Species Act, and the need to protect the endangered snail darter fish to block this project for a time. Eventually, the Tennessee congressional delegation (primarily former Senator Howard Baker) used the budget appropriations process to force construction funding despite endangered species concerns, and construction was completed in 1979. From today's perspective, there is little that is uplifting about this saga: many of the benefits projected for Lake Tellico failed to materialize, raising questions about the justification of the project; and the snail darter was eventually found in other streams in the region, raising questions about the use of the Endangered Species Act in opposition to the project.

7.   Major engineering and construction works continue, however, for river modification and lock-and-dam projects to promote navigation, but that is another story.

8.   For example, when conducting benefit–cost analyses of water projects and policies, federal water resources agencies still draw upon guidelines set up by the US Water Resources Council (1973), "Water and Related Land Resources: Establishment of Principles and Standards for Planning," *Federal Register* **38** (174), III (September 10): 4.

9.   The National Environmental Policy Act of 1969 is more commonly known as just the National Environmental Policy Act or NEPA.

10.   The specific EIA/EIS process the Agency must follow may change over time and each Agency may provide its own instructions to their employees in how to comply with the NEPA and the EIA/EIS process. The interested reader should do a web search for the EIA/EIS guidelines and formats used by a particular Agency (e.g., US Army Corps of Engineers, US Bureau of Reclamation, Tennessee Valley Authority).

11.   See Fred J. Hitzhusen (ed.) (2007), *Economic Valuation of River Systems*, Cheltenham, UK and Northampton, MA, USA: Edward Elgar Publishing.

Suggested reading: classic and contemporary

Baumol, W.J. (1977), "On the Proper Cost Tests for Natural Monopoly in a Multiproduct Industry," *American Economic Review* **67** (5): 809–22.

Dalhuisen, J.M., R.J.G.M. Florax, H.L.F. de Groot, and P. Nijkamp (2003), "Price and Income Elasticities of Residential Water Demand: A Meta-Analysis," *Land Economics* **79** (2): 292–308.

Griffin, R.C. (2001), "Effective Water Pricing," *Journal of the American Water Resource Association* **37** (5): 1335–47.

Johansson, R.C., Y. Tsur, T.L. Roe, R. Doukkali, and A. Dinar (2002), "Pricing Irrigation Water: A Review of Theory and Practice," *Water Policy* **4**: 173–99.

Rogers, P., R. de Silva, and R. Bhatia (2002), "Water is an Economic Good: How to Use Prices to Promote Equity, Efficiency and Sustainability," *Water Policy* **4**: 1–17.

PART VII

ENVIRONMENTAL ETHICS, RESOURCE CONSERVATION AND SUSTAINABILITY, AND THE FUTURE

19 Understanding sustainability: what can economics tell us about using and managing resources in a sustainable manner?

Whatever responsibilities economics and other scientific disciplines have for attaining sustainable development derive in large part from the responsibilities of society for sustainability. If society has no particular responsibilities in this direction, it is hard to see why scientists should be concerned. Likewise, society would bear no particular responsibility for sustainability if it were reasonably certain that the interworkings of the economic and ecologic systems assure sustainability. So, we must deal with the way the world works, as well as with ethical foundations, if we are to make progress in delineating the contribution of economics to sustainability. Economics does not have all the answers; it cannot map the prospects for sustainability with any assurance. But economic models can relate, in a fairly rigorous way, assumptions about the nature of the world and their consequences for sustainability. In this way, economics isolates the crucial questions, whose answers determine sustainability prospects. Economists also cannot escape dealing with ethical responsibilities when we participate in public discourse about sustainability.

Sustaining human welfare

One way to frame the sustainability question is to consider the prospects for sustaining human welfare through many generations. The Brundtland Commission defined sustainability as: "meeting the needs of the present without compromising the ability of future generations to meet their own needs."[1] This definition would surely be satisfied by any arrangement that succeeds in maintaining welfare for the indefinite future. By considering a sequence of highly abstract models, we can start to think systematically about sustainability prospects.

Model 1: pure bread-eating

Assume people consume only bread and the planet is a giant loaf. There are no production processes, and bread uneaten in a particular period neither grows nor deteriorates; it just sits there. The problem that must be solved is the optimal depletion of an endowment (see Chapter 7). Such models generate only one robust result: a society that discounts the value of future consumption will choose a consumption path declining with time. Within one's own life, such a choice might be termed myopic. In a multigenerational context, such selfish behavior can be supported only by a positional dictatorship of the present generation.[2]

From the perspective of sustainability, however, none of this is very interesting: a bread-eating universe is inherently unsustainable, and the world comes eventually to a bad end no matter how one slices the bread among generations. Of course, if society can be persuaded to eke out the endowment more frugally, more people and more generations can be supported until the eventual collapse. But it is not clear that a world in which more members of more generations barely subsist is more desirable ethically than one in which fewer members of fewer generations live decently well until the inevitable collapse.

Model 2: bread production and consumption

Bread (Y) is produced by combining a natural resource (D), capital (K), and labor (L). Following the early seminal work on sustainability by Solow, assume per capita consumption possibilities in each generation are governed by $Y_t = e^{(a-g)t} f(D_t, K_t)$ where Y, D, and K are in per capita terms, t denotes the generations, a is technological progress, and g is the growth rate of the human population.[3] Sustainability prospects now depend on the initial endowments of D and K, the regeneration rate of D, the substitutability of D and K, and the rates of population growth and technological progress.

Solow obtained an optimistic conclusion with the assumptions that D is a non-regenerating resource (e.g., a mineral), and D and K are perfect substitutes. In that case, human welfare is sustainable even as D approaches exhaustion, so long as technological progress and K accumulation are sufficient to compensate for population growth and declining D.

Abstract as it is, this model provides the foundation for conventional sustainability tenets found in the economic literature: the weak sustainability criterion, the Hartwick rule, and green accounting. Weak sustainability is attained when the stock of D and K (aggregated) per capita is maintained. The Hartwick rule requires that the scarcity rents from natural resource depletion be reinvested in reproducible capital, a sufficient condition for maintaining production and welfare so long as $a \geq g$.[4] An ideal system of green accounts would tell society whether it is satisfying the Hartwick rule.

Because this model generates one of the contending sets of sustainability policy prescriptions, it is important to look at its explicit and implicit assumptions. Solow grants special status to natural resources by assuming exhaustibility, but immediately revokes it by assuming perfect substitution of K for D; in the end, natural resources are nothing special in this model. Looking between the lines, welfare is maintained not just as K is substituted for D but also as the composition of both D and K change over time. Particulars do not matter so long as the aggregates are maintained. The goal of maintaining Y, aggregate consumption, has a couple of implications that deserve exposure. First, aggregation of Y permits a wide range of substitutions in consumption; particulars do not matter, so long as aggregate consumption maintains welfare. Second, people are assumed to be mobile, geographically and occupationally. Exhaustion of local natural resources does not matter, so long as the stock of natural and reproducible capital, aggregated, is maintained at the global level.

Challenges to Models 1 and 2

Natural resources and limits of substitution   Models 1 and 2 discussed above delineate the catastrophist and cornucopian extremes in the sustainability debate first discussed in this book in Chapter 3. Catastrophists call for vastly reduced per capita consumption of natural resources, and often identify positive discount rates as the fundamental evil that leads present generations (in wealthy countries) to live well at the expense of the future generations. Cornucopians place their faith in technology, substitution, and the human response to price signals that will induce and direct both. For the latter group, the future may be very different, but it will surely be better. For the former group, the future almost always looks bleak.

A major source of contention between catastrophists and cornucopians concerns the substitutability of *D* and *K*. Catastrophists see particular natural resources as essential to production – to use for raw materials or waste assimilation. Failure to conserve such resources would doom future human societies. Cornucopians see *D* and *K* as broadly substitutable, technology as capable of increasing the substitutability of *D* and *K*, and markets as self-regulating systems that respond to increasing scarcity with incentives for both conservation and technological innovation.

The problem of very long time horizons   In dealing with resource allocation problems that involve several consecutive time periods and in which actions taken in a given time period will influence the opportunity sets in later time periods, traditional economic theory assigns a crucial role to *r*, the rate of interest. It generally concludes that intertemporal efficiency requires that *r* = rate of time preference (*RTP*) = marginal efficiency of investment (*MEI*) and that the empirical magnitude of the social discount rate is best determined through judicious observation of market interest rates and their manipulation to correct obvious sources of the failure of market interest rates to reflect the social opportunity cost of capital (see Chapter 7). Yet market interest rates are determined in the market for capital investments that vary in duration from overnight to periods of seldom more than 20 to 40 years. Revenues accruing only two or three generations hence are reduced to trivial amounts when their present value is determined using social discount rates derived from market interest rates.

Some of the most serious and most intractable difficulties confronting society as it wrestles with intertemporal resource allocation problems are those in which the relevant time horizon is much more than a few years or decades. The half-life of certain kinds of nuclear residues is measured in the thousands of years. When a mineral deposit is entirely exhausted, it cannot be replaced in time periods of less than geological eras (which are measured in the millions and billions of years). It is reasonable to assume that when a living species becomes extinct, it is gone forever. More generally, the desire of human societies and civilizations to perpetuate themselves and their culture into the indefinite future is not easily analyzed with an economic theory that thinks in terms of years, or decades, at most.

Model 3: intergenerational markets

In this section, a model developed by Farmer and Randall[5] to address concerns related to these key issues is summarized. In this model, a sigmoid natural resource regeneration function is introduced. Sigmoid regeneration functions enjoy some support among biologists and have interesting implications for sustainability. In place of Solow's perfect *D–K* substitution, the model employs production functions that permit a broad range of substitutability but nevertheless penalize extreme factor specialization; such formulations treat natural resources as special without imposing unduly pessimistic technological expectations. So, natural resource regeneration and *D–K* substitution can be addressed with simple amendments to standard models. However, the issue of discounting and intergenerational equity can be understood only by breaking sharply with standard models.

In Models 1 and 2 discussed above, endowments are passed to future generations at the whim of the present. In the pure bread-eating model, the discount rate is chosen dictatorially by the present. In standard growth models (e.g., Model 2) the present bequeaths D and K to the future. In both cases, the future is dependent on the goodwill of the present, and policy prescriptions tend to involve a good deal of exhorting present generations to be nice to future generations. A very different picture emerges when intergenerational markets are more fully characterized and considered as in the models and approaches discussed below.

Assume each individual lives for three periods (young, middle-aged, and retired). At any given moment, three generations coexist. At the end of each period, each generation moves up one place: the retired die, the middle-aged retire, the young become middle-aged, and a new generation of young is born. The young and middle-aged consume bread and produce it by combining D, K and L. The retired just consume. The generations are differently endowed: the young start out with plenty of L, but no D and K; while the middle-aged have acquired D and K. The young are able to bid D and K away from the middle-aged; that is, they borrow K and buy D. The middle-aged willingly enter into these arrangements because next period, when they retire, they will be able to live on repaid principal and earned interest. Finally, assume individuals seek to equalize consumption in each period; that is, they are neither myopic nor selfishly dictatorial toward the unborn.

The model starts with initial endowments of D and K, and as the generations trade with each other and succeed each other, resource allocation, consumption, and prices are determined endogenously. Positive discount rates emerge endogenously in this model. Prospects for future welfare depend on what is assumed about initial endowments, the substitutability of D and K, and the regeneration of D. A considerable range of outcomes is possible: welfare may be increasing or decreasing over time; and, despite market forces that tend to stabilize the resource situation, resource crises may occur. The possibility of declining future welfare and resource crises may motivate policy interventions. The insights from this model enable us to critique several rather standard prescriptions for sustainability.

Discounting is not the problem, and discount rate repression is not the solution   In a pure bread-eating model, there is some validity to the notion that a society which discounts future production and costs *ipso facto* sacrifices future welfare, and therefore violates reasonable requirements for intergenerational equity. However, positive interest rates emerge endogenously as optimal in this model. The individuals in this model are not myopic – they seek to equalize consumption across the three life stages. So, the positive interest rates must be driven by something other than myopia. They arise because capital is scarce and productive, and the young have to buy (that is, borrow) it.

It might be tempting to blame declining welfare paths (in the particular cases where they emerge) on positive discount rates, and to prescribe discount rate repression in order to increase future welfare. But that would be the wrong diagnosis and the wrong prescription: regardless of whether the consumption path is increasing or decreasing, a policy of interest rate repression would only make things worse for the future. Why?

Because *K* matters: we could fail the future in not one but two ways – failing to save enough *D* and failing to save enough *K*.

Furthermore, this result has nothing to do with any positional dictatorship of the present generations. Unborn future generations would prefer that those living now face incentives to save, and to select only those investments that pass a net present value test.

Entitling future generations will help them less than one might think   A unique proposal for solving the sustainability problem is an appealingly simple yet effective instrument: a reassignment of property rights to future generations.[6] This approach would be effective: a future generation protected by property rights would have veto power over earlier-generation actions that might threaten its welfare. It would also be relatively simple in concept. The property rights reassignment to the future would be once and for all (although it would require a momentous public decision actually to make such a change), and enforcement of the reassigned property rights would proceed routinely, as does current enforcement of currently assigned property rights. As with the discount rate repression proposal, this proposal can be justified with models that do not fully characterize intergenerational trading opportunities.[7] With fully characterized intergenerational trade, however, it can be shown that property rights assignment to the future is unlikely to help and likely to harm the future itself.[8]

A bottom line on the rate of discount[9]

Discounting is, or should be, motivated by the productivity of capital – its purpose is to provide optimal incentives for saving and for allocating scarce capital efficiently. Discounting of utility itself makes little sense but, with productive capital, consumption will be discounted to reflect the reward for saving and investment. It follows that the appropriate rate of social discount is that rate that reflects the productivity of society. The question that remains is whether the social discount rate should reflect productivity of capital at the margin or for society as a whole – this is an important practical consideration because we might think in terms of about 3 or 4 percent (real) for the marginal productivity of capital and perhaps 2 percent for the long-run productivity of the whole economy. The choice of real social discount rate should reflect the size and timescale of the project under evaluation. For small projects with modest time horizons, *r* should reflect the marginal efficiency of capital. For large projects and very long time-horizons, *r* should reflect the real growth rate of the economy. In today's economy, these principles bound *r* within a quite narrow range of 3 to 4 percent real for small investment projects and 2 per cent real for policies with large and very long-term impacts.

Challenges to sustainability models

Risk and uncertainty

The future is inherently uncertain. This uncertainty is exacerbated when the period under consideration spans many generations into the future and when our ability to develop and implement new technologies outstrips our capacity to predict, monitor, and mitigate the adverse effects of those technologies.

When considering the long-term future, several types of uncertainty are significant.

Technological uncertainty is the lack of knowledge of the adverse impacts of new technologies (which may encourage their premature implementation) and the inability to foresee the new technologies that will be developed in the future. As an example of this latter kind of technological uncertainty, consider technologies that would permit more readily available resources to substitute for those exhaustible resources whose supplies are dwindling. Excessive optimism about the development of new technology will encourage excessively high rates of extraction of the exhaustible resource and its premature exhaustion, which would impose a high cost on future generations. On the other hand, excessively pessimistic expectations about future technology will result in extraction rates of exhaustible resources that are inefficiently low.

An additional type of technological uncertainty concerns the development of resource-using technologies. As discussed in Chapter 3, a resource was defined as something that is useful and valuable in the condition in which we find it in the environment. Thus technological developments may find valuable uses for things not currently considered valuable from an economic perspective, and new and highly valuable uses for those resources that are currently low-valued. For example, human history has been marked by the discovery of new medicinal uses for chemical compounds found in particular biological species – a process that continues to this day and can be expected to continue in the future. This is one of the reasons for the concern with the preservation of endangered species in order to maintain the world's gene pool (the reservoir of global genetic diversity): the possibility that by permitting the extinction of species that currently seem worthless, yet-to-be-discovered uses (medicinal and other) may be forever foreclosed.

The concept of a resource as something with economic value because it is useful and scarce suggests that in addition to technological uncertainty, demand uncertainty is a serious concern. The tastes and preferences of individuals in future generations may differ from those of current generations. In addition, it is not easy to predict the populations and per capita incomes of future generations. For these reasons, there is substantial uncertainty as to how future changes in patterns of demand will influence future scarcity relationships. Scarcity, of course, is influenced by both demand and supply conditions, and technology influences demand as well as supply. Technology introduces new commodities and amenities into opportunity sets, and an effective demand for those new commodities and amenities cannot arise until they exist.

Irreversibility

Many kinds of decision problems give the decision-maker the comfort and security of knowing that should they make in this time period a decision they later regret, they can minimize their losses over the long haul by changing direction, at some cost, in a future time period. Many of the items in today's opportunity set, even if not selected today, will remain in future opportunity sets. But there are some items that, if not selected from today's opportunity set, will be eliminated from future opportunity sets. The decision to eliminate these items from today's choice bundle is irreversible.

Although it offers a convenient shorthand to speak dichotomously of decisions as being either reversible or irreversible, such language is imprecise. The second law of thermodynamics indicates that the reversible–irreversible dichotomy is really a continuum and that the end points on that continuum will seldom be observed. No choice is reversible at zero cost, and many choices called irreversible may be reversed at a less than infinite cost. Nevertheless, the idea of irreversibility is useful because it draws our attention to those choices that can be reversed only at an extremely high cost.

The extinction of a biological species is in this sense irreversible. So is the creation, through genetic manipulation, of some new destructive (e.g., disease-causing) organism that proves to be nearly indestructible. Similarly, the generation of hazardous wastes (e.g., nuclear wastes and also various kinds of toxic synthetic chemicals) is irreversible: future generations may find effective ways of isolating these wastes and rendering them harmless, but they will always be obliged to bear the costs of so doing. The large-scale destruction of geological, hydrological, and ecological systems is also irreversible in the pragmatic sense in which we have been using that word. The vanishing wilderness is only expensively recreated. If a decision were made to divert that piece of real estate known as the Grand Canyon to some entirely different use, thereby effectively eliminating the Grand Canyon as we know it, its recreation in some later time period would be extremely, if not prohibitively, expensive.

Economics is all but silent when confronted with the need to analyze a decision involving, say, a truly catastrophic outcome with a very low probability at some future time. In recent years, economists have suggested several tentative approaches to the analysis of decision problems involving very long time horizons, extreme uncertainty, and/or irreversibility.

Economists' responses to these challenges

Extensions of the benefit–cost approach   Working with the traditional present value, or benefit–cost approach, some natural resource and environmental economists have attempted to expand or, if you will, perfect that approach. In application, the benefit–cost approach has typically resulted in the quantification and valuation (and, therefore, the explicit economic consideration) of only those benefit and cost items that are readily quantified and valued. In the last several decades, considerable progress has been made in incorporating benefits and costs associated with "non-market" goods and amenities (that is, those that are not marketed because of externality, indivisibility in consumption, and non-exclusiveness problems, individually or in some combination) into the quantitative benefit–cost analysis framework. This kind of approach has recently been extended to the valuation of fears, concerns, and sentiments that individuals in the current generation may have for the future. Care is taken to ensure that evidence of the growing demand for recreational and aesthetic amenities and for health and personal safety is recognized in benefit–cost analyses. Benefit–cost analysis has been extended to handle preservation issues, for example, by focusing on the total economic value of the environmental resource at issue.

Total economic value, as discussed in Chapter 13, includes use value and passive use value (or non-use value). In the context of the discussion in this chapter regarding sustainability, it is helpful to break use value into the following four components:

1.   Current use value that is generated by current use.
2.   Future use value that is expected to be generated by use in the future.

The distinction between current and future use value is not conceptually important but has implications for measurement: past and current use is *ex post* and (for some uses) is routinely recorded and available as secondary data, whereas future use is *ex ante* and probabilistic and subject to change as conditions change in unexpected ways. Future use must be projected from past use or inferred from, for example, survey data stating the *ex ante* intentions of the identifiable user population. The uncertainty of future use leads to two kinds of option values:

3. (Ordinary) option value. When risk attends the demand for the future use and/or the future availability of an environmental resource, risk-averse users may apply risk premiums and discounts. For example, a certain future demander facing an uncertain supply may rationally pay a premium to secure an option that guarantees future supply, hence the concept of option value. The problem is that uncertainty may cut both ways: a risk-averse and uncertain demander may expect a discount (not a premium) to compensate for the risk that a purchased option may not be used. In general, then, option value may be positive or negative.
4. Quasi-option value. If development is irreversible (for example, preservation in period 1 allows the choice of preservation or development in period 2, but development in period 1 preordains development in period 2) and one expects new information about the value of preservation to emerge after period 1 but before the second-period decision must be made, quasi-option value is positive. It is essentially the value of the emerging information conditioned on having made the first-period choice (preservation, in this case) that maximizes the second-period array of alternatives.

The concept of "real options" generalizes the value of keeping options open – the value of waiting, including the value of any learning that may occur while we wait – and thus includes ordinary option value and quasi-option value.[10] Real options theory adapts the theory and methods of valuing financial options to the real options case. One implication of real options theory is that any sunk cost or stranded investment introduces irreversibility. The real options concept of irreversibility parallels the thermodynamic concept, and highlights the temporal dimension of opportunity costs – if we do A there will be some costs sunk and some non-salvageable resources stranded if we then switch to B. Irreversibility in real options theory is continuous – it is just a cost, and some costs are greater than others – which makes sense. The irreversibility that concerns environmentalists most lies toward the high end of the cost continuum, where the post-change costs of reversion to the baseline state are prohibitively high.

One implication of real options theory is that the standard tools of risk management – insurance, self-insurance, and self-protection – may be conceptualized as purchasing real options to avoid uncertain and perhaps unlikely catastrophic harm. Of course, in the end, the real option is purchased if and only if the expected benefits (perhaps adjusted for the desired degree of risk aversion) exceed the costs.

As discussed in Chapter 13, passive use values include existence value which is derived from the knowledge that the environmental resource continues to exist. Individuals with an understanding and appreciation of natural systems and the important role that diversity plays in those systems may derive utility from the mere knowledge that those systems exist intact. The disappearance of a natural environment or the extinction of an individual species may, therefore, cause disutility for an individual who has never been observed "using" those natural resources. This utility from existence, or disutility from extinction or disappearance, provides the source of existence value. Because existence values are independent of current active use, expected future use, and the avoidance of risks related to future use, they must be derived from some form of caring. Caring can be directed to other people who may use or care about the biotic resource (the philanthropic motive), future generations who may use or care about the resource (the bequest motive), or to the biotic resource itself.

The total economic value approach to benefit–cost analysis recognizes all these various sources of value when conservation, preservation, and sustainability decisions are involved. There is a serious attempt to measure each or, alternatively, to estimate the total economic value directly. Because future use values and options, quasi-option, and passive use values may be problematical, it is likely that some components of the total economic value of the preservation option may be omitted or underestimated. At this point, proponents of the benefit–cost approach usually counsel that (in close decisions) the benefit of the doubt be extended to the preservation option.

A safe minimum standard of conservation   The concept of the safe minimum standard (SMS) was developed to analyze problems concerning endangered species but, it seems, could be adapted to many problems involving very long time horizons, massive uncertainty, and/or irreversibility. The SMS concept represents a partial retreat from the benefit–cost framework. It recognizes that regardless of the conceptual validity of the benefit–cost framework, it is, in application, often incomplete. Thus the SMS concept offers a decision criterion that is admittedly incomplete but that has the virtue of claiming no more completeness than it can deliver (a virtue that is not always apparent in applied benefit–cost analyses). The safe minimum standard of preservation for a given species is identified in terms of a population just large enough to ensure survival of the species; thus, the SMS is set just a little higher than the extinction threshold for a species discussed in Chapter 15.

In other words, the SMS is a level of conservation sufficiently high to reduce the probability of extinction (or irreversible loss) to a very low level. The expected costs of maintaining the SMS are then estimated, usually in terms of the present value of economic opportunities that would be forgone. Although there is often no direct, dollar for dollar, comparison of the economic value of maintaining the SMS versus the value of economic opportunities thus forgone, the decision-maker is encouraged to choose a risk-averse strategy. For any species, population should be permitted to fall below the SMS only if the value of economic opportunities forgone by maintaining the SMS is "too high" or "very high." The SMS decision criterion is clearly incomplete, but it is useful in that it draws attention to the huge and often unquantifiable uncertainties in irreversible change and to the desirability of a risk-averse decision strategy when considering such changes.

If our generic natural resource, *D*, regenerates in sigmoid fashion, it is possible that inadequate initial endowments or exogenous shocks could initiate a resource crisis from which the economy could not recover. An SMS policy would offer a direct approach, targeted to diagnosing the crisis and invoking a conservation constraint to avert it. To illustrate the principles involved, consider a simple two-period diagram (Figure 19.1).

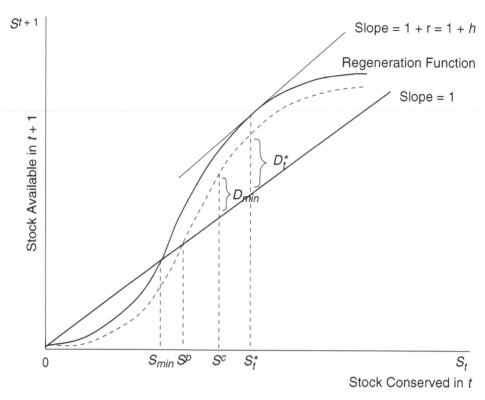

Figure 19.1   Setting the SMS

Assume *D* is renewable, that is, *D* withheld from production in one period regenerates in the next period. If S_t is the stock of *D* withheld from production in period *t*, the regeneration function traces the relationship between S_t and S_{t+1} (the amount of *D* available in the next period). In a two-period diagram, the line of slope = 1 starting from the origin is diagnostic: at points above the line, S_{t+1} exceeds S_t so that the natural resource is at least potentially sustainable; but at points below the line, the natural resource will eventually be exhausted even if none of it is used in production.

If less than S_{min} is withheld from production in each period, natural resource exhaustion is inevitable. The optimal stock to carry forward is S_t^* at which point the steady-state efficiency condition, $1 + r = 1 + h$ holds, where *r* is the marginal efficiency of capital, *h* is the marginal regeneration rate of the natural resource, and D^* may be used in production in each period. Interpreting S_{min} as the minimum standard (that is, the minimum carry-over stock to assure resource regeneration), the idea of a safe minimum standard invokes uncertainty. Assume that the regeneration function is stochastic and that its lower bound is traced by the dashed curve in Figure 19.1. If S^p, termed the safe minimum standard of preservation, is withheld from production in each period, resource exhaustion will be avoided even in the worst case with respect to resource regeneration. S^p is consistent with the classic meaning of the term safe minimum standard in the literature.[11]

S^p sustains the resource, which may satisfy some preservationists. But we have cast the issue as one of sustaining adequate consumption levels for the human population.

Assume that D_{min} is the minimum allocation of natural resources to production that is required to sustain adequate consumption. Let each time period, t, represent a generation of people. Then, any generation that uses less than D_{min} suffers extreme deprivation. S^c, termed the safe minimum standard of conservation, is the minimum stock withheld from production that will provide D_{min} for each succeeding generation; draws of D_{min} and regeneration of the stock are guaranteed.

Standard accounts of the SMS approach suggest that the SMS should be maintained unless the costs of so doing are "immoderate" or "intolerably high."[12] This escape clause recognizes that one cannot imagine a contract, freely entered and enforceable, between the present and the future that binds the present to observe the SMS. Rather, the SMS is a commitment that the present might undertake for ethical reasons. With only conscience to prevent the present from unilaterally voiding an SMS commitment, it is prudent to design an SMS policy that avoids requiring too much sacrifice on the part of any particular generation. To require consumption of less than D_{min} would clearly impose an intolerable cost on any generation.

A safe minimum standard policy capable of implementation must seek to conserve not S^p but S^c. That is, it must seek to avoid placing any present or future society in a position where it must choose between sacrificing itself and dooming subsequent societies. In practical terms a SMS policy would emphasize early warning, and early implementation of conservation policies that require only modest sacrifice on the part of each generation. Since unilateral withdrawal from any intertemporal obligation is always a possibility, conservationists have a strong interest in keeping the costs of conservation tolerably low.

Suppose particular natural resources matter   It can be argued that Model 3 takes a plausible middle ground regarding the substitutability of capital and natural resources: D and K are broadly substitutable, but extreme factor specialization is penalized. This would warn against allowing stocks of D to fall "too far." Even if one considers this middle-ground view to be a plausible broad-brush treatment, we may still worry that it omits the details, and the details are what matters. The issue here is aggregation: D is some index of aggregate natural resources, but what may really matter is particular natural resources.

Assume that people are bread-eaters, and particular natural resources are essential to the production of bread. Policy would logically be directed to sustaining these resources. One approach is to insist on sustaining D in aggregate while recognizing the fundamental distinction between renewable and exhaustible natural resources. El Serafy and Daly, among others, have proposed rules that exhaustible resources be exploited but no more rapidly than they can be replaced with renewable resources, while renewable resources are harvested at (economically) optimal sustainable rates.[13]

Barbier et al. propose a policy of compensating projects: a project involving non-sustainable exploitation of a particular natural resource in a particular place might be permitted, but only if coupled with a D-enhancing compensating project.[14] What counts as a compensating project is a difficult issue, as it is in US policies requiring compensation for damage to natural resources. Just doing something good for the environment may not really compensate, whereas "cut a tree, plant a tree" may be too stringent. Location, too, may matter. If the sustainability objective is articulated not at the global level (as we have been assuming) but locally, the compensating project would need to involve resources similar to those lost, and be located near the exploitative project.

It has been objected that these proposals are too restrictive. First, they all seek to maintain aggregate D, ignoring $D–K$ substitution possibilities. Second, the more stringent compensating projects proposals (e.g., in the extreme "cut a tree here, plant a tree here") make no allowance for mobility of people and resources or for substitutability within the categories of exhaustible and renewable resources. It makes no sense to assume that all exhaustible, and all renewable, resources are non-substitutable and equally scarce. As with a policy of discount rate repression, doing "too much" for sustainability of D will depress future welfare just as surely as doing too little will.

Although the SMS model described above uses an aggregate D, K model, we recognize that it is much more likely that the SMS will be applied to particular natural resources that exhibit substitutability and sustainability concerns. The SMS would serve as a constraint on business as usual, held in reserve until a sustainability alarm was triggered. In ordinary times, this would entail much less sacrifice of present and future welfare than would, say, a strict policy of compensating projects.

Accounting for the complexity of ecosystems   Some ecologists and more ecologically minded economists suggest that economic thinking about sustainability issues fails systematically to incorporate what ecologists know about how ecosystems work.[15] A couple of examples may serve to illustrate the point.

First, Model 3 described above and the SMS analysis (Figure 19.1) both assume sigmoid regeneration. Uncertainty is represented as a confidence band, and the more risk-averse among us can focus mainly on the lower boundary of that band. While for economists that is a considerable concession to existential uncertainty, many ecologists believe that in reality much less is known about the regeneration of natural populations. While economists seek point solutions identified by familiar tangents to regeneration curves, ecologists are more likely to examine the resiliency of the populations and to worry about what sorts of early warnings might alert us to impending regime switches.

Second, while many economists tend to discuss $D–K$ substitutability as a key question, but not literally an urgent one, ecologists are more inclined to see the limits of $D–K$ substitution as already upon us. For example, global climate change and depletion of atmospheric ozone are seen as clear cases where non-substitutable natural resources for waste assimilation are already being used beyond their capacity.

A society of bread-eaters would be well advised, the ecological economists say, to implement policies which recognize the complexity and importance of ecosystems. Such policies, for example, may emphasize the need to conserve a diversity of both renewable and non-renewable natural resources which contribute to ecosystem health. Rather than seeking to optimize, such policies may also recognize the uncertainty and unpredictability of ecosystems and the depth of human ignorance, and seek robust strategies that would do reasonably well under a wide range of conditions. Finally, such policies may promote adaptive management in which we use feedback information from economic and ecologic systems to make corrections and adjustments to keep things in reasonable balance.

The sustainability models (Models 1, 2, and 3) described above focus primarily on the economics of sustainability from a fairly standard neoclassical economics perspective. One of the limitations of this perspective, some may argue, is a failure adequately to consider ecological and ethical issues related to sustainability. We discuss some of these concerns and issues in this section.

Humans do not live by bread alone: sustaining particular ecosystems, places, and communities   In this chapter so far we have considered the implications for sustaining human welfare of various assumptions about the substitutability of reproducible capital for natural resources, the regeneration of natural resources and the structure of intergenerational financial and asset markets. But welfare has been defined quite narrowly. While we have used the bread metaphor, *Y* is actually an index of aggregate output, which implies that a broad range of substitution in consumption is permissible so long as welfare is maintained. If we combine this concept of welfare with the global level of analysis implied in sustainability Models 1, 2, and 3, we can readily imagine sweeping changes in what people consume, where they live, and how they relate to the natural environment, all without threatening the level of welfare thus defined.

Assume instead that people seek diversity in consumption, they value "natural" and "traditional" things more highly as they become rarer, they value "the natural world" for its own sake as well as for the pleasure it brings humans, and they respect place and all that it entails. Then policy would seek always to sustain human welfare and hence aggregate consumption levels. However, it would also be concerned with sustainability at the local level including the sustainability of particular habitats and ecosystems in particular places, and of particular human communities. Ecologists and economists would agree that, in general, these things matter. But they would also agree that it will be literally impossible, as well as of questionable desirability, to preserve things exactly as they are.

So, local sustainability or, as some call it, subsystem sustainability, can and often should be valued for its own sake; and policy should reflect this. In ordinary cases, however, assigning positive value does not settle the issue; the sacrifices required to guarantee subsystem sustainability may be greater than the benefits. Nevertheless, some particular species, habitats, geological formations, and human habitats may valued so highly as to be placed beyond the reach of ordinary trade-offs. Different people may well disagree as to how many and which ones should be accorded such status, leaving the issue to principled debate and/or political processes.

A sustainability case study

Many of the above concepts discussed with respect to sustainability are rather abstract. In this section we present a case study of sustainability to help explain sustainability concepts in more practical terms, and show how one region (in this case, a country) is measuring up to sustainability goals. The overall question addressed in this case study is: Is Australia on a sustainability path and how would we know?[16]

Genuine saving
One clue as to whether a country is on a sustainability path is net savings focusing on green accounting. An ideal system of green accounts would tell society whether it is satisfying the Hartwick rule.[17] Asheim and Weitzman show that growth in real net national product (where prices are deflated by a Divisia index of consumption prices) indicates

the change in welfare in the economy.[18] The implication is that negative levels of net saving reduce utility in future periods. Pezzey and Toman show that genuine saving (GS), an ideal account of net savings in a resource-using economy, provides a one-sided sustainability test in the Hartwick tradition – with negative GS, there must be negative welfare growth at any instant.[19] The opposite is not true in general – positive saving at a point in time does not indicate that future utility is everywhere non-declining. However, Hamilton and Hartwick show that positive genuine saving is a component of a feasible weak sustainability prescription.[20]

Genuine saving at any time t is the sum of the changes in stocks of each of the various kinds of natural and produced capital, each weighted by its virtual price:

$$GS_t = \sum p_{it} \cdot \Delta K_{it}, \tag{19.1}$$

where $i = (1, \ldots, n)$ is an exhaustive list of the various forms of capital with virtual prices p_i. Getting these virtual prices right matters – GS can provide a sustainability indicator only if it is calculated using the right prices. In this context, there are two dimensions to the concept of right prices: the familiar notion that observed prices should be adjusted to correct for market distortions, externalities and public goods; and the fundamental caveat that GS is a valid sustainability indicator only if it is based on sustainability prices, which can be observed only after sustainability has been achieved.[21] The K_i include gross national saving, net investment in human capital, depreciation, depletion of minerals and energy, net depletion of forests, net depletion of water resources in terms of quantity and quality), depletion of biodiversity, net pollution damage (including damage from greenhouse gases), and net degradation of soil.

Australia's adjusted net savings situation

There is a lot to be learned by consulting an ideal account of Australia's genuine savings. The World Bank has attempted to compile and maintain GS accounts for a broad array of countries.[22] The result is a downloadable spreadsheet of adjusted net savings (ANS) for 212 countries, with annual entries beginning in 1970 for many of them.[23]

Adjusted net savings includes gross national savings, educational expenditures, depreciation, mineral depletion, energy depletion, and damage from carbon dioxide and fine particulate emissions. It falls short of an ideal account of GS in several respects: educational expenditures is an unsatisfactory proxy for net investment in human capital; damage from CO_2 and fine particulate emissions captures only two among many categories of pollution damage; net forest depletion data are missing for most countries (including Australia); and there is no attempt to account for depletion of water, biodiversity, and soil.[24] Nevertheless, it is the best available accounting of GS in a form that facilitates cross-country comparisons.

For Australia (Figure 19.2), we see a secular decline in ANS since 1971, leveling out and perhaps recovering a little since 1990. ANS has followed roughly the pattern of gross national savings, but has been influenced also by some volatility in resource and environmental depletion (RED). Energy depletion and mineral depletion account for the bulk of RED (Figure 19.3), and show greater volatility than emissions (CO_2 and fine particulates).[25] The pattern of declining ANS in the last third of the twentieth century seems typical of wealthy countries, but for most of this period Australia leads a comparison

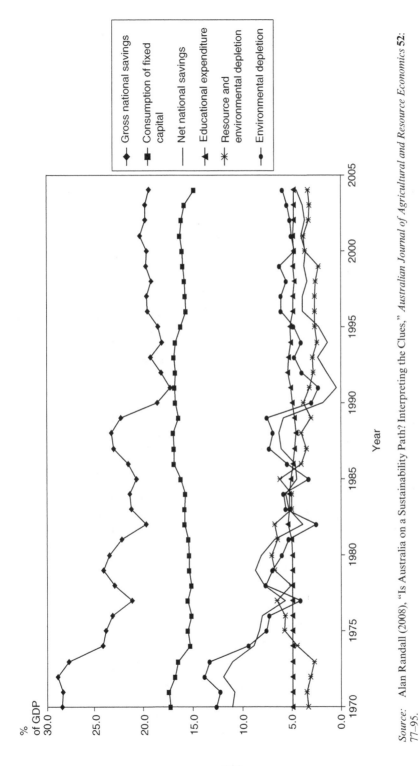

Source: Alan Randall (2008), "Is Australia on a Sustainability Path? Interpreting the Clues," *Australian Journal of Agricultural and Resource Economics* **52**: 77–95.

Figure 19.2   Composition of adjusted net savings, Australia, 1970–2004

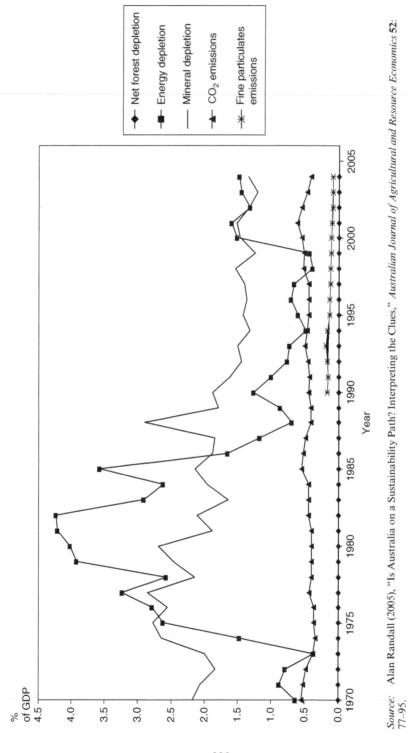

Source: Alan Randall (2005), "Is Australia on a Sustainability Path? Interpreting the Clues," *Australian Journal of Agricultural and Resource Economics* **52**: 77–95.

Figure 19.3   Composition of resource and environmental depletion, Australia, 1970–2004

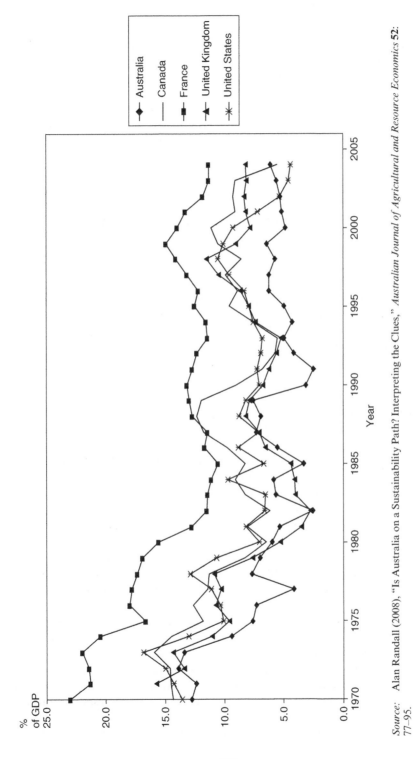

Figure 19.4 Adjusted net savings, selected OECD countries, 1970–2004

group that includes France, Canada, the United States, and the United Kingdom, in the extent of its relative decline (Figure 19.4).

Because ANS is in practice an imperfect sustainability indicator, this evidence of declining adjusted net saving should be interpreted cautiously. Nevertheless, it may be a warning signal, because ANS predicts future welfare.[26] Specifically, ANS in 1980 is positively correlated with the present value of changes in gross domestic product from 1980 to 2000, for a broad cross-section of countries. Ferreira and Vincent note that the correlation is better for non-OECD (Organisation for Economic Co-operation and Development) countries, and the fit improves as better measures of GS are tested.[27]

There is a strong negative correlation between dependency on exhaustible resources and adjusted net saving, to the extent that highly resource-dependent countries tend to have negative ANS.[28] If mineral- and energy-dependent economies were diligently investing their rents in other types of capital, as the Hartwick rule prescribes, then there should be no apparent link between resource dependence and genuine saving. Instead the evidence suggests a tendency to consume resource rents that increases with resource dependence.

Consider a more diverse comparison group that includes a rapidly growing lower-middle-income country (China), a middle-income country with a substantial oil extraction sector (Venezuela), and Saudi Arabia, which is highly dependent on oil extraction (Figure 19.5). To accommodate these countries, the range of the ANS axis has to be expanded. China has maintained ANS rates above 20 percent since 1993 and Saudi Arabia has experienced negative ANS in all but one year, with several observations below −30 percent. Venezuela, while exhibiting substantial volatility, has had mostly negative ANS since 1979.

Human, social, and institutional capital   The ANS accounts exhibit perhaps their greatest weakness in their treatment of intangible (that is, human, social, and institutional) capital, which they proxy by educational expenditures, a variable that performs poorly, as noted above. Contrast this with the World Bank's accounting of national wealth.[29] The characteristic pattern in wealthy countries is that intangible wealth accounts for more than 80 percent, and natural wealth less than 5 percent, of all wealth.[30] It seems scarcely credible that educational expenditures provide an adequate account of net additions to this vast stock of intangible capital. Yet, we know how important intangible capital is – accounting for technological change (which is generated by intangible capital) moved an account of Scotland's GS from an unsustainable reading to the sustainable range.[31]

France, the United Kingdom, and the United States exhibit the characteristic pattern of wealthy countries: intangible capital exceeds 80 percent of all capital, while natural capital accounts for less than 5 percent (Figure 19.6). Australia and Canada are more natural resource dependent than most wealthy countries, but natural capital is still less than 10 percent of all capital. Along with much lower wealth per capita, we see much lower proportions of intangible capital in China, Iran, and Venezuela.[32] The World Bank has quantified Australia's natural capital, in terms of subsoil assets (mainly minerals) which account for 47.5 percent of natural capital, farmland (the sum of cropland and pastureland) which accounts for 41.2 percent, and timber resources, non-timber forest resources, and protected areas, which account for the remainder. Unfortunately for our purposes, annual changes in these capital stocks are not captured in the ANS accounts.

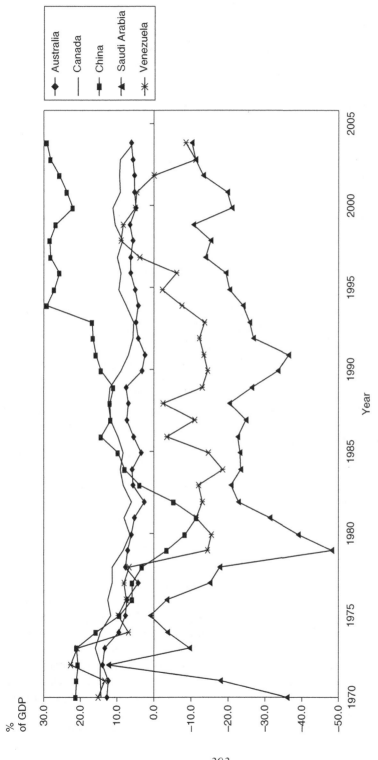

% of GDP

Source: Alan Randall (2008), "Is Australia on a Sustainability Path? Interpreting the Clues," *Australian Journal of Agricultural and Resource Economics* **52**: 77–95.

Figure 19.5   *Adjusted net savings, selected countries, 1970–2004*

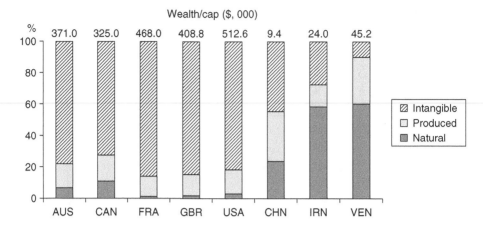

Source: Alan Randall (2008), "Is Australia on a Sustainability Path? Interpreting the Clues," *Australian Journal of Agricultural and Resource Economics* **52**: 77–95.

Figure 19.6   Composition of wealth, selected countries, 2000

In summary, from a weak sustainability viewpoint, the available data suggest that Australia is muddling along with ANS in the 5 percent range (Figure 19.4). It is doing better than many resource-exporting countries (the negative savers) but not so well as Canada, whose economy is similar in many respects: modern and diversified, but more dependent than many such countries on exports of natural resources and agricultural commodities. Canada's ANS has consistently exceeded Australia's, often by a substantial amount (although the two series appear to converge in 2004, the last year for which there is data).

Can Australia take comfort in its consistently positive, if small ANS rate? The evidence concerning this crucial question is far from complete. We know that the ANS data provide better measures for some kinds of saving than others (e.g., education expenditure is a poor measure of investment in intangible capital), and there are important omissions in the accounts of natural and environmental resources. To make progress, it is important to identify the missing categories and interpret the available evidence, fragmentary though it may be.

Adjusted net saving: tracking down the missing pieces
The obvious categories of natural and environmental resources that are missing in the ANS accounts are net depletion of forest resources (for many countries including Australia), net depletion of water resources (quantity and quality), depletion of biodiversity, most kinds of pollution damage (there are attempts to measure damage from CO_2 and fine particulate emissions), and net degradation/enhancement of soil resources. In practice, tracking down the missing pieces is mostly a matter of interpreting fragmentary evidence: looking for clues. Our search for clues focuses on agriculture, natural resources, and the environment, because these are the areas most under-represented in the ANS accounts.

The available evidence from natural resource assessments conducted in Australia[33] offers some clues that genuine savings in Australia are systematically lower than ANS. First, let us consider the "good news." Timber resources in aggregate do not appear to be experiencing net depletion, and the "ordinary" problems with atmospheric and soil resources (air pollution, soil erosion, and nutrient depletion) do not appear to be getting worse. So, the clues do not suggest that omission of these items distorts the genuine savings picture presented in the ANS accounts.

However, there is also bad news for us to consider. Water resources are overused, overcommitted, and of diminishing quality; and demand is growing exuberantly. Dryland salinity, and greenhouse gas (GHG) emissions and climate change, are increasing concerns and biodiversity (especially in eucalyptus and acacia ecosystems, wetlands, and riparian ecosystems) is diminishing. We appear to be on safe ground in concluding that omission of changes in water quantity and quality, dryland salinity, and biodiversity in the ANS accounts do in fact distort the picture of genuine savings. ANS attempts to account for GHG accumulation, but the difficulties of so doing tend to limit the confidence we can have in this accounting.

Policies for weak sustainability
The bottom line is that, while progress is clearly being made in resolving some long-standing market and government failures involving natural resources and environmental amenities, getting the prices systematically right is beyond reach for several reasons. Pigovian taxes are seldom on the political agenda, while regulation by design standards is losing rather than gaining momentum. Market-based incentives and "green payments" have potential, but there are important caveats. Cap-and-trade programs encounter political hurdles (caps are not always politically feasible). Conservation auctions of various kinds, and pollution trading networks that include farmers as sellers of credits, are popular because they deliver money (often to farmers), but delivery of environmental performance is less assured. For these reasons and more, we are likely always to stop short of getting all the prices completely right – and to stop short of achieving positive balances in the natural resources and environmental lines of our weak sustainability accounts.

Climate and GHGs, and dryland salinity, present particular challenges. The climate change issue cries out for global carbon or GHG taxes or, better yet, a global cap-and-trade system. However, global political capital presently falls far short of what would be needed to make that happen. Dryland salinity raises a different kind of challenge. First, it is an exhaustible-resource problem – even if the factor intensity of salinization in producing agricultural output was decreasing, it would mean only that we are "mining the soil" a little more slowly. Second, the extent of the market failures involved in dryland salinity is unclear.[34] Frankly, while certain salinity-controlling practices are profitable in particular cases, strong prevention and mitigation measures on a large scale are unprofitable at any realistic discount rate. For this reason, balancing the weak sustainability accounts may be a matter mostly of encouraging compensatory savings and investment elsewhere in the economy to compensate for the ongoing disinvestment in dryland soils.

Are weak sustainability policies enough?
For particular resource and environmental problems such as water supply, timber, soil erosion and nutrient depletion, air pollution, and the more tractable sorts of water

quality problems, it can be argued that getting the prices right would take us a long way toward weak sustainability. But it is well to remember that even weak sustainability asks us to do much more than we are doing now. For habitat conservation and biodiversity, getting the prices right is likely at best to be only a part of the solution. These problems are likely to require attention to specific resources in particular cases. For GHG and climate, we must recognize first that we are a very long way from systematically getting the prices right. The prices that matter include virtual prices for global public goods, and getting those prices right is no easy task for economics, politics, and diplomacy. Failing that, weak sustainability policies offer only the prospect of adapting to environmental and economic changes in ways that are unlikely to sustain welfare.

Dryland salinity highlights the distinction between weak and strong sustainability. Given the unprofitability of large-scale measures to control and mitigate dryland salinity, weak sustainability demands only that compensatory savings and investment elsewhere in the economy balance the disinvestment in dryland soils. Strong sustainability focuses not just on maintaining future welfare but also on maintaining the resource itself; for example, demanding that the soil be saved or (depending on the particular strong sustainability formulation) that losses in soil resources due to salinization be offset by compensating investments in soil improvements elsewhere.

The bottom line is that political impediments and challenges in mechanism design are so substantial that solutions in the real world are likely to involve some continuing shortfalls in getting the prices right, which will adversely affect the balances on the natural resource and environmental lines of the weak sustainability accounts. The policy matrix is likely to feature some continuing deviations from systematic efficiency (but perhaps fewer than we have now), shored up with piecemeal application of strong sustainability instruments, for example, precautionary instruments aimed at maintaining stocks of particular kinds of natural and environmental capital.

Concluding comment

As should be clear from the foregoing discussion, economics offers a way of organizing information and concepts, relating premises to consequences and generating policy insights. For two kinds of reasons, however, economics does not have the answers. First, the essential premises will include many matters of fact that are the proper province of other disciplines which are still working toward warrantable knowledge. Second, modern economics is founded on individualistic and utilitarian normative premises that are at best contenders, along with other quite different ethical systems, for human allegiance. Under these circumstances, economics cannot reasonably be charged with responsibility for saving the world by finding and promoting "correct" sustainability policies and practices. But, economists do have ethical obligations with respect to sustainability, and natural resource and environmental policy in general, which are more modest, but surely include the following.

Do economics well

Be concerned about aggregate human welfare, because it is hard to conceive of an ethical policy that sets objectives lower than sustaining human welfare. Given that preservation of especially treasured natural resources, ecosystems, and human artifacts enriches human existence, subsystem sustainability and preservation issues should also be taken seriously.

Continue to bring to the discussion the special insights of economics

Future human welfare will be diminished by showing too little respect for the natural world, but also by restricting human activity more than turns out to have been necessary. This implies a kind of symmetry – doing too much can be as bad as doing too little. In the extreme, however, asymmetry takes over: irreversible decline, unlike foregone consumption of life's little luxuries, cannot be made up later.

Practice humility and avoid economic tunnel-vision

Economists should show respect for the concepts, empirical knowledge, and perspectives of other disciplines. With respect to philosophy, in particular, economists should be open to policy dialogue based on philosophies other than a particular, utilitarian version of consequentialism. Finally, economists, especially in certain policy settings, can do more to acknowledge the virtue of community and the concomitant limits of individualism.

Questions for discussion

1. Colleges and universities are responsible for managing many types of capital, including natural resources such as the land and water, for the benefit of students. What would it mean for your college or university to manage capital at its disposal to meet the goal of weak sustainability?
2. Do you believe a "safe minimum standard" is needed for all endangered plants and animals? Why or why not? If budgets are limited, how would you prioritize which plants and animals to save first?
3. Some people argue that with increasing knowledge and technology, future generations will find ways to "take care of themselves," so present generations should not be so worried about sustainability measures and policy. What sustainability responsibilities do you think present generations have for future generations? What is the basis for your position?

Notes

1. Gro H. Brundtland (ed.) (1987), *Our Common Future: Report of the World Commission on Environment and Development*, Oxford: Oxford University Press.
2. John Ferejohn and Talbot R. Page (1978), "On the Foundations of Intertemporal Choice," *American Journal of Agricultural Economics* **60**: 269–75.
3. Robert M. Solow (1974), "Intergenerational Equity and Exhaustible Resources," *Review of Economic Studies* **41** (128): 29–46.
4. John M. Hartwick (1977), "Intergenerational Equity and the Investing of Rents from Exhaustible Resources," *American Economic Review* **67** (5): 972–4.
5. See Michael C. Farmer and Alan Randall (1997), "Policies for Sustainability: Lessons from an Overlapping Generations Model," *Land Economics* **73**: 608–22; Michael C. Farmer and Alan Randall (1998), "The Rationality of a Safe Minimum Standard," *Land Economics* **74**: 287–302.
6. Daniel W. Bromley (1989), "Entitlements, Missing Markets and Environmental Uncertainty," *Journal of Environmental Economics and Management* **17**: 181–94.
7. Richard B. Howarth and Richard B. Norgaard (1991), "Intergenerational Resource Rights, Efficiency, and Social Optimality," *Land Economics* **66**: 1–11.
8. Farmer and Randall, "Policies for Sustainability," op. cit.
9. See Randall (2006).
10. See Robert S. Pindyck (2007), "Uncertainty in Environmental Economics," *Review of Environmental Economics and Policy* **1** (1): 5–65.
11. See Siegfried von Ciriacy-Wantrup (1968), *Resource Conservation: Economics and Policies*, 3rd edn, Berkeley, CA: University of California Division of Agricultural Sciences; Richard C. Bishop (1978), "Endangered Species and Uncertainty: The Economics of a Safe Minimum Standard," *American Journal of Agricultural Economics* **60**: 10–18.
12. "Immoderate," in Ciriacy-Wantrup, *Resource Conservation*, op. cit; and "Intolerably High," in Bishop, "Endangered Species and Uncertainty," op. cit.
13. Salah El Serafy (1989), "The Proper Calculation of Income from Depletable Natural Resources," in *Environmental Accounting for Sustainable Development*, ed. Yusaf Ahmad, Salah El Serafy, and Ernst

Lutz, Washington, DC: World Bank; Herman Daly (1990), "Some Operational Principles of Sustainable Development," *Ecological Economics* **2**: 1–6.

14. Edward Barbier, Anil Markandya, and David W. Pearce (1990), "Environmental Sustainability and Cost–Benefit Analysis," *Environment and Planning* **22**: 1259–66.

15. Mick Common and Charles Perrings (1992), "Towards an Ecological Economics of Sustainability," *Ecological Economics* **6**: 7–34.

16. This case study is based upon Alan Randall (2008), "Is Australia on a Sustainability Path? Interpreting the Clues," *Australian Journal of Agricultural and Resource Economics* **52**: 77–95.

17. A fundamental concern relates to the argument raised by Pezzey and Toman that the Hartwick rule cannot offer an exact policy prescription for sustainability in the real world, because observed prices are not generated by an underlying sustainability objective function (to put it another way, sustainability prices can be observed only once sustainability has been achieved). See John Pezzey and Michael Toman (2002), "Progress and Problems in the Economics of Sustainability," in *International Yearbook of Environmental and Resource Economics 2002/2003*, ed. Tom Tietenberg and Henk Folmer, Cheltenham, UK and Northampton, MA, USA: Edward Elgar Publishing.

18. Geir B. Asheim and Martin L. Weitzman (2001), "Does NNP Growth Indicate Welfare Improvement?," *Economics Letters* **73** (2): 233–39.

19. Pezzey and Toman, "Progress and Problems," op. cit.

20. Kirk Hamilton and John M. Hartwick (2005), "Investing Exhaustible Resource Rents and the Path of Consumption," *Canadian Journal of Economics* **38** (2): 615–21.

21. Robert D. Cairns (2006), "On Accounting for Sustainable Development and Accounting for the Environment," *Resources Policy* **31** (4): 211–16; Pezzey and Toman, "Progress and Problems," op. cit.

22. R.C. Brown, J. Asafu-Adjaye, M. Draca, and A. Strastor (2005), "How Useful is the Genuine Savings Rate as a Sustainability Indicator for Regions within Countries? Australia and Queensland Compared," *Australian Economic Review* **38**: 370–88, provide a detailed discussion of the evolution of GS, its weaknesses and the improvements that can be (and in some cases have been) made in GS accounting. They also show what can, and cannot, be accomplished in disaggregating the Australian ANS accounts to the state (in their case, Queensland) level.

23. World Bank (2006), "Site Resources: Adjusted Net Savings 1970–2004," http://web.worldbank.org/WBSITE/EXTERNAL/TOPICS/ENVIRONMENT/EXTEEI/0,,contentMDK:20502388~menuPK:1187778~pagePK:148956~piPK:216618~theSitePK:408050,00.html.

24. In "Progress and Problems," Pezzey and Toman, op. cit., pp. 186–90 illustrate the challenges of applied sustainability accounting in a simple model economy, and the detailed attention required to do even a passably credible job.

25. A caveat: Common and Sanyal show that calculations of Australia's depreciation of non-renewable natural resources following different measures yield strikingly different results. See Mick Common and Kali Sanyal (1997), "Measuring the Depreciation of Australia's Non-Renewable Resources: A Cautionary Tale," *Ecological Economics* **26**: 23–30.

26. See Kirk Hamilton (2005), "Testing Genuine Saving," Policy Research Working Paper no. 3577, Washington, DC: World Bank; Susana Ferreira and Jeffrey Vincent (2005), "Genuine Savings: Leading Indicator of Sustainable Development?," *Economic Development and Cultural Change* **53** (3): 737–54; Kirk Hamilton and Katharine Bolt (2007), "Genuine Savings as an Indicator of Sustainability," in *Handbook of Sustainability*, ed. Giles Atkinson, Simon Dietz, and Eric Neumayer, Cheltenham, UK and Northampton, MA, USA: Edward Elgar Publishing.

27. Ferreira and Vincent, "Genuine Savings: Leading Indicator?," op. cit. With respect to this observation by Ferreira and Vincent, it is noteworthy that the adjustment for educational expenditure performs poorly.

28. Hamilton and Bolt, "Genuine Savings as an Indicator," op. cit.

29. World Bank (2006), *Where is the Wealth of Nations? Measuring Capital for the 21st Century*, Washington, DC: World Bank; World Bank (2006), "Site Resources: Wealth Estimates by Country, 2000," http://web.worldbank.org/WBSITE/EXTERNAL/TOPICS/ENVIRONMENT/EXTEEI/0,,contentMDK:20487828~menuPK:1187788~pagePK:148956~piPK:216618~theSitePK:408050,00.html.

30. However, it must be understood that intangible capital is measured by inference – the residual GDP that cannot be attributed statistically to other, more readily measurable factors is attributed to intangible capital, and is then capitalized.

31. John C.V. Pezzey, Nick Hanley, Karen Turner, and Douglas Tinch (2005), "Comparing Augmented Sustainability Measures for Scotland: Is There a Mismatch?," *Ecological Economics* **57**: 60–74.

32. Iran, rather than Saudi Arabia, represents the oil-rich countries in Figure 19.5. No sleight of hand is intended – the ANS data series is more complete for Saudi Arabia whereas the wealth data series is more complete for Iran.

33. Australian Government (2001), *Australian Agriculture Assessment 2001*, Canberra: National Land and

Water Resources Audit, Land and Water Australia; Australian Government (2000), *Australian Dryland Salinity Assessment 2000*, Canberra: National Land and Water Resources Audit, Land and Water Australia; Australian Government (2002), *Australian Terrestrial Biodiversity Assessment 2002*, Canberra: National Land and Water Resources Audit, Land and Water Australia; Australian Government (2001), *Australian Water Resources Assessment 2000*, Canberra: National Land and Water Resources Audit, Land and Water Australia.
34. Andrew Bathgate (2002), "Economic and Physical and Attributes of Dryland Salinity in NSW: A Review," Contributed Paper, 46th Annual Conference of the Australian Agricultural and Resource Economics Society, Canberra, Australian Capital Territory, February; David Pannell (2001), "Dryland Salinity: Economic, Scientific, Social and Policy Dimensions," *Australian Journal of Agricultural and Resource Economics* **45**: 517–46.

Suggested reading: classic and contemporary

Anton, W.R.Q., G. Deltas, and M. Khanna (2004), "Incentives for Environmental Self-regulation and Implications for Environmental Performance," *Journal of Environmental Economics and Management* **48**: 632–54.

Barnett, H. and C. Morse (1963), *Scarcity and Growth: The Economics of Natural Resource Availability*. Baltimore, MD: Johns Hopkins Press.

Bjornlund, H. and J. McKay (2002), "Aspects of Water Markets for Developing Countries: Experiences from Australia, Chile, and the US," *Environment and Development Economics* **7**: 769–95.

Brown, R.C., J. Asafu-Adjaye, M. Draca, and A. Straton (2005), "How Useful is the Genuine Savings Rate as a Sustainability Indicator for Regions within Countries? Australia and Queensland Compared," *Australian Economic Review* **38**: 370–88.

Common, M. and K. Sanyal (1998), "Measuring the Depletion of Australia's Non-Renewable Resources: A Cautionary Tale," *Ecological Economics* **26** (1): 23–30.

Dasgupta, P. and G. Heal (1979), *Economic Theory and Exhaustible Resources*, Cambridge: Cambridge University Press.

Harris, M. and I. Fraser (2002), "Natural Resource Accounting in Theory and Practice: A Critical Assessment," *Australian Journal of Agricultural and Resource Economics* **46**: 139–92.

Hartwick, J.M. (1977), "Intergenerational Equity and the Investing of Rents from Exhaustible Resources," *American Economic Review* **67** (5): 972–4.

Mallick, M., J.A. Sinden, and D.J. Thampapillai (2000), "The Relationship Between Environmentally Sustainable Income, Employment and Wages in Australia," *Australian Economic Papers* **39**: 232–44.

Randall, A. (2006), "Discounting Future Prospects, and the Quest for Sustainability," in *Economics and the Future: Time and Discounting in Private and Public Decision Making*, ed. D.J. Pannell and S.G.M. Schilizzi, Cheltenham, UK and Northampton, MA, USA: Edward Elgar.

Randall, A. (2007), "Benefits, Costs, and a Safe Minimum Standard of Conservation," in *Handbook of Sustainability*, ed. G. Atkinson, S. Dietz, and E. Neumayer, Cheltenham, UK and Northampton, MA, USA: Edward Elgar.

20 Economics and environmental ethics: what are the ethical implications of the economic approach to conservation and preservation and what can we learn from other ethical approaches?

We are frequently invited to consider the possibility that the principles for intertemporal optimization and sustainability developed in Chapters 14, 15, and 19, in which the discount rate plays an important role, simply fail to address the important issues in conservation and preservation decisions. It is sometimes argued that standard intertemporal economics legitimizes the premature exploitation of mineral resources to the detriment of future generations. With respect to the preservation of species and natural environments, for example, the objections to standard intertemporal economics may be considerably more broadly based and far-reaching. In this chapter, we introduce some of the issues that underlie the question: Does an economic approach utilizing the standard tools of economic theory adequately address the issues of conservation and preservation?

First, in order to illustrate the complexity of the issues, we consider the array of services provided by natural environments. Terrestrial environments, inland wetlands, and coastal marshes with substantially non-degraded ecosystems are, unfortunately, becoming increasingly rare. Nevertheless, these environments offer many services to people. For many kinds of wildlife, they provide a year-round habitat. For other species, they offer a nursery or migratory habitat. For still other kinds of wildlife, important links in the food chain are provided by species that use these environments as nursery or migratory habitats.

Thus, people may enjoy utility from fish and wildlife, via commercial harvest, sport hunting and fishing, or observation, in some cases by venturing into the natural environment and in other cases by encountering in other locales species that depend on natural environments for their survival. Those who enter substantially non-degraded natural environments for recreation enjoy more than the pleasures of hunting, observing, or fishing for a particular species. They enjoy a total aesthetic and recreational experience offered by the diversity of the non-degraded natural environment.

Among these environments one usually finds the few remaining significant habitats of endangered species, which is only to be expected, as species that are well adapted to intensively managed agricultural environments or urban environments are unlikely to become endangered in the modern world. Thus, natural environments are the best hope of preserving endangered species, which is thought desirable for several reasons: to preserve the natural heritage for the cultural and spiritual benefit of humanity, to maintain the diversity of nature's pool of genetic materials (e.g., biodiversity) to support ecosystem health, and because there is no assurance that species that seem of little use to humans today will not be recognized as useful in the future. The progress of science frequently provides examples of the last-mentioned phenomenon, when it is discovered that species previously considered to be useless play significant roles in the survival and productivity of valued species, and when science discovers important uses, medicinal and other, for chemical compounds produced by biological organisms.

Natural environments offer research and educational services associated with individual species that exist therein and with the ecological diversity of such environments. Ecologically diverse habitats provide the only opportunities for people to learn about the interactions in natural systems. Natural environments also offer a wide variety of services considered important by individuals who are not especially concerned with natural systems and ecological diversity per se. Terrestrial natural environments offer air quality enhancement through "greenbelt effects." Inland aquatic and wetland environments provide drainage, recharge of aquifers, floodwater retention, and buffering from flood damage. They provide silt retention that in the short term reduces expenditures for dredging streams, navigation locks, harbors, and the like, and in the long term assists the process of soil formation. Coastal estuarine and marsh environments have buffering effects, reducing damage from high winds, wave impact, and the accumulation of debris during violent weather. In addition, they help maintain the global chemical balance. As with inland wetlands, coastal environments help in drainage, floodwater retention, silt accumulation, and soil formation. Wetlands, whether inland or coastal, contribute to water-pollution control, by assimilating wastes and recycling chemicals.

Natural environments thus offer many goods and services (see Chapter 2 for more discussion), ranging from the mundane and commercial, through those that are clear and present but non-marketed, and those that may have non-exclusive benefits in some far-off and uncertain future, to those that most people would consider as categorically non-economic (e.g., those that contribute to cultural and spiritual well-being). Faced with the many kinds of services provided by natural environments, we observe some people making lists of different kinds of values served – commercial value, educational value, aesthetic value, cultural value, spiritual value, and so on. We are unconvinced by that approach – instead of many kinds of value, it makes more sense to think in terms of many different ways of valuing. Below, we consider some of the ways that people approach the ideas of goodness and value, starting with the mainstream approach as manifested, for example, in the benefit–cost and weak sustainability criteria.

Economic welfarism: the ethical foundations of the weak sustainability and benefit–cost criteria

Economists bring to the table a value system, and some technical tools for implementing it. The value system is one that considers the consequences of a proposed action, beneficial and adverse, and seeks to find a balance. Economic theories of value define individual good as the satisfaction of individual preferences. The resulting measures of value accurately reflect individual preferences, as intended, but have also the more controversial property that the preferences of the well-off count for more. Measures of benefit and cost for individuals are summed to calculate social welfare changes, in a modern and sophisticated attempt to implement Bentham's venerable idea of "the greatest good for the greatest number." This value system is a fairly coherent instantiation of a legitimate philosophy, utilitarianism (see Chapter 4). As Hubin notes, the benefit–cost analysis (BCA) criterion evaluates proposed actions by offering a reasonably good accounting of their prospective net contribution to the satisfaction of human preferences.

The kind of accounting represented by BCA and weak sustainability is axiological in that it treats goodness as a matter of value, consequentialist because outcomes are what is valued, welfarist in that benefits and costs (in money-metric utility terms) are aggregated across gainers and losers anonymously (that is, without consideration of who, and what sorts of people, stand to gain and lose), and utilitarian because individual preferences are the foundation of value.[1] So, the BCA criterion has coherent ethical foundations, but they are quite particular and when made explicit draw objections from utilitarians of other stripes and from adherents of competing ethical systems.

Controversies about economic welfarism

The weak sustainability criterion maintains human welfare over time while permitting changes in the composition of production and consumption – a stance that respects the modern experience of technical progress and increasing welfare even as substitution in production and consumption proceeds apace. In environmental matters, the BCA criterion gives voice in economic terms to human preferences for environmental goods and services that would likely be ignored or seriously undervalued in ordinary accounts of private gains and losses. Yet it remains controversial from several standpoints.[2]

Philosophical issues   When applied to environmental issues, the economic-welfarist ethic encounters objections that are founded in alternative ethical theories.

PREFERENCES MAY BE ILL-CONSIDERED AND EPHEMERAL (AS MAY COSTS WHICH, TOO, ARE SUBJECTIVE)   Decisions about environmental matters may commit society to long-lived outcomes (at worst, some natural entity may be lost forever), yet some critics worry that human preferences might be whimsical, ill-considered, and shaped by the past so that they travel poorly into the future. Economists, with their insistence on consumer sovereignty, bring some of this on themselves – the "utility swine" (a hypothetical individual who routinely prefers the most disgusting of the available alternatives) is a staple of undergraduate philosophy classes: should the preferences of such a person be accorded any ethical significance? The sense that preferences are impermanent may lead to a quest for some more enduring foundation for value.

VALUE MAY INVOLVE MORE THAN PREFERENCE   Immanuel Kant insisted that aesthetic judgments, while subjective, involve much more than preference – such judgments can make a claim to interpersonal agreement because they can be based on good reasons and shared experiences. The Kantian aesthetic leads to arguments that certain natural entities have intrinsic value – a good of their own, independent of human caring. Intrinsic value may be contrasted with instrumental value, in which value is derived from contribution to things people care about, as intermediate goods in the production of something valued, or as direct sources of utility. While instrumental values are entirely consistent with the utilitarian world-view, it is difficult to comprehend intrinsic value in a utilitarian framework.

THE GREAT MORAL QUESTIONS SHOULD BE ADDRESSED BY PRINCIPLES, NOT VALUES   Kant argued also that universal moral principles could be found to address the truly important decisions that human and social life requires, an argument that effectively relegates preferences to a set of issues that are morally less important. This perspective leads to a search for moral principles that imply human duties toward natural entities. These duties may be prohibitive (e.g., humans may be prohibited from taking harmful actions) and/or affirmative (e.g., humans may be required to take certain actions favoring the beneficiary of the duty). For those who take the study of ethics seriously, the major hurdle for a duty-based conservation or preservation ethic is explaining from whence the duty is derived. One explanation, offered by Donald Regan[3] in the more limited context of the preservation of species, proceeds as follows. Human beings have affirmative duties toward those things that are intrinsically good; knowledge is intrinsically good; the information encoded in the genes of any living species is a form of knowledge; and therefore it follows that there is an affirmative duty incumbent on humans to preserve any species, regardless of its utilitarian value to humans.

THE GREAT MORAL QUESTIONS ARE BEST ADDRESSED IN TERMS OF RIGHTS THAT MUST BE RESPECTED   Rights-based theories of the good offer an array of positions. For example, contractarians object to the potential Pareto improvement (PPI) criterion (see Chapter 8), arguing that hypothetical compensation is a kind of hypothesis, not a kind of compensation. Libertarians might argue that people's rights to enjoy nature oblige other people not to befoul it. Rights-based approaches must always explain the origin of the right that is claimed.

IT IS NOT JUST ABOUT HUMANS   Standard economics assumes, along with many other strands of philosophy, that humans are the only entities whose concerns matter. However, this position has been attacked from many quarters. There are utilitarians who argue that animal welfare matters, Kantian aesthetes who argue that natural entities may have intrinsic value, and rights-based deontologists who argue that rights should be extended to natural entities (intrinsic value may play a role in grounding such rights claims).

PERHAPS IT IS NOT ABOUT HUMANS AT ALL   The basic program of deep ecology, or ecocentrism, is to take any or all of the basic moral philosophy approaches and expand the set of entities that matter – that is, entities whose welfare counts, that have a good of their own, and/or that have rights – independently of human concern or patronage.

Issues that engage economists   The claim that BCA offers a reasonably good accounting of prospective welfare change invites a question: Perhaps so, but what are the caveats underlying the modifier "reasonably?"

THE PREFERENCES OF THE WELL-OFF COUNT FOR MORE   The PPI values and prices underpinning BCA and weak sustainability, willingness to pay (WTP) and willingness to accept (WTA), are consistent with the standard concepts of market value (buyer's best offer, seller's reservation price and, ideally at the margin, market price). This has evidentiary value in cases where market observations are available, and provides the underpinning to the claim that the BCA criterion is a filter for proposed actions that would increase the size of the game. However, because individual WTP is constrained by ability to pay, it has the unfortunate characteristic that the preferences of the well-off count for more. Economists have considered various valuation frameworks that overweight contributions to basic needs, or overweight gains to the worst-off households, but in the end consistency with the PPI criterion usually wins out.

TREATMENT OF RISK AND UNCERTAINTY   Issues of risky future outcomes typically are addressed by expressing benefits and costs in expected value terms, which is appropriate when probabilities can be specified and the decision maker is risk-neutral. Uncertainty is typically addressed via option values, and risk-aversion is sometimes introduced into the welfare calculations. All of this may be thought inadequate to deal with gross ignorance about the workings of environmental systems under increasing levels of anthropogenic stress, and some, but by no means all, economists are sympathetic to precautionary restraints invoked for threats beyond an appropriate threshold.

DISCOUNTING FUTURE BENEFITS AND COSTS   Calculating net present values discounts future prospects and serves as a lightning rod for critics who interpret this as in some sense devaluing future welfare. Discounting does in fact devalue future prospects in the "bread-eating" case, which is all about determining the ideal rate at which to consume an endowment. In a productive economy, however, even in the absence of utility discounting the equilibrium discount rate will be positive to reflect the productivity and scarcity of capital. As discussed in Chapter 19, suppressing the equilibrium discount will hurt rather than help the future by discouraging saving and investment.

Objections from environmentalists   Environmentalists, especially those who approach environmental issues primarily from non-economic perspectives, may express the following objections to BCA.

A TOOL OUT OF PLACE   Some environmentally concerned critics claim that BCA is an economic tool out of place in the environmental arena. There is not much substance to this criticism, we think. At best, it seems to be an expression of intuitions that the economy (and economics) is the problem, not the solution.

INAPPROPRIATE MONETIZATION   Environmentalists often object that BCA monetizes everything. But money is not the real issue: money, after all, is just a convenient token of value in exchange. The real issue is that monetization assumes that environmental entities are, at least in large part, fungible with ordinary produced goods and services. Opponents of the fungibility argument object to the implication of substitutability – that ordinary produced goods and services are (or should be) substitutable for natural entities, and that trade-offs across these two categories are meaningful. Non-fungibility arguments are arguments that trade-offs between natural entities and ordinary goods and services are inappropriate in general, or in particular circumstances that can be defined. Some environmental economists are sympathetic to the particular version of this argument.

ENVIRONMENTAL INJUSTICE   Environmentalists and other justice-minded people may raise the concern that the outcomes of a strict BCA may end up burdening certain segments of the population with outcome costs and/or restricting access to outcome benefits in an unjust or unfair manner. For example, BCA may recommend locating a municipal landfill in a less-developed section of a city or county because of lower land costs. However, lower land costs may also mean that the landfill will be located in an area of the city or county predominately surrounded by low-income households, perhaps mostly composed of a certain ethnic group. In this case, one might argue that an environmental injustice has occurred because this localized group of people must bear a disproportionately large portion of the total environmental costs of the landfill (e.g., noxious odors, surface and groundwater contamination). In addition, because of their relatively lower incomes and perhaps social standing in the community, the affected households are likely to be less empowered to resist the landfill location decision, leading to more exposure to environmental disamenities.

The same city or county which decided to locate the landfill near the low-income neighborhoods may also decide to locate a new public park on the other side of the city or county near high-income neighborhoods (e.g., because people living in the high-income neighborhoods express a relatively higher WTP for the new park). Due to the lack of affordable transportation options (e.g., the low-income neighborhood people cannot walk or ride bikes to the new park), the people living in the low-income neighborhoods may have more difficulty traveling to the new park, resulting in another environmental injustice – this one involving unjust or unfair restricted access to environmental amenities.[4]

These objections raise two quite distinct issues. First, BCA is responsible to some degree for these outcomes, because WTP and WTA overweight the preferences of the well-off. Second, in the real world a BCA rule is seldom the stand-alone social decision criterion. Environmental justice is one of several concerns, in addition to benefits and costs, that a society may choose to consider in social decision-making.

Environmental ethics
Beliefs and attitudes about how we should use and manage natural resources and the environment compose a person's environmental ethic. According to *Webster's Dictionary*, an "ethic" is a "set of moral principles or values" influencing what a person believes about what is good or bad and our moral duties and obligations. Thus, a person's particular environmental ethic refers to the moral principles or values he or she holds with respect to use and management of natural resources and the environment. A person's environmental ethic influences what he or she believes is good or bad about use and management of natural resources and the environment, and what our moral duties and obligations should be with respect to use and management of natural resources and the environment.

The preceding section has identified the key value commitments of the economic-welfarist ethic, and contrasted it with alternative ethical approaches based on duties, rights, the Kantian aesthetic, non-anthropocentrism, and ecocentrism. Philosophers have proven unable to define a single complete and coherent ethical system that dominates all others. Thus, the "ethical system" for many individuals may actually be a combination of many ethical systems. For that reason, different systems of environmental ethics are not mutually exclusive. For many individuals, their particular environmental ethic is likely to combine ideas, beliefs and practices from different environmental ethics systems.

In Western civilization, several major types of environmental ethics have been identified. We briefly discuss each of these below, focusing on guiding principles for use and management of natural resources and the environment, problem-solving methodology, and philosophical basis.

Conservationist approach
The conservationist approach emphasizes optimal use of natural resources and the environment over time generally from an economic returns perspective (e.g., maximization of net present value). Rational planning is the primary means for achieving optimal use over time. Theory and techniques for problem-solving are generally "reductionist and quantitative." Reductionist methodology seeks to understand and solve complex problems and relationships by breaking them into smaller, more manageable parts – that is, reductionists believe the whole can be understood from the parts. Quantitative methodology relies on mathematics, statistics, and models based on mathematical and statistical relationships to calculate optimal use and management of natural resources and the environment.[5]

The philosophical basis for the conservationist approach is generally utilitarianism, anthropocentrism, and perhaps humanitarianism. Utilitarianism, as discussed in Chapter 4, recognizes that social actions involves gains (benefits) and pains (costs) and therefore asserts that our goal with any action should be to provide "the greatest good for the greatest number of people." Anthropocentrism means a human-centered focus – that is, people are of central concern. Humanitarianism directs our concern toward the great mass of people and their welfare or well-being – the focus is on doing good for other people. The conservationist approach traditionally places high weight on use values (e.g., mineral extraction, timber harvest, recreational hunting and fishing), but at least in modern versions does not ignore passive or non-use values. The models for optimal extraction (depletion) of non-renewable resources and optimal harvest of biological renewable resources discussed in Chapters 14 and 15 basically follow the conservationist approach.

Preservationist approach
In the preservationist approach, guiding principles with respect to use and management emphasize preserving natural resources and the environment over time. In public discussions, there tends to be some confusion between conservation and preservation. For both words, standard definitions include terms such as "preventing exploitation, destruction, or neglect." Nevertheless, *Webster's Dictionary* recognizes a subtle distinction between the two words. Conservation has connotations of wise use, whereas one of the shades of meaning offered for preservation is "to keep intact."

There are points at which the affinity between the two words may dissolve into antagonism and conflict. In the case of a particular natural environment or ecosystem, a conservationist may seek an optimal plan of management over time in order to satisfy particular human purposes. On the other hand, a preservationist may well protest that management and human purposes are themselves intrusive and that the integrity of the natural environment or ecosystem should be maintained even at the cost of restricting human access. In contrast, there are cases such as endangered species in which preservation is surely a precondition to any kind of wise use that a conservationist might promote.

The problem-solving methodology in the preservationist approach is a combination of "reductionist and quantitative" and "holistic and qualitative." Holistic theory and techniques generally assert that the "sum of the parts is not equal to the whole."[6] Thus, holistic theory and techniques focus on studying and understanding the "whole" without necessarily trying to break things down into smaller parts. Although holistic theory and techniques make generous use of quantitative techniques, problem-solving methodology also includes qualitative techniques.

Qualitative techniques involve observation and interpretation of data without mathematics and statistics. For example, a qualitative approach to understanding the value of an endangered bird species may involve a researcher directly interviewing a small number of people and then reporting patterns in what people say about how they care about and value preservation of the bird (without analyzing these patterns mathematically or statistically). A quantitative approach may involve the researcher conducting a contingent valuation study (see Chapter 13) with a large number of respondents to measure willingness to pay to preserve the bird using mathematical and statistical analysis and models.

The philosophical basis for the preservationist approach is generally utilitarianism, romanticism, anthropocentrism, and humanitarianism. We have already discussed utilitarianism, anthropocentrism, and humanitarianism under the conservationist approach above. Romanticism, in contrast to a rational-planning "Age of Enlightenment" world-view, emphasizes a more emotional and intuitive world-view. Consider the decision of whether or not to preserve an endangered bird. A person with a rational planning world-view might say something like: "We should preserve the bird if the economic benefits to society are greater than the economic costs." A person with a romantic world-view might say something like: "We should preserve the bird because it is lovely to look at and sings a beautiful song that warms our hearts and uplifts our spirits." Romanticism is strongly embodied in the visual arts, music, and literature – with many applications to natural resources and the environment (e.g., environmental art, music, and literature).

For the above reasons, the preservationist approach generally de-emphasizes optimal consumption use of natural resources and the environment over time, as defined in the optimal extraction and harvest models discussed in Chapters 14 and 15. A relatively high weight is placed on passive use or non-use values. Use and management policies, for example, may emphasize permanent "set-asides" such as the US Wilderness Preservation System which restrict resource extraction from designated wilderness areas including logging and mining (hunting and fishing, however, are generally allowed in designated wilderness areas).

Ecocentrism and biocentrism
With respect to guiding principles for use and management, ecocentrism and biocentrism emphasize protecting ecosystem structure, processes, functions, and services. Relatively high weight is placed on passive use or non-use values. Consumptive and non-consumptive uses of natural resources and the environment are allowed, but maintaining ecosystem health and integrity takes priority. Biocentrism is a special case of ecocentrism which places relatively more emphasis on biotic resources (ecocentrism focuses on both biotic and abiotic resources). So, for example, biocentrism would be primarily concerned with the quantity and quality of plants and animals in a desert ecosystem, while ecocentrism would be equally concerned about the quantity and quality of plants, animals, and non-living components of the desert ecosystem including rocks, minerals, air, and water.

Because of the overarching concern about protecting the health and integrity of eco-systems as a whole, the problem-solving methodology in ecocentrism and biocentrism is holistic and quantitative, or holistic and qualitative. Philosophically, ecocentrism and biocentrism are consistent with a pantheistic worldview which asserts that the universe and all of its elements are essentially of one essence that cannot be separated into parts, as in a hierarchal manner. Ecocentrism and biocentrism traces its origins back to the "land ethic" discussed by the American biologist, ecologist, and forester, Aldo Leopold. This land ethic is often summarized by the following quote from Leopold's writings: "A thing is right when it tends to preserve the integrity, stability and beauty of the biotic community. It is wrong otherwise."[7]

"Deep ecology" approach
The "deep ecology" approach is similar to ecocentrism and biocentrism, but takes the focus on protecting the health and integrity of ecosystems and ecosystem components to a higher, more intense level. Guiding principles for use and management of natural resources and the environment assert that all living and non-living components of envi-ronmental systems (e.g., humans, wildlife, plants, rocks) must be given "equal rights" with policy and management actions developed and implemented accordingly. This "everything is equal in rights to exist" world-view places an emphasis on saving every-thing in the whole and the whole itself where plants, animals, and perhaps even inani-mate objects (e.g., unique rock formations) are given as much priority as people in policy and management decisions.

The problem-solving methodology in the "deep ecology" approach is generally holis-tic and qualitative. Like ecocentrism and biocentrism, the philosophical basis for the "deep ecology" approach is generally pantheism. The most well-known proponent (and originator) of the "deep ecology" environmental ethic is the late Norwegian philosopher Arne Naess.[8]

Stewardship ethic
Closely related to many of the concepts discussed above under other environmental ethics systems is the idea or concept of "stewardship" or "being a good steward." A "steward" is someone put in charge of taking care of something that does not belong to him or her. One is being a good steward when one takes careful care of what one has been entrusted with. The concept of stewardship is based on the concept of duty. The powers of humankind to dominate nature, including the "lesser" species, must not be used selfishly or negligently; rather, the stewardship ethic entails affirmative duties and responsibilities incumbent on humans to preserve the natural functions and services of the ecosystem and provide for the well-being of the sentient creatures therein.

The stewardship ethic emphasizes responsible and careful "caretaking" of natural resources and the environment which in the bigger picture are owned by another entity (perhaps a supreme being, or perhaps "the future"). One of the major goals of caretak-ing is to maintain the natural functions and services provided by natural resources and the environment, including use and passive (non-use) values. A farmer is practicing good stewardship when he or she farms in a way which preserves the natural functions and services provided by soil and water.

Theory and techniques for problem-solving under the stewardship ethic may be a combination of reductionist, holistic, quantitative, and qualitative. In Western civilization and the US in particular, the philosophical basis for the stewardship ethic is theism as reflected, for example, in Judeo-Christian teachings which claim the presence of a supreme being (God) who created and "owns" the universe and earth, and who expects people to be responsible caretakers or stewards of what has been entrusted to them. Although in the United States today most people and agencies probably practice stewardship from a secular perspective (e.g., the US Forest Service often refers to itself as stewards of the citizens' land), the philosophical roots of stewardship ideals can be found in religious beliefs regarding responsible caretaking.[9]

A concluding comment

With respect to conservation and preservation issues, the arguments are ultimately ethical. Although a base of sound scientific knowledge is essential to identify the possibilities and predict the outcomes of alternative actions, decisions must finally be made on ethical grounds. In this context, it is wise to remember that the standard economic-welfarist approaches, the weak sustainability and benefit–cost approaches, are derived from a particular utilitarian ethical system. No matter how carefully and effectively these approaches are implemented, they will encounter opposition, and reasonably so, from adherents of other ethical systems and positions.

Even for those who are convinced by the particular versions of utilitarian philosophy implemented in economic-welfarist approaches, the difficulties are not over. The present value and expected value concepts derived from standard economics have proved to be controversial and perhaps inadequate to resolve decision problems involving very long time horizons, massive uncertainty, and/or irreversibility. Common sense, combined with the little that economics can tell us, suggests caution, restraint, and risk aversion as appropriate responses to decision problems involving very long time horizons, massive uncertainty, and/or irreversibility. Options that involve even very low probabilities of catastrophic disaster at some future time should be approached with caution and restraint.

These words, caution, risk aversion, and restraint, are not precise economic terms. In fact, they sound suspiciously like some of the terminology used by those who take "conservationist" positions. We therefore conclude that for those intertemporal resource allocation problems whose outcomes will affect only the near-term future, and when the values of the various possible outcomes are of roughly the same order or magnitude, the intertemporal decision rules derived, or alluded to, in Chapters 7, 14, and 15 are viable. In these circumstances, conservation for conservation's sake is of no compelling importance. But, for decision problems involving very long time horizons, massive uncertainty, and/or irreversibility, the caution, risk aversion, and restraint suggested by different ethical systems and perspectives should be given careful consideration, and precautionary rules such as the safe minimum standard of conservation should be taken seriously.

Questions for discussion

1. What are the major differences between the conservationist approach, preservationist approach, ecocentrism, biocentrism, "deep ecology" approach, and stewardship ethic?
2. In his article, "The Historical Roots of our Ecological Crisis," the late Lynn White (Professor of History at Princeton, Stanford, and the University of California-Los Angeles) puts much of the blame for environmental degradation on the "Judeo-Christian ethic." In his article, "Ecology and Ethics: Relation

of Religious Belief to Ecological Practice in the Biblical Tradition," Calvin DeWitt (Professor of Environmental Studies at the University of Wisconsin-Madison) presents some counterpoints. What are your thoughts on this topic?

3. If there were available an acceptably reliable estimate of the cost of ensuring the survival of an endangered species (for example, the California condor or the bald eagle) of which the typical citizen is aware, how could the desirability of such an investment be determined? What kinds of information should be collected, and how should it be used? Is it likely that a reliable analysis of the benefits of such an investment could be made?

4. Three people are arguing about whether or not a particular wildlife species has intrinsic value. Compare and contrast the positions these people may take if one person bases their argument on a utilitarian stance, another on the idea of duties, and the third on a rights-based ethic. Is there any way to settle the argument?

5. In this chapter we argued: "Common sense, combined with the little that economics can tell us, suggests caution, restraint, and risk aversion as appropriate responses to decision problems involving very long time horizons, massive uncertainty, and/or irreversibility." Others have argued that excessive caution may be the most risky policy of all, as it would deprive society of the necessary capital to develop substitutes for resources approaching exhaustion and technology for environmental protection. The issues have been delineated. Proceed with the debate!

Notes

1. See Alan Randall (1999), "Taking Benefits and Costs Seriously," in Henk Folmer and Tom Tietenberg (eds), *The International Yearbook of Environmental and Resource Economics 1999/2000*, Cheltenham, UK and Northampton, MA, USA: Edward Elgar Publishing.
2. The discussion in this section is based on the encyclopedia article: Alan Randall (2008), "Cost Benefit Analysis," in *Encyclopedia of Environmental Ethics and Philosophy*, Woodbridge, CT: Macmillan Reference USA.
3. As stated in Brian G. Norton (ed.) (1986), *The Preservation of Species: The Value of Biological Diversity*, Princeton, NJ: Princeton University Press.
4. Susan L. Cutter (1995), "Race, Class and Environmental Justice," *Progress in Human Geography* 19 (1): 111–22.
5. An example is the USDA. Forest Service FORPLAN (Forestry Planning) model which is designed to calculate optimal US National Forest outputs (e.g., timber, minerals, recreation) with the general objective of maximizing net present value. It uses linear programming, interprogramming, mixed-integer programming, and goal programming techniques.
6. The late "father of ecology," Eugene Odum, was fond of this saying with respect to the study and understanding of ecosystems such as coastal wetlands.
7. Aldo Leopold (1949), *A Sand County Almanac*, Oxford: Oxford University Press.
8. Arne Naess (2003), "The Deep Ecology Movement: Some Philosophical Aspects," in Andrew Light and Holmes Rolston III (eds), *Environmental Ethics: An Anthology*, Malden, MA: Blackwell Publishing.
9. Richard Worrell and Michael C. Appleby (2003), "Stewardship of Natural Resources: Definition, Ethical and Practical Aspects," *Journal of Agricultural and Environmental Ethics* 12 (3): 263–77.

Suggested reading: classic and contemporary

Bishop, R.C. (1978), "Endangered Species and Uncertainty: The Economics of a Safe Minimum Standard," *American Journal of Agricultural Economics* 57: 10–18.

Ciriacy-Wantrup, S. von (1968), *Resource Conservation: Economics and Politics*, 3rd edn, Berkeley and Los Angeles, CA: University of California Press.

DeWitt, C.B. (1995), "Ecology and Ethics: Relation of Religious Belief to Ecological Practice in the Biblical Tradition," *Biodiversity and Conservation* 4: 838–48.

Hubin, D.C. (1994), "The Moral Justification of Benefit/Cost Analysis," *Economics and Philosophy* 10: 169–94.

Krutilla, J.V. (1967), "Conservation Reconsidered," *American Economic Review* 57: 777–86.

Krutilla, J.V. and A.C. Fisher (1975), *The Economics of Natural Environments*, Baltimore, MD: John Hopkins University Press.

White, Lynn, Jr (1967), "The Historical Roots of Our Ecological Crisis," *Science* 155: 1203–7.

21 Economic science, economic policy, and doing the best we can: how do we find our way forward?

We never said it was going to be easy. In Part I, the complexity of the natural and social systems that create the context for natural resource and environmental economics problems was emphasized. In Part II, we explained how economic systems ideally work to allocate natural resources efficiently to economic production and consumption. We also addressed the failure of economic theory to answer some fundamental questions about efficiency and equity in the static time-frame and in the intertemporal context. In Part III, it was seen that complex and fundamentally imperfect institutional arrangements are the norm. In Part IV, currently available techniques for empirical analyses were seen to be inadequate to analyze complex systems completely, and to be subject to serious data limitations when applied in the partial analyses that substitute for systems analyses. The economic concepts and tools discussed in Parts V and VI demonstrated the usefulness of natural resource and environmental economics for developing strategies for natural resource and environmental management and policy. The limitations of these concepts and tools were also addressed, indicating the inability of these concepts and tools to find "perfect solutions." Finally, in Part VII, we presented a broader discussion of sustainability, conservation, and preservation which demonstrates that natural resource and environmental economics does not have all the answers, suggesting the need to learn from and work with others with different perspectives and different sets of concepts and tools.

Nevertheless, natural resource and environmental economics can offer considerable insights into natural resource and environmental problems and solutions. Part I presented a useful perspective on the problems of economic growth, resource scarcity, and environmental degradation; and a perspective on the role of economic systems within the broader context of natural and social systems, and the function of economic science in analyzing that system. Part II presented the basic findings of economic science with respect to resource allocation, distribution, and economic well-being, in a static framework and in an intertemporal context. Part III discussed how economists evaluate public policies and deal with the problem of market failure and inefficiency. The theories presented are useful and reliable in predicting the behavior of individual economic actors in response to changes in the pattern of relative scarcity and in the structure of incentives as influenced by institutions. These theories were less successful in defining the "perfect society" and elucidating the rules by which such a social and economic state of grace may be achieved. A little thought leads to the conclusion that this failure was only to be expected: who could expect economics to succeed in 200 years when millennia of efforts in philosophy and theology have failed?

In Part III, we also elucidated the complex interrelationships among legal, political, and economic systems. If it succeeds, that section should increase the respect of lawyers and political scientists for economic relationships and warn the economists that they who deal only with "economic" variables are condemned forever to working with abstract systems. Practicing natural resource and environmental economists work within the institutional framework, though are always aware of the dynamism of that framework: thus they evaluate changes in the institutional framework in addition to predicting the response of individual economic actors to any existing or proposed institutional system. Parts IV, V, and VI demonstrated that natural resource and environmental economists are not without useful tools for empirical analysis. In the last several decades, these tools have been substantially improved, and there is no reason to expect that this process will not continue. In Part VII, it was shown that although natural resource and environmental economists never know all the answers, they are usually able to make useful suggestions with respect to long-term sustainability of our economy, environment and quality of life.

Economic science

There is a strong tradition in economics that seeks to establish economics as a science, by emulating some of the features of the natural sciences. Because it deals with complex systems, economics is often denied the possibility of controlled experimentation. But so is meteorology – a natural science.

In response to the complexities of the systems with which economics deals, the role of controlled experiments is limited (although economic experimentation, especially in subjects related to human decision-making, is becoming more prevalent). Economists have substituted the idea of the "natural experiment," that is, analyzing (often econometrically) the effects of exogenous shocks and /or discrete policy changes on real-world economic outcomes. With or without controlled experimentation, the notion of scientific objectivity[1] is central. Scientific objectivity is usually taken to mean the following: the scientist has the freedom and the responsibility to: (1) pose refutable and testable hypotheses; (2) test those hypotheses with relevant evidence; and (3) report the results in such a manner that they are accessible to any interested person. The idea of scientific objectivity thus includes the notions of positing relationships that could be proved invalid, testing the posited relationships with evidence, and exposing the posited relationship, the structure of the test, and the results of the test to criticism from within and without the economic discipline. It is scientific objectivity that provides the basis for any claim that economic analysis is more than mere speculation.

Economic policy

Natural resource and environmental economics deals with policy. Natural resource and environmental economists, functioning as scientists, test refutable propositions about the response of individual actors, and thus economic aggregates, to existing and alternative policies. Beyond this, they are often called upon to make policy recommendations, and it is a fact that natural resource and environmental economists sometimes rise to assume important roles in the decision-making process.

The processes of making recommendations and decisions go beyond science. The notion of scientific objectivity is a valuable element of quality control with respect to the information on which recommendations and decisions may be based, but it offers no instruction as to what should be recommended or decided. In making recommendations or decisions, economists simply go beyond the relatively secure confines of their science and into the thoroughly insecure world of normative policy.

It should be emphasized that economists, merely because they are economists, have no special and decisive qualifications for undertaking normative work. But although economists are no more qualified than others are for this kind of activity, neither are they less qualified. It would be ironic if economists, being overly conscious of the limitations of their science, withdrew from the policy arena, leaving it to others who have no more, and often less, of a scientific and philosophical basis on which to make policy recommendations and decisions.

Adaptive decision-making

In dealing with natural resource and environmental policy issues, which pertain to complex natural and social systems, natural resource and environmental economists can draw on the notion and processes of scientific objectivity as they apply to the generation of knowledge about those things that can be known, and the individualist ethic of modern welfare economics that gives them a healthy skepticism about proposals claimed to be in the "public interest" or for the "public welfare." These things, however, are seldom a sufficient basis for recommendations or decisions. Almost always, economists have inadequate information about the workings of the systems under study, in addition to an inadequate philosophical basis for determining the "best" solutions to policy problems.

Economists in the policy arena must eventually fall back on their intuition, best professional judgment, and some form of adaptive decision-making where feedback information is used to modify and improve policy dealing with natural resource and environmental policy issues. It is good that their adherence to the notion of scientific objectivity and the individualist ethic of their discipline should make economists modest, and even a little nervous, in this role. Such feelings are a good antidote to the self-importance that sometimes afflicts those active in the policy process. Nevertheless, these feelings should not lead economists to withdraw from the public policy process. They have too much to offer.

The market in ideas

There is an unfortunate notion, which is all too prevalent in economics, systems analysis, and operations research circles, that the role of "the analyst" is to provide information for "the decision-maker." We do not believe that "The Decision-Maker" exists, beyond the household and the classical capitalist firm, and our belief that he or she does not exist in the policy arena gives us considerable comfort. Rather, we conceptualize a complex policy-decision process, in which individual citizens, "experts" and subject-matter specialists, elected representatives, the personnel of bureaucratic agencies, the judiciary, and various organized interest groups all play significant roles.

Informational inputs, broadly defined to include statements on matters of fact and on normative propositions, play an important role in this decision process. However, informational inputs are not made directly (for example, from "analyst" to "decision-maker"), and they are not automatically taken as authoritative. Rather, informational inputs concerning both factual matters and normative propositions are evaluated by all parties in a "market in ideas," which is a subsystem of the complex system from which decisions eventually emerge. In such an environment, there is not much reason to fear that the value system of economists and their associated normative propositions will be imposed on society on the mere basis of the economist's authority. Instead, as Kenneth Boudling has written, considerable protection from that kind of outcome is provided through the market in ideas by "the criticism within the scientific community and the acute perception that we all have of the impact of the norms of others on their own thought, however blind we may be to the impact of our own norms on our own thought."[2]

The most important role of the natural resource and environmental economist, and of the other kinds of professionals who claim expertise on the basis of their education and intellectual development, is to participate actively in the market in ideas, while always endeavoring to keep that market open and competitive. The market in ideas provides the best protection of society against the entrenched power of established economic interests and against the growing army of "professional experts" that is attempting to establish itself as the new decision-making class.

Notes

1. See Karl Popper (1957), "Philosophy of Science: A Personal Report," in *British Philosophy in Mid-Century*, ed. C.H. Mace, London: George Allen & Unwin.
2. Kenneth Boulding (1977), "Prices and Other Institutions," *Journal of Economic Issues* 11: 809–21.

Name index

Abrams, R. 303
Ackerman, F. 242
Adamowicz, W. 272
Adams, J.S. 218
Aghion, P. 218
Ahmad, Y. 397
Akerlof, G.A. 176
Aldy, J.E. 271
Alonso, W. 350
Anderson, L.G. 303
Anton, W.R.Q. 399
Appleby, M.C. 410
Arbues, F. 371
Arrow, K.J. 127, 140, 146, 147, 148, 155, 163,
    175, 176, 242
Asafu-Adjaye, J. 398, 399
Asheim, G.B. 387, 398
Atkinson, G. 399
Ayres, R.U. 12, 39, 52

Banzhaf, H.S. 28, 271
Barber, N.L. 352
Barbier, E.B. 28, 105, 385, 398
Barnett, H.J. 49, 50, 52, 399
Bateman, I.J. 271
Bathgate, A. 399
Bator, F.M. 127, 205
Baumol, W.J. 10, 12, 163, 205, 270, 329, 372
Bayer, P. 271
Benitez, P.C. 303
Bentham, J. 61, 67, 155, 401
Berger, M.C. 262, 271, 272
Bergson, A. 59, 143, 147, 155, 163
Bergstrom, J.C. 23, 24, 28, 270, 272, 350
Berry, J.M. 218
Bertram, C. 67
Bhatia, R. 372
Bishop, R.C. 127, 176, 271, 397, 410
Bjornlund, H. 399
Blake-Hedges, L. 272
Blomquist, G.C. 262, 271, 272
Boadway, R. 163
Boardman, A.E. 242
Boerke, S. 303
Bohm, P. 329
Bolt, K. 398
Bolton, P. 218
Boulding, K. 414
Bovenberg, A.L. 329
Bowes, M.D. 303

Boyd, J. 28
Boyle, K.J. 28, 271, 272
Brajer, V. 329
Brennan, G. 218
Breton, A. 218
Bromley, D.W. 397
Brookshire, D.S. 242, 271
Brown, R.C. 24, 28, 398, 399
Brown, T.C. 23, 271, 371
Browning, M. 140
Bruce, J.P. 140, 163
Brueckner, L. 303
Brundtland, G.H. 375, 397
Bryant, W.R. 350
Buchanan, J.M. 60, 64, 67, 160, 163, 204, 205,
    218

Cairns, R.D. 290, 398
Cameron, T.A. 272
Carlsson, F. 271
Carson, R.T. 204, 271
Castle, E.N. 350
Champ, P.A. 271
Charles, A. 303
Chen, Y. 204, 205
Chestnut, L. 329
Cheung, S. 176
Chipman, J.S. 163
Chow, D. 303
Christiansen, G.B. 329
Christy, F.T. 205
Ciriacy-Wantrup, S. von 176, 410
Clawson, M. 255, 271, 348, 349, 350
Cline, W.R. 140, 163
Coase, R. 67, 198, 199, 201, 202, 204, 205
Colby, B.G. 329
Colome, S.D. 329
Common, M.S. 105, 398, 399
Commons, J.R. 174, 176, 218
Conklin, H.E. 350
Copes, P. 303
Cordell, H.K. 28, 270, 272
Covich, A.P. 28
Cropper, M.L. 205, 242
Crossley, T.F. 140
Cummings, R.G. 204
Cutter, S.L. 410

Dahlman, C.J. 67, 205
Daily, G.C. 28

415

Subject index